Fodor's
New
FIRST EDITION

The Rockies

MVFOL

MVFOL

D0375702

Fodor's Travel Publications, Inc.
New York • Toronto • London • Sydney • Auckland

First Edition

ISBN 0-679-02586-3

Fodor's The Rockies

Editor: Alison Hoffman with Andrea Lehman
Contributors: Brian Alexander, Robert Blake, Hannah Borgeson, Laura Kidder, Caroline Liou, Mike McClure, Geoffery O'Gara, Peter Oliver, Jim Robbins, Jordan Simon, Mary Ellen Schultz, Scott Warren
Creative Director: Fabrizio La Rocca
Cartographer: David Lindroth, Inc.; Eureka Cartography
Illustrator: Karl Tanner
Cover Photograph: Peter Guttman

Design: Vignelli Associates

Special Sales

Fodor's Travel Publications are available at special discounts for bulk purchases for sales promotions or premiums. Special editions, including personalized covers, excerpts of existing guides, and corporate imprints, can be created in large quantities for special needs. For more information, contact your local bookseller or write to Special Markets, Fodor's Travel Publications, 201 East 50th Street, New York, NY 10022. Inquiries from Canada should be directed to your local Canadian bookseller or sent to Random House of Canada, Ltd., Marketing Department, 1265 Aerowood Drive, Mississauga, Ontario L4W 1B9. Inquiries from the United Kingdom should be sent to Fodor's Travel Publications, 20 Vauxhall Bridge Road, London, England SW1 V 2SA.

Contents

Maps

Foreword

Every care has been taken to ensure the accuracy of the information in this guide. All prices and opening times quoted here are based on information supplied to us at press time. Hours and admission fees may change, however, and the prudent traveler will avoid inconvenience by calling ahead. The publisher cannot accept responsibility for errors that may occur.

Readers should also remember that adventure travel and outdoor vacations may entail certain risks. While the outfitters, trip operators, and tour guides mentioned in this book have been carefully selected, the publisher makes no warranties regarding their competence, reliability, and safety practices and disavows all responsibility for injury, death, loss, or property damage that may arise from participation in their trips.

The efforts of so many people have gone into the production of this book, but unfortunately, there are too many to list by name. However, we would like to thank their affiliated organizations: Colorado Division of Tourism, Colorado Ski Country, Aspen Skiing Company, Idaho Travel Council, Ski Utah, Utah Travel Council, Travel Montana, Wyoming Travel Commission, Continental Airlines.

Fodor's wants to hear about your travel experiences, both pleasant and unpleasant. When a hotel or restaurant fails to live up to its billing, let us know and we will investigate the complaint and revise our entries where the facts warrant it.

Send your letters to the editors of Fodor's Travel Publications, 201 East 50th Street, New York, NY 10022.

Highlights
and
Fodor's Choice

Highlights

Colorado

1993 was a tumultuous year for Colorado, which suffered repercussions from the late-1992 passage of Amendment 2, which outlawed civil rights legislation for special-interest groups. It was specifically targeted at gays, and in turn angered liberal groups who called for a boycott of the state. The move was moderately successful: Colorado lost over $100 million of convention business through 1995. However, its effects were ameliorated somewhat by an influx of right-wing convention business and, especially, by the finest ski season Colorado has had in years. Amendment 2 is expected to be declared unconstitutional in the courts.

Despite the fabulous winter season, ironically it was a difficult year for many in the ski industry. Small resorts such as Conquistador suspended operation; others such as Cuchara Valley struggled; and even established ski areas such as Purgatory-Durango suffered the pinch of the nationwide recession. The latter narrowly averted bankruptcy when NorWest Bank, which had sought a more favorable repayment schedule, decided not to foreclose, allowing Purgatory to stay open until at least the 1994/95 ski season. The gleaming new Doral at Telluride Spa and Resort went into receivership in 1993, and has been renamed The Peaks at Telluride. Meanwhile, the rich got richer. **Ralston Purina,** which already owned Summit County's Keystone and Arapahoe Basin, gobbled up Breckenridge as well. And an era came to a close when the "maverick" ski area, Aspen Highlands (a favorite of anti-establishment types) was purchased by the Aspen Skiing Company.

Lost amid the hubbub and hoopla was another development—one with frightening implications. This year Amendment 1 was passed—a legislation that eliminated the residents' tourism tax. Formerly, Coloradans had paid a 1¢ tax on every $100 dollars generated through tourism. The revenues enabled the Colorado Tourism Board and its regional arms to operate, as well as such admirable programs as the Colorado Welcome Centers, strategically located throughout the state to dispense information (and free coffee) to travelers. An ordinance repealing Amendment 1 is on the ballot for November 1993.

So far, there are no new developments for 1994: no major building, no imminent closures, no controversial amendments. But after the rollercoaster ride Coloradans took in 1993, they're staying tuned.

Idaho

As folks continue to look for the ever-shrinking last frontier, Idahoans are growing more and more protective of their state and its abundant natural resources. And why shouldn't they? Real estate prices are soaring, especially in Idaho's panhandle, which recently has been "discovered" by California city dwellers and others looking for their own piece of peace. Not only are people moving to Idaho, they're vacationing here by the droves. Tourism is now the third-largest industry in the state: In the past 10 years, hotel, motel, and private campground revenues have increased 66 percent.

Fortunately, however, there's plenty of Idaho to go around (although locals would disagree). The state is blessed with some of the best fly-fishing, white-water rafting, and canoeing waters in the country. Do the Salmon and Snake rivers ring a bell? How about Hells Canyon National Recreation Area? Increased activity on these waters continues to sustain the hospitality industry, as well as outfitters, guides, and outdoors-oriented retail stores.

Perhaps one of the most popular and lucrative areas on the Idaho map, however, is Sun Valley Resort, with its famed "Baldy" Mountain, reputed to be the best single ski mountain in the country. New for the '93–'94 season is an upgraded lift system to service 26,380 skiers per hour. Additionally, the resort has the largest computer-controlled snowmaking system in the world.

Baldy is tried and true, and will surely continue to attract skiers looking for good terrain within reach of a comfortable, if not posh, resort atmosphere. But be on the lookout for the up-and-coming Schweitzer Mountain, a favorite of locals.

When hiking, cycling, rafting, and skiing become mundane, Idaho is armed with the answer: Boise. Although this city is still "small town" by metropolitan standards, it's increasingly attracting attention. Major corporations are casting their votes of confidence in this little haven in the northwestern part of the state by planting their headquarters here, among the hundreds of square miles of nature.

Montana

Let's play word association. I say Montana; you say *A River Runs Through It*. Right? Fortunately, or unfortunately—depending on which side of the tourism fence you sit—the book by Norman Maclean and recent movie, directed by Robert Redford, have heightened peoples' awareness of this massive state—the fourth-largest in the country.

As is the case throughout the Rocky Mountain region, tourism—and real-estate prices—in Montana are on the rise.

The good news is that people are realizing there are few places left in the country with such resources and uninterrupted landscapes; the bad news is that Hollywood types and other bigwigs are flocking to the state; buying up huge ranches; and sending property values sky-high, making it difficult for old-timers and locals with modest incomes to afford their paradise.

Still, all the recent attention keeps the economy growing, and attractions such as Glacier National Park continue to post record visitation, with more than 2 million guests each summer.

Utah

Utah, like all the other Rocky Mountain states, boasts pristine lands, monstrous mountains, fertile streams, and lots of tourists trying to become one with nature. But what Utah has that the other states don't is historic Salt Lake City—home to Temple Square, the NBA's Utah Jazz, and hotels and restaurants that in recent years have come of age enough to rival those in big cities.

Conservative Salt Lake is stepping into the mainstream, despite its strong ties to the Mormon church, which at times has kept tourism development a beat behind that in other states. In fact, the once-impenetrable liquor laws are hardly obstacles now for those looking to party. This is good news for ski resorts whose guests' first question used to be: "Should I pack a fifth of vodka in my boot bag?"

It's wise to keep the ski resorts happy, for they are responsible for much of the state's tourism, especially after the record-breaking '92–'93 ski season, which saw more snow than it had in years. A lot of snow means a lot of money for the properties to put into developing their year-round facilities. Already many resorts, such as Snowbird, have begun to run lifts in the summer to make it easy for mountain bikers to access trails.

Wyoming

In the aftermath of the 1988 fire in Yellowstone National Park, which affected 36% of the land, an interesting phenomenon occurred: tourism increased. More than 3 million families, nature-lovers, and curious environmentalist-wannabes flocked here last year to hike, bike, raft, and climb. Perhaps they would have come even if the fire hadn't struck, or maybe they are visiting now, to assure themselves that nature really does heal itself. And it does, as evidenced by meadows of brilliant wildflowers and a flourishing of new plant life.

Needless to say, when the tourists come, the businesses in nearby towns thrive. Communities such as the well-positioned Jackson—in close proximity to Yellowstone and Grand Teton national parks—are reaping the benefits. But with such success, Jackson, as well as Casper and Cheyenne, are careful to monitor and control development.

Fodor's Choice

No two people will agree on what makes a perfect vacation, but it's fun and helpful to know what others think. We hope you'll have a chance to experience some of Fodor's Choices yourself while visiting the Rockies. For detailed information about each entry, refer to the appropriate chapters in this guidebook.

Colorado

Hotels	**The Broadmoor Hotel,** Colorado Springs (*Very Expensive*)
	Hotel Jerome, Aspen (*Very Expensive*)
	Saddle Ridge, Beaver Creek (*Very Expensive*)
	The Lodge at Cordillera, Vail Valley (*Expensive–Very Expensive*)
	Sonnenalp, Vail (*Moderate–Expensive*)
	Brown Palace, Denver (*Moderate–Expensive*)
	Hotel Boulderado, Boulder (*Moderate–Expensive*)
	Strater Hotel, Durango (*Inexpensive*)
Restaurants	**Alpenglow Stube,** Keystone (*Very Expensive*)
	The Flagstaff House, Boulder (*Very Expensive*)
	Renaissance, Aspen (*Very Expensive*)
	Syzygy, Aspen (*Very Expensive*)
	Soupçon, Crested Butte (*Expensive–Very Expensive*)
	Briarstone Manor, Colorado Springs (*Expensive*)
	Gorky Park, Steamboat Springs (*Expensive*)
	Sweet Basil, Vail (*Expensive*)
	Ski Tip Lodge, Keystone (*Moderate*)
	The Bluebonnet, Denver (*Inexpensive*)
	Janey's Chile Wagon, Cañon City (*Inexpensive*)
	Slogar, Crested Butte (*Inexpensive*)
Nightlife	**El Chapultepec,** Denver
	Diamond Belle Saloon, Durango
	The Mercury Café, Denver
	Mickey's, Vail
	One World Café, Telluride
	Sundance Saloon, Durango

The Tippler, Aspen

The Wynkoop Brewery, Denver

Views   First glimpse of Vail's (I–70 and the High Rockies) famous Back Bowls as you come off the lift

Pikes Peak (Southcentral) as seen through the gnarled spires of Garden of the Gods

Gazing down on the cliff dwellings at Mesa Verde (Southwest)

Idaho

Hotels   **Clark House on Hayden Lake,** Coeur d'Alene (*Expensive*)

The Lodge at Riggins Hot Springs, Riggins (*Expensive*)

The Cary House, Hagerman (*Moderate*)

Connie's Best Western, Sandpoint (*Moderate*)

Idaho Heritage Inn, Boise (*Moderate*)

The Idanha, Boise (*Inexpensive–Moderate*)

Restaurants   **Peter Schott's,** Boise (*Moderate–Expensive*)

The Bistro, Sandpoint (*Moderate*)

Buffalo Café, Twin Falls (*Inexpensive*)

Connie's Café, Sandpoint (*Inexpensive*)

Nightlife   **Shortbranch Bar,** Riggins

Views   Overlooking the Snake River as you drive across the Hanson Memorial or Perrine Bridge in Twin Falls

The hills in Hells Canyon that look like giant black pencils framing the Snake River

The pine-covered hills in Coeur d'Alene

Montana

Hotels   **Alley Cat,** Missoula (*Moderate*)

Goldsmith's Bed-and-Breakfast, Missoula (*Moderate*)

Kwa-Taq-Nuk, Polson (*Moderate*)

The Voss Inn, Bozeman (*Moderate*)

Fairmont Hot Springs, Butte (*Inexpensive*)

The Grand Hotel, Big Timber (*Inexpensive*)

The Murray Hotel, Livingston (*Inexpensive*)

The Sanders Bed and Breakfast, Helena (*Inexpensive*)

Restaurants   **Great Rocky Mountain Oyster Company at Yacht Basin,** Helena (*Inexpensive–Moderate*)

John Bozeman's Bistro, Bozeman (*Inexpensive*)

Rosario's, Townsend (*Inexpensive*)

Windbag Saloon & Grill, Helena (*Inexpensive*)

Nightlife **Billings Night Rodeo,** Billings

Views Any open field, at midnight, when the northern lights shine green and red against the black-velvet sky

The confluence of the Madison, Jefferson, and Gallatin rivers, forming the mighty Missouri River

Looking toward the snow-capped peaks of Glacier National Park from the adjacent village of Apgar

Watching mountain goats climb the rocky cliffs at Hidden Lake, at Logan Pass

Utah

Hotels **Alta Peruvian Lodge,** Alta (*Very Expensive*)

Brigham Street Inn, Salt Lake City (*Very Expensive*)

La Caille at Quail Run, Salt Lake City (*Very Expensive*)

The Cliff Lodge, Snowbird (*Very Expensive*)

The Homestead, Midway (*Very Expensive*)

Pack Creek Ranch, Moab (*Very Expensive*)

The Sundance Cottages, Sundance (*Very Expensive*)

Washington School Inn, Park City (*Very Expensive*)

Radisson Suite at Hotel Ogden, Ogden (*Expensive*)

Center Street Bed & Breakfast, Bear Lake (*Moderate*)

Green Gate Village Historic B&B Inn, St. George (*Moderate*)

Grist Mill Inn, Monticello (*Moderate*)

Little America Hotel & Towers, Salt Lake City (*Moderate*)

Radisson Hotel Airport, Salt Lake City (*Moderate*)

Seven Wives Inn, St. George (*Moderate*)

Restaurants **Glitretind,** Park City (*Very Expensive*)

Aerie, Snowbird (*Expensive*)

The Homestead, Midway (*Expensive*)

The Tree Room, Sundance (*Expensive*)

Bistro Royale, Park City (*Moderate*)

Cafe Terigo, Park City (*Moderate*)

Center Café, Moab (*Moderate*)

Great American Café, Vernal (*Moderate*)

Market Street Grill, Salt Lake City (*Moderate*)

Milt's Stage Shop, Cedar City (*Moderate*)

Café Pierpont, Salt Lake City (*Inexpensive*)

Frontier Grill, Roosevelt (*Inexpensive*)

Ray's Tavern, Green River (*Inexpensive*)

Squatter's Pub Brewery, Salt Lake City (*Inexpensive*)

Nightlife **The Blarney Stone,** St. George

The Dead Goat Saloon, Salt Lake City

The Green Parrot Café, Salt Lake City

Popular Place, Moab

Toones, Ogden

Views The sight of Temple Square in Salt Lake City

The Wasatch mountain range from any of the main thoroughfares

Bridal Veil Falls from the Skytram at Provo Canyon

The astounding Dinosaur Quarry at Dinosaur National Monument, with some 2,000 bones preserved in sandstone

Hundreds of petroglyphs etched into boulders and cliffs at Nine-Mile Canyon in Southeastern Utah

The 1,000-foot cliffs in Canyonlands National Park

Striking redrock spires, buttes, and mesas at the internationally recognized Monument Valley Tribal Park

Steep canyons, monumental monoliths, and spindly spires at Zion National Park

The series of amphitheaters carved into the eastern rim of the Paunsaugunt Plateau, at Bryce Canyon National Park

Wyoming

Hotels **Jenny Lake Lodge,** Grand Teton National Park (*Expensive*)

The Wort Hotel, Jackson (*Expensive*)

Lake Yellowstone Hotel, Yellowstone National Park (*Moderate–Expensive*)

Annie Moore's Guest House, Laramie (*Moderate*)

Parson's Pillow, Cody (*Moderate*)

Old Faithful Inn, Yellowstone National Park (*Inexpensive*)

Restaurants **The Blue Lion,** Jackson (*Expensive*)

The Bunnery, Jackson (*Moderate*)

Café Jacques, Laramie (*Moderate*)

Lexie's Café, Cheyenne (*Inexpensive*)

Views The magnificent Grand Canyon of the Yellowstone, where the water draining from Yellowstone Lake has cut deep into an ancient lava flow

Geysers erupting at Norris, the hottest, oldest geyser basin in Yellowstone

The sight of the Tetons from the Chapel of Transfiguration, near the end of Teton Park Road

Driving along Snowy Range Scenic Byway (west of Laramie), which passes through the Medicine Bow National Forest with 100 alpine lakes and streams

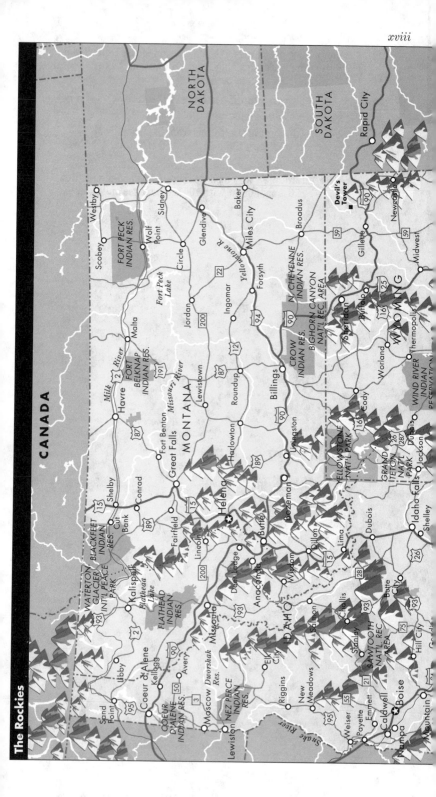

The Rockies

CANADA

NORTH DAKOTA

SOUTH DAKOTA

Rapid City

Westby

Scobey

FORT PECK INDIAN RES.

Wolf Point

Sidney

Baker

Devil's Tower

Newcastle

Glendive

Miles City

Broadus

Gillette

Midwest

Circle

Yellowstone R.

22

N. CHEYENNE INDIAN RES.

59

Fort Peck Lake

Jordan

Ingomar

94

CROW INDIAN RES.

BIGHORN CANYON NAT'L REC. AREA

90

Sheridan

WYOMING

25

Buffalo

16

Malta

200

12

Lewistown

87

Roundup

Billings

90

Worland

Thermopolis

WIND RIVER INDIAN RESERVATION

FORT BELKNAP INDIAN RES.

191

Milk River

2

Missouri River

Havre

Fort Benton

Great Falls

Fort Belknap

MONTANA

Harlowton

89

Livingston

16

Cody

26 287

YELLOWSTONE NAT'L PARK

GRAND TETON NAT'L PARK

Dubois

Jackson

Shelby

Conrad

15

Helena

Butte

Bozeman

Dillon

Lima

Dubois

Idaho Falls

Shelley

26

BLACKFEET INDIAN RES.

Cut Bank

87

89

Fairfield

Lincoln

200

Deer Lodge

Anaconda

Wisdom

15

28

WATERTON GLACIER INT'L PEACE PARK

93

2

Kalispell

Flathead Lake

FLATHEAD INDIAN RES.

Missoula

93

ELK CITY

Salmon

Challis

93

Stanley

75

SAWTOOTH NAT'L REC. AREA

Butte City

Sand Point

Libby

Kellogg

Coeur d'Alene

90

Avery

50

3

COEUR D'ALENE INDIAN RES.

95

Moscow

Dworshak Res.

NEZ PERCE INDIAN RES.

Lewiston

Riggins

New Meadows

IDAHO

21

Hill City

55

Weiser

Payette

Emmett

Caldwell

Nampa

Boise

Mountain

95

Snake River

The United States

World Time Zones

Numbers below vertical bands relate each zone to Greenwich Mean Time (0 hrs.).
Local times frequently differ from these general indications,
as indicated by light-face numbers on map.

Algiers, **29**
Anchorage, **3**
Athens, **41**
Auckland, **1**
Baghdad, **46**
Bangkok, **50**
Beijing, **54**

Berlin, **34**
Bogotá, **19**
Budapest, **37**
Buenos Aires, **24**
Caracas, **22**
Chicago, **9**
Copenhagen, **33**
Dallas, **10**

Delhi, **48**
Denver, **8**
Djakarta, **53**
Dublin, **26**
Edmonton, **7**
Hong Kong, **56**
Honolulu, **2**

Istanbul, **40**
Jerusalem, **42**
Johannesburg, **44**
Lima, **20**
Lisbon, **28**
London (Greenwich), **27**
Los Angeles, **6**
Madrid, **38**
Manila, **57**

Mecca, **47**
Mexico City, **12**
Miami, **18**
Montréal, **15**
Moscow, **45**
Nairobi, **43**
New Orleans, **11**
New York City, **16**

Ottawa, **14**
Paris, **30**
Perth, **58**
Reykjavík, **25**
Rio de Janeiro, **23**
Rome, **39**
Saigon (Ho Chi Minh City), **51**

San Francisco, **5**
Santiago, **21**
Seoul, **59**
Shanghai, **55**
Singapore, **52**
Stockholm, **32**
Sydney, **61**
Tokyo, **60**

Toronto, **13**
Vancouver, **4**
Vienna, **35**
Warsaw, **36**
Washington, D.C., **17**
Yangon, **49**
Zürich, **31**

Introduction

By Peter Oliver

Peter Oliver is a charmingly odd fellow. He is bright, amusing, and enigmatically handsome. He can bake bread, throw a knuckleball (with either a hardball or a softball), and type 80 words per minute. He takes milk in his coffee, and he doesn't snore. He is left-handed. Until 1992, he voted for five straight losers in presidential elections. He lives in New York and frequently writes for Fodor's, *among other publications.*

I caught my first trout as a kid in Colorado in the summer of 1966. It was a fish so small that I doubt it would have cast a shadow large enough to scare a chipmunk. Still, it was, undeniably, a fish, and as such emblematic of a victory of sorts. This, after an excruciating, stomach-churning ride in the back of a jeep, over some old, rutted logging road not far from Aspen and after coughing up dust and passing out briefly from the altitude, somewhere above 10,000 feet. This also after cheating, at least according to real-fisherman standards: I caught the thing with a spoon and a spinning rig. To real fishermen—*fly* fishermen—that's about as honorable as hunting squirrels with a cannon. Nevertheless, there I was holding my first-ever fish, a squirmy glob of quicksilver pinkness, shimmering in the mid-day sun. A life's first! No fishing purist can rob me of the right and pleasure to remember that occasion fondly.

I can also recall now that once I'd glossed over the puniness of the fish to appreciate it with a sense of grand achievement, once I'd gutted it to learn what fish in high-mountain lakes eat for lunch (lots of bugs), once my jeep-rattled stomach had settled and my altitude-fogged brain had cleared, I lifted my head to the hills (hackneyed as *that* sounds), smelled what can properly be described as the cleanness of the air, and thought: The Rocky Mountains are a very cool and righteous place. It wasn't just any old thought, mind you; it was a thought so intense that I swear I thought it *physically*, with my whole body, as if buzzed by a mild electrical shock. Once a thought like that gets into your system, it roots itself forever.

If there are three geographical features an American ought to see as a rite of citizenship, they are the Atlantic Ocean, the Pacific Ocean, and the Rocky Mountains. But beyond the dull obligations of democratic duty, the Rockies impress in other simple and profound ways: simple, in that they are, simply, big and beautiful; profound, in that they invoke a primordial spirit of wilderness and timelessness. The Rockies can inspire an appreciation that escapes logic, that comes on when alpenglow is the last light of day or when new snow highlights each feathered ledge in a band of rock cliffs. It occurs when the wild bloom of tundral, high-alpine meadows exceeds any fair description of color, or when you're standing around, above 10,000 feet, with a stupid grin on your face and a dead fish in your hand. The sentiment is something close to faith.

It is also something beyond accurate representation. On relief maps, the two-billion-year-old Rockies are often drawn as a single string of mountains—forming blisters on the page—and defined primarily by the dotted line of the Continental Divide. Granted, flying into Denver from the east, the Rockies *do* buck up west of Denver with a straight-line, dead-end finality. The plains are over and the mountains begin, and that's that.

But that's *not* that. The Rockies (and here things can get fuzzy, confused by which mountain ranges geologists choose to consider part of the Rockies) cut a swath several hundred miles wide in places and constitute multiple ranges and spurs, each with slightly or markedly differing characteristics. The Colorado Rockies are the highest of the bunch, with the most peaks exceeding 14,000 feet, but ironically they might not seem so because the timberline (the point above which trees won't grow) is unusually high. Lakes and large streams are more common in the northern Rockies, the result of years of snowmelt evaporating less quickly in the cooler climate. The various ranges are distinguished as being separate by rivers, broad basins, and geological history, and each range has its own physical idiosyncrasies, its own climate, even its own flora and fauna. In short, the Rockies aren't, as the maps might suggest, one big strip of interchangeable rock.

A**ll of these ranges do, however, share a similar history. Uplift (the pressure inflicted by the movements and swelling of ancient oceans through aeons of time) preyed upon weaknesses in the land mass (weaknesses known appropriately if unsympathetically as "faults"); the land squeezed thusly could go nowhere but *up*. Couple that phenomenon with volcanic activity—the egestion of magma through those faulty cracks in the earth's crust—and mountains were the result.

Thereafter came the sculpting effects of erosion, with water in various forms (ice, snow, rain, fog, and water falls) being the primary chisels. Over the long, long haul, the characteristic formations that we identify as elemental to mountain structure have taken shape: peaks, ridgelines, bowls, cirques, arêtes, scree slopes (those covered with loose stones or rocky debris), and so on, varying in shape and composition largely because of the rock involved—soft limestone, chippy shale, pumice, basalt, impervious granite. On lower slopes, depending on the quality and availability of soil as well as the harshness of weather, trees have grown: mainly cottonwoods and aspens (or "quakies," as cowboys dubbed them because of the shimmering illusion created by their leaves in the sun and wind); higher up, Douglas fir, lodgepole pine, and Engelmann spruce.

Although there are those rare events when the Earth shrugs and mountains heave with cataclysmic suddenness, the Rockies are essentially a stationary spectacle, or, as they appeared to settlers from the East in the 1800s, a stationary obstacle. One can only imagine the thoughts of the pioneers and railroaders on seeing the Rockies for the first time: A mix, presumably of awe and annoyance; inspired by the mountains' beauty yet flustered by the impending (and inevitable) difficulties in finding passage to the other side.

It is somewhat easier to tap the mindset of prospectors who, after word spread of the discovery of the Comstock lode in western Nevada in the 1850s, came to the Rockies with visions of vast wealth. I'm not sure whether the mountains imposed a ruggedness on the miners and railroad workers, the vanguard of settlement in the Rockies, or whether it was the other way around. Probably a bit of both. These were rowdy men in a rugged country, and I like their story: Civil War deserters, ex-cons, bushwhackers, and miners whose previous claims had come up empty in California, Nevada, or British Columbia. As Glenn Chesney Quiett put it in *They Built the West*, "It was a rough, dangerous, dirty, sweating, hard-working, hard-drinking, free-spending life."

I t was not a life made any more comfortable by Native American tribes residing in the mountains—the Cheyenne, the Crow, the Blackfoot, and others—whose homelands had been invaded by these interlopers pick-axing the countryside. Confrontations were numerous; Quiett relates one story in which the Natives killed a man by lighting a bonfire on his chest, suggesting—quite obviously— that some Natives were going around in very ill humor in regards to the whole idea of the white man's settlement.

Mining, railway construction, lawbreaking, opportunism: The early settlement of the Rockies began taking shape. The route of the railway dictated which Rocky Mountain outposts would become major cities and which wouldn't; that Denver, Colorado, rather than Cheyenne, Wyoming, became the central metropolis of the eastern slope of the Rockies was due largely to politicking by Denver's business elite. It was due also to the paying of a hefty sum to the railroad for the right to have the rail route pass through town. And as David Lavender puts it in his book, *The Rockies*, "The prime determinant of Rocky Mountain history has been the high country's non-ferrous metal mines, principally gold, silver, copper, and lead." Miners came, established towns, settled in (or some did, anyway), and left their mark and legacy. Indeed, towns that have become popular resorts in the latter half of the 20th century—Aspen, Breckenridge, and Telluride in Colorado and Park City in Utah, for example—have their roots in mining.

Unlike geology in its incomprehensible slowness, human activity in the Rockies has evolved and changed in a hurry. It has all transpired in little more than 100 years, which isn't even a hiccup's worth of geological time. As precious-metal mining has ebbed (due as much to a swoon in metal prices as a lack of ore) in the last few decades as a mainstay of the Rocky Mountain economy, a boom in tourism has more than filled the gap. Before the 1960s, visitors who spent time in the Rockies were likely to be bohemians, artists, die-hard sportsmen, and national-park visitors in Winnebagos and Airstreams; or passers-by broken down in transit—axle busted en route to California and the American Dream. Today the region hosts families and tourists of all means.

As much as any single event in the region, the creation of Vail (the ski resort 100 miles west of Denver) in 1964 issued an evangelical message to the world that tourism in the Rockies was for Everyman. In 1963, Vail was an empty valley; today it is a tourism machine generating more than $400 million a year in summer and winter business, but not including real-estate turnover, hardly small potatoes. No wonder other Rockies resorts, following the Vail model in varying degrees, have sprung up since the mid-1960s to tap the mighty tourism dollar.

An additional boost to tourism was the deregulation and "hubbing" of the airline industry in the '80s. Airfares plummeted, and Denver and Salt Lake City became major hubs. During an airfare war in the summer of 1992, I bought a non-stop, round-trip ticket from New York to Salt Lake City for $198. Why not take the trip? It was cheaper than renting a car to go to the Berkshires for the weekend. Visiting the Rockies, in short, has become convenient, comfortable, and relatively inexpensive.

It probably goes without saying, however, that the tourism boom has not gone over well with everyone. The presence of more people and more resort and tourist-service development, interfacing with other economic activity (agriculture, timbering, and in some places mining) and confronting varying levels of hostile environmentalist sentiment, has created a classic clash of interests and principles. There might not be Native Americans immolating trespassers on Main Street or lawbreakers shooting things up with vigilantes. The Rockies have become too civilized, and thank goodness for that. But political confrontation—now that's another story.

Anyone who spends any time in the Rockies is destined to be touched by the exquisite landscape supporting an intricately entwined network of ecosystems—and is subsequently destined to make judgments and establish values accordingly. I can remember, for example, discovering, on a south-facing slope in April, microscopic buds of wildflowers incubating under shards of warm shale. On north-facing slopes, the snow was still several feet deep. Something about that struck me: The land, severe as it is, takes care of itself. It regenerates all on its own. Things work. Far be it from me to butt in on a miracle like that, or to try to improve upon it. Unfortunately, once you accept the premise that you are in the presence of nature efficiently and dispassionately going about its own business—a premise that invariably comes in one form or another to anyone who visits or lives in the Rockies—you tend then to proceed to the next obvious question: What to do about it? Here, things turn troublesome.

In the last decade or so the Rocky Mountain states have become the political focus of land grabbers, tree huggers, civilization escapees, resort developers, ranchers, sportsmen, seasonal workers, the "Hollywood element." Each group has its own sense of righteous propriety and feelings about how the land should be best managed. For whatever reason—and a sheer, alpine beauty comes immediately to mind—almost everyone who comes to the Rockies for any length of time develops an instinctive (if imagined) sense of aboriginal belonging. It's funny: You hear people who have spent barely a year or two of their lives in the Rockies talk wistfully of "the way things used to be," as if their families had lived there for generations. Such reminiscence, of course, implies an attitude about the way things *ought* to be. The upshot is a messy collision of territorial imperatives: Each group is sure it *knows* what is best for the land, and how to defend it against the greed, shortsightedness, or hare-brained thoughtlessness of others. This can lead to such wacky scenarios as ardent wildlife preservationists stalking hunters, who in turn are stalking animals, the idea being that when the hunter gets lined up for a shot, the preservationists make a holy racket, alerting the animal and averting the kill. It is environmental politics right out of *Caddyshack*.

The issues are impossibly, hopelessly complex. In simplest terms the question is: What's the proper formula in balancing the interest of people, the integrity of the land and its resources, and the needs of wildlife? It is a question inevitably muddled in morality, pragmatism, science, self-interest, and the indisputable fact that nobody really knows for sure. As yet, there is no single, Grand Unifying Theory. The result, in part, has been a balkanized checkerboard: private land, wilderness areas, national parks, national forests, national monuments, state parks, state forests, wildlife preserves, Native American reservations. Tread carefully. The rules change from one land type to the next, and the borders aren't always obvious (except, mysteriously, to wild animals, who seem to know more accurately than surveyors where national-park borders are, within which hunting is prohibited). For example, hunting and campfires are legal in national forests but not in national parks; some private landowners are good sports about rights of way, some charge fees, some will have you arrested for just contemplating trespassing. And so on.

Needless to say, different land-use rules astride different land-management philosophies bring on many questions—none it seems, with a fully satisfactory answer. In several noteworthy cases such as with the buffalo and the grizzly, efforts to nurture dwindling species have been markedly successful. But more grizzlies have spiked a sharp rise in grizzly-human encounters in recent years, encounters in which the human, more often than not, gets the worst end of the deal. Nobody wants grizzlies wandering the streets of Kallispell, Montana, or Durango, Colorado, but other than that, what is the bear's rightful habitat? Is death or debilitating injury by bear-mauling a reasonable risk to impose on backcountry travelers for the sake of establishing a habitat for grizzlies? As for the buffalo, ranchers worry that a recent wave of brucellosis among buffalo will eventually infect their cattle. Is it right or wrong to shoot buffalo to save the lives of cows?

When 323,291 acres of forestland burned in Yellowstone in the summer of '88, fire control was a bitter issue: Would it be better to allow a fire to burn its natural course, even if it might threaten wildlife and human settlements? Fire, the argument goes, is part of a forest's natural way of replenishing itself. Or would it be more correct to fight the fire with every resource at one's disposal, snuffing it out as quickly as possible?

Are mountain resorts scars upon the landscape, as some environmentalists might suggest, or nodes of economic sustenance producing, in most respects, less environmental hazard and impact than mining, ranching, or lumbering? Do visitors to the resorts simply overpopulate an environmentally sensitive region? Or, inspired by the beauty of the land, does their visiting heighten their own environmental sensitivity? And do they then pass that new sensitivity on to others?

The ultimate question is: Who knows?

Fortunately, the Rockies are still big country. There is a lot of room for a lot of people to do a lot of shouting, hand-wringing, and placard-waving without upsetting, in any measurable way, the balance of universe. For all the shouting, for all the resort development that boomed in the '80s; for all the real-estate values gone haywire, riding a wave of second-home money; for all the ranchers fencing in land and upsetting animal migratory patterns; for all the sportsmen trekking into the wild and maybe or maybe not being conscientious wilderness citizens; for all the wildlife experts reinvigorating endangered species to good and bad effect; for all the Hollywooders moving to Aspen or Livingston, Montana, and wrecking the neighborhood, as some residents imply; for all the environmentalist militating against growth—for all of that, and above and beyond all of that, the Rockies remain relatively uncongested, undeveloped country, where the air above 12,000 feet is still clean.

The population density of Colorado, by far the most populous of the Rocky Mountain states, is about 32 people per square mile. Compare that, for example, with 190 people per square mile in California or more than 1,000 per square mile (gasp!) in New Jersey. There are more people living in the borough of Brooklyn than in the states of Idaho, Montana, and Wyoming combined.

It is easy to forget, for example, that for all the high-end growing Aspen has done in the last 15 years, the community is still surrounded on all sides by three large wilderness areas: Collegiate Peaks, Hunter/Fryingpan, and Maroon Bells/Snowmass. In all, there are more than 2.5-million acres of designated wilderness in Colorado, an area about twice the size of Delaware and representing only a fraction of the state's undeveloped backcountry. Every time a celebrity sneezes on Main Street, Aspen, national news is made, but none of that nonsense makes a whole heck of a lot of difference in the huge open spaces just beyond town.

Wandering around in those open spaces, one comes occasionally across the relics of human failure, most likely old mining encampments, now rotting and rusting on their slow way toward vanishing into total decay. They are small reminders that however abusive or misguided people are and have been in their use of this land—and in this regard, many of those old miners probably took the cake by digging holes, dumping tailings, and abandoning mining sites with little regard for clean-up—the land has the patience to heal itself. Patience that people, with lifespans of infinitesimal shortness in geologic terms, can't fathom. If the mountains had a voice in all the land-management yakkety-yak, they would be saying something like: "We can wait. We don't care."

And in the shorter term, the Rockies have one other ace in the hole in withstanding the incursion of man: their own magisterial presence, their ruggedness. The Rockies were the last part of the country to be "settled" and may be the only part of the country that will never be broadly developed. One doesn't build cities on 40-degree slopes raked by rockslides and avalanches. The land is too severe and the growing seasons too short to sustain viable commercial cultivation (except, to some degree, timber crops). In other words, the high-mountain wilderness is a great place to visit, but you wouldn't want to live there. And a great place, too, in the summer sun, when the thin air steals breath and the dust settles on old roads, to catch a fish.

1 Essential Information

Before You Go

Visitor Information

Contact the **Colorado Tourism Board** (1625 Broadway, Suite 1700, Denver 80202, tel. 303/592–5510 or 800/433–2656, fax 303/592–5406, ski reports 303/831–7669), the **TravelBank Colorado** (Box 200594, Denver 80220, tel. and fax 303/320–8550), the **Idaho Travel Council** (Department of Commerce, 700 W. State St., Boise 83720, tel. 208/334–2470 or 800/635–7820, fax 208/334–2631, ski reports 800/635–7820), **Travel Montana** (Department of Commerce, 1424 9th Ave., Helena 59620, tel. 406/444–2654 or 800/541–1447, fax 406/444–2808, ski reports 800/847–4868), the **Utah Travel Council** (Council Hall, Capitol Hill, Salt Lake City 84114, tel. 801/538–1030, fax 801/538–1399, ski reports 801/521–8102), and the **Wyoming Division of Tourism** (I–25 at College Dr., Cheyenne 82002, tel. 307/777–7777, fax 307/777–6904, ski reports 800/225–5996).

In Canada U.S. Travel and Tourism Office (480 University Ave., Suite 602, Toronto, Ontario M5G IV2, tel. 416/595–0335, fax 416/595–5211).

Tours and Packages

Should you buy your travel arrangements to the Rockies packaged or do it yourself? There are advantages either way. Buying packaged arrangements saves you money, particularly if you can find a program that includes exactly the features you want. You also get a pretty good idea of what your trip will cost from the outset. Generally, you have two options: fully escorted tours and independent packages. Escorted tours are most often via motorcoach, with a tour director in charge. They're ideal if you don't mind having limited free time and traveling with strangers. Your baggage is handled, your time rigorously scheduled, and most meals planned. Escorted tours are therefore the most hassle-free way to see a destination, as well as frequently the least expensive. Independent packages allow plenty of flexibility. They usually include airline travel and hotels, with certain options available, such as sightseeing, car rental, and excursions. Independent packages are often more expensive than escorted tours, but your time is your own.

While you can book directly through tour operators, you will pay no more to go through a travel agent, who will be able to tell you about tours and packages from a number of operators. Whatever program you ultimately choose, be sure to find out exactly what is included: taxes, tips, transfers, meals, baggage handling, ground transportation, entertainment, excursions, sports, or recreation (and rental equipment if necessary). Ask about the level of hotel used, its location, the size of its rooms, the kind of beds, and its amenities, such as pool, room service, or programs for children, if they're important to you. Find out the operator's cancellation penalties. Nearly everyone charges them, and the only way to avoid them is to buy trip-cancellation insurance (*see* Insurance, *below*). Also ask about the single supplement, a surcharge assessed to solo travelers. Some operators do not make you pay it if you agree to be matched up with a roommate of the same sex, even if one is not found by departure time. Remember that a program that has features you won't use may not be the most cost-wise choice.

Fully Escorted Tours Escorted tours are usually sold in three categories: deluxe, first class, and tourist or budget class. The most important differences are the price, of course, and the level of accommodations. Some operators specialize in one category, while others offer a range.

Contact **Maupintour** (Box 807, Lawrence, KS 66044, tel. 913/843–1211 or 800/255–4266) and **Tauck Tours** (11 Wilton Rd., Westport, CT 06881, tel. 203/226–6911 or 800/468–2825) in the deluxe category; **Bixler Tours** (Box 37, Hiram, OH 44234, tel. 216/569–3222 or 800/325–5087), **Domenico Tours** (751 Broadway, Bayonne, NJ 07002, tel. 201/823–8687 or 800/554–8687), **Gadabout Tours** (700 E. Tahquitz Way, Palm Springs, CA 92262, 619/325–5556 or 800/952–5068), **Globus-Gateway** (150 S. Los Robles Ave., Pasadena, CA 91101, tel. 818/449–0919 or 800/556–5454), and **Maitland Travel Services, Inc.** (38 2nd St. E, Kalispell, MT 59901, tel. 406/755–1032) in the first-class category.

Most itineraries are jam-packed with sightseeing, so you see a lot in a short amount of time (usually one place per day). To judge just how fast paced the tour is, review the itinerary carefully. If you are in a different hotel each night, you will be getting up early each day to head out, travel to your next destination, do some sightseeing, have dinner, and go to bed; then you'll start all over again. If you want some free time, make sure it's mentioned in the tour brochure; if you want to be escorted to every meal, confirm that any tour you consider does that. Also, when comparing programs, be sure to find out if the motorcoach is air-conditioned and has a rest room on board. Make your selection based on price and stops on the itinerary.

Independent Packages Independent packages are offered by airlines, tour operators who may also do escorted programs, and any number of other companies from large, established firms to small, new entrepreneurs.

Among the airlines offering independent packages are **America West** (tel. 800/247–5692), **American Airlines Fly AAway Vacations** (tel. 800/321–2121), **Continental Airlines' Grand Destinations** (tel. 800/634–5555), **Delta Dream Vacations** (tel. 800/872–7786), and **United Airlines' Vacation Planning Center** (800/328–6877). Other operators include **Caravan** (401 N. Michigan Ave., Suite 3325, Chicago, IL 60611, tel. 312/321–9800 or 800/227–2826) and **Gogo Tours** (available only through travel agents).

Their programs come in a wide range of prices based on levels of luxury and options—in addition to hotel and airfare, sightseeing, car rental, transfers, admission to local attractions, and other extras. Note that when pricing different packages, it sometimes pays to purchase the same arrangements separately, as when a rock-bottom promotional airfare is being offered, for example. Again, base your choice on what's available at your budget for the destinations you want to visit.

Special-Interest Travel Special-interest programs may be fully escorted or independent. Some require a certain amount of expertise, but most are for the average traveler with an interest and are usually hosted by experts in the subject matter. When the program is escorted, it enjoys the advantages and disadvantages of all escorted trips; because your fellow travelers are apt to be passionate or knowledgeable about the subject, they can prove as enjoyable a part of your travel experience as the destination itself. The price range is wide, but the cost is usually higher—sometimes a lot higher—than for ordinary escorted tours and packages, because of the expert guidance and special activities.

Biking **Backroads** (1516 5th St., Suite Q333, Berkeley, CA 94710, tel. 510/527–1555 or 800/245–3874) has escorted trips with camping or inn accommodations; **American Youth Hostels** (Box 37613, Washington, DC 20013-7613, tel. 202/783–6161) and **Bikecentennial** (Box 8308, Missoula, MT 59807, tel. 406/721–1776) have extensive programs for people of all ages and skill levels.

Camping Contact **AmeriCan Adventures** (79 Cherry Hill Rd., Pomfret Ct., CT 06259, tel. 203/974–3231) and **Trek America/Adventure Camping Tours** (Box 470, Blairstown, NJ 07825, tel. 908/362–9198 or 800/221–0596).

Nature The **National Audubon Society** (National Environmental Education Center, 613 Riversville Rd., Greenwich, CT 06831, tel. 203/869–2017) has a variety of natural-history camps and programs in the national parks, among them a winter ecology and nature-photography workshop in Yellowstone, and the **National Wildlife Federation** (1400 16th St. NW, Washington, DC 20036, tel. 703/790–4363 or 800/432–6564) runs weeklong national park seminars that include nature hikes, classes, and workshops. **Questers Worldwide Nature Tours** (275 Park Ave. S, New York, NY 10010, tel. 212/673–3120 or 800/468–8668) has naturalist-led luxury tours.

River Rafting Contact **O.A.R.S.** (Box 67, Angels Camp, CA 95222, tel. 209/736–4677) for a good selection of trips.

Other Outdoor Programs The **Sierra Club** (730 Polk St., San Francisco, CA 94109, tel. 415/776–2211) has volunteer trail-maintenance trips on its huge roster of varied programs. **Womantrek** (Box 20643, Seattle, WA 98102, tel. 206/325–4772 or 800/477–TREK) leads women on hiking, biking, and rafting trips to some of the region's national parks, while **Off the Beaten Path** (109 E. Main St., Bozeman, MT 59715, tel. 406/586–1311, fax 406/587–4147) custom-tailors weeklong tours ranging from hiking trips in Yellowstone to horse-pack and fly-fishing trips in Wyoming.

Tips for British Travelers

Government Tourist Office Contact the **U. S. Travel and Tourism Administration** (Box 1EN, London W1A 1EN, tel. 071/495–4466).

Passports and Visas British subjects need a valid 10-year passport. A visa is not necessary unless (1) you are planning to stay more than 90 days; (2) your trip is for purposes other than vacation; (3) you have at some time been refused a visa or refused admission to the United States or have been required to leave by the U.S. Immigration and Naturalization Service; or (4) you do not have a return or onward ticket. You will need to fill out the visa waiver form 1–94W, supplied by the airline.

To apply for a visa or to obtain more information, call the U.S. Embassy's visa information line (tel. 0891/200290; calls cost 48 pence per minute or 36 pence per minute cheap rate). If you qualify for visa-free travel but want a visa anyway, you must apply in writing, enclosing a self-addressed envelope, to the U.S. Embassy's Visa Branch (5 Upper Grosvenor St., London W1A 2JB), or, for residents of Northern Ireland, to the U.S. Consulate General (Queen's House, Queen St., Belfast BT1 6EO). Submit a completed nonimmigrant visa application (form 156), a valid passport, a photograph, and evidence of your intended departure from the United States after a temporary visit. If you require a visa, call 0891/234224 to schedule an interview.

Customs British visitors aged 21 or over may import the following into the United States: 200 cigarettes or 50 cigars or 2 kilograms of tobacco; 1 U.S. liter of alcohol; gifts to the value of $100. Restricted items include meat products, seeds, plants, and fruits. Never carry illegal drugs.

Insurance Most tour operators, travel agents, and insurance agents sell specialized policies covering accidents, medical expenses, personal liability, trip cancellation, and loss or theft of personal property. Some policies include coverage for delayed departure and legal expenses, winter sports, accidents, or driving abroad. You can also purchase an annual travel-insurance policy valid for every trip you make during the year in which it's purchased (usually only trips of fewer than 90 days). Before you leave, make sure you will be covered if you have a preexisting medical condition or are pregnant; your insurers may not pay for routine or continuing treatment, or they may require a note from your doctor certifying your fitness to travel.

The **Association of British Insurers**, a trade association representing 450 insurance companies, advises extra medical coverage for visitors to the United States. For advice by phone or a free booklet, *Holiday Insurance*, that sets out what to expect from a vacation-insurance policy and gives price guidelines, contact the Association of British Insurers (51 Gresham St., London EC2V 7HQ, tel. 071/600–3333; 30 Gordon St., Glasgow G1 3PU, tel. 041/226–3905; Scottish Provincial Bldg., Donegal Sq. W, Belfast BT1 6JE, tel. 0232/249176; call for other locations).

Tour Operators Among those companies you might consider as you plan your trip to the Rockies are **Cosmos** (Ground Floor, Dale House, Tiviot Dale, Stockport, Cheshire SK1 1TB, tel. 061/480–5799), **International Routes** (Clarendon House, Clarendon Rd., Eccles, Manchester M30 9AA, tel. 061/707–4404, fax 061/707–4403), **Kuoni Travel** (Kuoni House, Dorking, Surrey RH5 4AZ, tel. 0306/74222, fax 0306/740719), **Premier Holidays** (Premier Travel Center, Westbrook, Milton Rd., Cambridge CB4 1YQ, tel. 0223/355977, fax 0223/324373), **Ramblers Holidays, Ltd.** (Box 43, Welwin Garden, Hertfordshire AL8 6PQ, tel. 0707/331133, fax 0707/333276), and **Trek America, Ltd.** (Trek House, The Bullring, Deddington, Banbury, Oxon OX15 OTT, tel. 0869/38777, fax 0869/38846).

Airports and Airlines Service between Great Britain and the central areas of the United States has improved remarkably over the past couple of years. Airlines include **American Airlines** (tel. 0800/010151), **British Airways** (tel. 081/897–4000 or 0345/222111), **Continental** (tel. 0293/776464), **Delta Airlines** (tel. 0800/414767), **Northwest** (tel. 0293/28822), **TWA** (tel. 0800/22222), **United Airlines** (tel. 0800/888555), **USAir** (tel. 0800/777333), and **Virgin Atlantic** (tel.

0293/562000). Most serve at least the New York area, plus their own U.S. hubs, which include Chicago, Denver, and Salt Lake City. British Airways serves the largest number of U.S. cities, and those it doesn't can be reached on connecting flights from other carriers.

Fares on scheduled flights vary considerably. January to March are the cheapest months to fly, and midweek flights nearly always offer some reductions.

Thomas Cook Ltd. can often book you on very inexpensive flights. Call the branch nearest you at least 21 days in advance of your departure and ask to be put through to the Airfare Warehouse. Also check out the small ads in the Sunday newspapers and in magazines such as *Time Out*.

Car Rentals Make the arrangements from home to avoid inconvenience, save money, and guarantee yourself a vehicle. Major firms include **Alamo** (tel. 0800/272200), **Budget** (tel. 0800/181181), **EuroDollar** (tel. 0895/233300), **Europcar** (tel. 081/950–5050), **Hertz** (tel. 081/679–1799). In the United States you must be 21 to rent a car; rates may be higher for those under 25. Extra costs cover child seats, compulsory for children under five (about $3 per day); additional drivers (around $1.50 per day); and the all-but-compulsory collision damage waiver (*see* Insurance and Collision Damage Waiver, *below*). To pick up your reserved car, you will need the reservation voucher, a passport, a United Kingdom driver's license, and a travel-insurance policy covering each driver.

Travelers with Main information sources include the **Royal Association for Dis-**
Disabilities **ability and Rehabilitation** (RADAR, 25 Mortimer St., London W1N 8AB, tel. 071/637–5400), which publishes travel information for the disabled in Britain, and **Mobility International** (228 Borough High St., London SE1 1JX, tel. 071/403–5688), the headquarters of an international membership organization that serves as a clearinghouse of travel information for people with disabilities.

When to Go

Summer is one of the Rockies' two big seasons. Hotels in major tourist destinations book up early, especially in July and August, and hikers crowd the backcountry from June through Labor Day. Temperatures rarely rise into the 90s.

Winter is also prime time. Ski resorts buzz from December to early April, especially during Christmas and President's weeks.

If you don't mind sometimes-capricious weather, spring and fall are opportune seasons to visit; rates drop and crowds are nonexistent, so that you may enjoy a corner of Yellowstone all to yourself. Spring's pleasures are somewhat limited, since snow usually blocks the high country well into June, and mountain-pass roads such as the famous Going-to-the-Sun Road in Glacier National Park stay closed into June. But spring is a good time for fishing, rafting on rivers swollen with snowmelt, birding, and wildlife-viewing. In fall, aspen splash the mountainsides with gold, and wildlife come down to lower elevations. The fish are spawning, and the angling is excellent.

Climate Summer in the Rockies begins in late June or early July. Days are warm, with highs often in the 80s, while nighttime temperatures fall to the 40s and 50s. Afternoon thunderstorms are common over the higher peaks. Fall begins in September, often with a week of unsettled weather around mid-month, followed by four to six gorgeous weeks of Indian summer—frosty nights and warm days. Winter creeps in during November, and deep snows have arrived by December. Temperatures usually hover near freezing by day, thanks to the surprisingly warm mountain sun, dropping considerably overnight, occasionally as low as -60° F. Winter tapers off in March, though snow lingers into April on valley bottoms and into July on mountain passes. The Rockies have a reputation for extreme weather, but that cuts two ways: No condition ever lasts for long. What follows are the average daily maximum and minimum temperatures for the region.

Aspen, CO	**Jan.**	33F	1C	**May**	64F	18C	**Sept.**	71F	22C
		6	−14		32	0		35	2
	Feb.	37F	3C	**June**	73F	23C	**Oct.**	60F	16C
		8	−13		37	3		28	− 2
	Mar.	42F	6C	**July**	80F	27C	**Nov.**	44F	7C
		15	− 9		44	7		15	− 9
	Apr.	53F	12C	**Aug.**	78F	26C	**Dec.**	37F	3C
		24	− 4		42	6		8	−13

Boise, ID	**Jan.**	37F	3C	**May**	71F	22C	**Sept.**	75F	24C
		21	− 6		44	7		46	8
	Feb.	42F	6C	**June**	80F	27C	**Oct.**	64F	18C
		26	− 3		51	11		39	4
	Mar.	53F	12C	**July**	89F	32C	**Nov.**	50F	10C
		33	1		57	14		30	− 1
	Apr.	62F	17C	**Aug.**	87F	31C	**Dec.**	39F	4C
		37	3		55	13		24	− 4

Helena, MT	**Jan.**	28F	− 2C	**May**	62F	17C	**Sept.**	66F	19C
		12	−11		41	5		44	7
	Feb.	32F	0C	**June**	71F	22C	**Oct.**	55F	13C
		15	− 9		48	9		35	2
	Mar.	42F	6C	**July**	80F	27C	**Nov.**	41F	5C
		23	− 5		53	12		24	− 4
	Apr.	53F	12C	**Aug.**	78F	26C	**Dec.**	32F	0C
		33	1		53	12		17	− 8

Salt Lake City, UT	**Jan.**	35F	2C	**May**	73F	23C	**Sept.**	78F	26C
		17	− 8		44	7		48	9
	Feb.	41F	5C	**June**	82F	28C	**Oct.**	66F	19C
		24	− 4		51	11		39	4
	Mar.	51F	11C	**July**	91F	33C	**Nov.**	48F	9C
		30	− 1		60	16		28	− 2
	Apr.	62F	17C	**Aug.**	89F	32C	**Dec.**	39F	4C
		37	3		60	16		21	− 6

Sheridan, WY	**Jan.**	33F	– 1C	**May**	66F	19C	**Sept.**	71F	22C
		6	–14		39	4		41	5
	Feb.	35F	2C	**June**	75F	24C	**Oct.**	60F	16C
		10	–12		48	9		30	– 1
	Mar.	46F	8C	**July**	86F	30C	**Nov.**	46F	8C
		21	– 6		53	12		19	– 7
	Apr.	55F	13C	**Aug.**	84F	29C	**Dec.**	35F	2C
		30	– 1		50	10		10	–12

Altitude You may feel dizzy and weak and find yourself breathing heavily—signs that the thin mountain air isn't giving you your accustomed dose of oxygen. Take it easy and rest often for a few days until you're acclimatized; throughout your stay drink plenty of water and watch your alcohol consumption. If you experience severe headaches and nausea, see a doctor. It is easy, especially in Colorado, where highways climb to 12,000 feet and higher, to go too high too fast. The remedy for altitude-related discomfort is to go down quickly, into heavier air. Other altitude-related problems include dehydration and overexposure to the sun due to the thin air.

Information Sources For current weather conditions for cities in the United States and abroad, plus the local time and helpful travel tips, call the **Weather Channel Connection** (tel. 900/WEATHER; 95¢ per minute) from a Touch-Tone phone.

Festivals and Seasonal Events

Contact state tourism offices (*see* Visitor Information, *above*) for more on these events.

January The big events of the month are Denver's two-week **National Western Stock Show and Rodeo**, the world's largest livestock show, and the annual **Sundance Film Festival** in Park City, Utah, which lures film aficionados as well as industry executives to seminars, workshops, and previews of films from around the world. Meanwhile, throughout the Rockies, ski competitions such as the **Steamboat Springs Annual Northwest Bank Cowboy Downhill** and Breckenridge's **Ullr Fest and World Cup Freestyle,** both in Colorado, keep ski areas lively with races, torchlight skiing, and other events. Other snow towns stage winter carnivals such as the huge one in **McCall, Idaho,** where you'll find world-class ice sculptures along with the usual parades, fireworks, and on-the-snow competitions.

February In Colorado, the **Ice Fishing Contest** in Walden (tel. 303/723–4600) consists of fishing on four lakes for the nine largest fish. In Idaho, the **Lionel Hampton Chevron Jazz Festival** (tel. 208/882–3581) in Moscow attracts some of the world's top jazz musicians. Montana's **Race to the Sky** (tel. 406/442–2335) dogsled race in Helena is a 500-mile race along the Continental Divide; it's the longest in the lower 48 states. There is also a 250-mile race for public viewing at check-in sites. The **Western Montana Wine Festival** in Missoula features tastings of regional and West Coast wineries, accompanied by superb food. Wyoming's **Wild West Winter Carnival** (tel. 307/876–2796) at Boyston State Park has dog races, a demolition derby, softball, and golf, all on ice, as well as snowmobile races, and a "snowdeo."

March In Colorado, Springfield holds one of its two annual **Equinox Festivals** as the sun turns nearby Crack Cave into a sort of Stonehenge, highlighting the ancient Ogam calendar and writings of possible Celtic origin, dating to around 471. Pocatello, Idaho, is the site of the **Dodge National Circuit Finals Rodeo,** which draws the top two cowboys from each of 12 national circuits. **St. Patrick's Day** events occur in Butte and Lewiston, Idaho, and in Missoula, Montana; the latter's parade is one of the state's largest. And collectors from around the world attend the **C. M. Russell Auction of Original Art,** held in Great Falls, Montana.

April　On Easter, look around for nondenominational **Easter sunrise services;** Park City, Utah, mounts a big annual **Easter Egg Hunt.** Then there are the fun events such as **Kit Carson's Annual Mountain Man Rendezvous** in Kit Carson, Colorado; the citywide **Dogwood Festival** in Lewiston, Idaho. The annual **International Wildlife Film Festival** in Missoula, Montana, is one of two wildlife film festivals in the world.

May　Look into the **Fort Vasquez Fur Trappers Rendezvous,** in Platteville, Colorado, where fur-trading days return with demonstrations, contests, costumes, games, and Native American crafts and dances. Sandpoint, Idaho, celebrates summer's beginning with a **Waterfest,** including a sand-sculpture contest, a regatta, and waterskiing events. **Buzzard Day** celebrates spring and the return of turkey vultures to Makoshika State Park in Glendive, Montana. In Montana's cherry-growing country, Polson mounts a **Cherry Blossom Festival** and Big Fork does a laid-back **Cherry Blossom Weekend,** with a farmers' market, cherry desserts, and various competitions. In Miles City, Montana, rodeo stock for the upcoming season is auctioned off at the **Bucking Horse Sale.** The huge **Flaming Gorge Fishing Derby** in Rock Springs, Wyoming, draws 350 teams of anglers.

June　The **Silly Homebuilt River Raft Race,** held in Las Animas, Colorado, keeps spectators guessing which improbable floating contraptions will reach the finish line and which will explore the bottom of the Arkansas River. Meanwhile, the season of music festivals and cultural events gets into swing in Colorado with Telluride's weekend-long **Bluegrass Festival** (tel. 303/728–3041) and Boulder's **Colorado Shakespeare Festival** (tel. 303/492–1527), one of the top three in the country; in Idaho with Wieser's **Old-Time Fiddlers Contest,** which draws the nation's best to compete (tel. 208/549–0452); in Montana with Helena's **Montana Traditional Jazz Festival** (tel. 406/449–7969); and in Wyoming with the **Grand Teton Music Festival** in Teton Village (tel. 307/733–3050 or 307/733–1128). The **Statewide Idaho Women's Challenge** (tel. 208/344–7777) is the nation's premier cycling race for women. The **International Barbed Wire Show** in Miles City, Montana (tel. 406/232–0577), features contemporary and antique wire from all over the world. Also in Montana are the **Badlands Indian Celebration** at the Fort Peck Indian Reservation in Brockton (tel. 406/768–5151) and the **Custer's Last Stand Reenactment** in Hardin, involving more than 200 riders (tel. 406/665–1672). In Utah, look for Provo's **National Doll Festival** at the McCurdy Doll Museum (tel. 801/377–9935), and in Wyoming note the **Woodchoppers Jamboree** (tel. 307/326–8855) in Saratoga, where competitors vie for the title of Rocky Mountain Champion Lumberjack.

July　The Rockies celebrate an all-American Fourth of July. Among the largest celebrations is the **Fantastic Fourth** in Frisco, Colorado (tel. 303/668–5800) and the old-fashioned **Cody Stampede** (tel. 307/587–2297) in Buffalo Bill Cody's eponymous Wyoming hometown; also look into the **Fourth of July Parade and Pyrotechnic Extravaganza** (tel. 406/646–7701) in West Yellowstone, Montana.

Cheyenne Frontier Days (tel. 307/778–7200) in Cheyenne, Wyoming, is the world's largest outdoor rodeo. Other events commemorate the Rocky Mountains' past: in Utah, the monthlong **Days of '47** (tel. 801/254–2653) in Riverton and the **Railroaders Festival** (tel. 801/471–2209) in Ogden, where spike-driving and buffalo-chip-throwing contests and the Golden Spike Ceremony commemorate the completion of America's first transcontinental railroad; and in Wyoming, the **Green River Rendezvous** (tel. 307/367–4101) near Pinedale, a reenactment of mountain life in the 1830s. Thirty to 40 hot-air balloons are a colorful sight over the mountains at the **Teton Valley Hot-Air Balloon Races** (tel. 208/765–2500) in Driggs, Idaho. And don't miss the **Montana State Fair** (tel. 406/727–8900) in Great Falls.

August Who ever would have guessed that the largest outdoor Middle Eastern dance festival in the nation, featuring 200 dancers from around the country, would be held in Salt Lake City? But there you have it, the **Belly Dancing Festival** (tel. 801/486–7780). Rodeos are more typical late-summer fare; witness the **Pikes Peak or Bust Rodeo** (tel. 719/635–7506, 800/368–4748 outside the state) in Colorado Springs, Colorado's largest. Equally common are Native American events showcasing traditional songs, dances, and crafts, such as **Nez Percé Cultural Days** (tel. 208/843–2261) in Spalding, Idaho; the **Shoshone-Bannock Indian Festival** (tel. 208/785–0510) in Fort Hall, Idaho; and the **Crow Indian Fair and Rodeo** (tel. 406/638–2601) in Crow Agency, Montana, the self-styled tepee capital of the world. Boise's **Western Idaho Fair** (tel. 208/376–3247) is the state's biggest. Also note late August's **Cowboy Poetry Gathering** (tel. 800/548–3390) in Lewistown, Montana, where U.S. and Canadian performers share verses about a man and a horse following a cow.

September In Colorado, Cripple Creek's **Aspen Leaf Tours** (Cripple Creek Chamber of Commerce, tel. 719/689–2169), free trail tours by jeep through ghost towns and old gold mines, show off the brilliant mountain aspens, and the **Denver International Air Show** (tel. 303/892–1112), the country's largest such event, draws jet teams from around the world, antique aircraft, parachutists, high-tech military planes, and aerial acrobats. In Idaho, you'll find lumberjack competitions at the **Clearwater County Fair and Lumberjack Days** (tel. 208/476–4335) in Orofino and **Idaho Spud Day** (tel. 208/263–2161) in Shelley, with the World Spud-Picking Championship. Montana hosts the **"Running of the Sheep" sheep drive** (tel. 406/326–9911) in Reedpoint, an event comparable to Pamplona's running of the bulls but with hundreds of sturdy Montana-bred woollies charging down Main Street. There's also the big **Utah State Fair** (tel. 801/538–8440). Wyoming marks the season with the **Jackson Hole Fall Arts Festival** (tel. 307/733–3316), with concerts, art, poetry, dance, and crafts workshops and lectures throughout the valley.

October If the foliage doesn't provide color enough, try the **Flathead Balloon Festival** (tel. 406/756–9091 or 800/543–3105) in Kalispell, Montana. Billings's **Northern International Livestock Expo Cowboy Review** (tel. 406/246–2495) is Montana's largest such event. The **Microbrewery Beer Fest** (tel. 406/862–3000) at

Grouse Mountain Lodge in Whitefish, Montana, showcases the small-batch beers of local breweries.

November One of the most memorable events is the **eagle watch** (tel. 406/444–4720 or 406/444–4274) near Helena, Montana, where majestic bald eagles flock to the Missouri River to dive for kokanee salmon. Steelhead are the quarry at Idaho's **Great Snake Lake Steelhead Derby** (tel. 208/743–3531) in Lewiston. In Colorado, look for **Creede's Chocolate Festival** (tel. 719/658–2374 or 800/327–2102), which puts chocolates of every size, shape, and description in every corner of town.

December Christmas is the focus. Denver hosts the **World's Largest Christmas Lighting Display** (tel. 303/892–1112), with 20,000 floodlights washing civic buildings in reds, greens, blues, and yellows, while Silverton searches for a yule log at its **Yule Log Celebration** (tel. 303/387–5654 or 800/752–4494). In Idaho, Sandpoint becomes "Santapoint" for the **Hometown Christmas** (tel. 800/800–2106). In Montana, there's an **Old-Time Christmas Exhibit** (tel. 406/728–3476) in Missoula's historic fort, and Bozeman's **Christmas Stroll** (tel. 406/586–5421) features sleigh rides, carolers, hot-chocolate stands, holiday lights, and late shopping hours. Salt Lake City's show is the **Christmas Lights** ceremony (tel. 801/240–3318) at Temple Square. In Wyoming, the biggest deal is the opening of the **National Elk Refuge** (tel. 307/733–3316) in Jackson in late December—your opportunity to take a horse-drawn sleigh ride among a herd of elk numbering 8,000–9,000 strong. For the holidays, many ski areas throughout the Rockies mount **torchlight parades**, with large groups of torch-bearing ski instructors tracing patterns down the mountainside.

What to Pack

Clothing Informality reigns in the Rockies, and casual clothing is acceptable—even expected—in most places. Jeans, sport shirts, and T-shirts fit in almost everywhere, for both men and women. The few restaurants and performing-arts events where dressier outfits are required, largely in resorts and larger cities, are the exception.

If you plan to spend much time outdoors, and certainly if you go in winter, choose clothing appropriate for cold and wet weather. Cotton clothing, including denim—although fine on warm, dry days—can be uncomfortable when it gets wet and when the weather's cold. A better choice is clothing made of wool or any of a number of new synthetics that provide warmth without bulk and maintain their insulating properties even when wet.

In summer, you'll want shorts during the day. But because early morning and night can be cold, and high passes windy, pack a sweater and a light jacket, and perhaps also a wool cap and gloves. Try layering—a T-shirt under another shirt under a jacket—and peel off layers as you go. For walks and hikes, you'll need sturdy footwear. To take you into the wilds, boots should have thick soles and plenty of ankle support; if your shoes are new and you plan to spend much time on the trail, break them in at home. Bring a day pack for short hikes, along with a canteen or water bottle, and don't forget rain gear.

In winter, prepare for below-zero temperatures with good boots, warm socks and liners, long johns, a well-insulated jacket, and a warm hat and mittens.

If you attend dances and other events at Native American reservations, dress conservatively—skirts or long pants for women, long pants for men—or you may be asked to leave.

Miscellaneous Sunglasses and a sun hat are essential at high altitudes; the thinner atmosphere requires sunscreen with a greater SPF than you might need at lower elevations. Bring an extra pair of eyeglasses or contact lenses. If you have a health problem that may require you to purchase a prescription drug, pack enough to last the duration of the trip. And don't forget to pack a list of the addresses of offices that supply refunds for lost or stolen traveler's checks.

Luggage Free baggage allowances on an airline depend on the carrier,
Regulations the route, and the class of your ticket. In general, on domestic flights you are entitled to check two bags—neither exceeding 62 inches, or 158 centimeters (length + width + height), or weighing more than 70 pounds (32 kilograms). A third piece may be brought aboard as a carryon; its total dimensions are generally limited to fewer than 45 inches (114 centimeters), so it will fit easily under the seat in front of you or in the overhead compartment. As there are variations, ask in advance. The single rule, a Federal Aviation Administration safety regulation that pertains to carry-on baggage on U.S. airlines, requires only that carryons be properly stowed and allows the airline to limit allowances and tailor them to different aircraft and operational conditions. Charges for excess, oversize, or overweight pieces vary, so inquire before you pack.

Safeguarding Your Before leaving home, itemize your bags' contents and their
Luggage worth; this list will help you estimate the extent of your loss if your bags go astray. To minimize that risk, tag them inside and out with your name, address, and phone number. (If you use your home address, cover it so that potential thieves can't see it.) At check-in, make sure that the tag attached by baggage handlers bears the correct three-letter code for your destination. If your bags do not arrive with you, or if you detect damage, do not leave the airport until you've filed a written report with the airline.

Insurance In the event of loss, damage, or theft on domestic flights, airlines limit their liability to $1,250 per passenger. Excess-valuation insurance can be bought directly from the airline at check-in but leaves your bags vulnerable on the ground. Your own homeowner's policy may fill the gap, or you may want special luggage insurance. Sources include **The Travelers Companies** (1 Tower Sq., Hartford, CT 06183, tel. 203/277–0111 or 800/243–3174) and **Wallach and Company, Inc.** (Box 480, Middleburg, VA 22117, tel. 703/687–3166 or 800/237–6615), underwritten by Lloyd's, London.

Traveler's Checks

Although you will want plenty of cash when visiting small cities or rural areas, traveler's checks are usually preferable. The most widely recognized are **American Express, Barclay's, Thomas Cook,** and those issued by major commercial banks such as **Citibank** and **Bank of America.** American Express also issues Traveler's Cheques for Two, which can be signed and used by you or your traveling companion. Some checks are free; usually the issuing company or the bank at which you make your purchase charges 1% of the checks' face value as a fee. Be sure to buy a few checks in small denominations to cash toward the end of your trip, in case you don't want to be left carrying too much cash. Always record the numbers of checks as you spend them, and keep this list separate from the checks.

Getting Money from Home

Cash Machines   Automated-teller machines (ATMs) are proliferating; many are tied to international networks such as **Cirrus** and **Plus.** You can use your bank card at ATMs away from home to withdraw money from an account and get cash advances on a credit-card account (provided your card has been programmed with a personal identification number, or PIN). Check in advance on limits on withdrawals and cash advances within specified periods. Remember that on cash advances you are charged interest from the day you get the money from ATMs, just as you are from tellers. And note that transaction fees for ATM withdrawals outside your home turf will probably be higher than for withdrawals at home.

For specific Cirrus locations in the United States and Canada, call 800/424–7787 (for U.S. Plus locations, 800/843–7587) and press the area code and first three digits of the number you're calling from (or the calling area where you want an ATM).

American Express Cardholder Services   The company's **Express Cash** system lets you withdraw cash and/or traveler's checks from a worldwide network of 57,000 American Express dispensers and participating bank ATMs. You must enroll first (call 800/CASH–NOW for a form and allow two weeks for processing). Withdrawals are charged not to your card but to a designated bank account. You can withdraw up to $1,000 per seven-day period on the basic card, more if your card is Gold or Platinum. There is a 2% fee (minimum $2.50, maximum $10) for each cash transaction, and a 1% fee for traveler's checks (except for the Platinum card), which are available only from American Express dispensers.

At AmEx offices, cardholders can also cash personal checks for up to $1,000 in any seven-day period; of this, $200 can be in cash, more if available, with the balance paid in traveler's checks, for which all but Platinum cardholders pay a 1% fee. Higher limits apply to the Gold and Platinum cards.

Wiring Money   You don't have to be a cardholder to send or receive an **American Express MoneyGram** for up to $10,000. To send one, go to an American Express MoneyGram agent, pay up to $1,000 with a credit card and anything over that in cash, and phone a transaction reference number to your intended recipient, who needs only present identification and the reference number to the nearest MoneyGram agent to pick up the cash. There are MoneyGram agents in more than 60 countries (call 800/543–4080 for locations). Fees range from 5% to 10%, depending on the amount and how you pay. You can't use American Express, which is really a convenience card—only Discover, MasterCard, and Visa credit cards.

You can also use **Western Union.** To wire money, take either cash or a check to the nearest office. (Or you can call and use a credit card.) Fees are roughly 5%–10%. Money sent from the United States or Canada will be available for pickup at agent locations in the Rockies within minutes. (Note that once the money is in the system it can be picked up at *any* location. You don't have to miss your train waiting for it to arrive in City A, because if there's an agent in City B, where you're headed, you can pick it up there, too.) There are approximately 20,000 agents worldwide (call 800/325–6000 for locations).

What It Will Cost

Prices for dining and lodging in the Rockies are generally lower than in major North American cities in other areas. First-class hotel rooms in Denver, Salt Lake City, Boise, Missoula, and Cheyenne cost from $75 to $175 a night, although some "value" hotel rooms go for $40 to $60, and, as elsewhere in the United States, rooms in national budget chain motels go for around $30 nightly. Weekend packages, offered by most city hotels, cut prices up to 50% (but may not be available in peak winter or summer seasons). As a rule, costs outside the major cities are lower, except in some of the deluxe resorts. A cup of coffee costs between 50¢ and $1, the price for a hamburger runs between $3 and $5, and a beer at a bar generally is between $1.50 and $3.

Traveling with Cameras and Camcorders

Film and Cameras If your camera is new or if you haven't used it for a while, shoot and develop a few rolls of film before leaving home. Pack some lens tissue and an extra battery for your built-in light meter, and invest in an inexpensive skylight filter, to both protect your lens and provide some definition in hazy shots. Store film in a cool, dry place—never in the car's glove compartment or on the shelf under the rear window.

Films above ISO 400 are more sensitive to damage from airport-security X-rays than others; very-high-speed films, ISO 1,000 and above, are exceedingly vulnerable. To protect your film, don't put it in checked luggage; carry it with you in a plastic bag and ask for a hand inspection. Such requests are honored at American airports. Don't depend on a lead-lined bag to protect film in checked luggage—the airline may very well turn up the dosage of radiation to see what you've got in there. Airport metal detectors do not harm film, although you'll set off the alarm if you walk through one with a roll in your pocket. Call the Kodak Information Center (tel. 800/242–2424) for details.

Camcorders Before your trip, put new or long-unused camcorders through their paces, and practice panning and zooming. Invest in a skylight filter to protect the lens, and check the lithium battery that lights up the LCD (liquid crystal display) modes. As for the rechargeable nickel-cadmium batteries that are the camera's power source, take along an extra pair, so while you're using your camcorder you'll have one battery ready and another recharging.

Videotape Unlike still-camera film, videotape is not damaged by X-rays. However, it may well be harmed by the magnetic field of a walk-through metal detector. Airport-security personnel may want you to turn the camcorder on to prove that that's what it is, so make sure the battery is charged when you get to the airport.

Car Rentals

All major car-rental companies are represented in the Rockies, including **Avis** (tel. 800/331–1212, 800/879–2847 in Canada), **Budget** (tel. 800/527–0700), **Dollar** (tel. 800/800–4000), **Hertz** (tel. 800/654–3131, 800/263-0600 in Canada), and **National** (tel. 800/227–7368). **Alamo** (tel. 800/327–9633) and **Thrifty** (tel. 800/ 367–2277) often have the lowest rates, but may not have offices in some cities. Unlimited-mileage rates range from around $24 per day for an economy car to $47 for a large car; weekly unlimited-mileage rates range from $100 to $225.

Extra Charges Picking up the car in one city or state and leaving it in another may entail drop-off charges or one-way service fees, which can be substantial. The cost of a collision or loss-damage waiver (*see below*) can be high, also.

Cutting Costs If you know you will want a car for more than a day or two, you can save by planning ahead. Major companies have programs that discount their standard rates by 15%–30% if you make the reservation before departure (anywhere from two to 14 days), rent for a minimum number of days (typically three or four), and prepay the rental. Ask about these advance-purchase plans when you call for information. More economical rentals are those that come as part of fly/drive or other packages, even those as bare-bones as the rental plus an airline ticket (*see* Tours and Packages, *above*).

Other sources of savings are the several companies that operate as wholesalers—companies that do not own their own fleets but rent in bulk from those that do and offer advantageous rates to their customers. Rentals through such companies must be arranged and paid for in advance. Among them are **Auto Europe** (Box 1097, Camden, ME 04843, tel. 207/828–2525 or 800/ 223–5555) and **Connex International** (23 N. Division St., Peekskill, NY 10566, tel. 914/739–0066 or 800/333–3949, 800/843– 5416 in Canada). You won't see these wholesalers' deals advertised; they're even better in summer, when business travel is down. Always ask if unlimited mileage is available. Find out about any required deposits, cancellation penalties, and drop-off charges, and confirm the cost of the collision damage waiver (CDW).

One last tip: Remember to fill the tank when you turn in the vehicle, to avoid being charged a higher-than-usual price for refueling.

Insurance and Collision Damage Waiver The standard rental contract includes liability coverage (for damage to public property, injury to pedestrians, and so on) and coverage for the car against fire, theft (not included in certain countries), and collision damage with a deductible—most commonly $2,000–$3,000, occasionally more. In the case of an accident, you are responsible for the deductible amount unless you've purchased the CDW, which costs an average of $12 a day, although this varies depending on what you've rented, where, and from whom.

Because this adds up quickly, you may be inclined to say "no thanks"—and that's certainly your option, although the rental agent may not tell you so. Planning ahead will help you make the right decision. By all means, find out if your own insurance covers damage to a rental car while traveling (not simply a car to drive when yours is in for repairs). And check whether charging car rentals to any of your credit cards will get you a CDW at no charge. Note before you decline that deductibles are occasionally high enough that totaling a car would make you responsible for its full value. In many states, laws mandate that renters be told what the CDW costs, that it's optional, and that their own auto insurance may provide the same protection.

Traveling with Children

With dude ranches and many outdoor activities, the Rockies are tailor-made for family vacations. But plan ahead. Get your youngsters involved as you outline your trip. When packing, lay in a good supply of things to keep them busy in the car, on the airplane, on the train, or however you are traveling. Driving gives you the option of stopping frequently to let them get out and burn off energy.

On sightseeing days, try to plan some things that will be of special interest to your children. They may tolerate a museum and even show interest in a historic building or two, but put a zoo into the itinerary when you can. In addition, check local newspapers for special events mounted by public libraries, museums, parks, and YMCA/YWCAs.

Publications
Newsletter
Family Travel Times, published 10 times a year by **Travel with Your Children** (TWYCH, 45 W. 18th St., 7th floor tower, New York, NY 10011, tel. 212/206–0688; annual subscription $55), covers destinations, types of vacations, and modes of travel.

Books
Great Vacations with Your Kids, by Dorothy Jordon and Marjorie Cohen ($13; Penguin USA, 120 Woodbine St., Bergenfield, NJ 07621, tel. 800/253–6476) and *Traveling with Children—and Enjoying It,* by Arlene K. Butler ($11.95 plus $3 shipping per book; Globe Pequot Press, Box 833, Old Saybrook, CT 06475, tel. 800/243–0495, or 800/962–0973 in CT) help you plan your trip with children, from toddlers to teens. From the same publisher is *Recommended Family Resorts in the United States, Canada, and the Caribbean,* by Jane Wilford with Janet Tice ($12.95).

Tour Operators
GrandTravel (6900 Wisconsin Ave., Suite 706, Chevy Chase, MD 20815, tel. 301/986–0790 or 800/247–7651) offers international and domestic tours for grandparents traveling with their grandchildren. The catalogue, as charmingly written and illustrated as a children's book, positively invites armchair traveling with lap sitters aboard. **Rascals in Paradise** (650 5th St., Suite 505, San Francisco, CA 94107, tel. 415/978–9800 or 800/872–7225) specializes in programs for families.

Getting There
Airfares
On domestic flights, children under two not occupying a seat travel free, and older children currently travel on the "lowest applicable" adult fare.

Baggage
The adult baggage allowance applies for children paying half or more of the adult fare. Check with the airline for particulars.

Safety Seats
The FAA recommends the use of safety seats aloft and details approved models in the free leaflet *Child/Infant Safety Seats Recommended for Use in Aircraft* (available from the Federal Aviation Administration, APA–200, 800 Independence Ave.

SW, Washington, DC 20591, tel. 202/267–3479). Airline policy varies. U.S. carriers must allow FAA-approved models, but because these seats are strapped into a regular passenger seat, they may require that parents buy a ticket even for an infant under two who would otherwise ride free.

Facilities Aloft Airlines do provide other facilities and services for children, such as children's meals and freestanding bassinets (to those sitting in seats by the bulkhead, where there's enough legroom to accommodate them). Make your request when reserving. The annual February/March issue of *Family Travel Times* gives details of the children's services of dozens of airlines ($10; *see above*). "Kids and Teens in Flight" (free from the U.S. Department of Transportation, tel. 202/366–2220) offers tips for children flying alone.

Hints for Travelers with Disabilities

Local Information Colorado's **Wilderness on Wheels** (7125 W. Jefferson Ave., Lakewood 80235, tel. 303/988–2212) can help answer accessibility questions and plan outings. In Montana, contact **DREAM** (for "Disabled Recreation and Environmental Access Movement"; Northwest Montana Human Resources, 1st & Main Bldg., Box 8300, Kalispell 59715, tel. 406/752–6565). Wyoming's **Access Tours, Inc.** (3900 Smith Park Loop, Box 2985, Jackson 83001, tel. 307/733–6664) specializes in leisurely tours of several national parks. Contact the **Utah Travel Council** (tel. 801/538–1030) for statewide accessibility information and get the **Wyoming Tourist Commission**'s (tel. 307/777–7777) free *Wyoming Travel Guide (For the Person with a Handicap)*.

National Organizations Several organizations provide travel information for people with disabilities, usually for a membership fee, and some publish newsletters and bulletins. Among them are the **Information Center for Individuals with Disabilities** (Fort Point Pl., 27–43 Wormwood St., Boston, MA 02210, tel. 617/727–5540 or 800/462–5015 in MA between 11 and 4, or leave message; TDD/TTY tel. 617/345–9743); **Mobility International USA** (Box 3551, Eugene, OR 97403, voice and TDD tel. 503/343–1284), the U.S. branch of an international organization based in Great Britain (*see above*) and present in 30 countries; **MossRehab Hospital Travel Information Service** (1200 W. Tabor Rd., Philadelphia, PA 19141, tel. 215/456–9603, TDD tel. 215/456–9602); the **Society for the Advancement of Travel for the Handicapped** (SATH, 347 5th Ave., Suite 610, New York, NY 10016, tel. 212/447–7284, fax 212/725–8253); the **Travel Industry and Disabled Exchange** (TIDE, 5435 Donna Ave., Tarzana, CA 91356, tel. 818/368–5648); and **Travelin' Talk** (Box 3534, Clarksville, TN 37043, tel. 615/552–6670).

Travel Agencies and Tour Operators **Directions Unlimited** (720 N. Bedford Rd., Bedford Hills, NY 10507, tel. 914/241–1700), a travel agency, has expertise in tours and cruises for the disabled. **Evergreen Travel Service** (4114 198th St. SW, Suite 13, Lynnwood, WA 98036, tel. 206/776–1184 or 800/435–2288) operates Wings on Wheels Tours for those in wheelchairs, White Cane Tours for the blind, and tours for the deaf, and makes group and independent arrangements for travelers with any disability. **Flying Wheels Travel** (143 W. Bridge St., Box 382, Owatonna, MN 55060, tel. 800/535–6790 or 800/722–9351 in MN), a tour operator and travel agency, arranges international tours, cruises, and independent travel itineraries for people with impaired mobility. **Nautilus**, at the same address as TIDE (*see above*), packages tours for the disabled internationally.

Publications In addition to the fact sheets, newsletters, and books from the organizations mentioned above are several free publications available from the Consumer Information Center (Pueblo, CO 81009, tel. 719/948–3334): *New Horizons for the Air Traveler with a Disability*, a U.S. Department of Transportation booklet describing changes resulting from the 1986 Air Carrier Access Act and those still to come from the 1990 Americans with Disabilities Act (include Dept. 608Y in the address), and the Airport Operators Council's *Access Travel: Airports* (Dept. 5804), which describes facilities and services for the disabled at more than 500 airports worldwide.

Twin Peaks Press (Box 129, Vancouver, WA 98666, tel. 206/694–2462 or 800/637–2256) publishes the *Directory of Travel Agencies for the Disabled* ($19.95), listing more than 370 agencies worldwide; *Travel for the Disabled* ($19.95), listing some 500 access guides and accessible places worldwide; the *Directory of Accessible Van Rentals* ($9.95), for campers and RV travelers worldwide; and *Wheelchair Vagabond* ($14.95), a collection of personal travel tips. Add $2 per book for shipping. The Sierra Club (730 Polk St., San Francisco, CA 94109, tel. 415/776–2211) publishes *Easy Access to National Parks* ($16 plus $3 shipping).

Hints for Older Travelers

Organizations The **American Association of Retired Persons** (AARP, 601 E St. NW, Washington, DC 20049, tel. 202/434–2277) provides independent travelers the Purchase Privilege Program, which offers discounts on hotels, car rentals, and sightseeing, and the AARP Motoring Plan, provided by Amoco, which furnishes domestic trip-routing information and emergency road-service aid for an annual fee of $39.95 per person or couple ($59.95 for a premium version). The AARP also arranges group tours, cruises, and apartment living through AARP Travel Experience from American Express (400 Pinnacle Way, Suite 450, Norcross, GA 30071, tel. 800/927–0111); these can be booked through travel agents, except for the cruises, which must be booked directly (tel. 800/745–4567). The AARP membership is open to those 50 and over; annual dues are $8 per person or couple.

Two other membership organizations offer discounts on lodgings, car rentals, and other travel products, along with such nontravel perks as magazines and newsletters. The **National Council of Senior Citizens** (1331 F St. NW, Washington, DC 20004, tel. 202/347–8800) is a nonprofit advocacy group with some 5,000 local clubs across the United States; membership costs $12 per person or couple annually, and the clubs have no age requirement. **Mature Outlook** (6001 N. Clark St., Chicago, IL 60660, tel. 800/336–6330), a Sears Roebuck subsidiary with 800,000 members, charges $9.95 for an annual membership for those 50 and over.

Note: When using any senior-citizen identification card for reduced hotel rates, mention it when booking, not when checking out. At restaurants, show your card before you're seated; discounts may be limited to certain menus, days, or hours. If you are renting a car, ask about promotional rates that might improve on your senior-citizen discount.

Educational Travel **Elderhostel** (75 Federal St., 3rd floor, Boston, MA 02110, tel. 617/426-7788) is a nonprofit organization that has offered inexpensive study programs for people 60 and older since 1975. Programs take place at more than 1,800 educational institutions in the United States, Canada, and 45 countries overseas, and courses cover everything from marine science to Greek myths and cowboy poetry. Participants generally attend lectures in the morning and spend the afternoon sightseeing or on field trips; they live in dorms on the host campuses. Fees for programs in the United States and Canada, which usually last one week, run about $300, not including transportation.

Tour Operators **Saga International Holidays** (222 Berkeley St., Boston, MA 02116, tel. 800/343-0273), which specializes in group travel for people over 60, offers a selection of variously priced tours and cruises covering five continents. If you want to take your grandchildren, look into **GrandTravel** (*see* Traveling with Children, *above*).

Further Reading

History Jim Robbins's *Last Refuge: The Environmental Showdown in the American West* (William Morrow and Company, 1993) explores ways to preserve the region's resources by examining its past. *Bound for Idaho* is the 1864 Oregon Trail journal of the writer-explorer Julius Merril (University of Idaho Press). *Emigrant Trails of Southern Idaho* is a comprehensive guidebook (Bureau of Land Management in cooperation with the Idaho Historical Society, 3380 American Terr., Boise, ID 83706). *Across the Wide Missouri*, by Bernard De Voto (AMS Press), won the 1948 Pulitzer Prize; he also edited *The Journals of Lewis and Clark*, and when he died, the U.S. Forest Service saw to it that his ashes were scattered over Idaho's Bitterroot Wilderness. *Desert Solitaire* by Edward Abbey (University of Arizona Press), inspired by his experiences as a park ranger at Utah's Arches National Park, is said to rank among the greatest philosophy–natural history books ever written. *The Colorado Book*, edited by Eleanor Gehres et al. (Fulcrum Publishing) is, a compendium of reactions to the state by such writers as Stephen King, James Michener, Mark Twain, and Helen Hunt Jackson. Also see *A Lady's Life in the Rocky Mountains* by Isabella Bird (Trafalgar Square); *The Rocky Mountain Journals of William Marshall Anderson: The West in 1834*, edited by Dale Morgan and Eleanor Harris (University of Nebraska Press); and Duane A. Smith's *Rocky Mountains West: Colorado, Wyoming & Montana, 1895–1915* (University of New Mexico Native American Studies).

Fiction *A River Runs Through It and Other Stories*, by Norman Maclean (University of Chicago Press), is a lyrical reminiscence about growing up in Missoula, Montana, during the 1920s. Other works are *The Last Best Place: A Montana Anthology* by William Kittredge and Annick Smith (Falcon Press); *Montana on My Mind* by Michael Sample and Larry Mayer (Falcon Press); *This House of Sky: Landscapes of a Western Mind* by Ivan Doig (Harcourt Brace Jovanovich).

Natural History The **Peterson Field Guide** series (Houghton Mifflin Co.) includes *Western Birds, Rocky Mountain Wildflowers*, and *West-*

ern Butterflies, which are considered by many to be the bibles for identifying plant and wildlife in this part of the country.

Arriving and Departing

By Plane

Flights are either nonstop, direct, or connecting. A **nonstop** flight requires no change of plane and makes no stops. A **direct** flight stops at least once and can involve a change of plane, although the flight number remains the same; if the first leg is late, the second waits. This is not the case with a **connecting** flight, which involves a different plane and a different flight number.

Airports and Airlines
Each of the Rocky Mountain states has at least one major airport served by most of the major U.S. carriers. Denver's **Stapleton International Airport** (tel. 303/270–1300 or 800/247–2336) is served by American (tel. 800/433–7300), Continental (tel. 800/525–0280), TWA (tel. 800/221–2000), United (tel. 800/221–1212), and USAir (tel. 800/428–4322), with commuter airline links to smaller airports in the region. At press time, Stapleton is scheduled to be replaced by the new **Denver International Airport** (tel. 303/270–1900, TDD 800/688–1333). The airport is scheduled to open by January 1994 and will possess the best facilities for predicting and handling weather of any airport in the world. All airlines that serve Stapleton will serve Denver International. American, Continental, Delta (tel. 800/221–1212), SkyWest (tel. 800/453–9417), and several regional airlines fly from Denver and Salt Lake City into Jackson Hole, Wyoming, with additional service during ski season. Idaho's **Boise Air Terminal** (tel. 208/382–3110) is served by Delta, Empire (tel. 800/392–9233), Horizon (tel. 800/547–9308), Morris (tel. 208/383–3170), SkyWest, and United. In Montana, the **Missoula Airport** (tel. 406/543–7001) and **Glacier Park International Airport** (tel. 406/752–1028) in Kalispell are served by Big Sky (tel. 800/237–7788), Continental, Delta, Horizon, Northwest (tel. 800/225–2525), SkyWest, and United. Utah's **Salt Lake International Airport** (tel. 801/575–2400) is also an easy access point to Wyoming and Idaho, served by several domestic airlines, including Alaska Air (tel. 800/426–0333), American West (tel. 800/247–5692), American, Continental, Delta, Horizon, Morris, SkyWest, TWA, and United. **Jackson Hole Airport** (tel. 307/733–7682) in Wyoming has service by American, Continental, Continental Express (tel. 800/525–0280), Delta, SkyWest, and United Express/Mesa (tel. 800/662–3736).

Cutting Flight Costs
The Sunday travel section of most newspapers is a good source of deals. When booking, particularly through an unfamiliar company, call the Better Business Bureau to find out whether any complaints have been registered against the company, pay with a credit card if you can, and consider trip-cancellation and default insurance (*see* Insurance, *above*).

Promotional Airfares
All the less expensive fares, called promotional or discount fares, are round-trip and involve restrictions. The exact nature of the restrictions depends on the airline, the route, and the season and on whether travel is domestic or international, but usually you must buy the ticket—commonly called an APEX (advance purchase excursion) when it's for international trav-

el—in advance (7, 14, or 21 days are usual). You must also respect certain minimum- and maximum-stay requirements (for instance, over a Saturday night or at least seven and no more than 30, 45, or 90 days), and you must be willing to pay penalties for changes. Airlines generally allow some changes for a fee. But the cheaper the fare, the more likely the ticket is nonrefundable; it would take a death in the family for the airline to give you any of your money back if you had to cancel. The cheapest fares are also subject to availability; because only a certain percentage of the plane's total seats will be sold at that price, they may go quickly.

Consolidators Consolidators, or bulk-fare operators—also known as bucket shops—buy blocks of seats on scheduled flights that airlines anticipate they won't be able to sell. They pay wholesale prices, add a markup, and resell the seats to travel agents or directly to the public at prices that still undercut the airline's promotional or discount fares. You pay more than on a charter but ordinarily less than for an APEX ticket, and, even when there is not much of a price difference, the ticket usually comes without the advance-purchase restriction. Moreover, although tickets are marked nonrefundable so you can't turn them in to the airline for a full-fare refund, some consolidators sometimes give you your money back. Carefully read the fine print detailing penalties for changes and cancellations. If you doubt the reliability of a company, call the airline once you've made your booking and confirm that you do, indeed, have a reservation on the flight.

The biggest U.S. consolidator, C. L. Thomson Express, sells only to travel agents. Well-established consolidators selling to the public include **Council Charter** (205 E. 42nd St., New York, NY 10017, tel. 212/661–0311 or 800/800–8222), a division of the Council on International Educational Exchange and a longtime charter operator now functioning more as a consolidator; **Travac** (989 6th Ave., New York, NY 10018, tel. 212/563–3303 or 800/872–8800), also a former charterer; and **UniTravel** (Box 12485, St. Louis, MO 63132, tel. 314/569–0900 or 800/325–2222).

Charter Flights Charters usually have the lowest fares and the most restrictions. Departures are limited and seldom on time, and you can lose all or most of your money if you cancel. (Generally, the closer to departure you cancel, the more you lose, although sometimes you will be charged only a small fee if you supply a substitute passenger.) The charterer, on the other hand, may legally cancel the flight for any reason up to 10 days before departure; within 10 days of departure, the flight may be canceled only if it becomes physically impossible to operate it. The charterer may also revise the itinerary or increase the price after you have bought the ticket, but if the new arrangement constitutes a "major change," you have the right to a refund. Before buying a charter ticket, read the fine print for the company's refund policy and details on major changes. Money for charter flights is usually paid into a bank escrow account, the name of which should be on the contract. If you don't pay by credit card, make your check payable to the escrow account (unless you're dealing with a travel agent, in which case, his or her check should be payable to the escrow account). The Department of Transportation's Consumer Affairs Office (I–25, Washington, DC 20590, tel. 202/366–2220) can answer questions on charters and send you its "Plane Talk: Public Charter Flights" information sheet.

Charter operators may offer flights alone or with ground arrangements that constitute a charter package. Well-established charter operators include **Council Charter** (*see* Consolidators, *above*), now largely a consolidator, despite its name, and **Travel Charter** (1120 E. Long Lake Rd., Troy, MI 48098, tel. 313/528–3500 or 800/521–5267), with midwestern departures. **DER Tours** (Box 1606, Des Plaines, IL 60017, tel. 800/782–2424), a charterer and consolidator, sells through travel agents.

Discount Travel Clubs
Travel clubs offer their members unsold space on airplanes, cruise ships, and package tours at nearly the last minute and at well below the original cost. Suppliers thus receive some revenue for their "leftovers," and members get a bargain. Membership generally includes a regular bulletin or access to a toll-free telephone hot line giving details of available trips departing anywhere from three or four days to several months in the future. Packages tend to be more common than flights alone, so if airfares are your only interest, read the literature before joining. Reductions on hotels are also available. Clubs include **Discount Travel International** (114 Forrest Ave., Suite 203, Narberth, PA 19072, tel. 215/668–7184; $45 annually, single or family), **Moment's Notice** (425 Madison Ave., New York, NY 10017, tel. 212/486–0503; $45 annually, single or family), **Travelers Advantage** (CUC Travel Service, 49 Music Sq. W, Nashville, TN 37203, tel. 800/548–1116; $49 annually, single or family), and **Worldwide Discount Travel Club** (1674 Meridian Ave., Miami Beach, FL 33139, tel. 305/534–2082; $50 annually for family, $40 single).

Enjoying the Flight
Because the air aloft is dry, drink plenty of beverages while on board; remember that drinking alcohol contributes to jet lag, as do heavy meals. Sleepers generally prefer window seats to curl up against; restless passengers ask to be on the aisle. Bulkhead seats, in the front row of each cabin, have more legroom, but since there's no seat ahead, trays attach awkwardly to the arms of your seat, and you must stow all possessions overhead. Bulkhead seats are usually reserved for the disabled, the elderly, and people traveling with babies.

Smoking
Since February 1990, smoking has been banned on all domestic flights of less than six hours' duration; the ban also applies to domestic segments of international flights aboard U.S. and foreign carriers.

By Car

Major interstates crisscross the region, winding their way through accessible mountain passes. The busiest, but least scenic, east–west thoroughfare is **I-80,** which crosses southern Wyoming, passing through Cheyenne and Laramie in the southeast corner. To reach Yellowstone National Park, you must either make the long drive north from Rock Springs or come south from **I-90,** which crosses northern Montana. In Colorado, **I-70** runs east–west, cutting through Denver in the east and Grand Junction in the west and passing south of Rocky Mountain National Park. In Utah, Capitol Reef National Park can be reached off **I-70,** also known as U.S. 50, via Route 24. **Interstate 80** runs east–west, **I-215** circles Salt Lake City, and

I–15 runs north from Salt Lake City into Idaho and connects with I–84, which heads west to Boise and on to Portland. **Interstate 90** passes through Sheridan in northeast Wyoming before crossing Montana and northern Idaho; it comes within 100 miles of Glacier National Park, which can be reached by going north from Missoula on U.S. 93 and east on U.S. 2. **Interstate 15** goes along the east side of the park; you can reach Glacier by driving west on U.S. 89. **Interstate 25** comes up from New Mexico and passes through Colorado Springs and Denver in Colorado; Cheyenne and Casper in Wyoming; and then joins I–90 in Montana. Major attractions such as Glacier and Yellowstone national parks are well away from the interstates, requiring visitors to drive on scenic, two-lane highways to the entrances—and given the number of visitors that these major parks attract during their short season, the roads can be crowded.

By Train

Amtrak (tel. 800/872–7245) connects the Rockies to both coasts and all major American cities, with trains that run through Boise, Salt Lake City, and Denver, and other stops in between. Amtrak trains also run through northern Montana, with stops in Essex and Whitefish, along the southern border of Glacier National Park. Connecting motorcoach services are provided in the summer from Pocatello, Idaho, to Yellowstone National Park.

Canada's passenger service, **VIA Rail Canada** (tel. 800/665–0200), stops near the Canadian entrance to Waterton/Glacier International Peace National Park.

By Bus

Greyhound Lines (tel. 800/231–2222, 303/292–6111 in CO) operates bus service to the Rocky Mountain region from many points in the United States. There is extensive service throughout Colorado, with connections to major cities in the area, including Cheyenne, Boise, Pocatello, Missoula, and Salt Lake City. Canadian destinations are routed through Denver up to Regina and Moosejaw in Saskatchewan, or to Calgary via Salt Lake City, Idaho Falls, Bozeman, and Butte.

Staying in the Rockies

Getting Around

By Plane In the past few years, regional air travel has changed considerably in North America. Large national carriers have abandoned many of their shorter routes to secondary cities. Smaller regional companies, which are often owned by larger airlines or have joint marketing and reservation systems with them, have taken up the slack. Instead of operating jets, they often fly turboprop planes that hold 10–50 passengers. Following is a list of regional carriers.

Colorado Contact **Continental Express** (tel. 800/525–0820), **Great Lakes** (tel. 800/554–5111), **Mesa** (tel. 800/637–2247), **Midwest Express** (tel. 800/452–2022), and **United Express** (tel. 800/241–6522 or 800/662–3736).

Idaho Look into **Alaska Air** (tel. 800/426–0333), **Delta** (tel. 800/221–1212), **Empire** (tel. 800/392–9233), **Horizon** (tel. 800/547–9308), **Morris** (208/383–3170 or 800/466–7747), **United** (tel. 800/241–6522), and **United Express** (tel. 800/662–3736 or 800/241–6522).

Montana Carriers include **Big Sky** (tel. 800/237–7788), **Continental Express** (tel. 800/525–0280), **Horizon** (tel. 800/547–9308), **SkyWest** (tel. 800/453–9417), and **United Express/Mesa** (tel. 800/662–3736).

Utah In Salt Lake City, Continental, Delta, and TWA connect with **America West** (tel. 800/247–5692), **Horizon** (tel. 800/547–9308), **Morris** (tel. 800/466–7747), and **SkyWest/Delta Connection** (tel. 800/453–9417).

Wyoming At Jackson Hole Airport, American, Continental, and Delta connect with **Continental Express** (tel. 800/525–0280), **Mesa** (tel. 800/637–2247), **SkyWest/Delta Connection** (tel. 800/453–9417), and **United Express/Mesa** (tel. 800/662–3736).

By Car Before setting out on any driving trip, it's important to make sure your vehicle is in top condition. It is best to have a complete tune-up; at the least, you should make the following checks:

See that all the lights are working, including brake lights, backup lights, and emergency lights; make sure tires are in good shape (including the spare); check the oil; check the engine coolant; fill the windshield-washer bottle, make sure the washer blades are in good condition; and make sure the brakes are in good condition, too. For emergencies, take along flares or reflector triangles, jumper cables, an empty gas can, a fire extinguisher, a flashlight, a plastic tarp, blankets, and coins for phone calls.

The Rockies offer some of the most spectacular vistas and challenging driving in the world. Roads range from multilane blacktop to barely graveled backroad trails; from twisting switchbacks considerately marked with guardrails to primitive campgrounds with a lane so narrow that the driver has to back up to the edge of a steep cliff in order to make a turn. Scenic routes and lookout points are clearly marked, enabling visitors to slow down and pull over to take in the views.

You'll seldom be bored driving through the Rockies. The most mountainous terrain is in **Colorado**, but this state is also the most populated and accessible of those in the region. **Idaho** is home to the most rocky and rugged stretch of the mountains, with an extraordinarily wild beauty that may be too remote and desolate for most travelers. In fact, it is impossible to travel directly through the heart of the state—only two routes go from north to south. **Montana**'s interstate system is more driver-friendly, connecting soaring summits, rivers, glacial valleys, forests, lakes, and vast stretches of prairie, all capped by that endless "Big Sky." It is practically impossible to get around **Utah** without a car. There are more national parks here than in any other state, although their interiors are not always accessible by car, as are some other national park interiors. **Wyoming**'s interstate links classic, open-range cowboy country and mountain-range vistas of varying degrees of cragginess with the geothermal wonderland of Yellowstone National Park.

You'll find highways and the national parks to be crowded during the summer months (June, July, and August), and almost deserted (and occasionally impassable) in winter. Follow the posted speed limit, drive defensively, and make sure your gas tank is full, since distances between gas stations could make running on empty (or in the reserve zone) a not-so-pleasant memory of your trip.

A word to drivers: One of the more unpleasant sights along the highway are roadkills—animals struck by vehicles. Be aware that deer, elk, and even bears might be attempting to cross the road just as you're driving by. Exercise caution, not only to save an animal's life, but also to avoid possible extensive damage to your car.

Speed Limits The speed limit on U.S. interstate highways is 65 miles per hour in rural areas and 55 miles per hour in urban zones and on secondary highways.

Winter Driving Modern highways make mountain driving safe and generally trouble free even in cold weather. Although winter driving can occasionally present some real challenges, road maintenance is good and plowing is prompt. However, in mountain areas, tire chains, studs, or snow tires are essential. If you're planning to drive into high elevations, be sure to check the weather forecast beforehand. Even the mountain passes on main highways can be forced to close because of snow conditions. Each state highway department has a number to call for road conditions: **Colorado** (tel. 303/639–1111 within a 2-hour drive of Denver, 303/639–1234 statewide); **Idaho** (tel. 208/336–6600); **Montana** (tel. 406/444–6200 or 800/332–6171; 406/444–6339 for a recording); **Utah** (tel. 801/964–6000 in the Salt Lake City area; 800/492–2400 within Utah); and **Wyoming** (tel. 307/635–9966 or 800/442–7850). Be prepared for stormy weather by carrying an emergency kit containing warm clothes, a flashlight, some food, and perhaps a sleeping bag. If you do get stalled by deep snow, do not leave your car. Wait for help, running the engine only if needed, and remember that assistance is never far away.

Border Crossing Driving a car across the U.S.–Canadian border is a simple process. Personal vehicles are allowed entry into the neighboring country, provided they are not to be left behind. Drivers in rental cars should bring along a copy of the rental contract, bearing an endorsement stating that the vehicle is permitted to cross the border.

Auto Clubs The **American Automobile Association (AAA)** is a federation of state auto clubs that offers maps, route planning, and emergency road service to its members; members of Britain's Automobile Association (BAA) are granted reciprocal privileges. To join AAA, look in local phone directories under AAA for the nearest club, or contact the national organization (1000 AAA Dr., Heathrow, FL 32746-5063, tel. 407/444–7000 or 800/222–4357 in the U.S.; 800/336–4357 in Canada).

By Train **Amtrak** (tel. 800/872–7245) crisscrosses the region. Denver is on Amtrak's main east–west train route, with six arrivals and departures daily.

Scenic Train Trips Several Rocky Mountain states have restored unused stretches of track and refurbished turn-of-the-century touring cars. These give you the chance to scout out places beyond the reach of any four-lane blacktop.

In Colorado, the best-known journeys are to **Pikes Peak** on the highest cog railway in the world, and the celebrated **Durango-**

Silverton narrow-gauge mining-train trip along the Animas River. For details, contact the **Colorado Scenic Rails Association** (17155 W. 44th Ave., Box 641, Golden, CO 80402, tel. 800/866–3690).

In Utah, you can explore part of Bryce Canyon National Park in a restored limousine, a **1938 White Touring Car** (tel. 801/834–5361), and by early 1994, you should be able to catch the famous **Heber Creeper** (tel. 801/654–5601 or 800/982–3257), a turn-of-the-century steam train that rides the rails from Heber City across Heber Valley, alongside Deer Creek Reservoir, down Provo Canyon to Vivian Park and Bridal Veil Falls.

In Wyoming, one of the highest standard-gauge lines in the country, the **Wyoming/Colorado Railroad** (tel. 307/742–9612), chugs along through the scenic country from Laramie up into the Snowy Range Mountains, with a lunch stop in Centennial.

By Bus   **Greyhound Lines** (tel. 800/752–4841, 303/292–6111 in CO) operates regular intercity routes throughout the region, with connections from Denver to Cheyenne, Boise, Pocatello, and Missoula. Smaller bus companies provide service within local areas. Regional lines include **Springs Transit Management** in Colorado Springs (tel. 719/475–9733); **Boise-Winnemucca Stages** in Idaho (tel. 208/336–3302); **Intermountain Bus Company** (tel. 406/755–4011), **Karst Stages** (tel. 800/332–0504), and **Rimrock Stages** (tel. 406/254–5116 or 800/255–7655), all in Montana; and **Rock Springs Stages** (tel. 307/733–3133), **Targhee Express** (tel. 307/733–3101 or 800/443–8146), **Powder River Transportation** (tel. 307/635–1327), and **Karst Stages** (800/332–0504) in Wyoming.

Telephones

The telephone area codes for the Rocky Mountain region are 303 and 719 for Colorado; 208 for Idaho; 406 for Montana; 801 for Utah; and 307 for Wyoming.

Pay telephones cost 25¢ for local calls (except in Wyoming, where the cost is 35¢). Charge phones are also found in many locations. These phones can be used to charge a call to a telephone-company calling card, a credit card, or your home phone, or for collect calls.

Many hotels place a surcharge on local calls made from your room and include a service charge on long-distance calls. It may be cheaper for you to make your calls from a pay phone in the hotel lobby rather than from your room.

Opening and Closing Times

Throughout the Rockies, most retail stores are open from 9 or 9:30 until 6 or 7 daily in downtown locations and until 9 or 10 in suburban shopping malls. Downtown stores sometimes stay open later Thursday nights. Normal banking hours are weekdays 9–5; some branches are also open on Saturday morning.

Shopping

The Rocky Mountain region combines a frontier reverence for nature and the country's past with a fascination for ski resort glitz and a modern love for megamalls and discount outlet shopping centers. Boutiques, galleries, and malls are either right in or nearby the many resort towns and cities throughout all five states covered in this book.

Visit **Naatsilid Pottery** in the Canyonlands area near Blanding, Utah, and watch artisans create pottery that reflects their Navajo heritage. Native American jewelry can be bought throughout this part of the country—you can browse in shops for beautiful and unusual rings, necklaces, earrings, bolo ties, belts, and bracelets, crafted mostly of silver, often inlaid with coral, turquoise, or onyx. Most towns and resort areas have shops specializing in these crafts. Jackson, Wyoming, is a good source for sculpture and other collectible fine art as well as extraordinary handloomed Navajo rugs. Bargain if you dare, but don't expect giveaway prices. Throughout the area, Western wear—belts, fringed jackets, cowboy boots, and hats—will be well made, with price tags reflecting the quality. You'll be hard put to match the selection elsewhere in the United States.

For some good-natured, big-city shopping, Denver is the place to be, especially during its big Labor Day sales, when shops selling outdoor wear and sporting goods get a jump start on the approaching winter season and slash prices on new ski equipment.

Taxes The sales tax varies from state to state. It's 3% in Colorado and Wyoming, 5% in Idaho, and 6.25% in Utah. Montana has no sales tax.

If you are crossing the border into Canada, be aware of Canada's goods and services tax (better known as the GST). This is a value-added tax of 7%, applicable on virtually every purchase except basic groceries and a small number of other items. Visitors to Canada, however, may claim a full rebate of the GST on any goods taken out of the country as well as on short-term accommodations. Rebates can be claimed either immediately on departure from Canada at participating duty-free shops or by mail. Rebate forms can be obtained by writing to **Revenue Canada** (Visitor's Rebate Program, Ottawa, Ontario, Canada K1A 1J5, tel. 613/991–3346). Claims must be for a minimum of $7 worth of tax and can be submitted up to a year from the date of purchase. Purchases made during multiple visits to Canada can be grouped together for rebate purposes.

Sports and the Outdoors

Outdoor sports are a consuming, year-round passion in the Rockies. The months that are *least* appealing, and during which there are the fewest organized activities, are April, May, and November. Otherwise, the floodgate of activities is wide open.

Many ski resorts in the Rockies actively pursue summer-vacation business. Many also have working arrangements with airlines, notably American, Delta, and United. For reasonably priced recreational vacation packages—in winter or summer—start with the central reservation services at ski resorts.

Keep in mind that national parks tend to put the most restrictions on recreational use, specifically regarding camping, hunting, and vehicles. Also, national parks as well as other areas often require licenses or permits for specific activities, such as fishing, rafting, or climbing. It is best to check well ahead of time with park or forest-service rangers regarding the necessary permits for an activity in a particular area.

Many recreational activities, from backpacking to skiing, tend to be gear-intensive. Not to worry: Rental equipment for most activities is widely available, and sporting-goods stores, especially in resort towns, are numerous. Also, outfitters and trip organizers usually supply or rent necessary equipment. Except for very special clothing, such as helmets for climbing or boots for skiing, you are usually expected to bring the clothing and footwear appropriate for the sport and the weather.

One last matter to consider is insurance; emergency backcountry rescue may require special procedures, such as helicopter evacuation, that can be expensive. Check with your insurance company and/or outfitter to be sure you have the necessary coverage. Some outfitters and trip organizers offer special insurance packages. Many active vacations in the Rockies can be physically demanding, particularly so given the high elevations. If you are concerned about your fitness or have a medical condition (a heart or respiratory condition, for instance), be sure to check with your doctor before signing up for a trip.

Climbing and Mountaineering Climbing in its various forms—mountaineering, rock climbing, ice climbing—is a year-round sport in the Rockies. In many areas, especially in the national parks, climbing permits are required, primarily for safety reasons. Rangers want to be sure that you have the experience and skill necessary to undertake the challenge at hand.

Thus, it probably goes without saying that no one should attempt technical rock or mountain climbing without proper skills and equipment. Among the best climbing schools in the country are the **American Alpine Institute** (1515 12th St., Bellingham, WA 98225, tel. 206/671–1505) and the **Colorado Mountain School** (Box 2620S, Estes Park, CO 80517, tel. 303/586–5758). Both also lead trips in the Rockies.

Cycling Mountain biking, as a sport and cultural phenomenon, has its roots in the Rockies and is more popular in the region than touring on paved roads. Valley roads tend to be clear of snow by mid- to late-April. Roads and trails at higher elevations may not be clear until several months later, and may again be snow-covered by early October. Keep in mind that elevations in the Rockies are high, and exact their physical toll in an aerobically demanding sport such as cycling. Not only should you be physically fit, but you should be prepared to settle for riding shorter distances than you might be capable of handling at lower elevations.

Perhaps the best general source of information on bicycling in the Rockies—including detailed maps and information on trip organizers—is **Bikecentennial** (Box 8308, Missoula, MT 59807, tel. 406/721–1776).

Dude Ranches Dude ranches fall roughly into two categories: working ranches and guest ranches. Working ranches, in which guests participate in such activities as round-ups and cattle movements, sometimes require horsemanship experience. Guest ranches, with a wide range of activities in addition to horseback riding, rarely do.

For dude-ranch information, contact: the **Colorado Dude and Guest Ranch Association** (Box 300, Tabernash, CO 80478, tel. 303/887–3128 or 800/441–6060 outside of Colorado); the **Dude Ranchers Association** (Box 471, LaPorte, CO 80535, tel. 303/493–7623); or **Old West Dude Ranch Vacation,** c/o American Wilderness Experience (Box 1486, Boulder, CO 80306, tel. 800/444–3833).

Fishing Trout is the principal game fish in the Rockies. It is possible to fish year-round in fast-moving streams that don't freeze over. However, summer is by far the most popular fishing season. Fishing licenses, ranging in term from daily to annual, are required in each state: Be aware that a license in one state is not recognized in another. Licenses are available in many convenience stores and sporting-goods shops.

For information on fishing licenses and regulations, contact in each respective state: the **Colorado Division of Wildlife** (6060 Broadway, Denver, CO 80216, tel. 303/297–1192); the **Idaho Department of Fish & Game** (Box 25, 600 S. Walnut St., Boise, ID 83707, tel. 208/334–3700); the **Montana Department of Fish, Wildlife & Parks** (1420 E. 6th, Helena, MT 59620, tel. 406/444–2535); the **Utah Division of Wildlife Resources** (1596 W. North Temple, Salt Lake City, UT 84116, tel. 801/538–4700); or **Wyoming Game & Fish** (5400 Bishop Blvd., Cheyenne, WY 82002, tel. 307/777–7735).

Hiking There are literally thousands of miles of hiking trails in the Rockies. Hiking in the south, especially in the desert country of southern Utah, is usually best in spring, when water is plentiful and before the heat of summer sets in. July through September are the best months for hiking in the high mountains, although hikers should be alert to the dangers of summer thunderstorms at higher elevations.

Primarily for safety reasons, overnight hikers are usually expected to register with park or forest rangers. Rangers can also apprise you of, among other things, the availability of backcountry campsites and up-to-date forest-fire conditions. Permits for backcountry camping are usually free.

The Mountaineers (306 2nd Ave. W, Seattle, WA 98119) and **Sierra Club Books** (930 Polk St., San Francisco, CA 94109) are among the leading publishers of hiking guides for the Rockies. Topographical maps may be available in well-equipped outdoor stores (**REI** or **Eastern Mountain Sports,** for example). Maps are also available from the U.S. Geological Survey (Distribution Center, Denver, CO 80225). Be specific about the region you're interested in when ordering.

Horsepack Trips June through August is the peak period for horsepack trips. While horsemanship is usually not a prerequisite, at least some experience with horses is helpful. It is important before signing up with an outfitter, especially for a multiday trip, to know what sort of skills and experience will be expected of you.

Good sources of information on horsepack trips in the Rockies are: the **Colorado Outfitters Association** (Box 440021, Aurora, CO 80044, tel. 303/751–9274); the **Montana Outfitters & Guides Association** (Box 9070, Helena, MT 59604, tel. 406/444–3738); and **Utah Guides & Outfitters** (Box 111, Jensen, UT 84305, tel. 801/789–4952).

Skiing Ski resorts in the Rockies may open their lifts as early as October and close as late as June. However, the ski season typically runs from December until early April. Christmas through New Year's Day is the busiest period for most ski areas; often March is an active month as well. Conversely, the slower months of January and February are best for coming up with bargain vacation packages.

Cross-country trails in the valleys may close earlier because of lack of snow. On the other hand, April through June, when avalanche risks lessen, is one of the best periods for backcountry skiing. Ski resorts are generally the best sources of information on everything from lodging to snow conditions in a particular area.

Water Sports Spring, when rivers are flushed with snowmelt, is the best time of year for white-water enthusiasts. April through June is the best time to run rivers in the south; June through August are the principal months on rivers farther north. In general (except on dammed rivers) the later in the season, the less the flow of water. River runners seeking to maximize white-water thrills should come early; families and those who want a gentler float should come later.

To prevent overcrowding, almost all major rivers require rafters or kayakers to have permits. For individuals planning their own trips, permits on popular rivers (such as the Middle Fork of the Salmon or the Selway in Idaho) can be extremely hard to come by. Permits tend to be awarded first to reputable outfitters, and in almost all cases, signing up with an outfitter is the way to go about running a river.

A good general source of information on river and rafting outfitters in the Rockies is **American Outdoors** (2133 Yarrow St., Lakewood, CO 80227, tel. 303/377–4811).

National Parks

Fees and Hours National parks are open to the public 365 days a year, although winter weather renders some roads inaccessible. Most national parks charge entrance fees; generally, the admission is $3–$10 per car for a seven-day pass, and $1–$4 for a seven-day pass for bicycles, motorcycles, snowmobiles, and those who enter on foot.

Passes The **Golden Eagle Pass** can be a good deal if you plan to visit several parks during your travels. For $25, it entitles you and your companions to free admission to *all* parks for a year. It does not cover additional park fees such as those for camping or parking. Both the **Golden Age Passport**, for U.S. citizens or permanent residents 62 and older, and the **Golden Access Passport**, for travelers with disabilities, entitle holders to free entry to all national parks plus 50% off fees for the use of all park facilities and services except those run by private concessionaires. Both types of passports are free; you must show proof of disability or proof of age and U.S. citizenship or permanent residency (such as a U.S. passport, driver's license, or birth certificate). All three passes are available at all national park entrances.

More Information Contact the **National Park Service** national headquarters (Office of Public Inquiries, Box 37127, Washington, DC 20013, tel. 202/208–4747) or its Rocky Mountain regional office (12795 W. Alameda Pkwy., Lakewood, CO 80225, tel. 303/969–2000).

Fodor's *National Parks of the West* is a comprehensive guide covering 30 national parks and monuments in the western United States and Canada.

Major Parks   **Rocky Mountain National Park** is home to 355 miles of hiking
Colorado   trails and sweeping vistas of high-country lakes, meadows, brooks and rushing streams, pine forests, alpine tundra, and snow-dusted peaks dotted with small glaciers. The 265,200-acre park attracts over 2 million visitors annually; they come for rock climbing, fishing, golfing, horseback riding, and spectular hikes and drives. *Information: Rocky Mountain National Park Headquarters, Estes Park, CO 80517, tel. 303/ 586–2371. Campground reservations: tel. 800/365–2267. Backcountry permits: West Unit Office, tel. 303/586–4459. Camping facilities: 5 drive-in campgrounds with 577 drive- and hike-in sites in park, most sites with flush toilets, drinking water, and telephones, RV sites at 3 campgrounds. Reservations accepted at 2 campgrounds; contact park headquarters. 3 campgrounds open year-round, 1 late May–Labor Day, 1 late May–late Sept.*

Montana   **Glacier National Park** is dominated by the Continental Divide, where pure mountain streams form the headwaters of the Columbia and Missouri rivers. Glaciers, pine forests, craggy mountaintops, streams, flowers, and lush green meadows are home to bears, bighorn sheep, mountain goats, gray wolves, and more than 1,000 species of flowers. The narrow, curving, and popular Going-to-the-Sun Road provides a dizzying glimpse of the park's 1,600 square miles. Glacier National Park adjoins Canada's Waterton Lakes National Park; together, the parks are called Waterton/Glacier International Peace Park. *Information: Glacier Park Headquarters, West Glacier, MT 59936, tel. 406/888–5441, or Waterton Park, AB, Canada T0K 2M0, tel. 403/859–2224. Camping facilities: 5 drive-in campgrounds with 540 sites in Glacier Park, 3 drive-in campgrounds with 391 sites in Waterton Park, drinking water, fireplace/barbecue pits. One campground in Glacier open year-round; others open mid-May or early June–early to mid-Sept.*

Yellowstone National Park's 3,472 square miles comprise the world's largest thermal area, with 10,000 geysers, hot springs, fumaroles, and mud pots; landscapes around the areas of greatest thermal activity are otherworldly with their stunted pines and shrubs. On a high plateau ringed by mountains topping 10,000 feet, the park also includes scenery ranging from near-high desert to lodgepole-pine forests. The area is even more magical in winter, when the trees near the geysers and hot pools are hoary with thick layers of frost, the skeletons of trees killed by the heat glitter with icicles, and bison and elk forage in the low country. *Information: Yellowstone National Park, WY 82190, tel. 307/344–7381. Backcountry permits: tel. 307/ 344–7381, ext. 2294. Facilities: 9 hotels and lodges; contact TW Recreational Services, Inc., Yellowstone National Park, WY 82190-9989, tel. 307/344–7311. Camping facilities: 12 drive-in campgrounds with 2,198 sites; drinking water at most sites, 6 campgrounds with flush toilets, 5 with pit toilets, 3 with showers, 7 with telephones, 1 with RV hookups. Two campgrounds accept reservations (tel. 800/365–2267; RV reservations 307/ 344–7381). One campground open year-round; others early May to mid-June–mid-Sept. to late Oct.*

Utah **Arches National Park** preserves a 73,378-acre fantasy land-scape of red rock that glows fiercely in the hot summer sun, particularly at sunset; the stone has been carved by wind and water into 1,500 natural stone arches. A paved road leads to the major sites, and several hikes lead visitors to more remote areas, including the must-see Delicate Arch and Fiery Furnace, a labyrinth of canyons, passageways, and hidden arches. *Information: Arches National Park, Box 907, Moab, UT 84532, tel. 801/259–8161. Camping facilities: 1 drive-in campground with 54 sites; drinking water, flush and pit toilets, ranger station. Open year-round.*

Bryce Canyon National Park contains 35,835 acres of rock notable for its striking red, buff, tan, and pink colors. The land is stunning and best seen at dawn or sunset. Bryce is a relatively quiet place, easily seen from paved roads leading to all the major overlooks. Still, it is imposing: Ebenezer Bryce, the Mormon settler for whom the park is named, is said to have exclaimed that this was "a hell of a place to lose a cow!" *Information: Bryce Canyon National Park, Bryce Canyon, UT 84717, tel. 801/834–5322. Facilities: lodge (tel. 801/586–7686 for reservations, 801/772–3213 to reach lodge, fax 801/586–3157). Camping facilities: 2 drive-in campgrounds with 218 sites; drinking water, flush toilets, telephones, 1 campground with showers and ranger station, both with RV sites. One campground open year-round, other early May–mid-Oct.*

Canyonlands National Park offers views down to the white-water rapids of the Green and Colorado rivers, and up to red rock pinnacles, cliffs, and spires. The park is a haven for adventure-sports enthusiasts; much of the park can be explored only by foot, mountain bike, or four-wheel-drive vehicle, or on a white-water river trip. *Information: Canyonlands National Park, 125 W. 200 S, Moab, UT 84532, tel. 801/259–7164. Camping facilities: 2 drive-in campgrounds with 38 sites; 1 with drinking water, pit toilets. Open year-round.*

Capitol Reef National Park is an inviting wilderness of sandstone formations and cliffs in Utah's desert country. A striated reeflike wall soars a thousand feet up to the sky, with domelike features reminiscent of the U.S. Capitol. Visitors can pick fruit at the park's large orchards, hike down into the canyons to visit the 1,000-year-old Fremont Petroglyphs, or take a 25-mile scenic drive along the "reef" itself. *Information: Capitol Reef National Park, Torrey, UT 84775, tel. 801/425–3791. Camping facilities: 3 drive-in campgrounds with 70 sites; drinking water, flush toilets, 1 campground with telephones. Open year-round.*

Zion National Park, one of the nation's oldest national parks, is famous for sheer sandstone walls reaching 2,000 feet into the sky and a complex desert ecology. Zion can be seen from a car, although anyone who ventures away from canyon roads will find a great variety of wildflowers and wildlife; the 147,035-acre park is home to 120 types of flowers and 270 different birds, as well as deer, lizards, and mountain lions. *Information: Zion National Park, Springdale, UT 84767, tel. 801/772–3256. Facilities: lodge (tel. 801/586–7686 for reservations, 801/772–3213 to reach lodge, fax 801/586–3157). Camping facilities: 3 drive-in campgrounds with 416 sites; 2 with drinking water, flush toilets, and telephones, 1 with pit toilets. One* *campground open year-round, others mid-Apr. or early June–mid-Oct.*

Wyoming The focal point of 310,000-acre **Grand Teton National Park** is the trio of distinctively shaped mountains that French trappers called Les Trois Tetons (the Three Breasts). You'll find two stunning high-mountain lakes, Jenny Lake and Jackson Lake, as well as rugged wilderness crisscrossed by hiking trails. There is boating and fishing on the lakes, rafting on Snake River, and plenty of hiking and climbing opportunities. *Information: Grand Teton National Park, Drawer 170, Moose, WY 83012, tel. 307/733–2880 or 307/543–2851. Facilities: 3 lodges, 2 log cabin complexes; contact Grand Teton Lodge Company, Box 240, Jenny Lake Rd., Moran, WY 83013, tel. 307/543–4647 or 800/628–9988, fax 307/543–2869). Camping facilities: 4 drive-in and 1 RV campground with 1,019 sites; drinking water, flush toilets, 2 campgrounds with showers, 4 with boat access, 5 with telephones. Open early to late May–Oct.*

There are five main entrances to **Yellowstone National Park** (*see above*); two of them are in Wyoming, east of Cody and just north of Grand Teton National Park.

Dining

Ratings Unless otherwise noted, Dining ratings throughout the book follow either the Cities and Resorts or Towns and Country price chart.

Restaurants are divided into the following price categories: Very Expensive, Expensive, Moderate, and Inexpensive. Prices are per person for a three-course dinner, not including drinks, tax, and tip.

Highly recommended restaurants in each price category are indicated by a star ★.

Category	Cities and Resorts	Towns and Country
Very Expensive	over $40	over $30
Expensive	$30–$40	$25–$30
Moderate	$20–$30	$15–$25
Inexpensive	under $20	under $15

In 1944, a Denver drive-in owner named Louis Ballast grilled a slice of cheese on top of a hamburger and became famous for patenting his invention, the cheeseburger. It has been suggested that Rocky Mountain cuisine consists of the three Bs: beef, buffalo, and burritos. While these items certainly will appear on menus throughout the region, restaurant chefs rise to the challenge and head to market to round out the offering with seasonal and local specialties.

In addition to mouthwatering steak and tender lamb, this is prime hunting and fishing territory, so antelope, elk, venison, and grouse are among the offerings. Rainbow trout, salmon, and bass practically leap from rivers and lakes into the skillet and then onto your plate. Colorado's Rocky Mountain oysters (fried bull testicles) are famous (some would say infamous) for their size and taste.

Colorado's sugar-sweet Rocky Ford cantaloupe has passionate admirers. Utah's raspberries, Montana's huckleberries, and Idaho's and Utah's cherries bake up into tasty pies. Apples, peaches, and pears are delicious purchased from roadside stands or transformed into luscious desserts. And don't forget about potatoes—natives will tell you that if it's not from Idaho, it's just a spud. Idahoans are also proud of their sugar beets, corn, mint, beans, and onions.

While the emphasis is on enjoyment of all this hearty regional fare, ethnic foods are becoming popular. Tex-Mex, Greek, and Asian cuisines are increasingly well represented, especially in resort areas.

As for regional beverages, portions of the area possess excellent vineyards, and local wines are often featured in the best restaurants. Treasure Valley in Idaho is home to the award-winning Ste. Chapelle and Weston wineries, and the industry is one of the fastest-growing in Colorado. Beer is also popular, and microbreweries are enjoying increasing recognition throughout the Rockies. Often located in or connected with a local pub, some of these breweries produce only enough specialty beers (called microbrews) for their own establishments. Colorado has more microbreweries than any other state, and some of their brews, such as Elk, Venison, and Trout, are available from regular beer outlets.

Lodging

Ratings Unless otherwise noted, Lodging ratings throughout the book follow either the Cities and Resorts or Towns and Country price chart.

Lodgings are divided into the following price categories: Very Expensive, Expensive, Moderate, and Inexpensive. Prices are for a standard double room in high season, not including tax and service.

Highly recommended lodgings in each price category are indicated by a star ★.

Category	Cities and Resorts	Towns and Country
Very Expensive	over $325	over $200
Expensive	$225–$325	$140–$200
Moderate	$125–$225	$80–$140
Inexpensive	under $125	under $80

For comprehensive statewide accommodation information, contact the **Colorado Hotel and Lodging Association** (999 18th St., Suite 10472, Denver, CO 80202, tel. 303/297–8335); **Idaho Division of Travel Promotion** (Idaho Department of Commerce, 700 W. State St., Boise, ID 83720, tel. 800/635–7820), **Travel Montana** (Department of Commerce, 1424 9th Ave., Helena, MT 59620, tel. 406/444–2654 in MT, 800/541–1447 out of state), **Utah Hotel/Motel Association** (9 Exchange Pl., Suite 715, Salt Lake City, UT 84114, tel. 801/359–0104), **Wyoming Division of**

Tourism (I–25 at College Dr., Cheyenne, WY 82002, tel. 307/777–7777). For information about hotels near national parks, contact tourism offices and the various parks' superintendents' offices (*see* National Parks, *below*).

Hotels Most big-city hotels cater primarily to business travelers, with such facilities as restaurants, cocktail lounges, swimming pools, exercise equipment, and meeting rooms. Room rates often reflect the range of amenities offered. Most cities also have less expensive hotels that are clean and comfortable but have fewer facilities. A new accommodations trend is all-suite hotels, which give travelers more room for their money and are gaining popularity with business travelers; examples include **Courtyard by Marriott** (tel. 800/321–2211) and **Embassy Suites** (tel. 800/362–2779).

Many properties offer special weekend rates, sometimes up to 50% off regular prices. However, these deals are usually not extended during peak summer months, when hotels are normally full.

All five states covered in this book have experienced hotel building booms during the past 10 years. **Doubletree** (tel. 800/528–0444), **Four Seasons** (tel. 800/332–3442), **Holiday Inn** (tel. 800/465–4329), **Marriott** (tel. 800/228–9290), **Ramada** (tel. 800/228–2828), **Red Lion Hotels and Inns** (tel. 800/547–8010), **Sheraton** (tel. 800/325–3535), **Stouffer** (tel. 800/468–3751), and **Westin** (tel. 800/228–3000) have properties in Denver (Colorado); Boise, Coeur d'Alene, and Ketchum (Idaho); Helena, Bozeman, and Billings (Montana); Salt Lake City and Park City (Utah); or Cheyenne, Jackson, and Sundance (Wyoming).

Motels The once-familiar roadside motel is fast disappearing from the American landscape. In its place are chain-run motor inns that are strategically located at highway intersections. Some of these establishments offer very basic facilities; others provide restaurants, swimming pools, and other amenities.

Nationally recognized chains include **Best Western** (tel. 800/528–1234), **Days Inn** (tel. 800/325–2525), **La Quinta Inns** (tel. 800/531–5900), **Motel 6** (tel. 505/891–6161), **Quality Inn** (tel. 800/228–5151), **Rodeway Inn** (tel. 800/221–2222), **Super 8 Motel** (tel. 800/848–8888), and **Travelodge** (tel. 800/255–3050). **Shilo Inn** (tel. 800/222–2244), **Red Lion Inn** (tel. 800/547–8010), and **Skyline Motor Inn** (tel. 800/843–8809) are regional chains.

Inns Charm is the long suit of these establishments, which generally occupy a restored older building with some historical or architectural significance. They're generally small, with under 20 rooms, and located outside cities. Breakfast may be included in the rates. For complete lists, contact professional associations such as **Distinctive Inns of Colorado** (Box 10472, Colorado Springs, CO 80932, tel. 800/866–0621), **Montana Innkeepers Association** (Box 1272, Helena, MT 59624, tel. 406/449–8408), **Bed and Breakfast Inns of Utah, Inc.** (Box 3066, Park City, UT 84060, tel. 801/645–8068).

Bed-and-Breakfasts Bed-and-breakfasts are private homes whose owners welcome paying guests. They usually have anywhere from two to 10 rooms, some with private baths and some with shared facilities, and always serve breakfast at no extra charge. The decor and the hospitality definitely reflect the personalities and tastes of the B&B's owners to an even greater degree than at inns. Sometimes you can book directly through the B&B; arrangements at others must be made through a reservation system such as **Bed & Breakfast Rocky Mountains** (906 S. Pearl, Denver, CO 80209, tel. 303/744–8415 or 800/733–8415); **Bed & Breakfast Western Adventure** (Box 20972, Billings, MT 59104, tel. 406/259–7993), covering Montana, Wyoming, and Idaho; the **Montana Bed & Breakfast Association** (5557 Hwy. 93 S, Somers, MT 59932, tel. 800/453–8870); and **Bed & Breakfast Inns of Utah** (Box 3066, Park City, UT 84060, tel. 801/645–8068.

Guest Ranches   If the thought of sitting around a campfire after a hard day on the range makes your heart beat faster, consider playing dude on a guest ranch. These range from wilderness-rimmed working ranches that accept guests and encourage them to pitch in with chores and other ranch activities to luxurious resorts, on the fringes of a small city, with an upscale clientele, swimming pools, tennis courts, and a lively roster of horse-related activities such as breakfast rides, moonlight rides, all-day trail rides, and the like. Rafting, fishing, tubing, and other activities in the surrounding wilderness are usually available, and at working ranches, guests may be able to participate in a cattle roundup. In winter, cross-country skiing and snowshoeing keep guests busy. Lodgings can run the gamut from charmingly rustic cabins to the kind of deluxe quarters you expect at a first-class hotel. Meals may be gourmet or plain but hearty. Many ranches offer packages and children's and off-season rates. For lists of ranches, contact **Bed & Breakfast Western Adventure** (Box 20972, Billings, MT 59104, tel. 406/259–7993), a reservation system for Idaho, Montana, and Wyoming; the **Colorado Dude/Guest Ranch Association** (Box 300, Tabernash, CO 80478, tel. 303/887–3128 or 800/441–6060 outside the state); the **Dude Ranchers' Association** (Box 471, LaPorte, CO 80535, tel. 303/223–8440); and the various state tourism offices.

Resorts   Rockies resorts range from fishing lodges to luxury turn-of-the-century showplaces. Ski resort towns throughout the Rockies are home to dozens of resorts in all price ranges; the activities lacking in any individual property can usually be found in the town itself, in summer as well as winter. Off the slopes, there are wonderful rustic-luxurious resorts in the national parks: **Jackson Lake Lodge** and **Jenny Lake Lodge** in Grand Teton National Park, and **Old Faithful Lodge** in Yellowstone. The **Broadmoor**, in Colorado Springs, is a grand old property dating from the late 19th century. Northwestern Montana is home to Flathead Lake, the largest freshwater lake west of the Mississippi, and **Averill's Flathead Lake Lodge**, a deluxe 2,000-acre rustic Western property that spices up its spring season with a rodeo-training school.

Home Exchange   This is obviously an inexpensive solution to the lodging problem, because house swapping means living rent free. You find a house, apartment, or other vacation property to exchange for your own by becoming a member of a home-exchange organization, which then sends you its annual directories listing available exchanges and includes your own listing in at least one of them. Arrangements for the actual exchange are made by the two parties involved, not by the organization. Principal clearinghouses include **Intervac U.S./International Home Exchange** (Box 590504, San Francisco, CA 94159, tel. 415/435–3497), the oldest, with thousands of foreign and domestic homes for exchange in its three annual directories; membership is $62, or $72 if you want to receive the directories but remain unlisted. The **Vacation Exchange Club** (Box 650, Key West, FL 33041, tel. 800/638–3841), also with thousands of foreign and domestic listings, publishes four annual directories plus updates; the $50 membership includes your listing in one book. **Loan-a-Home** (2 Park La., Apt. 6E, Mount Vernon, NY 10552, tel. 914/664–7640) specializes in long-term exchanges; there is no charge to list your home, but the directories cost $35 or $45 depending on the number you receive.

Apartment and Villa Rentals If you want a home base that's roomy enough for a family and comes with cooking facilities, a furnished rental may be the solution. It's generally cost-wise, too, although not always—some rentals are luxury properties (economical only when your party is large). Home-exchange directories (*see above*) do list rentals—often second homes owned by prospective house swappers—and there are services that can not only look for a house or apartment for you (even a castle if that's your fancy) but also handle the paperwork. Some send an illustrated catalogue and others send photographs of specific properties, sometimes at a charge; up-front registration fees may apply.

Among the rental companies are **Overseas Connection** (31 N. Harbor Dr., Sag Harbor, NY 11963, tel. 516/725–9308) and **Rent a Home International** (7200 34th Ave. NW, Seattle, WA 98117, tel. 206/789–9377 or 800/488–7368). **Hideaways International** (767 Islington St., Box 4433, Portsmouth, NH 03802, tel. 603/430–4433 or 800/843–4433) functions as a travel club. Membership ($79 yearly per person or family at the same address) includes two annual guides plus quarterly newsletters; rentals are arranged directly between members, not by the club staff.

Camping Camping is an invigorating and inexpensive way to tour the Rockies. Colorado, Idaho, Montana, Utah, and Wyoming are full of state and national parks and forests with sites that range from rustic, with pit toilets and cold running water, to campgrounds with full hookups, bathhouses with hot showers, and paved trailer pads that can accommodate even jumbo RVs. Fees vary, from $6 to $10 a night for tenters up to $21 for RVs, but are usually waived once the water is turned off for the winter. Sometimes site reservations are accepted, and then only for up to seven days (early birds reserve up to a year in advance); more often, they're not. Campers who prefer a more remote setting may camp in the backcountry; it's free but you'll need a permit, available from park visitor centers and ranger stations. If you're visiting in summer, plan well ahead. *The National Parks: Camping Guide* (Superintendent of Documents, U.S. Government Printing Office, Washington, DC 20402; $3.50) may be helpful.

In addition, you'll find privately operated campgrounds; their facilities and amenities are usually more extensive (swimming pools are common), reservations are more widely accepted, and nightly fees are higher: $7 and up for tents, $23 for RVs.

Credit Cards

The following credit card abbreviations are used: AE, American Express; D, Discover; DC, Diners Club; MC, MasterCard; and V, Visa.

2 Special-Interest Vacations: Winter

By Peter Oliver

The special-interest winter activity in the Rockies is, of course, downhill skiing, there being (at last count) more than 60 ski areas in the region—each with at least a 1,000-foot vertical rise. The fastest-growing special interest might be snowboarding, which has exploded in popularity over the last 10 years. Despite that growth, however, snowboarders still represent only about 10% of the people on the trails on any given day. They are, after all, still called *ski* areas.

Because space is limited, only the 20 most prominent ski areas are described in this chapter, meaning that some smaller but very worthy resorts, such as Purgatory, Colorado, didn't make the cut. Also, there are numerous virtual unknowns out there where you can experience fine, crowd-free skiing.

In addition to offering you the rundown on ski areas, we've included information on other activities offered at resorts and surrounding areas. Cross-country skiing (of which there is plenty), dogsledding, snowmobiling, fishing, hot-air ballooning, paragliding, and even golf in some locations late in the season are among the possibilities.

Nevertheless, downhill skiing remains far and away Activity #1, and in an effort to keep things that way, resorts in recent years have been bending over backward to offer programs for special-interest groups. Almost all of the major resorts now have some form of children's program, women's program, snowboarding program, disabled-skier program, and recreational-racing program. Again for the sake of space, only unique or exemplary programs at each resort are described below. If you're looking for a program to suit your particular interests, call ahead or check at the main ski-school desk; chances are pretty good that you'll find what you're looking for.

The skiing season runs approximately from mid-November to mid-April, depending on the resort and the location. The best package deals usually apply early and late in the season; for packages, check not only with each resort but also with major airlines (American, Continental, Delta, and United) that service the Rockies. Many resorts open late and shut down early not for lack of snow but for lack of business. In fact, some of the best backcountry skiing can be had in late April and May, when avalanche risks subside and the firmer, sun-baked snow is easier to walk and climb on than midwinter powder. Just because the ski resorts give up on skiing doesn't mean you have to.

A few notes: terrain ratings (i.e., beginner, intermediate, advanced) are approximate and may vary considerably from one ski area to the next. In other words, an intermediate trail at one area might be rated as expert elsewhere; rating trails is a matter of judgment rather than science. Thus, the terrain ratings might give you a rough idea of the ratio of beginner versus advanced options at a particular area, but are of much less use in comparing areas with one another. Also, prices were accurate as of spring '93.

The Rockies Ski Areas

CANADA

NORTH DAKOTA

SOUTH DAKOTA

MONTANA

WYOMING

IDAHO

Rapid City

Newcastle

Midwest

Gillette

Buffalo

Sheridan

Devils Tower

N. CHEYENNE INDIAN RES.

BIGHORN CANYON NATL REC. AREA

CROW INDIAN RES.

Worland

Thermopolis

WIND RIVER INDIAN

Cody

Billings

Livingston

YELLOWSTONE NATL PARK

GRAND TETON NATL PARK

Jackson Hole

Idaho

Jackson

Westby

Wolf Point

Sidney

Glendive

Circle

Miles City

Forsyth

Jordan

Roundup

FORT PECK INDIAN RES.

Fort Peck Lake

Malta

Havre

FORT BELKNAP INDIAN RES.

Milk River

Missouri River

Yellowstone R.

Great Falls

Shelby

Conrad

Fairfield

Helena

Butte

Bozeman

Big Sky

Lima

Deer Lodge

Anaconda

Wisdom

Butte City

Salmon

Challis

Stanley

SAWTOOTH NATL. REC. AREA

Sun Valley

WATERTON-GLACIER INT'L PEACE PARK

Big Mountain

Kalispell

Flathead Lake

FLATHEAD INDIAN RES.

Missoula

Elk City

Dworshak Res.

NEZ PERCE INDIAN RES.

Lewiston

Moscow

Coeur d'Alene

COEUR D'ALENE INDIAN RES.

Sand Point

Snake River

Payette

Caldwell

Boise

Nampa

BLACKFEET INDIAN RES.

NEBRASKA

Julesburg
80
Sterling
385
59
Burlington
76
Sterling
Greeley
Lamar
50
40
287
Arkansas River
La Junta
Cheyenne
Fort Collins
Denver
70
Colorado Springs
350
10
Trinidad
Boulder
Summit County
25
NEW MEXICO
Casper
Wheatland
Laramie
Winter Park
24
Leadville
Pueblo
Walsenburg
Alamosa
26
487
Vail/ Beaver Creek
82
COLORADO
285
Continental Divide
Steamboat Springs
Gunnison
287
Rawlins
Craig
40
Aspen/ Snowmass
133
Crested Butte
84
Lander
28
Colorado River
Glenwood Springs
50
Montrose
Durango
Pinedale
189
191
80
Rock Springs
Meeker
70
Telluride
160
Silverton
S. UTE INDIAN RES.
Farson
30
139
Grand Junction
Montpelier
FLAMING GORGE NAT'L REC. AREA
Dinosaur
DINOSAUR NAT'L MON.
UTE MTN. INDIAN RES.
Rawlins

NEVADA

Twin Falls
51
93
Home
86
84
Pocatello
15
Preston
Logan
30
Evanston
Ogden
Great Salt Lake
Salt Lake City
Park City/ Deer Valley
Alta/ Snowbird
Provo
UTAH
Nephi
Fillmore
15
Vernal
UINTAH & OURAY INDIAN RES.
Price
Green River
Moab
ARCHES NAT'L PARK
CANYONLANDS NAT'L PARK
CAPITOL REEF NAT'L PARK
GLEN CANYON NAT'L REC. AREA
Bluff
Cedar City
BRYCE CANYON NAT'L PARK
ZION NAT'L PARK
St. George

ARIZONA

N

KEY
—— Amtrak Lines

150 miles
225 km
0

Colorado

Aspen/Snowmass

Aspen is as much a national icon as it is a town—forever in the news as a litmus test of the American public's tolerance of radical-chic politics, conspicuous consumption, and conspicuous love affairs. It is a scriptless, cinema-verité soap opera: part resort town, part ski area, part cultural retreat, part New-Age-politics–thirtysomething-hedonistic-excess comic strip. It is a place where celebrities have affairs and locals have dogs and mountain bikes. It is weird.

In Aspen, high-end clothing boutiques have been known to serve free Campari and soda après-ski, a practice so brazenly elitist that there's a certain charm to it. At the same time, it's a place where people actually live, send their kids to school, and work real jobs that may or may not have to do with skiing. It is, arguably, America's original ski-bum destination, a fact that continues to give the town's character an underlying layer of humor and texture. People can come to Aspen, dress much too expensively, and loudly make fools of themselves, as Donald Trump and Barbra Streisand (among others) have done. But a person can also come to Aspen and have a reasonably straightforward, enjoyable ski vacation, because once you've stripped away the veneer, Aspen is not a bad town or a bad place to ski.

Snowmass was built in 1967 as Aspen's answer to Vail—a ski-specific resort—and although it has never quite matched the panache or popularity of Vail, it has gained a certain stature with age. It used to be that if you stayed at Snowmass, your dining and entertainment choices were pretty much either cooking in your condo or driving the 15 or so miles to Aspen. In recent years, an effort has been made to breathe a little life and pizzazz into Snowmass Village, and the effect has been noticeable. Better restaurants and a livelier après-ski scene in recent years have lured people into the village after the lifts close. In years past, the tendency was to make quick tracks back to your hotel or condo.

In general, Snowmass is the preferred alternative for families with young children, leaving the town of Aspen to a more hard-partying, up-at-the-crack-of-noon kind of crowd. The selling points of Snowmass as an alternative to Aspen are lots of on-slope, ski-in/ski-out lodging, a slow pace, and quiet.

Visitor Information Central reservations: tel. 800/262–7736 for Aspen, 800/332–3245 for Snowmass. General information: **Aspen Skiing Company** (Box 1248, Aspen 81612, tel. 303/925–1220 or 800/525–6200); **Aspen Visitors Center** (425 Rio Grande Pl., Aspen, CO 81611, tel. 303/925–1940). Snow reports: tel. 303/925–1221.

Getting There Both **Continental Express** (tel. 303/925–4350 or 800/525–0280) and **United Express** (tel. 303/925–3400 or 800/241–6522) have frequent flights between Denver and Aspen. United Express also has nonstop flights from Chicago, Dallas, and Los Angeles. Many major airlines (including Continental and United) have numerous flights to and from Denver. **Avis, Budget,** and **Hertz,** among others, rent cars from the Aspen airport. **Aspen Limo** (tel. 800/222–2112) and **High Mountain Limo** (tel. 800/528–

8294) provide service to Aspen from Denver and Glenwood Springs.

Generally speaking, driving to Aspen from Denver in the winter is more trouble than it's worth, unless you are on an extended vacation and plan to stop at other resorts such as Vail. With Independence Pass closed in the winter, the drive takes more than three hours at best, depending on road and weather conditions. On the other hand, the drive from the west is relatively easy, with no high-mountain passes to negotiate. Take the Route 82 exit off I–70 at Glenwood Springs.

Getting Around A rental car is unnecessary in either Aspen or Snowmass, since both are geared as much for pedestrians as cars; in many cases it's easier getting around on foot. Furthermore, the Aspen/Snowmass area has perhaps the best free shuttle-bus system (tel. 303/925–8484) in ski-dom, its main drawback being that buses stop running after about 5 PM. The free shuttles are backed up by a county bus system (tel. 303/925–8484), which does continue service late into the night. As an alternative means, hitchhiking between Aspen and Snowmass is still considered an acceptable form of transportation, but you should use your judgment.

Downhill Skiing Aspen and Snowmass are really four ski areas rolled into one resort. Three—Aspen (or Ajax) Mountain, Tiehack, and Snowmass—are owned by the Aspen Skiing Company and can be skied on the same ticket. Aspen Highlands, the fourth, has always been the loner with a perplexing character, although it recently came under the umbrella of Aspen Skiing Company; it has the greatest vertical rise (3,800 feet) of the four Aspen mountains but, in terms of skiable acreage, it may have the least amount of skiing.

Aspen Mountain is considered a mogul skier's dreamland, and from its Bell Mountain chairlift, that's certainly true. However, most Aspen Mountain skiers spend much of their time on intermediate trails off the upper-mountain quad. They also spend their lunchtime on the deck of Bonnie's, the midmountain restaurant, which on a sunny day is one of the great people-watching scenes in the world of skiing. Aspen Mountain's biggest drawback is that too many trails funnel into Spar Gulch, making the end-of-the-day rush to the bottom chaotic and often dangerous.

Tiehack—a place where it is virtually impossible to get into trouble—is terrific for lower intermediates and kids. It's a low-key, lighthearted sort of place, an antidote to the kind of skiing macho you might encounter at Aspen Mountain. Among its featured attractions is a hangout for kids named Fort Frog—a name that ought to tell you something about how seriously Buttermilk takes itself. If you're looking for an escape from the Aspen bustle, spend a day at Tiehack, with its supposed expert cluster of trails, although "expert" is an extremely relative term.

Snowmass is a huge sprawl of a ski area, best known for Big Burn, itself a great sprawl of wide-open, intermediate skiing. In general, Snowmass is one of the best ski areas in the Rockies for intermediates. The route variations down Big Burn are essentially inexhaustible, but still, there are many, many other places on the mountain for intermediates to find entertainment. Not so for experts: Although there are some truly challenging chutes and glades—such as Hanging Valley—they are too often either closed or the snow conditions virtually unskiable. On the other side of the coin, the novice and lower-intermediate terrain on the lower part of the mountain makes Snowmass a terrific place for young kids.

Aspen Highlands is essentially a long, long ridge with trails dropping off to either side. Unfortunately the management of Highlands has let the area grow ragged around the edges, especially regarding its antiquated lift system. Highlands does, however, have some superb expert terrain; its Steeplechase cluster of trails and small bowls is one of the best places to be in the Aspen area on a powder day. The payback is the long, slow lift ride back to the summit, but at least once there you are treated to one of the best summit views in American skiing.

Lessons and Programs For all four mountains: Two-hour adult group lessons start at $35, but a noteworthy deal is the three-day learn-to-ski or learn-to-snowboard package at Tiehack, which includes lessons and lift tickets for $99. All-day children's programs start at $48 per day. Among Aspen's more interesting special programs is the Vic Braden Ski College (based at Snowmass), a four-day program designed for novices and intermediates having difficulty breaking through to the next level of skiing. For more advanced skiers, the Cooper-Tache Race Program, under the direction of former U.S. Ski Team members Mark Tache and Christin Cooper, uses racing techniques to help skiers improve recreational and racing skills.

Facilities Aspen Mountain: 3,267-foot vertical rise; 625 skiable acres; 35% intermediate, 35% advanced, 30% expert; 1 4-passenger gondola, 1 high-speed quad chair, 2 quad chairs, 4 double chairs. Tiehack: 2,030-foot vertical rise; 410 skiable acres; 35% beginner, 39% intermediate, 26% advanced; 6 double chairs. Snowmass: 10% beginner, 51% intermediate, 18% advanced, 21% expert. Aspen Highlands: 3,800-foot vertical rise; 550 acres skiable terrain; 25% beginner, 50% intermediate, 25% advanced; 9 double chairs, 2 surface lifts.

Lift Tickets $42 adults, $24 children 7–12, children under 7 and adults over 70 free. Savings of less than 10% on multiday tickets. Note: Lift tickets are included in some lodging prices.

Rentals Numerous ski shops in Aspen and Snowmass rent equipment. One of the best and most conveniently located is **Sport Stalker,** at the Aspen Mountain gondola base (tel. 303/925–5773) and in Snowmass Village (tel. 303/923–6111). Rentals are also available at the Tiehack base lodge. Rental packages (skis, boots, poles) start at around $15 per day, although bargain shopping at stores around town may turn up lower-priced deals.

Cross-Country Skiing
Backcountry Skiing The **10th Mountain Hut and Trail System,** named in honor of the U.S. Army's skiing 10th Mountain Division, includes 10 huts along the trail connecting Aspen and Vail. The main trail follows a generally avalanche-safe route in altitudes that vary between 8,000 and 12,000 feet. This translates to a fair amount of skiing along tree-lined trails and a good bit of high-alpine up and down. You must be in good shape, and some backcountry skiing experience is extremely helpful. The accommodations along the trail are the Hiltons of backcountry huts, supplied with precut wood for wood-burning stoves, mattresses and pillows, and propane stoves and utensils for cooking. Each hut generally sleeps 16 (more if you're willing to cuddle). *1280 Ute*

Ave., Aspen 81612, tel. 303/925–5775. Hut fees: $22 per person per night. Reservations required at least a month in advance.

The **Alfred A. Braun Hut System** is Aspen's other major backcountry network. The trailhead leads from the Ashcroft Touring Center (*see* Track Skiing, *below*) into the Maroon Bells/Snowmass Wilderness, and generally covers terrain more prone to avalanche possibilities than the 10th Mountain Division Trail. Huts sleep 6–9 people. *Box 7937, Aspen 81612, tel. 303/925–7345. Hut fees: $14 per person per night. Reservations required at least a day in advance, considerably earlier for weekends and peak-season periods.*

If you're unfamiliar with either hut system or inexperienced in backcountry travel, you should hire a guide. One reliable recommendation is **Aspen Alpine Guides** (Box 5122, Aspen 81612, tel. 303/925–6680 or 800/643–8621). In Aspen, the best stores for renting backcountry gear (including ski equipment, climbing skins, packs, sleeping bags, and mountaineering paraphernalia) are **The Hub** (315 E. Hyman Ave., tel. 303/925–7970) and **Ute Mountaineer** (308 S. Mill St., tel. 303/925–2849).

Track Skiing There is something to be said for a wealthy tax base. Subsidized by local taxes (in most towns, public cross-country ski trails would be considered a fiscal extravagance), the Aspen/Snowmass Nordic Council charges no fee for the 80 kilometers (49½ miles) of maintained trails (not all interconnected) in the Roaring Fork Valley. Probably the most varied, in terms of scenery and terrain, is the 30-kilometer (18½-mile) Snowmass Club trail network.

For a longer ski, try the Owl Creek Trail, connecting the Snowmass Club trail system and the Aspen Cross-Country Center trails. More than 16 kilometers (10 miles) long, the trail provides both a good workout and a heavy dosage of woodsy beauty, with many ups and downs across meadows and aspen-gladed hillsides. Lessons and rentals available at the **Aspen Cross-Country Center** (39551 Hwy. 82 at the Aspen Golf Course, tel. 303/925–2145). Diagonal, skating, racing, and light touring setups available. Open daily 8:30–4:30. Lessons and rentals are also available at the **Snowmass Club Touring Center** (0239 Snowmass Club Cir., tel. 303/923–5600) and the **Hub of Aspen** (315 E. Hyman Ave., tel. 303/925–7970). Open daily 9–8.

Twelve miles from Aspen, the **Ashcroft Touring Center** is sequestered in a high alpine basin up Castle Creek, which runs between Aspen Mountain and Aspen Highlands. The 30 kilometers (over 18½ miles) of groomed trails are surrounded by the high peaks of the Maroon Bells/Snowmass Wilderness. It is truly one of the more dramatic cross-country sites in the Rockies. *Ashcroft Touring Unlimited, Castle Creek Rd., tel. 303/925–1044.*

Other Activities
Dogsledding **Krabloonik** (1201 Divide Rd., Snowmass, tel. 303/923–4342), with more than 250 dogs at its disposal, can put on a good half-day ride (beginning at 9:30 AM or 1 PM). The ride is preceded or followed by lunch at the Krabloonik restaurant, among the best in the Aspen/Snowmass area.

Paragliding Skiing or running off a mountainside with a parachute attached to your back is the sort of thing you'd expect to be popular in adventure-crazed France, and it is. In the United States, however, paragliding is still a relatively fledgling sport, and Aspen is one of the few places in the country where you can get your ya-ya's out this way. The **Aspen Paragliding School** (Box 2432, Aspen, CO 81612, tel. 303/925-7625) offers everything from single rides to four-day courses. Single rides are in tandem with a pilot; four-day courses ($375) lead up to solo flights.

Snowcat Skiing **Aspen Mountain Powder Tours** (tel. 303/925-1227) provides access to 1,500 acres on the back side of Aspen Mountain. Most of the terrain is negotiable by confident intermediates, with about 10,000 vertical feet constituting a typical day's skiing. Reservations are required at least a day in advance. Allow more time during peak season. Tours cost about $200.

Crested Butte

Crested Butte has traditionally presented itself as the promised land of ski towns: After you've sold your soul in the Sodom and Gomorrah of Aspen and Vail, you pass through pearly gates and enter Crested Butte. No pretensions. No resort bluster. No fur, except for that worn by living animals. An honest, down-to-earth Rocky Mountain ski town.

The truth is, Crested Butte is more than *one* ski town, and there *are* similarities to the two big shots: There's Crested Butte, a former mining town (not unlike Aspen), and Mount Crested Butte, a recently built resort town (not unlike Vail). But Crested Butte's relaxed, earthy atmosphere is genuine. Its generally youngish and politically left-leaning populace tends toward being "granola," as they say in the West. In other words, things like natural foods, natural-fiber clothing, and a rugged outdoor spirit are commonplace. For athletic purists, Crested Butte lays claim to sparking the resurgence of telemark skiing about 20 years ago and the emergence, more recently, of mountain biking. You know you're an authentic Crested Butte-ite when you own not one but two mountain bikes: a town bike for hacking around and a performance bike for *serious* hacking around.

One other thing the people at Crested Butte have done in recent years that is very unlike Aspen or Vail—very un-American, for that matter—is that they've let people ski for nothing. No kidding—free lift tickets up until the week before Christmas. The thinking was that the freebies would drum up business for local lodging and dining establishments during a traditionally slow period for ski areas. In the first year the idea was tried, a lot of skinflint ski bums showed up, and a lot of the local business proprietors were dubious. Since then, the idea has caught on with families and ski clubs; it is one of the few ways for a family of four or more to go on a relatively inexpensive ski vacation these days.

Visitor Central reservations: tel. 800/544-8448. General information:
Information **Crested Butte Mountain Resort** (12 Snowmass Rd., Box A, Mount Crested Butte, tel. 303/349-2281); **Crested Butte Chamber of Commerce** (Old Town Hall, Box 1288, Crested Butte, tel. 303/349-6438). Snow report: tel. 303/349-2323.

Getting There **American Airlines** (tel. 800/433-7300) offers direct flights to Gunnison (30 miles from Crested Butte) from Chicago and Dallas/Fort Worth. **Delta** (tel. 800/221-1212) has direct flights to Gunnison from Atlanta. **Continental Express** (tel. 800/525-

0280) and **United Express** (tel. 800/241–6522) have regular service from Denver. **Alpine Express** (Box 1250, Gunnison 81230, tel. 303/641–5074) offers van service from Gunnison to Crested Butte.

Crested Butte is 230 miles southwest of Denver.

Getting Around There is reliable shuttle-bus service between the town of Crested Butte and the resort village, which are about 3 miles apart. However, because most lodging is at the resort village and the better restaurants, shopping, and general atmosphere are in town, you can expect to make many resort-to-town trips, and a car makes the going much easier. You can rent a car at the Gunnison airport.

Downhill Skiing Crested Butte skiing has a split personality, a judgment that is easily made by checking out the skiers who come here. One side of its personality is the primary trail network, characterized by long intermediate and lower-intermediate runs. This is the sort of skiing that attracts vacationers and families, mostly from the Southwest and Texas. They take advantage of, among other things, a wonderful expanse of easy terrain from the Keystone lift—not just a trail network but instead rolling, tree-dotted meadows with plenty of opportunities to poke around off the beaten track.

The other side of Crested Butte's personality is the so-called Extreme Limits, several hundred acres of steep bowls, gnarly chutes, and tight tree skiing. This is an attraction for extreme skiers (and extreme-skiing wannabes), so it's not surprising that Crested Butte is the site of the national extreme-skiing championships each year.

The best skiing on the main trail network is on the front side of the mountain. The new high-speed quad (open for the '92–'93 season) has been a great addition, making 2,000 vertical feet available with just one quick lift ride. Unfortunately this has made the long, slow lift on the Paradise Bowl side seem that much longer and slower, although it accesses some of the mountain's best intermediate terrain.

The Extreme Limits is quirky terrain, capable of being sensational, horrible, or (more often than a lot of experts would like) closed. A few years ago, the only way to get to it was to climb over the ridgeline from the top of the Paradise lift. Although the installation of a poma changed that, it also brought more skiers, some of whom are over their heads on that side of the mountain. This means the fresh snow gets skied up earlier than it used to, especially in those gnarly chutes. Face it: Terrain as steep and rocky as this really requires superb snow conditions to make it truly pleasurable. Otherwise, it can be rough going, and even hazardous.

Lessons and Two-hour group lessons start at $26; two-hour special work-
Programs shops begin at $37. One special program of note is Kim Reichhelm's Women's Ski Adventures. Reichhelm, a former world extreme-skiing champion, leads four-day workshops aimed at "breakthrough" experiences for women of all abilities. Call or write Women's Ski Adventures (237 Post Rd. W, Westport, CT 06880, tel. 800/992–7700) for dates and details. Call the ski school (tel. 303/349–2251) for information on other programs.

Facilities 2,775-foot vertical rise; 877 skiable acres; 27% beginner, 53% intermediate, 20% advanced for the main trail network; 100% expert for the Extreme Limits; 1 high-speed quad chair, 3 triple chairs, 5 double chairs, 4 surface lifts.

Lift Tickets $39 adults, $24 children; children under 12 free when an adult purchases a ticket. Free lift tickets from Thanksgiving week until the week before Christmas.

Rentals Full rental packages (including skis, boots, poles) are available through **Crested Butte Ski Rental** (tel. 303/349–2241) and start at $13 per day for adults, $9 children under 11. Substantial discounts available for multiday rentals.

Cross-Country Skiing
Backcountry Skiing Considerable avalanche hazards notwithstanding, Crested Butte abounds with backcountry possibilities, from deep-woods touring to above-tree-line telemarking. Keep in mind that this is high-mountain country (the town itself is around 9,000 feet, and things go up from there) and that skiing in certain areas under certain weather conditions can be nothing short of suicidal. To play it safe, your best bet is to arrange a guided tour with the **Crested Butte Nordic Ski Center** (*see below*).

Another possibility is to spend a few days at **Irwin Lake Lodge,** located in a high basin about 12 miles from town. In winter, snowcats carry Alpine as well as telemark skiers to a ridge rendering terrific views of the 14,000-foot peaks of the Maroon Bells/Snowmass wilderness. From here, it's more than 2,000 vertical feet of bowl and tree skiing back to the lodge. Equally enjoyable is touring on your own (or with a guide) from the lodge. If there is a drawback, it is that this area is popular with snowmobilers (in fact, the lodge also operates a snowmobile guide service), and you may from time to time find your high-mountain solitude interrupted by the buzzing sounds of machinery. *Box 457, Crested Butte 81224, tel. 303/349–5140 or 303/349–7423. Prices vary according to activities, time of season, and length of stay.*

At the base of the ski area, **Crested Butte Ski Rental and Repairs** (tel. 303/349–2241) rents touring and telemark equipment. In town, **The Alpineer** (419 6th St., tel. 303/349–5210) is not only a good backcountry equipment source but can also provide information on backcountry routes and snow conditions.

Track Skiing Three track networks totaling 29 kilometers (18 miles) are maintained by the **Crested Butte Nordic Ski Center**. The largest of the three, the Red Lady Loop, covers mostly flat and rolling terrain across the meadows and through the aspen groves of the valley floor. Views of distant peaks are stunning. The 9 kilometers (about 5½ miles) of the Bench network include a steep loop through the trees of Gibson Ridge—close to town but seemingly far away in the woods. The 9-kilometer (5½-mile) system set on the Skyland Golf Course, 3 miles out of town, is probably the least interesting of the three, although its worth is enhanced considerably by its on-site restaurant. *2nd St., Box 1269, Crested Butte 81224, tel. 303/349–6201. Trail fee: $6 adults, $3 children 12 and under. Lessons: 2-hour group lessons start at $18; all-day tours start at $40. Rental packages (including skis, boots, poles) start at $10 a day. The Nordic Ski Center can also arrange backcountry tours for skiers of all ability levels.*

Other Activities The conditions must be just right, but on a clear windless
Hot-Air Ballooning morning, this wide-open basin, surrounded on all sides by
mountain ranges, must surely be one of the country's best
places to be aloft in a balloon. For information, contact **Bighorn
Balloons** (tel. 303/349–6335). Flights are $100 per person.

Snowmobiling *See* Irwin Lake Lodge in Cross-Country Skiing, *above.*

Steamboat Springs

Perhaps more than any other ski resort in the United States,
Steamboat has linked its identity to a single person: Billy Kidd,
the preeminent U.S. ski racer of the '60s. The everlasting image is of Kidd blasting through the powder with a big grin on
his face and a cowboy hat that must be glued to his head since it
never blows off. That's how Steamboat projects itself: Cowboy
living and deep-snow skiing—new resort meets the Old West.
In large part, Steamboat pulls it off, even if the cowboy business gets a little hokey at times. It is the sort of hokeyness,
though, that works for families, which represent Steamboat's
major target market.

This is not to suggest that there is no legitimacy to Steamboat's
cowboy image, which dates back to the 1800s when the first
ranching communities took root. In fact, these early settlers
were also responsible for the advent of skiing in the area, as
they strapped wooden boards (vaguely resembling skis) to
their feet so they could get around the neighborhood in winter.
Later, Steamboat was one of the first ski areas to be developed
in the West.

Steamboat carries the banner of "Ski Town, USA," which is simultaneously descriptive and misleading: In reality, this is a
modern resort area, sprawling around the base of the ski lifts,
and an older town (Steamboat Springs) located 2 miles away.
The older town indeed has the kind of verve and funkiness you
would expect in a real ski town; the resort area, where a good
many Steamboat visitors stay, is too spread out—or still too
new—to have developed much ski-town character.

Visitor Central reservations: tel. 800/922–2722. General information:
Information **Steamboat Ski & Resort Corporation** (2305 Mt. Werner Circle,
Steamboat Springs 80487, tel. 303/879–6111); **Steamboat
Springs Chamber Resort Association** (Box 774408, Steamboat
Springs 80477, tel. 303/879–0740). Snow report: tel. 303/879–
7300.

Getting There **American** (tel. 800/433–7300), **Continental** (tel. 800/525–0280),
Northwest (800/225–2525), and **United** (800/241–6522) offer
service from several U.S. cities to Yampa Valley Airport, 22
miles from Steamboat. **Continental Express** and **United Express**
have connecting service from Denver's Stapleton Airport to
the Steamboat Springs Airport. Rental cars are available at
both airports. **Alpine Taxi** (tel. 303/879–3400), **Steamboat Taxi**
(tel. 303/879–6800), and **Panorama Coaches** (tel. 303/879–3335)
provide transportation from the airport to lodging within the
resort community. For rental-car and airport-shuttle information, call central reservations (*see* Visitor Information, *above*).
Steamboat Express offers daily bus service from Denver's
Stapleton Airport to Steamboat. For schedules and information, call central reservations (*see* Visitor Information, *above*).

Steamboat is about a three-hour drive from Denver via I–70 west and Route 40 north. The route traverses high-mountain passes, so it's a good idea to check road conditions (tel. 303/639–1234) before you travel.

Getting Around Steamboat's public bus system is a regular and reliable network that gets you around town and to and from the resort community. Skiers staying in town may find a rental car unnecessary; those staying in the more spread-out resort may appreciate the convenience of having one.

Downhill Skiing Steamboat is perhaps best known for its tree skiing and "cruising"—the latter term referring to intermediate skiing on wide, groomed runs. The abundance of cruising terrain has made Steamboat immensely popular with intermediates and families who ski only a few times a year and who aren't looking for diabolical challenges to overtax their abilities. Set on a predominantly western exposure—most ski areas are situated on north-facing exposures—the resort benefits from intense sun, which contributes to the cruising quality. Moreover, one of the most extensive lift systems in the West allows skiers to take a lot of fast runs without having to spend much time in line. The Storm Peak and Sundown high-speed quads, for example, each deliver about 2,000 vertical feet in less than seven minutes. Do the math, and you can figure that a day of more than 60,000 vertical feet is entirely within the realm of diehards.

All this is not to suggest, however, that Steamboat lacks challenge entirely. A number of runs, such as Concentration, are not groomed regularly, and while the pitch might not be extraordinarily steep, big moguls can make the going pretty rugged. There are also some real steeps, such as Chute One, but they're few and not especially long. If you're looking for challenging skiing at Steamboat, take on the trees. The ski area has done an admirable job of clearing many gladed areas of such nuisances as saplings, underbrush, and fallen timber, making Steamboat tree skiing a much less hazardous adventure than it can be at some areas. The trees are also where advanced skiers—as well as, in some places, confident intermediates—can find the best of Steamboat's ballyhooed powder. Ironically the resort that is renowned for its "champagne powder" doesn't receive significantly more snow statistically than other major Colorado resorts. At least on the top half of the mountain, however, the snow does tend to retain an unusual lightness and freshness.

Lessons and Programs Two-hour adult lessons begin at $32. Mogul, powder, racing, snowboarding, and telemark clinics are available, and intensive two- and three-day "training camps" are offered in racing and advanced skiing through the Billy Kidd Center for Performance Skiing (tel. 303/879–6111, ext. 543). Children's programs (lessons and/or day care) are offered for kids 6 months to 15 years old through the Kids' Vacation Center (tel. 303/879–6111, ext. 218). Rates begin at $30 per half day, $42 per day. For general ski school information, call 303/879–6111, ext. 531.

Facilities 3,685-foot vertical rise; 2,500 skiable acres; 15% beginner, 54% intermediate, 31% advanced; 1 8-passenger gondola, 2 high-speed quad chairs, 1 quad chair, 6 triple chairs, 7 double chairs, 2 surface lifts.

Lift Tickets	$39 adults, $23 children; children under 13 free with an adult buying a multiday ticket for 5 days or more (1 child per adult). Savings of 5% or less on multiday tickets.
Rentals	Equipment packages are available at the gondola base as well as at ski shops in town. Packages (skis, boots, poles) average about $16 a day; less for multiday rentals. Call central reservations, *above* for rental information.

Cross-Country Skiing
Backcountry Skiing The most popular area for backcountry skiing is Rabbit Ears Pass southeast of town, the last pass you must cross if you drive from Denver to Steamboat. Much of its appeal is the easy access to high country; trails emanate from the Route 40 roadside. There are plenty of touring routes possible, with limited telemarking opportunity. Arrangements for backcountry tours can be made through the **Steamboat Ski Touring Center** (*see* Track Skiing, *below*).

Another popular backcountry spot is Seedhouse Road, north of the town of Clark and about 25 miles north of Steamboat. A marked trail network covers rolling hills, with good views of distant peaks. For maps, trail suggestions, and information on snow conditions and stability, contact the **Hahn's Peak Ranger Office** (57 10th St., Box 1212, Steamboat Springs 80477, tel. 303/879–1870).

Touring and telemarking rentals are available at various ski shops in the Steamboat area. One of the best is the **Ski Haus** (Rte. 40 and Pine Grove Rd., tel. 303/879–0385).

Track Skiing The main center for cross-country skiing is the **Steamboat Ski Touring Center,** where most of the 30-kilometer (18½-mile) trail network—laid out on or alongside the Sheraton Steamboat Golf Club—is relatively gentle. The inspiration behind the center is Sven Wiik, a seminal figure in the establishment of cross-country skiing in the United States. A good option for a relaxed afternoon of skiing is to pick up some eats at the Picnic Basket in the touring center building and enjoy lunch alfresco at the picnic area along the Fish Creek Trail, a 5-kilometer (3-mile) loop that winds through pine and aspen groves. *Box 772297, Steamboat Springs 80477, tel. 303/879–8180. Trail fee: $9 adults per day, $7.50 after 1 PM; $5 children. Rental packages (skis, boots, poles): $10 per day, $8.50 half day.*

Some guest ranches in the area also have groomed track networks. **Home Ranch** (Box 8221, Clark 80428, tel. 303/879–9044), 20 miles north of Steamboat, has 40 kilometers (25 miles) of groomed tracks. **Vista Verde Guest Ranch** (Box 465, Steamboat Springs 80477, tel. 303/879–3858 or 800/526–7433) also has a groomed trail network, as well as access to adjacent national-forest land for touring.

Other Activities Outdoor activities—including dogsledding, hot-air ballooning, and snowmobiling—can be arranged by calling the activities department at **Steamboat Central Reservations** (tel. 800/922–2722, ext. 372).

Bobsledding The term "bobsledding" might be stretching things, since this isn't quite the 80-mile-per-hour rush down a twisting gutter of ice that you've seen at the Olympics. However, when riding a soft-shelled, four-person sled down the course at Howelsen Hill (tel. 303/879–2170), the ski-jumping hill just outside town, it's possible to reach speeds of nearly 50 miles per hour—plenty fast for most people. The cost is $8 per run.

Ice Driving Here's one for anyone who's either been intimidated by snowy roads or gotten teenage thrills from executing doughnuts on icy shopping-mall parking lots. The **Jean-Paul Luc Ice Driving School** (tel. 303/879–6104) offers ½- to 1½-hour clinics that include classroom instruction as well as driving on a snow- and ice-covered track.

Sleigh Rides Several ranches in the area offer horse-drawn sleigh rides, dinner rides being the most popular. Call the central reservations number (*see* Visitor Information *above*) for details. **Windwalker Ranch** (Box 5093, Steamboat Springs 80477, tel. 303/879–8065) also offers daily afternoon sleigh rides to view elk herds that winter in the area.

Snowcat Skiing Buffalo Pass, northeast of Steamboat, is reputed to be one of the snowiest spots in Colorado, and that's where **Steamboat Powder Cats** (Box 2468, Steamboat Springs 80477, tel. 303/879–5188) operates. The basics are included: open-meadow skiing, deep snow, and a maximum of only 11 skiers. Snowcat skiing is the "poor man's" version of helicopter skiing, although at more than $150 a day, it's not exactly skiing for the lunch-pail crowd. One advantage over helicopters: Cats don't have to worry about landing and can get to places in bad weather that would be inaccessible by helicopter.

Summit County: Arapahoe Basin, Breckenridge, Copper Mountain, Keystone

Summit County is a hard place to get a fix on: four ski areas, three resorts, three towns in between . . . and Vail just over the pass. Where do you start? This multiplicity is both Summit County's bounty and its curse. It is a curse in that the area seems to have developed without much unified focus or sense of direction. The three major resorts—Breckenridge, Copper Mountain, and Keystone—are caught in that peculiar bind of establishing their own identities, while still maintaining an association with the others.

Frisco, Dillon, and Silverthorne—those three towns in between—have accepted their mandate as calling for function over character. They provide moderately priced lodging and dining at approximately equal distances to the ski areas and are close to the highway. The fact is that many Summit County skiers are weekenders from Denver looking for a few days of respite from the city, not a fancy, full-service vacation.

The multimountain, multitown mishmash is not without irony. The one resort with solid historical roots is Breckenridge, built around the Main Street of an old mining town. Yet Breckenridge has become so built up over the years (close to 25,000 beds) that it comes off as the most thoroughly developed resort of the three, rather than the quaintest. The area that *does* have a legitimately unique character is the odd man out here, Arapahoe Basin, which really hasn't made any effort to buff up an image. Arapahoe is pretty much the ski area it was 20 years ago and is popular with a generally younger crowd and especially visited late in the season—April into June. Arapahoe's late-season, on-mountain partying spirit has become legendary.

What does it all add up to? Very briefly: Breckenridge is generally the choice of a young, lively crowd. The skiing focuses mainly on cruising, and so does the nightlife. Copper Mountain is best for skiers committed to skiing. The terrain is the best and most varied in Summit County, but the resort village expresses an angular, antiseptic functionality—a suburban cluster at the mountain base. Keystone is a quiet and, by the often slapdash standards of ski-lodging construction, well-built place. It's popular with families and probably wins the Summit County prize as the most genuine mountain resort.

Visitor Information Central reservations: tel. 800/221–1091 for Breckenridge; tel. 800/458–8386 for Copper Mountain; tel. 800/222–0188 for Keystone (condos), tel. 800/541–0346 (lodge). General information: **Breckenridge Ski Corporation** (Box 1058, Breckenridge 80424, tel. 303/453–5000); **Copper Mountain Resort** (Box 3001, Copper Mountain 80443, tel. 303/968–2318); **Keystone Resort** (Box 38, Keystone 80435, tel. 303/426–2316; **Ski the Summit** (Box 98, Dillon 80435, tel. 800/441–3533). Snow reports: tel. 303/453–6118 for Breckenridge; tel. 303/968–2100 for Copper Mountain; tel. 303/468–4111 for Keystone/Arapahoe Basin.

Getting There Summit County is approximately 75 miles west of Denver on I–70. Most major carriers fly into Denver. **Resort Express** (tel. 800/334–7433) provides van service between the airport and the resorts.

Getting Around Although there is free shuttle-bus service within Summit County, a car is almost essential if you plan to do much traveling between your resort of choice and other points in Summit County. For anyone trying to avoid renting a car, Breckenridge, with the widest array of services and a town shuttle bus, is probably the best place to set up shop.

Downhill Skiing Let's see . . . close to 5,000 skiable acres, 60-some lifts, more than 300 marked trails. What you need in Summit County isn't a lift ticket but a calculator. Despite their proximity, the four ski areas do have distinctly different characters. A quick summary: For the most part, Breckenridge is the sort of area where you can close your eyes and let your skis run; intermediate cruising is the name of the game. It is ideal for people who like a relaxed day on the slopes without having to worry about overworking the challenge meter. Still, there is some more adventurous, above-tree-line bowl skiing, accessible either by hiking or by a hard-to-ride T-bar. When that high-country skiing is good, it's great, but because of Breck's exposure to stormy weather, conditions can often be less than ideal.

Breckenridge's chief drawback is its horizontal layout, spreading across the flanks of three main peaks, named—with great imagination—Peaks 8, 9, and 10. Want to get from the base of Peak 8 to the summit of Peak 10? A couple of lift rides are necessary, and navigational aids would be helpful.

As mentioned, Copper Mountain has perhaps the best variety of skiing among the Summit County areas. Good, long cruisers, satisfying mogul runs, above-tree-line bowl skiing, tight tree skiing, and a terrific cluster of lower-intermediate terrain. Furthermore, the layout is such that there's minimal contact (literally) between skiers of differing abilities; you don't have fast skiers sharing the same terrain as beginners, as you do at some areas.

One reason for this is that Copper, like Breckenridge, is a horizontal spread, with novice skiers tending toward the right, intermediates in the middle, and experts toward the left. It's a great choice for a family or group of friends with widely varying skills; there's skiing to keep everyone entertained. Copper used to have a cross-mountain navigational problem similar to Breckenridge's, but the well-placed installation of a couple of high-speed quad chairs a few years back improved the situation considerably.

Keystone is hard to get a good read on at first, especially since the slopes you see from the base lodge look quite steep—and they are—but they are not indicative of the rest of the trails. About 90% of Keystone Mountain is geared toward novice and lower-intermediate skiing. Yet Keystone Mountain isn't all there is to Keystone. Slip off the back side, and you've got North Peak and the Outback, with skiing for more skilled intermediates and advanced skiers. None of it, though, is real knock-your-socks-off expert terrain, but Keystone has never tried to market itself as an expert's ski area. It's great for families or for people who ski once or twice a year. Better skiers prefer to toss the boards in the car and head for either Copper or Arapahoe, 6 miles up the road.

They *won't* head for Arapahoe, however, on bad-weather days. What can make Arapahoe delightful is also what damns it in bad weather: its elevation. The *base* elevation is almost 10,800 feet, so that most of Arapahoe's skiing is above tree line. When a storm moves in, you can't even tell which way is up or down at Arapahoe, and when the storm passes, skiing can be limited because of avalanche problems.

But if that sounds dreadful, consider the other side of the coin: On sunny spring days, Arapahoe is probably *the* place to be skiing in Colorado. It feels more like skiing in the Alps than Summit County, Colorado, with craggy peaks surrounded by treeless, rolling terrain. Intermediates can have a great time here, although "A-Basin" is best known for its expert challenges: the East Wall, a steep open face with great powder-skiing possibilities; Pallavicini, a wide, steep, tree-lined gutter of a run; and the West Wall cornice, from which young bucks, with varying degrees of bravado and sobriety, like launching themselves. A typical spring day at Arapahoe: Ski frantically hard in the morning; kick back, catch rays, and swill beers in the afternoon.

Lessons and Programs All four areas offer a variety of instructional programs, from half-day group lessons to special clinics, notably mogul clinics and women's seminars. Among the better bargains is the $36 all-day group-lesson rate at Breckenridge. One of the better children's programs is at Keystone, with day care and ski groups for kids from two months to 16 years old. Rates for all-day kids' camps (3–16, grouped by age), which include lift tickets, lessons, rentals, and lunch, start at $55 per day. A special program of note is the Mahre Training Center at Keystone, intensive three- or five-day clinics held at various dates during the season and hosted by either Phil or Steve Mahre, both Olympic medalists.

Facilities Arapahoe Basin: 1,670-foot vertical rise; 425 skiable acres; 10% beginner, 50% intermediate, 40% advanced; 1 triple chair, 4 double chairs. Breckenridge: 3,398-foot vertical rise; 1,600 skiable acres; 20% beginner, 32% intermediate, 48% advanced; 4 high-speed quad chairs, 1 triple chair, 8 double chairs, 3 surface lifts. Copper Mountain: 2,760-foot vertical rise; 1,550 skiable acres; 25% beginner, 40% intermediate, 35% advanced; 2 high-speed quad chairs, 6 triple chairs, 8 double chairs, 4 surface lifts. Keystone: 2,340-foot vertical rise; 1,200 skiable acres; 10% beginner, 59% intermediate, 31% advanced; 2 gondolas, 3 high-speed quad chairs, 1 quad chair, 3 triple chairs, 6 double chairs, 4 surface lifts.

Lift Tickets Tickets cost $38–$40, depending on the resort; children under 6 and adults over 70 ski free. Multi-day ticket savings can exceed 20%. Multiday, multi-area coupon booklets are also available, beginning with a 4-day, 4-area booklet for $132 adults, $68 children.

Rentals Rental shops are located at the bases of all four ski areas, with rental packages (skis, boots, poles) starting at $12 per day. Considerable savings can be found by bargain shopping at ski stores in Breckenridge, Dillon, Frisco, and Silverthorne.

Cross-Country Skiing
Backcountry Skiing Despite widespread development in Summit County, there are still plenty of opportunities to escape into the backcountry and get away from it all. They don't call it Summit County for nothing; mountain passes above 10,000 feet allow for relatively easy access to high-country terrain and good, high-country snow. This recommendation comes, however, with a word of caution; avalanche-related deaths are all too common in Summit County (more often involving snowmobilers than skiers). Easy access often attracts backcountry travelers whose snow-safety awareness is not what it should be. For information on snow conditions, contact the **Dillon Ranger District Office** (Box 620, 135 Rte. 9, Silverthorne 80498, tel. 303/468–5400 or 303/468–5434).

Among the easier, and safer, touring routes is the trip to Boreas Pass, just south of Breckenridge. The trail (about 20 kilometers [12 miles] round-trip) follows a former rail route, with good views of distant peaks along the way. Summit County is also developing a system of backcountry huts that will link in with Aspen's 10th Mountain Hut and Trail System. The first of these huts is Janet's Cabin, about a 10-kilometer (6-mile) ski in from the trailhead off I–70 west of Copper Mountain. For information and reservations, contact the **10th Mountain Trail System** (1280 Ute Ave., Aspen 81612, tel. 303/925–5775). (Also *see* Cross-Country Skiing in Aspen/Snowmass, *above*.)

Track Skiing The **Breckenridge Nordic Center** (tel. 303/453–6855), with 30 kilometers (18½ miles) of groomed tracks; the **Copper Mountain Cross-Country Center** (tel. 303/968–2882, ext. 6342), with 25 groomed kilometers (15½ miles); the **Frisco Nordic Ski Center** (tel. 303/668–0866), with 35 groomed kilometers (21½ miles); and the **Keystone Cross-Country Center** (tel. 303/468–4275), with 30 groomed kilometers (18½ miles), are Summit County's main areas for track skiing. Of these, the Breckenridge terrain is probably the most gentle, the Copper Mountain terrain the most challenging. All offer lessons and rentals.

Other Activities A range of nonskiing activities—dogsledding, sleigh rides, snowmobiling—can be arranged through the central reservation services at Breckenridge, Copper, and Keystone (*see* Visitor Information, *above*).

Ice-Skating Keystone claims to have the largest outdoor maintained rink in the country. Actually it is not a true rink but a pond regularly resurfaced by maintenance machinery. At the center of Keystone Village, it is great for a leisurely postski skate and is open (and lit in the evening) daily 10–10, with skate rentals available.

Telluride

There are at least two Tellurides: Telluride Past and Telluride Future. That leaves the question: Where is Telluride Present? Telluride's distant past—dating to the late 1800s—revolved around mining; more recently, the town had the reputation of being a kind of societal escape hatch. Stuck in a box canyon in Colorado's southwest, Telluride was hard to find and even harder to access. As such, it was a perfect (and perfectly beautiful) hole in the wall of the San Juan Mountains for political and societal recalcitrants (most young and college educated) who'd had it up to here with the status quo. They weren't bothered too much by the few straggling skiers who made their way to Telluride, and from those roots a ski town developed with a distinctively hip, back-to-nature edge.

Telluride Future has to do with the development of a resort village on the other side of the mountain. The concern is how its existence will mesh with Telluride's already established character. The current centerpiece of the resort village is the Doral Hotel, which—depending on whom you talk to—is defined as either the luxury hotel Telluride has long needed or an ostentatious sore thumb. As plans for Telluride Future are beginning to be realized, a number of longtime residents say that the writing is on the wall: Telluride as a ski resort has been "discovered." Real estate values are escalating, encouraging many old-time Telluriders to sell out and move elsewhere. Effectively, some purists believe that Telluride can never again be what it was.

A couple of things are certain. First, thanks to very strict zoning ordinances, the old town of Telluride still looks as it always has—a turn-of-the-century mining town against an exquisite backdrop—even if the cost of housing has gone through the roof. However, the village is still a work in progress, and a final judgment on its aesthetic look and character wait for Telluride Future to assert itself fully.

Visitor Information Central reservations: tel. 800/525–3455. General information: **Telluride Chamber Resort Association** (666 W. Colorado Ave., Box 653, Telluride 81435, tel. 303/728–3041); **Telluride Ski Resort** (562 Mountain Village Blvd., Box 11155, Telluride 81435, tel. 303/728–7404). Snow report: tel. 303/728–3614.

Getting There Telluride is notorious for being one of the hardest ski resorts in the country to fly into, mainly because its airport elevation is well above 9,000 feet. A little bumpy air, a few clouds, and the next thing you know, you're landing in Montrose, 65 miles away, and taking a van to Telluride. Be patient.

Continental Express (tel. 800/525–0280) and **United Express** (tel. 800/241–6522) have frequent connecting flights from Denver's Stapleton Airport. **Delta** (tel. 800/221–1212) offers service from Salt Lake City and **Mesa Airlines** (tel. 800/637–2247) from Albuquerque and Phoenix.

Telluride is 330 miles southwest of Denver.

Getting Around While the separation of the resort village from the town of Telluride has kept the town's historic integrity intact, it has also created a transportation headache: how to get easily from village to town? The completion by early 1994 of a 2½-mile, over-the-mountain gondola (to run in the evening as well as the day) should solve that problem.

The gondola will make a car unnecessary; both the village and the town are pedestrian-friendly. However, for any out-of-town excursions—and a drive through the spectacular San Juan Mountains is well worthwhile—**Avis, Budget, Dollar,** and **Thrifty** rent from the Telluride Airport.

Downhill Skiing Another split image: Telluride is really two ski areas in one. For many years, it had a reputation as being an experts-only ski area. Indeed, the north-facing trails on the town side are impressively steep and long, and by springtime, the moguls are humongous. When the snow is good, this is the site of some of the most outrageous mogul skiing in the world. So reputations are made.

But then there is the other side—literally—of the ski area, the west-facing village, with long, gentle runs. Despite the annoyance of a slow and inefficiently laid out lift system, this is still a terrific place for lower-intermediate skiers and young kids. It's as good as it gets in the West, really.

What Telluride lacks is much in between the super gentle and the super steep. There is the aptly named See Forever, a great, long cruiser, but in order to do it top to bottom, you must also ride lifts forever (or more than 25 minutes, anyway, which on a cold day seems like forever). There are a few good intermediate runs from Lift 5, but they are, unfortunately, short and have nagging flat spots. The ski area's management hopes that a planned expansion will eventually solve the intermediate shortage.

Lessons and Programs Half-day group lessons begin at $35. First-time beginner lessons are available for Alpine and telemark skiers, as well as snowboarders. Including lessons, rentals, and restricted beginner lift tickets, beginner packages start at $45.

Facilities 3,522-foot vertical rise (3,165 feet lift serviced); 1,050 skiable acres; 21% beginner, 47% intermediate, 32% advanced; 1 high-speed quad chair, 2 triple chairs, 6 double chairs, 1 surface lift.

Lift Tickets $39 adults, $22 children 6–12, children under 6 free. Adult daily rate as low as $34 on multiday tickets (up to 6 of 7 days).

Rentals Rental packages (skis, boots, poles) are available from **Olympic Sports** (tel. 303/728–4477 or 800/828–1547) with locations at the Mountain Village and Oak Street base areas, as well as at 150 W. Colorado St. Rentals are also available from ski shops in town. Packages start at around $12.

Cross-Country Skiing *Backcountry Skiing* Among the better backcountry skiing routes in Colorado is the **San Juan Hut System,** leading toward Ridgeway along the Sneffels Range. Five huts in the system are each about 11 kilometers (7 miles) apart and are well equipped with beds, blankets, wood-burning stoves, and cooking stoves. Previous backcountry experience is not essential (though highly recommended). *224 E. Colorado Ave. or Box 1663, Telluride 81435, tel. 303/728–6935. $17 per person per night; rental equipment* *available. Reservations recommended at least 2 weeks in advance.*

About an hour's drive by car from Telluride (though only a few miles as the crow flies) is **St. Paul Lodge** (Box 463, Silverton 81433, tel. 303/387–5494), a terrific find for anyone enchanted by remote high country. Above 11,000 feet and about a half-hour ski-in from the summit of Red Mountain Pass between Ouray and Silverton, the lodge (a converted mining camp) provides access to a series of above-tree-line bowls and basins. Included in the lodge rates are guide service (essential in this potentially hazardous area), ski equipment, and telemark lessons if necessary, along with meals and lodging.

The San Juan Hut System (*see above*) offers a day-guiding service as an introduction to backcountry skiing. The best place for backcountry equipment rentals in Telluride is **Telluride Mountaineer** (219 E. Colorado Ave., tel. 303/728–6736).

Track Skiing The **Telluride Nordic Association** is really three Nordic centers under the same aegis, totaling 50 kilometers (31 miles) of groomed track. The three are distinctly different. The 12-kilometer (7½-mile) track along the San Miguel River on the valley floor is relatively flat and good for those who like to develop momentum and rhythm in their skiing. The 5 kilometers (3 miles) of track on the golf course by the Doral Hotel are more rolling. For distinctly backcountry flavor, try the groomed trails in the Prospect Basin area, reached from the top of Lift 10. In fact, many skiers who go into this area wear sturdy touring or telemarking gear and branch off from the groomed tracks. However, caution is advised here: Parts of the Prospect Basin area are notoriously prone to avalanches. *Box 1784, Telluride 81435, tel. 303/728–6911 or 303/728–7570. No trail fee, although a 2-ride ticket for Lift 10, to reach Prospect Basin, is $10. Rentals (skis, boots, poles): $14 per day, $9 half day. Lessons: $25, although less for package programs. Half-day and full-day track tours (including snowshoe tours) range between $30 and $65.*

Other Activities **Telluride Outside** (666 W. Colorado Ave., Telluride 81435, tel. 303/728-3895 or 800/831-6230) organizes a variety of winter activities in the Telluride area, among them hot-air ballooning, sleigh rides, snowmobile tours, and even winter fly-fishing excursions.

Glider Rides For an unusual look at the San Juans, **Telluride Soaring** (tel. 303/728–5424) operates out of the Telluride Airport. Rates are about $75 per half hour, $120 per hour, and rides are offered daily, weather permitting.

Heli-Skiing Among the unusual activities offered by **Telluride Helitrax** (Box 1560, Telluride 81435, tel. 303/728–4904) are helicopter-assisted Nordic tours and late-season corn-snow skiing in the La Sal Mountains southeast of Telluride. Otherwise, a typical run-of-the-mill day of helicopter skiing includes five runs totaling about 12,000 feet. The cost is $425 per person. Reservations should be made at least two days in advance, and up to two weeks in advance for holiday periods.

Ice Climbing Having your body suspended for any extended length of time on a frigid wall of ice would be considered a form of torture by some. For those who think it can be fun, **Fantasy Ridge Alpin-**

ism (Nugget Bldg., Suite 204, Box 1679, Telluride 81435, tel. 303/728–3546) offers introductory ice-climbing courses.

Vail/Beaver Creek

Vail is American skiing's big kahuna, the king of the hills. It is either the most, as they used to say in beatnik talk, or too much, depending on your tastes. Vail logs more "skier days" (the ski industry's measure of ticket sales) than any other resort in the country. You don't do that without being big, both as a ski area and as a resort, and Vail—by ski-resort standards—is enormous. It is astounding how much developers have been able to cram into the relatively narrow Vail Valley—and all the more astounding when you consider that a chunk of the valley floor is taken up by a major interstate highway (I–70).

Of course, one valley can only absorb so much, and by the beginning of the '80s, when it became obvious that Vail development had almost maxed out, the satellite resort of Beaver Creek sprang up. "The Beave," as locals call it, has quickly become a substantial resort in its own right—a low-key (relatively speaking) alternative to Vail itself.

Vail and Beaver Creek score high marks on two counts: the total amount of skiing (more than 5,000 skiable acres) and resort amenities. The two combine as the very definition of full-service resort, a well-oiled service machine that must take care of a bed base of roughly 40,000: restaurants, posh lodging, even ski concierges who will help you put on your skis in the morning. Lacking is a sense of soulful character, but what would you expect with an interstate highway running right through town? The original resort village was developed with a neo-Tyrolean theme, which subsequent development practically ignored. Vail today has more of a neosuburban atmosphere. You come to Vail and Beaver Creek to ski, eat, and be pampered, but certainly not to have your soul reclaimed by the splendor of the wilderness.

Visitor Information Central reservations: tel. 800/525–2257. General information: **Vail Associates, Inc.** (Box 7, Vail 81658, tel. 303/949–5750 or 800/525–2257). Snow reports: tel. 303/476–4888 or 303/476–4889.

Getting There **American Airlines** (tel. 800/433–7300) has nonstop flights from Chicago, Dallas, and New York to Eagle County Airport, 35 miles west of Vail. **America West Airlines** (tel. 800/247–5692) has nonstops from Los Angeles, Phoenix, and San Francisco.

Vail and Beaver Creek are about 100 miles from Denver's Stapleton Airport, via I–70.

Getting Around **Vans to Vail** (tel. 303/476–4467) and **Vail Valley Taxi** (tel. 303/476–8294) provide transportation between Vail/Beaver Creek and both the Eagle County Airport and Denver. **Budget, Dollar, Hertz, National,** and **Thrifty** rent cars in the Vail valley. A public shuttle-bus service is also available within Vail and between Vail and Beaver Creek.

Downhill Skiing Vail is perhaps best known for its back bowls, a vast expanse (nearly 3,000 acres) of open-bowl skiing that can be sensational on powder days but generally only so-so at other times, after the fresh snow has been tracked up and worked on by sun and wind. For the most part, the back bowls are not extraordinarily steep, and thus are good places for intermediates to learn how to ski powder.

Skiing on the front side of the mountain is a markedly different experience. There's lots of wide-trail skiing, heavily skewed toward groomed intermediate runs. Vail is an ideal mountain for those in the intermediate- and advanced-skier audience who ski a week or two a season and want to be reminded each year that they do know how to turn a ski. Vail skiing has a way of boosting egos. There are a few steep and long mogul runs for experts, but Vail's true expert terrain represents a relatively small chunk of the huge Vail pie.

Beaver Creek has even less expert terrain. The addition a couple of years ago of the Grouse Mountain chair did add steep stuff to the Beaver Creek package, but no one really comes to Beaver Creek in search of killer steeps. In fact, it is perhaps one of the best ski areas in America for lower intermediates. The top third of the mountain features a large trail cluster of almost exclusively easy-going stuff, and any skier who doesn't feel up to the slightly steeper lower section of the mountain can ride the lift down to the base. Beaver Creek has a noteworthy advantage over Vail: a single, central base area. It's hard to get lost (not so at Vail), something for families with small, losable children to consider.

Lessons and Programs Half-day group lessons start at $45; full-day lessons start at $50. The ski schools at Vail and Beaver Creek are among the best in the country, with several specialty classes and excellent children's programs. For more information, call the Vail and Beaver Creek Ski School (tel. 303/476–3239).

Facilities Beaver Creek: 3,340-foot vertical rise; 1,050 skiable acres; 18% beginner, 39% intermediate, 43% advanced; 2 high-speed quad chairs, 4 triple chairs, 4 double chairs. Vail: 3,250-foot vertical rise; 3,992 skiable acres; 32% beginner, 35% intermediate, 32% advanced on the front side; 36% intermediate, 64% advanced in the back bowls; 1 gondola, 7 high-speed quad chairs, 2 regular quads, 3 triple chairs, 6 double chairs, 5 surface lifts.

Lift Tickets $42 adults, $29 children. Multiday tickets (up to 7 days) available, although per-day savings are minimal. Tickets are good at Vail and Beaver Creek.

Rentals Full rental packages (skis, boots, poles) starting at $16 per day are available at Beaver Creek Sports in the Beaver Creek Resort Village. For Beaver Creek rental reservations, tel. 303/949–2310. In Vail, packages are available at rental shops operated by Vail Associates at the Golden Peak and Lionshead base areas. Performance packages, snowboards, and monoskis are also available for rental. For Vail rental reservations, tel. 303/479–2050.

Cross-Country Skiing
Backcountry Skiing The 10th Mountain Hut and Trail System reaches far into Vail's backcountry; one route continues to Aspen (*see* Cross-Country Skiing in Aspen/Snowmass, *above*). Maps, equipment, and other information are available from the 10th Mountain Hut and Trail System (1280 Ute Ave., Aspen 81612, tel. 303/925–5775). Hut reservations should be made at least a month in advance.

If you aren't familiar with the trail system, hiring a guide is highly recommended. In Vail, contact **Paragon Guides** (Box 130-O, Vail 81658, tel. 303/926–5299).

Track Skiing To reach Beaver Creek's cross-country trail network, **McCoy Park,** you must ride the Strawberry Park chairlift. This is a bonus, for it gets you far enough from the resort village that you get a rare sense (around Vail, anyway) that you're in a pristine mountain environment. The 30 kilometers (18½ miles) of groomed tracks have a fair amount of ups and downs—or perhaps because the elevation is above 9,500 feet, it just seems that way. The cross-country skiing at the Vail Nordic Center is less inspiring—a network laid out on what in the summer is a golf course. *McCoy Park, tel. 303/845–5313. Trail fee: $15 adults, $7 children for full day; $11 adults, $5 children for half day. Lesson and tour packages begin at $32, with snowshoe tours and rentals also available. Daily rental rates range between $15 and $20, depending on equipment.*

Other Activities The **Activities Desk of Vail** (tel. 303/476–9090) or the **Activities Desk at Beaver Creek** (tel. 303/949–9090) can arrange a variety of nonskiing activities, including dogsledding, hot-air ballooning, and snowcat skiing.

Bobsledding Vail's on-mountain bobsled run, a 2,900-foot course, begins below Mid-Vail (the large restaurant about halfway up the mountain). Neither the course nor the sleds are quite up to an Olympic standard, but speeds of up to 50 miles per hour are still possible. The sleds hold up to four people, and cost $12 per person.

Snowmobiling Twelve-mile snowmobile tours are conducted at **Piney River Ranch** (Box 7, Vail, CO 81658, tel. 303/476–3941), just north of Vail. Rates include helmets, snowmobile suits and boots, and sometimes meals, and range from $72 to $135 per person.

Winter Park

There is no more aptly named ski area in America than Winter Park. Technically the area—a public park—is owned by the city of Denver and is frequented primarily by skiers who drive 1½ hours from the city for a winter's day or weekend. Its close proximity to Denver affects Winter Park's character in a variety of ways. For one thing, it is still at heart a day-skier resort, despite efforts by the Winter Park area to spruce up lodging, dining, and other amenities to attract longer-term vacationers.

There's no spiffy resort village, and the après-ski scene, while it can be vibrant, tends to peter out on the early side, since all those day skiers beat their way back to Denver. What this means, too, is that Winter Park tends to be most crowded on weekends, and fairly uncrowded on weekdays: It's often the reverse at resorts such as Aspen or Vail, which usually see a guest turnover on weekends (Saturdays especially).

Winter Park isn't Colorado's most scenic resort; the front-range mountains lack the dramatic rocky structure of, say, the San Juans in Colorado's southwest. In large part, that's because proximity to Denver, rather than scenic drama, was most important in choosing the location of the resort. Not that Winter Park is *ugly* by any means; it's all relative.

Finally, Winter Park can attract an unusually eclectic crowd. On any given day, you might have the U.S. Ski Team in training (the 1993 U.S. National Skiing Championships were held here), a large corps of disabled skiers (Winter Park has the best disabled-skier program in the country), and busloads of school kids from the Denver area, most of them throwing snowballs at one another.

Visitor Central reservations: tel. 800/453–2525. General information:
Information **Winter Park Resort** (Box 36, Winter Park 80482, tel. 303/726–5514); **Winter Park/Fraser Valley Chamber of Commerce** (Box 3236, Winter Park 80482, tel. 303/726–4118). Snow report: 900/950–5550.

Getting There Most major airlines fly into Denver International Airport. **Home James Transportation** provides van service from the airport to the resort; airport-shuttle arrangements can be made by calling central reservations (*see above*) or tel. 303/726–5587.

Winter Park is about 70 miles west of Denver via I–70 west and Route 40 north. However, if you drive, be forewarned that Berthoud Pass on Route 40 can be treacherous when winter storms blow in.

Winter Park is the only ski resort in the Rockies with train service right to the slopes. In winter, the **Winter Park/Rio Grande Ski Train** (tel. 303/296–4754) provides round-trip weekend service from Denver's Union Station to the ski area. **Amtrak's** (tel. 800/872–7245 or 800/533–0363) *California Zephyr* also provides daily service to Winter Park from Chicago and the West Coast; some ski packages are available.

Getting Around A free shuttle-bus service runs between most lodges in the Winter Park area and the ski area, but because things are fairly spread out in the Fraser Valley, having a car is preferable.

Downhill Skiing Winter Park is really three interconnected ski areas: Winter Park flanked by Mary Jane and Vasquez Ridge. That's both good and bad: It's good in that it spreads skiers out on those busy weekend days; it's bad in that it spreads skiers out. In other words, it's easy to lose your skiing partners at Winter Park, and once that happens, it's hard to find them.

The skiing at Winter Park and Vasquez Ridge leans heavily toward ultrawide, groomed intermediate trails. It's terrific skiing for families, groups, and schussboomers who enjoy testing the ski patrol's resolve by skiing too fast. On busy weekends, Vasquez Ridge is the best place for escaping crowds, partly because it's difficult to figure out how to get there.

Mary Jane is 1,800 vertical feet of unrelenting moguls, with a couple of groomed runs; if you want groomed, though, there are more choices at Winter Park. One nice addition to Winter Park for the '92–'93 season was the Timberline lift behind Mary Jane, providing access to the above-tree-line skiing of Parsenn Bowl. The pitch is moderate, making the bowl a terrific place for intermediates to try their luck at powder and crud-snow skiing.

Lessons and For adults, 1½-hour lessons start at $25; 3-hour workshops
Programs start at $40. All-day children's programs, which include lunch, start at $50. Free beginner snowboarding lessons (4½ hours) are offered when you purchase an adult daily ticket.

Facilities 3,060-foot vertical rise; 1,300 skiable acres; 21% beginner, 58% intermediate, 21% advanced; 4 high-speed quad chairs, 4 triple chairs, 12 double chairs.

Lift Tickets $36 adults, $15 children 6–13, children under 6 free. Adult multiday-ticket savings are considerable: $30 per day for 2-

to 6-day tickets. Lower-priced, limited-lift tickets are also available.

Rentals Rental equipment is available at the bases of Winter Park and Mary Jane. Slightly lower-priced rental packages (as low as $8 per day) are available at the **Ski Exchange** (tel. 303/726–9240), ⅓ mile from the Winter Park base on Winter Park Dr. Rental equipment is also available from several shops in downtown Winter Park.

Cross-Country Skiing
Backcountry Skiing When last we looked, the ski area at the summit of Berthoud Pass—which has been in and out of operation over the last few years—was not in business. For backcountry telemarkers, that's a bonus because you can use the precut ski trails for easy climbing and skiing. Be cautious: The above-tree-line terrain around Berthoud is prone to quick and severe weather changes, as well as avalanches. One popular thing to do among locals is to drive to the top of the pass and ski down one of many possible routes on either side; whoever draws the short straw has to drive the car down for pickup.

The **Idlewood Nordic Center** (*see* Track Skiing, *below*) leads six-hour backcountry tours.

Track Skiing The closest groomed tracks to Winter Park are the **Idlewood** and **Devil's Thumb** cross-country centers, an interconnected trail system totaling more than 100 kilometers (62 miles). The closer is Idlewood, half a mile from Winter Park on Route 40, with skiing mostly along tree-lined trails. Devil's Thumb (7 miles from Winter Park) is the larger of the two, with more ups and downs and more open views. *Box 1364, Winter Park 80482, tel. 303/726–8231 or 303/726–5632. Trail fee: $8 adults, $6 children under 13. Rentals, lessons, and backcountry tours available. Lodging and restaurant at Devil's Thumb.*

Somewhat farther afield is **Snowy Mountain Ranch,** located 12 miles northwest of Winter Park in Tabernash. The 60-kilometer (37-mile) trail system includes 3 kilometers (almost 2 miles) lit for night skiing. The ranch is a YMCA facility (with discounts for YMCA members) that has such added bonuses as a sauna, a gym, and an indoor pool. *Box 169, Winter Park 80482, tel. 303/887–2152. Trail fee: $7 adults, $3 children, $2 evening. Lessons, rentals, and on-site lodging available.*

Other Activities
Dogsledding **Dogsled Rides of Winter Park** (tel. 303/726–5527) offers one-hour rides in the area.

Snowmobiling Rentals and guided tours are available from **Trailblazer Snowmobile Tours** (Box 3437, Winter Park, CO 80482, tel. 303/726–8452 or 800/669–0134). Rates range from $35 for a one-hour ride to $105 for a four-hour ride.

Snow Tubing A lift-serviced snow-tubing hill? Yes, and it's lit at night, no less. The **Fraser Snow Tubing Hill** (tel. 303/726–5954) has two lifts, groomed trails, and a warming hut to make your experience of riding an inner tube down a snowy hill most enjoyable. The rate is $8 per hour before 6 PM, $9 per hour after 6 PM.

Idaho

Sun Valley

Before there was Aspen, there was Sun Valley. Long before there were such movies as *Aspen Extreme* (1993) to take Hollywood skiing, there was *Sun Valley Serenade* (1941). Sun Valley's celebrity lineup of yesteryear—Gary Cooper, Claudette Colbert, Erroll Flynn, and Ernest Hemingway, among others—makes Aspen's present-day luster seem dull in comparison. A lot of this can be attributed to the power of astute marketing: When W. Averell Harriman, chairman of the Union Pacific Railroad in the 1930s, decided that the railroad company needed some Western attraction to fill train-car seats with tourists, he had visions of the St. Moritz of the Rockies. The location of choice was an old mining town named Ketchum, and imagine how alluring a destination Harriman might have had with a name like that. But his PR team came up with the much sexier name of Sun Valley, flew in a host of Hollywooders for the 1936 opening, and the rest is skiing history.

Sun Valley can still summon up its share of Hollywood glamour; among its regulars are Clint Eastwood, Brooke Shields, and a few folks (e.g., Mariel) named Hemingway. But it would be misleading to suggest that this is what Sun Valley is all about. If anything, it is antiglitter, a place where the stardust settled long ago. Today it is a resort of balanced proportions: well developed but not (yet) overdeveloped, the town of Ketchum (and its Harriman-inspired satellite, Sun Valley) effectively mixing an air of elegance (and the aura of past glory) with ski-town funkiness.

The ski area is also a well-proportioned mix of trail and open-bowl skiing, easy skiing and tough stuff. The unfortunate rap on Sun Valley has been a lack of snow; not lying in a natural snowbelt and with parts of the mountain exposed to too much of that Sun Valley sun, the ski area has been more likely than most other Western resorts to suffer snow shortages. Recent snowmaking improvements have gone a long way toward solving the problem, but Sun Valley is still not the best choice for powder-skiing addicts.

Visitor Information Central reservations: tel. 800/786–8259. General information: **Sun Valley Company** (Sun Valley 83353, tel. 208/622–4111). Snow report: tel. 800/635–4150.

Getting There **Horizon Air** (tel. 800/547–9308) and **SkyWest** (800/453–9417) offer connecting service primarily from Boise and Salt Lake City, respectively, to Hailey, 12 miles south of Sun Valley. **Sun Valley Bell Service** provides complimentary transportation to the resort (arrangements made through central reservations, *see above*).

By car, Sun Valley is about 160 miles (2½ hours) east of Boise via I–84 and Routes 68 and 93. It is about 80 miles north of Twin Falls via Routes 93 and 75. **Avis, Hertz,** and **National** rent from the Boise airport and offer one-way options to Sun Valley, in addition to the regular daily and weekly rates.

Getting Around A free shuttle-bus system for the Sun Valley-Ketchum area makes a car unnecessary. However, because the resort community sprawls over several square miles, a car may be a welcome convenience, especially for those staying in outlying condos in the Elkhorn or Warm Springs areas.

Downhill Skiing Dollar Mountain (with separate facilities from those listed below) is Sun Valley's original ski hill (although its amenities are not included in Facilities for the resort, below), and when you compare it with Bald Mountain—"Baldy" for short—you get a good idea of how far skiing has come in almost 60 years. Dollar alone was enough to lure celebrities in the '30s and '40s, but it's a short beginner's hill by today's standards, utterly dwarfed by Baldy's 3,400 vertical feet.

Two Baldy attributes are the resort's most noteworthy pluses. One is that its vertical is continuous and so are its ski runs (not interrupted by cat tracks, long traverses, or extra lift rides). For example, from the Challenger quad alone, you can cover more than 3,000 vertical feet—a rarity in U.S. skiing. The second plus is Sun Valley's diverse terrain: plenty of good skiing for novices, intermediates, and experts.

Trails reach down three Baldy exposures (east, north, and west), and the art to skiing Sun Valley (at least on sunny days) is to follow the sun around the mountain. The best skiing for novices and lower intermediates is from the Seattle Ridge quad chair, a nice pod of easy skiing set apart from Sun Valley's more challenging terrain. The best skiing for intermediates is long— *very* long—cruisers such as River Run. For experts, Sun Valley's mogul skiing is famous; Exhibition has long been regarded as one of the premier mogul runs in America, although the real mogul action tends to be on the Warm Springs side of the mountain, under the afternoon sun. The quality of Sun Valley bowl skiing can vary dramatically according to snow conditions. After a storm, the skiing—about 1,500 vertical feet of wide-open terrain—can be absolutely exhilarating. Otherwise, depending on the time of day, the snow can be soft, crusty, mushy, or slick.

Lessons and Programs Three-hour group lessons start at $39, and four-hour children's programs start at $52. A pre-ski children's program, offered weekdays for children under 3, costs $16 per hour. Race, snowboarding, and women's clinics are also offered. For more information, call the ski school (tel. 208/622–2248).

Facilities 3,400-foot vertical rise; 2,000 skiable acres; 38% beginner, 45% intermediate, 17% advanced/expert; 3 high-speed quad chairs, 3 quad chairs, 4 triple chairs, 2 double chairs.

Lift Tickets $42 adults, $23 children under 12; up to 15% savings on multi-day tickets.

Rentals Equipment can be rented at a number of shops in Ketchum or Sun Valley.

Cross-Country Skiing The nearby **Sawtooth National Recreation Area** offers plenty of backcountry opportunity, with one potential drawback: The term "recreation area"—unlike "park"—means snowmobiling is permitted. Tours for skiers of all abilities, from first-time tourers to telemarkers, can be arranged through the **Sun Valley Nordic Center** (*see* Track Skiing, *below*).

Track Skiing The **Sun Valley Nordic Center** grooms 40 kilometers (24½ miles) of track on the flatlands and rolling meadows of the valley. Scenic beauty (the trail system doesn't venture far from the resort's developed areas) and challenge (ups and downs are minimal compared with trail systems at many other resorts) are not the strong points here, but the groomers do an excellent job of maintaining the tracks, and instruction is first-rate. One other noteworthy feature: The Nordic center sets some tracks specifically for children—leaving less space between left- and right-ski tracks to account for smaller legs. Because of the open-valley exposure, late-season (late March and onward) trail conditions can be iffy. *Tel. 208/622–2250. Trail fee: $11 adults per day, $9 half day (after 1 PM); $6 children 6–12, $5.50 half day; children under 6 free. Full-day rental packages start at $13, half day at $11.*

Other Activities Sure, many resorts have a skating rink or two, but the rink at
Ice-Skating the Sun Valley Lodge is special. The original rink dates back to 1937 and has been a training and performance spot for skaters from Sonja Heine to Kristi Yamaguchi. Katarina Witt has reportedly named this her favorite place to skate. Shows featuring some of the world's great skaters are still staged here regularly (mainly in the summer); when they aren't being staged, the ice is open to the public. For information, call the **Sun Valley Sports Center** (tel. 208/622–2231).

Montana

Big Mountain

Big Mountain (officially named The Big Mountain) has aspirations of bigness beyond the mountain itself. It would like to be *the* big resort, too, and has been trying aggressively to develop its base area and sell real estate to make this happen. But for the moment, Big Mountain is still a little resort, and that's probably something to be thankful for.

Despite ski-area roots that date back to 1936, why hasn't Big Mountain grown much? Perhaps for lack of a sexy name, for starters: Big Mountain, near Whitefish, in Flathead National Forest . . . how enticing does that sound? Also, Whitefish is still a relatively small, remote town, perhaps best reached by train, that forgotten form of travel. (If you want to check out a curious slice of American life, drop by the Whitefish train station at 6 AM, as a sleepy collection of farmers, cowboys, skiers, and seedy-looking dirtballs awaits the arrival of Amtrak's *Empire Builder*, en route from Seattle to Chicago.) Whitefish isn't a bad town, mind you: Folks are quite friendly, but it hasn't stirred up a swankiness or sizzle in the manner of, say, Colorado resort towns. That, too, might be something to be thankful for.

The ski resort is 8 miles from town up a windy mountain and remains comfortably small, popular among train travelers from the Pacific Northwest and the upper Midwest and others simply seeking more of an escape than an event in their ski vacation.

Visitor Central reservations: tel. 800/858–5439; for nonresort lodging,
Information call the **Flathead Convention and Visitors Association** (tel. 800/543-3105). General information: Box 1400, Whitefish 59937, tel. 406/862–3511. Snow report: tel. 406/862–7669.

Getting There **Delta** (tel. 800/221–1212), **Horizon Air** (tel. 800/547–9308), and **United Express** (tel. 800/241–6522) offer service to Glacier Park

International Airport in Kalispell, 20 miles from the Big Mountain.

Amtrak (tel. 800/872–7245 or 800/533–0363 for ski packages) offers daily service to Whitefish from Chicago and Seattle, as well as other points en route.

By car, Big Mountain is 8 miles from Whitefish and 135 miles north of Missoula via Route 93.

Getting Around Having a car is virtually essential at Big Mountain; there is no adequate public transportation between the resort and Whitefish.

Downhill Skiing At Big Mountain, snowboarders like running into trees. This says more about the nature of Big Mountain's terrain than it does about the sanity of snowboarders (which may or may not be suspect). Its most distinctive feature is the widely spaced trees that, when they become encased in snow, are known as snow ghosts. Snowboarders seem to think sideswiping snow ghosts is quite a lot of fun.

Big Mountain claims to have 4,000 skiable acres. Although that figure seems inflated, there is indeed a lot of terrain to explore and many different lines to discover among those widely spaced trees. The pleasures of exploration and discovery—such as the finding of a fresh cache of powder many days after a snowstorm—are perhaps the main reason to ski Big Mountain.

In general, the pitch is in the intermediate to advanced-intermediate range; there's not a whole lot of supersteep or a whole lot of supereasy skiing. A sameness in pitch, however, doesn't mean a sameness in skiing. With trails falling away on all sides of the mountain, there is a tremendous variation in exposure and hence in snow texture; also take into consideration the number of trees to deal with and the views (the best being northeast toward Glacier National Park).

One of Big Mountain's best features is its bottom-to-top high-speed quad (the "Glacier Chaser"), meaning that runs using the mountain's full 2,200-foot vertical are interrupted by less than 10 minutes of lift-riding time. A negative is weather; foggy days are not uncommon, and that's when you're thankful that those snow ghosts are around as points of visual reference.

Lessons and Programs Group instruction in downhill is offered for about $20 for a half day; cross-country, telemark skiing, and snowboarding lessons are also available for about $20 per person. A half-day snowcat powder-skiing lesson (includes lesson and transportation) costs about $60. Specialty clinics such as racing and mogul techniques are provided, as well as children's programs. For information call the ski school office (tel. 406/862–3511, ext. 431 or 432).

Facilities 2,200-foot vertical rise; 4,000 skiable acres; 25% beginner, 55% intermediate, 20% advanced. 1 high-speed quad chair, 4 triple chairs, 1 double chair, 2 surface lifts.

Lift Tickets $30 adults, $23 juniors (13–18) and senior citizens (over 62), $16 children 7–12, children under 7 free. Night skiing (Wed.–Sun., 4:30–10): $9 adults, $7 juniors and senior citizens, $6 children.

Rentals Full rental packages (skis, boots, poles) per day: $15 adults, $7.50 children under 7. Snowboard rental: $25 per day. Equipment can also be rented in Whitefish at **Silvertip** (33 Baker Ave., tel. 406/862-2600).

Cross-Country Skiing
Backcountry Skiing

Because of an unusually liberal policy regarding skiing out-of-bounds, backcountry tours are possible from the top of Big Mountain. For the most part, the Big Mountain ski patrol does not prevent skiers from crossing ski-area boundary ropes, although if you do so and get into trouble, you're responsible for paying rescue costs. While the avalanche danger (*very* relatively speaking) is usually not high around Big Mountain, the chances of getting lost are. It is very easy to ski too far down the wrong drainage, creating the prospect of a tiring and excruciating bushwhack back to the base.

Guide service for backcountry tours (with some telemarking) in Glacier National Park costs $60–$80 per person per day. Excursions are best made on a clear day, since the mountain views are what make the trip. Contact the **Izaak Walton Inn** (*see* Track Skiing, *below*) or **Glacier Park Ski Tours** (tel. 800/926–8688). Backcountry equipment rentals are available in Whitefish at **Silvertip** (*see* Rentals, *above*).

Track Skiing

There are two track systems in the Whitefish area: 15 groomed kilometers (9 miles) at **The Big Mountain Nordic Center** and another 15 kilometers (9 miles) at the **Glacier Nordic Touring Center** at Grouse Mountain Lodge in Whitefish. Both systems serve their purpose well enough, but don't expect inspiring views or a sense of wilderness seclusion. One advantage that Glacier Nordic Touring Center has is its 5 kilometers (3 miles) of groomed trail for night skiing. Arrangements for cross-country lessons can be made through the ski school office (*see* Lessons and Programs, *above*). *Daily trail fee for The Big Mountain Nordic Center (tel. 406/862–3511): $5 adults, $2 youths 13–18, $1 children 7–12. Rentals (skis, boots, poles): $14 per day. No trail fee for the Glacier Nordic Touring Center (tel. 406/862–4369), but a $2-per-person donation is suggested. Group lessons: $15. Private lessons: $20 per hour. Rentals available at Grouse Mountain Lodge (tel. 406/862–3000, ext. 436).*

Farther afield, the 30 kilometers (18½ miles) of groomed track at **Izaak Walton Inn,** 62 miles east at the edge of Glacier National Park, *do* combine nicely the pleasures of groomed-trail skiing with the spirit of backcountry skiing. Originally built in 1939 for railroad crews, the inn is now devoted almost exclusively to housing cross-country skiers during the winter. Because it's alongside the railroad tracks, it is also accessible from Whitefish by train. *Box 653, Essex 59916, tel. 406/888–5700. Track, touring, and telemark rentals available. Multiday packages including skiing, lodging, and meals available.*

Other Activities
Dogsledding

Dog Sled Adventures (Box 34, Olney 59927, tel. 406/881–2275) leads 12-mile tours in Stillwater State Forest, a few miles northwest of Whitefish.

Ice Fishing

Dangling a line through a sawed hole in the ice isn't the world's most aerobic sport, but because of the many lakes in the Whitefish area, it's a popular pastime. Whitefish Lake is the obvious place to start; the **Tally Lake Ranger District** (tel. 406/862–4451) can recommend other lakes. The best place for ice-fishing gear in Whitefish is **Sportsman & Ski Haus** (105 Baker Ave., tel. 406/862–3111).

Snowmobiling There are more than 200 groomed snowmobile trails in the Flathead region. **Columbia Saw & Ski-doo** (30 9th St., Columbia Falls, tel. 406/892–2195 or 800/221–5098) rents machines and clothing and also leads guided tours.

Big Sky

Lone Peak, the mountain that looms over Big Sky, is an appropriate metaphor for the resort conceived 25 years ago by the renowned TV newscaster Chet Huntley: Big Sky is a solitary node of civilization in otherwise undeveloped country. Rugged wilderness areas, huge open ranches, and Yellowstone National Park are the main features of this part of Montana. But amid all that wide, empty space, there's Big Sky, which could be considered as much a full-service outpost as a full-service resort. It is the sort of place where locals are used to driving nearly 50 miles to Bozeman for such simple pleasures as a fresh head of lettuce.

This is not to suggest that Big Sky is uncivilized. Indeed, being just 25 years old and still growing, the resort is quite modern in its design and amenities. It's not as if you can't get a daily newspaper, cable TV, or a substantial, well-prepared meal. Still, the fact remains that Big Sky is one of the most isolated major ski resorts in the country.

This can be both good and bad. It's bad if you're someone who puts a premium on convenient travel arrangements. Getting to Big Sky invariably means at least one plane change en route to Bozeman and about an hour's drive to the resort. It's great, though, if you're someone who appreciates a pervading spirit of the surrounding wilderness and a lack of crowds without having to give up the creature comforts of a warm bed and a good meal.

Recent land transactions around Big Sky have many local people worrying about major real-estate development in the near future that could impinge upon that resort-in-the-wild atmosphere. For the moment, there's a lot more speculation than development activity. It should be some time before hordes of tourists begin descending on Big Sky.

Visitor Information Central reservations: tel. 800/548–4486. General information: **Big Sky Ski and Summer Resort** (Box 160001, Big Sky 59716, tel. 406/995–4211 or 800/548–8096). Snow report: tel. 406/995–2526.

Getting There **Continental** (tel. 800/525–0280), **Delta** (tel. 800/221–1212), **Northwest** (tel. 800/225–2525), and **Horizon Air** (tel. 800/547–9308) offer service to Bozeman, about 45 miles north of Big Sky. **City Taxi** (tel. 406/586–2341) provides van service to the resort. **Avis, Budget, Hertz, National,** and **Thrifty** rent cars from the airport.

By car, Big Sky is 45 miles south of Bozeman and 50 miles north of West Yellowstone on Route 191.

Getting Around Although there is free shuttle-bus service, it's best to have a car at Big Sky. The resort comprises two developments, the Meadow Village and the Mountain Village, about 6 miles apart. A car is pretty much essential for exploring beyond the resort area (in Yellowstone National Park, for example).

Downhill Skiing For many years, the attitude of more advanced skiers toward Big Sky was "big deal." There wasn't nearly enough challenging skiing to keep expert skiers interested for long, certainly not for an entire ski week. As a remedy, the Big Sky people strung up the Challenger chairlift, one of the steepest in the country, and figured the problem was solved. Not quite: Big Sky still has the reputation of being a mountain best suited to less skilled skiers, keeping many experts away and keeping the Challenger chair skiing remarkably underpopulated. It's not a huge amount of terrain, but with a nice variety of open-face skiing and tree-and-rock-lined chutes, it *seems* like a lot when you're virtually the only person skiing it. And if you're looking for more, you can hike up to additional chutes and a very serious couloir.

Now, about that easy-skiing reputation: It wasn't built on thin air. There is, indeed, a good deal of intermediate and lower-intermediate terrain, a combination of wide-open bowl skiing higher up and trail skiing lower down. And as on the Challenger terrain, the skiing on these slopes is pretty unpopulated. To go on any further about the lack of crowds being one of Big Sky's great assets would be belaboring the point.

The other plus about skiing Big Sky is that there is a wide variety of exposures. Ski areas tend to be built on north-facing slopes where snow usually stays fresher longer, protected from the sun. In addition to these, Big Sky also has plenty of runs facing south and east, and the differing snow textures as a result make for more interesting skiing.

Lessons and Programs Half-day group-lesson rates are $20; a learn-to-ski package (half-day lesson, equipment rentals, and restricted lift ticket) is $30. Racing, powder, mogul, and snowboarding clinics are also available and start at $20 per person.

Facilities 3,030-foot vertical rise; 2,000 skiable acres; two 4-passenger gondolas, 1 high-speed quad, 2 triple chairs, 3 double chairs.

Lift Tickets $35 adults, children under 11 free; night-skiing ticket (Fri. and Sat. 4–9), $16; Super Ticket (9–9), $42. Multiday tickets (up to 6 of 7 days) available, with savings of $1–$2 per day.

Rentals At the base of the mountain, **Boyne Country Sports** (in the Mountain Mall, tel. 406/995–4211) offers rental packages (skis, boots, poles) at $19 per day for adults, $14 children. More moderate rental packages (starting at $12.95 per day for adults, $8 children) are available from **Mad Wolf Ski & Sport** (Rte. 91, 8 mi from ski area, tel. 406/995-4369).

Cross-Country Skiing **Lone Mountain Ranch** (*see* Track Skiing, *below*) offers guided tours in the nearby backcountry as well as in Yellowstone National Park. Tours near Big Sky tend to cover steeper terrain, with opportunities for telemarking, and are best for experienced skiers. Tours in Yellowstone generally cover flat or gently rolling terrain, for which little or no cross-country skiing experience is necessary. In some cases, snowcoaches (essentially, snow "buses") are used to take skiers from West Yellowstone to scenic parts of the park for skiing.

Track Skiing **Lone Mountain Ranch,** a full-service cross-country resort located about 6 miles down the road from the downhill-ski resort, is a rare bird in cross-country circles. Not only are there 75 kilometers (46½ miles) of groomed trails but also lodging and dining facilities for 50 guests. The trail network is superb, with everything from a flat, open golf-course layout to tree-lined trails with as much as 1,600 feet of elevation gain (and loss). Much of the trail network provides a genuine sense of woodsy mountain seclusion. If there is a drawback, it is that moose sometimes wander onto the tracks, causing pockmarked tracks and occasional moose-skier confrontations. The things a skier must put up with . . . . *Box 160069, Big Sky 59716, tel. 406/ 995–4644. Trail fee: $8 per day adults, children under 13 free. Rentals (skis, boots, poles): $10 per day adults, $8 children. Weekly lodging/cross-country skiing packages are available.*

Other Activities

Fishing   On almost any day of the year, no matter how bitter or nasty the weather, there are usually a couple of diehard anglers laying out lines in the Gallatin River, which runs along Route 191. Rivers such as the Madison (one valley west), the Yellowstone (one valley east), and the Gallatin have made southwestern Montana famous among fly fishermen, most of whom visit during the nonwinter months. However, that's not to say the trout stop biting in winter.

Tackle, equipment rentals, and clothing are available at **Gallatin Riverguides** (Box 160212, Big Sky, tel. 406/995–2290), half a mile south of the Big Sky entrance on Route 191. A state fishing license, sold at many local stores, is required. Rental equipment is also offered at **Lone Mountain Ranch** (*see* Cross-Country Skiing, *above*).

Snowmobiling   Far and away the most popular nonskiing activity in the region is snowmobiling into Yellowstone National Park. West Yellowstone (50 miles south of Big Sky) prides itself on being the "Snowmobile Capital of the World," and in winter there are at least as many snowmobiles in town as cars.

The most popular excursion is the 60-mile round-trip between West Yellowstone and Old Faithful. Sightings of buffalo and elk are a certainty along the way, and while you'll have to share the track with plenty of other snowmobilers, the scene is nothing like the crowds that descend upon the park in summer.

Several businesses in West Yellowstone rent snowmobiles on a daily basis. Among the best are **Two Top Snowmobile** (645 Gibbon Ave., tel. 406/646–7802 or 800/522–7802) and **Yellowstone Tour & Travel** (211 Yellowstone Ave., tel. 800/221–1151). Rates per machine start around $75 per day; a helmet, suit, and glove rental package is about $15 a day. Guide service is available.

Utah

Alta/Snowbird

What strange canyon mates Alta and Snowbird make: The two are such close neighbors in Little Cottonwood Canyon that it's possible to ski from one area into the other and back (though not, unfortunately, on the same lift ticket). Yet they are, in almost every way but the quality of their snow, antipodal in character.

Alta is devotionally retro, the sort of place where if the lifts creak (as they often do), the creaks are apt to be revered as part of the Alta legend rather than oiled. Duct tape on ripped nylon overpants is Alta chic, and trail signs are exceedingly rare, since only interloping tourists don't know their way around.

Alta is so retro that it is one of the few ski areas left in the country that disallows snowboarding, basically because snowboarding seems to Alta skiers just too MTV-nouveau and faddish. Alta also prides itself in being a preternaturally local ski area, a pride shared by Alta skiers. It's a pride worn so openly on fraying wool sleeves that even those skiers who aren't Alta locals have a peculiar habit of dressing the part and pretending they are.

Snowbird, on the other hand, is Euro-modern, its fast tram quietly whisking skiers in stylish powder suits to the summit. Not only does Snowbird have plenty of trail signs, but most come with Japanese translations. Its concrete-and-steel base facilities express an angular, urban efficiency, the most conspicuous structure being the Cliff Lodge, with a ritzy spa in it, no less. A Cliff Lodge–style complex will be built at the base of Alta sometime after the moon falls out of the night sky.

What the two share is snow—lots of it, with a lightness and quantity that is legendary. For the winter of '92–'93, Snowbird got about three or four seasons' worth at many resorts. (Alta's figure was approximately the same.) Short of heli-skiing, powder skiing in America gets no better on a consistent basis. It had better be good, because skiing is pretty much all there is to do in the winter in Little Cottonwood Canyon. That's why many Alta and Snowbird visitors lodge 30 minutes away in Salt Lake City, where there are—despite rumors to the contrary—things to do at night.

Visitor Information Central reservations: tel. 801/942–0404 for Alta; tel. 800/453–3000 for Snowbird. General information numbers: **Alta,** tel. 801/742-3333; **Snowbird,** tel. 801/742-2222. **Ski Utah** (150 W. 500 South St., Salt Lake City 84101, tel. 801/534–1779) is an excellent source of information on Utah skiing. Call 800/754–8824 for a free **Utah Winter Vacation Planner.** Snow reports: tel. 801/521–8102.

Getting There Salt Lake City International Airport is a major hub for **Delta** (tel. 800/221–1212), with frequent nonstop flights from several U.S. cities. Most other major carriers also fly into Salt Lake.

By car, Alta and Snowbird are about 30 miles from the airport. Take I–215 to the 6200 South Street exit and follow signs for Alta and Snowbird. Keep in mind that all that wonderful snow can make driving in the canyon treacherous. **Canyon Transport** (tel. 801/255–1841 or 800/255–1841) and **Lewis Bros. Stages** (tel. 801/359–8347 or 800/826–5844) provide individual and group transportation service to the resorts. Also, the **Utah Transit Authority** (tel. 801/287–4636) has regular bus service into Little Cottonwood Canyon.

Getting Around If you're staying at Alta or Snowbird, there's not much need for a car unless you're planning frequent visits to Salt Lake City or Park City. The **Utah Transit Authority** public bus service (tel. 801/287–4636) between Salt Lake City and the canyon is excellent, the drawback being that buses stop running around 5 PM. Parking at the mouth of the canyon and hitchhiking to the ski areas is a standard mode of transport for many locals. If you do wish to rent a car, most major agencies operate from the Salt Lake airport.

Downhill Skiing The common denominator is snow, but the differences in the skiing experience at Alta and Snowbird are otherwise significant. While Snowbird presents itself unambiguously with 3,100 vertical feet of in-your-face steepness, Alta is an enigma. Within 15 minutes, by riding the tram and simultaneously scoping out more than 1,000 acres of skiable terrain, you can get a pretty good idea of what Snowbird is all about. On the other hand, you can return to Alta year after year and still discover places to ski you never knew existed before.

Snowbird is an expert's dream and a novice skier's nightmare. Its open bowls, such as Little Cloud and Regulator Johnson, are challenging, while chutes from the Upper Cirque and the Gad Chutes can be positively hair-raising. They're certainly not for skiers in any way doubtful of their skills. On deep-powder days—not uncommon at the 'Bird—those chutes can also be exhilarating for skiers who like that sense of a cushioned free fall with every turn. If you're looking for intermediate cruising runs, however, there's the long, meandering Chips, a few runs from the Gad chairlifts. For lower-intermediate skiers and down, Snowbird is a waste of time. Head for Alta.

Alta devotees (of which there are many) believe in this version of Creation: On the first day, God created Heaven and Earth; on the second, He created Alta. (Some, in fact, even question those priorities.) On your first couple of visits to Alta, you might wonder why people feel this way. You must give Alta time to grow on you; inevitably it will.

Alta is a ski area made to be explored but hard to get around; as mentioned, there are few trail signs. The lift system seems antiquated and poorly laid out, and a lot of trails seem to flatten out quickly or lead nowhere. This is a complex package of terrain, and the more you explore Alta, the richer your rewards.

Alta sprawls across two large basins, Albion and Wildcat, comprising mostly open bowls and meadows but with some trail skiing, too. There is no clear, easily readable fall line as there is at Snowbird; fall lines drop and roll away in many directions and angles. Furthermore, much of the best skiing (for advanced or expert skiers) requires finding obscure traverses or some hiking.

The only solution is simply to stick with it. One day—one run, even—will be your epiphany, and suddenly Alta will explode upon you with possibilities. On the lower slopes of Albion Basin, Alta has a terrific expanse of novice and lower-intermediate terrain. Rolling meadows combine as perhaps the best place in the country for lesser-skilled skiers to learn to ski powder.

Lessons and Programs At Alta, half-day group lessons for adults and chilren are available. Special workshops for teens and adults are available, in addition to children's programs. For information, call the ski school (tel. 801/742–2600). At Snowbird, three-hour lessons begin at $40; children's programs, which last from four hours to all day, start at $36. Of note is Snowbird's Mountain Experience Program, a combination of guidance and instruction for advanced skiers in challenging, off-slope terrain and variable snow conditions. Full-day workshops start at $65.

Facilities Alta: 2,050-foot vertical rise; 2,000 skiable acres; 25% novice, 40% intermediate, 35% advanced; 6 double chairs, 2 triple chairs. Snowbird: 3,100-foot vertical rise; 2,000 skiable acres;

20% novice, 30% intermediate, 50% percent advanced. 125-passenger tram, 7 double chairs.

Lift Tickets Alta: $23 per day; Snowbird: $38 for tram and chairs for adults, $23 children 12 and under; $31 chairs only, $18 children 12 and under.

Rentals Any of several ski shops in the Salt Lake City area offer reasonably priced rental packages, some as low as $5 a day for skis, boots, and poles. Equipment can also be rented at ski shops at Alta and Snowbird; rates range between $8.50 and $25 per day, depending on equipment and store location. Advance rental reservations are available from **Breeze Ski Rentals** (tel. 800/525–0314), with seven stores in the Salt Lake City area, including one at Snowbird's Upper Tram Plaza.

Cross-Country There are no groomed tracks in Little Cottonwood Canyon,
Skiing largely because the canyon configuration is too narrow and steep. Track junkies can go either toward Park City (*see* Cross-Country Skiing in Park City/Deer Valley, *below*) or to Solitude ski area (tel. 801/272–7613), with 20 kilometers (12 miles) of groomed trails in Big Cottonwood Canyon. The bottom line for anyone who puts a high premium on logging lots of track mileage is that Alta and Snowbird are poor destination choices.

Telemarking Not surprisingly given its retro-ness, Alta has been a center in the resurgence of telemark skiing. The guided **Ski Utah Interconnect** tour (*see* Cross-Country Skiing in Park City/Deer Valley, *below*) is a combination of lift-serviced and backcountry skiing that connects Utah's three major skiing canyons: Parley's, Big Cottonwood, and Little Cottonwood. The trip can be negotiated either on telemark skis or regular Alpine gear. For the most part, however, avalanche risks make backcountry skiing in this area ill-advised for all but those with the proper safety equipment and considerable backcountry experience.

Other Activities Because the lift-serviced powder skiing at Alta and Snowbird
Heli-Skiing can be so good, heli-skiing here can often be a real extravagance. On the days when you must go farther afield to find powder, or simply for the blessed solitude of the backcountry, **Wasatch Powderbird Guides** has permits for several thousand acres of skiable terrain, mostly in the basins and drainages on the periphery of Alta and Snowbird. The company guarantees seven runs a day (weather permitting), though it doesn't necessarily guarantee the quality of the snow. In general, heli-skiing is an experience most enjoyable for strong intermediate skiers and better. *Box 920057, Snowbird 84092, tel. 801/742–2800. Cost: $315–$385 per day, depending on the season. Reservations required at least a day in advance, more during busy periods; a $200 advance deposit guarantees a seat for a specific day. Custom tours available.*

Park City/Deer Valley

Park City and Deer Valley combine as Utah's one true full-service resort, with an old mining town tossed into the package. The skiing might not be as dramatic as elsewhere (i.e., Alta and Snowbird) and the natural snow not quite as plentiful (about 300 inches a winter, compared with about 500 in neighboring Big Cottonwood and Little Cottonwood canyons), but there is a lot of skiing for all levels and much to do besides ski. In large part this has been made possible by the Park City area's geography. While the Cottonwood canyons have a more dramatic beauty, they are too steep and narrow to accommodate much development. Not so in the more rolling and wide-open spaces around Park City, where there are plenty of hotels, restaurants, nightlife, and outdoor activities such as cross-country skiing and snowmobiling.

Park City—sprawling over several square miles—isn't quite a city, as its name implies, but it's no petite resort, either. Main Street, a protected historic district, adds character to an otherwise rather ordinary-looking collection of hotels, condos, restaurants, and businesses. It's not particularly unattractive, but not really inspiring, either.

Deer Valley, 2 miles up the road, was created about 20 years ago as the resort that would be skiing's final word in style. The slopes were groomed with a manicurist's attention to detail. Chairlifts had padded seats. Ski "valets" helped you unload your skis. Mountainside lodges actually served something that could be legitimately considered a gourmet lunch. Lots of posh condos and lodges surrounded the resort. The topper was the presence of skiing's master of style and verve, Stein Eriksen.

Some stumbling blocks appeared on the way: A few real estate investors lost their shirts, and many people were turned off by Deer Valley's priciness and the aura of country-club snobbishness. But on the whole, Deer Valley has worked out more or less as planned—perhaps not *the* final word in style and panache, but certainly a notable statement. The buffet at the Silver Lake Lodge may indeed make for the best on-mountain lunch in U.S. skiing.

Visitor Information
Central reservations: tel. 800/424-3337 for Deer Valley; tel. 800/222-7275 for Park City; tel. 801/649-0493 elsewhere in Utah. General information: **Deer Valley** (Box 3149, Park City 84060, tel. 801/649-1000); **Park City Ski Area** (Box 39, Park City 84060, tel. 801/649-8111); **Park City Chamber of Commerce** (Box 1630, Park City 84060, tel. 801/649-6100 or 800/453-1360. **Ski Utah** (150 W. 500 South St., Salt Lake City 84101, tel. 801/534-1779) is an excellent source of information on Utah skiing. You can get a free **Utah Winter Vacation Planner** from Ski Utah (tel. 800/754-8824). Snow reports: tel. 801/649-2000 for Deer Valley; tel. 801/649-9571 for Park City.

Getting There
Salt Lake City International Airport is a major hub for **Delta** (tel. 800/221-1212), with frequent nonstop flights from several U.S. cities. Most other major carriers also fly into Salt Lake.

By car, Park City and Deer Valley are just under 40 miles from Salt Lake City. Take I-80 east to the Park City exit. **Canyon Transport** (tel. 801/255-1841 or 800/255-1841) and **Lewis Bros. Stages** (tel. 801/359-8347 or 800/826-5844) provide individual and group transportation service to the resorts.

Getting Around
Because of a free shuttle-bus system, a car is not essential when staying at Park City and Deer Valley. But the layout is fairly spread out—it's 6 miles from Deer Valley to Parkwest, another ski area—so a car can be helpful. Most major rental-car companies operate from the Salt Lake City airport.

Downhill Skiing
The rap on Park City has always been that it lacks legitimate expert skiing. Unfair: The east face of Jupiter Peak features some truly hairy, rock-lined chutes, and Portuguese Gap is an elevator shaft lined by trees. The problem is finding these

places; the east face requires about a 20-minute traverse and hike from the top of the Jupiter chair.

Park City's main drawback isn't lack of steepness but lack of length; despite a vertical rise of 3,100 feet, it's hard putting together a run of more than about 1,400 vertical feet. The ski area is laid out as a series of segments rather than a single unit. That said, however, Park City probably has the best overall terrain mix of any ski area in Utah, enough to keep skiers of all abilities happy for several days.

Deer Valley, on the other hand, *is* short on legitimate expert terrain: Its forte is wide, meticulously groomed intermediate runs. It is a ski area for those who want to believe that they can ski with the grace of Stein Eriksen; the moderate pitch of the terrain and the quality of the grooming leads to skiing's version of ballroom dancing. Deer Valley is not for skiing's hardcore, but then it was never intended to be. Many a Deer Valley skier's day includes a two- to three-hour midday interlude of feasting on the Silver Lake Lodge buffet and catching major rays on the snow-covered meadow in front of the lodge—an area known appropriately as McHenry's Beach. The skiing experience, in other words, fits right in with the resort's overall image. After a while, however, a certain sense of sameness can set in; that's why it's nice having Park City right next door.

Lessons and Programs At Park City, a two-hour adult group lesson starts at $31; a four-hour Youth School lesson for children seven–13 starts at $38; an eight-hour ski school lesson for children three–six is $59, with lunch included. Call 800/227–2754 for information. Park City also has an excellent instructional program for disabled skiers. At Deer Valley, five-hour adult group lessons start at $55; six-hour children's group lessons start at $60.

Facilities Park City: 3,100-foot vertical rise; 2,200 skiable acres; 17% beginner, 48% intermediate, 35% advanced; 1 4-passenger gondola, 1 high-speed quad chair, 1 quad chair, 5 triple chairs, 5 double chairs. Deer Valley: 2,200-foot vertical rise; 1,000 skiable acres; 15% beginner, 50% intermediate, 35% advanced; 1 high-speed quad chair, 9 triple chairs, 1 double chair.

Lift Tickets Park City: $40 adults, $18 children under 13; night skiing (4–10): $8 adults, $5 children. Deer Valley: $43 adults, $28 children 4–12, $19 children under 4; holiday rates: $46 adults, $31 children 4–12.

Rentals Several shops in the Park City and Salt Lake City area rent equipment packages, some for as little as $6 a day. Advance rental reservations are available from **Breeze Ski Rentals** (tel. 800/525–0314), with seven stores in the Salt Lake City area, including one in Park City at the resort center. Rates range between $8.50 and $25 per day, depending on equipment and store. **Jans Mountain Outfitter** (1600 Park Ave., Park City, tel. 801/649–4949 or 800/745–1020) offers not only equipment packages ($10–$50 per day) but also clothing-rental packages, starting at $25 per day.

Cross-Country Skiing *Backcountry Skiing* The **Ski Utah Interconnect** is a good trip for Alpine skiers who want to get a taste of the backcountry experience. The guided tour covers the three major skiing canyons of the Wasatch Range—Parley's Canyon (in which Park City is located), Big Cottonwood (Brighton and Solitude), and Little Cottonwood (Alta and Snowbird). Ski-area lifts provide uphill transport, and about half of the skiing is within ski-area boundaries. The trip can be negotiated on regular Alpine equipment (or on telemark gear) and is recommended only for strong intermediates or better. *Ski Utah Interconnect, c/o Ski Utah, 307 W. 200 South St., Salt Lake City 84101, tel. 801/534–1907. Daily rates for the 5-area tour from Park City to Snowbird are $95, per person, with return transportation to Park City provided. Reservations are recommended.*

Skiers who want to do some unguided skiing on their own can climb the Guardsman's Pass Road, which is between Deer Valley and Park City and is closed to traffic in winter. Also worth checking out are trails in Iron Canyon near Parkwest.

Track Skiing The only set tracks in the Park City area are at the **White Pine Ski Touring Center,** between Park City and Parkwest. The 10 groomed kilometers (6 miles) are on a flat golf course that's nothing special as far as either scenery or terrain variation is concerned, but adequate for anyone seeking a quick aerobic workout. *Box 680393, Park City 84068, tel. 801/649–8710 or 801/649–8701. Trail fee: $3 adults, children under 12 free. Lessons and rentals available.*

Other Activities **Utah Powderbird Guides** offers daily helicopter skiing in the
Heli-Skiing mountains surrounding Park City and guarantees seven runs a day. For the most part, skiers should be at least strong intermediates with some powder-skiing experience, although Powderbird Guides does have a learn-to-ski-powder program. *Box 1760, Park City 84060, tel. 801/649–9739. Rates range from $315 to $385 per person per day, depending on the terrain covered. A limited number of guaranteed reservations (deposit required) are available.*

Hot-Air Ballooning On a clear day, when the wind is low, it is common to see a hot-air balloon rising above Park City. **Balloon Biz** (Box 17601, Salt Lake City, tel. 801/278–3051 or 800/448–2138) offers half-hour scenic flights and trips up to two hours. Most flights are just after sunrise, when winds are most predictable.

Snowmobiling The Park City location of **Action Snowmobile Tours** (512 E. 2750 North St., Provo, tel. 801/649–3866 or 801/222–0882) is a mile east of town on Highway 224. Hourly, half-day, and full-day tours are available; proper clothing and gear can be rented here, as well.

Wyoming

Jackson Hole

Jackson Hole is potentially the best ski resort in the United States. The expanse and variety of terrain utterly awe the imagination. There are literally thousands of ways of getting from top to bottom, and not all of them are hellishly steep, which is Jackson's reputation.

There are two reasons why Jackson might not *absolutely* be the country's best ski resort. The first has to do with the base village, a functional but rather ordinary cluster of buildings with limited lodging. Surrounded by protected land (Grand Teton National Park), Teton Village (as it's called) has only limited expansion possibilities. All things considered, this is probably a plus. Still, this is not a good excuse for leaving the existing base layout unimproved; the new management group has pledged to remedy this situation over the next few years. The main alternative to staying in Teton Village is staying in the town of Jackson, about 20 minutes away. All in all, it's not a bad town, but one that has been somewhat hoked up primarily for the sake of the many summer tourists on their way to Grand Teton and Yellowstone national parks.

Jackson's second drawback can be snow, or inconsistency thereof. Because of its location on the eastern flanks of the Tetons, it gets on average about 20 feet less snow in a season than does Grand Targhee, a much smaller resort on the western slope. That predominantly eastern exposure often results in snow conditions (at least on the lower half of the mountain) that are less than ideal, either mushy or crusty.

But when the snow is right, this is truly one of the great skiing experiences in America. Jackson is a place to appreciate both as a skier and a voyeur: Every so often you can witness an extreme skier skiing a line that's positively dazzling in its drama and risk. A glimpse of that alone is worth the price of a lift ticket.

Visitor Information Central reservations: tel. 307/733–1286 or 800/443–6931. General information: **Jackson Hole Ski Corporation** (Box 290, Teton Village 83025, tel. 307/733–2292); **Jackson Hole Visitors Council** (532 N. Cache St., Box 982, Jackson, WY 83001, tel. 307/733–0355 or 800/782–0011). Snow report: tel. 307/733–2291.

Getting There **American** (tel. 800/433–7300) has daily flights from Chicago and Dallas/Fort Worth to Jackson. **Continental** (tel. 800/525–0280) and **Delta** (tel. 800/221–1212) also have flights to Jackson, connecting through Denver or Salt Lake City, respectively. **A-1 Taxi** (tel. 307/733–5809) and **Tumbleweed Taxi** (tel. 307/733–0808) can provide transportation to and from the airport; many lodging facilities also offer free airport shuttle-bus service. **Avis, Budget, Hertz**, and **National** rent cars at the airport.

Getting Around **START Public Shuttle Bus** (tel. 307/733–4521) offers service between Jackson and Teton Village (the resort village at the ski-area base). Nightly shuttle-bus service is provided by **All Star Transportation** (tel. 307/733–2888). Given the distances between Teton Village, the town of Jackson, and other points of interest in the area, renting a car is a good idea.

Downhill Skiing Skiing Jackson is a process of imagination as much as the physical process of turning skis. On the trail map, about 60 squiggly lines have been drawn in and designated as named trails, but this does not even begin to suggest the thousands of different skiable routes from top to bottom. The resort claims 2,500 skiable acres, a figure that seems unduly conservative. And while Jackson is best known for its advanced to extreme skiing, it is also a place where imaginative intermediates can go exploring and have the time of their lives.

The tram to the summit of Rendezvous Peak provides access to 4,139 vertical feet of skiing, the most in the United States. If there is a drawback to Jackson skiing, it is that the immediate possibilities from the top are somewhat limited: The choice is either Rendezvous Bowl, wide open and moderately steep; or Corbett's Couloir, perhaps the most famous extreme run in America. You must jump into Corbett's or rappel in by rope. If you don't make that first turn, you don't make any; it can be a long and injurious slide to the bottom. Needless to say, the vast majority of skiers choose Rendezvous Bowl. Thereafter, many, many possibilities unfold. In fact, there is so much skiing (most of it expert and advanced) that one whole side of the mountain (the Hobacks) is generally opened only on fresh powder days.

Most of Jackson's intermediate skiing is from Après Vous Mountain and in Casper Bowl, between Rendezvous and Après Vous. Casper Bowl tends to attract more skiers, but Après Vous is surprisingly underskied (in part because the chair is long and slow). Après Vous is a great place for intermediates to ski groomed runs and to explore off the beaten track. From the chairlifts on Rendezvous Mountain, Gros Ventre (known by locals simply as GV) is flat-out one of the best intermediate runs in the country—about 2,800 vertical feet of big-turn cruising, with a good, consistent pitch most of the way.

Jackson is not a good place for novice skiers. A small cluster of trails near the base is serviceable, but that's about it. The only way novices get to see the summit is to ride the tram to the top, take in the view (which on a clear day is awesome), and ride the tram down.

Lessons and Programs Two-hour group lessons start at $30. A two- to four-hour (depending on group size) Mountain Experience Program for advanced and expert skiers—at $50 per person—is a good introduction to Jackson's challenging terrain. Mogul, racing, women's, and performance clinics are also offered. The Jackson ski school features extensive children's programs, including day care and lessons for kids two months to 14 years old. Of note are "extreme skiing" clinics, offered by Doug Coombs, two-time winner of the World Extreme Skiing Championships.

Facilities 4,139-foot vertical rise; 2,500 skiable acres; 10% beginner, 40% intermediate, 50% expert; 1 aerial tram, 1 quad chair, 1 triple chair, 5 double chairs, 2 surface lifts.

Lift Tickets $39 adult (all chairlifts), $19 junior (under 15) and senior citizens (65 and older); tram $2 per ride. Savings of more than 15% for 5- to 7-day tickets.

Rentals Equipment can be rented at **Jackson Hole Ski Shop** (tel. 307/733–2292, ext. 189), with full-package rates starting at around $11 per day for adults, $10 children 6–14, $7 "mini" for children under 6. Equipment can also be rented at **Teton Village Sports** (tel. 307/733–2181) and **Wilderness Sports** (tel. 307/733–4297) in Teton Village and at ski shops in the town of Jackson.

Cross-Country Skiing
Backcountry Skiing Few areas in North America can compete with Jackson Hole when it comes to the breadth, beauty, and variety of backcountry opportunities. For touring skiers, one of the easier areas (because of flatter routes) is along the base of the Tetons toward Jenny and Jackson lakes. In summer, this area can become crowded with national park visitors; solitude is more the order of things in winter. Telemark skiers (or even skiers on Alpine gear) can find numerous downhill routes by skiing in from Teton Pass, snow stability permitting. In summer, easy day trips to multiday expeditionary trips (with winter camping involved) along the Teton Crest trail represent the range of backcountry possibilities around Jackson. A guide isn't required for tours to the national park lakes but might be helpful for those unfamiliar with the lay of the land; trails and trail markers set in summer can become obscured by winter snows.

When you are touring elsewhere, a guide familiar with the area and avalanche danger is a virtual necessity, for the sake of navigation and safety. The Tetons are big country, and the risks are commensurately big as well.

The **Jackson Hole Nordic Center** (*see* Track Skiing, *below*) leads tours of varying length and difficulty. **Alpine Guides** also leads half-day and full-day backcountry tours into the national parks and other areas near the resort, for more downhill-minded skiers. Arrangements can also be made through the **Jackson Hole Ski School. Jackson Hole Mountain Guides & Climbing School** (Box 7477T, Jackson 83001, tel. 307/733–4979) leads more strenuous backcountry tours.

Track Skiing The **Jackson Hole Nordic Center** is located at the ski-resort base. The 22 kilometers (13½ miles) of groomed track is relatively flat; scenery rather than heavy aerobic exertion is the main feature. A nice option offered here—because the Nordic Center and the downhill ski area are under the same management—is that downhill skiers with multiday passes can switch over to Nordic skiing in the afternoon for no extra charge. *Tel. 307/733–2292, ext. 129. Trail fee: $8 adult per day, $5 half day; $5 children and senior citizens per day, $3 half day. Rentals (diagonal, skating, touring, and telemark packages available) start at $12 per day adults, $7 children and senior citizens. Lessons (trail fee included) start at $25 adults, $12 children and senior citizens.*

Other Activities Dogsledding excursions are available through either **Freebird**
Dogsledding **Alaska Adventures** (tel. 307/733–7388) or **Washakie Outfitting** (tel. 307/733–3602).

Heli-Skiing Daily trips can be arranged through **High Mountain Helicopter Skiing** (tel. 307/733–3274), located in Teton Village Sports. In general, a good time to go is when there has been relatively little recent snowfall. For two or three days after a storm, good powder skiing can usually be found within the ski area.

Ice Climbing Among North American climbers, the Tetons are considered a must before hanging up one's ropes and pitons. The mountaineering action continues into winter. Anyone interested in climbing, or learning to climb, can contact **Jackson Hole Mountain Guides & Climbing School** (*see* Cross-Country Skiing, *above*). Offerings range from half-day lessons to multiday trips.

Sleigh Rides The largest herd of elk in North America can be found in winter in the **National Elk Refuge** (tel. 307/733-8084), just north of the town of Jackson. Sleigh rides into the refuge last about 45 minutes and leave the Elk Refuge Visitor Center daily, 10–4, about every 20 minutes. Dinner sleigh rides are also offered at **Spring Creek Resort** (tel. 307/733–8833 or 800/443–6139), with dinner at the resort's Granary Restaurant.

Snowmobiling Numerous companies in the Jackson area rent snowmobiles. **Flagg Ranch** (Box 187, Moran 83013, tel. 307/733–8761 or 800/ 443–2311), a 1½-hour drive north of Jackson via Route 89, is particularly well situated to take advantage of much of the region's most spectacular terrain. Located between Grand Teton and Yellowstone national parks, the ranch offers guided and unguided tours of both parks.

3 Special-Interest Vacations: The Outdoors

Choosing Your Vacation

By Peter Oliver

It's hard to imagine vacationing or living in the Rockies without becoming hooked on some kind of outdoor recreation. Any excuse *not* to partake in the outdoors is a lousy excuse, seeing as there is a form of recreation to suit anyone's needs or physical condition. Floating gently down a river on a raft, fishing a fast-flowing stream, riding horseback on a pack trip through the high mountains, climbing 14,000-foot peaks or 1,000-foot rock walls—the range of opportunities is endless.

Outdoor activities in the Rockies are not only plentiful but also easily accessible. Within an hour of leaving their homes and offices, outdoor jocks can be doing their recreational thing, whatever it might be, in the midst of an exquisitely beautiful backcountry environment. These are people who regard the Rockies as America's greatest open-air playground, and their thinking isn't far off the mark.

Under each heading in this chapter, descriptions of suggested trips are included. These activities are among the best the Rockies have to offer, and they have been chosen to give you ideas for planning an off-the-beaten-path vacation. However, these are *not* complete lists. The Rocky Mountain area is immense, and there is simply not enough space to mention all the recreational opportunities the region holds. If one of the listings doesn't quite fit your specifications, contact the outfitter for other itineraries. Local and regional chambers of commerce are also good sources of information about trip organizers or outfitters operating in a particular area. Another consideration is not to feel limited to a single activity. Many organized trips combine activities: Rafting and fishing is an obvious combination; rafting and mountain biking is a less obvious combo.

Going with a Group

Hiking, pack trips, and river rafting are the recreational activities probably best suited to group travel in the Rockies. Individuals or small groups (four people or fewer), on the other hand, tend to prefer such activities as fishing or mountaineering. Group sizes for organized trips vary considerably, depending on the organizer and the activity. Many trip organizers offer discounts of 10% or more for larger groups, so be sure to inquire. Often, if you are planning a trip with a large group, trip organizers or outfitters are willing to customize. For example, if you're with a group specifically interested in photography or in wildlife, trip organizers have been known to get professional photographers or naturalists to join the group. Recreating as a group gives you leverage with the organizer, and you should use it.

One way to travel with a group is to join before going. Conservation-minded travelers might want to contact the **American Forestry Association** (1516 P St. NW, Washington, DC 20005, tel. 202/462–3088 or 800/323–1560), a nonprofit organization. An educational alternative is to join a working group; hiking trails tend, for example, to be maintained by volunteers (generally local hiking clubs) that are always recruiting. Park or forest rangers are the best source of information for groups involved in this sort of work. **American Youth Hostels** (Box 37613, Washington, DC 20013, tel. 202/783–6161) provides service for recreational travelers of all ages (despite the name) and is an especially helpful organization for road cyclists.

Two organizations that teach groups and individuals a variety of wilderness skills—from white-water paddling to mountaineering—are the **Colorado Outward Bound** (945 Pennsylvania St., Denver, CO 80203, tel. 303/837–0880 or 800/477–2627) and **National Outdoor Leadership School** (Dept. R, 288 Main St., Lander, WY 82520, tel. 307/332–6973).

Trip Organizers Many trip organizers specialize in only one type of activity; however, a few companies guide a variety of active trips in the Rockies. (In some cases, these larger companies also act essentially as a clearinghouse or agent for smaller trip outfitters.) At last count, there were something like 5,000 "adventure travel" outfitters operating in North America, a good many of which are here-today, gone-tomorrow operations. Be sure to sign on with a reliable outfitter; getting stuck with a shoddy operator can be disappointing, uncomfortable, and even dangerous. Some sports—white-water rafting and mountaineering, for example—have organizations that license or certify guides, and you should be sure that the guide you're with is properly accredited.

The following are among the most reliable companies that organize active adventures in the Rockies: **American Wilderness Experience** (Box 1486, Boulder, CO 80306, tel. 800/444–0099); **Mountain Travel/Sobek** (6420 Fairmount Ave., El Cerrito, CA 94530, tel. 510/527–8100 or 800/227–2384); **The Road Less Traveled** (Box 8187–Q16, Longmont, CO 80501, tel. 303/678–8750); **Sierra Club Outings** (730 Polk St., San Francisco, CA 94109, tel. 415/923–5522).

Canoeing and Kayaking

For individual paddlers (as opposed to rafters), the streams and rivers of the Rockies tend to be better suited to kayaking than canoeing. Steep mountains and narrow canyons usually mean fast-flowing water in which the maneuverability of kayaks—especially their ability to roll over and be righted in rough water—is a great asset. A means of transport that has become increasingly popular in recent years for less experienced paddlers is the inflatable kayak.

For true white-water thrill-seekers, June is usually the best month to take on undammed rivers. Before then, high water due to snowmelt runoff can make many rivers dangerous; later in the summer, dwindling flow reduces white-water thrills and exposes rocks. The flow of dammed rivers, of course, can vary at any time of year, according to dam release schedules. Central Idaho and southern Colorado and Utah are where the best rivers for kayaking enthusiasts are found.

It may go without saying that many of the rivers that are good for rafting are also suitable for kayaking and/or canoeing. (For other recommended rivers, *see* Rafting, *below.)*

Before You Go When planning any vacation on a river, it's important to understand that rivers change, presenting different challenges depending on precipitation and the time of year. To help characterize a river's potential, a class system has been established: A Class I river, for example, is as calm as pond water; a Class V river churns with rapids that can summon all of the mayhem of a washing machine gone haywire. Like any subjective rating system, this one isn't perfect: Conditions can vary dramatically. For example, a river that earns a Class V rating during the spring runoff may be an impassable trickle by late summer. Nevertheless, the rating system gives you an approximate idea of what sort of thrills or hazards to expect. Anything above a Class II river is probably unsuitable for small children.

Expect to get wet; it's part of the fun. Outfitters often provide waterproof containers for cameras, clothing, and sleeping bags, but passengers remain exposed to the elements. If you don't like getting wet, don't go canoeing or kayaking. Also, bring a good hat and sunblock as well as warm clothing for overnight trips. The sun on the river can be intense, but once it disappears behind canyon walls, the temperature can drop 30° or more. The best footwear is either a pair of water-resistant sandals or old sneakers. Outfitters provide life jackets and, if necessary, paddles and helmets.

To minimize environmental impact as well as ensure a sense of wilderness privacy (riverside campgrounds are often limited to one party per night), a reservation policy is used for many rivers of the West. Often, the reserved times—many of the *prime* times—are prebooked by licensed outfitters, limiting your possibilities if you're planning a self-guided trip. For those rivers with restricted-use policies, you're well advised to write for reservations several months or more in advance. Also, try to be flexible about when and where to go; you might find that the time you want to go is unavailable, or you may find yourself closed out altogether from your first river of choice. If you insist on running a specific river at a specific time, your best bet is to sign on with a guided trip.

The rivers of the Rockies are fed by snowmelt, meaning that the water can be cold, especially early in the summer. Plan accordingly; having warm, dry clothing to change into can mean the difference between a pleasurable and a miserable trip. (Dammed rivers, for which chilled, subsurface water from reservoirs is squeezed through dams, can remain cold throughout the summer.) Figure on spending about $100 a day for a guided trip.

Organizers and Outfitters   **Dvorak Kayak & Rafting Expeditions** (17921-O U.S. Hwy. 285, Nathrop, CO 81236, tel. 800/824–3795) leads trips on the rivers of southwestern Colorado and Utah. **River Travel Center** (Box 6-U, Point Arena, CA 95468, tel. 800/882–7238) guides trips in Idaho and Utah, among other destinations.

Suggested Trips

Colorado   **Black Canyon of the Gunnison River.** The 12-mile stretch of the Gunnison River through the Black Canyon (Superintendent, 2233 E. Main St., Box 1648, Montrose 81402, tel. 303/249–7036) is so narrow and steep that in some sections the distance from rim to rim at the top is less than the distance from the elevation of the rim to the river. In fact, the Black Canyon—a national monument—earned its name because in places very little sunlight reaches the canyon floor. The stretch of the Gunnison through the canyon is one of the premier kayak challenges in North America, with Class IV and V rapids and portages required around bigger drops. It is a section of river that early visitors to the canyon declared unnavigable, and the fact that a few intrepid kayakers are able to make the journey today still stretches belief. This part of the river is only for hardy and experienced paddlers. However, once outside this area designated as a national monument, the canyon opens up, the rapids ease considerably, and the trip becomes more of a quiet float. *Trip organizer: **Gunnison River Expeditions** (Box 315, Montrose, CO 81402, tel. 303/249-4441). Dates: June–Oct. River rating: Class IV–Class V for the upper Gunnison, Class I–Class III for the lower Gunnison.*

Idaho **Salmon River.** The Salmon River is not one river but several. As far as kayakers and rafters are concerned, the two Salmons of greatest interest are the Middle Fork (*see* Rafting, *below*) and the Main. The Main is that 80-mile stretch of water with as good a nickname as a river can have: "River of No Return." While the rapids of the Main are somewhat less fierce or frequent than the rapids on the Middle Fork, the scenery is possibly even more breathtaking. The Main runs through one of the deepest canyons in the country—narrower, certainly, and in places deeper than the Grand Canyon. Running through the heart of the largest wilderness area in the country, the Salmon is a great river for kayakers who appreciate natural beauty and wildlife as much as white-water conquest. *Trip organizer: **Salmon River Outfitters** (Box 307, Columbia, CA 95310, tel. 209/532-2766). Dates: Apr.–Oct. River rating: Class III (possibly Class IV in spring).*

Selway River. Idaho is famous for its white-water rivers, including the Lochsa, the Payette, the Salmon, and the Snake. But perhaps the river that out–white-waters them all—the one that licensed Idaho boaters generally consider the ultimate test of their skill—is the Selway. All the elements that go into making white water come into play here: a steep drop (up to 125 feet per mile), a shallow riverbed, and a narrow passageway. When the snowmelt feeds the river in earnest in June, the Selway can offer true Class V action. By July, it has usually toned down its act to something more like Class IV. Thereafter, the river can become impassably shallow in places. Running through the Selway-Bitterroot Wilderness Area, this is wild country; the two things you can generally count on from the Selway are that you'll get very wet and that you'll see wildlife. Perhaps the biggest challenge of the Selway, though, is simply getting on it. Permits are issued on a lottery basis, and kayaking groups might have to wait a couple of years before landing a prized permit. (Another possibility is that one of the licensed raft companies that runs the river will agree to allow kayakers to accompany a trip, if space is available.) By all accounts, the wait is well worth it. *Trip organizer: Kayakers interested in booking a space on a raft trip should contact the **River Travel Center** (see Organizers and Outfitters, above). Dates: June–July. River rating: Class III–Class V in early summer.*

Utah **Cataract Canyon.** Timing is everything on the section of the Colorado River that runs through Cataract Canyon. Come in spring, and the rapids can rise with Class V force; come in August or September when the river settles back to a Class II or III, and you'll wonder what all the fuss is about. Whatever time of year you come, traveling by kayak (or raft) is one of the best ways to experience Canyonlands National Park (125 W. 200 South, Moab 84532, tel. 801/259-7164). Not all of the trip, of course, is a battle against white water; gently flowing stretches of the river allow for exploration of Native American ruins and the canyon's dramatic rock formations. *Trip organiz-er: Dvorak Kayak & Rafting Expeditions* (see *Organizers and Outfitters,* above).

Instruction **Cascade Kayak School** (Box 60, Garden Valley, ID 83622, tel. 800/292–7238) features Idaho river trips and instruction by a former U.S. national kayak team coach. **Dvorak Kayak & Raft-ing Expeditions** (*see* Organizers and Outfitters, *above*) con-ducts clinics for kayakers of all abilities on the Green River. **Mountain Sports Kayak School** (Box 1986, Steamboat Springs, CO 80488, tel. 303/879–8794 or 303/879–6910) offers classes pri-marily for kayakers with previous experience.

For the Family In general, rafting, which does not necessarily require the pad-dling skills that kayaking does, is a better way for young chil-dren to experience and appreciate river travel (*see* Rafting, *below*).

Resources **American Outdoors** (2133 Yarrow St., Lakewood, CO 80227, tel. 303/377–4811) is a good source of general information on Rocky Mountain Rivers.

Cycling

The Rockies, not surprisingly, are the land of the mountain bike. In fact, a mountain bike in these parts is as much a cultur-al statement as it is a recreational vehicle. Not that road bikes are obsolete in the Rockies; several good multiday road tours are possible in the region, although the paved back roads and country inns that make road touring so popular in the North-east are harder to find in the Rockies.

The mountain bike, on the other hand, has opened up vast stretches of terrain to two-wheelers. A number of ski resorts that run lifts in the summer for sightseers have made arrange-ments to accommodate mountain bikes, and a popular summer activity for bikers is to launch themselves down ski trails at breakneck speed. The mountain bike has also provided a new means for exploring the backcountry, a fact that doesn't always sit well with hikers. Mountain bikes are prohibited on many trails, especially in national parks, to limit biker-hiker confrontations, but this still leaves thousands of miles of trails and old logging and mining roads to explore.

Before You Go High, rugged country puts a premium on fitness. Even if you can ride 40 miles at home without breaking a sweat, you might find yourself struggling terribly on steep climbs and in eleva-tions often exceeding 10,000 feet. If you have an extended tour in mind, you might want to come a couple of days early and try some shorter rides, just to acclimatize yourself to the altitude and terrain. Also, it probably goes without saying that engag-ing in a little pretrip conditioning is likely to make your trip more enjoyable.

On tours where the elevation may vary 4,000 feet or more, the climate can change dramatically. While the valleys may be scorching, high-mountain passes may still be lined with snow in summer. Pack clothing accordingly. (Bicycle racers often stuff newspaper inside their jerseys when descending from high passes to shield themselves from the chill.) While you shouldn't have much problem renting a bike (trip organizers can usually arrange rentals), it's a good idea to bring your own pair of sturdy, stiff-bottomed cycling shoes to make riding easier, and your own helmet to make riding safer. Summer and early fall are the best times to plan a trip; at other times, snow and ice may still obstruct high-terrain roads and trails.

Guided bike trips generally range in price between $80 and $150, depending on lodging.

Organizers and Outfitters **Kaibab Mountain Bike Tours** (Box 339, Moab, UT 84532, tel. 800/451–1133) specializes mainly in mountain-bike touring in Colorado and Utah. **The Road Less Traveled** (Box 8187–Q16, Longmont, CO 80501, tel. 303/678–8750) and **Timberline Bicycle Tours** (7975 E. Harvard, No. J, Denver, CO 80231, tel. 303/759–3804) have extensive lists of bike tours in the Rocky Mountain region.

Suggested Trips

Colorado **Pearl Pass.** Mountain-bike historians—if there is such a breed —say that this is the route that got the mountain-biking craze started almost 20 years ago. A couple of guys, sitting around in Crested Butte without much to do, decided that a great way to entertain themselves would be to ride the rough old road over Pearl Pass to Aspen. Jeeps did it, so why not bikes? They hopped on board their clunky two-wheelers—a far cry from the sophisticated machinery of today—and with that, a sport was born. Today Crested Butte is probably *the* mountain-biking center of the Rockies (vying with Moab, Utah, for the title), a place where there are more bikes than cars, and probably more bikes than residents, too. It is home each July to **Fat Tire Bike Week** (Box 782, Crested Butte 81224, tel. 303/349–6817), a week of racing, touring, silly events, and mountain-biker bonding.

The 40-mile trip over Pearl Pass can be done in a day, but you must be in excellent condition to do it. Altitude is the chief enemy of fitness here; the pass itself is close to 13,000 feet. Unless you want to ride back from Aspen, you'll need to make return shuttle arrangements by car or by plane.

San Juan Mountains. The San Juans offer opportunities for both road cyclists and mountain bikers, although in both cases the going can be pretty rugged. For road cyclists, the more-than-200-mile loop linking Durango, Cortez, Ridgway, Ouray, and Silverton is as beautiful a ride as there is in the country, from the mountains to the mesas and back into the mountains. With several high-mountain passes (Red Mountain Pass is above 11,000 feet), however, there is a good deal of high-altitude climbing involved, along with some steep, tricky descents. For mountain bikers, the **San Juan Hut System** (Box 1663, Telluride 81435, tel. 303/728–6935), used by skiers in winter, creates a 215-mile backcountry link, mostly on old logging and mining roads, between the San Juan Mountains and the canyon country of southeastern Utah. The huts are rustic— without electricity or running water—but with bunk beds and cooking facilities, they're comfortable enough.

Utah **Slickrock Trail.** For mountain bikers, this is as much of a shrine as it is a trail. In this regard, the 12-mile trail, originally used by motorcyclists, is a bit like Yankee Stadium: There might be other places like it to strut your stuff, but there is a special aura about strutting your stuff here. The route across polished sandstone demands good balance and bike-handling skills, and erring far from the trail can lead to cliff edges to test one's nerve. Take in the beauty of southern Utah's arid canyon country, and hold on tight. Once you've conquered Slickrock, there are numerous other rides worth checking out in the area, especially in Canyonlands National Park (although before setting out, be sure that bikes are permitted on your trail of choice). If you want company, come in October, when the **Canyonlands Fat Tire Festival** (tel. 801/259–5333) is in session, an event that attracts mountain-bike junkies from around the country. *Trip organizer: **Rim Tours** (94 W. 1st N, Moab, 84532, tel. 801/259–5223).*

Instruction A few ski resorts now have mountain-biking schools in the summer, with the opportunity to ride and learn ski trails. Among the resorts with good instructional programs is **Snowbird** (Snowbird Ski and Summer Resort, Snowbird 84092, tel. 801/742–2222).

For serious road riders, especially racers, the **Carpenter/Phinney Cycling Camp** (Beaver Creek 81620, tel. 303/949–5750) at Vail/Beaver Creek is conducted by 1984 Olympic road champion Connie Carpenter and her husband, Davis Phinney, also an Olympic medalist and professional racer. One-week sessions focus on riding technique, training methods, and bicycle maintenance.

For the Family Multiday tours, as well as the trips listed above, are generally not good recreational choices for families with small children. The riding can be strenuous—made all the more so by the altitude—as well as hazardous, on the road and off. Short half-day or full-day trips with plenty of flat riding are, however, possible at many major Rocky Mountain resorts, where bike rentals in summer are easy to come by. Among the better resorts for this sort of riding are **Aspen** and **Steamboat Springs**, in Colorado; **Sun Valley,** Idaho; and **Park City,** Utah. All are located in fairly broad, flat valleys although surrounded—obviously—by mountains. Ask at local bike shops for recommended rides for children. Again, keep in mind that the altitude can be even more taxing on small lungs than on adult lungs, so be conservative in choosing a ride with children.

Resources **American Youth Hostels** (Box 37613, Washington, DC 20013, tel. 202/783–6161) has a strong focus on lodging and tours for cyclists of all ages. **Bikecentennial** (Box 8308, Missoula, MT 59807, tel. 406/721–1776) is the nation's largest nonprofit recreational cycling organization and is a good source of information on (among other things) bike-tour organizers.

Dude Ranches

Wyoming is obviously not the only Rocky Mountain state in which to find dude ranches, but Wyomingites might want you to think so. No state in the Union exalts cowboy life as Wyoming does, and cowboy life is at the heart of what dude ranching is all about. Wyoming can boast more dude ranches—more than 80 at last count—than any other state.

It was in Wyoming (around Sheridan) that the first dude ranches were open for business in the early 1900s, which in all likelihood makes dude ranching the earliest form of organized recreational tourism in the Rockies. The dude ranch was originally conceived as a true East-meets-West phenomenon: Wealthy easterners curious about the mythic ruggedness of the West accounted for the "dude" part; ranchers eager to cultivate the money of wealthy tourists as well as their own crops and livestock accounted for the ranch part. Railroad companies in turn were happy to have their seats filled, going both west and east. It's no wonder the idea took hold.

The original concept was to give those easterners a taste of real ranch and cowboy life—horseback riding, cattle roping, nights spent in bedrolls by the chuck wagon, and so on. A few dude ranches still promote the working-ranch aspect of the experience, but most have come to realize that there is a larger market in a "softer" ranching experience. In other words, most ranch guests prefer a comfortable bed to sleep in, something more inviting for dinner than jerky and hardtack around the campfire, and recreation other than (or at least in addition to) ranching-related activities. Hence, we get the more modern term "guest ranch." A few old-time dude-ranch owners might insist that there's a difference between a legitimate dude ranch and a guest ranch, but the differences in many cases are more a matter of opinion than definition. In general, though, those ranches that call themselves dude ranches put a heavy emphasis on horseback riding and ranching activities; at guest ranches, such activities share the billing with others, and real ranching is often not part of the mix at all.

The slate of possible activities can vary widely from ranch to ranch. Horseback riding obviously remains Activity #1, and at most ranches guests will be given some taste of the working-ranch experience with demonstrations of cowboy (rodeo) skills and the like. Fishing tends to be given second priority, with large ranches usually having access to private waters that otherwise see relatively little fishing activity. After that, almost anything goes: hiking, hunting, mountain biking, tennis, swimming, river rafting (on or off the ranch), and so on. Most ranches try to retain a semblance of ranch life, and at a typical dude ranch, guests stay in log cabins and are served meals family style (everyone eats at the same time, at long tables) in a larger lodge or ranch house. "Family," incidentally, is an important concept here; a dude ranch (or guest ranch) vacation is one of the best ways for a family of widely varying ages and interests to have a shared experience of the Rockies.

Before You Go Most dude ranches don't require any previous experience with horses, although a few working ranches reserve weeks in spring and fall—when the chore of moving cattle is more intensive than in summer—for experienced riders. No special equipment is necessary, although if you plan to do much fishing, you're best off bringing your own tackle (some ranches have tackle to loan or rent). Be sure to check with the ranch for a list of items you might be expected to bring. If you plan to do much riding, a couple of pairs of sturdy pants, a wide-brimmed hat to shield you from the sun, and outerwear as protection from the possibility of rain or chill should be packed. Casual dress is the norm, for day and evening. Expect to spend at least $110 per day. Depending on the activities you engage in, as well as accommodations, the price can go up as high as $250 a day or more.

Organizers and **Colorado Dude and Guest Ranch Association** (Box 300,
Outfitters Tabernash, CO 80478, tel. 303/887–3128 or 800/441–6060 out-

side CO), the **Dude Ranchers Association** (Box 471, Laporte, CO 80535, tel. 303/493–7623), and **Old West Dude Ranch Vacations** (c/o American Wilderness Experiences, Box 1486, Boulder, CO 80306, tel. 800/444–3833).

Suggested Trips

Colorado   **Focus Ranch, Slater.** This ranch, located in the high-mesa country near the Colorado–Wyoming border, is the real thing: a dude ranch that emphasizes ranching and has been steadfast in maintaining its working-ranch character. If you don't like riding, go elsewhere; the predominant activity is working in small groups with professional cowboys to move cattle from one grazing ground to the next. For guests who need another diversion, there is also good fishing. While activities in summer are skewed toward family business, spring and fall are periods reserved for experienced riders and fishermen. Accommodations in five cabins are for 30 guests. *Slater 81653, tel. 303/583–2410. Open year-round.*

Wind River Ranch, Estes Park. Any ranch that advertises "modern comfort" and "fine wines" as being among its principal selling points is likely to be more of a guest ranch than a dude ranch, and so it is with Wind River. Not that the ranch lacks historical authenticity: The original homestead dates back more than 100 years. The homesteaders knew what they were doing; this is a spectacular plot of land at the doorstep of Rocky Mountain National Park. The log cabin accommodations are pretty elegant by ranch standards, and the activity roster tends to be skewed away from horseback riding toward hiking, climbing, and fishing. As for eating, the food here could be called gourmet, a word normally not found in the rancher's lexicon. *Box 3410D, Estes Park 80517, tel. 303/586–3341 or 800/ 523–4212. Accomodations for 55. Open June–mid-Sept.*

Wyoming   **H F Bar Ranch, Saddlestring.** There is something special about being the original, and this ranch can lay claim to being one of the oldest dude ranches in the West. The emphasis is on horseback riding and fishing, accommodations are in cabins, and meals are served family style in the ranch house. In other words, H F Bar follows the dude-ranch book of rules. Another feature here is a remote camp—a destination for horse-pack trips in summer and hunting trips in the fall—located 15 miles from the ranch in the Big Horn Mountains. *Saddlestring 82840, tel. 307/684–2487.*

R Lazy S Ranch, Jackson. Jackson Hole, with the spectacle of the Tetons in the background, is true dude-ranch country. Although a number of the "ranches" in the state stretch the ranch concept, the R Lazy S does not. One of the largest in the Jackson area, it has been owned for more than 40 years by the family that is now co-owner of the Jackson Hole Ski Resort. Horseback riding and instruction (for adults and children) is emphasized; the secondary emphasis is fishing in private waters on the ranch and in other rivers and streams in the area. Accommodations are in the dude-ranch tradition—in log-cabin guest cottages, with meals served in the large main lodge. *Box 308, Teton Village 83025, tel. 307/733–2655. Accommodations for 45. Open mid-June–Sept.*

For the Family   Although most dude ranches are ideal for children of all ages, not all feature the same types of activities; some ranches (more likely to be guest ranches), for example, focus more on fishing and river sports than ranching activities, which are usually of less interest to children. Be sure you know not only the activities a ranch offers but also which are emphasized before booking your vacation.

Resources *Farm, Ranch, and Country Vacations* (Farm, Ranch, and Family Vacations, Inc., Box 698, Newfoundland, NJ 07435, tel. 602/596–0226; $12), by Pat Dickerman, is a good source of information on ranch vacations. State tourism offices can provide lists of dude and guest ranches in the Rocky Mountain region. For other sources of information that can help in selecting a ranch to match your interests, *See* Organizers and Outfitters *above*.

Fishing

Fishing in the Rockies is more than a form of recreation; it is for many a secular religion. It breeds the kind of devotion that leads otherwise sane people to stand waist-deep in 35° water in January for hours at a time, or to discuss at length among one another the intricate and intimate details of bug gestation, or to lose their eyesight (as flytiers) fiddling around with pieces of string and lint. It strains marriages. However, when you consider that the thousands of cold streams and lakes of the Rockies are ideal habitats for trout—cutthroats, browns, rainbows, and lake trout—you can understand why people get so enthusiastic. As Brigham Young said about Salt Lake City, so it could be said among trout fishermen about the Rockies: This is the place.

It is hardly an undiscovered place, though; no longer can you toss a line into almost any Rocky Mountain stream and expect a hit within minutes. Nor is this necessarily trophy-fish country. The fish may be plentiful and lively, especially in stocked waters, but considerable fishing activity assures that most of the older, bigger fish are long gone. A partial remedy is that many popular rivers now have catch-and-release stretches, a measure taken to sustain fish populations and to help smaller fish survive to become bigger fish.

Serious fishermen spend a lot of time observing streams to "match the hatch"—that is, to study the insects along a body of water and their state of maturity, then come up with flies from their tackle box that are approximately similar. Less serious anglers can shortcut the process simply by asking tackle-shop proprietors what sort of flies have been working best for a particular area at a particular time and buy flies accordingly. Any angler can make the whole business much, much easier by hiring a knowledgeable guide or signing on with an outfitter.

Before You Go Fishing licenses, available at tackle shops and a variety of local stores, are required in all Rocky Mountain states. The fishing season may vary from state to state, and from species to species. A few streams are considered "private" streams, in that they are privately stocked by a local club, so be sure you know the rules before making your first cast.

For information on fishing regulations and licenses, contact the following: in Colorado, the **Colorado Division of Wildlife, Central Regional Office** (6060 Broadway, Denver 80216, tel. 303/297–1192); in Idaho, the **Department of Fish and Game** (600 S. Walnut St., Box 25, Boise 83707, tel. 208/334–3700); in Montana, the **Montana Department of Fish, Wildlife and Parks** (1420 E. 6th, Helena 59620, tel. 406/444–2535); in Utah, the **Utah Division of Wildlife Resources** (1596 W. North Temple, Salt Lake City 84116, tel. 801/538–4700); in Wyoming, **Wyoming Game and Fish** (5400 Bishop Blvd., Cheyenne 82002, tel. 307/777–7735).

Rocky Mountain water can be cold, especially at higher elevations and especially in spring and fall (and winter, of course). You'd do well to bring waterproof waders or buy them when you arrive in the region. Outfitters and some tackle shops rent equipment, but you're best off bringing your own gear. Lures are another story, though: Whether you plan to fish with flies or other lures, local tackle shops can usually give you a pretty good idea of what works best in a particular region, and you can buy accordingly.

Organizers and Outfitters Local guide services generally provide the best trip leadership when it comes to fishing. In addition, fishing tends not to be a group activity, although it does tend to be a popular peripheral activity on organized river trips (*see* Canoeing and Kayaking, *above*, and Rafting, *below*) and on pack trips (*see* Pack Trips and Horseback Riding, *below*). Perhaps the most noteworthy organizer of fishing-specific trips is **Orvis** (Rte. 7A, Manchester, VT 05454, tel. 802/362–1300).

Needless to say, in a region with such a wealth of fishing, there are many guide services and outfitters. For a complete listing of guides or outfitters in a region, probably your best bet is contacting a local or regional chamber of commerce (*see* individual state chapters throughout the book). For state associations of outfitters and guides, also *see* Resources, *below*.

Suggested Trips

Colorado **Dolores River.** The recently built McPhee Dam has changed the character of the Dolores River—changed it for the better, many local anglers would argue. The reservoir formed by the dam has been heavily stocked with rainbow trout by the Colorado Division of Wildlife. The best reservoir fishing, unfortunately, is by boat, which is not the case for the river below the dam. The dam has had a couple of positive influences on fish life in the river: Fish apparently appreciate the nutrients that spill out during regulated dam releases, and the dam also maintains a flow of cool water throughout the summer, something trout enjoy. Here the San Juan Mountains meet mesa country, and it is a pretty place to fish as well as one that is relatively undiscovered (by Colorado standards) when compared with streams and lakes closer to major resorts and population centers. *Trip organizer:* **Outfitter Sporting Goods** *(410 Railroad Ave., Dolores 81323, tel. 303/882–7740) can provide equipment and information on current fishing conditions.*

Montana **The Southwest.** This is the land of *A River Runs Through It*, the acclaimed book (by Norman Maclean) and the movie with trout fishing as a central theme. In fact, several rivers run through the region, notably the Madison, Gallatin, and Yellowstone, which run more or less parallel to one another between Yellowstone National Park and Bozeman, as well as the Big Hole River to the west. All are easily accessible from major roads, which can mean that in summer you might have to drive a ways to find a hole to call your own. However, stream fishing in these parts is a year-round enterprise. Just where the fishing is best along these rivers will vary considerably depending on the source of local knowledge you tap into, but such disagreement no doubt confirms a wealth of opportunity. The Gallatin near Big Sky resort; the Madison south of Ennis as well as at its confluence with the Missouri near Three Forks; the Yellowstone south of Livingstone: These are among the spots that get mentioned most often, though it is hard to go wrong in these parts. And even if you never catch a fish, the mountain ranges that separate these rivers (or vice versa) are among the most beautiful in the Rockies. Just being in this part of the world ought to be enough satisfaction; catching a fish is a bonus. *Trip organizers:* ***Blue Ribbon Flies*** *(Box 1037, West Yellowstone 59758, tel. 406/ 646–7642);* ***East Slope Anglers*** *(Box 160261, Big Sky 59716, tel. 406/995–4369). The* Montana 1993 Recreation Guide *lists more than 150 fishing guides who work in this region.*

Utah **Provo Canyon.** Provo Canyon has a reputation as having one of the great trout streams in North America—a reputation that many local fishermen regard dubiously. They claim to know better places in Utah to fish, and they complain that the reputation has resulted in overfishing in Provo Canyon. Maybe they're right, but driving through the canyon at any time of year, and in almost any kind of weather, you're assured of seeing believers in the reputation out there in their waders, laying out lines. They are presumably pulling something out of the river to make that immersion in cold water worthwhile. Wilderness seclusion is not the thing here. A heavily used road parallels the river through the canyon, and its location just a few miles from downtown Provo makes this the sort of river where businesspeople can pull on waders over suit trousers and make a few casts after work. But if there is indeed substance to that reputation, this is one of the great places in the Rockies to catch trout.

Wyoming **Wind River Range.** For good reason, most visitors to the Jackson Hole area cast their attention westward to the Tetons, as attention-grabbing as any mountain range can be. For that reason, such waters as Jackson and Jenny lakes and the Snake River are heavily fished, especially in the height of the summer tourist season. That's why many local fishermen prefer heading eastward into the Wind River Mountains. Numerous lakes and more than 800 miles of streams in Bridger National Forest, which encompasses the Wind Rivers, make for abundant fishing. This is high country—including Gannett Peak, at 13,804 feet the highest point in Wyoming—meaning that some lakes may remain partially frozen even into July. If the Wind Rivers have a drawback, it is ease of access. No roads lead through the region, only to it; for the best fishing, you should be prepared to do some hiking. Check at tackle shops in Jackson or Pinedale for recommended fishing spots, although don't necessarily expect to get a straight answer. These are waters Wyomingites would prefer to keep for themselves. *Trip organizer:* ***Skinner Brothers Guides and Outfitters*** *(Box 859, Pinedale 82941, tel. 307/367–2270 or 307/237–9138).*

Instruction **Orvis Fly Fishing Schools** (Rte. 7A, Manchester, VT 05255, tel. 802/362–3622) runs one of the most respected fishing instructional programs in the country and endorses instructional programs around the country. Contact Orvis for a list. Good instruction in the Rocky Mountain region is also offered through **Bud Lilly's Trout Shop** (39 Madison Ave., Box 698

West Yellowstone, MT 59758, tel. 406/646–7801) and **Telluride Outside** (666 W. Colorado, Box 685, Telluride, CO 81435, tel. 303/728–3895 or 800/831–6230).

For the Family Despite the noble effort of *A River Runs Through It* to project an image of fishing as a family sport, the nuances of fishing, especially the patience required, are often lost on children. Perhaps lakes and reservoirs are better choices than streams and rivers as sites for taking the family fishing, because of the possible alternative activities: swimming, boating, or simply exploring the shoreline.

A couple of good choices along the family lines are **Grand Lake,** the largest natural lake in Colorado and not far from Rocky Mountain National Park, and **Jackson Lake** in Grand Teton National Park.

Resources In Montana, you can contact the **Montana Outfitters & Guides Association** (Box 9070, Helena 59604, tel. 406/444–3738); in Utah, **Utah Guides & Outfitters** (Box 111, Jensen 84035, tel. 801/789-4952). *Field and Stream,* published by Times Mirror magazines, is a leading source of information on fishing travel, technique, and equipment.

Hiking and Backpacking

Hiking is the easiest and least expensive way to experience the Rockies; all you need are a sturdy pair of shoes and a desire to explore. (Even a sturdy pair of shoes isn't essential if you stay on well-maintained trails; hikers have been known to travel comfortably for miles in tennis shoes.) There are literally thousands of miles of marked trails in the Rockies, and they are free of any user's fees, as are most backcountry campgrounds (although permits and/or reservations may be required in some places).

It is surprising, then, how few people take advantage of this wealth of recreational opportunity. Each year, visitor surveys in national parks indicate that less than 5% of all visitors venture more than a mile from paved roads. Use of hiking trails outside the national parks is even less, and one can only thank the volunteer efforts of local outdoor clubs as well as national organizations for maintaining trails despite (apparently) such little interest among visitors in using them.

There are a couple of things to keep in mind, however. Not all trails are simply hiking trails. On a great many, especially those outside the national parks, don't be surprised to encounter horseback riders, mountain bikers, or even motorized vehicles. Such confrontations can be not only intrusive but also hazardous. Bears, especially in the northern Rockies, present an increasing danger (bear populations have been growing in recent years). Take all bear precautions seriously, and be extra careful traveling in the backcountry in fall, when bears tend to be out foraging in preparation for winter.

Before You Go In areas (such as national parks) where hiking trails are well marked and well maintained, detailed topographical maps are unnecessary. Rudimentary trail-system maps are usually available at visitor centers or ranger stations for free or for a minimal fee. A good guidebook for the specific region you plan to hike in, however—no matter how well marked the trails—can be extremely helpful. Most guidebooks for hikers provide fairly detailed trail descriptions, including length and elevation gains involved and recommended side trips. Guidebooks to larger areas—a state, for instance—may be helpful in deciding where to go, but they don't serve as well as actual trail guides (*see* Resources, *below*).

If you plan to do much scrambling or bushwhacking, or traveling where trails might not be well marked or maintained, you'll need maps and a compass. Topographical maps are available from the **U.S. Geological Survey** (Distribution Section, Federal Center, Denver, CO 80225). When ordering, be as specific as possible about the area through which you plan to hike; good topographical maps can be expensive. Many local camping, fishing, or hunting stores also carry detailed maps of the surrounding region. One other hiking advantage: It's relatively cheap. Organized-trip costs can be as little as $30 a day. Costs can reach $100 a day for llama trekking.

Organizers and Outfitters
Sierra Club Outings (930 Polk St., San Francisco, CA 94109, tel. 415/923–5522) and **Wild Horizon Expeditions** (West Fork Rd., Dept. B, Danby, MT 59829, tel. 406/821–3747) have extensive listings of guided trips in the Rocky Mountain region. One option backpackers might consider is llama trekking, where the beasts bear the burden. A couple of examples: **Teton Llamas** (673N 4200 East, Rigby, ID 83442, tel. 208/745–6706) leads trips in the Teton area; **High Uinta Llamas** (1010 E. Upper Loop Rd., Kamas, UT 84036, tel. 801/783–4480) leads trips in the Uintas, Utah's highest mountain range.

Suggested Trips

The following recommended areas for hiking are rated from easy to strenuous. Easier hiking areas involve little climbing—a rarity in the Rockies. Strenuous hiking may involve as much as 5,000 vertical feet in a day's hike, with steep trail sections included.

Idaho
Sawtooth Mountains. About 20 years ago, the Sawtooths were in line to become a national park, but it didn't happen: In its zeal to create as much bureaucracy as possible, Congress instead divvied the land up into two parcels—a wilderness area and a national recreation area, each with different regulations. This has not, however, detracted significantly from the beauty of the landscape of rough-edged peaks (hence the name), and perhaps *because* this is not a national park, much of the backcountry here is barely visited, even in the summer. There are 180 lakes, but only the two or three most accessible receive much visitor traffic, mostly locals from the nearby Sun Valley area. Because this is technically national forest, not national park, don't be surprised to encounter mountain bikes and horses on some trails. On many trails, however, don't be surprised if you don't see much of anyone at all. *For information and permits, write* **Sawtooth National Forest**. *Trip length: 5–30 mi. Dates: around July–Sept., when trails are generally clear of snow. Difficulty: moderate. Guidebook:* Trails of the Sawtooth and White Cloud Mountains, *by Margaret Fuller.*

Montana
Absaroka-Beartooth Wilderness. While summer visitors swarm into Yellowstone National Park just to the south, relatively few (except for dedicated backcountry travelers) come to the Absaroka-Beartooth Wilderness. One reason is that, unlike

Yellowstone, the wilderness area has no paved roads leading into it, although a four-wheel-drive vehicle is not essential for access.

Montana's highest mountains, including 12,799-foot Granite Peak, are encompassed by the wilderness boundaries; because of that, the prime hiking season is relatively short. High-mountain lakes may remain partially frozen even into August. Perhaps the most popular hiking is in the East Fork–Rosebud Creek area, featuring numerous lakes in high-alpine basins above 9,000 feet. One warning: This is bear country. *For information and permits, write* **Custer National Forest** *(2602 1st Ave. N, Box 2556, Billings 59103, tel. 406/657–6361);* **Gallatin National Forest** *(Federal Bldg., Box 130, Bozeman 59771, tel. 406/587–6701). Trip length: One-way from East Rosebud Creek to Cooke City is 35 mi. Difficulty: moderate–strenuous. Dates: Aug. is best. Guidebook:* Hiker's Guide to Montana *(Falcon Press).*

Utah   **Capitol Reef National Park.** While summer visitors crowd the other national parks of southern Utah—Arches, Bryce Canyon, Canyonlands, and Zion—Capitol Reef is the park few people seem to know about. This is, literally, a reef in Utah's desert country—a giant fold in the earth that stretches for more than 100 miles. White rock domes, multicolored cliffs, deep canyons, and natural bridges are the park's physical features, through which the Fremont River has managed to find its course. In summer, hiking on and through all of this rock can be brutally hot (albeit spectacular); a better time to visit is in spring, when days are warm and nights cool, when side-canyon creeks are still full of water, and when wildflowers and cacti are in bloom. Hikes can range from a couple of miles to a couple of days, although in order to get to some of the more remote side canyons or trailheads, a four-wheel-drive vehicle may be helpful. *For information and permits, write* **Capitol Reef National Park** *(Superintendent, Torrey 84775, tel. 801/425–3791). Trip length: 2–15 mi. Difficulty: moderate. Dates: Apr.–June is best. Guidebook: Trail guide and topographical maps available at the visitor center.*

Wyoming   **Teton Range.** A good deal here is that much of the uphill legwork can be dispensed with by aerial tram, the same one that carries Jackson Hole skiers upward in winter. From the top, you can walk through high-mountain basins filled with wildflowers in summer, or along cliff-line ridges, all the while with the stunning facade of the Tetons as a backdrop. A loop of about 30 miles can be made by joining with the Teton Crest Trail, then branching off on the Death Canyon trail. Longer hikes are also possible. Don't necessarily expect solitude; most of the time you're in Grand Teton National Park, an exceedingly popular tourist destination. However, this route keeps you well away from the visitor crush at the park's main gate, so you aren't likely to encounter hiker traffic jams, either. *For information and permits, write* **Grand Teton National Park** *(Drawer 170, Moose 83012, tel. 307/733–2880). Trip organizer:* **Jackson Hole Mountain Guides** *(Box 7477T, Jackson 83001, tel. 307/733–4979). Trip length: 30 mi. Dates: July–Aug. are best for weather and wildflowers. Difficulty: moderate. Guidebook:* Hiking the Teton Backcountry, *by Paul Lawrence (Sierra Club Books).*

For the Family Several ski resorts in the Rockies run lifts in the summer for sightseers, hikers, and mountain bikers. Riding a lift up and hiking down—or taking short hikes along ridgelines—can be a relatively easy way for a family to experience both the beauty of the high country and the joys of hiking. Descents are typically between 2 and 5 miles. For other short day hikes, national parks tend to be good places to find short, well-marked trails that lead quickly to spectacular scenery, although such routes usually see plenty of traffic in summer. Some trip organizers arrange backpacking outings specifically geared toward families with small children, especially for family groups of eight or more.

Resources The **American Hiking Society** (Box 20160, Washington, DC 20041, tel. 703/385–3252) is a general source of hiking information. **The Mountaineers** (306 2nd Ave. W, Seattle, WA 98119) and **Sierra Club Books** (930 Polk St., San Francisco, CA 94109) offer a good selection of Rocky Mountain hiking guides. ***Backpacker*** magazine (Rodale Press) is the leading national magazine that focuses on hiking and backpacking. Those interested in llama trekking might want to contact the **Colorado Llama Outfitters and Guides Association** (Box 1394, Carbondale, CO 81623).

Pack Trips and Horseback Riding

As movies and lore will not let us forget, the horse was the animal that enabled settlement of the West. Despite the use of everything from motorcycles to helicopters, ranches continue to rely on horses as a means of transportation. But horses are also an excellent way to get to the Rocky Mountain backcountry, as they can carry loads and travel distances that would be impossible for hikers. (What backpacker, for example, would carry a heavy iron skillet?) In other words, traveling by horseback is a terrific way to experience the big spaces of Rocky Mountain backcountry—the reason there are hundreds of outfitters that guide pack trips throughout the region.

The length, difficulty, and relative luxury of a pack trip can obviously vary considerably, although anyone who expects true luxury is obviously missing the point. Most pack-trip outfitters try to retain the rough edges that are traditionally a part of the pack-trip experience, and that's as it should be. In other words, tents are the usual overnight accommodations (although backcountry lodges or cabins may be used). Morning coffee is traditionally made from grinds dumped in a big pot of hot water and is powerful enough to keep your eardrums ringing for the rest of the day.

Before You Go Horsemanship is not a prerequisite for most trips, but it is helpful. If you aren't an experienced rider (and even if you are), you can expect to experience some saddle discomfort for the first day or two. If you're unsure of how much of this sort of thing you can put up with, sign up for a shorter trip (one to three days) before taking on an adventure of a week or longer. Another option is to spend a few days at a dude or guest ranch (*see* Dude Ranches, *above*) to get used to life in the saddle, then try a shorter, overnight pack trip organized by the ranch.

Clothing requirements are minimal. A sturdy pair of pants, a wide-brimmed sun hat, and outerwear to protect against rain are about the only necessities. Ask your outfitter for a list of items you'll need. You might be limited in the gear (extra clothing) or luxuries (alcoholic beverages) an outfitter will let you bring along; horses and pack mules are strong but can still carry only so much. Check with your outfitter before showing up at the saddle-up with a trunk full of accessories. Trip costs typically range between $120 and $180 per day.

Organizers and Outfitters Pack trips tend to be organized by local outfitters or ranches rather than national organizations. Local chambers of commerce can usually provide lists of outfitters who work in a particular area. (*See* Resources, *below*, for additional information sources.)

Suggested Trips

Colorado **Aspen.** The T Lazy 7 Ranch outside of Aspen is a good place to find out if pack tripping is for you, before committing yourself to a multiday ride. The ranch rents horses by the hour and by the day (with instruction, if you want). The T Lazy 7's convenient location, on Maroon Creek Road, enables short rides into one of the prettiest, and certainly the most photographed, valleys in Colorado's central Rockies, capped by the twin peaks of the Maroon Bells. If that appeals to you, you can sign up for an overnight pack trip, organized by the ranch, into one of Aspen's surrounding wilderness areas. If you want to find out if you can hack some of the cowboy culture that inevitably comes with pack tripping (both the real thing and show-off stuff put on for tourists), combine a ride with a steak dinner at the ranch, enlivened by country musicians. *Trip organizer: **T Lazy 7 Ranch** (3129 Maroon Creek Rd., Aspen 81612, tel. 303/925–7040 or 303/925–4625; open for horseback riding Memorial Day–mid-Oct.).*

Steamboat Springs. The Yampa and Elk River valleys around Steamboat have a long and continuing ranching history. Indeed, Steamboat has successfully used its cowboy heritage as a way of promoting tourism; the area is full of not only real cowboys but also visitors trying to act the part. Horseback riding is a spectator as well as a participant sport here; every weekend in summer, rodeos are held in the evening at the Steamboat Rodeo Grounds. Riding, instruction, and extended pack trips are offered at a number of ranches in the area, although some require minimum stays of a week, for example. One ranch that offers the full gamut, from hour-long rides to rides of several days into the surrounding mountains, is Del's Triangle 3 Ranch, about 20 miles north of Steamboat. Dinner rides are a good choice for those who want to get a feeling for the life-on-the-trail character of pack tripping before signing on for an overnighter. *Trip organizer: **Del's Triangle 3 Ranch** (Box 333, Clark 80428, tel. 303/879–3495 or 303/879–4109).*

Montana **Bob Marshall Wilderness.** Known by locals simply as "the Bob," this wilderness has remained wild enough to have become popular with bears (including a large grizzly population), mountain goats, bighorn sheep, and elk, as well as pack trippers. It is the largest expanse of roadless land in Montana, and while there are trails to be hiked in the Bob, horse-pack trips are a better way to penetrate this huge wilderness. This tends to be big-country riding, best for (though not restricted to) experienced riders, with stretches of more than 20 miles a day common. Among the highlights of the Bob are wildflowers as well as wildlife, mountain scenery (of course), fishing, and the Chinese Wall, a 120-mile-long, reef-like stretch of cliffs, a kind of natural monument to the powers of tectonic forces. *Trip organizer:* **Snowy Springs Outfitter** *(720 Main St., Kalispell 59903, tel. 406/752–7278). There are dozens of other outfitters who guide horse-pack trips in the Bob. For a list, contact the* **Montana Outfitters & Guides Association** *(Box 1339, Townsend 59644, tel. 406/266–2652). Dates: July–Aug.*

Wyoming   **Pinedale.** Pinedale combines with Jackson as twin headquarters of the dude-ranch center of the universe. Not surprisingly, this region is also a center for pack tripping. There are mountains to explore in almost every direction (except due south)—the Tetons being the most obvious (and most populated), the Gros Ventres and the Wind Rivers less famous but no less worthy as pack-trip destinations. And, of course, the wonders of Yellowstone lie to the north. While Pinedale shares a good bit of Jackson's real and faux Western architecture, it isn't nearly as overcome by the inundation of touristy schlock that is Jackson's summertime curse. In other words, Pinedale's authentic cowboy roots tend to be more apparent, making it a good starting point for pack trips into the Wind River Mountains, in particular. There are several ranches and outfitters in the Pinedale area; half-day trail rides, multiday pack trips, spring or fall hunting expeditions—all are possible. *Trip organizer:* **Bridger Wilderness Outfitters** *(Box 561T, Pinedale 82941, tel. 307/367–2268 or 307/367–2928). Dates: June–Sept. for trail rides and pack trips.*

Instruction   Most ranches and outfitters offer instruction on Western-style riding for those who want it (*also see* Dude Ranches, *above.*)

For the Family   Even for adults, an extended pack trip is something best worked up to gradually. That's especially advisable for children. Before launching off on a long trip with younger children (or even teenagers), it's probably a good idea to spend a few days at a dude ranch to find out how well your kids take to horses and riding. The T Lazy 7 Ranch, Bridger Wilderness Outfitters, and Del's Triangle 3 Ranch (*see above* for all) can arrange short rides and instruction for children.

Resources   Local and regional chambers of commerce (*see* individual state chapters throughout the book) are good sources of information on ranches and outfitters. You can get additional information from the **Colorado Outfitters Association** (Box 440021, Aurora CO 80044, tel. 303/751–9274), the **Montana Outfitters & Guides Association** (Box 9070, Helena, MT 59604, tel. 406/444–3738), and **Utah Guides & Outfitters** (Box 111, Jensen, UT 84035, tel. 801/789–4952).

Rafting

River rafting is truly one of the great ways to experience the Rockies. It is a relatively easy way to get into the backcountry, whether on a half-day float or a two-week white-water adventure. For most trips, no special skills or physical conditioning is necessary, although you'll probably want to be in good enough shape to make short hikes to explore side canyons along the way. One bonus of river travel is that, by backcountry standards, you can live—or more accurately, you can *eat*—in relatively high style. Heavy food-and-drink items such as beer, soda, refrigerated meats—items that might be cumbersome on a backpacking or horse-pack trip—are easily stashed and carried along on rafts. But don't expect too much luxury: For extended trips, accommodations in virtually all cases are in tents on riverside beaches.

Note: Raft trips are also run through Cataract Canyon in Utah and on the Selway River in Idaho (*see* Canoeing and Kayaking, *above*).

Before You Go Rivers are rated according to the ferocity of their water. (For an explanation of class and challenge level, *see* Before You Go in Canoeing and Kayaking, *above*.)

"Raft" can mean any of a number of things: an inflated raft in which passengers do the paddling; an inflated raft or wooden dory in which a licensed professional does the work; a motorized raft on which some oar work might be required. Be sure you know what kind of raft you'll be riding—or paddling—before booking a trip. Day trips typically run between $30 and $60 per person. Expect to pay between $80 and $120 for multiday trips.

Organizers and Different companies are licensed to run different rivers, al-
Outfitters though there may be several companies working the same river. Some organizers combine river rafting with other activities: pack trips, mountain-bike excursions, extended hikes.

The following companies offer a variety of Rocky Mountain river trips: **Adrift Adventures** (Box 577, Moab, UT 84532, tel. 801/259-8594 or 800/874-4483); **ARTA River Trips** (24000 Casa Loma Rd., Groveland, CA 95321, tel. 800/323-2782); **Glacier Raft Company** (Box 218A, West Glacier, MT 59936, tel. 406/888-5454 or 800/332-9995); **Mountain Travel/Sobek** (6420 Fairmount Ave., El Cerrito, CA 94530, tel. 510/527-8100 or 800/227-2384); **OARS** (Box 67, Angels Camp, CA 95222, tel. 209/736-4677).

Suggested Trips

Colorado **Dolores River.** Beginning in the San Juan Mountains of southwestern Colorado, the Dolores runs north for more than 100 miles before joining the Colorado River near Moab, Utah. This is one of those rivers that tend to flow madly in spring and diminish considerably by midsummer, and for that reason trips are usually run between April and June. Sandstone canyons, Anasazi ruins, and the spring bloom of wildflowers and cacti are trip highlights. For the most part, this is a float, interrupted by rapids that—depending on the flow level—can rate a Class V. *Trip organizer: OARS* (see *Organizers and Outfitters*, above). Trip length: 6 or 10 days. Dates: late Apr.–June. River rating: Class II–Class V.

Idaho **Middle Fork, Salmon River.** The Middle Fork is a true rafting legend. Other than running the Colorado River through the Grand Canyon, the Middle Fork offers perhaps the preeminent rafting experience in North America. It is known less, perhaps, for the seriousness of its rapids (mostly rated Class III and IV, although possibly Class V in spring) than for the quantity of rapids. Designated a "wild and scenic river," the 100-

mile-plus Middle Fork is not only undammed but undeveloped; despite the number of river runners who come here each summer, the signs of civilization along the way are exceedingly rare. Steep, tree-studded mountainsides, hot springs, and wildlife are trip highlights—along with all those rapids, of course. *Trip organizers: **Custom River Tours** (Box 7071, Boise 83707, tel. 208/343-3343); **OARS** or **Sobek** (see Organizers and Outfitters, above). Trip length: 6 days. Dates: June–Sept. River rating: Class III–Class IV (higher in June, lower in Sept.).*

Utah **Green River.** The Green River is more of a float than a whitewater adventure; while there are plenty of rapids, the most serious rate only a Class III. Floating the Green can be a terrific way to experience Utah's canyon and desert country in midsummer, when the midday heat can brutalize land-bound visitors. The principal geologic features along the way are Desolation and Gray canyons; side trips include visits to Native American ruins and pictographs and a ranch where Butch Cassidy once holed up. Several outfitters run day trips on the Green, but a day trip is hardly worth the effort; the four- or five-day, 80-plus-mile ride is the only way to go. *Trip organizers: **Adrift Adventures** or **OARS** (see Organizers and Outfitters, above). Trip length: 4 or 5 days. Dates: May–Sept. River rating: Class II–Class III.*

Wyoming **Snake River.** The Snake has earned a strange footnote in history as the river that Evel Knievel tried (and failed miserably) to jump over on a rocket-powered motorcycle. It deserves better. The Snake is a river for river runners who value scenery over white-water thrills. For the most part, floating rather than taking on rapids is the theme of running the Snake (with trips usually incorporating Jackson Lake); as such, it is a good choice for families with younger children. What makes the trip special is the Teton Range, looming as much as 8,000 feet above the river. *Trip organizers: **Mad River Float Trips** (Box 2222, Jackson 83001, tel. 307/733-6203); **OARS** (see Organizers and Outfitters, above). Trip length: 1–5 days. Dates: June–Sept. River rating: Class I–Class II.*

For the Family Any river can be dangerous, and it is thus not advisable to bring children under seven on any extended river trip. Before taking an extended trip with your children, you might want literally to test the waters with a half-day or one-day excursion. Several outfitters run short trips out of Moab, Utah. For families with younger children, trips aboard larger, motorized rafts are probably safest. Among the trips described here, floating the gentle Snake River is best for young children. The Green is also a fairly gentle river in most places; not so the Dolores or the Middle Fork of the Salmon. Outfitters designate some trips as "adults only," with the cutoff usually being 16 years old.

Resources A good general source of information on rivers and rafting outfitters in the Rockies is **American Outdoors** (2133 Yarrow St., Lakewood, CO 80227, tel. 303/377-4811).

Rock Climbing and Mountaineering

There are two basic things to know about climbing in the Rockies: (1) The Rockies offer almost unlimited climbing opportunities, as you might expect; (2) bad things happen to ill-prepared climbers. The first is stated with great appreciation, and the second is not necessarily stated with great foreboding. It is just a fact. There is one good rule in climbing: If you are unsure of your skills or ability to take on a particular climb, don't do it.

That basic precaution given, the question is: What can you expect when climbing in the Rockies? Not all of the climbing requires great technical skills, if any. Many high peaks, such as Long's Peak in Colorado (*see* Rocky Mountain National Park in Suggested Trips, *below*) are walk-ups. At the same time, of course, there are numerous highly technical climbs, ranging from rock climbing in the mesa and canyon country of southern Colorado and Utah to alpine-style ascents of the mountains of northern Montana. Rare, however, are the sort of big rock faces a climber might encounter in Yosemite or extensive glaciers similar to those found in the Canadian Rockies or in Alaska. Expeditionary climbers, looking for life-on-the-edge challenges or first ascents, go elsewhere.

Before You Go Climbing in the Rockies is for some hardcore alpinists a year-round sport. Certainly rock climbing in the southern region and ice climbing wherever there are stable icefalls are reasonable wintertime sports. Realistically, though, avalanche risks can persist even into May at higher elevations, and winter can begin in earnest by October. The best months, weather-wise, are June and July; the risk of afternoon thunderstorms (also possible earlier in the summer) throw an additional hazard into August climbing.

Generally speaking, the Rockies do not call for great expeditionary preparation. The range is very accessible and the climbs, by alpine standards, relatively short. In other words, long hikes with heavy packs in order to establish a base are rare, and climbs that typically involve less than 6,000 vertical feet are not like dealing with the 10,000 or more vertical feet involved in climbing, say, Mt. Rainier in Washington. There are few major climbs in the Rockies that can't be accomplished in a day or two.

Guide services usually rent technical gear such as helmets, pitons, ropes, and axes. A good guide service can also provide a gear list of necessary items; be sure to ask for one. Some mountaineering stores also rent climbing equipment. As for clothing, temperatures can fluctuate dramatically, even in summer, at higher elevations. Bringing several thin layers of clothing, including a sturdy, waterproof/breathable outer shell, is the best strategy for dealing with weather variations.

Before you sign on with any trip, be sure to clarify to the trip organizer your climbing skills, experience, and physical condition. Climbing tends to be a team sport, and overestimating your capabilities can endanger not only yourself but other team members. A fair self-assessment of your abilities also helps a guide choose an appropriate climbing route; routes (not unlike ski trails) are rated according to their difficulty. The way to a summit may be relatively easy or brutally challenging, depending on the route selected.

Trip costs when going on an organized climb can vary considerably, depending on group size, length of climb, instruction rendered, and equipment supplied. (Outfitters usually rent equipment on a per-item per-day basis.) Count on spending at least $80 a day. However, the cost of a small-group multiday instructional climb can push $200 a day.

Organizers and Outfitters
The **American Alpine Institute** (1212 24th, M-39, Bellingham, WA 98225, tel. 206/671–1505) leads trips around the world, ranging from training climbs to expeditionary first ascents. It is one of the most respected climbing organizations in the country.

Suggested Trips

Colorado
Rocky Mountain National Park. There are 78 peaks in the park that rise above 12,000 feet, several of which require no technical skills in order to reach the summit. Via the easiest route, for example, the summit of Long's Peak, the highest point in the park at 14,255 feet, is one of these. This makes the park a good learning and training area for novices.

Climbing in Rocky Mountain National Park has its pros and cons. The pros are variety and ease of access: There are climbs for novices as well as for experienced mountaineers, and most are easily reached from roads leading to and through the park. The cons are (again) ease of access, which can make the park relatively crowded in summer; as many as 800 hikers and climbers have registered to ascend Long's Peak on a single day. Another con is elevation: Not only can the elevation of the park steal one's breath away, but with mountain bases above 9,000 feet, ascents of even the 14,000-footers become relatively short climbs. *For information and permits, write* **Rocky Mountain National Park** *(Estes Park 80517, tel. 303/586–2371 or 303/ 627–3471). Trip organizer:* **Colorado Mountain School** *(Box 2620S, Estes Park 80517, tel. 303/586–5758). Guidebook:* Rocky Mountain National Park: Classic Hikes and Climbs, *by Gerry Roach (Fulcrum).*

San Juan Mountains. From the mesas of southcentral Colorado, the San Juans appear to rise up with startling vertical upthrust, and the trip from Montrose to Ouray, less than 50 miles, is like a trip from one planet to another. Whether the San Juans are Colorado's most dramatic mountains is obviously a matter of debate, but a strong case can certainly be made on their behalf. Not surprisingly, this dramatic verticality lends itself to climbing of various sorts: alpine ascents, rock climbing (notably the Ophir Wall near the small town of Ophir), and ice climbing in winter on waterfalls near Ouray and Telluride. The dominant mountain of the range is Mt. Sneffels, 14,150 feet high, although there are several other peaks that rise above 14,000 feet. Because of the San Juans' southerly location, the climbing season (that is, nonwinter climbing) can last somewhat longer than in the northern Rockies. *For information and permits, write* **San Juan National Forest** *(701 Camino del Rio, Room 301, Durango 81301, tel. 303/247–4874). Trip organizer:* **Fantasy Ridge Alpinism** *(Nugget Bldg., Suite 204, Box 1679, Telluride 81435, tel. 303/728–3705).*

Wyoming   **Grand Teton National Park.** In many ways, the 13,770-foot Grand Teton is the most obvious U.S. mountain to climb: 8,000 vertical feet of jagged, exposed rock—more photographed, perhaps, than any other mountain in the nation. It is far from the easiest mountain to climb, however, and requires at least two days of steep rock to deal with on the ascent and rappels of 100 feet (or more) to negotiate on the descent. It is hard to believe that a fellow named Bill Briggs actually skied down the Grand Teton. Fortunately for less experienced climbers, there are other good options in the park, notably 12,325-foot Teewinot Mountain, a more moderate challenge that combines rock, ice, and scrambling. Regardless of the mountain (or route) chosen, the views are as good as they come in the Rockies. *For information and permits, write **Grand Teton National Park** (Drawer 170, Moose 83012, tel. 307/733–2880). Trip organizer: **Jackson Hole Mountain Guides** (Box 7477T, Jackson 83001, tel. 307/733–4979). Guidebook:* Climber's Guide to the Tetons *(Grand Teton Natural History Association).*

Wind River Mountains. Much of the appeal of the Wind River range is the relatively difficult access to major peaks, the most significant of which is Gannett Peak, at 13,804 feet the highest mountain in Wyoming. The trip into the base of the mountain can take two days, with considerable ups and downs and stream crossings that can be dangerous in late spring and early summer. The reward for such effort, however, is seclusion: Climbing Gannett Peak might not be as dramatic as climbing the Grand Teton to the west, but you won't have to face the national park crowds at the beginning or end of the climb. The Wind Rivers are a world of granite and glaciers, the latter (though small) being among the last active glaciers in the U.S. Rockies. Other worthy climbs in the Wind Rivers are Gannett's neighbors, Mt. Sacajawea and Fremont Peak. *For information and permits, write **Bridger-Teton National Forest** (Box 1888, Jackson 83001, tel. 307/733–2752). Trip organizer: **Jackson Hole Mountain Guides** (Box 7477T, Jackson 83001, tel. 307/733–4979).*

Instruction   The **American Alpine Institute** (*see* Organizers and Outfitters, *above*), the **Colorado Mountain School, Fantasy Ridge Alpinism,** and **Jackson Hole Mountain Guides** (*see* Suggested Trips, *above*, for last three references) have instructional programs for novices as well as experienced climbers. One other reputable climbing school in the Jackson area is **Exum School of Mountaineering** (Box 56–O, Moose 83012, tel. 307/733–2297). Also, climbing walls (both indoor and outdoor) have opened in many places in the United States, and some offer instructional programs, which are helpful preparation for a trip to the Rockies.

Resources   For technical climbers interested in detailed route descriptions, *The Climber's Guide to North America,* by John Harlin III, is one of the best books on the subject. The **American Alpine Club** (113 E. 98th St., New York, NY 10028, tel. 212/722–1628) can provide information on guides, guide accreditation, and climbing schools.

4 Colorado

by Jordon Simon

Jordan Simon defected to the world of journalism in 1987. The former contributing editor of Taxi *magazine has also written for such publications as* Elle, Travel and Leisure, Modern Bride, International Entertaining, Wine Country International, California, *and* Fodor's *Caribbean and Fodor's* Virgin Islands. *He is food and wine editor of* Ski Impact, *author of the upcoming* Gousha/USA Today Ski Atlas, *and director of the International Ski Film & Video Festival, held annually in Crested Butte.*

Teddy Roosevelt spoke of Colorado as "scenery to bankrupt the English language." Walt Whitman wrote that its beauty "awakens those grandest and subtlest elements in the human soul." For more than 200 years, pioneers, poets, and presidents have rhapsodized over what an increasing number of "out-of-towners" are learning: that Colorado is one of America's prime chunks of real estate.

Colorado is a state of sharp, stunning contrasts. The Rockies create a mountainous spine that's larger than Switzerland, with 52 eternally snowcapped summits towering higher than 14,000 feet. Yet its eastern third is a sea of hypnotically waving grasslands; its southwest, a vibrant multihued desert, carved with pink and mauve canyons, vaulting cinnamon spires, and gnarled red-rock monoliths. Its mighty rivers, the Colorado, Arkansas, and Gunnison, etch deep, yawning chasms every bit as impressive as the shimmering blue-tinged glaciers and jagged peaks of the San Juan, Sangre de Cristo, and Front ranges. Add to this glittering sapphire lakes and jade forests, and you have an outdoor paradise second to none.

Much of the state's visual appeal can also be attributed to the legacy of the frontier and mining days, when gold, silver, and railroad barons left an equally rich treasure trove of Victorian architecture in the lavish monuments they built to themselves. The Old West comes alive in Colorado, where you're practically driving through the pages of a history book. The first Europeans to explore were the Spanish, who left their imprint in the lyrical names and distinctive architecture of the southern part of the state. They were followed by trappers, scouts, and explorers, including some of the legendary names in American history—Zebulon Pike, Kit Carson, Stephen Long, and William Bent—intent on exploiting some of the area's rich natural resources, including vast lodes of gold and silver. In so doing they displaced—and often massacred—the original settlers, Pawnee, Comanche, Ute, and Pueblo, whose ancestors the Anasazi fashioned the spectacular, haunting cliff dwellings of Mesa Verde National Park.

The controversy and contentiousness live on. In 1992, Colorado made national headlines when it passed Amendment 2, carefully worded (some say deliberately vague) legislation designed to outlaw antidiscrimination bills. In reality, the amendment was aimed directly at homosexuals and sought to reverse existing local gay-rights ordinances (Aspen, Boulder, and Denver were among the first communities in the nation to pass such ordinances).

In response to the legislation a boycott was called (and has since been canceled) by liberal and gay/lesbian groups nationwide, with mixed results. The state picked up almost as much convention business from conservative organizations as it lost, and a superb 1992–93 snow season brought skiers in droves. The constitutionality of Amendment 2 is currently being debated in court; most observers feel it will die there. Indeed, despite the Amendment 2 controversy, Colorado has its progressive side: It was the first state to send a Native American to the Senate in 1992—Ben "Nighthorse" Campbell, himself a figure of controversy for his flamboyant style and mannerisms.

Along with feisty independence, be it right- or left-wing, Coloradans have always displayed an eccentric, even ostentatious, streak. State history is animated by stories of fabulous wealth and equally spectacular ruin in the bountiful precious-metal mines. Discovery of gold in 1859 spurred the first major settlement of Colorado, followed by the inevitable railroad lines for transport. When the lodes petered out, many of the thriving communities became virtual ghost towns, until the discovery of black gold in the oil-shale reserves of northwest Colorado and, especially, white gold on the ski slopes.

Today Colorado is a state of unabashed nature lovers and outdoors enthusiasts. Though most people associate the state with skiing, residents have a saying, "We came for the winters, but we stayed for the summers." In addition to skiing and snowmobiling in winter, they climb, hike, bike, fish, and camp in the summer, making Colorado one of America's premier four-seasons destinations.

Essential Information

Visitor Information

Contact the **Colorado Tourism Board** (1625 Broadway, Suite 1700, Denver 80202, tel. 303/592–5510 or 800/433–2656, fax 303/592–5406, ski reports 303/831–7669) to speak to a representative about the state, and the **TravelBank Colorado** (Box 200594, Denver, CO 80220, tel. and fax 303/320–8550) for information via modem.

In Canada Contact the **U.S. Travel and Tourism Office** (480 University Ave., Suite 602, Toronto, Ontario M5G IV2, tel. 416/595–0335, fax 416/595–5211).

Emergencies

Unless otherwise noted, dialing 911 will summon police, fire, and ambulance services throughout the state of Colorado.

Tour Groups

General-Interest Tours
Gray Line of Denver (Box 38667, Denver 80238, tel. 303/289–2841) offers two- to five-day tours of the surrounding areas. **Maupintour** (Box 807, Lawrence, KS 66044, tel. 913/843–2121 or 800/255–4266) runs an eight-day tour that takes in Denver, Estes Park, Vail, Grand Junction, Durango, and Colorado Springs. They also offer an 11-day rail tour that includes parts of New Mexico. **Tauck Tours** (11 Wilton Rd., Westport, CT 06880, tel. 203/226–6911 or 800/468–2625) offers several seven- to 15-day tours throughout the state. For a slight surcharge, you can choose to complete only part of the tour (at least 50%) if your time is limited or the entire tour itinerary doesn't appeal to you.

Special-Interest Tours
Camping and Wilderness
American Adventures (79 Cherry Hill Rd., Pomfret, CT 06259, tel. 203/974–3231) runs tours throughout the Rockies, with itineraries geared specifically toward 18- to 35-year-olds. **Colorado Outfitters Association** (Box 440021, Aurora 80044, tel. 303/368–4731) provides a list of specific wilderness treks throughout the state.
Colorado Llama Outfitter and Guide Association (30361 Rain-

bow Hill Rd., Golden 80401, tel. 303/526–0092) offers unique multiday tours into Colorado's backcountry.

Skiing **Aspen Alpine Guides** (Box 659, Aspen 81612, tel. 303/925–6618) designs customized, multiday, backcountry, cross-country treks along the 10th Mountain Trail (Aspen to Vail) and Alfred A. Braun Hut System (Aspen to Crested Butte).

Colorado Heli-Ski (Box 64, Frisco 80443, tel. 303/668–5600 or 800/HELISKI) arranges multiday heli-skiing tours of the unspoiled, untracked Colorado wilderness.

White-water Rafting **Colorado River Outfitters Association** (Box 502, Westminster 80030, tel. 303/220–8640) provides a list of 40 member outfitters whose excursions range in duration from ½ day to two weeks. Many also offer guided fishing trips.

Package Deals for Independent Travelers

American Airlines, United Airlines, and **Continental Airlines** all offer fly/drive packages that originate in Denver or a major ski resort, as well as various fly/stay deals.

When to Go

Colorado is a four-season destination. In fact, while most people associate the state with skiing, locals have a saying, "We came for the winters, but we stayed for the summers." Fabled ski resorts such as Aspen, Vail, Telluride, and Steamboat Springs are equally delightful in summer, with a wealth of festivals and superb hiking, mountain biking, horseback riding, and fishing. Best of all, rates plummet by as much as 50% in the "off season." Skiers will usually find excellent snow in January, when high-season rates are lowest at the various ski areas. Early December and early April comprise the shoulder season, when conditions are variable; several resorts offer enticing incentives, such as Crested Butte's annual "Ski Free" promotion mid-November–mid-December (free lift tickets, no restrictions).

Many national parks and monuments are either wholly or partially closed from October through May. Access varies according to the prevailing weather conditions. High season at Rocky Mountain National Park, Mesa Verde National Park, and summer resorts such as Durango, Estes Park, Colorado Springs, and Glenwood Springs, runs from June through September.

Spring and, especially, autumn are also fine times to visit. The weather usually remains temperate and tours can be cheaper (and crowds smaller) in the leading destinations. Fall is becoming increasingly popular, thanks to the spectacular fireworks display of the turning aspen and birch leaves.

Climate Coloradans are fond of quipping, "If you don't like the weather, just wait 10 minutes!" But if you're unprepared, it's no joke. The weather *is* changeable. Sudden thunderstorms crackle unexpectedly across the mountain faces during the spring and summer, often causing rock slides. Moreover, the wide range in topography, from mountains to prairie to semiarid desert, further complicates matters. Adequate preparation is vital when planning an extensive driving or camping trip.

The harsh winters can be devastatingly cold, with sub-zero temperatures frequent on the Western Slope of the Rockies.

Unlike the damp chilly coastal regions, it's a dry cold, but occasional whipping winds can drive anyone inside for the duration. The mountain weather is the most unpredictable and dramatic, but extremes are not uncommon even in Denver. One thing you can count on: Despite its snow-bound reputation, Colorado is one of the sunniest states in the union, averaging more than 300 days of sunshine a year.

Spring and fall are usually quite pleasant, with temperatures reaching the 70s. In summer the mountain air is bracing, with the thermometer rarely reaching 90 degrees. (Remember, though, that the high altitude makes the sun even stronger.) Evenings are much cooler, with temperatures plunging into the 50s, even 40s.

Denver, protected by the Front Range of the Rockies, enjoys a generally milder, drier climate, with less than 15 inches of precipitation annually. Summer temperatures rarely exceed 95 degrees; winter evenings almost never drop below 10 degrees.

For up-to-date weather reports, call 303/398-3964 (Denver) and 303/893-4492 (statewide). Colorado Ski Country (tel. 303/831-SNOW) offers a snow report hotline. If you're driving long stretches, it's a good idea to call the Highway Patrol (303/639-1111 or 303/639-1234) for road conditions.

Festivals and Seasonal Events

January: This is the time for winter carnivals, as well as World Cup and professional ski, freestyle, mogul, extreme skiing, and snowboarding races (scheduled throughout the winter) at various prominent resorts.

February: This is the month for Chinese New Year and Mardi Gras celebrations, including those at Aspen/Snowmass, Breckenridge, Georgetown (called "Fasching Days," after the German equivalent of Mardi Gras); as well as Winter Park's Cajun Ski Week and Steamboat's Winter Carnival, the oldest continuous such event west of the Mississippi.

March: Charity and celebrity events are the scene, foremost among them the Crested Butte American Airlines Celebrity Ski to Benefit the Cystic Fibrosis Foundation, the Colorado Special Olympics at Copper Mountain, Jimmy Heuga's Mazda Ski Express (raising money to fight MS) at various areas, and the Beaver Creek American Ski Classic hosted by former president Gerald Ford.

April: Spring events, celebrations, and festivals include the John Elway Celebrity Ski Race at Copper Mountain, the Annual Taste of Breckenridge and Taste of Vail, Crested Butte's Flauschink (German for "flushing out" the winter) and assorted spring-break tomfoolery.

May: Memorial Day and colorful Cinco de Mayo festivals abound throughout the state. The season at Denver's Opera Colorado, starring internationally acclaimed artists, continues.

June: Aspen hosts the world-famous Aspen Music Festival (for nine weeks), as well as a highly regarded Air Show, the Food and Wine Classic, and the prestigious International Design Conference. Snowmass boasts an impressive mass ascension at its Hot Air Balloon Festival, which concludes with the Taste of

Snowmass. Historical re-enactments dominate Colorado City's Heritage Days, Fort Morgan Museum's Living History Day, the Grand Lake Day in 1915, Pagosa Springs' Mountain Man Rendezvous, and Steamboat Springs' Western Weekend (with rodeo events, a Country Music Festival, Cowboy Poetry gathering, chili cook-off, gunslinging competition and more).

July: Fourth of July lights up celebrations statewide, including rodeo and cowboy roundups and parades. Arts events galore continue throughout the summer, including the renowned Dance Aspen, Boulder's Colorado Music and Shakespeare Festivals, the Breckenridge Music Institute Concert Series, Denver's Black Arts and Asian Arts Festivals and Colorado Indian Market, Steamboat's Strings in the Mountains Chamber Music Festival, Vail/Beaver Creek's Bravo! Colorado Music Festival and Vail Arts Festival, and the Winter Park Jazz and American Music Festivals.

August: Top arts events include the Estes Park Folks Festival, Loveland's Bluegrass Festival and Corn Roast, the Music in Ouray Chamber Concert Series, the Telluride Jazz Celebration, and the Bolshoi Ballet's annual visit to Vail. Food commands center stage during Winter Park's Rocky Mountain Food and Wine Festival, Denver's Taste of Colorado and the Telluride Wild Mushroom Festival.

September: Oktoberfests get an early start in Denver's Larimer Square and in Vail. Fall-foliage fireworks are featured in celebrations throughout the state. Most notable are those in Aspen/Snowmass, Colorado City, Glenwood Springs, Keystone, and Steamboat Springs. Major film festivals take place in Aspen, Breckenridge, and Telluride (one of the world's leading showcases for independent and foreign cinema). The sound of music continues to filter through the Rockies during Boulder's Blues and Bluegrass Festivals. Daredevils take to the air during the Hot Air Balloon Classic in Colorado Springs and the Telluride Hang Gliding Festival.

October: Oktoberfests and harvest celebrations dominate the calendar. Carbondale hosts an Annual Potato Days; Haxtun a Corn Festival, Cedaredge and Penrose Applefests. The Denver International Film Festival attracts suitably jet-set audiences, Durango's Cowboy Gathering a more down-home crowd.

November: The Yuletide season is rung in with spectacular Christmas-tree lightings and parades in Denver, Cañon City, Estes Park, and other tours across the state.

December: Christmas extravaganzas, each designed to take advantage of its unique setting, continue in Denver, Durango, Boulder, Cañon City, and throughout Colorado.

What to Pack

Whenever you travel, be sure to pack warm clothes, as nights can be nippy even in July and August. If you're a skier, fisherman, or hiker, bring the appropriate clothing and gear, although there are numerous sporting goods stores and rental shops throughout the state. Layering, especially in winter, is a good idea, starting with thermal underwear and ending with a wind- and waterproof jacket or coat. Sunglasses with UV lenses and sunscreen are imperative, whatever the season, as the high-altitude sun is deceptively strong.

Locals are casual and practical, dressing for the elements first, then style. Jackets and ties for men and dresses for women are required only in the toniest restaurants. An air of casual-chic prevails at the glitzy resorts such as Aspen, Vail, and Telluride, but even here the countercultural influence is strong. It's not uncommon to see frosted dreadlocks, overalls, or birkenstocks alongside neon high-tech jumpsuits on the slopes and in town.

Traveling with Children

Ever since the ski industry experienced a stagnant period in the 1980s, resorts have outdone themselves in devising ways to attract the entire family. Colorado ski areas such as Vail/Beaver Creek, Telluride, Copper Mountain, Keystone, Steamboat, and especially Winter Park, to name just a few, have pioneered innovative children's programs and activities. Day-care centers and children's ski schools are de rigueur throughout the state. In summer, programs such as the Telluride Kids' Academy allow children to experience the romance of the Old West, by goldpanning, rockclimbing, and spending the night in an authentic tepee. Many communities hold "Little Britches Rodeos" throughout the summer. Children adore the special events held throughout the state, from winter carnivals to county fairs; as a bonus, these can provide numerous educational opportunities to introduce kids to other cultures and lifestyles. If you plan your itinerary around some of these festivals, you'll never lack for things to do.

Hints for Travelers with Disabilities

The Rockies are in the vanguard of providing greater accessibility to the physically challenged at various tourist attractions. The wheelchair symbol specifically denotes parking, toilets, ramps, and camping for the physically challenged traveler. Most chambers of commerce, convention and visitors bureaus, and park services publish special material detailing services for the disabled in their respective areas. The larger ski areas all offer excellent instruction for the disabled, led by the forerunner in the field, Winter Park.

The Breckenridge Outdoor Education Center (Box 697, Breckenridge 80424, tel. 303/453–6422) is pioneering adventure travel for the physically and mentally challenged. While the focus is international, they run trips within Colorado, such as whitewater rafting on the Gunnison. Excursions can also be custom designed.

The **Denver Commission for People with Disabilities** (303 W. Colfax, Suite 875, Denver 80204, tel. 303/575–3056) helps put out an access guide to outdoor recreation for the disabled, *Colorado on Wheels*.

Wilderness on Wheels (7125 W. Jefferson Ave., #155, Lakewood 80235, tel. 303/988–2212) is constructing a "model facility" 60 miles southwest of Denver, including an 8-foot wide, mile-long boardwalk that will eventually attain the summit of a 12,300-foot peak.

Getting Around Colorado

By Plane The big news is the enormous (twice the size of Manhattan) new *Denver International Airport,* which is scheduled to replace the old Stapleton facility by January 1994. All major U.S. carriers fly into Denver, and a large jet service flies into Aspen (United), Colorado Springs (Delta, TWA), Gunnison (American), Steamboat Springs (American, Northwest), and Vail (American, America West). Continental Express, United Express and American Eagle serve smaller airports throughout the state.

By Car The U.S. Interstate highway network provides quick and easy access to Colorado despite imposing mountain barriers. Denver is served by I–25, running north-south through Colorado Springs and Pueblo; I–70, running east-west via Vail, Glenwood Springs, and Grand Junction; and I–76, running northeast from Denver via Fort Morgan into Wyoming. U.S. 666 flirts with the southwest corner of the state. U.S. 160 traverses the southern part of Colorado, while U.S. 40 accesses its northwest section.

By Train **Amtrak** (tel. 800/USA–RAIL), the U.S. passenger rail system, has daily service to Denver's Union Station. The railroad, of course, helped to shape and develop the American West, and it's still a marvelous way to see the state at leisure. The westbound route cuts through the spectacular Glenwood Canyon.

By Bus **Greyhound/Trailways** (tel. 800/752–4841) connects all major towns and cities in Colorado, utilizing Denver as its interstate gateway.

Shopping

You'll find outlets of many top designers in Denver's malls and department stores, as well as in chic resorts such as Aspen and Vail. But the real buys in Colorado, of course, are indigenous artifacts, crafts and specialties; Western and Native American art galleries, ceramics and jewelry shops, and stores specializing in Western memorabilia and cowboy clothing dot the landscape, especially in the southwest. Beware of the numerous "authentic trading posts" lining the roads: while fun and kitschy, they're usually tourist traps with second-rate merchandise.

Sports and the Outdoors

Fishing Fishing in Colorado's numerous rivers, lakes, and streams is an equally popular activity. Among the abundant cold-water sport fish are several species of trout, including cutthroat, rainbow, lake, and brook, and kokanee salmon and mountain whitefish. Cool-water varieties are walleye, yellow perch, and northern pike. Warm-water sport fish include channel catfish, white crappie, and white, largemouth and smallmouth bass. Fishing is legal year-round (though several restrictions apply in Rocky Mountain National Park), but you must obtain a license. Fees for nonresidents are $40.25 annually, $18.25 for a five-day period, and $5.25 for a single day. For more information, including the *Fishing Hotspots* and *Watchable Wildlife* booklets, contact the **Colorado Division of Wildlife** (6060 Broadway, Denver 80216, tel. 303/297–1192).

Golf   Golf is the other major warm-weather activity and golfers especially love Colorado's superlative championship courses—for
the combination of stunning mountain scenery and the additional loft on their drives. For more information, see the regional sports listings, or contact the **Colorado Golf Association**
(5655 S. Yosemite, Suite 101, Englewood 80111, tel. 303/779-
4653); **Colorado Golf Country USA** (559 E. 2nd Ave., Castle
Rock 80104, tel. 303/688-8262); or the **Colorado Golf Resort Association** (1407 Larimer Sq., Suite 300, Denver 80202, tel. 303/
770-0100).

Hiking and   Hikers and backpackers should contact the U.S. Bureau of
Backpacking   Land Management, and the U.S. Forest Service (Box 25127,
Lakewood 80225, tel. 303/236-9431) for information on
Colorado's sterling trekking opportunities. The Colorado Trail
is an incredibly scenic 465-mile route that winds its way from
Durango to Denver and is popular with both bikers and hikers.
For more information, contact **The Colorado Trail** (548 Pine
Song Trail, Golden 80401, tel. 303/526-0809). Take the same
precautions outlined above for bikers, and always carry emergency supplies in your backpack: Proper equipment includes a
flashlight, a compass, waterproof matches, a first-aid kit, water, extra food, a knife, and a light plastic tarp for shelter. Never drink from streams or lakes, unless you boil the water first,
or purify it with tablets. Giardia, an intestinal parasite, may be
present.

Mountain Biking   Mountain biking is zooming in popularity, and thousands of
people challenge the same Colorado slopes in summer that skiers do in winter. More and more ski areas are opening their
chairlifts to bikers and hikers, and actively promoting themselves as summer destination resorts. There are numerous
trails winding through the mountain passes, with arduous ascents and exhilarating descents. For more information, contact
your resort of choice, the cycling/fat tire associations listed under regional sports headings, or **Bicycle Colorado** (Box 3877,
Littleton 80161, tel. 900/288-BIKE). For a free trail map, send
a SASE to **Colorado Plateau Mountain Bike Trail Association**
(Box 4602, Grand Junction 81502, no tel.). You can also obtain
brochures and maps from the Colorado State Office of the U.S.
Bureau of Land Management (Dept. of the Interior, 2850
Youngfield St., Lakewood 80215, tel. 303/236-6639). Remember: know your limits! Many trails are between 7,500 and 11,000
feet, where oxygen is scarce. They're also frequently desolate;
always bring along some food and a canteen of water, as dehydration is a common occurrence at high altitudes. Weather can
have a tremendous impact on outdoor activities. Always check
the condition of roads and trails, and get the latest weather reports before setting out. Take precautions against heat stroke
or exhaustion by resting frequently in shaded areas, and
against hypothermia by layering clothing in winter. Ultimately, good physical conditioning is the strongest guard against
the elements.

Rafting   The other classic Colorado watersport is white-water rafting.
Rivers such as the Colorado, Arkansas, and Animas abound in
Level IV and V rapids, as well as a gentler stretches for begin-
ners. For more information, contact the **Colorado River
Outfitters Association** (Box 1662, Buena Vista 81211, tel. 303/
369-4632).

Skiing   Colorado is virtually synonomous with skiing. In fact, 20% of all skier visits throughout the United States in 1991 were recorded in Colorado. Residents and travelers alike claim that Colorado snow—champagne powder—is the lightest and fluffiest anywhere. World-famous resorts such as Aspen/Snowmass, Vail/Beaver Creek, Crested Butte, Telluride, Steamboat Springs, Purgatory, Winter Park, Breckenridge, Keystone/Arapahoe and Copper Mountain are legendary for the variety of their terrain and their consistently superb conditions. But don't overlook the so-called "Gems of Colorado"—smaller resorts that would be considered quite sizable almost anywhere else—such as Wolf Creek, Monarch, Loveland, Ski Sunlight, and Eldora that offer the same pristine snow and far smaller crowds. For complete information on Colorado's more than 30 ski areas, contact **Colorado Ski Country, USA** (1560 Broadway, Suite 1440, Denver 80202, tel. 303/836–0793).

More adventuresome types may want to contact **Heli-Ski USA** (Box 1560, Telluride 81435, tel. 303/728–6990) or one of the heli- or snowcat-skiing operators listed under regional sports headings. If Nordic is more your speed, contact the **Colorado Cross-Country Ski Association** (Box 1336, Winter Park 80482, tel. 303/887–2152), which can recommend one of the dozens of great ski-touring centers in Colorado. If you head out on your own for some backcountry skiing, take the proper gear (repair and first-aid kits, blankets, an avalanche beacon and a lightweight shovel). Call the U.S. Forest Service Colorado Avalanche Information line in your region for the latest snowpack and weather conditions.

Snowmobiling   Snowmobiling is another superb way to explore virgin terrain. For more information, contact the **Colorado Snowmobile Association** (Box 1260, Grand Lake 80447, tel. 800/235–4480).

Beaches

Believe it or not, there *are* beaches in Colorado: sandy stretches adorn some of the larger lakes, such as Grand Lake, abutting Rocky Mountain National Park, and Lake San Cristobal in the southcentral part of the state. Even in summer the water is far too cold for swimming without a wetsuit, though the beaches are nice for sunning on a pleasant afternoon.

National Parks and Forests

National Parks   Colorado boasts two glorious national parks, **Rocky Mountain** (north of Denver) and **Mesa Verde,** in the southwest corner (but not included in this chapter). The former celebrates Colorado's sublime wilderness scenery, full of glowering glaciers, glittering alpine lakes, meadows woven with wildflowers and majestic stands of aspen and evergreens. The latter contains an awe-inspiring collection of hauntingly beautiful ancient cliff dwellings, abandoned by the Anasazi centuries ago, set amid exquisite sandstone and red-rock formations.

National Forests   Colorado's 11 national forests (though not all included in this chapter), comprising over two thirds of the state—**Arapaho, Roosevelt, Grand Mesa, Gunnison, Pike, Rio Grande, Routt, San Isabel, San Juan, Uncompahgre,** and **White River**—abound in recreational and sightseeing activities for tourists.

Dining

The dining scene in Colorado is quite sophisticated, especially in Denver and the resort towns. Still, restaurants in smaller areas such as Crested Butte rank among the country's most vibrant and creative. Of course, beef, buffalo, and burritos appear in many of the restaurants throughout the state, but a dazzling range of international cuisine from southwestern to classic French, Italian, and Thai can be found just as easily.

For ratings, *see* either the Resorts and Cities or Towns and Country price charts (as specified) in Chapter 1, Essential Information.

Lodging

Take your pick from the numerous selections across the state: resorts, chain hotels, dude ranches, bed-and-breakfasts, guest houses. Colorado has all sorts of accommodations to match any budget.

For ratings, *see* either the Resorts and Cities or Towns and Country price charts (as specified) in Chapter 1, Essential Information.

Denver

Denver's buildings jut jaggedly into the skyline, creating an incongruous setting in a state that prides itself on its pristine wilderness. But for all the high-powered, high-rise grandeur displayed downtown, Denver is really a cow town at heart. Throughout the 1960s and '70s, when the city mushroomed on a huge surge of oil and energy revenues, Denverites hustled to discard evidence of its Western past and prove its modernity. The last decade, however, has brought an influx of young, well-educated professionals—Denver has the second-largest number of college graduates in the country—lured by Colorado's outdoor mystique and encouraged by the megalopolis's business prospects.

Most Denverites are unabashed nature lovers whose weekends are often spent skiing, camping, hiking, biking, or fishing. For them, maintaining the environment and the city's rich mining and ranching heritage are of equally vital importance to their quality of life. Areas like LoDo—the historic lower downtown—now buzz with jazz clubs, restaurants, and art galleries housed in carefully restored century-old buildings. Recently, the culturally aware populace celebrated the Denver Art Museum's centennial. The expert acting troupe of the Denver Center Theater Company is at home in both traditional mountings of classics and more provocative contemporary works.

The Rocky Mountains make a spectacular backdrop behind the otherwise flat Denver, and those who don't know Denver are in for a few big surprises. While one of its monikers is the "Mile High City," another is "Queen City of the Plains." Although Denver is within arms' reach of the high Rocky Mountain peaks, the city itself has a delightfully mild climate. Denverites do not spend their winters digging out of fierce snowstorms and skiing out their front doors. They take advantage of a comfortable climate, historic city blocks, a cultural center, and sky's-the-limit outdoor adventures just minutes from their homes. All of these factors make this appealing city more than just a layover between home and the Rockies.

Important Addresses and Numbers

Tourist Information The **Denver Metro Convention and Visitors Bureau** (225 W. Colfax Ave., Denver, CO 80202, tel. 303/892–1112 or 800/888–1990), open weekdays 8–5 and Saturdays 9–1, is located across from the City and County Building and provides information and free maps, magazines, and brochures. **Travelers Aid Society** (1245 E. Colfax Ave., tel. 303/832–8194) offers the same assistance.

Emergencies For nonemergency police assistance, call 303/575–3127.

Emergency Rooms **Rose Medical Center** (4567 E. 9th Ave., tel. 303/320–2121) and **St. Joseph Hospital Emergency Room** (1835 Franklin St., tel. 303/866–8000) are both open 24 hours.

Doctors **Downtown Health Care** (1860 Larimer St., No. 100, tel. 303/296–2273) is a full medical clinic. **Rose Medical Center** (*see above*) refers patients to doctors, 8–5:30. **Med Search St. Joseph's Hospital** (1835 Franklin St., tel. 303/866–8000) is a free referral service.

Dentists **Metropolitan Denver Dental Society** (3690 S. Yosemite St., tel. 303/488–0243) offers referrals to dentists; **Centre Dental Associates** (1600 Stout St., No. 1370, tel. 303/592–1133) is open 8–6, with emergency after-hours care available.

Late-Night Pharmacies **Walgreens** (2000 E. Colfax Ave., tel. 303/331–0917) is open daily, 24 hours.

Arriving and Departing by Plane

Airports and Airlines Denver International Airport (tel. 800/AIR–2–DEN), or DIA, is scheduled to open by early 1994 and will serve as the hub for Continental and United. Until then, Stapleton International Airport (tel. 303/AIR–2–DEN) will handle flights from most of the major domestic carriers and many international ones, including **Alaska Airlines** (tel. 800/426–0333), **American** (800/433–7300), **America West** (tel. 800/247–5692), **Continental** (tel. 800/525–0280), **Delta** (tel. 800/221–1212), **SkyWest** (tel. 800/453–9417), **Mesa** (tel. 800/637–2247), **Northwest** (tel. 800/225–2525), **TWA** (tel. 800/221–2000), **United** (tel. 800/241–6522), and **USAir** (tel. 800/425–4322).

Between the Airport and Downtown **By Bus** The **Airporter** (tel. 303/321–3222) serves downtown and southeast Denver Tech Center hotels, with 15-minute scheduled departures daily between 6AM and 10:15 PM to downtown, and 30-minute departures to southeast Denver. **People's Choice Transportation** (tel. 303/777–2388) serves downtown and several nearby ski areas. There is a transportation center in the airport just outside baggage claim.

By Taxi Taxis to downtown cost about $12 from Stapleton and $15 from Denver International. Call **Metro Taxi** (tel. 303/333–3333), **Yellow Cab** (tel. 303/777–7777), or **Zone Cab** (tel. 303/444–8888).

By Limousine Contact **Admiral Limousines** (tel. 303/741–6464 or 800/828–8680), **Colorado Limousine Service** (tel. 303/832–7155), **Mile Hi Limousine** (tel. 303/373–1974), or **Sterling Limousine Service**

(tel. 303/366–5466 or 800/366–5416). Rates average $20 and up, depending on the type of car.

Rental Car **Alamo** (tel. 303/321–1176 or 800/327–9633), **Avis** (tel. 303/839–1280 or 800/331–1212), **Budget** (tel. 303/341-2277 or 800/222-6772), **Dollar** (tel. 303/398–2323 or 800/228–9987), **General** (tel. 303/320–1244 or 800/327–7607), and **Hertz** (tel. 303/355–2244 or 800/654–3131) all have airport and downtown locations.

Arriving and Departing by Car, Train, and Bus

By Car Reaching Denver by car is fairly easy, except during rush hour when the interstates (and downtown) get congested. Interstate highways I–70 and I–25 intersect near downtown; an entrance to I–70 is just outside the airport.

By Train **Union Station** (17th Ave. at Wynkoop, downtown, tel. 303/524–2812) has Amtrak service.

By Bus The **Greyhound/Trailways** depot/bus station is located at 1055 19th Street (tel. 303/292–6111).

Getting Around

In downtown Denver, free shuttle-bus service operates about every 10 minutes until 11 PM, running the length of the 16th Street Mall (which bisects downtown) and stopping at two-block intervals. If you plan to spend much time outside downtown, a car is advised, although buses and taxis are available. Even downtown, parking spots are usually easy to find; try to avoid driving in the area during rush hour, when traffic gets heavy.

By Bus The region's public bus service, **Regional Transportation District** (RTD, tel. 303/299–6000 for route and schedule information; 303/299–6700 for other inquiries), is comprehensive, with routes throughout the metropolitan area. The service also links Denver to outlying towns such as Boulder, Longmont, and Nederland. Buy bus tokens at grocery stores or with exact change on the bus. Fares vary according to time and zone. Within the city limits, buses cost $1 during peak hours (6 AM–9 AM, 4 PM–6 PM), 50¢ at other times. You can also buy a **Cultural Connection Trolley** (tel. 303/299–6000) ticket for $1 at several convenient outlets throughout downtown, from the trolley driver, or via most hotel concierges. The trolley operates daily, every half hour 9–6, linking 18 prime attractions from the Denver Performing Arts Complex downtown to the Denver Natural History Museum in City Park. Tickets are good for one stop.

By Taxi Cabs are available by phone and at the airport and can generally be hailed outside major hotels. Companies offering 24-hour service include **Metro Taxi** (tel. 303/333–3333), $1.40 minimum, $1.40 per mile, and **Yellow Cab** (tel. 303/777–7777), $1.40 minimum, $1.20 per mile.

Opening and Closing Times

Most stores open at 9 or 10 and close at 5 or 6 during the week; hours on weekends may be shorter. Banks are open weekdays 9–3. The **First Interstate Bank of Denver** branch at 633 17th Street (corner of California) is open Monday–Thursday 7:30–5, Friday 7:30–5:30. **American Express Travel Service** (555 17th

St., Anaconda Tower, tel. 303/298–7100) is open weekdays 8:30–5.

Guided Tours

Orientation **The Gray Line of Denver** (tel. 303/289–2841) offers a three-hour city tour, a Denver mountain parks tour, and a mountain casino tour. Tours range from $15–$30 per person.

Walking Tours The preservation group **Historic Denver** (1330 17th St., tel. 303/534–1858) offers tours of old Denver for a $5 fee. Self-guided walking-tour brochures are available through the Denver Metro Convention and Visitors Bureau (225 W. Colfax Ave., tel. 303/892–1112).

Highlights for First-Time Visitors

City Park, Tour 2
Civic Center, Tour 1
Denver Art Museum, Tour 1
Denver Museum of Natural History, Tour 2
Golden, Off the Beaten Track
Museum of Western Art, Tour 1
16th Street Mall, Tour 1

Tour 1: Downtown

Numbers in the margin correspond to points of interest on the Colorado and Denver maps.

Denver presents its official face to the world at the Civic Center, a three-block-long park, with lawns, gardens, and a Greek amphitheater that together form a serene backdrop for the
❶ **state capitol** built in 1894, constructed with mostly indigenous materials from Colorado, including marble, granite, and rose onyx. Especially inspiring is the gold-leafed dome, a reminder of the state's mining heritage. Visitors can climb to the balcony for a panoramic view of the Rockies, or merely to the 13th step, which is exactly 1-mile high (above sea level). *1475 Sherman St., tel. 303/866–2604. Open Mon.–Sat. 9–4; tours available on the half hour. Admission free.*

❷ Just off the Civic Center is the **Colorado History Museum,** a vibrant depiction of the state's frontier past and how the cultures have collided here. Changing exhibits highlight different eras such as the Jazz Age and the Gay '90s; permanent displays include Conestoga wagons, great old touring cars, and an extraordinary time line called the Colorado Chronicle 1800–1950, which depicts the state's history in amazing detail. The display stretches 112 feet, 6 inches, and dedicates 9 inches to each year. It's crammed with artifacts from rifles to land-grant surveys and old daguerreotypes. *1300 Broadway, tel. 303/866–3682. Admission: $3 adults, $1.50 senior citizens and children. Open Mon.–Sat. 10–4:30, Sun. noon–4:30.*

❸ The **Denver Art Museum,** also off Civic Park, was recently remodeled for its 1993 centennial and boasts uniquely displayed, superlative holdings in Asian, pre-Columbian, and Spanish-Colonial art. A model of museum design, with dazzling mountain views as a bonus, the museum is intelligently laid out, highly accessible (providing just enough information while emphasizing the aesthetics), and thoughtfully lit. Children will love the imaginative "touchables" hands-on exhibits and video corners. If there's a flaw here, it's that the fine European collection, now exhibited on a rotating basis, has been temporarily displaced until enough funding is acquired to build a new wing. *100 W. 14th Ave., tel. 303/575–2793. Admission free; donation recommended. Open Tues.–Sat. 10–5, Sun. noon–5.*

4 Close by is the **Byers-Evans House,** an elaborate redbrick Victorian built in 1883 and restored to its pre–World War I splendor. It serves as the **Denver History Museum,** and offers exciting interactive video programs and history about the city. *1310 Bannock St., tel. 303/620–4933. Admission: $2.50 adults, $1.25 children and senior citizens. Open Wed.–Mon. 11–3.*

5 A few blocks away is the source of all those coins stamped with a *D*—The Denver **U.S. Mint.** Free tours take guests around the facility, where more than 5 billion coins are minted yearly, and where the nation's second-largest hoard of gold is displayed. *W. Colfax Ave. and Cherokee St., tel. 303/844–3582. Admission free. Tours weekdays 8:30–3, except during inventory (usually the last 2 weeks in June).*

6 A fascinating detour is to the **Denver Firefighters Museum,** which occupies the space of Denver's first firehouse. All the original items of the trade are displayed here, including uniforms, nets, fire carts and trucks, bells, and switchboards. *1326 Tremont Pl., tel. 303/892–1100. Admission: $2. Open weekdays 11–2.*

7 From here, it's one block up to the tranquil **Trianon Museum and Art Gallery,** and its marvelous collection of 18th- and 19th-century European furnishings and objets d'art. The museum also houses a rare-gun collection, with pieces dating from the 16th century onward. Guided tours are offered. *335 14th St., tel. 303/623–0739. Admission: $1. Open Mon.–Sat. 10–4.*

Walk up to the 16th Street Mall to pick up one of the free shuttle buses that run the length of downtown, providing a good, quick tour. These buses are the only vehicles allowed on the otherwise pedestrianized street, which features shady trees, outdoor cafés, historic buildings, and tempting shopping.

8 Hop off at Tremont Place and walk a block to the **Museum of Western Art,** set in a converted frontier-era bordello (on the National Register of Historic Places). It now houses works by those artistic heroes of the Western mythos: Remington, Bierstadt, and Russell, and latter-day masters such as O'Keeffe. The collection is highly distilled; all the vividly composed works on display are considered by experts to be among the artists' finest and most representative pieces. *1727 Tremont Ave., tel. 303/296–1880. Admission: $3. Open Tues.–Sat. 10–4:30.*

9 Catercorner from the museum is the majestic **Brown Palace Hotel** (321 17th St.), Denver's hotel empress, built in 1892 and still considered the city's most prestigious address. Reputedly this was the first atrium hotel in the United States: Its ornate lobby and nine stories are crowned by a stunning Tiffany stained-glass window. (*See* Lodging, *below.*)

10 As you head back down the mall toward lower downtown, you'll see the 330-foot-tall **Daniels and Fisher Tower** (16th and Arapahoe Sts.), built to emulate the campanile of St. Mark's Cathedral in Venice. Head a block east to Curtis, then south about **11** two blocks to the **Denver Center for the Performing Arts** (14th

Colorado

WYOMING

Flaming Gorge
National Recreation
Area

318

Dinosaur
National
Monument

Yampa

Craig

40

Steamboat
Springs
29

River

Walden

MEDICINE BOW MOUNTAINS

PICEANCE BASIN

White

13

64

Meeker

River

131

Rocky
Mount
Nationa
Park

40

Hot Sulphur
Springs

ROAN PLATEAU

Rifle

6

Glenwood
Springs
30

70

Eagle

River

Vail
28

Winter
Park
23

24

FRONT

GORE RANGE

Copper
Mountain
27 **26**

25 Keyst
Arape

Breckenr

UTAH

70

Colorado

River

GRAND MESA

Redstone

Snowmass
32

82

Aspen
31

Mt Elbert

24

Leadville

Fairplay

Colorado
National
Monument

Grand
Junction

Gunnison

Delta

River

133

Crested
Butte
33

ELK MTNS

SAWATCH RANGE

Buena
Vista
63

285

UNCOMPAHGRE PLATEAU

Dolores

141

50

Black Canyon of
the Gunnison
National Mon

Montrose
35

Gunnison
34

Curecanti National
Recreation Area

50

Salida
64

50

SANGRE

River

141

145

Ouray
41

Lake
City
42

Saguache

285

Dove
Creek

666

145

Telluride
36

Silverton
40

550

River

Creede

149

SAN

JUAN

Del
Norte

Great Sa
Dune
Nation
Monum

SAN LUIS VALLEY

Hovenweep
National
Monument

Cortez
37

Mancos
38

Durango
39

Mesa Verde
National Park

MOUNTAINS

Pagosa
Springs

160

Alamosa

285

Grand

160

666

San Juan

Aztec

Animas

River

84

Conejos

Rio

N

and Curtis Sts. , tel. 303/893–4000), a huge, impressively high-tech complex of theaters connected by a soaring, glass archway to a futuristic symphony hall. Guided tours are available, but times vary so you must call ahead.

12 Return to Arapahoe and go one block to the **Tabor Center,** a festive shopping mall with more than 60 stores and attractions, including fast-food eateries, strolling troubadours, jugglers and fire-eaters, and splashing fountains. Across from Tabor Center
13 is **Writer Square,** whose shops line the entrance to the arched
14 redbrick courtyards of historic **Larimer Square** (Larimer and 15th Sts.), Denver's most charming shopping district, where some of the city's oldest retail buildings and classiest specialty shops do business. Larimer Square—actually a street—was saved from the wrecker's ball by a determined preservationist in the 1960s, when the city went demolition crazy in its eagerness to present a more youthful image.

Larimer roughly marks the boundary of **LoDo,** an equally historic, but quirkier, district just northwest with art galleries, nightclubs, and restaurants that range from Denver's most upscale to its most down-home. This part of town was once the city's thriving retail center, then fell into disuse, slid into slums, and is now undergoing a vigorous revival spearheaded not just by avant-garde artists and retailers, but by loft dwellers who have taken over old warehouses.

A little outside the downtown loop (west on 15th St., just past the confluence of the South Platte River and Cherry Creek) is
15 the wonderfully odd **Forney Transportation Museum.** Resem-

bling an abandoned auto yard, the property outside is littered
with peeling carriages, corroding cabooses, and classic cycles;
inside, in the not-quite-thought-out exhibit rooms, are an 1898
Renault coupe, Teddy Roosevelt's tour car, Aly Khan's Rolls,
and a Big Boy steam locomotive, among other collectibles.
Strangely enough, there's also a room dedicated to 18th-
century military uniforms. Anyone who grew up on model cars
or Lionel trains will wander this eccentric museum in a happy
daze. *1416 Platte St., tel. 303/433–3643. Admission: $4 adults,
$2 children 12–18, $1 children 5–11. Open Mon.–Sat. 10–5,
Sun. 11–5.*

Tour 2: East of Downtown

A car is recommended on this tour, as it covers an area more
spread out than downtown.

⑯ The **Molly Brown House,** on Pennsylvania Street between East
12th and 13th streets, not far from the capitol, is a Victorian
confection that celebrates the life and times of the scandalous,
"unsinkable" Molly Brown, heroine of the *Titanic* who coura-
geously saved several lives and continued to provide assistance
to survivors back on terra firma. Costumed guides and original
furnishings in the museum (including flamboyant gilt-edged
wallpaper) evoke the bygone days. *1340 Pennsylvania St., tel.
303/832–4092. Open Mon.–Sat. 10–4, Sun. noon–4.*

⑰ A few blocks down the street, the Beaux Arts–style **Grant-
Humphreys Mansion** is a grandiose, 42-room testament to the
proper Denver society that looked down on Molly at the turn of
the century. *770 Pennsylvania St., tel. 303/894–2506. Admission: $3 adults, $1.50 children 6–17. Open Tues.–Fri. 10–2.*

⑱ Head east on 8th Avenue to the **Denver Botanic Gardens,** a flow-
ering respite from the urban hustle and bustle. A conservatory
looms above; among its displays is a re-creation of a tropical
rain forest; outside are a Japanese garden, a rock garden, gaze-
bos and arboretums, and gorgeous horticultural displays (at
their peak during summer). *1005 York St., tel. 303/331–4010.
Admission: $3 adults, $1.50 senior citizens, $1 children. Open
daily 9–4:45.*

Northeast of downtown, between Colorado Boulevard and
York Street, along 17th Avenue, is **City Park,** Denver's largest
public space of its kind, with rose gardens, lakes, a golf course,
tennis courts, and two of the city's most popular attractions:
the Denver Zoo and the Denver Museum of Natural History. A
shuttle runs between the two.

⑲ The engaging **Denver Zoo** features a nursery for new, baby animals; a polar bear exhibit, where visitors can watch the animals
swim underwater; seal shows; educational programs on endangered species; and the "Zooliner" train, which snakes through
the property as guests are given a safari lecture. *E. 23rd St.,
between York St. and Colorado Blvd., tel. 303/331–4110. Admission: $4 adults, $2 senior citizens and children. Open daily
10–6.*

⑳ The seventh-largest museum in the United States, the **Denver
Museum of Natural History,** offers a rich combination of traditional collections—dinosaur remains, a mineralogy display, an
Egyptology wing—and intriguing hands-on exhibits such as
the Hall of Life, where you can test your health and fitness on

various contraptions. The massive complex includes an **IMAX** movie theater and the Gates Planetarium. *2001 Colorado Blvd., tel. 303/322–7009. Admission to museum: $4 adults, $2 senior citizens and children; to IMAX: $5 adults, $4 senior citizens and children; to planetarium: $3.50 adults, $2.50 senior citizens and children. Open daily 9–5.*

㉑ Return to City Park, and exit north along York Street, then turn west on 30th Avenue to the **Black American West Museum and Heritage Center,** with its revealing collection of documents that depict the vast contributions African-Americans made to opening up the West. Nearly a third of the cowboys and many pioneer teachers and doctors were African-Americans. *3091 California St., tel. 303/292–2566. Admission: $2 adults, $1.50 senior citizens, 75¢ youths 12–17, 50¢ children under 12. Open Wed.–Fri. 10–2, Sat. 10–5, Sun. 2–5.*

Denver for Free

Denverites enjoy strolling the **16th Street Mall** (*see* Shopping, *below*), window-shopping and people watching along the way. It doesn't cost any money to look, and this meandering will pleasantly fill up any extra time your itinerary allows.

Tours of the imposing **U.S. Mint** and **state capitol** are free, as is sitting in **City Park** admiring the disparate, yet harmonious, architectural styles of the surrounding buildings. (*See* Tour 1, *above.*)

Denver is proud of what may be the largest parks system in the United States, which includes 205 individual parks, 150 tennis courts, and six public golf courses (Denver Parks Dept., tel. 303/698–4900). In total, there are more than 20,000 acres of green space in the city and surrounding mountains. The most popular with residents is **Washington Park** (east of Downing St., between Virginia and Louisiana)—filigreed with lakes and flower beds, shaded by cottonwoods and willows—where active Denverites go to in-line skate, bike, run, hike, play volleyball, tennis, and just hang out.

What to See and Do with Children

The **Denver Children's Museum** is one of the finest of its kind in North America, offering constantly changing hands-on exhibits that lure children into discovery. The biggest attraction is a working television studio, replete with weather station, news desk, and a viewing booth where kids can videotape each other and watch the results on "byte"-size monitors. Other interesting aspects of the museum include the "Indians of the Northwest" display, where children can build their own totem poles, and the outdoor park with climbing equipment, a year-round ski instruction hill, and a trolley ($2 for adults, $1 for children) that clatters and clangs the 2 miles down the South Platte River to the Forney Transportation Museum. *2121 Crescent Dr., tel. 303/433–7444. Admission: $3 adults, $1.50 senior citizens over 60, $4 children. Open June–Aug., daily 10–5. Sept.–May, Tues.–Sun. 10–5.*

The Denver Zoo (*see* Tour 2, *above*).

Elitch Gardens Amusement Park is a Denver family tradition, with three hair-raising roller coasters (one ranked in the nation's top 10), a carousel, log flume, high-dive show, summer stock theater, and botanical gardens. *4620 W. 38th St., tel. 303/455-4771. Admission: $13.95 unlimited ride pass weekdays, $14.95 weekends; chaperone pass (no rides) $7 weekdays, $8 weekends. Open mid-Apr.–May, weekends; June–Labor Day, daily. Hours vary so call ahead.*

Tiny Town is the oldest kid-size village in the United States, with more than 100 colorful structures and a coal-fired steam train. *6249 S. Turkey Creek Rd., Morrison (5 min. west of the C–470 interchange on U.S. 285; turn left at Tiny Town sign), tel. 303/790-9393. Admission: $2 adults, $1 senior citizens and children. Open June–Sept., daily 10–7; May–Oct., weekends 10–5.*

Shopping

Denver may be the best place in the country for recreational gear and fashions of all stripes. Sporting goods stores hold legendary ski sales around Labor Day.

Shopping Districts and Malls The **Cherry Creek** shopping district, Denver's finest, is located 2 miles from downtown in a pleasant, predominantly residential neighborhood. On one side of 1st Avenue at Milwaukee Street is The Cherry Creek Shopping Mall, a classy granite-and-glass behemoth that houses some of the nation's top retailers, among them: Abercrombie & Fitch, Bally, Banana Republic, Burberry's, Laura Ashley, Lord & Taylor, Louis Vuitton, Neiman Marcus, Polo/Ralph Lauren, and Saks Fifth Avenue. On the other side of 1st Avenue lies Cherry Creek North, an open-air development of tree-lined streets and shady plazas, with still more art galleries, specialty shops, and fashionable restaurants.

Historic **Larimer Square** (14th and Larimer Sts.), downtown, houses another set of distinctive shops and restaurants, as does adjoining **Writer Square.** Nearby is the **Tabor Center** (16th Street Mall), a light-filled atrium whose 60 specialty shops include upscale retailers such as Brooks Brothers and Crabtree & Evelyn, and others that showcase uniquely Coloradan merchandise. It also contains a Bridge Market filled with pushcarts selling everything from Ecuadorian sweaters to endearingly tacky souvenirs. The **Tivoli** (900 Auraria Pkwy., corner of 9th Ave. and Larimer) is a restored historic brewery, with its original pipes and bricks exposed, that houses several moderately priced specialty stores and restaurants.

South of Denver, **Castle Rock Factory Shops** (exit 184 off I–25), offers 25%–75% savings on everything from appliances to apparel at its more than 50 outlets.

Department Stores In addition to those districts listed above, you'll find value at **Joslins** (16th and Curtis Sts.), Denver's oldest department store, and the eight **May D & F Department Stores** throughout metropolitan Denver.

Specialty Stores
Antiques South Broadway between 1st Avenue and Evans Street, as well as the side streets radiating off this main drag, is chockablock with dusty antiques stores, where patient browsing could net some amazing bargains.

The **Antique Mall of Lakewood** (9635 W. Colfax Ave.) features more than 200 dealer showrooms.

Arts and Crafts **LoDo** is the area to hunt for the trendiest galleries, many located in restored Victorian warehouses. **Soho West** (1730 Wazee St., tel. 303/242–9475) specializes in functional and wearable art. **Hassel-Haeseler** (1743 Wazee St., tel. 303/295–6442) exhibits Colorado's up-and-coming artists.

For Native American arts and crafts, head for **Native American Trading Company** (1301 Bannock St., tel. 303/534–0771), which has an outstanding collection of weavings, pottery, jewelry, and regional painting. The **Mudhead Gallery** (555 17th St., in the Hyatt, tel. 303/293–0007; and 321 17th St., in the Brown Palace, tel. 303/293–3377) features museum-quality southwestern art, with an especially fine selection of Santa Clara and San Ildefonso pottery and Hopi kachinas.

Beer Colorado is considered the center of home brewing, and Denver has five brew pubs, each with its own distinct ambience. If you're feeling heady, stop by **The Wine and Hop Shop** (705 E. 6th Ave., tel. 303/831–7229) for beginner beer- and wine-making kits and a virtual field of fresh hops and grains, or to goggle at the "wall of malt."

Books **The Tattered Cover** (1st Ave. at Milwaukee St., tel. 303/322–7727) is a must pilgrimage for all bibliophiles. It may be the best bookstore in the United States, not only for the near-endless selection of volumes (more than 400,000 on four stories) and helpful, knowledgeable staff, but for the incomparably refined atmosphere: overstuffed armchairs, reading nooks, and afternoon readings, lectures, and musicales.

Sporting Goods **Gart Brothers Sports Castle** (1000 Broadway, tel. 303/861–1122) is a huge, multistoried shrine to Colorado's love of the outdoors. Entire floors are given over to a single sport at this and the many other branches located throughout Denver.

Western Wear and Collectibles **Cry Baby Ranch** (1428 Larimer, tel. 303/623–3979) has a rambunctious assortment of '40s and '50s cowboy kitsch. **Denver Buffalo Company** (1109 Lincoln St., tel. 303/882–0884) has wonderful Western duds and high-quality souvenirs, not to mention a restaurant specializing in buffalo—low in fat and cholesterol. There's also a gourmet deli with BuffDogs, corned buffalo, and other such specialties. **Miller Stockman** (16th Ave. and California, tel. 303/825–5339) is an old-line Denver retailer selling the real McCoy.

Sports and the Outdoors

Cycling and Jogging **Platte River Greenway** is a 20-mile in-line skating, bicycle, and jogging path that follows Cherry Creek and the Platte River, much of it through downtown Denver. Paved paths wind through the lovely **Matthews-Winters Park,** dotted with plaintive pioneer graves amid the sun-bleached grasses, thistle, and columbine. **The Denver Parks Department** (tel. 303/698–4900) has more suggestions for biking and jogging paths throughout the metropolitan area's 205 parks, including the popular Cherry Creek and Chatfield Lake State Recreation areas.

Golf Six courses are operated by the city of Denver and open to the public: **City Park** (E. 25th Ave. and York St., tel. 303/295–4420), **Evergreen** (29614 Upper Bear Creek, Evergreen, tel. 303/674–4128), **Kennedy** (10500 E. Hampden Ave., tel. 303/751–0311), **Overland Park** (S. Santa Fe Dr. and Jewell Ave., tel. 303/698–4975), **Wellshire** (3333 S. Colorado Blvd., tel. 303/692–

5636), and **Willis Case** (W. 50th Ave. and Vrain St., tel. 303/458–4877).

Arrowhead Golf Club (10850 W. Sundown Trail, Littleton, tel. 303/973–9614), located 45 minutes from downtown in Roxborough State Park, was designed by Robert Trent Jones and is set impressively among red sandstone spires. **Plum Creek Golf and Country Club** (331 Players Club, Castle Rock, tel. 303/688–2611) is an 18-hole Pete Dye–designed championship course.

Health Clubs Denver has more fitness clubs per capita than any other American city. The state-of-the-art **International Athletic Club** (1630 Welton St., tel. 303/623–2100), is a 65,000-square-foot, full-service facility featuring over 65 aerobics classes weekly, cardiovascular equipment, weight room, racquetball, squash, massage, basketball, and running track. Guest arrangements are available through major hotels.

Hiking Just 15 miles west of Denver, **Red Rocks Park and Amphitheater** (just off U.S. 285 or I–70), is a breathtaking, 70-million-year-old wonderland of vaulting oxblood- and cinnamon-colored sandstone spires; the outdoor music stage is set in a natural 8,000-seat amphitheater (with perfect acoustics, as only nature could have designed) that has awed even the likes of Leopold Stokowski and the Beatles. Tickets to concerts are stratospheric, but hiking in this metro Denver park is free.

Mt. Falcon Park (off Hwy. 8, Morrison exit, or U.S. 285, Parmalee exit) looks down on Denver and across at Red Rocks. It's amazingly tranquil, laced with meadows and streams and shaded by conifers. The trails are very well marked.

In-line Skating *See* Platte River Greenway, in Cycling and Jogging, *above.*

Tennis The city has 28 parks with tennis courts. For information call the **Parks Department** (tel. 303/331–4047).

Water Sports Both **Cherry Creek Marina** (Cherry Creek State Park, Aurora, tel. 303/779–6144) and **Chatfield Marina** (Chatfield State Park, Littleton, tel. 303/791–7547) rent sailboats, powerboats, and Windsurfers, April to October.

Spectator Sports

Auto Racing **Bandimere Speedway** features NHRA Championship Drag Racing April–September. *3051 S. Rooney Rd., Morrison, tel. 303/697–6001.*

Baseball The **Colorado Rockies,** Denver's National League expansion team, plays April–October. *Mile High Stadium, just west of downtown across I–25, tel. 303/ROCKIES.*

Basketball Denver's NBA franchise team, the **Denver Nuggets,** plays October to April. *McNichols Arena, just west of downtown across I–25, tel. 303/893–3865.*

Football **Denver Broncos,** the city's NFL team, plays September to December. *Mile High Stadium, just west of downtown across I–25, tel. 303/433–7466.*

Horse Racing **Arapahoe Park** (26000 E. Quincy Ave., tel. 303/690–2400) is the venue for pari-mutuel racing May through September.

Dining

As befits a multiethnic crossroads, Denver offers a dizzying range of eateries: Head for LoDo or 17th Street for the more inventive kitchens, Federal Street for cheap ethnic eats—especially Thai and Vietnamese. Throughout Denver, however, you'll find many trendy restaurants offering New American cuisine, which emphasizes indigenous regional ingredients, with a light, healthful preparation. For price ranges, *see* Resorts and Cities price chart in Chapter 1, Essential Information.

Highly recommended restaurants are indicated by a star ★.

Downtown and Environs
American

Strings. This light, airy restaurant with its wide-open kitchen is a preferred hangout for Denver's movers and shakers. The food is billed as casual contemporary; one specialty is spaghetti with caviar, asparagus, and champagne cream sauce. *1700 Humboldt St., tel. 303/831-7310. Reservations required. Dress: neat but casual. AE, D, DC, MC, V. Closed for lunch Sun. Expensive.*

★ **Zenith American Grill.** This attractive space sports a cool high-tech look—track lighting, striking artwork, black-and-white tables—that contrasts with the conservative design of most Denver establishments. Chef Kevin Taylor produces creative variations on the southwestern theme and cleverly lightens the traditional meat-and-potatoes bent of Colorado cuisine. Standouts include a velvety yet fiery smoked corn soup with avocado salsa; Texas venison with caramelized apples; sweet potato custard and spicy sun-dried cherries; and "kick-ass" swordfish with Texas BBQ, chili stir-fry, and cilantro-lime butter. *1750 Lawrence St., tel. 303/820-2800. Reservations required. Dress: neat but casual. AE, MC, V. No lunch weekends. Expensive.*

Wazee Supper Club. Denverites flock to this hip hole for hot jazz and the best pizza in town—crisp yet gooey and bursting with flavor. Some grouse the Wazee has less ambience since it moved down the street, but the exposed brick walls, jet-black tables, and maroon Naugahyde chairs still convey its ultracool tone. *1600 15th St., tel. 303/623-9518. No reservations. Dress: casual. AE, MC, V. Inexpensive.*

★ **The Wynkoop.** This trendy yet unpretentious local institution, located in a converted building, was Denver's first brew pub, and it's still the best. Try the terrific shepherd's pie or grilled marlin sandwich; wash it down with wilderness wheat ale or sagebrush stout; then repair to the gallery, pool hall, and cabaret for a full night of entertainment. *1634 18th St., tel. 303/297-2700. Reservations for 6 or more during the week; no reservations on weekends. Dress: casual. AE, DC, MC, V. Inexpensive.*

Chinese

★ **Imperial Chinese.** Papier-mâché lions greet you at the entrance of this sleek Szechuan stunner, probably the best Chinese restaurant in a 500-mile radius. Seafood is the specialty; try the steamed sea bass in ginger or the spicy, fried Dungeness crab. *1 Broadway, tel. 303/698-2800. Reservations advised. Dress: casual. AE, DC, MC, V. Closed Sun. for lunch. Moderate.*

Continental

★ **Cliff Young's.** Many Denverites' first choice for a showcase dinner is this property, presided over by Cliff Young himself. The owner runs his refined Art Deco restaurant with meticulous care and showers diners with attention. New head chef James van Dyk has introduced a sly Asian gloss to the menu with specialties such as scallops crowned with shiitake caps. Still, the New American standbys are here for devoted regulars, including gorgeous Colorado rack of lamb and free-range veal. *700 E. 17th Ave., tel. 303/831–8900. Reservations advised. Dress: neat but casual. AE, D, DC, MC, V. No lunch weekends. Expensive.*

European Café. Housed with panache in a converted loft that now gleams with polished brass and crystal, the European Café is a favorite for those attending downtown events. Many of the dishes pay homage to French master chefs such as Georges Blanc and Paul Bocuse, and all are beautifully presented. Try the lamb chops with shiitake mushrooms in Madeira glaze. *1515 Market, tel. 303/825–6555. Reservations advised. Dress: neat but casual. AE, D, DC, MC, V. No lunch weekends. Moderate–Expensive.*

French **Cache Cache.** Chef Jack Goldsmith is a practitioner of cuisine *minceur*—no butter or cream is used in his preparations. But the sunny flavors of Provence explode on the palate, thanks to the master's savvy use of garlic, tomato, eggplant, fennel, and rosemary. The lamb loin sandwiched between crisp potato galettes on a bed of spinach and ratatouille is sublime, as are the sensational salads. *265 Detroit St., tel. 303/394–0044. Reservations advised. Dress: neat but casual. AE, MC, V. Closed Sun. Expensive.*

Tante Louise. This long-time Denver favorite, situated just 15 minutes from downtown by car, resembles an intimate French country home. One-third of the menu is French, one-third is New American, and one-third features low-fat dishes. Try the delicate angel-hair pasta and grilled salmon in beurre blanc, or the superlative rack, loin, or shank lamb specials. *4900 E. Colfax Ave., tel. 303/355–4488. Reservations advised. Dress: neat but casual. AE, D, DC, MC, V. Closed Sun.; no lunch except Fri. Expensive.*

Le Central. This homey bistro calls itself "Denver's affordable French restaurant." While the preparation can be inconsistent, old standbys such as cassoulet, bouillabaisse, and steak au poivre are dependable. *112 E. 8th Ave., tel. 303/863–8094. Reservations for 5 or more at dinner. Dress: casual. No credit cards. Closed Sat. for lunch; open Sun. for brunch. Moderate.*

Italian **Barolo Grill.** This restaurant looks like a chichi farmhouse, as if
★ Laura Ashley went gaga over an Italian count, yet it's exquisite: There are dried flowers in brass urns, hand-painted porcelain, and straw baskets everywhere. The food isn't precious in the least, however: It's more like Santa Monica meets San Stefano—bold yet classic, healthful yet flavorful. Choose from wild boar stewed with apricots; risotto croquettes flavored with minced shrimp; or smoked salmon pizza. The wine list is well considered and fairly priced. *3030 E. 6th Ave., tel. 303/393–1040. Reservations advised. Dress: neat but casual. AE, MC, V. Closed for lunch and Sun. and Mon. Moderate.*

Mexican **The Bluebonnet Café and Lounge.** Its location out of the tourist
★ loop, in a fairly seedy neighborhood southeast of downtown, doesn't stop the crowds from lining up early for this restaurant. The early Western, Naugahyde decor and fantastic jukebox set an upbeat mood for killer margaritas and the best burritos and green chili in town. *457 S. Broadway, tel. 303/778–0147. No reservations. Dress: casual. No credit cards. Inexpensive.*

Las Delicias. Aficionados claim the food here is better—at least more authentic—than at the Bluebonnet (no Anglos work here). It could be true, because people certainly don't line up here for the decor or service. Try to go on weekends, when the chef makes delicious *carnitas*—tender pork simmered with green chili. *419 E. 19th St., tel. 303/839–5675. Reservations only for early lunch and dinner. Dress: casual. MC, V. Inexpensive.*

Steaks/Western **The Buckhorn Exchange.** If hunting makes you queasy, don't
★ enter this Denver landmark, a shrine to taxidermy where 500 Bambis stare down at you from the walls. The handsome men's-club decor—with corrugated tin ceilings, burgundy walls, red-checkered tablecloths, rodeo photos, shotguns, and those trophies—probably looks the same as it did when the Buckhorn first opened in 1893. Rumor has it Buffalo Bill was to the Buckhorn what Norm Peterson was to *Cheers*. The dry-aged, prime-grade Colorado steaks are huge, juicy, and magnificent, as is the game. For an appetizer, try the smoked buffalo sausage or black bean soup. *1000 Osage St., tel. 303/534–9505. Reservations advised. Dress: casual. AE, D, DC, MC, V. Closed weekends for lunch. Expensive.*

Lodging

Denver has lodging choices from the stately Brown Palace to the YMCA, with options such as bed-and-breakfasts and business hotels in between. Unless you're planning a quick escape to the mountains, consider staying in or around downtown, where most of the city's attractions are within walking distance. For price ranges *see* the Resorts and Cities price chart in Chapter 1, Essential Information.

Highly recommended lodgings are indicated by a star ★.

★ **Brown Palace.** This grande dame of Colorado lodging has housed numerous public figures from President Eisenhower to the Beatles. The details are exquisite: A dramatic nine-story lobby is topped with a glorious stained-glass ceiling, and rooms are decorated with Victorian flair, using sophisticated wainscoting and Art Deco fixtures. The Palace Arms, its formal restaurant, has won numerous awards, including one from *Wine Spectator* magazine. *321 17th St., tel. 303/297–3111 or 800/321–2599, fax 303/293–9204. 205 rooms, 25 suites. Facilities: 4 restaurants, 2 bars, concierge, access to local health club, parking. AE, D, DC, MC, V. Moderate–Expensive.*
Burnsley. Since its face-lift in the 1980s, this 16-story, Bauhaus-style tower has been a haven for executives seeking peace and quiet close to downtown. The tastefully appointed accommodations are all suites and feature balconies and full kitchens. The swooningly romantic restaurant is a perfect place to pop the question or let someone down easily. *1000 Grant St., tel. 303/830–1000 or 800/231–3915, fax 303/830–7676. 82 suites. Facilities: restaurant, bar, outdoor pool, parking. AE, DC, MC, V. Moderate.*
Cambridge Club Hotel. This 1960s-era luxury-suites hotel is one block from the state capitol on a tree-lined street convenient to downtown. All suites are decorated differently, but each has a firm bed and cozy reading chairs. Local lobbyists, politicos, and CEOs favor the bar. *1560 Sherman St., tel. 303/831–1252 or 800/877–1252; fax 303/831–4724. 27 suites. Facilities: restaurant, bar, parking. AE, D, DC, MC, V. Moderate.*

Holiday Inn Denver Southeast. This large hotel caters predominantly to business travelers and is one of the nicer properties in the Denver Tech Center/Cherry Creek area. Oversize rooms are comfortably furnished and have most standard amenities. *3200 S. Parker Rd., tel. 303/695–1700; fax 303/745–6958. 475 rooms. Facilities: restaurant, lounge, indoor pool, complimentary airport shuttle. Moderate.*

★ **Loews Giorgio.** The 12-story steel-and-black glass facade conceals the unexpected and delightful Italian Baroque motif within. Rooms are spacious and elegant, with teal colors and blond wood predominating, and such Continental touches as fresh flowers, fruit baskets, and Renaissance-style portraits. The only drawback of this property is its location: halfway between downtown and the Denver Tech Center, with little in the immediate vicinity. *4150 E. Mississippi Ave., tel. 303/782–9300 or 800/345–9172; fax 303/758–6542. 200 rooms, 19 suites. Facilities: restaurant, bar, access to nearby health club, complimentary Continental breakfast, complimentary airport shuttle. AE, D, DC, MC, V. Moderate.*

Warwick Hotel. This stylish business hotel, ideally located on the edge of downtown, offers oversize rooms and suites and features brass and mahogany Thomasville antiques reproductions. Most rooms contain wet bars, full refrigerators, and private balconies. *1776 Grant St., tel. 303/861–2000 or 800/525–2888; fax 303/832–0320. 145 rooms, 49 suites. Facilities: restaurant, lounge, gift shop, outdoor pool, concierge, complimentary breakfast buffet, complimentary health club privileges, complimentary shuttle to downtown and Cherry Creek, parking. AE, DC, MC, V. Moderate.*

Castle Marne. This historic bed-and-breakfast, just east of downtown in a shabbily genteel area, presents a dramatic facade with a four-story turret, intricate stone and woodwork, and balconies. On the inside, rooms are richly decorated with antiques and artworks. A full gourmet breakfast served in the dining room is included in room rate, as is afternoon tea. *1572 Race St., tel. 303/331–0621 or 800/926–2763; fax 303/331–0623. 9 rooms. Facilities: game room, parking. AE, D, DC, MC, V. Inexpensive–Moderate.*

★ **Oxford Hotel.** During the Victorian era this charming hotel was an elegant Denver fixture, and it has been restored to its former turn-of-the-century glory. Rooms are uniquely furnished with French and English period antiques, while the bar re-creates an Art Deco ocean liner. Its location in is perfect for those seeking a different, artsy environment. Complimentary shoeshines, afternoon sherry, and morning coffee and fruit are among the civilized touches offered here. Although the Oxford is a notch down from the Brown Palace in most respects, it's also less expensive and can boast **McCormick's Fish and Oyster House,** Denver's premier seafood restaurant. *1600 17th St., tel. 303/628–5400 or 800/228–5838; fax 303/628–5413. 81 rooms. Facilities: restaurant, 2 bars, beauty salon, valet parking, free limousine service downtown. AE, DC, MC, V. Inexpensive–Moderate.*

★ **Queen Anne Inn.** The Queen Anne is set in two adjacent Victorians north of downtown in the regentrified Clements historic district (some of the neighboring blocks have yet to be reclaimed). This delightful property is a romantic, pampering getaway for bed-and-breakfast mavens, with fresh flowers daily, antique armoires, carved four-poster or brass beds, and bay or stained-glass windows. All rooms have phone and private bath. A full breakfast is offered every morning. *2147 Tremont Pl., tel. 303/296–6666; fax 303/296–2151. 10 rooms, 4 suites. Facilities: parking. AE, D, MC, V. Inexpensive–Moderate.*

Red Lion. This is the closest hotel to the airport, making it a good option if you plan to sidestep Denver and head directly for the mountains. The rooms are unexceptional but comfortable, the service efficient. *3203 Quebec St., tel. 303/321–3333 or 800/547–8010; fax 303/355–0103. 567 rooms. Facilities: 2 restaurants, 2 bars, exercise room, indoor pool, parking. AE, D, DC, MC, V. Inexpensive–Moderate.*

Comfort Inn/Downtown. The advantages to this well-worn hotel are its reasonable rates and its location in the heart of downtown. As a bonus, rooms were recently given a face-lift and those corner rooms high up feature wraparound floor-to-ceiling windows with stunning panoramic views. *401 17th St., tel. 303/296–0400 or 800/221–2222; fax 303/297–0774. 229 rooms. Facilities: valet parking, complimentary Continental breakfast. Inexpensive.*

Holiday Chalet. Stained-glass windows and homey touches throughout make this Victorian brownstone exceptionally charming. It's also conveniently situated in Capitol Hill, the neighborhood immediately east of downtown. A kitchenette in each room is stocked with breakfast foods. *1820 E. Colfax Ave., tel. 303/321–9975 or 800/626–4497. 10 rooms. Facilities: parking. AE, D, DC, MC, V. Inexpensive.*

YMCA. Here's a respectable old standby with clean, basic rooms, some with private baths. The downtown location can't be topped, and a newer section is coed. *25 E. 16th Ave., tel. 303/861–8300. 185 rooms. Facilities: restaurant, health club. MC, V. Inexpensive.*

The Arts

Friday's *Denver Post* and *Rocky Mountain News* publish calendars of the week's events, as does the slightly alternative *Westword*, which is free and published on Tuesdays. **Ticketmaster** (tel. 303/290–8497) sells tickets by phone to major events, tacking on a slight service charge; the **Ticket Bus** (no tel.), on the 16th Street Mall at Curtis Street, sells tickets from 10 until 6 weekdays, and half-price tickets on the day of the performance.

Dance **Colorado Ballet** (tel. 303/298–0677) specializes in the classics; **Colorado Contemporary Dance** (tel. 303/892–9797) brings national dance companies to Denver.

Music The **Colorado Symphony Orchestra** performs at Boettcher Concert Hall (13th and Curtis Sts., tel. 303/893–3272); the **Denver Chamber Orchestra** (18th Ave. and Broadway, tel. 303/825–4911) usually plays at historic Trinity Methodist Church, downtown. The **Paramount Theater** (1621 Glenarm Pl., tel. 303/623–0106) is the site for many large-scale rock concerts. The exquisite **Red Rocks Amphitheater** (tel. 303/572–4704) and **Fiddler's Green** (tel. 303/741–5000) are the primary outdoor concert venues.

Opera **Opera Colorado** (tel. 303/778–6464) offers spring and fall seasons, often with internationally renowned artists, at the Performing Arts Complex. **Central City Opera** (621 17th St., Central City, tel. 303/292–6700), housed in an exquisite Victorian opera house, has the finest of settings.

Theater The **Denver Center for the Performing Arts** (13th and Curtis Sts., tel. 303/893–3272) is a modern complex that houses most of the city's large concert and theater venues. The **Denver Center Theater Company** (tel. 303/893–4100) offers high-caliber repertory theater, including new works by promising playwrights; **Robert Garner Attractions** (tel. 303/893–4100) brings Broadway road companies to Denver. Among the provocative fringe theaters are **Spark Artists Cooperative** (1535 Platte St., tel. 303/744–3275), which also has a gallery space; **Euclipion, Inc. Cultural Center** (2715 Welton St., tel. 303/295–6814), which presents plays by and with African-Americans; **Hunger Artists Ensemble Theater** (1553 Platte St., tel. 303/893–5438); and **Teatro Tonight** (4925 High St., tel. 303/296–0219).

Nightlife

Downtown and **LoDo** are where most Denverites make the scene. Downtown features more mainstream entertainment, whereas LoDo is home to fun, funky rock clubs, and small theaters. Remember that Denver's altitude can intensify your reaction to alcohol.

Cabaret The **Wynkoop Cabaret** (1634 18th St., downstairs in The Wynkoop Brewpub) offers everything from top-name jazz acts to up-and-coming stand-up comedians, including cabaret numbers.

Comedy Clubs **Comedy Works** (1226 15th St., tel. 303/595–3637) is where Denver comics hone their skills. Well-known performers often drop by.

Country and Western The **Grizzly Rose** (Exit 215 at I–25, tel. 303/295–1330) has miles of dance floor, national bands, and offers two-step dancing lessons. **Cactus Moon** (10001 Grant St., tel. 303/451–5200) is larger than most venues and offers "Food, Firewater, Dancin'."

Dinner Theater The **Country Dinner Playhouse** (6875 S. Clinton St., tel. 303/799–1410) serves a meal before the performance, which is usually a Broadway-style show. In Golden, the **Heritage Square Music Hall** (tel. 303/279–7800) has a buffet to go along with an evening of old-fashioned melodrama.

Bars and Clubs **Club Infinity** (900 Auraria Pky., in the Tivoli Mall, tel. 303/534–
Discos 7206) nearly lives up to its name, with five bars and an enormous dance floor swept by laser beams.

Gay Bars **Charlie's** (900 E. Colfax Ave., tel. 303/839–8890) offers country-and-western atmosphere and music at the hottest gay bar in town.

Jazz **El Chapultepec** (20th and Market Sts., tel. 303/295–9126) is a depressing, flourescent-lit, bargain-basement Mexican dive. Still, the Harleys and limos parked outside hint at its enduring popularity: This is where visiting musicians, from Ol' Blue Eyes to the Marsalis brothers, jam after hours. **Serf's Jazz Pub** (1620 Wazee St., tel. 303/534–3188) is a good place to check out local talent.

Rock and Roll There are a number of smoky hangouts in this city, the most popular being the down-home **Herman's Hideaway** (1578 S. Broadway, tel. 303/778–9916), showcasing local and national acts, with a smattering of reggae, blues, and alternative music thrown in to keep things lively. Also popular are **The Broadway** (1082 Walnut St., tel. 303/860–7558), *the* heavy metal and alter-

native club; **The Mercury Café** (2199 California St., tel. 303/
294–9281), which triples as a marvelous health food restaurant
(sublime tofu fettuccine), fringe theater, and rock club specializing in acoustic sets, progressive, and newer wave music. **23
Parrish** (2301 Blake St., tel. 303/292–0816) features several
clubs, including The Garage, a local institution.

Singles **Rock Island** (Wazee and 15th Sts., tel/ 303/572–7625) caters to
the young, hip, and restless. Denver's five brew pubs are always hopping: **Rock Bottom Brewery** (1001 16th St., tel. 303/
534–7616) is the flavor-of-the-month, thanks to its rotating
special brews and reasonably priced pub grub.

I–70 and the High Rockies

Interstate 70 is the major artery that fearlessly slices the Continental Divide, weaving its way through many of Colorado's
most fabled resorts and towns: Aspen, Vail, Breckenridge,
Steamboat, Keystone, Snowmass, Copper Mountain, Beaver
Creek, Winter Park. True powder hounds intone those names
like a mantra to appease the snow gods, speaking in hushed
tones of the gnarly mogul runs, the wide-open bowls on top of
the world. Here is the image that lingers when most people
think of Colorado: a Christmas paperweight come to life, with
picture-postcard mining towns and quasi-Tyrolean villages
framed by cobalt skies and snowcapped peaks. To those in the
know, Colorado is as breathtaking the rest of the year, when
meadows are woven with larkspur and columbine, the maroon
mountains flecked with the jade of juniper and the ghostly
white of aspen.

Like most of Colorado, the High Rockies region is a blend of old
and new, of tradition and progress. It is historic towns such as
Leadville, whose muddy streets still ring with the lusty laugh-
ter from saloons, of flamboyant millionaires who built grandiose monuments to themselves before dying penniless. It's also
modern resorts such as Vail, whose history began a mere 30
years ago, yet whose founding and expansion involved risk-
taking and egos on as monumental a scale. The High Rockies is
fur trappers and fur-clad models, rustlers, and Rastafarians,
heads of cattle and heads of state. One thing links all the players together: a love of the wide-open spaces, and here, those
spaces are as vast as the sky.

Important Addresses and Numbers

Tourist **Aspen Chamber Resort Association** (328 E. Hyman Ave., tel.
Information 303/925–5656; and 425 Rio Grande Pl., tel. 303/925–1940);
Breckenridge Resort Chamber (309 N. Main St., tel. 303/453–
6018); **Georgetown Visitor Center** (404 6th St., tel. 303/569–
2555; and 613 6th St., tel. 303/569–2888); **Glenwood Springs
Chamber Resort Association** (1102 Grand Ave., tel. 303/945–
6589 or 800/221–0098); **Leadville Chamber of Commerce** (809
Harrison St., tel. 719/486–3900); **Steamboat Springs Chamber
Resort Association** (1201 Lincoln Ave., tel. 303/879–0880 or
800/922–2722); **Summit County Chamber of Commerce** (Main
St., Frisco, tel. 303/668–5000); **Vail Valley Tourism and Convention Bureau** (100 E. Meadow Dr., tel. 303/476–1000; and a tourist information center in the Vail Village and Lionshead
parking structures).

Hospitals For Aspen/Snowmass: **Aspen Valley Hospital** (0200 Castle Creek Rd., tel. 303/925–1120); Glenwood Springs: **Valley View Hospital** (6535 Blake St., tel. 303/945–8566); Summit County: **Summit Medical Center** (Hwy. 9 and School Rd., Frisco, tel. 303/668–3300); Vail Valley: **Vail Mountain Medical** (181 W. Meadow Dr., Vail, tel. 303/476–5695); **Beaver Creek Village Medical Center** (1280 Village Rd., Beaver Creek, tel. 303/949–0800).

Arriving and Departing by Plane

Airports and Airlines Most of the I–70 corridor is served via Denver and its airports (*see* Arriving and Departing by Plane in Denver, *above*). There's an extensive list of Denver-based companies that specialize in transportation to the mountain resorts (*see* Between Airports and the Resorts, *below*).

Continental Express offers daily service from Denver; United has flights from Denver (via Aspen Aviation), as well as nonstop service to Los Angeles, Dallas, Phoenix, and Chicago in ski season. Delta flies from Salt Lake City.

Aspen/Snowmass' **Aspen Airport** (tel. 303/920–5385) is served daily by Continental Express (tel. 800/525–0280) and is served United Express (tel. 800/241–6522).

Steamboat Springs Airport (tel. 303/879–1204) is served daily by Continental Express. American (tel. 800/433–7300), America West (tel. 800/247–5692), Northwest (tel. 800/255–2525, and United fly nonstop from various gateways during ski season.

The Vail Valley is served by **Eagle County Airport** (Gypsum, tel. 303/524–9490), 35 miles west of Vail. During ski season, American and Delta offer direct nonstop from several gateways, as well as connecting flights.

Between Airports and the Resorts
By Bus or Van
To and from Aspen/Snowmass: **Roaring Fork Transit Agency** (tel. 303/925–8484) provides bus service from Aspen Airport to the Ruby Park bus station in Aspen. **Aspen Limousine and Bus Service** (tel. 303/925–9400) runs trips to Denver, Glenwood Springs, and Vail. **Colorado Mountain Express** (tel. 303/949–4227) runs trips to Vail and Aspen.

To and from Summit County (Breckenridge, Copper Mountain, Dillon, Frisco, Keystone): **Resort Express** (tel. 303/468/7600 or 800/334–7433) and **Skier's Connection** (tel. 303/668–0200 or 800/824–1004) have regular service to and from Denver airports.

To and from Steamboat Springs: **Alpine Taxi** (tel. 303/879–2800) offers service from the airport, as well as special rates to Vail, Boulder, and Denver. **Steamboat Express** (tel. 303/879–3400) also services Denver airports.

To and from Vail/Beaver Creek: **Airport Transportation Service** (tel. 303/476–7576); **Colorado Mountain Express** (tel. 303/949–4227); **Vans to Vail** (tel. 303/476–4467 or 800/222–2212).

To and from Winter Park: **Vanex** (tel. 303/726–4047 or 800/521–5401) and **Home James** (tel. 303/726–5050) offer service from Denver. **Greyhound/Trailways** (tel. 800/752–47841) runs from Denver to Winter Park.

Arriving and Departing by Car, Bus, and Train

By Car If you're entering Colorado from the north or south, take I–25, which intersects with I–70 in Denver. If you're entering from the east or west, I–70 bisects the state. Idaho Springs, Summit Country, the Vail Valley, and Glenwood Springs are all on I–70. Winter Park is north of I–70, on U.S. 40, which has several hairpin turns. Leadville and Ski Cooper are south of I–70 along U.S. 24 or U.S. 91. Steamboat Springs is most easily reached via CO. 131, north from I–70. Aspen/Snowmass can be reached via CO. 82, south from I–70.

By Train **Amtrak** (800/USA–RAIL) offers service from Denver's Union Station to the Winter Park Ski Area Station in nearby Fraser (where shuttles to the area are available). Glenwood Springs is on the *California Zephyr* route.

The nonstop *Denver Rio Grande Bud Light Ski Train* (tel. 303/296–4754) leaves Denver's Union Station every Sunday morning, chugging through stunning scenery and 29 tunnels before depositing passengers only 50 yards from Winter Park's lifts.

By Bus **Greyhound/Trailways** (tel. 800/752–4841) offers regular service from Denver to several towns along I–70.

Getting Around

By Bus or Shuttle For intercity bus service try **Greyhound** (call local listings). Free shuttles serving the resorts are offered throughout the area.

Aspen/Snowmass: Within Snowmass there is free shuttle service; five colored flags denote the various routes. The **Roaring Fork Transit Agency** (tel. 303/925–8484) provides free shuttle service within Aspen and between Aspen and Snowmass.

Steamboat: **Steamboat Springs Transit** (tel. 303/879–3717) provides transportation between the mountain and the town and costs 50¢ per trip.

Summit County: **Summit Stage** (tel. 303/453–1241) links Breckenridge, Frisco, Copper Mountain, Dillon, Silverthorne, and Keystone for free. **Breckenridge Free Shuttle and Trolley** (tel. 303/453–2368) runs through town and up to the ski area. The **Frisco Flyer** (tel. 303/668–5276) provides service throughout Frisco. Keystone offers regular free shuttles between the Keystone and Arapahoe Basin ski areas.

Vail Valley: **Avon Beaver Creek Transit** (tel. 303/949–6121) runs free shuttles the length of the valley, daily, between 7 AM and 1:30 AM, every 10 minutes.

Winter Park: The **Winter Park Lift** (tel. 303/726–4163) is the area's free shuttle service.

By Car Interstate 70 is a fast, convenient superhighway that is remarkably well maintained. All major sights in this tour are either on I–70 or on clearly marked side routes.

By Taxi Aspen/Snowmass: **Aspen Limousine** (tel. 303/925–2400) and **High Mountain Taxi** (tel. 303/925–8294); Glenwood Springs: **Glenwood Taxi** (tel. 303/945–2225); Steamboat Springs: **Alpine Taxi** (tel. 303/879–TAXI); Summit County: **Around Town Taxi** (tel. 303/453–6425) and, in Dillon, **Summit Taxi Service** (tel. 303/468–8294); Vail Valley: **Vail Valley Taxi** (tel. 303/476–8294).

Guided Tours

Orientation   A romantic way to orient yourself to Aspen is by taking the **T Lazy 7 Ranch** (tel. 303/925–4614) stagecoach tour of its downtown area.

In Breckenridge, the **Breckenridge Historical Society** (tel. 303/453–9022; tours run Wed.–Sat. 11 AM) offers lively 1½-hour tours of Colorado's largest National Historic District.

Several tour companies include Idaho Springs on their itineraries, and the **Idaho Springs Visitor Information Center** (2200 Miner St., tel. 303/567–4382) can supply information.

Special-Interest   In summer, narrated bus tours from Aspen to the spectacular
Tours   **Maroon Bells** are available (tel. 303/925–8484). Steamboat's **Sweet Pea Tours** (tel. 303/879–5820) and **Peak Experience** (tel. 303/879–8125) visit nearby hot springs.

Exploring I–70 and the High Rockies

Numbers in the margin correspond to points of interest on the Colorado map.

Most visitors on their way to the magnificent ski resorts accessed by I–70 whiz through the Eisenhower Tunnel and cross the Continental Divide without paying much attention to the extraordinary engineering achievements that facilitate their journey. Interstate 70 and the tunnel are tributes to human ingenuity and endurance: Before their completion in the 1970s, crossing the High Rockies evoked the long, arduous treks of the pioneers.

Idaho Springs, just outside of Denver, is your first stop on I–70, although a more spectacular drive is along Highway 6, which parallels the interstate and winds through Clear Creek Canyon. In autumn, the quaking aspens ignite the roadside, making this an especially scenic route.

㉒   **Idaho Springs** was the site of Colorado's first major gold strike, which occurred on January 7, 1859. Today, the quaint old town recalls its mining days, especially along downtown's National Historic Landmark District **Miner Street,** the main drag whose pastel Victorians will transport you back a century without too much imagination.

During the Gold Rush days, ore was ferried from Central City via a 22,000-foot tunnel to Idaho Springs. The **Argo Gold Mill** explains the milling process and runs public tours. *2350 Riverside Dr., tel. 303/567–2421. Admission: $3. Open mid-May–mid-Oct., daily 9–5.*

Just outside town is the **Phoenix Gold Mine,** still a working site. A seasoned miner leads visitors underground, where they can wield 19th-century excavating tools and dig or pan for gold. Whatever riches guests find are theirs to keep. *Off Trail Creek Rd., tel. 303/567–0422. Admission: $5 adults, $3 children under 12. Open daily 10–6.*

Idaho Springs presently prospers from its **Hot Springs,** at Indian Springs Resort (302 Soda Creek Rd., tel. 303/567–2191). Around the springs, known to the Ute natives as the "healing waters of the Great Spirit," are geothermal caves that were used by several tribes as a neutral meeting site. Hot baths and a mineral-water swimming pool are the primary draws for the resort, but the scenery from here is equally fantastic. **Bridal Veil Falls,** within sight of the resort, is spun out as delicately as lace on the rocks. Also close by is the imposing **Charlie Tayler Water Wheel**—the largest in the state—constructed by a miner in the 1890s who attributed his strong constitution to the fact that he never shaved, took baths, or kissed women.

Drive 2 miles west up Fall River Road to **St. Mary's Glacier,** a vision of alpine splendor. In summer the sparkling sapphire lake makes a pleasant picnic spot; in winter, intrepid extreme skiers and snowboarders hike up the glacier and bomb down.

For even more glorious surroundings, take the Mt. Evans Scenic and Historic Byway—the highest paved auto road in America—to the summit of the 14,264-foot-high **Mt. Evans.** The pass winds through scenery of incomparable grandeur: past several placid lakes, one after another every few hundred feet, and vegetation galore, from towering Douglas firs to stunted dwarf bristlecone pines.

West on I-70, then north on U.S. 40 (along the glorious ㉓ Berthoud Pass) is **Winter Park,** a place that Denverites have come to think of as their own personal ski area. Although it's owned by the city of Denver and makes a favorite day trip— only 67 miles away—it deserves consideration as a destination resort on its own. Winter Park is easily accessible, the skiing and setting are superb, and it offers the best value of any major ski area in the state. It's also equally popular in summer for hiking and biking. Since the glory of the area is its natural setting, and most people come here specifically to enjoy the resources, Winter Park otherwise has few tourist attractions.

The three interconnected mountains—Winter Park, Mary Jane, and Vasquez Ridge—offer a phenomenal variety of terrain. Head to Vasquez Ridge for splendid intermediate cruising; Mary Jane for some of the steepest thrilling bumps in Colorado; and Winter Park for a pleasing blend of both.

Just east of the Continental Divide, and just west of the I-70/ ㉔ U.S. 40 junction is **Georgetown,** also close enough to be a day trip from Denver, but its quiet charms warrant more than a hurried visit. Georgetown rode the crest of the silver boom during the second half of the 19th century. Most of its elegant, impeccably maintained brick buildings, which comprise a National Historic District, date back to that period. Fortunately, Georgetown hasn't been tarted up at all, so it provides a true sense of what gracious living meant in those rough-and-tumble times. You can wander the five-square-block downtown on your own, or explore it on horse-drawn trolley, courtesy of the **Rutherford Carriage Service** (tel. 303/569-2675), which runs half-hour tours in the summer, daily between 11 and 4.

The **Hamill House,** home of the silver magnate William Arthur Hamill, is a Gothic Revival beauty that displays most of the original wall coverings and furnishings; there's also a unique curved glass conservatory. *3rd and Argentine Sts., tel. 303/ 569-2840. Admission: $2. Open summer, daily 10-5; rest of year, Wed.-Sun. noon-4.*

The elaborate **Hotel de Paris,** built almost single-handedly by Frenchman Louis Dupuy in 1875, was one of the Old West's preeminent hostelries. Now a museum, the hotel depicts how luxuriously the rich were accommodated: Tiffany fixtures, lace curtains, and hand-carved furniture re-create an era of opulence. *6th and Griffith Sts., tel. 303/569-2311. Open Memorial Day–Oct. 1, daily 9–5; Oct.–Memorial Day, Tues.–Sun. noon–4.*

Hop on the **Georgetown Loop Railroad,** a 1920s narrow-gauge steam locomotive that connects the town with the equally historic community of **Silver Plume.** The 6-mile round-trip excursion takes about 70 minutes and winds through vast stands of pine and fir, before crossing the 95-foot-high Devil's Gate Bridge, where the track actually loops over itself to gain elevation. In Silver Plume, you can tour the **Lebanon Silver Mill and Mine.** *100 Loop Dr., tel. 303/569-2403. Train operates Memorial Day–Labor Day, daily 10–4; Labor Day–early Oct., weekends 10–4.*

Now get in the car and drive the 20-mile loop of the Guanella Pass Scenic Byway (C.R. 381 and 62) for stunning vistas of the **Mt. Evans Wilderness Area.** Then park yourself at the **Wildlife Viewing Station** by Georgetown Lake, from where you can catch a glimpse of the state's largest herd of rare bighorn sheep.

The western slope of the Rockies (past the Continental Divide) is where the most—and fluffiest—snow falls. As you travel west along I-70, you'll reach one of world's engineering marvels, the 8,941-foot-long **Eisenhower Memorial Tunnel.** Most people who drive through take its presence for granted, but until the first lanes were opened in 1973, the only access route west was the perilous **Loveland Pass,** a twisting, turning roller coaster of a ride. Snow, mud, and a steep grade proved the literal downfall of many an intrepid motorist. In truly inclement weather, it was impassable, and the east and west slopes were completely cut off from one another.

Authorities first proposed the Eisenhower in 1937 (under a different name, of course). At that time, most geologists warned about unstable rock; for more than three decades their direst predictions came true as rock walls crumbled, steel girders buckled, and gas pockets caused mysterious explosions. When the project was finally completed, more than 500,000 cubic yards of solid granite had been removed from Mt. Trelease. The original cost estimate in 1937 was $1 million. By the time a second bore marked its completion in 1979, the cost had skyrocketed to $340 million.

A string of superb ski areas now greets you. First is unassuming **Loveland** (*see* Sports and Outdoor Activities, *below*), a favorite of locals who appreciate the inexpensive lift tickets and short lines. More popular, however, is **Summit County,** a few miles farther on I-70, where four mega-areas—Keystone/Arapahoe Basin (A-Basin), Breckenridge, and Copper Mountain—market themselves under the umbrella "Ski the Summit." Special multiday lift tickets allow you to mix and match, for those seeking a universal ski experience. There's a saying among Summit County residents: Copper for skiing, Breck for lodging, and Keystone for food. The adage is accurate.

Though the resorts are marketed together, they are not all owned by the same company. Ralston Purina, which owns Keystone/A-Basin, recently purchased Breckenridge, and plans are afoot to link those three areas even more closely. So popular is Summit County, thanks to its incomparable setting, incredible variety of ski terrain, multitude of summer activities, and easy accessibility from Denver, that it welcomes more visitors annually than Aspen and Vail combined. Unfortunately, this creates terrible snarls along I–70, especially on weekends and holidays.

In many respects, Summit County serves as a microcosm of Colorado. It's a combination of grand old mining towns and ultramodern developments, of salty old-timers and Yuppies. (Indeed, the county attracts so many young technocrats and professionals it's being touted as the new Silicon Valley.)

Dillon, just off I–70 on U.S. 6 east, was founded in the 1870s as a stagecoach stop and trading post for miners, but its location has changed twice since the town's conception. Only a decade after it was founded, Dillon was moved closer to the railroad line. Then, in 1955, plans were drawn up to dam the Blue River, hence forming a reservoir to quench Denver's growing thirst. Dillon would end up submerged under 150 feet of water. Once again the town was moved. Foresighted residents decreed that no building in the new location would be higher than 30 feet, so as not to obstruct the view of the reservoir—now gratefully called Dillon Reservoir, or Lake Dillon. The potential tragedy turned into a boon and a boom for the reborn town, stunningly set on pine-blanketed hills mirrored in the sapphire water. There's no pretension to Dillon, just nature lovers and sports enthusiasts who take advantage of all the recreational opportunities their idyllic home affords.

Continue along U.S. 6 to the first two great ski areas of Summit County, **Keystone** and **Arapahoe Basin**. Arapahoe, the farther of the two areas, was the first to be built in Summit County, in the late '40s. Some say it hasn't changed since; the dig refers, in part, to some of Colorado's notoriously slowest lifts. Still, most of A-Basin's dedicated skiers wouldn't have it any other way. It's also America's highest ski area, with a *base* elevation of 10,780 feet. Most of the runs are above timberline, giving it an almost otherworldly feel. Aficionados love the short lift lines, the literally breathtaking views (and altitudes), the whopping 90% intermediate and expert terrain, and the wide-open bowls that stay open into June. Keystone Corporation bought A-Basin in the late '70s, but, aside from upgrading some facilities, has kept it true to its resolutely unchic, gnarly self.

Keystone is another matter. Designed to be cruisers' nirvana, with just enough flash to compete with the glamorous resorts, it compares favorably with the stylish if sterile mega-developments of the Alps—such as France's Les Arcs. For the most part, its planners were sensitive to the environment, favoring mountain colors and materials that blend inconspicuously with the natural surroundings. Keystone has pursued an aggressive policy of expansion, recently opening the tougher terrain on North Peak (mogul heaven) and the Outback (glade skiing) in an attempt to change its "easy" reputation and provide a balanced ski experience. Keystone is becoming a magnet in summer, too, with a small lake for water sports, a top-ranked golf course, and the same premium service visitors can expect in winter.

Double back on U.S. 6 west until it merges with CO 9 south. In a few miles you'll reach **Breckenridge,** a town that many consider the state's prettiest. In 1859, the first gold was discovered here, springing the town to life. For the next several decades Breckenridge experienced the attendant ups and downs, as the lodes of gold and then silver petered out. Still it's the oldest continuously occupied town on the western slope, and fortunately, its architectural legacy from the mining era has remained stable.

The downtown comprises one of Colorado's largest National Historic Districts, with 254 buildings in the National Register of Historic Places. The district is roughly a compact 12 square blocks, bounded by Main and High streets, Washington Avenue, and Wellington Road. The **Breckenridge Activity Center** (201 S. Main St., tel. 303/453–5579) and **Summit Historical Society** (309 N. Main St., tel. 303/453–9022) publish guided tours of more than 40 prominent structures, which range from simple log cabins to false fronts to lacy Victorian gingerbreads, all lovingly restored and painted.

Time Out   Step back to the '50s, and stop by **Glory Days Café** (311 S. Main St., tel. 303/453–9495), a tribute to all that is deliriously retro hip from the Eisenhower years, with an authentic 1952 jukebox (and 45s), and cholesterol-laden '50s favorites.

The skiing at Breckenridge, which opened as a resort in 1961, is wonderfully varied over Peaks 8, 9, and 10 of the Tenmile Range. The only downside is the strenuous poling required between Breck's three mountains. There are marvelous bowls and chutes on Peak 8, which is above timberline; gentle sweeping runs on Peak 9; and roller-coaster steeps on Peak 10. Consistent with the town's proud heritage, many runs are named for the old mines, including Bonanza, Cashier, Gold King, and Wellington. Nonetheless, Breck has developed a reputation for embracing the new: One of the first areas to permit snowboarding, it now holds the annual World Snowboarding Championships. Also, for one week each January the town declares itself an independent kingdom during the wild revel called Ullr Fest, which honors the Norse god of snow.

Back on I-70, just past CO 9, lies the funky, low-key town of **Frisco,** an odd hodgepodge of strip malls near the interstate, with a charming downtown district trimmed with restored bed-and-breakfasts and hell-raising bars. Frisco is a good, moderate (and sane) alternative to the glitzier, pricier resorts in the county, and it's worth exploring even if you're staying elsewhere. The **Frisco Historic Park** (Main and 2nd Sts., tel. 303/668–3428; admission free; open Tues.–Sat. 11–4) recreates the boom days with a fully outfitted one-room schoolhouse, jail, and log chapel, among the seven authentic 19th-century buildings.

㉗ A few miles farther, off I-70, is **Copper Mountain,** another major ski area. Copper is even more self-contained than Keystone and is dedicated to skiing, although it's picking up as a summer resort. Many skiers think the award-winning design, perfectly contoured to the natural terrain, is one of the world's best. The layout is ideal: Beginner runs are concentrated on the right side (facing the mountain) of the area, intermediate runs in the center, and expert terrain to the left. Weaker skiers can't get into trouble unless they look for it. Accommodations here are uniformly excellent, the nightlife lively for singles and younger couples, and the variety of activities and programs perfect for families.

Just a hop, skip, and a jump west of Summit County on I–70 is one of America's leading destinations, a playground of former presidents (and vice-presidents), consistently ranked the finest ski resort in America, if not the world: **Vail.** The four-letter word means Valhalla for skiers and conjures up images of the rich and famous enjoying their privileges. Actually, Vail is one of the unlikelier success stories in skiing. Seen from the village, the mountain doesn't look all that imposing. There are no glowering glaciers, no couloirs and chutes slashed from the rock, not even an Olympian summit shrouded in clouds. Even local historians admit that the Gore Creek valley in which Vail regally sits was an impoverished backwater, too isolated to play a prominent or colorful role in Colorado history, until the resort's opening in 1962.

In truth, the men who lent their names to the valley and resort deserved more notoriety than notice. Sir St. George Gore (a regrettably appropriate name) was a swaggering, filthy rich, drunken lout of a baronet who went on a three-year bacchanal in the 1850s and butchered every herd of elk and buffalo in sight. Charles Vail, the otherwise obscure chief engineer of the Colorado Highway Department from 1930–45, was—according to townspeople who dealt with him—an ornery cuss who was rumored to accept kickbacks from contractors.

Then, two visionaries appeared on the scene: Pete Seibert, a veteran of the 10th Mountain Division that prepared for alpine warfare in the surrounding Gore and Sawatch ranges during World War II; and Earl Eaton, a uranium prospector who had grown up in and surveyed these very ranges. In 1957 they ascended the mountain now known as Vail and upon attaining the summit discovered what skiers now salivate over: the Back Bowls, 4,000 acres of open glades formed when the Ute Indians set "spite fires" to the timberland in retaliation for being driven out by ranchers and miners. After five years of bureaucratic red tape and near-financial suicide, Seibert's dream became reality, and Vail resort was created.

Former owner George Gillett calls Vail "one of God's special works," and in reality it is an almost perfect example of mountain-and-village design. The development is remarkably compact, divided into the residential East Vail, the upscale Vail Village, and the more modest utilitarian Lionshead. Vail resembles a quaint Bavarian hamlet, with homey inns and lodges nestled against cozy A-frame chalets and clock towers. This, along with a heavy European bias among both the population and clientele, gives Vail perhaps the most international flavor and flair of any Colorado resort. It's crafted to anticipate a guest's every need, so you'll find a wealth of dining, shopping, and entertainment options at your fingertips. Everyone here is thoroughly professional: friendly without being familiar, knowing their business but not yours. Despite its tony reputation, the resort has actively courted the family trade in recent years. Children love the kids-only amusement parks at the ski area, with 15 acres of ski-through tepee villages, gold mines, and Fort Whippersnapper!

While the mountain has the sheer exhilarating edge in size over nearly every other North American ski area, it's brilliantly and clearly linked by a well-placed network of lifts and trails. There are 1,220 acres of immensely varied runs on the front side alone, but the Back Bowls are truly skiers' heaven: More than twice the skiable terrain accessed from the front, the back side has eye-popping expanses of fluffy white snow that make both intermediates and experts feel they can ski for days and not run into a single soul. Those same slopes have become a mecca for mountain-bike fanatics in summer, and the village now hosts a wide variety of festivals year-round.

Time Out   The **Hubcap Brewery and Kitchen** (Crossroads Shopping Ctr., tel. 303/476–5757) is Vail's only microbrewery, offering five regular beers (Vail Pale Ale and Beaver Tail Brown Ale are standouts) and rotating specials. Decor is upscale diner, with gleaming chrome hubcaps and a fire-engine-red chassis adorning the walls. The food is mostly superior pub grub such as calamari, chicken wings, and quesadillas. But this *is* Vail, so Vail Quail—three bite-size halves of range-fed birds, "nestled on a bed of wild rice"—also graces the menu.

At cosmopolitan Vail the emphasis is on luxury, although the prefab buildings are beginning to show their age. The best sightseeing is window-shopping, ogling the deluxe merchandise and the consumers—a delightful rather than daunting experience. While you're here, there are two tourist attractions worth visiting. **The Betty Ford Alpine Gardens** (183 Gore Creek Dr., tel. 303/476–0103; donations accepted; open Memorial Day–Labor Day, daily 9–7) is an oasis of forsythia, heather, wild roses, and shrubs and has the distinction of being the highest, public alpine gardens in the world. **The Colorado Ski Museum/Ski Hall of Fame** (15 Vail Rd., tel. 303/476–1876; donations accepted; open Tues.–Sat. 9–5) traces the development of the sport throughout the world, with an emphasis on Colorado's contributions. Fascinating displays include century-old skis and tows, early ski fashions, and an entire room devoted to the 10th Mountain Division.

The rest of Vail Valley is composed of solid working-class towns such as **Avon, Minturn, Eagle,** and **Edwards.** There is, however, one exception—**Beaver Creek,** constructed opposite Avon. Beaver Creek is an exclusive four-season development that gives even Utah's ultraposh Deer Valley a run for its cash flow. It's been open since 1980 and is finally emerging from big sister Vail's shadow. The rap used to be that Beaver Creek was even more immaculately groomed than its soigné clientele. However, when Beaver Creek developed the 110-acre Grouse Mountain in 1991, the resort's reputation changed. With more than 40% of its terrain now rated advanced, skiers flock here on powder days to seek out Grouse and famed runs such as Birds of Prey. Beginners and intermediates can still find the same pampering on the slopes they receive elsewhere in the resort, which is often blissfully uncrowded even on Vail's most congested days.

Beaver Creek's sublime setting, luxurious accommodations, gourmet restaurants, and world-class golf course designed by Robert Trent Jones, make the resort equally popular in summer, especially with families and couples. Elegant without being ostentatious, Vail's quietly glamorous little sister appeals to a select settled crowd, and everything at Beaver Creek lives up to its billing, from the billeting to the bill of fare.

A few miles west, past the town of Edwards, the narrow, winding Highway 131 squirrels north from I–70 through the **Yampa Valley.** The lush, wide-open spaces and vistas are both gorgeous and lonely, relieved only by the occasional odd rock formation thrusting up from the ground. This is cattle country, a land of jade forests, jagged outcroppings, and streams silvered by the sun and skirting the **Flat Tops Wilderness Area,** a high, flat mountain top crowned with a lava dome that glaciers have sculpted into a stunning series of steep cliffs and deep gashes.

Time Out **Antlers Café** (Main St., Yampa, no tel.) is owned by Mike Benedict, who, by his own admission, is a crusty old codger. Women couldn't sit at the handsome old bar until 1970 ("This ain't no brothel," Mike growled, "and I ain't got no cabaret license."). There's no question where some of his sympathies lie: Amid the trophies, potbellied stove, antique jukebox, and cash register are such signs as "If you're hungry and out of work, eat an environmentalist." Mike's an equal-opportunity insulter, though, with a delightfully sly grin ("Never mind the dog," reads another sign, "beware of owner."). He'll say you owe him 25 bucks for a photo: He means it!

After driving another 30–40 minutes north on Highway 131, **㉙** you'll arrive at **Steamboat Springs,** followed closely by **Steamboat Mountain Village.** Steamboat is aptly nicknamed Ski Town, U.S.A., since the town has "sent" the most Olympic athletes of any resort in America to the Winter Olympics. Presently, the tally is over 30, the most famous probably being silver medalist (in the 1972 slalom) Billy Kidd, whose irrepressible grin and 10-gallon hat are instantly recognizable. When he's around, Kidd conducts daily tours of the mountain.

Speaking of the mountain, keep in mind that the part that's visible from the base area is only the tip of the iceberg, and much more terrain lies concealed in back. Steamboat is famed for its eiderdown-soft snow; in fact, the term "champagne powder" was coined here to describe the area's unique feathery dumps, the result of Steamboat's fortuitous position between the arid desert to the west and the moisture-magnet of the Continental Divide to the east, where storm fronts duke it out.

The modern Mountain Village at Steamboat is attractive enough, if lacking in personality: a maze of upscale condos, boutiques, and bars. To its credit, though, this increasingly "hot" destination has retained its down-home, Western friendliness, providing the trappings while avoiding the trap of a premium resort. That may have to do with Steamboat Springs itself, a mere 10-minute drive away, where Stetson hats are sold for use and not for souvenirs. Steamboat originated not as a mining town but as a ranching and farming community, setting it apart from a Breckenridge or an Aspen. It has its share of Victorian buildings, most of them fronting Lincoln Avenue, the main drag, but they were built to be functional rather than ornamental.

The Tread of Pioneers Museum, located in a beautifully restored federal building, is an excellent spot to bone up on local history and includes ski memorabilia dating back to the turn of the century, when Carl Howelsen opened Howelsen Hill, still the country's preeminent ski-jumping facility. *8th and Oak*

Sts., tel. 303/879-2214. Admission: $2.50 adults, $1 children 6-12. Open daily 11-5.

The entrance to Steamboat from the mountain is roughly marked by the amusingly garish '50s neon sign from the Rabbit Ears Motel, and the unmistakable stench of sulfur. The town got its name from French trappers who, after hearing the bubbling and churning hot springs, mistakenly thought a steamboat was chugging up the Yampa River.

There are more than 100 hot springs in the immediate vicinity; the **Steamboat Visitor Center** (12th St. and Lincoln Ave., tel. 303/879-4301) publishes a fun and informative walking tour guide that describes many of the spots. The two most famous are the **Steamboat Springs Health and Recreation Hot Springs** (Lincoln Ave., tel. 303/879-1828; admission: $5; open daily 7 AM-8 PM) in town and the **Strawberry Park Natural Hot Springs** (Strawberry Park Rd., tel. 303/879-0342; admission: $5; open daily 8 AM-midnight), 7 miles out of town. The springs may not be as restorative as legend claims, but the inspiring views of the surrounding pristine forest certainly are.

In summer, Steamboat serves as the gateway to magnificent **Routt National Forest,** which offers a wealth of activities from hiking to mountain biking to fishing. Among the nearby attractions are the 283-foot **Fish Creek Falls** and the splendidly rugged **Mt. Zirkel Wilderness Area.** To the north, two sparkling man-made lakes, **Steamboat** and **Pearl,** offer a variety of water sports, including fishing and sailing.

Return the way you came and head west on I-70 to reach the natural and man-made 15-mile-long **Glenwood Canyon.** Nature began the work as the Colorado River carved deep buff-tinted granite, limestone, and quartzite gullies—brilliantly streaked with lavender, rose, and ivory. This process took a half-billion years. Then man stepped in, seeking a more direct route west. In 1992, the work on I-70 through the canyon was completed at a cost of almost $500 million. Much of the expense was attributable to the effort to preserve the natural landscape as much as possible. When contractors blasted cliff faces, for example, they stained the exposed rock to simulate nature's weathering. Biking trails were also created, providing easy access to the hauntingly beautiful **Hanging Lake Recreation Area.** Here Dead Horse Creek sprays ethereal flumes from curling limestone tendrils into a startlingly turquoise pool, as jet-black swifts dart to and fro. It's perhaps the most transcendent of several idyllic spots now reachable on bike or foot. The intrepid can scale the delicate limestone cliffs, pocked with numerous caverns embroidered with pastel-hued gardens.

Interstate 70 snakes through the canyon on its way to a famed spa that forms the western apex of a triangle with Vail and Aspen. Once upon a time **Glenwood Springs** was every bit as tony as those chic resorts are today, attracting a faithful legion of the pampered and privileged who came to enjoy the waters (the world's largest natural hot springs), said to cure everything from acne to rheumatism.

Today the entrance to town and its once-splendid prospects of a fertile valley fringed by massive peaks is marred by the proliferation of malls, motels, and fast-food outlets. Remnants of her glory days can still be seen in the grand old **Hotel Colorado** (526 Pine St., tel. 303/945-6511), regally commanding the vaporous pools from a patrician distance. Modeled after the Villa de Medici in Italy, the property opened its doors in 1893 to become the fashionable retreat of its day. Teddy Roosevelt even made it his unofficial "Little White House" in 1905, and so began the Teddy Bear craze, when a chambermaid stitched together tatters for the president after he returned empty-handed from an exhausting hunt.

The **Yampah Hot Springs,** situated near the hotel, were discovered by the Ute Indians (*yampah* is Ute for "big medicine"), and are still popular today. Even before the heyday of the Hotel Colorado, Western notables from Annie Oakley to Doc Holliday came to take the curative waters. In Doc's case, however, the cure didn't work, and six months after his arrival in 1887 he died broke, broken-down, and tubercular. (He lies in Linwood Cemetery, a half mile east of town.) The smaller pool is 100 feet long and maintained at 104°; the larger is more than two city blocks long (405 feet) and contains in excess of a million gallons of constantly filtered water that is completely refilled every six hours and maintained at a soothing 90°. *Pine St., tel. 303/945–6571. Admission: $6 adults, $3.75 children 3–12, children under 3 free. Open Memorial Day–Labor Day, daily 7:30 AM–10 PM; Labor Day–Memorial Day, 9 AM–10 PM.*

Two blocks down the street, the **Yampah Spa and Vapor Caves** is a series of three natural underground steam baths. The same 124° springs that supply the pool flow under the cave floors. Each chamber is successively hotter than the next; you can scoop mud from the walls for a cleansing facial, as you purify your body (and soul, according to Ute legend). A variety of spa treatments from massages to body wraps is also available. *709 E. 6th St., tel. 303/945–0667. Admission: $6.75 for caves alone, more for various treatments. Open daily 9–9.*

Twenty minutes south of Glenwood Springs, off CO 82 along C.R. 117, is another Colorado gem, the small but satisfying **Ski Sunlight,** a favorite of locals who enjoy the varied terrain, sensational views, and lack of pretension. The ratio of shredders (snowboarders) to downhillers here is quite high, as Sunlight has a reputation for "radical air."

At **Carbondale,** CO 82 splits, and CO 133 veers south on its way to **Redstone,** a charming artists' colony whose streets are lined with pretty galleries and boutiques and whose boundaries are ringed by impressive sandstone cliffs from which the town draws its name. Its history dates back to the late 19th century when J.C. Osgood, director of the Colorado Fuel and Iron Company, built **Cleveholm Manor** (now known as **Redstone Castle**) to entertain the other titans of his day, such as John D. Rockefeller, J. P. Morgan, and Teddy Roosevelt. Among the home's embellishments are gold-leaf ceilings, maroon velvet walls, silk brocade upholstery, marble and mahogany fireplaces, Persian rugs, and Tiffany chandeliers. Today, the hotel is in the National Register of Historic Places and is open to the public. Stay a night amid baronial splendor in one of the rooms favored by a Roosevelt or a Rockefeller. *58 Redstone Blvd., tel. 303/963–3408.*

Osgood's largesse extended to his employees, for whom he constructed one of the first planned communities, a utopian model in its day. The **Redstone Inn** (0082 Redstone Blvd., tel. 303/963–2526), designated a National Historic Place, is a fine example of the magnate's generosity. Though this structure pales in comparison to the castle, its flourishes include a Tudor bell tower and sumptuous Victorian furnishings. You can also stay overnight at the cozy, relaxing inn.

Meanwhile, CO 82 continues southeast and skirts the Roaring Fork River on its way to Aspen, one of the world's fabled resorts and practically a byword for glitz, glamour, and glorious skiing. To the uninitiated, Aspen and Vail are virtually synonymous. To residents, a rivalry exists, despite the current détente that led to the formation of the Aspen/Vail Premier Passport (an interchangeable ski pass that includes a one-way transfer). Comparisons are admittedly odious and at best superficial, though a few instructive generalizations can be made.

The most obvious distinction is the look: Vail is a faux-Bavarian development, Aspen an authentic Victorian mining town. Vail is a lower-key, discreet, relaxed, and relaxing retreat. In see-and-be-seen Aspen, the only bad press is no press (the season doesn't seem to begin without some tabloid scandal). Vail is politicians—where Gerald Ford, Dan Quayle, and John Sununu fled to escape the cares of state. Aspen is rock stars and Hollywood—where Don Johnson and Melanie Griffith remarried and Barbra Streisand took a stand against the controversial Amendment 2.

③ **Aspen** is a slave to fashion, so much so that the term "Aspen formal" was coined to describe the combination of dressing for the elements (ski hat, wool mittens) and for success (dinner jacket, evening gown). Locals tend to be either violently beautiful or merely wealthy, but fashionable takes on many meanings in Aspen. It's always been a magnet for cultural and countercultural types. After all, gonzo bad-boy journalist Hunter S. Thompson is one of the more visible citizens; and one of Aspen's most beloved figures is unrepentant hippie John Bennett, who tools around in his "Ultimate Taxi" (it's plastered with 3-D glasses, crystal disco balls, and neon necklaces and redolent of dry ice and incense). You'll find everyone from "social X rays" with *Vogue* exteriors and vague interiors to long-haired musicians in combat boots and fatigues. To be fair, most Aspenites couldn't care less: Theirs is a freewheeling, tolerant town that welcomes diversity of personal expression. It's all part of the Aspen mystique. Ultimately, it doesn't matter what you wear here, as long as you wear it with conviction.

Before entering Aspen you'll pass through several communities and satellite ski resorts, starting with **Woody Creek,** a determinedly unchic part of the valley that's most famous as the residence of Hunter S. Thompson. He isn't the only unique contribution to this area, though; if the snow's not too deep you might catch a glimpse of an Aspen landmark, the **Finger House.** Its roof sports an enormous middle finger, painted in Day-Glo colors—the owner's gesture to his wife after a particularly acrimonious divorce.

Time Out A perfect example of this hip anomie is the **Woody Creek Tavern** (0002 Woody Creek Plaza, tel. 303/923–4585), which has the temerity to sit next to a trailer park. It features pool tables, knotty-pine decor, TVs broadcasting sporting events, great burgers, nachos, and BBQ—and Hunter, who has been known to shoot target practice here every now and then. Don Henley's another habitué, though he usually keeps a low profile.

Continue southeast along CO 82, and you'll see the turnoffs **32** (Brush Creek or Owl Creek Rds.) to **Snowmass,** one of four ski areas owned by the Aspen Skiing Company. Snowmass Village has its share of chic boutiques and eateries, but is more affordable and down-to-earth than Aspen and predominantly caters to families. These differences apply equally to the development and the mountain itself. Aspen Mountain is a rigorous ski experience; Snowmass is Aspen Skiing Company's family resort, with 51% of its 2,500 skiable acres designated intermediate, including the renowned classic cruiser runs off Big Burn lift, the stuff of ego massage. However, don't overlook that Snowmass is four times the size of Aspen Mountain and has triple the black and double black diamond terrain of its famed sister, including several fearsomely precipitous gullies and Hanging Valley, accessible by a short hike. More and more skiers are discovering Snowmass's other personality, although Aspen Mountain remains the definitive test of skiing ability.

The next area, accessed by West Buttermilk Road, is **Tiehack,** known as Aspen's "learning" mountain. It's often dissed and dismissed as a beginners' area, but the Tiehack section on the east contains several wonderfully cut advanced runs (though nothing truly expert), as well as sweeping views of Maroon Creek valley. It also boasts superb powder, and deep snow sticks around longer because so few serious skiers realize what they're missing.

Aspen Highlands is the next mountain you'll reach off Maroon Creek Road, and until 1993, it was the only area not owned by the Aspen Skiing Company. This, alone, made the Highlands a favorite of anti-establishment types; it can no longer play on its independence by billing itself as the "maverick ski area." But, locals ski here for other reasons as well, including the best views among the four mountains, comparatively short lift lines, and some heart-pounding runs. While not quite as hairy as Aspen Mountain, the Highlands offers thrilling descents at Steeplechase and Olympic Bowl, as well as a lovely wide-open bowl called Thunder, where intermediates play. While you're here, enjoy Aspen Highlands' anything-goes spirit, evidenced by special events such as the freestyle contests every Friday, and the now-legendary Ski Patrol Jump, over the deck—and over startled skiers—at the Cloud Nine Picnic Hut. It's held every day at noon, weather permitting.

Continue back on CO 82, and you'll finally reach **Aspen.** Originally called Ute City (after its displaced former residents), it was founded in the late 1870s during a silver rush. The most prominent early citizen was Jerome Wheeler, who in 1889, at the height of Aspen's prosperity, opened two of Aspen's enduring landmarks: the sturdily elegant redbrick **Jerome Hotel** (330 E. Main St., tel. 303/920–1000), whose ornate lobby, bar, and restaurant today re-create fashionable turn-of-the-century living, and the elegant **Wheeler Opera House** (320 E. Hyman Ave., tel. 303/925–2750). In 1893, however, silver crashed and Aspen's population dwindled from 15,000 to 250 people by the Depression era.

In the late 1930s, the region struck gold when Swiss mountaineer and ski consultant Andre Roche determined that Aspen

Mountain would make a prime ski area. By 1941 it had already landed the U.S. Nationals, but Aspen was really put on the world map by Walter Paepcke, who developed the town as a cultural mecca. In 1949, he helped found the Aspen Institute for Humanistic Studies and organized an international celebration to mark Johann Wolfgang von Goethe's 200th birthday. This event paved the way for such renowned annual festivities as the Aspen Music Festival and the International Design Conference.

Downtown Aspen is easily explored on foot; it's best to wander without a planned itinerary, although the Aspen Historical Society puts out a walking-tour brochure. You can spend an afternoon admiring the sleek window displays and graceful Victorian mansions and gingerbreads, many of which now house fine boutiques and restaurants.

You can obtain great insight into Victorian high life at the **Wheeler-Stallard House Museum,** which displays period memorabilia collected by the Aspen Historical Society. *620 W. Bleeker St., tel. 303/925-3721. Admisson: $2. Open mid-June-Sept., daily 1-4; mid-Dec.-Apr., weekends 1-4.*

Your next stop should be the **Aspen Art Museum,** where top local and national artists in varied disciplines are exhibited. The complimentary wine-and-cheese session-cum-gallery tour, held Thursdays at 5:30, is a lot of fun. *590 N. Mill St., tel. 303/925-8050. Admission: $3 adults, $2 senior citizens and students, children under 12 free. Open Tues.-Sun. noon-6, Thurs. noon-8.*

Between galleries, museums, international conferences, and events, there's so much going on year-round that even in winter many people come to "do the scene" and don't even ski. Still, **Aspen Mountain** (also known as Ajax) is the standard by which many good skiers test themselves. Aspen is not for beginners (there are no green runs); in fact, a black diamond here might rank as a double diamond elsewhere. The narrow mountain is laid out as a series of steep unforgiving ridges with little room for error. Those wanting cruisers ski the ridge tops or valleys: Ruthie's Run, Buckhorn, and International are the classics. Bell Mountain provides some of the best bump skiing anywhere, followed by Walsh's Gulch, Hyrup's, and Kristi's. If you don't like catching air, or don't want your knees to get a workout, go elsewhere!

Aspen is equally popular in summer, with marvelous hiking and biking throughout the **White River National Forest.** One favorite jaunt is to the majestic **Maroon Bells,** twin fourteeners so colorful, thanks to mineral streaking, you'd swear they were blanketed with primrose and Indian paintbrush. It's one of the most photographed spots in the state. Cars are only allowed part way, but Roaring Fork Transit provides shuttle buses that leave regularly in the summer from the Aspen Highlands parking lot.

What to See and Do with Children

Aspen Center for Environmental Studies (Hallam Lake Wildlife Sanctuary, 100 Puppy Smith St., Aspen, tel. 303/925-5756) is a research center and wildlife sanctuary, where children and adults alike can take refuge. The facility sponsors snowshoe walks with naturalist guides in winter and backyard-wildlife workshops that teach children to create a minisanctuary in their own yard. In summer there are bird-watching hikes and Special Little Naturalist programs for 3–5- and 5–7-year-olds, which include nature walks and arts and crafts.

Amaze 'N' Breckenridge (710 S. Main St., tel. 303/453–7262) is a maze that confounds and delights adults and children alike.

Shopping

Needless to say, you can find anything in these glamorous resorts, except bargains. Still, window-shopping can be fun, as can a splurge every now and then.

Shopping Districts and Malls Downtown Aspen is an eye-popping display of conspicuous consumption. Among the malls with ultrachic stores are **Hyman Street Mall, Cooper Street Mall, Ute City Building,** and **Mill Street Plaza.**

Breckenridge also offers high-end shopping in the **Lincoln West Mall,** the **Main Street Mall,** and **Four Seasons Plaza.**

In Frisco, **The Mining Exchange Building** (313 Main St.) has several shops specializing in Americana, antiques, and collectibles.

Glenwood Springs Mall, in Glenwood, offers everything from K-Mart and JC Penney to factory outlets and specialty shops.

Keystone features several top shops in the **Argentine Plaza.**

Silverthorne Factory Stores Complex, in Summit County, has developed a reputation for discount shopping for Adolfo, Geoffrey Beene, Liz Claiborne, Evan Picone, Bass Shoe, Royal Doulton, Nike, and many others.

Steamboat's **Old Town Square** is a collection of upscale boutiques and retailers, such as Benetton.

To some, Vail is one large upscale mall, but for the best of the best, head for **Gateway Plaza, Crossroads Shopping Center,** and, of course, the **Beaver Creek Promenade.**

The top boutiques and galleries in Winter Park are concentrated downtown in **Cooper Creek Square** and **Crestview Place Mall.**

Specialty Stores
Antiques **Cheap Shots** (303 E. Main St., Aspen, tel. 303/925–6888) sells antiques and stylish secondhand threads in a darling Victorian house. **Fetzer Antiques** (305 S. Hunter St., tel. 303/925–5447), carries Aspen's finest antiques and specializes in 18th- and 19th-century English and Continental goods.

In Georgetown, the **Georgetown Antique Emporium** (501 Rose St., tel. 303/569–2727) specializes in oak and brass items.

Art Galleries **Amer-Indian Gallery** (747 Lincoln Ave., Steamboat Springs, tel. 303/879–7116) is owned by North American native-culture expert Mark St. Pierre (Pulitzer-nominated for his *Madonna Swan: A Lakota Woman's Story*). A wide range of native art from Alaska to Mexico is featured. **Hill Gallery of Photography** (205 S. Mill St., Aspen, tel. 303/925–1836) captures nature's artistry in works by leading American photographers. **Olla Podrida Gallery** (100 E. Meadow Dr., Vail, tel. 303/476–6919) specializes in contemporary and antique American folk art and craft work. **Red Men Hall** (Hwy. 40, Empire, tel. 303/569–3243), located a few miles from Georgetown, showcases Native American art, including jewelry, paintings, and exquisite hand-painted kachina jackets. **Stars Memorabilia** (521 E. Cooper St., Aspen, tel. 303/920–2920) offers every kind of celebrity memorabilia, from Lincoln's autograph to Pete Townshend's smashed guitar. **White Hart Gallery** (843 Lincoln Ave., Steamboat Springs, tel. 303/879–1015) is a magnificent clutter of Western and Native American paintings and objets d'art. **Windwood Galleries** (151 Main St., Minturn, tel. 303/827–9232) specializes in Colorado artists, as well as ceramics and artifacts.

Books   **Off the Beaten Path** (56 7th St., Steamboat, tel. 303/879–9127) is a throwback to the beat generation, with poetry readings, lectures, and concerts. It has an excellent selection of new-age works, in addition to the usual best-sellers and guides.

Boutiques   **Amallama** (Old Town Sq., Steamboat, tel. 303/879–9127) offers folk art, jewelry, and clothing from around the world, including Dhurrie, Afghan, and Kashmir rugs and Balinese cradle watchers. You can make your own earrings at the bead counter. **Kirk's Kritters** (806 Lincoln Ave., in the Shirt Stop, Steamboat Springs, tel. 303/879–1288) offers a zany selection of jewelry and hand-knit sweaters.

Boogie's (534 E. Cooper Ave., Aspen, tel. 303/925–6111) sells kitschy clothes and jewelry; you can grab a bite in their diner, too. **Chepita's** (525 E. Cooper Ave., Aspen, tel. 303/925–2871) calls itself a "toy store for adults," and the whimsy continues with kinetic clothing and wood-carved sartorially resplendent pigs, to complement the standard designer watches and jewelry.

Gorsuch (263 Gore Creek Dr., Vail, tel. 303/476–2294; 70 Promenade, Beaver Creek, tel. 303/949–7115) is far more than a boutique or a sporting goods store; it offers everything from alpaca sweaters to buffalo coats and pottery to potpourri. **Gracy's** (202 E. Main St., Aspen, tel. 303/925–5131) has first-class second-hand clothing. **Gypsy Woman** (223 E. Main St., Aspen, no tel.) has everything from antique skis to leather vests in this cramped space. **Old Town Leather** (929 Lincoln Ave., Steamboat Springs, tel. 303/879–3558) offers every conceivable leather item, most of them handmade. **Scandinavian Designs** (607 E. Cooper Ave., Aspen, tel. 303/925–7299) features some of Aspen's finest hand-knit sweaters, as well as everything Scandinavian from Swedish clogs to Norwegian trolls to Finnish Arabia.

Limited Additions (205 S. Mill St., Aspen, tel. 303/925–7112) features unique wearable art, handwoven or painted garments, and handcrafted jewelry.

Ceramics   **Aspen Potters** (231 E. Main St., tel. 303/925–8726) offers the latest designs from local artisans.

Crafts   **Hunter Hogan Tapestries** (520 W. Main St., Aspen, tel. 303/925–8842) is named for the designer of the weavings that are sold here. Most prints have been adapted from African patterns. **Quilts Unlimited** (Silvertree Plaza Mall, 100 Elbert La., Snowmass, tel. 303/923–5467) sells superb handmade antique and contemporary quilts, as well as various regional handicrafts.

Undercover Quilts (Westhaven Dr., Vail, tel. 303/476–0559; by appointment only) celebrates the art of hand-stitched and pieced quilts, with special emphasis on traditional Amish and Mennonite designs. Custom orders also available.

Curios and Collectibles **The Ore Rock Cart Shop** (324 S. Main St., Breckenridge, tel. 303/453–1567) carries unique gifts made from stone, minerals, and precious metals: gold-nugget jewelry, agate bookends, crystals, even fossils and dinosaur bones.

Silver 'n Threads (509 Rose St., Georgetown, tel. 303/569–2965) offers a remarkable range of items, from silver ornaments, coins, and jewelry to handcrafted dolls and animals to rare tins and Navajo rock statues.

The **Watersweeper and the Dwarf** (717 Grand St., Glenwood Springs, tel. 303/945–2000) sells handicrafts and Americana fashioned from silver, gold, clay, wood, glass, stone, wool, wax, and patience.

Sporting Goods **Aspen Sports** (408 E. Cooper Ave., tel. 303/925–6331; 303 E. Durant Ave., tel. 925–6332; Snowmass Mall, tel. 303/923–6111; Snowmass Center, tel. 303/923–3566; Silvertree Hotel, tel. 303/923–6504).

Sport Stalker (Ski Time Square, Steamboat, tel. 303/879–2445).

Western Wear and Accessories **F.M. Light and Sons** (830 Lincoln Ave., Steamboat Springs, tel. 303/879–1822), owned by the same family for four generations, caters to the Marlboro man in us all. If you're lucky you'll find what you're looking for cheap—how about cowboy hats for $4.98!

Happy Trails (725 Grand St., Glenwood Springs, tel. 303/945–6076) has lots of Western-themed goods, much of it on consignment.

Into the West (8th St. off Lincoln Ave., Steamboat Springs, tel. 303/879–8377) is owned by Jace Romick, a former member of the U.S. ski team and a veteran of the rodeo circuit. He crafts splendid, beautifully textured lodgepole furniture and sells anything tasteful to do with the West: antiques (even ornate potbellied stoves), collectibles, cowhide mirrors, and new handicrafts such as Indian drum tables and fanciful candle holders made from branding irons.

Sports and the Outdoors

Camping Call the U.S. Forest Service for complete information on camping in the following national forests: **Arapahoe** (tel. 303/444–6001), **Routt** (tel. 303/879–1722), and **White River** (tel. 303/945–2521).

Cycling **Blazing Pedals** (Aspen, tel. 303/925–5651 or 303/923–4544 or 800/282–7238) offers downhill bicycle tours through Aspen and the surrounding countryside.

Steamboat Ski Area (tel. 303/879–6111) has expanded its trail service. **Routt National Forest** has numerous routes in its 1.5-million-acre wilderness. **White River National Forest** boasts the Rio Grande, Richmond Ridge, and the more strenuous Vail Pass and Independence Pass trails, among many others. **Arapahoe National Forest** offers Boreas Pass, Loveland Pass, Blue

River Bikeway, and Tenmile Canyon National Recreation Trail.

Winter Park is one of the leading cycling destinations in the Rockies, thanks to the 660-mile trail system created by **Winter Park Fat Tire Society** (Box 1337, Winter Park 80482, no tel.). **Mad Adventures** (tel. 303/726–5290 or 800/451–4844) offers instruction and guided bike tours.

Fishing Among the region's leading destinations are **Dillon Lake** and the **Blue** and **Snake rivers,** in Summit County; **Black Lakes** and the **Eagle River** in Vail Valley; the **Elk** and **Yampa rivers, Dumont Lake,** and **Steamboat Lake,** near Steamboat Springs; and the **Frying Pan** and **Roaring Fork rivers** around Aspen. You'll find loads of trout, bass, walleye, pike, and others.

Aspen Outfitting Co. (tel. 303/925–3406) runs a fly-fishing guide service to local waterways. **Buggywhips Fish and Float Service** (Steamboat Springs, tel. 303/879–8033) arranges trips on the Elk and Yampa rivers. **Mountain Anglers** (Breckenridge, tel. 303/453–HOOK) organizes trips throughout Summit County. **Oxbow Outfitting Co.** (Aspen, tel. 303/925–1505) runs trips for anglers. **Roaring Fork Anglers** (Glenwood Springs, tel. 303/945–1800) leads wade and float trips throughout the area. **Summit Guides** (Dillon, tel. 303/468–8945) offers full- and half-day trips. **Vail Fishing Guides** (tel. 303/476–3296) provides gear as well as guided tours.

The Fraser Valley was a favorite angling spot of Ike's. For information about fishing in Winter Park and the surrounding region, call the **Arapaho National Forest** (tel. 303/887–3331).

Fitness **Aspen Athletic Club** (720 E. Hyman Ave., tel. 303/925–2531) is fully equipped and includes a steam room, tanning salon, and massage therapy.

Breckenridge Recreation Center (Kingdom Park, tel. 303/453–1734) is a state-of-the-art, 62,000-square-foot facility that has a fully equipped health club, two swimming pools, and indoor tennis and racquetball courts.

Cascade Club (Cascade Village, next to Westin, Vail, tel. 303/476–7400) and **Vail Athletic Club** (352 E. Meadow Dr., tel. 303/476–7960) are full-service facilities and include spas.

Copper Mountain Racquet and Athletic Club (tel. 303/968–2882) features full-service fitness rooms, racquetball, tennis, aerobics, saunas, and tanning booths.

Hot Springs Athletic Club (401 N. River Rd., Glenwood Springs, tel. 303/945–7428) offers Nautilus, saunas, tanning beds, and racquetball.

Golf **Beaver Creek Golf Course** (tel. 303/949–7123), befitting the resort's reputation, is a 6,400-yard, par-70 stunner designed by Robert Trent Jones.

Breckenridge Golf Club (tel. 303/453–9104), the only Jack Nicklaus–designed course in America, is a 7,279-yard, par-72 beauty. Dramatically situated, it resembles a nature reserve, with woods and beaver ponds lining the fairways.

Copper Creek Golf Club (Copper Mountain, tel. 303/968–2339), at 9,650 feet, is America's highest course. Designed by Pete and Perry Dye, the par-70, 6,094-yard course follows the twisting, narrow, natural terrain of Copper's valley.

Eagles Nest Golf Club (tel. 303/468–0681), renowned as the country's most mountainous course, is a par 70 with 6,698 yards and has several daunting challenging tee-to-green elevation shifts.

Keystone Ranch Course (Silverthorne, tel. 303/468–4250) is listed as one of the top-50 resort courses in America by *Golf Digest*. The 7,090-yard, par-72 course, designed by Robert Trent Jones, winds through stunning mountain scenery.

Sheraton Steamboat Golf Club (tel. 303/879–2220) is a 6,906-yard, par-72, 18-hole championship course designed by Robert Trent Jones, Jr.

Singletree Golf Course (Edwards, Vail Valley, tel. 303/926–3533), a 7,059-yard, par-71 course, is another perennial top-50 resort course, according to *Golf Digest*.

Snowmass Lodge and Golf Club Links (tel. 303/923–3148) is an 18-hole, 6,900-yard championship course designed by Arnold Palmer and Ed Seay.

In Winter Park, the par-72, 7,000-yard, 18-hole **Pole Creek Golf Club** (tel. 303/726–8847), designed by Gary Player and Ron Kirby, is consistently ranked in the top-75 public courses by *Golf Digest*.

Hiking Near Steamboat, **Routt National Forest** offers miles of trail through aspen and conifer forests, mountain meadows, lakes, and the thunderous 283-foot cascade, Fish Creek Falls. Rabbit Ears Pass is especially beautiful, including the eroded volcanic pinnacles of Rabbit Ears Peaks. The Devil's Causeway is a vertiginous narrow isthmus along the massive ramparts of **Flat Tops Wilderness**. The **Arapahoe** (especially the Wheeler National Recreational Trail and Eagles Nest Wilderness) and **White River national forests** (including the famed Rio Grande Trail, Sunnyside Trail, Hanging Trail, and the Maroon Bells and Collegiate Peaks wilderness areas) offer a similar range of scenic trails. For further information, call the **U.S. Forest Service** (Arapahoe, tel. 303/444–6001; Routt, tel. 303/879–1722; White River, tel. 303/945–2521).

Hiking opportunities in Winter Park include **Byer's Peak** and **Devil's Thumb**, but for more information contact the **Winter Park/Fraser Valley Chamber of Commerce** (tel. 303/726–4118) or **Arapaho National Forest** (tel. 303/887–3331).

Horseback Riding Riding trails are generally easy and wind through stunning alpine scenery. Rates begin at $12 an hour. For outfitters try **A.J. Brink Outfitters** (Sweetwater, north of Vail off Exit 133 of I–70, tel. 303/524–9301); **Aspen Canyon Ranch** (Parshall, Summit County, tel. 303/725–3518); **Beaver Stables** (Winter Park, tel. 303/726–9247); **Breckenridge Stables** (tel. 303/453–4438); **Canyon Creek Ranch** (I–70, 7 mi west of Glenwood to Exit 109, tel. 303/984–2000); **Continental Arabians** (Steamboat, tel. 879–8974); **Steamboat Lake Outfitters** (tel. 303/879–4404); **Steamboat Stables** (tel. 303/879–2306); and **T Lazy Seven** (Aspen, tel. 303/925–4614).

Rafting **Adventures Wild** (Steamboat, tel. 303/879–8747) runs excursions to various rivers. Half-day to two-week trips are offered for all levels. Rates start at $30 a person. **Aspen Whitewater/ Colorado Riff Raft** (tel. 303/925–5405 or 800/759–3939) offers mild to wild excursions on the Shoshone, Upper Roaring Fork, and lower Colorado. **Blazing Paddles/Snowmass Whitewater** (tel. 303/923–4544 or 800/282–RAFT) runs trips to various rivers and canyons in the area and beyond. **Blue Sky Adventures** (Glenwood Springs, tel. 303/945–6605) offers rafting on the Colorado and Roaring Fork rivers. Also, try **Colorado River Runs** (State Bridge, Summit County, tel. 303/653–4292 or 800/826–1081). **Mad Adventures** (Winter Park, tel. 303/726–5290 or 800/451–4844) lets you shoot the rapids of the North, Platte, Colorado and Arkansas rivers. **Rock Garden Rafting** (Glenwood Springs, tel. 303/945–6737) runs trips down the Colorado and Roaring Fork rivers. **Whitewater Rafting** (Glenwood Springs, tel. 303/945–8477) also runs trips throughout the region.

Skiing
Cross-Country

Ashcroft Ski Touring (Aspen, tel. 303/925–1971) features 40 kilometers (25 miles) of groomed trails in the White River National Forest. **Aspen/Snowmass Nordic Trail System** (tel. 303/923–3148) contains 81 kilometers (50 miles) of trails through the Roaring Fork Valley. **Breckenridge Nordic Ski Center** (tel. 303/453–6855) maintains 31 kilometers (19 miles) of trails in its system. **Copper Mountain/Trak Cross-Country Center** (tel. 303/968–2882) offers 26 kilometers (16 miles) of groomed track and skate lanes. **Devil's Thumb Ranch/Ski Idlewild** (Devil's Thumb is 10 mi north of Winter Park; Ski Idlewild, in Winter Park, tel. 303/726–5564) are full-service resorts with 53 miles of groomed trails between them. **Frisco Nordic Center** (1121 N. Summit Blvd., tel. 303/668–0866) has nearly 40 kilometers (25 miles) of one-way loops. **Keystone Nordic Center at Ski Tip Lodge** (tel. 303/468–4275) provides 29 kilometers (18 miles) of prepared trails and 56 kilometers (35 miles) of backcountry skiing winding through Arapahoe National Forest. **Steamboat Ski Touring Center** (tel. 303/879–8180) has trails on the golf course. **Vail/Beaver Creek Cross-Country Ski Centers** (tel. 303/476–5601, ext. 4390) provide information on the many trails in the Vail Valley.

Downhill

Arrowhead at Vail. West down the Vail Valley lies Arrowhead, a small mountain with only one chair—a high-speed quad—that accesses gently rolling beginner and intermediate terrain. This is an ideal place for families who just want to get away from the madding crowds for a day. *Tel. 303/926–3029 or 800/332–3029. Open mid-Dec.–early Apr., 9–3:30.*

Aspen Highlands. Nine chairs and two pomas access 500 acres of terrain with a dizzying 3,800-foot vertical drop. *Tel. 303/925–3491. Open late Nov.–early Apr., 9–4.*

Aspen Mountain. Eight lifts, including a high-speed gondola, service the 625 acres of challenging terrain, spanning a vertical of 3,267 feet. *Tel. 800/262–7736. Open late Nov.–mid-Apr., 9–3:30.*

Beaver Creek Resort. With 50 trails, 1,050 skiable acres, a 3,400-foot vertical, and 10 lifts (including two high-speed quads), uphill capacity is tremendous at this still-uncrowded, upscale winner. *Tel. 303/949–5750. Open late Nov.–mid-Apr., 8:30–3:30.*

Breckenridge. Seventy miles of trails, across 1,600 skiable acres, and a 3,398-foot verticle drop, are served by 16 lifts (including four speedy "SuperChair" quads). It offers just under 50% expert terrain. *Tel. 303/453–3000. Open mid-Nov.–mid-Apr., 8:30–3:45.*

Copper Mountain Resort. Copper offers 1,330 acres of skiing on 96 trails and four back bowls, with a 2,760-foot vertical, serviced by 20 lifts. The area also provides the "Extreme Experience" on 350 acres of guided adventure skiing. *Tel. 303/968–2882. Open mid-Nov.–late Apr., 8:30–4.*

Howelsen Ski Area. This tiny historic area located right in Steamboat Springs is Colorado's oldest. Its three lifts, 10 trails, and 440-foot vertical aren't impressive, but it *is* the largest and most complete ski-jumping complex in America, and a major Olympic training ground. Howelsen also offers the "Champagne of Thrills" bobsled course, open daily in season 6 PM–10 PM. *Howelsen Ski Area, Steamboat Springs, tel. 303/879–2043. Open Dec.–Mar., weekdays noon–10; weekends 9 AM–10 PM.*

Keystone/Arapahoe Basin. Three mountains—Keystone, North Peak, and the new Outback—comprise Keystone Resort, with Arapahoe Basin (a.k.a. A-Basin) available on the same lift ticket. A-Basin offers predominantly intermediate and expert terrain (90% of the 30 trails), with a 1,670-foot vertical drop, serviced by five lifts. In all, there are two high-speed gondolas, three high-speed quads, 15 other chairs, and four surface lifts to connect this monstrous area, which just keeps growing. *Keystone/Arapahoe Basin, I–70 to Exit 205 onto Hwy. 6, tel. 800/222–0188. Keystone open late Oct.–mid-Apr., daily 8:30 AM–10 PM; North Peak open mid-Nov.–mid-Apr.; Outback open mid-Dec.–mid-Apr., 9–3; A-Basin open early Nov.–early June, 8:30–4.*

Loveland Ski Area. Loveland is considered small-fry, but only because of its proximity to the megaresorts of Ski the Summit. Actually, Loveland—the nearest ski area to Denver (just above the Eisenhower Tunnel, 56 mi from Denver)—offers a respectable 830 acres, serviced by 10 lifts, spread out over two mountains: Loveland Valley for beginners, and Loveland Basin for everyone else. Basin boasts some excellent glade and open-bowl skiing, with a 1,680-foot vertical drop. Best of all, it opens early and usually stays open later than any other area, except A-Basin. *Tel. 303/569–3203. Open mid-Oct.–May, weekdays 9–4; weekends 8:30–4.*

Ski Cooper. Seventy percent of the 350 skiable acres is rated beginner or intermediate, but the area—with a 1,200-foot vertical drop—also runs snowcat tours into 1,800 acres of pristine backcountry powder. *Off Hwy. 24, tel. 719/486–2277. Open late Nov.–early Apr., 9–4.*

Ski Sunlight. Yet another of Colorado's affordable gems, Ski Sunlight has 38 trails serviced by four lifts with 2,010 vertical feet. The new East Ridge will add four more trails of super-steep glade skiing. *Off C.R. 117, tel. 303/945–7491 or 800/445–7931. Open late Nov.–early Apr.*

Snowmass. This is a sprawling mountain, with five clearly defined skiing areas totaling 2,500 acres and a 4,015-foot vertical, accessed by 16 lifts. As at Breckenridge, it's a good idea to plan your route carefully, especially if you're meeting someone on the mountain. *Tel. 800/598–2005. Open late Nov.–mid-Apr., 8:30–3:30.*

Steamboat Ski Area. Twenty lifts, including two high-speed quads and a gondola, access 102 trails (2,500 acres), roughly half of them intermediate, with a 3,600-foot vertical drop. *Tel. 303/879–6111. Open late Nov.–mid-Apr., 9–4.*

Tiehack. This is Aspen's "learning" area, and it offers plenty of wide, gently rolling slopes for beginners and intermediates, over 410 acres with 45 trails and a vertical of 2,030 feet. *Just off Hwy. 82, tel. 303/925–9000. Open mid-Dec.–early Apr., 9–4.*

Vail. Vail has an embarrassment of riches: 20 lifts, including a gondola and seven high-speed quads, with an uphill capacity of 39,920 per hour (and they need it—20,000 is the average skier day!), a vertical of 3,200 feet, nearly 4,000 acres of skiing on 121 runs, divided fairly evenly (32% beginner, 36% intermediate, 32% advanced/expert). *Tel. 303/949–5750. Open late Nov.–mid-Apr., 8:30–3:30.*

Winter Park/Mary Jane. There are 1,300 skiable acres with a vertical of 3,060 feet. The resort's hub is at the base of Winter Park. Twenty chair lifts (including four high-speed quads) and 112 trails connect the three mountains and high alpine bowl. *U.S. 40, 67 mi from Denver, tel. 303/726–5514. Open mid-Nov.–mid-Apr., weekdays 9–4; weekends 8:30–4.*

Heli-Skiing/Snowcat Skiing **Colorado Heli-Ski** (Frisco, tel. 303/668–5600 or 800/HELISKI) arranges tours into the backcountry.

Steamboat Powder Cats (tel. 303/879–5188) runs snowcat tours.

Ski Touring **Aspen Alpine Guides** (tel. 303/925–6618) arranges customized multiday tours along the 10th Mountain Trail System connecting Aspen and Vail and the Alfred A. Braun Hut System connecting Aspen and Crested Butte, as do **Elk Mountain Guides** (Aspen, tel. 303/927–4272) and **Paragon Guides** (Avon, tel. 303/949–4272). You can also contact the **10th Mountain Hut and Trail System** (tel. 303/925–5775) and **Alfred A. Braun Hut System** (tel. 303/925–7345) directly.

Snowboarding Most ski areas permit at least limited snowboarding; many offer special half pipes for performing tricks, in addition to their skiable terrain. Aspen and Keystone do not allow snowboarding.

Snowmobiling The following companies run tours throughout the High Rockies region: **Good Times** (Breckenridge, tel. 303/453–7604, and Frisco, tel. 303/668–0930); **Hahn's Peak Guest Ranch** (Steamboat, tel. 404/879–5878); **High Mountain Snowmobile Tours** (Steamboat, tel. 303/879–9073); **Nova Guides** (Vail/Beaver Creek, tel. 303/949–4232); **Steamboat Lake Outfitters** (tel. 303/879–4404); **Piney River Ranch** (Vail, tel. 303/476–3941); **T Lazy Seven** (Aspen, tel. 303/925–4614); **Tiger Run Tours** (Breckenridge, tel. 303/453–2231); **Trailblazers Snowmobile Tours** (tel. 303/726–8452 or 800/669–0134); **2 Mile Hi Ski-Doo** (Leadville, tel. 719/486–1183 or 800/933–1183).

Water Sports Canoeing, kayaking, windsurfing, and sailing are done on many lakes and reservoirs, most notably Dillon (Dillon Yacht Basin, tel. 303/468–2396, and Frisco Bay Yacht Club, tel. 303/668–3022) in Summit County.

Dining

Colorado is a melting pot of cuisines, and nowhere is that diversity and artistry better reflected than at the state's top resorts. Talented young American and European chefs are attracted to resort restaurants because of the diverse clientele and demand for variety on the menus. You can find super sushi in Aspen, terrific tajine in Vail, blissful blinis in Steamboat. All you have to do is follow your nose.

The downside, however, is that the price for this expertise can be stratospheric. As an indicator, the McDonald's in Aspen and Vail are, respectively, the third and fourth most expensive in the world (Hong Kong and Moscow beat them out). A fun, relatively new trend being offered at several resorts, such as Keystone and Copper Mountain, is a "dine around progressive dinner," which encourages guests to take in a different course at several restaurants. For rates *see* Resorts and Cities price chart in Chapter 1, Essential Information.

Highly recommended restaurants are indicated by a star ★.

Aspen/Snowmass   **Piñons.** The food is sublime, the muted ranch decor—with a leather bar and enormous brass bowls brimming with tortillas—exquisite. Unfortunately, the waitstaff seems oh-so-above-it-all most of the time; maybe they think the attitude is what you're paying for. Still, the cuisine is exotic: Try pheasant quesadillas or lobster strudel (complemented by morels and chanterelles in phyllo) for an appetizer; then segue into elk tournedos sautéed in ginger and pink peppercorn sauce or roasted Colorado striped bass in potato crust swimming on a bed of red onion sauce. *105 S. Mill St., 2nd fl., tel. 303/920–2021. Reservations advised. Dress: neat but casual. AE, MC, V. Closed for lunch. Very Expensive.*

★ **Renaissance.** The decor of this stunner, which is among the Rockies' finest eateries, is a coolly seductive, abstract rendition of a sultan's tent. Owner/chef Charles Dale apprenticed as chef saucier to his mentor, Daniel Boulud, at New York's trendiest mineral watering hole, Le Cirque, before opening Renaissance in 1990. He dubs his cuisine "the alchemy of food," and he probably could transform leftovers into culinary gold, thanks to his magical artistry in blending tastes and textures. Opt for his *menu degustation*—six courses matched with the appropriate glass of wine. The menu changes seasonally, as well as the style of preparation for many signature dishes. Among his standouts are *ravioli à la Monegasque* (ravioli with pistachio-nut pesto), freshwater striped bass with fennel-tomato marmalade, and a roast rack of Australian lamb perfectly accompanied by asparagus, morels, and mint salsa. *304 E. Hopkins St., Aspen, tel. 303/925–1402. Reservations advised. Dress: neat but casual. AE, D, MC, V. Closed for lunch. Very Expensive.*

★ **Syzygy.** Another stunner with smart decor, this posh establishment is painted peach and accented by black lacquer chairs and translucent water walls. "Syzygy" means the alignment of three or more heavenly bodies in the solar system, and the name was chosen to reflect personable owner Walt Harris's attempt to provide a harmony of expressive cuisine, fine service, and elegant atmosphere. He succeeds, thanks to a sterling, unusually helpful waitstaff and the assured, sublimely seasoned creations of chef Alexander Kim. Kim is clearly impatient with the inevitable meat-and-potatoes bent of the ski crowd, thus assuring that adventurous palates won't be disappointed. His food is crisply flavored and sensuously textured, floating from French to Oriental to southwestern influences without skipping a beat. Standouts include the pheasant spring roll and ahi tartare to start, followed by such main courses as rack of lamb with juniper glaze over polenta and sweet potato puree, or gulf prawns barbecued with achiote and jicama. The patient and knowledgeable will find a few good buys on the extensive wine list. *520 E. Hyman Ave., Aspen, tel. 303/925-3700. Reservations advised. Dress: neat but casual. AE, MC, V. Closed for lunch. Very Expensive.*

★ **Krabloonik.** A dogsled whisks you from Snowmass Village to this cozy rustic-elegant cabin (or you can ski there for lunch), where you'll dine sumptuously on some of the best game in Colorado, perhaps elk loin with marsala and sun-dried cherry glaze; pheasant breast with Gorgonzola; or wild boar medallions sautéed in apple cider. The Western decor features ski memorabilia and throw rugs. *4250 Divide Rd., Snowmass, tel. 303/923-3953. Reservations required. Dress: neat but casual. AE, MC, V. Expensive-Very Expensive.*

Pine Creek Cookhouse. You cross-country ski or board a horse-drawn sleigh to this homey log cabin—Krabloonik's main competition—where the emphasis is less on game and more on Continental favorites with an Oriental or southwestern twist. *11399 Castle Creek, Aspen, tel. 303/925-1044. Reservations required for dinner. Dress: casual. MC, V. Expensive-Very Expensive.*

Kenichi. For some reason, Aspen doesn't boast many good Oriental restaurants, with the exception of a Thai and two Japanese spots. Kenichi was started by two "defectors" from one of the Japanese favorites. It gets the nod as much for its elegant spacious setting as for the delectable bamboo salmon and Japanese rack of lamb. *533 E. Hopkins St., Aspen, tel. 303/920-2212. Reservations advised. Dress: casual. AE, MC, V. Expensive.*

Anguilla. The decor is a bit more Santa Fe than St. Bart's, but the light nouvelle American fare, tinged with Creole and Jamaican influences, satisfies on all counts. Don't miss the spicy whole red snapper, Calypso chicken, and mango-berry pie. *205 S. Mill St., Aspen, tel. 303/920-1527. Reservations accepted. Dress: casual. AE, MC, V. Closed for lunch. Moderate-Expensive.*

★ **Farfalla.** The food is quite good and the scene spectacular at this northern Italian winner. This slick, sleek L.A.-style eatery, well lit and adorned with fine artworks, was all the rage in 1993; go off peak—at lunch when it's deserted. Specialties include tortellini with asparagus and ham in walnut pesto, and deboned quail in vegetable sauce on a bed of polenta and beans. *415 E. Main St., Snowmass, tel. 303/925-8222. Reservations only accepted for parties of 6 or more (lines form early). Dress: casual. AE, D, MC, V. Moderate-Expensive.*

Il Poggio. This spirited trattoria suits all moods, with a light lively café and a quieter, more romantic back room. Chef Chris Blachly is a whiz at the wood-burning oven, turning out delicious grilled items such as rosemary, garlic, and cambozola pizzette; free-range chicken; and duck breast with polenta in honey balsamic sauce. *Elbert La., Snowmass, tel. 303/923-4292. Reservations advised (for back room). Dress: casual. MC, V. Closed for lunch. Moderate.*

★ **Lauretta's Mexican Kitchen.** Little more than a coffee shop, Lauretta's is jazzed up with colorful artworks, brick walls, and a fireplace. Her food includes magical *posole* and *pollo en mole*, and attracts the country's leading southwestern chefs, such as Bobby Flax and Brendan Walsh, when they're in town.

Lauretta's is open for breakfast, too. *333 E. Durant Ave., in the Moutain Chalet, tel. 303/920–4525. Reservations accepted. Dress: casual. MC, V. Inexpensive–Moderate.*

Little Annie's Eating House. Everything at this charming place is ultrasimple, from the wood paneling and red-and-white-checked tablecloths to the fresh fish, BBQ ribs and chicken, and Colorado lamb. Annie's is a big favorite with locals who like the relaxed atmosphere, dependable food, and reasonable prices. *517 E. Hyman Ave., Aspen, tel. 303/925–1098. Reservations accepted. Dress: casual. MC, V. Inexpensive–Moderate.*

The Flying Dog Brew Pub and Grille. This local hangout, with exposed brick walls and wood beams, has a pleasant ambience. The solid pub grub is a bonus, but mostly customers howl for the wonderful home-brewed beers. Try the sweet and smooth Old Yeller, the gold medal–winning Doggie-Style amber, or the malty Rin Tin Tin. *424 E. Cooper St. (downstairs), Aspen, tel. 303/925–7464. Reservations accepted. Dress: casual. MC, V. Inexpensive.*

The Main Street Bakery. This light, airy place has been a favorite local standby for ages. The fresh-baked pastries and powerful cappuccinos are the draw, of course, but don't discount the scrumptious soups, sandwiches, and pastas available during lunch. *201 E. Main St., tel. 303/925–6446. No reservations. Dress: casual. MC, V. Open Mon.–Sat. 7 AM–9 PM and Sun. 7 AM–4 PM. Inexpensive.*

The Popcorn Wagon. Only in Aspen would this concession be possible. The wagon is a classic: an original 1913 Cretor's Special Model D. Popcorn only whets the appetite, though. Follow it with surprisingly good crepes, plump juicy hot dogs, or gourmet sandwiches. Best of all, it's open every day from before lunch through to the wee hours of the morning. The lack of tables is a minor inconvenience. *305 S. Mill Ave., Aspen, tel. 303/925–2718. No reservations. Dress: casual. No credit cards. Inexpensive.*

Glenwood Springs   **Florinda's.** The russet-and-salmon-pink walls of this handsome space are graced by changing exhibits of local artists. Although most items on the menu are Neapolitan—all garlic and attitude—the chef has a deft hand with more creative fare such as veal chops delicately sautéed with shiitake mushrooms in marsala, garlic, sun-dried tomatoes, and topped with Romano cheese. *721 Grand St., tel. 303/945–1245. Reservations accepted. Dress: casual. AE, MC, V. Closed for lunch and Sun. Inexpensive–Moderate.*

★ **The Bayou.** "Food so good you'll slap yo' mama," trumpets the menu at this casual eatery, whose most distinctive attribute is its frog awning (two bulbous eyes beckon you in). Choose from "pre-stuff, wabbit stuff, udder stuff," such as lip-smacking gumbo that looks like mud (and is supposed to), étouffée, and blackened fish as well as lethal Cajun martinis and jalapeño beers. On summer weekends live music is played on the patio. *52103 Hwy. 6 at Hwy. 24, tel. 303/945–1047. Reservations accepted. Dress: casual. AE, MC, V. Inexpensive.*

The Loft. The decor here is soothingly southwestern, with rough-hewn columns and lintels contrasting pleasingly with pastel linens, hanging plants, stained glass, Native American artworks, and elegant banquettes. The Mexican food is better and cheaper than the southwestern specialties. Black-bean burritos are especially tasty and tangy. *720 Grand St., tel. 303/*

945–6808. *Reservations accepted. Dress: casual. AE, MC, V. Inexpensive.*

Idaho Springs **Buffalo Bar.** No surprise as to the specialty here: steaks, burgers, fajitas, chili, Philly steak sandwiches—all made with choice buffalo. It's all part of the Western theme, with walls jam-packed with frontier artifacts and memorabilia, and the ornate bar that dates from 1886. There's often great live music that lures people from as far as Summit County. *1617 Miner St., tel. 303/5467–2729. No reservations. Dress: casual. AE, MC, V. Inexpensive.*

Steamboat Springs **L'Apogee.** This expert French restaurant is Steamboat's most intimate, with rose-colored walls, flickering candlelight, and hanging plants. The classic food is lovely, especially the Oysters Hercules, accentuated by a delicate mustard sauce and salmon caviar, or the house rack of lamb. Still, the menu takes a backseat to the admirable wine list. Oenophile alert: owner Jamie Jenny is a collector whose magnificent wine cellar—cited annually by the *Wine Spectator* as one of America's best—contains more than 750 labels (10,000 bottles); cellar master Doug Enochs is knowledgeable and enthusiastic. *911 Lincoln Ave., tel. 303/879–1919. Reservations advised. Dress: casual. AE, MC, V. Expensive.*

★ **Gorky Park.** This opulent restaurant is done up in burgundy, salmon, and mauve with stone walls, stained glass, and a painted tin roof. Marvelous haute czarist cuisine, such as wondrously light, flaky piroshki and blini with caviar, are served here, as well as a knockout list of almost 30 homemade vodkas, steeped for weeks in everything from thyme to vanilla. The main attraction, however, is owner Joey Kay, a lovable blond Brit. "It's not a gourmet experience, darling," she confides candidly in a quiet moment to the strains of a balalaika, "but it gives you the chance to let your hair down in an atmosphere that's exhilarating but not too rowdy." Then she sits in a client's lap, exclaiming, "I'm too old to be a boy toy." If Joey herself doesn't have time to tell you her life story, you can buy or browse through the hilarious *Behind the Rose-Coloured Curtain,* a book about her life. *57½ 8th St., tel. 303/879–9939. Reservations advised. Dress: neat but casual. AE, D, DC, MC, V. Closed for lunch. Moderate–Expensive.*

Mattie Silk's. Named after a notorious turn-of-the-century madam, this plush split-level charmer, all velour and lace, looks like a prim wife had loosened her corset and redecorated in an effort to win back her man. Chef Dee Conder's sauces, with fresh pungent herbs and very little butter, are assertive and zippy. Try the tender lemon-pepper veal, pounded thin, breaded, then sautéed in a fragrant lemon-cognac sauce. *Ski Time Square, Steamboat Mountain Village, tel. 303/879–2441. Reservations advised. Dress: casual. AE, MC, V. Closed for lunch. Moderate–Expensive.*

Yama Chan's. Most people think you can't get good sushi in Colorado: wrong. Somehow, the fish tastes fresher in the crisp mountain air at this simple, superlative Japanese restaurant. The rest of the menu is equally well presented and prepared. *Old Town Square, tel. 303/879–8862. Open Tues.–Fri. for lunch, Tues.–Sun. for dinner. Reservations advised. AE, MC, V. Closed weekend lunch and Mon. Moderate.*

★ **Harwig's Grill.** This popular eatery is just next door to L'Apogee and run by the same team. You can order from the neighboring wine list, and the bar offers 40 vintages by the glass, including many lesser-known labels. The menu here reflects owner Jamie Jenny's love of travel, with confidently prepared specialties from around the world: Colorado smoked trout to raclette, tandoori chicken to jambalaya, jerk chicken to *shu mei dim sum*. The desserts are predictably sinful. *911 Lincoln Ave., tel. 303/879-1980. Reservations accepted. Dress: casual. AE, MC, V. Closed for lunch. Inexpensive–Moderate.*

★ **La Montana.** This Mexican/southwestern establishment is probably Steamboat's most popular restaurant. The kitchen is wonderfully creative, incorporating indigenous specialties into the traditional menu. Among the standouts are red chili pasta in a shrimp, garlic, and cilantro sauce; mesquite-grilled braided sausage, interwoven strands of elk, lamb, and chorizo sausage; enchiladas layered with Monterey Jack and goat cheese, roasted peppers, and onions; and elk loin crusted with pecan nuts and bourbon cream sauce. *Après Ski Way and Village Dr., tel. 303/879-5800. Reservations advised. Dress: casual. D, MC, V. Closed for lunch. Inexpensive–Moderate.*

Riggio's. This unpretentious Italian restaurant has two sections: a pubby lounge with jazz piano nightly and a sleek contemporary dining room. Wherever you sit, you'll receive well-prepared standards such as chicken cacciatore, saltimbocca, and fettuccine Alfredo. *709 Lincoln Ave., tel. 303/879-9010. Reservations advised. Dress: casual. D, MC, V. Closed for lunch. Inexpensive–Moderate.*

Steamboat Smokehouse. The loud, raucous scene, brick and wood decor, and occasional live music might fool you into thinking this joint is just a bar. Once you try the phenomenal barbecue or hickory-smoked brisket and turkey, however, you'll realize this is a place where they really know their beans about home cooking. *912 Lincoln Ave., tel. 303/879-5570. Reservations accepted. Dress: casual. MC, V. Inexpensive.*

Summit County

★ **Alpenglow Stube.** Without a doubt this is the finest on-mountain dining establishment in Colorado. The decor is warmly elegant, with exposed wood beams, stone fireplace, antler chandeliers, and floral upholstery. Dinner is a six-course extravaganza, starting with the signature pinecone paté, followed perhaps by scrumptious venison carpaccio or scampi in Pommery cream, fresh tangy wild green salad, and such Stube specialties as smoked saddle of rabbit in tricolored peppercorn sauce or rack of boar in Poire William sauce. Lunch is equally delectable, with particularly fine pasta specials. The gondola rides at night that you must take to get here are alone worth the cost of the meal. *North Peak, The Outpost, Keystone, tel. 303/468-4130. Reservations advised. Dress: neat but casual. AE, MC, V. Closed for lunch in summer. Very Expensive.*

★ **Keystone Ranch.** This glorious 1880s log cabin was once part of an actual working cattle ranch, and memorabilia is strewn throughout the restaurant, nicely blending with stylish throw rugs and Western craft work. The gorgeous and massive stone fireplace is a cozy backdrop for sipping an aperitif or after-dinner coffee. Chef Mark Martin's rotating, seasonal six-course menu emphasizes farm-raised game and fresh fish. He has an especially deft hand with lamb: You're in luck if the menu includes mignons of lamb *decatur* (loin encased within a herb, pear, and cranberry glaze in truffle sauce); rack of lamb encrusted with hazelnuts and served with a red onion and apple marmalade; and Gorgonzola flan. *Keystone Ranch Golf Course,* *tel. 303/468–4130. Reservations advised. Dress: neat but casual. AE, MC, V. Closed for lunch in winter. Very Expensive.*

Café Alpine. This bright, cheerful place offers terrific soups, salads, and sandwiches at lunch, and more substantial Continental fare with Oriental flair at dinner. At the tapas bar (served after 4) you can sample succulent offerings from around the world, including eggplant crepes, marinated quail breast, blackened tuna sashimi, and lamb chops Szechuan. The moderately priced wine list, favoring Australian and Chilean selections, is particularly well thought out. *106 E. Adams Ave., Breckenridge, tel. 303/453–8218. Reservations not necessary. Dress: casual. AE, D, MC, V. Moderate.*

Gassy Thompson's. Imagine a sports bar crossbred with a hunting lodge, and you'll get an idea of the ambience and decor of this popular mountain-base hangout. The Continental cuisine is solid if not inspired: Grilled items are best, including honey-mustard chicken breast and pork medallions. *Mountain House, Keystone, tel. 303/468–4130. No reservations. Dress: casual. AE, MC, V. Closed summer. Moderate.*

Pesce Fresco. The fish is as fresh as advertised at this engaging spot, where a jazz pianist plays most nights during ski season. The decor is upscale coffee shop, but the menu is creative, with salmon-dill linguine, wasabi tuna, and mixed seafood grill the winners. Breakfast is served here, as well as lunch and dinner. *Mountain Plaza Bldg., Copper Mountain, tel. 303/968–2882, ext. 6505. Reservations advised. Dress: casual. AE, DC, MC, V. Moderate.*

Rackets. This split-level, high-tech restaurant is Copper's best and serves predominantly southwestern cuisine. Start with the calamari breaded with blue cornmeal; smoked duck and piñon sausage over capellini; or southwestern ravioli (oozing Monterey Jack and green chili); then follow with tender baked cilantro-lime scallops or Rocky Mountain trout in bourbon-pecan sauce. Rotisserie items are also good bets. *Racquet & Athletic Club, Copper Mountain, tel. 303/968–2882, ext. 6386. Reservations advised. Dress: casual. AE, MC, V. Closed for lunch in winter. Moderate.*

The Blue Moose. Locals flock here for the hearty breakfasts, with menu highlights such as the Mexican Moose—a tortilla crammed with pork, green chili, cheese, sour cream, and scallions. Lunch and dinner are equally satisfying; chicken vermouth and drunken chicken (marinated with tequila, lime, tomato, green chili, and jalapeño) are particularly noteworthy, as is Mother's fettuccine al pesto. *540 S. Main St., Breckenridge, tel. 303/453–4859. Reservations accepted. Dress: casual. No credit cards. Inexpensive.*

Frisco Bar & Grill. You'll find no frills here, just juicy burgers (nine varieties), hellacious nachos, buffalo wings, and a lively crowd in this classic pub with neon signs on the walls and sawdust on the floors. *720 Granite Boardwalk Blvd., Frisco, tel. 303/668–5051. No reservations. Dress: casual. AE, MC, V. Inexpensive.*

The Vail Valley **Beano's Cabin.** Perhaps the ultimate wilderness dining experience is traveling in a snowcat-drawn sleigh to the restaurant of this tasteful, assured Beaver Creek hunting lodge. Once there, you'll choose among seven seasonally rotating entrées and six courses. Ever since chef Chad Scothorn left to start his own restaurant, Beano's has seen a succession of competent chefs, but they lacked their predecessor's imagination and panache.

His tradition of witty pizzas has remained a constant, however, and the convivial setting is unmatched. *Larkspur Bowl, Beaver Creek, tel. 303/949–9090. Reservations required. Dress: casual. AE, MC, V. Very Expensive.*

★ **Chadwick's.** Even the people at Vail Associates call this ultraposh eatery the height of decadence, probably because of the marble columns and statuary and custom-made Italian linens that adorn the tables. Owner/chef Chad Scothorn (who ran Beano's Cabin for several years) has an earthy playful touch, artfully blending country-French, Tuscan, and Western influences. His signature pizzas change daily and make the perfect starter before such inventive preparations as roasted veal tenderloin with shiitake ragout and lemon grass–infused veal sauce; smoked duck breast with three-grain risotto and pears; and grilled cured salmon on a bed of linguine, spinach, chives, and portobello mushrooms. Pastry chef Sheila Geere excels at such standards as crème brûlée. *17 Chateau La., Beaver Creek, tel. 303/845–8808. Reservations advised. Dress: neat but casual. AE, MC, V. Closed for lunch. Expensive–Very Expensive.*

L'Ostello. The severe minimalist decor contrasts effectively with the richly textured menu at this superlative Italian eatery. Innovative variations on Italian regional favorites come out of the kitchen, where the chef creates unusual specialties such as penne-and-goat-cheese terrine; porcini linguine with roasted monkfish and tomato cream sauce; Maryland crabmeat ravioli in ginger-carrot broth; salmon roulade with sorrel and Star anise sauce. The lodge offers nicely appointed very reasonable rooms as well. *705 W. Lionshead Cir., Vail, tel. 303/476–2050. Reservations advised. Dress: casual. Closed for lunch. AE. Expensive–Very Expensive.*

Alpen Rose Tea Room. Claus Fricke's establishment started as a tearoom and bakery in 1976. He's still in the kitchen every evening, cooking feverishly until midnight; and he can still bake truly magnificent pastries. This is rich, luscious, love-handle cuisine with tons of calories and drowned in butter: so good and so bad for you. The schnitzels, steak tartare, and fresh seafood specials are all home cooking at its best. The pink, frilly decor is similarly sugar coated. Except on Tuesdays, Alpen Rose Tea Room is open for breakfast and lunch; it's open every evening for dinner. *100 E. Meadows Ave., Vail, tel. 303/476–3194. Reservations advised. Dress: casual. AE, MV, V. Closed Tues. for breakfast and lunch. Expensive.*

Left Bank. This cozy bistro, with homey touches such as family antiques and paintings, has been a Vail fixture for nearly a quarter century. Liz and Luc Meyer are the gracious hosts who consistently pamper their clientele with fresh adroitly prepared bistro fare. How they can make the airy soufflés so fluffy at this altitude is nothing short of miraculous. *Sitzmark Lodge (not affiliated), 183 Gore Creek Dr., Vail, tel. 303/476–3696. Reservations advised. Dress: neat but casual. No credit cards. Closed Wed. and for lunch. Expensive.*

Michael's American Bistro. This very sleek, stylish boîte overlooks the atrium of the Gateway Mall, but the space is dramatic: fancifully carved wood columns, lacquered black tables, and striking—almost disturbing—photographs and art on the walls. The hip atmosphere is further accentuated by the cool jazz echoing through the room and the slinky waitstaff garbed entirely in black. They're extremely attentive and will often let you know what the chef thinks is particularly good that day. You could make a meal of the openers alone: grilled smoked quail with orange chutney; gourmet spicy shrimp pizza with roasted-onion sauce; vegetable terrine with three pestos. If you can't decide, order the tapas plate, an assortment of three appetizers that changes daily. All courses are superbly presented, with festive colors springing from the plate—giving equal weight to the palette and palate. The fine, extensive wine list (predominantly American, natch!) has several bargains under $25. Michael's is also Vail's latest power spot for breakfast. *12 S. Frontage Rd., Vail, tel. 303/476-5353. Reservations advised. Dress: neat but casual. AE, D, DC, MC, V. Expensive.*

★ **Mirabelle.** From the crackling fireplace to the burgundy and pink linens, and fine details, this restaurant has achieved the ultimate in romantic, French-country decor. Belgian Daniel Joly is the superb chef who offers the closest to classic French haute cuisine as you'll get in Colorado. His preparations combine the perfect blend of colors, flavors, and textures. Try the escargots baked in puff pastry with Stilton in Madeira sauce, or shrimp and lobster mousseline accompanied by sautéed shiitakes and chives to start; follow with shrimp nestled in spinach with tapioca caviar and bell-pepper coulis, or free-range chicken breast bursting with brie and hazelnuts, in orange hollandaise sauce. Fairly priced wine recommendations are listed beneath each entrée. Desserts are sheer heaven, with caramelized cinnamon pear tarte kissed with passion-fruit sorbet and vanilla ice cream, the crowning achievement. *Entrance to Beaver Creek, tel. 303/949-7728. Reservations advised. Dress: casual. No credit cards. Closed Mon. and for lunch. Expensive.*

★ **Sweet Basil.** Don't be fooled by the unassuming teal-and-buff, upscale, coffee-shop decor enlivened by towering floral arrangements and abstract artworks. Chef David Walford, who apprenticed at northern California's Auberge du Soleil and Masa's, is a master of the New American cuisine, borrowing merrily from several different traditions. He is equally adept at turning out a Provençale-tinged yellowfin tuna with olives, tomatoes, and saffron sauce; a salmon paillard with bok choy, sesame potato puree, and tomato-cilantro sauce; roast chicken in Moroccan lemon-basil sauce; and pork chops with spinach, apple-smoked bacon, shiitake mushrooms, and maple-mustard vinaigrette. The menu changes seasonally, and the daily specials are invariably brilliant. *193 E. Gore Creek Dr., Vail, tel. 303/476-0125. Reservations advised. Dress: neat but casual. AE, MC, V. Expensive.*

TraMonti. This breezy trattoria in the Charter at Beaver Creek showcases the vibrant progressive cuisine of chef Cynde Arnold. She loves experimenting with bold juxtapositions of flavors and is most successful with her gourmet pizzas, such as shrimp, goat cheese, braised scallions, and black olives, and pastas (penne with wild boar and veal bolognese; ravioli stuffed with lobster, mascarpone, sun-dried tomatoes, and basil in saffron cream). *The Charter at Beaver Creek, tel. 303/ 949-5552. Reservations advised. Dress: casual. AE, MC, V. Closed for lunch. Moderate–Expensive.*

Blu's. This fun, casual, constantly hopping place is a Vail institution, with an eclectic affordable menu. The food is always fresh and zippy, from smoked duck, onion, and sage pizza to kick-ass California chicken relleño. Blu's is open for all three meals. *193 E. Gore Creek, Vail, tel. 303/476-3113. No reservations. Dress: casual. D, MC, V. Moderate.*

Covered Bridge Café. No item on this menu is above $10—an almost unheard-of deal for Beaver Creek, which explains how this cavernous space gets packed nightly with customers. Sports memorabilia decorate the interior, which is filled with mementos donated by famous athletes such as Jack Nicklaus and Bobby Rahal (and their groupies—such as former president Gerald Ford). The all-American truck-stop dishes are first-rate. *50 Promenade Dr., Beaver Creek, tel. 303/845-5752. No reservations. Dress: casual. AE, MC, V. Inexpensive.*

Minturn Country Club. This rustic, homey joint is a favorite hangout of racers during World Cup ski competitions, when they literally hang from the rafters. Steaks, prime rib, fish, and chicken preparations vary wildly, but you have only yourself to blame if you wanted it medium rare and it comes out well done: you cook everything yourself. *Main St., Minturn, tel. 303/827-4114. No reservations. Dress: casual. MC, V. Closed for lunch. Inexpensive.*

Winter Park **Gasthaus Eichler.** This is Winter Park's most romantic dining
★ spot, with quaint Bavarian decor, antler chandeliers, and stained-glass windows, all glowing in the candlelight as Strauss rings softly in the background. Featured are veal and grilled items, in addition to scrumptious German classics such as sauerbraten, *kassler rippchen*, and *rindsrollaten*. The *rahmschnitzel*—tender veal dancing in a delicate, wild mushroom and brandy cream sauce—is extraordinary, as are the feathery light potato pancakes. The Eichler also offers 15 inexpensive cozy Old World rooms, with down comforters, lace curtains, armoires, cable TV, and Jacuzzi tubs. *Winter Park Dr., tel. 303/726-5133 or 800/543-3899. Reservations advised. Dress: neat but casual. AE, D, MC, V. Closed for lunch. Moderate–Expensive.*

The Peck House. This snug, red-and-white, barnlike inn, Colorado's oldest continually operating hostelry, is actually located in the quirky town of Empire, on U.S. 40 a few miles north of I-70. It began in 1860 as a boarding house built for wealthy mine investors, and the dining room is crammed with period antiques and evocative tinted lithographs, including the original etched-glass, gaslight lampshades from the state capitol. Game is the house specialty: expertly prepared quail and venison (try it in the cabernet sauce) are among the standouts. The Peck House also offers 11 charming inexpensively priced rooms (not all with private bath), awash in Victorian splendor. A Sunday brunch is offered. *Just off U.S. 40, Empire, tel. 303/ 569-9870. Reservations advised. Dress: neat but casual. AE, MC, V. Moderate–Expensive.*

Deno's Mountain Bistro. In many ways Deno's is an anomaly; it seems like a casual drinking establishment (there's a sizable selection of beers from around the world) and is by far the liveliest spot in town, yet it also boasts an impressive international wine list that's comprehensive and fairly priced. The wine is as much a labor of love as a folly in this unpretentious area, thanks to Deno himself, a charismatic, energetic powerhouse. The menu is as eclectic as the wine list, from spicy Szechuan beef eggroll to Cajun BBQ shrimp to veal marsala, all well prepared and served by a friendly staff, most of whom have been working here for years. *Winter Park Dr., tel. 303/726-5332. Reservations not necessary. Dress: casual. AE, D, MC, V. Moderate.*

The Last Waltz. This very homey place is festooned with hanging plants and graced with a crackling fireplace and tinkling piano. The huge menu jumps from bagels and lox to burritos without missing a beat. The south-of-the-border dishes are best: zesty *calientitas* (fried jalapeños filled with cream cheese served with a devilish salsa) and black-bean tostadas are especially noteworthy. Breakfast and brunch will power you for those mogul runs. *Winter Park Dr., tel. 303/726–4877. No reservations. Dress: casual. AE, DC, MC, V. Inexpensive–Moderate.*

Lodging

Lodging options range from humble motor inns in towns outside the main resorts to Beaver Creek's $400 (per person per night) Trapper's Cabin, a luxury rustic retreat that comes replete with private chef and activity director. Winter is high season in Aspen, Vail, Summit County, Winter Park, and Steamboat. Prices often drop as much as 50% in summer, despite the wealth of activities, events, and festivals. As a spa resort, Glenwood is the lone exception, with higher rates in the summer months.

Winter Park offers affordability, comfort, even luxury—but don't expect the "poshness" that the other top resorts offer. In this area, inns customarily serve both breakfast and dinner family style, enabling guests to socialize easily. Most of the lodging is more than a mile from the mountain, but a free shuttle service runs throughout the area.

Unless otherwise noted, all accommodations include standard amenities such as phones, cable TV, and full baths in the rooms. For rates *see* the Resorts and Cities price chart in Chapter 1, Essential Information.

Highly recommended lodgings are indicated by a star ★.

Hotels
Aspen/Snowmass

Hotel Jerome. One of the state's truly grand hotels since 1889, this is a treasure trove of Victoriana and froufrou. The sumptuous public rooms alone sport five kinds of wallpaper, antler sconces, and more than $60,000 worth of rose damask curtains. Each luxurious room and suite is individually decorated in soft pastel hues with period furnishings such as carved cherrywood armoires, with minibar and cable TV; the huge bathrooms include oversize marble baths, many with Jacuzzis and separate showers. *330 E. Main St., Aspen 81611, tel. 303/920–1000 or 800/331–7213; fax 303/925–2784. 44 rooms, 50 suites. Facilities: 2 restaurants, bar, heated pool, 2 Jacuzzis, complimentary airport and ski-slope transfers. AE, MC, V. Very Expensive.*

★ **Little Nell.** Built to be the last word in luxury, the Nell is the only truly ski-in/ski-out property in Aspen, and that alone is worth something. The handsomely appointed rooms (all in mountain colors and abounding with wildlife prints) have every conceivable amenity and comfort, including fireplace, patio, marble bath, safe, cable TV, down comforters, and minibar. Equally superior is the waitstaff who anticipate your every need. The restaurant, under new executive chef George Mahaffey, is one of the best in town. *675 E. Durant Ave., Aspen 81611, tel. 303/920–6200 or 800/525–6200; fax 303/920–4670. 86 rooms, 11 suites. Facilities: 2 restaurants, deli, bar, ski rental, outdoor heated pool and Jacuzzi, bookstore, health club, complimentary Snowmass shuttle. AE, DC, MC, V. Very Expensive.*

★ **Ritz-Carlton.** The redbrick building seems more appropriate to Harvard's hallowed halls than Aspen, and although it's a tad less stately than other Ritz-Carltons, this one is still imposing, even by Aspen's exacting standards. In the august reception area, for example, are elegant burnished hickory walls, crystal chandeliers, Colorado green-granite floors, antique grandfather clocks and secretaries, and a $5 million art collection highlighted by commissioned sculptures and faux-18th-century landscapes and portraiture. The mostly peach-colored rooms are more casual than the lobby, with cherrywood furnishings, luxuriant marble bath, and three phones, among other amenities. The property is ski-out, though not quite ski-in. *315 E. Dean St., Aspen 81611, tel. 303/920–3000 or 800/241–3333; fax 303/920–8724. 231 rooms, 26 suites. Facilities: 2 restaurants; 2 bars; meeting facilities; outdoor heated pool; indoor and outdoor Jacuzzis; sauna/steam room; fitness room; beauty salon; gift shop; boutique; complimentary airport transfers, morning paper, and shoe shines. AE, DC, MC, V. Very Expensive.*

★ **Snowmass Club.** If you like Ralph Lauren's Polo style, you'll love this elegant property with English hunting-lodge decor: rose-and-jade color schemes, with handsome rustic armoires and writing desks, some with rocking chairs and four-poster beds. The club is equally popular with sportspeople: The Ed Seay–designed 18-hole championship golf course doubles as a fine cross-country ski center in winter, and there's a fully equipped health and racquet club on the premises. For families this resort is well-suited: children stay free in their parents' rooms, and there's a fine day-care center. Four Corners Grill is the standout restaurant, featuring executive-chef Scott Phillip's sterling "Contemporary Ranchlands" cuisine. *Box G-2, Snowmass Village 81615, tel. 303/923–5600 or 800/525–0710; fax 303/923–6944. 76 rooms, 60 villas. Facilities: restaurant, lounge, 18-hole championship golf course, 11 tennis courts, racquetball and squash, sauna/steam room, 2 outdoor heated pools, cross-country touring center, hot tubs, fitness room, spa, complimentary airport and ski-area shuttle, ski rental, ski concierge. AE, DC, MC, V. Expensive–Very Expensive.*

★ **Aspen Club Lodge.** This refined, intimate ski-in hotel has a delightfully European flavor and was extensively remodeled in 1991. The rooms are tastefully outfitted in burgundy and royal blue or forest green, with polished pine woodwork and beams, French doors opening onto the balcony, and down comforters. The plush ZG Restaurant affords stunning views of Ajax and marks the return of Gordon Naccaroto and his "high-altitude cuisine" to the Aspen dining scene. The management also runs several top-notch condominiums. *709 E. Durant Ave., Aspen 81611, tel. 303/920–2000 or 800/882–2582; fax 303/920–2020. Facilities: restaurant; lounge; heated outdoor pool and Jacuzzi; ski concierge; ski rental; use of Aspen Club International health club (and complimentary transportation) with weight room, pool, Jacuzzi, sauna/steam room, tennis courts, squash and racquetball courts, complimentary airport shuttle. AE, MC, V. Expensive.*

★ **Hotel Lenado.** This ravishing B&B is Aspen's most romantic property. The smallish but quaint rooms contain either intricately carved applewood or Adirondack ironwood beds (*lenado* is Spanish for "wood," and the motif appears throughout the hotel), antique armoires, even wood-burning stoves, in addition to modern amenities such as cable TV and tile bath. Gracious and graceful, the Lenado is Aspen at its considerable best. *200 S. Aspen St., Aspen 81611, tel. 303/925–6246 or 800/*

321–3457; fax 303/925–3840. 19 rooms. Facilities: lounge, breakfast room, hot tub. AE, DC, MC, V. Expensive.

Sardy House. If the Lenado is full, head down the block to this equally sumptuous property, under the same management. The tiny reception area opens onto an inviting parlor, with bay windows and dripping with chintz and lace. A narrow winding staircase with magnificent oak balustrade leads to the precious rooms, decorated in aubergine, mauve, and rose, with Axeminster carpets from Belfast, cherrywood armoires and beds, wicker furniture, and such welcome touches as Laura Ashley bedclothes and duvets, heated towel racks, and whirlpool tubs. The new wing scrupulously duplicates the authentic Victorian feel of the original house. The Sardy is straight out of a novel, the kind you read curled up by the fire on a frosty night. *128 E. Main St., Aspen 81611, tel. 303/920–2525 or 800/321–3457; fax 303/920–4478. 14 rooms, 6 suites. Facilities: restaurant, pool, hot tub, sauna. AE, DC, MC, V. Expensive.*

Silvertree Hotel. This ski-in/ski-out property is actually built into Snowmass Mountain. It's sprawling, with virtually everything you need on-site. Rooms and suites feature subdued attractive decor, with all the expected amenities of a first-class hotel. Condominium units are also available, with full use of facilities. *Box 5009, Snowmass Village 81615, tel. 303/923–3520 or 800/525–9402; fax 303/923–5192. 262 rooms, 15 suites. 200 condo units. Facilities: 3 restaurants, lounge, shopping arcade, meeting facilities, health club and spa, cabaret, 2 outdoor heated pools and Jacuzzis, shopping arcade, ski rental. AE, D, DC, MC, V. Moderate–Expensive.*

Boomerang Lodge. This comfortable, functional property offers a wide range of accommodations, from standard, somewhat drab hotel rooms to smartly appointed studios and deluxe rooms to three-bedroom apartments. There's even a log cabin. The nicest lodgings are the deluxe units, decorated in earth tones and with a southwestern flair, balcony, enormous marble bath, fireplace, and wet bar. The staff is most hospitable. Continental breakfast is included in the rate. *500 W. Hopkins Ave., Aspen 81611, tel. 303/925–3416 or 800/992–8852; fax 303/925–3314. Facilities: breakfast room, heated outdoor pool and Jacuzzi, sauna. AE, MC, V. Moderate.*

Snowflake Inn. This is another property with wildly divergent accommodations, all quite comfortable and decorated mostly in tartans or bright colors. The rustic lobby with its stone fireplace and wood beams is a convivial gathering place for the complimentary Continental breakfast and afternoon tea. *221 E. Hyman Ave., Aspen 81611, tel. 303/925–3221 or 800/247–2069; fax 303/925–8740. 38 units. Facilities: heated outdoor pool and Jacuzzi, sauna, laundry facilities. AE, MC, V. Moderate.*

Skier's Chalet. This is arguably Aspen's best bargain. The location—100 feet from the ticket office and #1A chairlift—can't be beat. Basic but snug rooms all have cable TV, private bath and phone, and the staff and fellow clientele are unfailingly congenial. A complimetary Continental breakfast is served every morning. *233 Gilbert St., Aspen 81611, tel. 303/920–2037. 20 rooms. Facilities: restaurant, heated outdoor pool. MC, V. Closed late Apr.–late Nov. Inexpensive.*

Breckenridge **Breckenridge Hilton.** This ski-in/ski-out property, the only full-service hotel in Breckenridge, was originally intended as a condo development, but management ran out of financing. This pays dividends in the enormous bedrooms, which feature pleasing contemporary southwestern decor in teal, salmon, mauve, and maroon. A half-million dollars was recently spent on refurbishment; however, one surprising omission is air-conditioning, although it's rarely necessary. Swans, on the property, is one of the town's more highly regarded restaurants. *550 Village Rd., tel. 303/453-4500; fax 303/453-0212. 208 rooms. Facilities: restaurant, lounge, health club, ski rental, indoor pool, 2 indoor Jacuzzis, meeting facilities. AE, D, MC, V. Moderate.*

The Lodge at Breckenridge. This special property has the disadvantage of being outside town, though shuttle service is provided to the town and ski area. The compensation is the breathtaking panoramas of the TenMile Range from nearly every angle; huge strategically placed picture windows allow full vantage. The look is mountain chalet, with a rustic-modern decor. The well-lit, spacious rooms all have cable TV and full bath; minisuites also feature fireplace and kitchenette. The complete spa and health club facility is a bonus. *112 Overlook Dr., tel. 303/453-9300 or 800/736-1607; fax 303/453-0625. 45 units. Facilities: restaurant, spa, health club, indoor pool, 2 indoor Jacuzzis, 2 outdoor Jacuzzis, racquetball court, pro shop. AE, D, MC, V. Moderate.*

River Mountain Lodge. The cozy units in this fine property range from studios to two-bedroom suites. Each is decorated with natural-pine furnishings and soothing earth tones and includes a kitchen, private terrace, cable TV, full bath, and washer-dryer. River Mountain also has a fine location—two blocks from Main Street, and right on the ski-shuttle route. *100 S. Park St., tel. 303/453-4711 or 800/325-2342. 49 units. Facilities: lounge, exercise room, 2 outdoor Jacuzzis. AE, D, MC, V. Moderate.*

Village at Breckenridge. The word "village" puts it mildly, at this sprawling, self-contained resort, spread-eagled over 14 acres and offering several varieties of accommodations from lodge-style rooms to three-bedroom condominiums. The decor runs from southwestern color schemes to gleaming chrome-and-glass units. Studios and efficiencies feature fireplaces and kitchenettes. *Box 8329, Breckenridge 80424, tel. 303/453-2000 or 800/800-7828; fax 303/453-1878. 455 units. Facilities: 9 restaurants, 3 bars, shopping arcade, ski rental, 2 health clubs, sauna, 2 indoor pools, 2 outdoor heated pools, 12 hot tubs, 2 medical clinics, 32,000 sq. ft. of meeting space, rental-car station. AE, D, MC, V. Moderate.*

★ **Williams House.** Innkeepers Fred Kinat and Diane Jaynes spent a year restoring this intimate, cobalt-blue, 1885 miner's cottage, then expanded it with utmost care. From the cozy front parlor, done up in pink and ultramarine, with a crackling, mantel fireplace and floral spreads, to the exquisite dollhouse-like accommodations, the Williams House is a dream bed-and-breakfast. The individually decorated rooms are romantic as can be, with chintz or lace curtains, Laura Ashley and Ralph Lauren comforters and linens, mahogany beds, walnut wardrobes or cherry armoires, old framed magazine covers, hand-blown globe lamps, fresh flowers and sachets, and footed tubs. Best of all are the affable hosts: Avid skiers ("cold cereal on powder days," they warn), they take guests to their secret stashes and on hikes in summer. Diane's muffins, quiches, and *huevos rancheros* (eggs with salsa) are addictive. *303 N. Main*

St., tel. 303/453–2975. 4 rooms. Facilities: none. AE. Inexpensive.

Georgetown **The Hardy House B&B Inn.** This 1877 Victorian has been lovingly restored by owner Sarah Schmidt, whose welcome couldn't be warmer (nor could the potbellied stove that greets you in the parlor). The cozy rooms, all with private bath, are furnished comfortably with antiques and period reproductions, as well as down comforters. *605 Brownell St., Box 0156, Georgetown 80444, tel. 303/569–3388. 4 rooms. Facilities: none. MC, V. Inexpensive.*

Glenwood Springs **Hotel Colorado.** The exterior of this building, on the National Historic Register, is simply exquisite, with graceful sandstone colonnades and Italianate campaniles. The impression of luxury continues in the imposing, yet gracious, marble lobby and public rooms. Unfortunately, the sunny, individually decorated rooms and suites—most with high ceilings, fireplaces, gorgeous period wainscoting, and balconies affording superlative vistas—are a little threadbare and oddly configured. But everyone, whether notable or notorious, from Doc Holliday to Al Capone, stayed here in its halcyon days. *526 Pine St., tel. 303/945–6511 or 800/544–3998; fax 303/045–7030. 96 rooms, 26 suites. Facilities: 2 restaurants, lounge, health club, meeting facilities, beauty salon, sporting goods store. AE, DC, MC, V. Inexpensive.*

★ **Hotel Denver.** Although this hotel was originally built in 1806, its most striking features are the numerous art deco touches throughout. Most rooms open onto a view of the springs or a three-story New Orleans–style atrium bedecked with colorful canopies. The accommodations are ultraneat, trim, and comfortable and are decorated predominantly in maroon and teal. There are plenty of homey touches, such as fresh-baked cookies upon your arrival (the cordial owner also runs the best bakery in town—The Daily Bread). The Daily Bread Too is the excellent hotel restaurant. *402 7th St., tel. 303/945–6565; fax 303/945–2204. 60 rooms. Facilities: restaurant, lounge, fitness room, beauty salon, meeting facilities. AE, D, MC, V. Inexpensive.*

Hot Springs Lodge. This lodge is perfectly located right by the springs, which are used to heat the property. The attractive rooms, decorated in jade, teal, buff, and rose, stress the southwestern motif. Deluxe rooms contain a minifridge and tiny balcony, in addition to standard conveniences, such as cable TV and full bath. *401 N. River Rd., tel. 303/945–6571. 107 rooms. Facilities: restaurant, lounge, discount to springs, Jacuzzi, game room, laundry facilities, health club (at spa). AE, D, DC, MC, V. Inexpensive.*

Ramada Inn. This pleasant, centrally located (two blocks from the springs) property is the best on the strip in terms of comfort and facilities. Fair-size rooms are decorated in '50s earth tones (burnt orange and muddy brown), and most have exposed brick walls. Studios and suites have fireplaces and kitchenettes. *124 W. 6th St., tel. 303/945–2500 or 800/228–2828; fax 303/945–2530. 123 rooms, 9 suites. Facilities: restaurant, lounge, pool, complimentary use of gym across street, meeting facilities. AE, D, DC, MC, V. Inexpensive.*

Sunlight Inn. This charming traditional ski lodge a few hundred feet from the Ski Sunlight lifts brims with European ambience, from the delightful lounge (with a marvelous carved fireplace and wrought-iron chandeliers) and fine German restaurant, to the cozily rustic rooms, all with pine-board walls and rough-hewn armoires. Sunlight is a true get-away-from-it-all place, with no TVs or phones in the rooms. *10252 C.R. 117, tel. 303/ 945–5225. 24 rooms (5 share baths). Facilities: restaurant, bar, Jacuzzi. MC, V. Inexpensive.*

Keystone **Keystone Lodge.** The ugly cinder-block structure gives no hint
★ of the gracious living within. The lodge is a pampering place, and a member of Preferred Hotels. Rooms are on the small side, but beautifully appointed in rich mountain colors, with all the amenities. There are lovely thoughtful touches, like a jar of fresh-baked cookies with your turndown service. *Keystone Resort, Box 38, Keystone 80435, tel. 303/468–4242 or 800/222–0188; fax 303/468–4343. 152 rooms. Facilities: 4 restaurants, lounge, fitness center, indoor pool and Jacuzzi, 2 indoor tennis courts, day-care center, conference center, grocery, shopping arcade, complimentary ski-area shuttle. AE, DC, MC, V. Moderate–Expensive.*

★ **Ski Tip Lodge.** This charming, elegant log cabin is an agreeable hostelry whose rooms have quaint names, such as Edna's Eyrie, and are uniquely decorated with homespun furnishings, including several four-posters, and accessories such as quilts and hand-knit throw rugs. Breakfast and lunch are included in the room rate, and as the kitchen vies for best in Summit County with the Alpenglow Stube and Keystone Ranch, you won't be sorry if you take advantage of the deal. You might start with pheasant, caribou, and buffalo ravioli in roasted-red-pepper sauce, followed with salmon swimming in cilantro-pineapple salsa or baked pheasant breast dusted with crushed pecans, hazel nuts, and sage. Be sure to adjourn to the cozy lounge for the decadent desserts and special coffees. Fortunately, nonguests as well can dine on a limited basis. *Keystone Resort, Box 38, 80435, tel. 303/468–4242 or 800/222–0188; fax 303/468–4343. 24 rooms. Facilities: restaurant, complimentary ski shuttle. AE, DC, MC, V. Moderate.*

Steamboat Springs **Sheraton Steamboat Resort & Conference Center.** This bustling deluxe hotel is Steamboat's only true ski-in/ski-out property. Rooms are Sheraton standard, fair size with muted decor and most comforts. The hotel also handles Sheraton Plaza (not ski-in/ski-out), economy units with kitchens and cable TV, whose guests enjoy full hotel privileges. *Box 774808, 80487 tel. 303/ 879–2220 or 800/848–8878; fax 303/879–7686. 270 rooms, 3 suites (26 units in Sheraton Plaza). Facilities: 2 restaurants, 2 lounges, heated outdoor pool, 2 hot tubs, steam room/sauna, ski rental, gift shop, 25,000 sq. ft. of meeting space, children under 17 stay free. AE, D, DC, MC, V. Expensive.*

Ptarmigan Inn. Convenience and comfort are the keynotes of this appealing property, situated on the slopes. The modest rooms, decorated in pleasing pastels and earth tones, feature cable TV, balcony, and full bath. *Box 773240, 80487 tel. 303/ 879–1730 or 800/538–7519; fax 303/879–6044. 78 rooms. Facilities: restaurant, lounge, ski rental, outdoor hot tub and pool, sauna. AE, MC, V. Moderate.*

Overlook Lodge. This slightly frayed but welcoming hotel, perched between the ski area and downtown, lives up to its name, with smashing sweeping views of the mountains from most rooms. Rooms, decorated in mountain colors, are plain but comfortable and homey, and the staff is especially friendly. *1000 High Point Dr., 80487, tel. 303/879–2900 or 800/752–5666; fax 303/879–7641. 101 rooms, 16 suites. Facilities: restaurant,* *lounge, heated indoor pool and hot tub, sauna, gift shop, ski rental, complimentary shuttle service, complimentary buffet breakfast during ski season. AE, MC, V. Inexpensive–Moderate.*

★ **Sky Valley Lodge.** This homey property is located a few miles from downtown, amid glorious scenery that contributes to the get-away-from-it-all feel of the inn. Warm English country-style rooms are decorated in restful mountain colors and feature touches such as fruits and dried flowers. *31490 E. Hwy. 40, 80477, tel. 303/879–7749 or 800/538–7519; fax 303/879–7749. 24 rooms. Facilities: hot tub, ski shuttle. AE, MC, V. Inexpensive–Moderate.*

The Alpiner. This basic but pleasant Bavarian-style property is conveniently located a block from the hot springs, for those who want to be where the downtown action is (there's a free shuttle to the ski area). Rooms are spacious, but the full bath is a tight squeeze. Guests have full use of the facilities at the Ptarmigan (*see above*). *424 Lincoln Ave., 80487, tel. 303/879–1430 or 800/538–7519; fax 303/879–0054. 32 rooms. Facilities: complimentary ski shuttle, access to all Ptarmigan facilities. AE, MC, V. Inexpensive.*

★ **Harbor Hotel and Condominiums.** This charming, completely refurbished 1930s hotel is smack in the middle of Steamboat's historic district. The inviting brick and wood-paneled lobby sets the tone, further emphasized by the nifty artifacts, such as the old switchboards, that dot the interior of the property. Each room is individually decorated with period furniture, combined with modern amenities for comfort. The property also runs an adjacent motel and condo complex. *703 Lincoln Ave., 80477, tel. 303/879–1522 or 800/543–8888; fax 303/879–1737. 62 units (another 23 in the motel and 24 condos). Facilities: 2 indoor hot tubs, sauna/steam room, ski storage, laundry facilities, gift shop, shuttle pass, complimentary Continental breakfast during ski season (coffee the rest of the year). Inexpensive.*

Rabbit Ears Motel. You won't find a motel that feels more like the '50s than this one, where a neon Bugs Bunny sign welcomes its guests. The location is ideal for those who want the springs (across the street), ski area (the town bus stops outside), and downtown shops, bars, and restaurants. All the clean attractive rooms have been recently spruced up, and most boast a view of the Yampa River. *201 Lincoln Ave. 80477, tel. 303/879–1150 or 800/828–7702. 65 rooms. Facilities: complimentary Continental breakfast, discounts to pool and health club. AE, D, DC, MC, V. Inexpensive.*

The Vail Valley
★ **Hyatt Regency Beaver Creek.** Because this slopeside hotel has been carefully crafted for guests' maximum comfort, it is considered a model accommodation. The lobby, with a magnificent antler chandelier as the centerpiece and huge oriel windows opening onto the mountain, manages to be both cozy and grand. Rooms are sizable and decorated in an appealing French-provincial style, and all of them have the usual amenities and welcome extras such as coffeemakers and heated towel racks. Maintaining Beaver Creek's tradition of excellent children's programs, the Camp and Rock Hyatt day-care centers make this resort wildly popular with families. Conventioneers like the full spa and health club, ski-in/ski-out ease, and nearby golf course. *136 E. Thomas Pl., Beaver Creek, tel. 303/949–1234 or 800/233–1234; fax 303/949–4164. 295 rooms, 3*

suites, 26 condo units. Facilities: 3 restaurants, deli, 2 lounges, spa and health club, pool, 6 outdoor Jacuzzis, 5 tennis courts, ski concierge, shopping arcade, day-care center, 23,000 sq. ft. of meeting space. AE, D, DC, MC, V. Very Expensive.

The Lodge at Vail. The first hotel to open in Vail remains one of the swanker addresses in town. As they say in the hotel business, it has "location, location, location," which translates to ski-in/ski-out status. The medium-size rooms are frilly and floral, a riot of pastels, with mahogany and teak furnishings and marble baths. The 40 suites are individually owned and decorated, but must meet rigorous standards set by management. The Wildflower Inn restaurant, a splendiferous space with vaulting floral arrangements and flowered banquettes, serves "postmodern Hebrew cuisine," jokes chef Jim Cohen, but it's really solidly regional American. Mickey's piano bar is still a favored après-ski spot. *174 E. Gore Creek Dr., tel. 303/476-5011 or 800/331-5634; fax 303/476-7425. 60 rooms, 40 suites. Facilities: 2 restaurants, lounge, spa, sauana, fitness room, heated outdoor pool, Jacuzzi, ski rental. AE, D, DC, MC, V. Very Expensive.*

★ **Saddle Ridge.** This resplendently rustic property is a series of tastefully done, classic American West villas, as reinvented by Naomi Leff, who designed New York's Ralph Lauren Polo store. The accommodations are plush yet unpretentious, with river-rock fireplaces, Ralph Lauren furnishings, superb Western artwork and antiques, Native American bedspreads and pottery, and a full kitchen and bath with steam showers and whirlpool tubs. In a nutshell: This is like vacationing at a friend's ranch. Available to guests who pay the $1,000 annual membership fee is the stylish saloon restaurant (it's also open on a limited basis to guests of other top-of-the-line properties). Executive chef Jim Dotsch uses indigenous and organic ingredients whenever possible, with an emphasis on fresh game and fish. The menu rotates depending on the season, but standouts might include a roasted-corn-and-chili chowder; hickory-glazed prawns; and a mixed grill of pheasant, quail, and free-range chicken breast with peach-and-onion chutney in a roasted-red-pepper sauce. *44 Meadow La., Beaver Creek, tel. 303/949-4108 or 800/352-7557; fax 303/845-9228. 12 villas. Facilities: restaurant, lounge, fitness room, indoor/outdoor pool, Jacuzzi, conference facilities. AE, MC, V. Very Expensive.*

★ **The Lodge at Cordillera.** This exquisite property is purposely isolated from all the activity in the valley. Surrounded by a pristine wilderness area—nearly half the property's 3,100 acres has been designated as wildlife reserve—the lodge offers privacy and spectacular sweeping vistas. The rooms are decidedly Old World, done up in mountain colors—burgundy, buff, and hunter green—with burled pine furnishings and balconies or transom windows to enjoy the views. An air of quiet luxury prevails throughout this secluded palatial retreat: prints by Picasso and Miró adorn the pine-paneled or exposed-brick walls, and ceilings are of carved recessed wood. You can luxuriate in the spa after a hard day's hiking or cross-country skiing, then sit down to a gourmet repast in the superlative Picasso restaurant. Belgian chef Fabrice Beaudoin weaves subtle magic with the healthy spa cuisine, and glorious views ensure a romantic evening out. An 18-hole Hale Irwin–designed golf course is scheduled for completion by summer 1994. Nordic enthusiasts will appreciate the miles of trails in winter. The lodge operates a shuttle to the lifts. *Box 1110, Edwards 81632, tel. 303/926-*

2200 or 800/548-2721; fax 303/926-2486. 28 rooms. Facilities: restaurant, lounge, spa and health club, cross-country ski center, shuttle to Beaver Creek and Vail, outdoor/indoor pool and Jacuzzi, meeting facilities. AE, MC, V. Expensive-Very Expensive.

★ **Beaver Creek Lodge.** An atrium centerpiece highlights this all-suites property that's charmingly decorated in European style. The units graciously maintain a sky blue-and-forest-green color scheme, and all feature a kitchenette and gas-burning fireplace among the usual amenities. The casually elegant Black Diamond Grill offers an inventive new American menu, which includes the highly touted scallop bisque and the buffalo carpaccio garnished with rattlesnake. *26 Avondale La., Beaver Creek, tel. 303/845-9800. 70 suites, 16 condo units. Facilities: restaurant, lounge, spa and health club, indoor/outdoor pool and Jacuzzi, boutique, ski rental, meeting facilities. AE, MC, V. Expensive.*

★ **Sonnenalp.** This property amid a pseudo-Bavarian village impresses as the real thing, and for good reason: the owning Fassler family has been in the hotel business in Germany for generations. Each of the three buildings offers a distinct look and ambience: the Swiss Chalet is quaint, with Bavarian pine armoires and secretaries and down comforters; the Austria Haus is a tad more rustic, with rough-hewn wood walls, stone floors, intricate ironwork, and Bavarian antiques throughout the public rooms; and the Bavaria Haus suites sport a modern lodge look. The superb restaurants include the delightful Stueberl (tiny rooms with wood paneling and sconces), the Western saloon Bully Ranch (great BBQ), and the elegant Continental Ludwig's. *20 Vail Rd., tel. 303/476-5656 or 800/654-8312; fax 303/476-1639. 36 rooms (Austria Haus), 70 rooms (Swiss Chalet), 80 suites (Bavaria Haus). Facilities: 4 restaurants, 3 lounges, spa, fitness center, outdoor heated pool and Jacuzzi, 2 indoor pools and Jacuzzis, day-care center. AE, MC, V. Expensive.*

Westin Vail. Down-to-earth yet glamorous is the best way to describe this ski-in/ski-out hotel that manages—despite its fairly large size—to maintain an intimate feel, thanks to the expert staff. Rooms in the older wing sport mountain colors, those in the newer wing have a lighter touch. Alfredo's, the hotel's restaurant, has long been one of the best Italian restaurants in the valley. *1300 Westhaven Dr., tel. 303/476-7111; fax 303/479-7025. 290 rooms, 28 suites. Facilities: 2 restaurants, lounge, meeting facilities, privileges at adjoining Cascade Athletic Club (including indoor and outdoor tennis, racquetball, squash, Nautilus and free-weight rooms), outdoor heated pool, 2 Jacuzzis, ski concierge, 2 ski shops. AE, DC, MC, V. Expensive.*

Christie Lodge. The property looks unprepossessing, rather like an upscale dorm or YMCA. But the suites, though cramped, are quite serviceable, including all the basics and kitchenette, balcony, and fireplace. There are also plenty of facilities on site. *Box 1196, Avon 81620, tel. 303/949-7700 or 800/551-4326. 280 suites. Facilities: restaurant, lounge, 2 heated outdoor pools, 2 saunas, 3 Jacuzzis, video game room, sports rental. AE, DC, MC, V. Moderate.*

Gasthof Gramshammer. Pepi Gramshammer, a former Austrian Olympic ski racer, is one of Vail's most beloved, respected citizens whose labor of love—Wedel Weeks—ranks among the country's best intensive ski programs. His charming rooms are done up in pastels, with original oil paintings and fluffy down comforters. Pepi's and Antlers, the property's two fine restaurants, reflect European ambience, with stucco walls, wood-beamed ceilings, and waitresses in dirndls. *231 E. Gore Creek Dr., tel. 303/476-5626; fax 303/476-8816. Facilities: 2 restaurants, lounge, ski rental. AE, MC, V. Moderate.*

★ **Roost Lodge.** Situated on I-70 and advertising economical rates, comfortable rooms, and a heated pool, this accommodation is true to its promise—and then some, considering the price. The airy rooms are pleasing, many with four-poster beds, all with basic amenities. The staff is helpful and ingratiating, and complimentary Continental breakfast and afternoon wine and cheese are served daily in ski season. *1783 N. Fontage Rd., tel. 303/476-5451. 72 rooms, 3 suites. Facilities: heated pool, Jacuzzi, sauna, shuttle service to ski area and village. AE, MC, V. Inexpensive.*

Winter Park **Iron Horse Resort Retreat.** This ski-in/ski-out hotel/condominium complex is the deluxe address in Winter Park. All units except the lodge rooms feature a full kitchen, Jacuzzi bath, and sun deck and are furnished in an attractive modern rustic style, with individual touches. *Box 1286, 80482, tel. 303/726-8851 or 800/621-8190. 130 1- and 2-bedroom units. Facilities: restaurant, lounge, rental shop, health club, pool, game room, complimentary local shuttle. AE, D, DC, MC, V. Moderate-Expensive.*

Hidden Mountain Lodge. The only downside of this first-rate property is its location, 20 minutes from the ski area by private shuttle (provided by the lodge). Cross-country skiing is also available in this secluded spot surrounded by the national forest. The pleasing rooms include fireplace, king-size bed, sitting room, microwave, minifridge, balcony, and plush carpeting. What really sets this property apart is the innovative kitchen under the management of chef Chris Lightfoot. His menu changes daily, but might highlight blackened mahimahi, yellowfin tuna in roasted-pepper beurre blanc, or Texas baby back ribs. The restaurant is open on a limited basis to nonguests with 24-hour notice. Room rates include breakfast, dinner, and lift ticket. *Box 177, 80482, tel. 303/726-9266 or 800/221-9125. 18 units. Facilities: restaurant, hot tub, game/TV room, complimentary shuttle to area/town. AE, MC, V. Inexpensive-Moderate.*

Timber House Ski Lodge. This family-run property is as congenial as can be, and the staff makes you feel as though you're staying in someone's sprawling, though slightly disordered, home. The tiny rooms in the old wing have shared bath and rustic decor, with brightly colored curtains and spreads. Smallish rooms in the newer wing have private bath and huge picture windows opening onto the mountains. Dorm rooms and bunk rooms are also available. All-you-can-eat breakfast and dinner are served family style. *Box 32, 80482, tel. 303/726-8417. 35 rooms. Facilities: dining room, hot tub, sauna, rec room, TV lounge. AE, MC, V. Inexpensive-Moderate.*

Vintage Hotel. This well-run hotel/condo complex is Winter Park's other premier resort, offering spacious, comfortable units mostly decorated in soothing earth or mountain tones. Configurations range from standard, inexpensive hotel rooms (with kitchenette and gas fireplace) and studios (with kitchen) to three-bedroom condos. *Box 1369, 80482, tel. 303/726-8801 or 800/472-7017; fax 303/726-9230. 118 units. Facilities: restau-*

rant, lounge, ski shop, Jacuzzi, sauna, pool, free shuttle. AE, D, DC, MC, V. Inexpensive–Moderate.

Sundowner Motel. This is probably the nicest motel on the strip, and a great bargain considering the free shuttle to the ski area. The rooms, decorated in muted earth tones, are slightly threadbare but feature the standard amenities. It's right on the main drag and convenient to restaurants and shops. *Box 221, 80482, tel. 303/726–9451; fax 303/726–5452. 22 rooms. Facilities: hot tub. AE, DC, MC, V. Inexpensive.*

Condominiums   Condominiums often represent an excellent alternative to the pricier hotels, especially for families and groups. All the companies listed below represent top-notch properties, usually on or within walking distance of the slopes (or major activities in summer). All have full kitchen and cable TV, most with pool and/or hot tub access.

Aspen/Snowmass   Call **Aspen Central Reservational Travel** (tel. 800/26–ASPEN) and **Snowmass Resort Association** (tel. 800/598–2005). Among the recommended management companies are **Coates, Reid & Waldron** (720 E. Hyman Ave., Aspen 81611, tel. 303/925–1400 or 800/222–7736; fax 303/920–3765); **Condominium Rental Management** (747 S. Galena St., Aspen 81611, tel. 303/925–2260 or 800/321–7025; fax 303/925–2264); **Aspen Alps Condominium Association** (700 Ute Ave., Aspen 81611, tel. 303/925–7820 or 800/228–7820; fax 303/925–2528); **Aspen Classic Properties** (600 E. Main St., Aspen 81611, tel. 303/925–5759 or 800/642–4210; fax 303/920–3279); **McCartney Properties** (421-G Aspen Airport Business Center, tel. 303/925–8717 or 800/433–8465; fax 303/920–4770); **Dolomite Management** (650 S. Monarch, Aspen 81611, tel. 303/925–7624 or 800/332–1060; fax 303/925–7624). In Snowmass, contact **Snowmass Lodging Company** (Box 6077, Snowmass Village 81615, tel. 303/923–5543 or 800/365–0410; fax 303/923–5740) and **Village Property Management** (Box 5550, Snowmass Village 81615, tel. 800/525–9402; fax 303/923–5192).

Breckenridge   In addition to the resorts listed above, **Breckenridge Accommodations** (Box 1931, Breckenridge 80424, tel. 303/453–9140 or 800/872–8789), **Breckenridge Vacation Rentals** (Box 7909, Breckenridge 80424, tel. 800/433–9217; fax 303/453–6600), **AMR Lodging** (400 N. Park Ave., No. 6A, Breckenridge 80424, tel. 800/334–9162 or 303/453–0833; fax 303/453–4432), **Breckenridge Central Lodging** (Box 709, Breckenridge 80424, tel. 303/453–2160 or 800/858–5885), and **Colorado Mountain Lodging** (Drawer 1190, Breckenridge 80424, tel. 303/453–4121 or 800/627–3766; fax 303/453–0533) are a few of the reputable rental agencies. You can also call the **Breckenridge Resort Chamber Central Reservation System** (tel. 800/221–1091 or 303/453–6018).

Copper Mountain   **Copper Mountain Resort** (tel. 303/968–2882 or 800/458–8386) runs all 22 lodging facilities, ranging from hotel-style units to condos. All are either on the slopes or serviced by shuttles.

Keystone   **Keystone Resort Corporation** (tel. 800/222–0188) operates all the lodging facilities at the resort, which range from hotel-style accommodations at Keystone Lodge (*see above*) to various condominium properties.

Steamboat   **Steamboat Premier Properties** (1855 Ski Time Sq., Steamboat Springs 80487, tel. 303/879–8811 or 800/228–2458; fax 303/879–8485) lives up to its name, with the finest condominium units,

from studios to three-bedroom units, in three deluxe properties: The Torian Plum, Bronze Tree, and Trappeur's Crossing.
Steamboat Resorts (Box 2995, Steamboat Springs 80477, tel.
800/525–5502; fax 303/879–8060) and **Mountain Resorts** (2145
Resort Dr., No. 100, Steamboat Springs 80487, tel. 800/525–
2622; fax 303/879–3228) also represent top properties.

Vail/Beaver Creek **Vail/Beaver Creek Reservations** (tel. 800/237–0643) can handle
all calls, requests, and bookings. Among the recommended Vail
properties are Cascade Village, Manor Vail, Vail Village Inn,
and Simba Resort (all of which boast several extras including
restaurants and shops on site). Top Beaver Creek facilities,
also with the above extras, include the Poste Montane, St.
James Place, and The Charter.

Winter Park The condominiums at Winter Park are an especially good value,
particularly those managed by **Winter Park Vacations** (Box
3095, Winter Park 80482, tel. 303/726–9421 or 800/228–1025;
fax 303/726–9421, ext. 119). They are all excellent and feature
recreational centers (including pool and hot tub) and laundry
facilities, and they run the gamut in price.

The Arts

Dance **Dance Aspen** (210 AABC, tel. 303/925–7718) presents a Summer Festival and various internationally acclaimed performers.

Film All the towns listed have at least one theater screening first-
run films. Aspen hosts a highly regarded film festival in late
September.

Music The various chambers of commerce will have information on
upcoming events. Aspen's **Wheeler Opera House** (tel. 303/925–
2750) is the venue for big-name acts, especially in summer. The
Aspen Music Festival, featuring chamber music to jazz, runs
late June to September.

Theater **Snowmass/Aspen Repertory Theatre** (Snowmass Village Mall,
tel. 303/923–3773) offers performances.

Nightlife

Bars and Lounges In Aspen, **The Tippler** (535 E. Dean St., tel. 303/925–4977) is
Aspen affectionately nicknamed The Crippler for the happy customers staggering out after a long night. Tuesday is '70s Night, a
must for all fans (and detractors) of diva disco. **Legends** (325 E.
Main St., tel. 303/925–5860) is a sports bar that attracts a lively
crowd of frat brothers and sorority babes. **Shlomo's** and **Little
Nell's Bar** (675 E. Durant Ave., tel. 303/920–4600), **Bentley's at
the Wheeler** (328 E. Hyman Ave., tel. 303/920–2240), and the
Jerome Bar (330 E. Main St., tel. 303/920–1000) are the civilized choices for après-ski. There's also that hardy perennial,
Hard Rock Café (210 S. Galena St., tel. 303/920–1666).

Breckenridge In Breckenridge, the two hot après-ski spots in town are the
Breckenridge Brewery (600 S. Main St., tel. 303/453–1550) with
its six premium homemade beers, and **Hearthstone** (130 S.
Ridge St., tel. 303/453–1148), set in a former bordello, with maroon velour walls and lace curtains. This is a congenial hangout
where locals scarf down the addictive happy-hour special,
jalapeño-wrapped shrimp.

Copper Mountain In this town **Double Diamond Bar and Grill** (Base of B Lift, tel. 303/968–2882) and **Farley's** (Snowflake Bldg., tel. 303/968–2577) are hot spots for lunch and happy hour, as is the frequently raucous **Sports Bar at O'Shea's** (base of American Eagle, tel. 303/968–2882, ext. 6504). The best après-ski scene is at the always-packed **Kokomo's** (Copper Commons, tel. 303/968–2882, ext. 6591).

Frisco Frisco hops during ski season at **Casey's** (Best Western, 1202 Summit Blvd., tel. 303/668–5094) and **Frisco's** (720 Granite St., tel. 303/668–5051).

Keystone **Gassy Thompson's** and **Ida Belle's** (both base area, tel. 303/468–4130) are popular hangouts after hitting the slopes.

Steamboat Springs The **Old Town Pub** (601 Lincoln Ave., tel. 303/879–2101) has juicy burgers and local flavor, with some great live bands. On the mountain, **Mattie Silk's** (*see* Dining, *above*) is a favorite après-ski hangout.

Vail/Beaver Creek The coolest, hottest Vail hangout is **Palmo's** (Gateway Plaza, tel. 303/476–0646), with eye-catching decor that was designed and carved by Menzel, who utilizes gorgeously textured 200-year-old wormwood (visible throughout the mall; notice the wild stairways) to dazzling effect. The tables reputedly cost $3,000 each. There's a wonderful selection of hot drinks, brandies, and single malts.

In Beaver Creek, the Hyatt's **Crooked Hearth Tavern** (tel. 303/949–1234, ext. 2260) is a wonderful place to wind down after attacking the moguls, usually to the strains of a folk guitarist.

Cabaret The **Crystal Palace** (300 E. Hyman Ave., tel. 303/925–1455) is an Aspen fixture, offering two seatings nightly with fine food and a fiercely funny up-to-the-minute satirical revue.

In Steamboat, **Club Majiks** (tel. 303/879–5848) offers dinner and various cabaret acts.

Country and Western In Aspen/Snowmass, **Cowboys** (Silvertree Hotel, tel. 303/923–5249) usually has live country-western music and dancing nightly, as does **Shooters Saloon** (Galena and Hopkins Sts., tel. 303/925–4567).

In Steamboat, **The Saloon** (Sundance Plaza, tel. 303/879–6303) is in no-man's-land behind a Wendy's, but it's a real cowboy joint that offers two-step lessons early in the evening.

In the Vail Valley, **Cassidy's Hole in the Wall** (82 E. Beaver Creek Blvd., Avon, tel. 303/949–9449) is a saloon offering live C&W bands nightly, to go with the authentic mouthwatering barbecue.

Discos In Aspen, **Ebbe's** (312 S. Galena St., tel. 303/925–5249) provides a dance space beneath a skylight.

In Breckenridge, **Tiffany's** (tel. 303/453–6000, ext. 7914) has a DJ and dancing nightly. **Johsha's** (tel. 303/453–4146) offers live bands, a dance floor, pool tables, and cheap eats.

Jazz Clubs Aspen's **Ritz-Carlton Club Room** (315 Dean St., tel. 303/920–3300) presents live jazz nightly in season. In Snowmass, **La Brasserie** (Snowmass Village Mall, tel. 303/923–6804) showcases leading artists nightly in season.

Copper Mountain's **Pesce Fresco** (Mountain Plaza Bldg., tel. 303/968–2882, ext. 6505) offers jazz piano Wed.–Sun. nights in season.

In Vail, **Babau's Café** (L'Ostello Lodge, Lionshead Cir., tel. 303/476–2050) is a piano jazz club with fine Italian specialties as a plus.

Rock Clubs   In Steamboat (on the mountain), **The Tugboat** (Ski Time Sq., tel. 303/879–7070) always features live loud acts. **Heavenly Daze** (Ski Time Sq., tel. 303/879–8080) has three levels: the ground floor a brew pub, the second floor a restaurant, and the third floor a combination billiards parlor/rock club/disco.

Singles   In Aspen, **Eric's** (315 E. Hyman Ave., tel. 303/920–1488), under the same ownership as the Su Casa restaurant across the way, is always jammed and jammin' with a lustily youthful crowd.

Southwest Colorado

"Colorado" is a Spanish word meaning "ruddy" or "colorful"— adjectives that clearly describe many regions of the state, but particularly the Southwest, with the Four Corners region and the San Juans. A wide variety of terrain rests here, from yawning black canyons and desolate monochrome lunarscapes to pastel desert and mesalands to shimmering sapphire lakes and 14,000-foot glaciers. It's so rugged in the Southwest that a four-wheel-drive vehicle is necessary to explore the wild and beautiful backcountry.

The region's history and people are as colorful as the landscape, from the mysterious Anasazi (meaning "ancient ones") who constructed impressive cliff dwellings in Mesa Verde National Park to notorious outlaws such as Butch Cassidy, who embarked on his storied career by robbing the Telluride Bank in 1889. Even today, the more ornery, independent locals, disgusted with the political system, periodically talk of seceding. They're as rough as the country they inhabit.

Southwest Colorado offers such diversity that depending on where you go, you can have radically different vacations, even during the same season. Visit the world-class resorts of Crested Butte, Purgatory, and Telluride for quality ski and golf holidays; then move on to the Old West railroad town of Durango, followed by a pilgrimage to the Anasazi ruins dotting the area. Even for Colorado, the combination of recreational, historical, and cultural opportunities is unbeatable.

Important Addresses and Numbers

Tourist Information   **Cortez Area Chamber of Commerce** (925 S. Broadway, 81321, tel. 303/565–3414 or 800/346–6528); **Crested Butte–Mt. Crested Butte Chamber of Commerce** (7 Emmons Loop, tel. 303/349–6438 or 800/545–4505); **Durango Chamber Resort Association** (111 S. Camino del Rio, 81302, tel. 303/247–0312 or 800/525–8855); **Gunnison County Chamber of Commerce** (500 E. Tomichi Ave., 81230, tel. 303/641–1501 or 800/274–7580); **Lake City Chamber of Commerce** (306 N. Silver St., 81235, tel. 303/944–2527); **Mesa Verde National Park** (Supt. Mesa Verde Nat'l. Park, 81330, tel. 303/529–4465); **Montrose Chamber of Commerce** (550 N. Townsend Ave., tel. 800/873–0244) and **Visitor**

Information Center (2490 S. Townsend Ave., 81401, tel. 303/ 249–1726); **Ouray County Chamber** (1222 Main St., 81427, tel. 303/325–4746 or 800/228–1876); **Pagosa Springs Chamber of Commerce** (402 San Juan St., 81147, tel. 303/264–2360 or 800/ 252–2204); **San Luis Valley Information Center** (Box 165, 1st St. and Jefferson Ave., Monte Vista 81144, tel. 719/672–3355); **San Luis Visitor Center** (Box 9, San Luis 81152, tel. 719/672–3355); **Silverton Chamber of Commerce** (414 Greene St., 81433, tel. 303/387–5654 or 800/752–4494); **Telluride Chamber Resort Association** (666 W. Colorado Ave., 81435, tel. 303/728–3041).

Hospitals   Cortez: **Southwest Memorial Hospital** (1311 N. Mildred St., tel. 303/565–6666); Durango: **Mercy Medical Center** (375 E. Park Ave., tel. 303/247–4311); Gunnison: **Gunnison Valley Hospital** (214 E. Denver Ave., tel. 303/641–1884); Montrose: **Montrose Memorial Hospital** (800 S. 3rd St., tel. 303/249–2211); **San Luis Valley: San Luis Valley Regional Medical Center** (106 Blanca Ave., Alamosa, tel. 719/589–2511); Telluride: **Telluride Medical Center** (500 W. Pacific Ave., tel. 303/728–3848).

Arriving and Departing by Plane

Airports and   Durango: The **Durango–La Plata Airport** (tel. 303/247–8143)
Airlines   receives daily flights from America West (tel. 800/247–5692), Continental Express (tel. 800/525–0280), Mesa Airlines (tel. 800/637–2247), and United Express (tel. 800/241–6522).

Gunnison: Continental Express and Delta (tel. 800/221–1212) as well as United Express and American (tel. 800/433–7300) fly nonstop from Chicago, Dallas, and San Jose into **Gunnison County Airport** (tel. 303/641–2304), which also serves Crested Butte.

Montrose: **Montrose Airport** (tel. 303/249–3203) is served by Continental Express and United Express.

Telluride: **Telluride Regional Airport** (tel. 303/728–5313) welcomes flights from Continental, Delta, Mesa Airlines (tel. 800/ MESA–AIR), Skywest (tel. 800/453–9417), and United Express.

Between the   Crested Butte: **Alpine Express** (tel. 303/641–5074 or 800/822–
Airport and the   4844); Durango: **Durango Transportation** (tel. 303/259–4818);
Resort   Montrose: **Western Express Taxi** (tel. 303/249–8880); Telluride:
By Shuttle   **Skip's Taxi** (tel. 303/728–6667) and **Telluride Transit** (tel. 303/ 728–6000). Shuttles average $15–$20 per person.

Arriving and Departing by Car and Bus

By Car   If you're entering Colorado from the south, both U.S. 550 and U.S. 666 access the Four Corners region. From the east or west, I–70 (U.S. 6) intersects U.S. 50 south in Grand Junction, to reach the San Juans and Four Corners area. From the north, I–25 intersects in Denver with I–70, for a long drive to U.S. 50. Alternatively, U.S. 40 enters northwest Colorado from Utah, connecting with CO 64 in Dinosaur, then CO 139 south in Rangely, to I–70 east to Grand Junction.

San Luis Valley can be reached via U.S. 160 from both the west (direct from Durango) and the east (via I–25), or via U.S. 285 from New Mexico.

By Bus Greyhound/Trailways (tel. 800/752–4841) serves most of the major towns in the region via Salt Lake City, Denver, or Albuquerque/Santa Fe.

Getting Around

By Car The main routes are CO 135 between Crested Butte and Gunnison; U.S. 50 linking Poncha Springs, Gunnison, Montrose, and Delta; CO 149 between Gunnison, Lake City, and Creede; U.S. 550 from Montrose to Ridgway; CO 62 and CO 145 linking Ridgway with Telluride, Dolores, and Cortez; CO 110 running from Ridgway through Ouray and Silverton to Durango; and U.S. 160, the closest thing to a major highway in the area, from Cortez to Durango via the Mesa Verde entrance.

By Bus or Shuttle In Crested Butte, the **Crested Butte Shuttle** (no tel.) runs regularly between the town and the ski area.

In Durango, **Durango Lift** (tel. 303/247–5438) has regular bus service up and down Main Street, as well as to Purgatory Ski Area during ski season.

In Telluride, **San Miguel Transit Service** (tel. 303/728–4191) offers free shuttle service between the town of Telluride and Telluride Ski Village.

By Taxi In most cases you'll need to call for a cab; taxis are plentiful and the wait is only about 15 minutes. **Durango Transportation** (Durango, tel. 303/259–4818); **Montrose Taxi** (Montrose, tel. 303/249–8880); **Skip's Taxi** (Telluride, tel. 303/728–6667); and **Telluride Transit** (Telluride, tel. 303/728–6000).

Guided Tours

Orientation **ARA Mesa Verde Company** (Mancos, tel. 303/529–4421) runs three- and six-hour tours into Mesa Verde National Park.
Durango Transportation (tel. 303/259–4818) arranges tours of Mesa Verde, Chaco Canyon, and the San Juan Skyway.
San Juan Jeep Tours (tel. 303/325–4444) explores the high country in open vehicles that allow unobstructed views.
Sierra Vista Tours (tel. 719/379–3277) offers tours of the area, including the Great Sand Dunes.

Special-Interest Tours
Native-Heritage Programs **Crow Canyon Archaeological Center.** The center exists to foster greater understanding and appreciation of Anasazi culture by guiding visitors through excavations and botanical studies in the region. Also included in the weeklong programs are day trips to isolated canyon sites and hands-on lessons in weaving and pottery making with Native American artisans. Day programs are also available on a reservation-only basis to families and groups. *23390 C.R. K, Cortez 81321, tel. 303/565–8975 or 800/422–8975.*

Ute Mountain Tribal Park. Native American guides lead grueling hikes into this dazzling primitive repository of Anasazi ruins, including the majestic Tree House cliff dwelling and enchanting Eagle's Nest petroglyphs. It's also a wonderful opportunity to learn more about the Ute tribe's culture and customs. Tours usually start at the Ute Mountain Pottery Plant, 15 miles south of Cortez, on Highway 666. Overnight camping can also be arranged. *Towoac 81334, tel. 303/565–3751, ext. 282.*

Exploring Southwest Colorado

The San Juans This tour spirals from the towering peaks of the San Juan range to the plunging Black Canyon of the Gunnison, taking in Colorado's most stunning alpine scenery along the way, as well as the spectral remains of old mining towns.

Numbers in the margin correspond to points of interest on the Colorado map.

㉝ **Crested Butte** is literally just over the mountain from Aspen, but a 15-minute scenic flight or one-hour drive in summer turns into a four-hour trek by car in winter, when Kebler Pass is closed. The town of Crested Butte was declared a National Historic District and, like Aspen, it was once a quaint mining center whose exquisite pastel Victorian gingerbreads remain. Unlike Aspen, however, Crested Butte never became chic, as attests a recent controversial ad campaign about its ski area (3 mi from town): "Aspen like it used to be, and Vail like it never was."

That adage might make the locals seem crustier than they are; they're just proud and independent, with a puckish sense of humor. In fact, in a state that prides itself on hospitality, Crested Butte just may be the friendliest ski town of them all. (If you want the dope, stop by the Conoco Station and ask Tony. Well into his eighties, he's a font of information about the place—some unprintable.) A sense of warmth and whimsy pervades the area, most evident in the hot pink, magenta, and chartreuse facades of the buildings along Elk Avenue, the main drag.

Crested Butte Mountain Resort is a trailblazer and renegade in many respects: it initiated a daring—and wildly successful—venture in which everyone skis free the first four weeks of the season, and first timers get free lessons. While many resorts are limiting their "out-of-bounds" terrain due to increasing insurance costs and lawsuits, Crested Butte is thumbing its nose at the establishment by steadily increasing its extreme-skiing terrain, which now speaks for 550 ungroomed acres. The Extreme Limits and the North Face could send chills down the spine of any mere expert, but still, there are plenty of cruisable trails for recreational skiers. In the summer, mountain bikers increasingly challenge the same slopes, which are blanketed with columbine and Indian paintbrush.

Crested Butte is considered the quintessential ski bum's town: Friendly, reasonably priced, cute as hell, great bars, impressive restaurants, and a gnarly mountain that remains far less crowded than its better-known neighbors.

The CO 135 scenic loop goes west from Crested Butte over Kebler Pass to **Paonia**, and south through banks of cottonwoods **㉞** (which usually attract several swooping bald eagles) to **Gunnison**. Situated at the confluence of the Gunnison River and Tomichi Creek, Gunnison has been a fishing and hunting community ever since the Utes adopted it as their summer hunting grounds. It provides economical lodging for those skiing Crested Butte, and for backpackers, mountain bikers, and fishermen in summer.

The **Gunnison County Chamber of Commerce** (500 E. Tomichi Ave., tel. 303/641–1501) issues an informative historical walking-tour brochure of downtown. Those interested in the region's history can also stop by the **Pioneer Museum,** a living-history complex that includes several buildings and relics dating back to the late 19th century. *Hwy. 50 and S. Adams St., tel. 303/641–4530. Admission: $3 adults, $1 children 6–12. Open Memorial Day–Labor Day, Mon.–Sat. 9–5, Sun. 1–5.*

Aside from its easy access to Crested Butte, Gunnison is recognized for two other things. Its Western State College, the local seat of higher learning, boasts a 320-foot by 420-foot white-washed rock, shaped like a W, and located on Tenderfoot Mountain, just to the north of campus. Ostensibly, this is the largest collegiate insignia in the world. Gunnison's other claim to fame is that the town has recorded some of the coldest temperatures ever reported in the continental United States.

Nine miles west of Gunnison is the **Curecanti National Recreation Area** (tel. 303/641–2337), set amid a striking eroded volcanic landscape and stretching for more than 60 miles. The area was created in the '60s by a series of dams that resulted in three reservoirs, including **Blue Mesa**—the state's largest body of water. The reservoirs provide a wealth of aquatic recreational opportunities, as well as fine camping and hiking. At the western entrance of the **Cimarron Visitor Center** (tel. 303/249–4074; open daily 9–5) are vintage locomotives, an 1882 trestle listed on the National Register of Historic Places, and a reconstruction of a railroad stockyard.

Once liberated from the restrictions of Curecanti, the Gunnison River slices through one of the West's most awe-inspiring sights, the **Black Canyon of the Gunnison National Monument,** a vivid testament to the powers of erosion. This 2,500-foot-high gash in the earth's crust is 1,300 feet wide at its top and only 40 feet wide at the bottom. The canyon received its name because so little sunlight penetrates its depths, the eternal shadows permitting scant plant growth on the steep narrow walls. The Black Canyon lies 60 miles west of Gunnison, on CO 347 north, off Highway 50. The fine **Visitor Center** (tel. 303/249–1915 or 303/249–7036; open Apr.–Sept., daily 9–5) includes exhibits on the region's geology, history, and flora and fauna, and schedules nature walks to the canyon's forbidding rim.

③⑤ **Montrose,** the self-described "Home of the Black Canyon" is another 7 miles west along Highway 50. Though it sits amid glorious surroundings, it is an otherwise nondescript town with little more than a collection of truck stops, trailer parks, and strip malls. However, Montrose is perfectly placed for exploring Curecanti and the Black Canyon to the east, the San Juans to the south, the world's largest flattop mountain, Grand Mesa to the north, and the fertile Uncompahgre Plateau to the west.

If you're interested in learning more about the original residents of the area, stop by the excellent **Ute Indian Museum,** a mile south of town on U.S. 550. The venue contains several dioramas and the most comprehensive collection of Ute materials and artifacts in Colorado. *17253 Chipeta Dr., tel. 303/249–3098. Admission: $2. Open mid-May–Sept., Mon.–Sat. 10–5 and Sun. 1–5.*

The Four Corners and the Million Dollar Highway   Head south on U.S. 550 to Ridgway, notable mainly for its strategic location at the junction of U.S. 550 and CO 62. These two routes fan out from the town to form one of the country's most stupendously scenic drives, the **San Juan Skyway**, which weaves through a series of fourteeners (a Rockies term for peaks reaching more than 14,000 feet) and picturesque mining towns. U.S. 550 continues through historic Ouray and Silverton to Durango. CO 62 and CO 145 reach Durango via the extraordinary Anasazi cliff dwellings of Mesa Verde National Park.

Take CO 62 to its juncture with CO 145 east, to one of Colorado's hottest destinations. Tucked like a jewel in a tiny valley caught between azure sky and gunmetal mountains is **③ Telluride,** once so inaccessible that it was a favorite hideout for desperadoes such as Butch Cassidy, who robbed his first bank here in 1889. Some locals claim the town is named not after the mineral Tellurium, but the saying "To hell you ride."

The savage but beautiful terrain now attracts mountain people of a different sort—alpinists, telemarkers, snowboarders, freestylers, mountain bikers, and freewheeling four-wheelers—who attack any incline, up or down, with consummate abandon. As one local quips, "The Wild Bunch is alive and well."

The ski area, too, is not for the faint of heart. Telluride poses the ultimate test for skiers, with one legendary challenging run after another. Terrain accessed by Chair 9, including the famed "The Plunge" and "Spiral Staircase," is for experts only (although one side of "The Plunge" is groomed for advanced skiers). Telluride has also expanded its "ultimate skiing" terrain to include more than 400 acres on Gold Hill. Forgotten in the excitement of all the challenge is that Telluride has a superb beginners' and learners' area; it's middle-of-the-road intermediates who may find themselves between a rock and a hard place.

The town's independent spirit is shaped not only by its mining legacy, but by the social ferment of the '60s and early '70s. Before the ski area opened in 1971, Telluride had been as remote as it was back in Cassidy's day. It was even briefly included on the Ghost Town Club of Colorado itinerary, but that was before countercultural types moved in, seeking to lose themselves in the wilderness. By 1974 the town's orientation had changed so radically that the entire council was composed of hippies. Today there is one holdover—Councilman Rasta Stevie (he's white, but his waist-length dreadlocks might have made even Bob Marley green with envy)—who cheerfully admits, "I came to power through the dirtbags." Regardless of future development, Stevie defends an enduring Telluride tradition called the Swap Corner (Pine St. and Colorado Ave.), where indigent residents can sort through and take whatever used clothing and appliances they need.

Indeed, more and more locals are finding they can no longer afford to live here. Things were fine when the town was isolated, but thanks to the construction of the Telluride Regional Airport in the late 1980s it's become quite accessible. Today Telluride is positioning itself as an upscale alternative to Vail and Aspen, and celebrities who need only be identified by their first names (Arnold and Oprah, for example) are purchasing homes.

Telluride is chic—and not everyone's happy about it. Many townies deplore the mushrooming Telluride Mountain Village development at the base of the ski area, and they bitterly resent the glamorous new The Peaks at Telluride Resort and Spa. When the owners overextended themselves and the property went into receivership, locals merely snickered. Well, what did they expect? Telluride is just too gorgeous for its own good. Every corner of the town yields stunning prospects of the San Juans, which loom both menacingly and protectively, depending on the lighting.

The 425-foot liquid diamond **Bridal Veil Falls,** Colorado's highest cascade, tumbles lavishly just a short hike from the end of Colorado Avenue, the main street. The town itself offers one pastel Victorian residence or frontier trading post after another, as well as the 1883 **San Miguel County Courthouse** and the 1895 **New Sheridan Hotel and Opera House.** (*Telluride Magazine* prints an excellent historic walking tour in its "Visitors' Guide" section). Today it's hard to believe that those lovingly restored shops and restaurants once housed gaming parlors and saloons known for the quality of their "waitressing."

That party-hearty spirit lives on, evidenced by the numerous annual events held here. Highly regarded wine and wild mushroom festivals alternate with musical performances celebrating everything from bluegrass to jazz to chamber music. And the Telluride Film Festival is one of the world's leading showcases for the latest releases of top independent and foreign directors.

Time Out **The House** (131 N. Fir St., tel. 303/728–6207) is set in a building once dubbed "The Freak House," for the colorful characters who lived here in the '70s and '80s. These days the atmosphere is more refined—likened to a European "social hub" by owner Tom Wirth—with fine ales on tap, along with cribbage, backgammon, Trivial Pursuit, and chess.

This portion of the tour winds through striking desert scenery, taking in the superlative Anasazi ruins and the Old West town of Durango along the way. Continue southwest along CO 145, which follows the course of the lovely Dolores River. In 1968, construction of an irrigation dam was authorized, forming the **McPhee Reservoir,** a haven for boaters and fishermen. An environmental-impact study was mandated by law and concluded that hundreds of potentially valuable archaeological sites would be flooded. This led to massive, federally funded excavations and the creation of one of the West's model museums, the Anasazi Heritage Center, 3 miles west of Dolores.

The Anasazi were a mysterious and talented people who thrived until 1300 and, far from being a vanished race, were probably the ancestors of present-day Pueblo tribes. They left behind a legacy of stunning ruins, both freestanding pueblos and ingenious cliff dwellings. No one knows for sure why they abandoned their homes, although most anthropologists surmise a combination of drought and overfarming sent them off in search of greener pastures.

The first white explorers to stumble upon Anasazi ruins were the Spanish friars Dominguez and Escalante, who set out in 1776 from Santa Fe to find a safe overland route to Monterey, California. The two major ruins at the **Anasazi Heritage Center** (CO 184, tel. 303/882–4811; admission free; open daily 9–5) are named for them. The Dominguez site, right next to the parking lot, is unimpressive, although of great archaeological interest because extremely rare evidence of a "high-status burial" was found here. The Escalante site, a half-mile hike away, is a 20-room masonry pueblo standing eerie guard over McPhee Reservoir.

The state-of-the-art facility houses the finest artifacts culled from more than 1,500 excavations, as well as a theater, library, gift shop, and full-scale replica of an Anasazi pit-house dwelling that illustrates how the Anasazi lived around 850. The complex is particularly notable for its Discovery Center, a series of hologrammatic, hands-on, and interactive displays that enable visitors to weave on a Navajo loom, grind corn, even generate an Anasazi village on a computer.

Continue south along CO 145, passing through **Dolores** and its enchanting **Galloping Goose Museum** (5th St. and Hwy. 145, tel. 303/882–4018), a replica of a Victorian train station that contains an original narrow-gauge locomotive. The gentle rising hump to the southwest is **Sleeping Ute Mountain,** which resembles the reclining silhouette of an Indian replete with headdress. The site is revered by the Ute Mountain tribe as a great warrior god who, mortally wounded in a titanic battle with the evil ones, lapsed into eternal sleep, his flowing blood turning into the life-giving Dolores and Animas rivers.

③⑦ At the juncture of CO 145 and U.S. 160 is **Cortez,** dominated by the northern escarpment of Mesa Verde and the volcanic blisters of the La Plata Mountains to the west. The sprawling town is an unrelieved tedium of Days Inns, Dairy Queens, and Best Westerns, its architecture seemingly determined by neon-sign and aluminum-siding salesmen of the '50s. Hidden among these, however, are fine galleries and a host of pawn shops that can yield surprising finds.

There is a **Colorado Welcome Center** here (160 E. Main St., tel. 303/565–4048), as well as the excellent **Cortez/Colorado University Center,** its exterior painted to resemble the cliff dwellings of Mesa Verde. Inside the University Center are changing exhibits of regional artists and artisans, displays from the Ute Mountain branch of the Ute tribe, and interpretive exhibits on various periods of Anasazi culture. On summer evenings Native American dances; sandpainting, rug-weaving, and pottery making demonstrations; and storytelling events are organized. The related **Cultural Park** contains an authentic Navaho hogan and Ute tepee. *Park, 25 N. Market St., tel. 303/565–1151. Admission free; donations accepted. Open daily 9–5.*

Time Out   **Earth Song Haven** (34 E. Main St., tel. 303/247–0470) is a fine bookstore, with an espresso bar and tearoom in back. Cortez seems an unlikely spot for this European touch, but the café makes wonderful coffees, sandwiches, and high-calorie desserts such as peanut-butter cream pie.

Cortez is the gateway to **Mesa Verde National Park,** 80 square miles forming one of America's most riveting attractions. From the 1850s through the 1870s, surveying and geological teams had explored parts of the vast Mesa Verde (Spanish for "green table"), discovering some isolated ruins. In 1888, two ranchers—Richard Wetherill and Charlie Mason—set off in search of stray cattle and stumbled upon the remarkable and perfectly preserved **Cliff Palace,** apartment-style cliff dwellings built into the canyon walls. By the next day's end they had discovered two more major sites: Spruce Tree House and Square Tower House. Excitement over their find eventually led to the 1906 creation by Congress of the national park, the first of its kind set aside to preserve the works of humankind (though nature, in its photogenic transition from high desert to subalpine ecosystems, plays a juicy bit part).

Mesa Verde is one of Colorado's highlights, but consider going off-season (though many of the ruins are closed) or overnighting in the park (after the tour buses have departed) to appreciate its full effect, without the crowds. The entrance, where you can pick up information on the park's attractions and accommodations, is 10 miles east of Cortez on U.S. 160. From here a 15-mile drive corkscrews up the mesa, skirting canyons and plateaus, to the **Far View Visitor Center.** *Tel. 303/529–4461 or 303/529–4475. Admission to park: $5 per vehicle. Visitor center open daily 8–6.*

From the visitor center, you can head in one of two directions within the park. Your first option is to take the scenic route to **Wetherill Mesa** (open Memorial Day–Labor Day), which affords spectacular vistas of the Shiprock Formation in New Mexico, and Monument Valley in Arizona and Utah. A minitram departs every half hour between 8:55 AM and 4:55 PM from the Wetherill parking lot, on a 4-mile loop to view the ruins, or there are self-guided and ranger-led tours of Long House, the second-largest dwelling in the park. The other Far View route, **Ruins Road,** accesses the major sites on Chapin Mesa in two 6-mile loops. If you don't want to hike down into the canyons to view the ruins up close, this drive offers several strategic overlooks.

The first stop on the Ruins Road is the park's informative archaeological museum, which traces the development of Anasazi/Pueblo culture. It's a short walk from the museum to one of the most extraordinary sites, **Spruce Tree House,** the only ruin open year-round. Here you can climb down into an excavated kiva (Native American ceremonial structure, usually partly underground), symbolic of the womb of Mother Earth, for a better sense of how the Anasazi worshiped.

From the museum trailhead, one loop leads to the most famous ruin, **Cliff Palace,** the largest dwelling of its kind in the world (accessible by a moderately strenuous 15-minute hike), and to the more remote **Balcony House** (an arduous trek into the canyon below). Ranger-guided tours are available. The other loop accesses two major ruins, **Sun Temple** and **Square Tower House,** both involving a significant amount of walking and climbing.

Cortez is also convenient to other spectacular Anasazi sites, **Lowry Pueblo** and **Hovenweep National Monument,** which straddles the Utah-Colorado border (*see* Other Points of Interest, *below*).

Driving east on U.S. 160 from Mesa Verde will take you past an endearing bit of classic American kitsch, **The Mud Creek Hogan** (Hwy. 160, tel. 303/533–7117). More than a dozen enormous arrows stuck in the ground mark the spot of this hokey trading post and museum (where you get the feeling everything is for sale), with tepees and a giant plastic horse. Beside the shop is a re-creation of a frontier town, replete with saloon, hotel, bank, jail, and livery station. Don't breathe too hard or you'll blow the town over: The "buildings" are only fronts.

The highway winds through the lush Mancos Valley, passing
through the small and charming town of **Mancos,** which exudes
Old West ambience. There are several excellent crafts shops
that offer everything from saddles to 10-gallon hats, and a cute
Cowboy Museum (100 Bauer St., tel. 303/533–7563), in a restored mansion that also houses a B&B and the Old Mesa Verde
Inn restaurant. The **Mancos State Recreation Area** offers a
wealth of activities, including **Ski Hesperus** (*see* Sports and the
Outdoors, *below*), a small ski area a few miles farther east.

U.S. 160 now approaches a classic Western town, **Durango,** of
which Will Rogers once observed, "It's out of the way and glad
of it." His crack is a bit unfair, considering that as a railroad
town Durango has always been a cultural crossroads and melting pot (as well as a place to raise hell). It was founded in 1879
by General William Palmer (president of the all-powerful Denver & Rio Grande Railroad), when nearby Animas City haugh-
tily refused to donate land for a depot; within a decade Durango
had absorbed its rival completely. The booming town quickly
became the region's main metropolis and a gateway to the
Southwest. A walking tour of the historic downtown bears eloquent witness to Durango's prosperity in the late 19th century.
The northern end of Main Street offers the usual assortment of
cheap motels and fast-food outlets, as present-day Durango
serves as the major hub for tourism in the area.

At 13th Avenue and Main Street—the beginning of its National
Historic District—the tenor changes dramatically, with old-
fashioned gas lamps gracing the streets and a superlative collection of Victorians boasting chic galleries, restaurants, and
brand-name outlet stores. The 1882 **Train Depot** (4th St. and
Main Ave.), the 1887 **Strater Hotel** (7th St. and Main Ave.), and
the three-story sandstone **Newman Building** (8th St. and Main
Ave.) are among the elegant edifices restored to their original
grandeur. Stop in the **Diamond Belle Saloon** (in the Strater Hotel)—awash in velour and lace, with a player piano, gilt-and-
mahogany bar, and scantily clad Gay '90s waitresses—for a
wonderfully authentic re-creation of an old-time honky-tonk.

The **Third Avenue National Historic District** (known simply as
The Boulevard), two blocks east of Main Avenue, offers one of
America's most outstanding displays of Victorian residences,
ranging from the imposing mansions of railroad and smelting
executives to more modest variations erected by well-to-do
merchants. The delightful hodgepodge of styles veers from
Greek Revival to Gothic Revival to Queen Anne to Spanish Co-
lonial and Mission designs.

In Durango, the most entertaining way to relive those halcyon
days is to take a ride on **The Durango & Silverton Narrow Gauge
Railroad,** an eight-hour, round-trip journey along the 45-mile
railway. You'll travel in comfort in restored 1882 parlor cars
and listen to the train's shrill whistle as the locomotive chugs
along the fertile Animas River valley and, at times, clings precariously to the hillside. *479 Main St., tel. 303/247–2733. Admission: $37.15 adults, $18.75 children. Operates Apr.–Oct.,
and late Nov.–Jan. 1 daily; times vary.*

At the junction of U.S. 50 and U.S. 160 you have two options:
Pick up U.S. 550 north and continue the tour, or follow U.S. 160
east for a 35-mile excursion to **Chimney Rock,** distinctive, twin-
rock spires that architecturally are more closely related to the

Chaco Canyon Anasazi sites in New Mexico than to those in Mesa Verde. Anthropologists debate the rocks' purpose, whether they served as a trading post or an astronomical observatory of great religious significance. Whatever the origin, many believe the mystical ruins retain tremendous power and resonance. Access to the site is only possible with a forest service guide; reservations are mandatory for the free tour. For information contact the **Pagosa Springs Forest Ranger District** (tel. 303/264–2268).

If you choose to continue on the tour's direct route, take U.S. 550 north along the section of the San Juan Skyway that's otherwise known as the **Million Dollar Highway.** Depending on whom you talk to, it earned the moniker because of: the million dollars' worth of gold and silver mined each mile along the stretch; the low-grade ore from the tailings used to pave the road; the cost of the construction; or the million-dollar views.

Time Out   Seven miles north of Durango lies the **Trimble Hot Springs** (U.S. 550, follow signs, tel. 303/247–0111), a great place to soak your aching bones, especially if you've been doing some hiking.

Fifteen and 25 miles north (respectively) from the U.S. 160 and U.S. 550 junction are two famous recreational playgrounds: the ravishing golf course and development at **Tamarron** (*see* Lodging, *below*) and the **Purgatory Ski Area.** Purgatory is about as down-home as it gets, with clientele that runs toward families, cowboys, and college kids on break. Purgatory's ad campaign proudly tells it like it is: "No movie stars here" and "You don't have to be a celebrity to be treated like a star."

What's unique about Purgatory is its stepped terrain: lots of humps and dips, steep pitches followed by virtual flats. This profile makes it difficult for skiers to lose control. There are some great powder days on the mountain's back side, which will convince anyone that Purgatory isn't just "Pleasant Ridge," as it's derisively known in Crested Butte and Telluride. Unfortunately, the resort has had some financial problems recently, and in 1993 it narrowly avoided bankruptcy when Norwest Bank sought a more favorable repayment schedule. However, a deal was worked out that will enable the area to operate as usual, at least until the 1994–95 season.

The tortuous northern route begins a dizzying series of switchbacks as it climbs over the Molas Pass, yielding splendid vistas of the Grand Turks, the Needles Range, and Crater Lake. This is prime mountain-biking and four-wheeler territory. On the ❹ other side of the pass you'll reach **Silverton,** an isolated, unspoiled old mining community ringed by glorious peaks. It reputedly got its name when a miner exclaimed, "We ain't got much gold but we got a ton of silver!" The entire town is a National Historic Landmark District. The chamber of commerce (414 Greene St., tel. 303/387–5654) has issued a fact-filled walking-tour brochure that describes—among other things— the most impressive buildings lining Greene Street: **Miners' Union Hall,** the **Teller House, Town Hall, San Juan County Courthouse,** and the **Grand Imperial Hotel.** These structures hold historical significance, but more history was probably made in the raucous red-light district along Blair Street.

Silverton has always been a rowdy town with a hardy populace, and that spirit has remained. Every summer evening at 5:30, gunfights are staged at the corner of Blair and 12th streets. In no way are these events hokey; residents take their heritage seriously. If you look north toward Anvil Mountain, you'll see the community's touching tribute to miners—**The Christ of the Mines Shrine**—built in the '50s out of Carrara marble.

41 **Ouray,** 23 miles north, over Red Mountain Pass, is a town trapped in a narrow steep-walled valley in the bullying shadow cast by soaring peaks. The ravishing setting amply explains the town's nickname, "The Switzerland of America." It was named for the great Southern Ute chief Ouray, labeled a visionary by the U.S. Army and branded a traitor by his people because he attempted to assimilate the Utes into white society. The mining town is yet another National Historic Landmark District, with a glittering array of lavish old hotels and residences. More than 25 classic edifices are included in the historic walking-tour brochure issued by the chamber of commerce (1222 Main St., tel. 303/325-4746); among the points of interest are the grandiose **Wright's Opera House; Beaumont, Western, and St. Elmo hotels;** and **Elks Lodge.**

Ouray's architecture is notable, but the town's ultimate glory lies in its surroundings, and it has become an increasingly popular destination for climbers (both mountain and ice varieties), fat-tire fanatics, and hikers. One particularly gorgeous jaunt is to **Box Canyon Falls and Park,** just south of town, off U.S. 550. The turbulent waters of Clear Creek (part of the falls) thunder 285 feet down a narrow gorge. A steel suspension bridge and various well-marked trails afford breathtaking panoramic vistas.

Other natural wonders are the various hot springs in the area. It's hard to tell which is more revivifying: the 104° waters or the views of surrounding peaks at the **Ouray Hot Springs Pool.** *U.S. 550 at the north end of town, tel. 303/325-4638. Admission: $4 adults, $3.50 students 13-17, $2.75 children 5-12 and senior citizens. Open June-Sept., daily 10-10; Oct.-May, Mon.-Wed. noon-9.*

From Ouray, you can continue north for 13 miles on U.S. 550 on your return to Ridgway, where this tour began; or follow the four-wheel-drive **Alpine Loop Scenic Byway** (*see* Four-Wheel Driving in Sports and the Outdoors, *below*), which shimmies through stunning scenery on its way to Lake City, 45 miles south and east.

42 **Lake City** is noted for the superb hiking and fishing in Uncompahgre National Forest, especially at Lake San Cristobal. The town—with its collection of lacy gingerbreads and false-front Victorians—also has the largest National Historic Landmark District in Colorado. But Lake City is best known for the lurid history surrounding a notorious gentleman by the name of Alferd Packer. Packer was a member of a party of six prospectors who camped near Lake San Cristobal during the winter of 1874. That spring, only Packer emerged from the mountains, claiming to have been deserted, and to have subsisted on roots and rabbits. Soon after, a Ute came across a grisly scene: strips of human flesh and crushed skulls. Packer protested his innocence and fled, but a manhunt ensued; Packer was finally caught nine years later, tried, and sentenced to life (he was convicted of manslaughter because of a technicality). As one wag noted at the time, "There were but six dimmocrats in Hinsdale County and he et five of 'em." To this day the event is commemorated by an Alferd Packer Barbecue, held annually in June.

The San Luis Valley At 8,000 square miles, the San Luis Valley is the world's largest alpine valley, stunningly nestled between the San Juan Mountains to the west and the Sangre de Cristo range to the east. Despite its average altitude of 7,500 feet, its sheltering peaks help create a relatively mild climate. The valley is one of Colorado's major agricultural producers, with huge annual crops of potatoes, carrots, canola, barley, and lettuce. It's so self-sufficient that in the '50s local businessmen threatened to secede to prove their point that the state couldn't get along without the valley and its valuable produce.

Watered by the mighty Rio Grande and its tributaries, the San Luis Valley also supports a magnificent array of wildlife, including flocks of sandhill and even whooping cranes. The range of terrain is equally impressive, from the soaring fourteener Mt. Blanca to the stark lunarscape of the Wheeler Geologic Area to the tawny, undulating Great Sand Dunes National Monument.

The area was settled first by the Ute, then by the Spanish, who left their indelible imprint in the town names and local architecture. The oldest town (San Luis), the oldest military post (Fort Garland), and the oldest church (Our Lady of Guadalupe in Conejos) in the state are in this valley. It's no surprise that the area is a highly religious, traditional area, whose many rewards unfold gradually as you unwind under its spell.

Travel east on CO 149 from Lake City to **Creede,** which once earned a reputation as Colorado's rowdiest mining camp and was immortalized in an evocative poem by the local newspaper editor, Cy Warman: "It's day all day in daytime, and there is no night in Creede." Every other building was a saloon or bordello. Bob Ford, who killed Jesse James, was himself gunned down here; other notorious residents included Calamity Jane and Bat Masterson. As delightful as the town is, its location is even more glorious, with the pristine **Weminuche Wilderness** and the **Wheeler Geologic areas,** where the unusual rock formations resemble playful abstract sculptures or an Escher creation.

The Creede Museum, occupying the original Denver & Rio Grande Railroad Depot, paints a vivid portrait of those rough-and-tumble days. Highlights include an underground firehouse and mining museum. *6th and San Luis Sts., tel. 719/658-2374. Admission: $3. Open Memorial Day–Labor Day, daily 10-4.*

Continue along CO 149—declared the Silver Thread National Scenic Byway—on its impossibly beautiful journey east through South Fork (where CO 149 joins with U.S. 160) and through the **Rio Grande National Forest** to **Del Norte.** The route flirts with the Rio Grande, passes near the majestic North Clear Creek Falls, and ambles through numerous ghost towns along the way. In and around the town are several historic sites, such as an original 1870s stage station on the **Barlow-Sanderson Stagecoach Line.**

The **Rio Grande County Museum and Cultural Center,** in town, celebrates the region's multicultural heritage with displays of petroglyphs, mining artifacts, early Spanish relics, and rotating shows of contemporary art. *580 Oak St., tel. 719/657-2847.*

Admission: $2. Open mid-May–Labor Day, Mon.–Sat. 10–5;
Labor Day–mid-May, weekdays 10–4.

Just west of town is the gaping **Penitente Canyon,** which is usually crawling with climbers. Several miles north of town, off CO 112, near La Garita, is another marvel—the towering rock formation, **La Ventana Natural Arch.**

About 20 miles farther east at the junction of U.S. 160 and U.S. 285 is **Alamosa,** the valley's major city, best known as the Olympic high-altitude training center for long-distance runners. Just outside town are the important **Alamosa and Monte Vista wildlife refuges,** whose natural and man-made wetlands—an anomaly amid the arid surroundings—are a sanctuary for the nearly extinct whooping crane and its cousin the sandbill. *9383 El Rancho La., tel. 719/589–4021. Admission free. Open daily 9–sunset.*

The attractive **Adams State College** complex (in town, along Main Street) contains several superlative examples of 1930s WPA-commissioned murals in its administrative building. The admirable **Luther Bean Museum and Art Gallery** (Richardson Hall, Main St., tel. 719/589–7151; admission free; open weekdays 1–5), on campus, displays European porcelain and furniture collections in a handsome, wood-paneled 19th-century drawing room, and changing exhibits of regional arts and crafts.

Alamosa also serves as the gateway to the **Great Sand Dunes National Monument,** 35 miles northeast and reached via U.S. 160 and CO 150. Created by windswept grains from the Rio Grande floor, the sand dunes—which catapult up to 700 feet— are an improbable, unforgettable sight, silhouetted against the sagebrush plains and looming forested slopes of the San Juans. The dunes, as curvaceous as Rubens' nudes, stretch for 55 square miles and are painted with light and shadow that shift through the day. Their very existence seems tenuous, as if they might blow away before your eyes, yet they're solid enough to withstand the stress of hikers and skiers. The sand is as fine and feathery as you'll find anywhere; it's a place for contemplation and repose, the silence broken only by sobbing birds and the faint rush of water from the Medano Creek.

If you travel south from Alamosa on U.S. 285, you'll reach the little town of Romeo. From here pick up CO 142 east to **Manassa,** about 15 miles away, the birthplace of Jack Dempsey, one of the greatest heavyweight boxing champions of all time. Dempsey (nicknamed Manassa Mauler) is commemorated in the **Jack Dempsey Museum.** *401 Main St., tel. 719/843–5207. Admission: $2 adults, $1 children under 12. Open Memorial Day–Labor Day, Mon.–Sat. 9–5.*

Continue east along the scenic byway to the junction of CO 142 and CO 159 to reach **San Luis,** founded in 1851, the oldest incorporated town in Colorado. Its Hispanic heritage is celebrated in the superb **San Luis Museum and Cultural Center,** with its extensive collection of santos (exquisitely decorated figures of saints used for household prayer), *retablos* (paintings on wood), and *bultos* (carved religious figures). Wonderful murals retelling famous stories and legends of the area adorn the town's gracious tree-lined streets. A latter-day masterpiece is the *Stations of the Cross Shrine,* created by renowned local sculptor Huberto Maestas. Perched above town on a mesa called La

Mesa de la Piedad y de la Misericordia (Hill of Piety and Mercy), its 15 figures dramatically depict the last hours of Christ's life. The trail culminates in a tranquil grotto dedicated to the Virgin Mary. *402 Church Pl., tel. 719/672–3611. Admission: $3. Open Memorial Day–Labor Day, weekdays 8–4:30 and weekends 10–3.*

Eighteen miles farther north, in the Sangre de Cristos ("Blood of Christ," after the ruddy color of the peaks at dawn), is **Fort Garland,** the site of Colorado's first military post that was originally established in 1856 to protect settlers. The legendary Kit Carson commanded the outfit, and the six original adobe structures are still around, comprising the **Fort Garland State Museum.** The venue features a re-creation of the commandant's quarters, various period military displays, and a rotating local folk-art exhibit. *U.S. 159, south of 160, tel. 719/379–3512. Admission: $2. Open Memorial Day–Labor Day, Mon.–Sat. 10–5, Sun. 1–5.*

Consider visiting a portion of the Santa Fe Trail by continuing east on U.S. 160 to the town of Walsenburg. From Walsenburg you can either go south on I–25 to the town of Trinidad, or travel north, passing through Pueblo and winding up in Colorado Springs (*see* Southcentral Colorado, *below*).

What to See and Do with Children

Anasazi Heritage Center (*see* The Four Corners in Exploring Southwest Colorado, *above*) features educational, hands-on displays and computer games.
Doo Zoo (635 Main St., Durango, tel. 303/241–5225), a children's museum, offers constantly changing hands-on exhibits.
The **Durango & Silverton Narrow Gauge Railroad** (*see* The Four Corners in Exploring Southwest Colorado, *above*).

Other Points of Interest

Four Corners Monument. A stone slab marks the only spot where four states—Colorado, Arizona, Utah, and New Mexico—meet. Of course, this is photo-op country, so smile and say "cheese"! Snacks and souvenirs are sold by Native Americans. To get here, travel south from Cortez on Highway 160 for about 40 miles: You can't miss the signs. *Hwy. 160 (follow signs). Admission: $1 per vehicle. Open daily 7 AM–8 PM.*
Hovenweep National Monument. This site—whose literal translation from Ute means "deserted valley"—contains several major ruins, including such imposing square, oval, and circular towers as Holly, Cajon, Hackberry, and Horseshoe, all of which are accessible only on foot. The most impressive ruin, called The Castle, underscores the site's uncanny resemblance to a medieval fiefdom. Hovenweep is approached via Highway 160 west to C.R. G (McElmo Canyon Rd.), which enters the spectacular red-walled McElmo Canyon along the way. *McElmo Canyon Rd., tel. 303/529–4465 (Mesa Verde National Monument HQ). Admission free; camping entry fee $3. Open daily sunrise–sunset.*
Lowry Pueblo. Small in comparison to Hovenweep, the Lowry site has only eight kivas and 40 rooms and may have been a "suburb" of larger communities in the area during its occupation from about 800 to 1110. Of particular note are the Great Kiva, one of the largest such structures ever discovered, and a

painted kiva, providing a fascinating insight into Anasazi decorative techniques. A brochure, which details the self-guided tour, is available at the entrance of the site. *Hwy. 666, 9 mi west of Pleasant View, no tel. Admission free. Open daily 9–5.*

Shopping

Southwest Colorado is the best place to pick up Western and Native American art and artifacts. Although there are malls and factory outlets in Durango housing the usual retailers, the following list includes only shops and boutiques with unique merchandise.

The San Luis Valley offers superb examples of folk crafts, such as Norwegian rosemaling and Hardanger lacework, and basketry, embroidery, weaving, and beadwork adapted from Native American traditions.

Specialty Stores
Antiques **Buckskin Trading Co.** (636 Main St., Ouray, tel. 303/325–4044) sports an array of mining, railroading, Native American, and cowboy collectibles.
Treasures of Time (Pacific and Davis Sts., Telluride, tel. 303/728–3383) carries a selection of Western memorabilia, including frontier-style furnishings.

Art Galleries **Golden West Indian Arts/Jan Cicero Gallery** (101 W. Colorado Ave., Telluride, tel. 303/728–3664) stocks a superb selection of southwestern, Native American, and Hispanic artworks.
Goodman Gallery (3rd St. and Elk Ave., upstairs, Crested Butte, tel. 303/349–5470) displays and sells southwestern artwork from regional artisans.
Hellbent Leather and Silver (209 E. Colorado Ave., Telluride, tel. 303/728–6246; 741 Main Ave., Durango, tel. 303/247–9088) is a fine source for Native American arts and crafts.
Toh-Atin Gallery (149 W. 9th St., Durango, tel. 303/247–8277) is probably the foremost Western, Native American, and Southwestern art gallery in Colorado, offering a wide-ranging selection of paintings, pottery, prints, records, foodstuffs, clothing, and jewelry.

Alamosa offers some of the best galleries in the region. Among them are **Firedworks Gallery** (608 Main St., tel. 719/589–6064), **Gallery West** (718 Main St., tel. 719/589–2275), **This That and the Other** (717 Main St., tel. 719/589–6417), and **The Turquoise Shop** (423 San Juan Ave., tel. 719/589–2631). In Manassa, **Something Pewter** (419 Main St., tel. 719/843–5702) fashions seemingly everything from bolos to belts, charms to figurines—all in pewter. **Casa de Madera** (680 Grand St., tel. 719/657–2336), in Del Norte, sells marvelous regional wood carvings.

Books **Between the Covers Bookstore and Coffee House** (224 W. Colorado Ave., Telluride, tel. 303/728–4504) offers the perfect ambience for browsing through the latest titles while sipping a cappuccino.
Maria's Books (928 Main Ave., Durango, tel. 303/247–1438) specializes in regional and southwestern literature and nonfiction.

Boutiques **Blair Street Cottage** (1342 Blair St., Silverton, tel. 303/387–5735) specializes in silk batik, with lovely scarves, ties, camisoles, and wall hangings.
Circumstance Leatherworks (306 6th Ave., Ouray, tel. 303/325–

7360) is the venue for leather custom-craft designs by Rob and Jane Holmes.

North Moon (109 W. Colorado Ave., Telluride, tel. 303/728–4145) features exquisite, contemporary Native American jewelry.

Unicas Southwest (Ft. Smith Saloon Bldg., Ridgway, tel. 303/626–5723; 215 E. Colorado Ave., Telluride, tel. 303/728–4778; 703 Main Ave., Ouray, no tel.) delivers on its advertising promises of "worldly styles" and "fun, fashion, funk, and folk art."

Western Outfitters (960 Main St., Durango, tel. 303/247–0260) outfits men, women, and children from head to toe in everything from Stetson hats to Tony Lama Boots.

Ceramics **Creekside Pottery** (126 Elk Ave., Crested Butte, tel. 303/349–6459) showcases local artist Mary Jursinovic's pottery and landscape lamps.

Mesa Verde Pottery (27601 Hwy. 160 E, Cortez, tel. 303/565–4492) offers a comprehensive sampling of ceramics from most Southwest tribes.

The Potter's Wheel (221 E. Colorado Ave., Telluride, tel. 303/728–4912) has a wide selection of both decorative and functional pottery crafted by local artisans.

Ute Mountain Pottery Plant (Jct. Hwys. 160 and 666, Towaoc, tel. 303/565–8548) invites customers to watch the painstaking processes of molding, trimming, cleaning, painting, and glazing, before adjourning to the showroom to buy pieces straight from the source.

Zappa Pottery (688 Spring Creek Blvd., Montrose, tel. 303/249–6819) showcases the fine stoneware designs of Nick and Joan Zappa.

Crafts and Collectibles **The Candle Shop** (Blair St., Silverton, tel. 303/387–5733) sells not only handmade candles, but wind chimes, hurricane lamps, and local crafts.

Cortez Curiosity Shop (30 E. Main St., Cortez, tel. 303/565–4856) sells everything from scented candles to tinctures to astrology charts to crystals.

The Train Store (501 Main St., Durango, tel. 303/259–2145) offers unique train and railroad memorabilia, toys, models, books, T-shirts, and videos.

Flea Markets **Kellogg's Corner** (24 Everett St., Durango, tel. 303/247–2500) is a daily flea market.

Food **Adobe Milling Co.** (Main St., Dove Creek, tel. 303/677–2620) is located in the self-styled Pinto Bean Capital of the World and vends Anasazi beans, Dos Gringos spices, piñon nuts, and other products.

Honeyville Station (33633 Hwy. 550 N, Hermosa, tel. 800/676–7690) sells jams, jellies (try the chokecherry), condiments, and, of course, honey. You can watch how the bees make honey (in glass hives) and may be treated to a lecture by a fully garbed beekeeper.

The San Luis Valley is noted for its produce. Mycophiles should stop by the **Alamosa Mushroom Farm** (10719 S.R. 5 S, tel. 719/589–5881). **Mountain Maid Jelly** (710 2nd St., Saguache, tel. 719/655–2824) offers a variety of unusual and delicious flavors. **Haefeli's Honey Farms** (0041 S.R. 1 E. Monte Vista, tel. 303/852–2301) sells delectable mountain-bloom honeys.

Jewelry **The Enameling Shop** (1249 Greene St., Silverton, tel. 303/387–5442) features original enamel works by Gary and Robert Richardson, who make buckles, earrings, and bolo ties.

Sporting Goods **Olympic Sports** (150 W. Colorado Ave., Telluride, tel. 303/728–4477) has a plethora of equipment and clothing for all seasons.

Western Wear **O'Farrell Hat Company** (598 Main St., Durango, tel. 303/259–2517) makes hats to custom fit your head: They've fitted heads such as former presidents Bush and Reagan's.

Sports and the Outdoors

Camping The glorious wilderness area of the San Juans and Sangre de Cristos offers a plethora of camping activities. Contact the **Bureau of Land Management** (Durango, tel. 303/247–4082), the **San Juan National Forest** (Durango, tel. 303/247–4874), the **Curecanti National Recreation Area** (Montrose, tel. 303/641–2337), and the **Uncompahgre and Gunnison national forests** (Delta, tel. 303/874–7691) for more information. Campsites are also available in Mesa Verde and Hovenweep; contact the **National Park Service at Mesa Verde National Park** (CO 81330, tel. 303/529–4465).

Canoeing **Shorty's** (Bayfield, tel. 303/884–2768) and **Mountain Marina** (Bayfield, tel. 303/884–9450) rent canoes on Vallecito Lake. **Beaver Creek Marina** (Cortez, tel. 303/882–2258) rents canoes and boats on McPhee Reservoir. **San Juan Skyway Marina** (Ouray, tel. 303/626–5480) rents boats at the Ridgway State Recreation Area (Hwy. 550, 12 mi north of town). You can also call the **Curecanti National Recreation Area** (Montrose, tel. 303/641–2337), **Elk Creek Marina** (Montrose, tel. 303/641–0707), and **Ridgway Reservoir** (Ridgway, tel. 303/626–5822) for more information about boating.

Climbing **Fantasy Ridge Alpinism** (Telluride, tel. 303/728–3546) and **SouthWest Adventures** (Durango, tel. 303/259–0370) are two climbing clubs in the region. Ouray is gaining fame in ice-climbing circles, with its abundance of frozen waterfalls.

World-class climbing can be found outside Del Norte, in the **Penitente Canyon,** as well as in the **San Juans,** and the **Wheeler Geologic Area,** outside Creede.

Cycling Durango/Purgatory has good cycling trails, such as **Hermosa Creek** and **La Plata Canyon Road.**

Mountain Bike Specialists (340 S. Camino del Rio, Durango, tel. 303/259–6661) arranges tours throughout the Four Corners region.

Crested Butte Mountain offers several miles of scenic trails. **Signal Peak Loop** and **Rage in the Sage Track** outside Gunnison are also popular.

Top Telluride trails include **Ilium Road** and **Sawpit Road.** The entire **San Juan Skyway,** many of whose ascents are quite steep, is a favorite for cyclists.

Routes around Silverton run through ghost towns and mining trails.

The Cortez area is popular for the Anasazi ruins.

Fishing For information on fishing in the region contact the **Colorado Division of Wildlife** (2300 S. Townsend Ave., Montrose 81401, tel. 303/249–3431); the **Bureau of Land Management** (701 Camino del Rio, Durango 81301, tel. 303/247–4082); the **San Juan National Forest** (Durango, tel. 303/247–4874); and the **Uncompahgre and Gunnison National Forests** (Delta, tel. 303/874–7691).

One of the finest sources of prime trout and bass in Colorado is the **McPhee Reservoir.** The second-largest body of water in the state, it reputedly has the best catch record in Southwest Colorado. Other well-stocked reservoirs in the area include **Jackson, Joe Moore, Taylor,** and **Groundhog.** The **Dolores, Gunnison** and **Mancos rivers,** and **Taylor** and **Bear creeks** are other big locales. North of Durango are Lakes **Haviland, Lemon,** and **Vallecito.** Outside Gunnison, the **Blue Mesa Reservoir** in the Curecanti National Recreation Area (tel. 303/641–2337) is another top choice, as is Lake San Cristobal.

The **Rio Grande River**—between Del Norte and South Fork—teems with rainbows and lunker browns.

The following operators run trips to various areas within the region: **Colorado Fishing Adventures** (Pagosa Springs, tel. 303/264–4168); **Duranglers** (Durango, tel. 303/385–4081); **Telluride Outside** (tel. 303/728–3895).

Four-Wheel Driving The inspiring **Alpine Loop Scenic Byway** joins Lake City with Ouray and Silverton. This circle is only open in summer and is paved, except for the dirt roads over Cinnamon and Engineer passes. However, this is four-wheel heaven, dizzily spiraling from 12,800-foot passes to gaping valleys and whizzing past haunting ghost towns.

Golf **Conquistador Golf Course** (2018 N. Dolores St., Cortez, tel. 303/565–9208) is an 18-hole public course with sweeping views of Mesa Verde and Sleeping Ute Mountain.
Dalton Ranch and Golf Club (7 mi north of Durango, on U.S. 550, tel. 303/247–7921) is a Ken Dye–designed 18-hole championship course with inspiring panoramas of red-rock cliffs. Also, the **Hillcrest Golf Course** (2300 Rim Dr., tel. 303/247–1499) is an 18-hole public course perched on a mesa. **Tamarron Resort** (40292 Rte. 550 N, tel. 303/259–2000) is an 18-hole, 6,885-yard course, frequently ranked among *Golf Digest*'s top 75 resort courses.
Dos Rios Golf Club (Hwy. 50, 2 mi west of Gunnison, tel. 303/641–1482) has lovely views; water comes into play on 17 holes.
Skyland Country Club (385 Country Club Dr., tel. 303/349–6127) is a ravishing 18-hole course designed by Robert Trent Jones, Jr.
Fairfield Pagosa Resort (Hwy. 160, 3 mi west of Pagosa Springs, tel. 303/781–4141) offers both an 18-hole and a 9-hole course.
Telluride Golf Club (Telluride Mountain Village, tel. 303/728–3856) boasts breathtaking views of Mt. Wilson and Mt. Sunshine, which dominate this 7,009-yard course.

In the San Luis Valley, **Alamosa Golf Course** (6678 River Rd., tel. 719/589–5330) is an 18-hole championship course. **Cattails Golf Course** (State St., tel. 719/589–9515), also in Alamosa, is an 18-hole course that wraps scenically around the Rio Grande. **Great Sand Dunes Country Club** (5303 Hwy. 150, Mosca, tel. 719/378–2357) is an 18-hole course with billowing dunes as a backdrop.

Hiking For general information about hiking in Southwest Colorado, contact the **Bureau of Land Management** (701 Camino del Rio, Durango 81301, tel. 303/247–4082) or the **San Juan National Forest Ranger Districts** (100 N. 6th St., tel. 303/882–7296 in Dolores; 41595 E. Hwy. 160, tel. 303/533–7716 in Mancos).

In the Needles Range of the San Juans, picturesque, fairly strenuous hikes include **Molas Pass** to **Crater Lake, Engineer Peak,** and the **Grand Turks.** Trails abound throughout the region, skirting waterfalls and mining ruins. The **Lizard Head Wilderness Area,** dominated by the eerie rock tooth of the same name, showcases the region's alpine scenery at its best.

The **Great Sand Dunes** are a favorite hike. The **Rio Grande National Forest** offers over a million acres of pristine wilderness.

Horseback Riding **Fantasy Ranch** (Crested Butte, tel. 303/349–5425), **Southfork Stables** (3 mi east of Durango, tel. 303/259–4871), and **Telluride Outside** (tel. 303/728–3895) provide horses for riding tours, which range from one-hour walks to overnight excursions; rates begin at $20.

Llama Rides In Durango, **Buckhorn Llama** (tel. 303/259–5965) and **Turnbull Llama** (tel. 303/259–3773) both offer gourmet lunch treks.

Rafting River tours can last for an afternoon or for 10 days, depending on the arrangements. Rates begin at $30. **Durango Rivertrippers** (tel. 303/259–0289) runs expeditions down the Animas River. **Gunnison River Expeditions** (Montrose, tel. 303/249–4441) specializes in Gunnison River tours. **Telluride Whitewater** (tel. 303/728–3895) explores down the Gunnison, Dolores, Colorado, and Animas rivers.

Skiing **Crested Butte Nordic Center** (tel. 303/349–6201) has a 48-mile, *Cross-Country* groomed track system and also offers guided tours into the backcountry.

Purgatory-Durango Cross-Country Center (tel. 303/247–9000) offers 26 miles of machine-groomed scenic trails just outside the ski area.

Telluride Nordic Center (tel. 303/728–5989) provides almost 80 miles of pristine trails.

Downhill **Crested Butte Mountain Resort.** 85 trails; 13 lifts; 1,160 acres; 2,775-foot vertical. Good beginner and extreme terrain. *CO 135, tel. 303/349–2222. Open late-Nov.–early Apr., daily 9–4.*

Purgatory-Durango. 50 trails; 9 chairs; 675 acres; 2,029-foot vertical. A lot of intermediate runs and glade and tree skiing. *U.S. 550, tel. 303/247–9000 or 800/525–0892. Open late Nov.– early Apr., daily 9–4.*

Ski Hesperus. 18 trails; 2 lifts. This is a small, family ski area close to Durango. The Navajos regarded the mountain as a sacred peak and used it as a directional landmark. Hesperus offers 100% night skiing. *U.S. 160, tel. 303/259–3711. Open Dec.– early Apr., Sat.–Tues. 9–4, Wed.–Fri. 4:30–9:30.*

Telluride. 62 trails; 9 chairs and a poma; 1,060 acres; 3,165-foot vertical (3,522-ft. vertical if you hike to the highest ridge). *CO 145, tel. 303/728–3856 or 800/525–3455. Open late Nov.–early Apr., 9–4.*

Wolf Creek. 50 trails; 5 lifts; 700 acres; 1,425-foot vertical. This is one of Colorado's best-kept secrets and a powder hound's dream: it's uncrowded with no lift lines and gets phenomenal snow (averaging more than 450 in. a year). The 50 trails run the gamut from wide-open bowls to steep glade skiing. *U.S. 160, at*

the top of Wolf Creek Pass, Pagosa Springs, tel. 303/264-5629. Open early Nov.–mid-Apr., daily 9–4.
Snowboarding is also permited at all the above ski areas.

Heli-Skiing **Telluride Helitrax** (tel. 303/728–4904) offers thrilling touring through the New Eastern Powder Circuit.

Ski Touring **San Juan Hut System** (Telluride, tel. 303/728–6935) connects Telluride with Ridgway. There are five huts equipped with beds, blankets, and stoves. Huts are about 7 miles apart.

Tennis The following parks offer free, public courts and reservations are advised: **Crested Butte** and **Mt. Crested Butte Town** parks (no tel.); **Durango City Park** (tel. 303/247–5622); **Ouray Hot Springs Pool** (no tel.); **Telluride Town Park** (tel. 303/728–3071).

Dining

Colorado's Southwest is one of those regions in the good ol' U.S. of A. that has made truck stops and their fare an indelible part of our tradition. What you'll also find here is sensational southwestern-style cooking, especially around Durango, and superb gourmet dining in Crested Butte, about which a journalist from the *Denver Post* once opined, "There are more fine restaurants per capita in Crested Butte than anywhere else in America." Telluride isn't far behind, befitting its status as unofficial rival to Vail and Aspen. For rates *see* Towns and Country price chart in Chapter 1, Essential Information.

Highly recommended restaurants are indicated by a star ★.

Alamosa **True Grits.** This is a handsome steak house, its exposed brick walls and wood beams alive with hanging plants. The cuts are predictably good, but that's not the real draw: As the name implies, the restaurant is really a shrine to John Wayne. His portraits hang everywhere: The Duke in action; The Duke in repose; The Duke lost in thought. *Jct. Hwys. 160 and 17, tel. 719/589–9954. Reservations accepted. Dress: casual. MC, V. Moderate.*

★ **Ace Inn and Old Town Bar.** The decor is rough hewn: wood-paneled walls adorned with dried chilies and assorted kitsch, such as antique pepper mills and cheesy Eiffel Tower ceramics of uncertain taste. You should definitely bring an empty stomach to this superior Mexican restaurant, for heaping portions of stuffed *sopaipilla* (beans, rice, and beef smothered in red and green chili), burritos, and chile relleños. Save room for the sopaipilla sundae drowned in cinnamon wine sauce. Even the margaritas are daunting: The small one is 28 ounces! *326 Main St., tel. 719/589–9801. Reservations accepted. Dress: casual. MC, V. Inexpensive.*

Cortez **M & M Family Restaurant and Truckstop.** Semis and RVs jammed into the parking lot attest that M & M is the real McCoy as truck stops go. If chicken-fried steak, enchiladas, and huge breakfasts (served 24 hours a day) are your fancy, you'll be thrilled to eat here. There are posher restaurants in town, but none better—certainly not for these prices. *7006 Hwy. 160 S, tel. 303/565–6511. No reservations. Dress: casual. AE, MC, V. Inexpensive.*

Crested Butte **Le Bosquet.** This charming Western-style Victorian bistro is the only game in town if game is what you're hankerin' for. However, if sublime elk medallions in cabernet reduction or a venison special doesn't appeal to you, feast on the first-rate ginger salmon or hazelnut chicken. *2nd and Elk Aves., tel. 303/ 349-5808. Reservations advised. Dress: neat but casual. AE, MC, V. Closed weekend lunch. Expensive–Very Expensive.*

★ **Soupçon.** Soupçon ("soup's on," get it?) occupies a delightful log cabin—and a cozier place, with its two intimate rooms, doesn't exist in this town. Mac Bailey, the impish owner-chef (women fall in love nightly: "He's so cute," they gush when he trundles out from the kitchen), brings innovative variations to classic bistro cuisine. His roast duckling, usually topped with an impeccably balanced Michigan cherry sauce, may be the best in the state. The fish dishes he prepares are sublime: Try petrale (sole lightly breaded in cornmeal, glistening with black bean, ginger, and sake sauce). Desserts, however, are where Mac really shines: Order any soufflé, Jack Daniels bread pudding, or hazelnut ice-cream cake. *Just off 2nd St., behind the Forest Queen, tel. 303/349-5448. Reservations advised. Dress: neat but casual. AE, MC, V. Closed for lunch. Expensive– Very Expensive.*

Timberline. This handsome, cozy split-level restaurant is set in a restored Victorian home. Among the top starters are fettuccine Alfredo with smoked trout and goat-cheese terrine. Poached salmon au jus or herb-crusted veal chops might make a perfect second course. The weekly prix-fixe menus are good-value options. In summer, a pleasant Sunday brunch is offered. *21 Elk Ave., tel. 303/349-9831. Reservations advised. Dress: neat but casual. AE, MC, V. Closed for lunch. Expensive– Very Expensive.*

Penelope's. Mac, the owner of Soupçon (*see above*), also manages this local favorite, whose Victorian ambience is complemented by a pretty greenhouse. Everything on the menu is solid and dependable, from the Colorado rack of lamb to the roast apricot duck. Sunday brunch here is a Crested Butte institution. *120 Elk Ave., tel. 303/349-5178. Reservations advised. Dress: neat but casual. AE, MC, V. Closed for lunch. Expensive.*

★ **Powerhouse.** This is an enormous rough-hewn, barnlike structure, with a delightful Gay '90s bar. The cuisine is haute Mexican, with scrumptious standards such as tacos and burritos, and more exotic dishes such as delectable mesquite-roasted *cabrito* (kid)—a true delicacy. The margaritas are the best in town. *130 Elk Ave., tel. 303/349-5494. No reservations. Dress: casual. AE, MC, V. Closed for lunch. Moderate–Expensive.*

Swiss Chalet. The owners duplicate the true alpine experience, right down to a *bierstube* with Paulaner on tap. The *kalbsgeschnetzeltes* (veal loin sautéed with mushrooms and shallots in white-wine cream sauce), raclette, and fondue are luscious, as are such hard-to-find specialties as *buendnerfleisch* (savory air-dried beef). *621 Gothic Rd., on the mountain, tel. 303/349-5917. Reservations advised. Dress: casual. AE, MC, V. Closed for lunch in summer. Moderate.*

The Artichoke. From the deck of this simple bustling establishment you can watch the skiers come down the mountain while you nibble on "high-altitude diner cuisine," with a Cajun slant. Artichokes are obviously a specialty and are prepared in various ways. Among entrée favorites are popcorn shrimp, chicken pot pie, cat's meow catfish, gumbo, and Philly cheese steak —all of which should satisfy even the heartiest appetites. *Treasury Ctr., on the mountain (upstairs), tel. 303/349-6688.*

Reservations accepted. Dress: casual. AE, DC, MC, V. Inexpensive–Moderate.

Donita's Cantina. This down-home Mexican restaurant is hard to miss since it's the one in the hot-pink building. The fare isn't nearly as showy: simply good, solid standards such as fajitas and enchiladas, and a rollicking salsa. It may be due to either the bargain prices or the killer margaritas, but the crowds here are always jovial. *330 Elk Ave., tel. 303/349–6674. No reservations. Dress: casual. MC, V. Closed for lunch. Inexpensive.*

★ **Slogar.** Set in a lovingly renovated Victorian tavern awash in lace and stained glass, this restaurant—also run by Mac Bailey of Soupçon (*see above*)—is just plain cozy. In the gastronomic equivalent of prestidigitation (a cleverly executed trick), Mac turns out some of the plumpest, juiciest fried chicken west of the Mississippi. The fixings are just as sensational: flaky biscuits, creamy mashed potatoes swimming in hearty chicken gravy, and the unique sweet-and-sour coleslaw from a Pennsylvania Dutch recipe dating back nearly two centuries. All that and more, including homemade ice cream, for $10.95! *2nd and Whiterock Sts., tel. 303/349–5765. Reservations advised. Dress: casual. MC, V. Closed for lunch. Inexpensive.*

Durango/Purgatory   **Café Cascade.** Many locals' choice for the best restaurant on the mountain, if not in the region, this intimate split-level eatery features the southwestern stylings of chef Tom Hamilton. Cajun BBQ rock shrimp, fried alligator, and pheasant ravioli are his sterling appetizers; fresh grilled swordfish brushed with piñon cilantro butter, and New Zealand red deer in porcini mushroom sauce are among the standout entrées. *50827 Hwy. 550 N (1 mi north of Purgatory), Cascade Village, tel. 303/259–3500. Reservations advised. Dress: casual. AE, D, DC, MC, V. Closed for lunch. Very Expensive.*

Ariano's. This popular Italian place occupies a dimly lit room plastered with local artworks. It offers exceptional pizzas (try the pesto) and pastas, and the best fried calamari in the Four Corners. Next door, under the same ownership, is Pronto, a bright and noisy trattoria where you can get the same pastas for less money. *150 E. 6th St., Durango, tel. 303/247–8146. Reservations advised. Dress: casual. AE, MC, V. Closed for lunch. Moderate–Expensive.*

Ore House. Durango is a meat-and-potatoes kind of town, and this is Durango's idea of a steak house, where the aroma of beef smacks you in the face as you walk past. This classic rough-hewn eatery offers enormous slabs of aged Angus—cholesterol heaven hand-cut daily. *147 E. 6th St., Durango, tel. 303/245–5707. Reservations advised. Dress: casual. AE, D, DC, MC, V. Moderate–Expensive.*

The Red Snapper. If you're in the mood for fresh fish, head to this congenial place, decorated with more than 200 gallons' worth of saltwater aquariums. Of course, steaks and prime rib are also available. The salad bar includes more than 50 items. *144 E. 9th St., Durango, tel. 303/259–3417. Reservations advised. Dress: casual. AE, MC, V. Closed for lunch. Moderate–Expensive.*

★ **Sow's Ear.** It's a toss-up between the Ore House and this Purgatory watering hole for the "best steak house award." The Sow's Ear gets the edge, though, for its rustic but elegant decor, with a huge fireplace, hanging plants, and—okay—statues of urinating cowboys. The mouthwatering, fresh-baked seven-grain bread and creative preparations such as blackened fillets and the daunting hodgeebaba—an 18-ounce rib eye smothered with sautéed mushrooms and onions—are a few more reasons Sow's Ear leads the pack. There's a brightly painted climbing wall at the bar for those who need to burn calories (or wait for their table). *Hwy. 55 N, Purgatory, tel. 303/247–3527. Reservations advised. Dress: casual. AE, D, DC, MC, V. Closed for lunch. Moderate–Expensive.*

Carver's Bakery and Brew Pub. This microbrewery run by the "Brews Brothers," Bill and Jim Carver, offers about eight beers at any given time, including flavors such as Raspberry Wheat Ale (which brewmaster Patrick Keating nicknamed "Seduction Ale"), Zolly's Nut Brown Ale honey lager, as well as barley wine. The front room is a well-lit coffeehouse/bakery and the back a more subdued sports bar. No matter when you visit, the place is always hopping, from breakfast (delicious muffins) to the wee hours. (Try the bratwurst; brew-jitas, which are chicken or sirloin strips pan-fried in tequila and salsa; or specials such as shrimp and pecan chilaquiles.) *1022 Main St., Durango, tel. 303/259–2545. No reservations. Dress: casual. AE, D, MC, V. Inexpensive–Moderate.*

Olde Tymer's Café. Locals flock to this former drugstore that still drips with atmosphere from the bygone days: The balcony, pressed-tin ceiling, and walls plastered with artifacts and locals' photos lend a '20s dance-hall look to the place. You can get cheap draft beer, great burgers, and $5 blue-plate specials. *1000 Main St., Durango, tel. 303/259–2990. No reservations. Dress: casual. AE, MC, V. Inexpensive.*

Mancos **Millwood Junction.** Folks come from four states (no fooling) for the 25-item salad bar and phenomenal Friday-night seafood buffet. Steaks and seafood are featured in this upscale Red Lobster/Sizzler–style eatery. *Jct. Hwy. 160 and Main St., tel. 303/533–7338. No reservations. Dress: casual. AE, DC, MC, V. Moderate.*

Montrose **The Whole Enchilada.** You'll get the whole enchilada and then some at this lively place. Portions are gargantuan, and the food goes down easily, especially the tasty chimichangas, blue-corn enchiladas, and homemade pies. The patio is a pleasant place to sit in summer. *44 S. Grand St., tel. 303/249–1881. Reservations accepted. Dress: casual. AE, MC, V. Inexpensive–Moderate.*

Sally's Café. Warm comfort food is served here, in plentiful portions, and drowned in glutinous brown gravy. The menu has it all, from Mexi-burgers, patty melts, chicken-fried steak, and grilled PB & J sandwiches to Duncan Hines cakes and dull-as-dirty-dishwater coffee. Gum-cracking waitresses and tables covered in red vinyl and set up in Sally's living room hint at what you can expect to find here: Sally revels in the tacky, from a Christmas moose to an astounding collection of hand-painted china ("I like my dishes," says Sally with typical understatement). Sally's Café is a treat, especially first thing in the morning for breakfast. *715 S. Townsend Ave., tel. 303/249–6096. Reservations accepted. Dress: casual. Closed Sun. for dinner and Wed., Thurs. No credit cards. Inexpensive.*

Pagosa Springs/Wolf Creek **Elkhorn Café.** Filling and fiery Mexican fare (try the stuffed sopaipillas), as well as robust American standards such as meat loaf and pot roast, draws people from miles around. Breakfast burritos will help propel you down the Wolf Creek bowls in record time. *438 Main St., tel. 303/264–2146. Reservations accepted. Dress: casual. AE, MC, V. Inexpensive–Moderate.*

Silverton **Handlebars Food and Saloon.** This relaxed eatery occupies the oldest brick building (dating back to the 1850s) on the Western Slope. Barbecued pork ribs, steaks, and burgers are featured. *117 E. 13th St., tel. 303/387–5395. Reservations accepted. Dress: casual. AE, MC, V. Inexpensive–Moderate.*

Telluride **La Marmotte.** Ambience can't get much more romantic than at
★ this warm bistro that seems transplanted from Provence, with its brick walls, lace curtains, and flowerpots of fresh geraniums. The fish specials, such as delicate flaky salmon in dill sauce, are particularly splendid. *150 W. San Juan Ave., tel. 303/728–6232. Reservations advised. Dress: neat but casual. AE, MC, V. Closed for lunch. Very Expensive.*

Evangeline's. This intimate boîte has only 30 seats, providing an intimate and private mood for this rather formal dining room dressed in primrose and mint. Chef Moore's food is haute Cajun; specialties include oysters Rockefeller, ravioli, and a classic shrimp Creole. The $29 prix-fixe meal is a sensational buy. *646 Mountain Village Blvd., tel. 303/728–9717. Reservations advised. Dress: neat but casual. AE, MC, V. Expensive–Very Expensive.*

★ **The PowderHouse.** Tony Clinco (a former Golden Gloves winner who found another use for his hands) bills his food as "Rocky Mountain Cuisine." In reality, this is classic Italian married to wild game. Among the winners are pheasant ravioli; smoked buffalo sausage; and the game special—stuffed quail, venison chop, and marinated elk, each in its own sauce. *226 W. Colorado Ave., tel. 303/728–3622. Reservations advised. Dress: neat but casual. AE, MC, V. Expensive–Very Expensive.*

221 South Oak Bistro. It had to happen that a Telluride restaurant would finally include "bistro" in its title. This one is very pretty, too, with high-tech southwestern decor, spot-lit peach walls, and a blond-wood bar. Soft jazz wafts through the casually elegant space. The menu sounds exciting—for example, cured salmon, potato, and walnut ravioli—but fails to deliver on its promise in execution. Stick to the simpler dishes such as free-range chicken with herb fettuccine and winter squash, or crispy salmon medallions with yummy roast-garlic potatoes and braised napa cabbage. *221 S. Oak St., tel. 303/728–9507. Reservations advised. Dress: casual. AE, MC, V. Expensive.*

Leimgruber's Bierstube and Restaurant. Christel Leimgruber's hangout is arguably Telluride's most popular après-ski bar. The wonderful Bavarian ambience is enhanced by barmaids in dirndls right out of "The Student Prince" and a clientele that seems on the verge of launching into "The Drinking Song." The fine, traditional alpine food includes mixed German and wild-game sausage plates, mouth-puckering sauerbraten, and, of course, apple strudel. If you only want a brew, stop by to down a Paulaner or hoist a glass boot, which holds more than a liter of beer. *573 W. Pacific Ave., tel. 303/728–4663. Reservations advised. Dress: casual. AE, MC, V. Closed for lunch. Moderate–Expensive.*

Athenian Senate. This restored bordello has seen its share of history: World-champion heavyweight Jack Dempsey even washed dishes here once, when he was down on his luck. The ambience is warm and homey, and owner/chef Angel Chakeres serves tasty Greek and Italian specialties, from moussaka to eggplant parmigiana. Traditional Greek dancing, ouzo, and plate-smashing have been known to end evenings. *123 S.*

Spruce St., tel. 303/728–3018. No reservations. Dress: casual.
AE, MC, V. Closed for lunch in winter. Moderate.

Floradora. This Telluride institution, the longest single-owned
eating and drinking establishment in town, is named for two
turn-of-the-century ladies of the evening (although locals call it
Howie's, after the owner). The rafters are draped with pennants contributed by patrons over the years. Southwestern and
Continental specials include southwest pizza (with three
cheeses, sun-dried tomatoes, roasted red peppers, oregano,
garlic, and salsa), blackened catch of the day, and tropical
chicken. *103 W. Colorado Ave., tel. 303/728–3888. Reserva-*
tions accepted. Dress: casual. AE, MC, V. Inexpensive–
Moderate.

Roma Bar and Café. In operation since 1897, this restaurant offers tremendous value and an incomparable air of history. The
1860 Brunswick bar, with marvelous 12-foot-high mirrors, has
seen everything, including cowboys riding their mounts up to
the stools, and flappers brewing rotgut whiskey in the cellar
during Prohibition. The pasta specials are terrific, as are the
burgers. *133 E. Colorado Ave., tel. 303/728–3622. Reserva-*
tions accepted. Dress: casual. AE, MC, V. Inexpensive–
Moderate.

Eddie's. This ultracasual spot serves up heaping helpings of
pastas, homemade soups and stews, and gourmet pizzas
(choose from more than two dozen toppings). *300 W. Colorado*
Ave., tel. 303/728–5335. Reservations accepted. Dress: casual.
AE, MC, V. Closed Mon. Inexpensive.

Lodging

Whatever your lodging preference, you'll be able to find a suitable property in Southwest Colorado: from motor inns in Durango and elegant Telluride bed-and-breakfasts to upscale
resort developments such as Tamarron, outside Purgatory/Du-
rango, and the Doral in Telluride. Winter is high season in
Crested Butte, Purgatory, and Telluride (with rates dropping
as much in 50% in summer despite the wealth of festivals and
events). Properties in Durango, Ouray, Silverton, and the
Mesa Verde area work in the opposite fashion, with many accommodations closing all or part of the winter. Recently, properties in outlying communities such as Ouray, Ridgway,
Montrose, and Gunnison began offering half-price lift tickets
for guests who plan to ski. Unless otherwise noted, rooms have
a full bath and include cable TV and phones.

Condominiums throughout Colorado generally represent excellent value, especially for families. All the companies listed in
the Lodging section represent top-notch properties, usually
within walking distance of the slopes in winter (or major activities in summer). All have full kitchen and cable TV, most with
Jacuzzi and/or pool access, among other amenities.

For rates *see* Towns and Country price chart in Chapter 1, Essential Information.

Highly recommended accommodations are indicated by a star
★.

Alamosa **Best Western Alamosa Inn.** This sprawling, well-maintained
complex, scattered over several blocks, is the best hotel bet in
town. Rooms are spacious and offer the standard amenities.
1919 Main St., 81101, tel. 719/589–4943. 121 rooms. Facilities:

restaurant, lounge, indoor pool. AE, D, DC, MC, V. Inexpensive–Moderate.

★ **Cottonwood Inn B&B.** This pretty cranberry-and-azure house was built in 1898 and lovingly refurbished by an Adams State professor and his wife. Public rooms feature original Stickley woodwork and furnishings; regional artworks (most of them for sale), from pastels to serigraphs, grace the walls. The four sunny rooms have country-French washed walls, some with handpainted florettes, framed knits, weavings, dried flowers, lace curtains, Art Deco fixtures, and predominantly wicker furnishings. There are also two apartments with wonderful oak floors and clawfoot tubs. A complimentary breakfast is provided for guests. *123 San Juan Ave., 81101, tel. 719/589–3882. 4 rooms, 2 with private bath; 2 apartments. Facilities: gallery, gift counter. DC, MC, V. Inexpensive.*

Antonito **Conejos River Guest Ranch.** Located on the Conejos River, this peaceful family-friendly retreat offers private fishing and wagon rides. The recently remodeled cabins—all fully equipped— and guest rooms are pleasantly outfitted. A complimentary breakfast is provided. *25390 Hwy. 17, 81120, tel. 719/376–2464. 6 cabins, 8 rooms. Facilities: restaurant, private fishing, stables. No credit cards. Inexpensive.*

Cortez **Anasazi Motor Inn.** This is definitely the nicest hotel on the strip, mostly because air-conditioned rooms are spacious and pleasantly decorated in southwestern colors. Children under 18 stay free in their parents' room. *666 S. Broadway, 81321, tel. 303/565–3773 or 800/972–6232; fax 303/565–1027. 89 rooms. Facilities: restaurant, lounge, outdoor pool, hot tub, meeting facilities, airport transfers. AE, D, DC, MC, V. Inexpensive.*

Creede **Creede Hotel.** A relic of the silver days, this charming 1890s structure has been fully restored, and the rooms offer the usual Victoriana. The gracious dining room serves excellent meals, aside from the complimentary gourmet breakfast. *1892 Main St, tel. 719/658–2608. 4 rooms. Facilities: restaurant. D, MC, V. Closed winters. Inexpensive.*

Crested Butte **Crested Butte Club.** This quaint, stylish inn is a Victorian
★ dream: Each sumptuous, individually furnished room contains a brass or mahogany bed, Axeminster carpets, and cherrywood antiques or good-quality reproductions. All have spacious modern bathrooms and little extras such as footed copper and brass tubs or gas fireplaces. The downstairs bar is similarly delightful, but best of all is the full health club on the property, so you don't have to go far to soothe your weary muscles after a hard day's hiking or skiing. *512 2nd St., 81224, tel. 303/349–6655; fax 303/349–6654. 7 rooms. Facilities: lounge, health club (including heated lap pool, 2 steam baths, 3 hot tubs, weight room, racquetball court), Nordic ski center, pro shop, complimentary Continental breakfast. AE, MC, V. Moderate.*

★ **Grande Butte Hotel.** This ski-in/ski-out property offers all the amenities and facilities of other luxury hotels at down-to-earth prices. Huge rooms are decorated in muted earth and pastel tones and feature a wet bar, whirlpool tubs, and private balcony. The public spaces are dotted with towering plants, regional paintings and sculptures, and oversize, overstuffed armchairs and sofas. Giovanni's, the gourmet restaurant, is excellent: Oddly enough, conventional fare such as saltimbocca is far surpassed by such creative adventurous dishes as ravioli in raspberry sauce and penne with duck breast. *Box 5006, Mt. Crested*

Butte, 81225, tel. 303/349–7561 or 800/642–4422; fax 303/349–
6332. 210 rooms, 53 suites. Facilities: 3 restaurants, 2 lounges,
indoor heated pool, sauna, outdoor hot tub, game room, 11,000
sq. ft. of meeting space, laundry facilities. AE, D, MC, V.
Moderate.

★ **Irwin Lodge.** The Irwin touts itself as "the best-kept secret in
the Rockies," and it's no idle boast. Talk about seclusion: In
winter you must take a thrilling snowmobile ride around several switchbacks to reach this aerie, nearly 1,000 feet above (and
8 miles from) Crested Butte. The lodge sits 10,700 feet above
sea level, on a remote ridge overlooking Lake Irwin and the
Sangre de Cristo range. Several cozy lounge areas circle a magnificent stone fireplace at the entrance. The smallish, charmingly rustic rooms are tastefully appointed, with pine walls and
mahogany furnishings. A hearty breakfast is included in the
rate; fine Continental lunch and dinner, served family style,
available at a nominal surcharge. The repeat clientele knows
this is the premier place in America to learn powder skiing, as
the surrounding area boasts an average of 500 inches of fluffy
white stuff a year. A snowcat will take you up to 12,000 feet,
with a 2,000-foot vertical. (Nonguests can make arrangements
on a limited basis.) Summer activities include fishing, horseback riding, and mountain biking. With no phone or TV, just a
shortwave radio to civilization, the Irwin represents the ultimate in total isolation. Box 457, Crested Butte 81224, tel. 303/
349–5308. 24 rooms, 1 suite. Facilities: restaurant, lounge,
snowcat skiing, snowmobiling, horseback riding, fishing, hiking, cycling. AE, MC, V. Moderate.

Condominiums Crested Butte Vacations (Box A, Mt. Crested Butte 81225, tel.
800/544–8448; fax 303/349–2250) can make arrangements for all
condominiums on the mountain.

Durango/Purgatory **Tamarron.** This handsome development, nestled on 750 acres of
★ protected land surrounded by the San Juan National Forest
and situated about 10 miles north of Durango, harmonizes
beautifully with the environment; the main lodge seems an extension of the surrounding cliffs. Units are an attractive blend
of frontier architecture and southwestern decor, and nearly all
feature fireplace, full kitchen, and terrace. Tamarron is famed
for one of the country's most ravishing championship golf
courses, and tennis and horseback riding are also available. Le
Canyon, the gourmet restaurant, is a romantic spot that specializes in table-side pyrotechnics. Drawer 3131, Durango
81302, tel. 303/259–2000 or 800/678–1000; fax 303/259–0745.
411 units. Facilities: 3 restaurants, 2 lounges, 18-hole golf
course, 3 tennis courts, riding stables, health club and spa, in-
door/outdoor swimming pools, hot tub, shopping arcade, "Zoo
Crew" child-care center. AE, D, DC, MC, V. Expensive–Very
Expensive.

★ **Purgatory Village Hotel.** This luxurious ski-in/ski-out property
offers both hotel rooms and condos, all decorated with southwestern flair, including Native American rugs and prints. The
condos include full kitchen, private balcony, washer/dryer,
whirlpool bath, in-room sauna, and wood-burning fireplace.
Box 2062, Durango (but located in Purgatory) 81302, tel. 303/
247–9000 or 800/879–7974; fax 303/385–2116. 271 units. Facilities: restaurant, lounge, weight room, hot tubs, sauna and
steam room, outdoor heated pool. AE, D, DC, MC, V. Moderate–Expensive.

★ **Strater Hotel.** This Victorian beauty originally opened in 1887 and has been lovingly restored to its full glory. Public rooms, including Henry's restaurant and the Diamond Belle Saloon, sport crystal chandeliers, beveled windows, original oak beams, flocked wallpaper, and plush velour curtains. The individually decorated rooms are swooningly exquisite: After all, the hotel owns the largest collection of Victorian walnut antiques in the world, and it even has its own wood-carving shop on site to create exact period reproductions. All rooms feature intricate tracery and wainscoting, hand-carved armoires and beds, brass lamps, and down pillows. Your room might have entertained Butch Cassidy, Gerald Ford, Francis Ford Coppola, Louis L'Amour (he wrote *The Sacketts* here), JFK, and Marilyn Monroe (the latter two at separate times). *699 Main St., Durango 81301, tel. 303/247-4431 or 800/247-4431; fax 303/259-2208. 93 rooms. Facilities: restaurant, lounge, hot tub. AE, MC, V. Moderate.*

Comfort Inn. This is one of the nicer properties along Durango's strip because it's clean, comfortable, and has sizable rooms decorated in subdued mountain colors. *2930 N. Main St., Durango 81301, tel. 303/259-5373. 48 rooms. Facilities: hot tub, outdoor pool. AE, D, DC, MC, V. Inexpensive.*

Condominiums   In addition to **Tamarron** and **Purgatory Village Hotel** (*see above* for both), there are fine condo units at **Cascade Village** (50827 Hwy. 550 North, Durango (but located in Purgatory) 81301, tel. 303/259-3500 or 800/525-0896).

Gunnison   **Mary Lawrence Inn.** This restored Victorian is an unexpected and welcome delight in Gunnison. The oversize rooms are furnished with tasteful antiques and Victorian touches such as lace curtains and potpourri. A complimentary gourmet breakfast is offered each morning, along with a smile and advice for the day's adventures from owner Jan Goin. *601 N. Taylor St., tel. 303/641-3343. 5 rooms, 4 with shared bath. No facilities. MC, V. Inexpensive–Moderate.*

Lake City   **Old Carson Inn.** This peaceful log cabin is nestled among banks of towering aspen and spruce. Don and Judy Berry offer five nicely appointed rooms with down comforters, private bath, and brimming with rustic charm. The complimentary country breakfast, served family style, should get you off to a good start. *C.R. 30, Hinsdale 81235, tel. 303/944-2511. 5 rooms. Facilities: hot tub. MC, V. Inexpensive–Moderate.*

Mesa Verde   **Far View Lodge.** The rustic rooms at this lodge include private balconies with panoramas of Arizona, Utah, and New Mexico. Soothing southwestern pastels predominate. Another draw here is the hotel's enthusiasm in arranging guided tours. They even provide a multimedia show on the Anasazi for guests. *Box 277, Mancos 81328, tel. 303/529-4421. 150 rooms. Facilities: restaurant, gift shop. AE, D, DC, MC, V. Open mid-Apr.– mid-Oct. Inexpensive.*

Montrose   **Best Western Red Arrow Motor Inn.** This fully outfitted property is one of the nicest in the area, mainly because of the large, prettily appointed rooms, adorned in mountain colors with handsome mahogany furnishings. The full baths include jetted tubs. *1702 E. Main St., tel. 303/249-9641 or 800/468-9323; fax 303/249-8380. 60 units. Facilities: restaurant, lounge, meeting facilities, fitness center, hot tub, laundry, ski storage. AE, D, DC, MC, V. Inexpensive–Moderate.*

Red Barn Motel. This friendly property offers pleasing, fair-size rooms with all the usual motel amenities, including a coffeemaker. Apart from the Red Arrow, the Red Barn boasts the most facilities in town, at a considerably lower rate than the competition. Children under 12 stay free in their parents' room. *1417 E. Main St., tel. 303/249–4507. 70 units. Facilities: 2 restaurants, lounge, heated outdoor pool, hot tub, sauna, exercise room. AE, D, DC, MC, V. Inexpensive.*

Ouray **The Damn Yankee.** The balconies of this charming inn offer views of several soaring peaks surrounding the narrow valley in which Ouray is situated. The gracious parlor holds a baby-grand piano and wood-burning fireplace, and informal musicales by guests are not uncommon. Rooms are a pleasing blend of period antiques and modern comfort, and all include beds draped with down comforters. The third-floor sitting room is always stocked with snacks and soft drinks. In the morning a complimentary gourmet breakfast is provided for guests. *100 6th St., tel. 303/325–4219 or 800/845–7512. 8 rooms. Facilities: hot tub. AE, MC, V. Moderate–Expensive.*

Box Canyon Lodge and Hot Springs. The attraction here is the private mineral springs, used first by the Ute, then by Coger Sanitarium (formerly on site). Soak away your cares in two redwood tubs full of steaming 103°–107° water, with the stunning mountain views around you. The rooms are nondescript, but modern and comfortable, with all amenities. *45 3rd St., tel. 303/327–5080. 40 rooms. Facilities: 2 natural hot tubs. AE, DC, MC, V. Moderate.*

St. Elmo Hotel. This tiny 1898 hostelry was originally a haven for "miners down on their luck," thanks to its former owner Kitty Heit, who couldn't resist a sob story. Her son's ghost reputedly hovers about protectively. The rooms are awash with polished wood, brass, stained glass, and antiques. Complimentary breakfast buffet is served in a sunny parlor. The Bon Ton restaurant, the best in this town—serves fine Continental cuisine with Italian flair. *426 Main St., tel. 303/325–4951. 10 rooms, 1 suite. Facilities: restaurant, outdoor hot tub, sauna. D, MC, V. Inexpensive–Moderate.*

Pagosa Springs **Davidson's Country Inn B&B.** This three-story log cabin is located on a 32-acre working ranch in the middle of Colorado's stunning San Juan Mountains. The location is perfect, just 20 minutes from Wolf Creek Ski Area (which has no lodging of its own). Rooms are comfortable and crammed with family heirlooms and antiques. In the morning a complimentary full breakfast is served. *E. Hwy. 60, 81147, tel. 303/264–5863. 8 rooms, 4 with shared bath. Facilities: game room. MC, V. Inexpensive.*

Silverton **Wingate Guest House.** The worldly Judy Graham (she hails from Wisconsin, has lived in New York, Chicago, and northern California and taught at two universities) is the genial hostess of this quaint inn. A prominent landscape artist, her works and those of her friends adorn the walls, along with family photos dating back to the Civil War, creating an ambience that is an appealing cross between sophisticated and homey. The breezy front porch overlooks a majestic thirteener. Large sunny rooms are filled with antiques and sport down pillows and comforters, as well as an eclectic library culled from Judy's journeys. A complimentary breakfast is served. *1045 Snowden St.,* *tel. and fax 303/387–5520. 5 rooms with shared bath. No facilities. No credit cards. Inexpensive.*

Wyman Hotel. This wonderful, 1902, red-sandstone building has 24-inch-thick walls, cathedral ceilings, and arched windows. The attractive rooms all contain period antiques and pretty wallpaper, brass lamps, and a VCR. If the Wyman is full, the owners also run the **Alma House** (220 E. 10th St., tel. 303/387–5336; open year-round), a charming B&B set in a restored 1902 stone house with neat, tasteful rooms and an excellent restaurant. *1371 Greene St., tel. 303/387–5372. 18 rooms. No facilities. AE, MC, V. Closed mid-Oct.–early May. Inexpensive.*

Telluride **The Peaks at Telluride Resort and Spa.** The pastel-colored prisonlike exterior and lapses in service can be excused at this ski-in/ski-out would-be luxury resort, thanks to its invigorating, revitalizing spa facilities. The setting is glorious, dominated by fourteener Mt. Wilson (the peak on the Coors can). Rooms have balconies and are sizable, if somewhat sterile, in Norwegian wood and muted mountain colors, with all amenities, including VCR, minibar, and full bath with dual marble vanities and hair dryer. The Doral has spared no expense in the pampering spa (muds and waters for hydrotherapy and facials are imported from Italy's Terme di Saturnia) and fitness center. Extras include a cardiovascular deck and climbing room. In fact, so much money was sunk into the resort, it went into receivership the following year. The primary effect seems to be the Continual turnover of staff (few of them locals) who, while eager, have difficulty answering the simplest questions about the area. *Country Club Dr., tel. 303/728–6800 or 800/223–6725; fax 303/728–6567. 145 rooms, 32 suites. Facilities: 2 restaurants, lounge, full spa (including 44 separate treatment rooms and offering massage, facials, various treatments), beauty salon, 5 tennis courts, 1 squash court, 1 racquetball court, full Cybex-equipped weight room, indoor/outdoor swimming pool, Jacuzzis, water slide, dry sauna, climbing wall, cardiovascular deck. AE, D, DC, MC, V. Very Expensive.*

★ **Pennington's Mountain Village Inn.** This secluded, exclusive inn features huge rooms in varying color schemes, with smashing mountain views from private decks, brass beds with cushy down comforters, handcrafted furniture, and stocked minifridges. The pampering includes concierge service, gourmet breakfast, and afternoon hors d'oeuvres. *100 Pennington Ct., off Mountain Village Blvd., tel. 303/728–5337 or 800/543–1437. 9 rooms, 3 suites. Facilities: lounge, steam room, hot tub, game room, guest laundry. AE, MC, V. Expensive–Very Expensive.*

San Sophia B&B. Rooms are on the small side, but luxurious and contemporary—eschewing Victorian frills save for brass beds. The amiable staff is extremely helpful. The inn is known for its fabulous gourmet breakfasts and après-ski treats. *330 W. Pacific St., tel. 303/728–3001 or 800/537–4781. 16 rooms. Facilities: hot tub, underground parking. AE, MC, V. Expensive–Very Expensive.*

New Sheridan Hotel. William Jennings Bryan delivered his rousing "Cross of Gold" speech here in 1896, garnering a presidential nomination in the process. (He was later defeated by McKinley.) The rooms remain a funky blend of period elegance and no-frills economy, despite a recent face-lift. A favorite local spot is the gorgeous Victorian bar here; the Continental food in the restaurant is well above average, even for Telluride. *231 W. Colorado Ave., tel. 303/728–4351. 24 rooms, 14 with shared bath, 1 suite. Facilities: restaurant, bar. AE, MC, V. Inexpensive–Moderate.*

Condominiums **Telluride Central Reservations** (tel. 800/525–3455) handles all properties at Telluride Mountain Village, and several in town. **Resort Rentals** (Box 1278, Telluride 81435, tel. 800/LETS–SKI) offers several top-notch accommodations in town.

The Arts

Film The Telluride Film Festival, in September, is considered one of the world's leading showcases for foreign films.

Music The **Montrose Pavilion** (1800 Pavilion Dr., tel. 303/249–7015) includes a 602-seat auditorium where name acts, dance companies, and regional orchestras often perform.

Telluride offers numerous festivals during the summer, including the monstrous jazz and bluegrass festivals.

Theater In Durango, the **Diamond Circle Theater** (699 Main Ave., tel. 303/247–4431) stages rip-roaring melodramas, and the **Durango Lively Arts Co.** (Durango Arts Ctr., 835 Main Ave., tel. 303/259–2606) presents fine community-theater productions.

In Silverton, **A Theatre Group** (Miners Union Theatre, Greene St., tel. 303/387–5337) presents a varied repertory season.

Nightlife

Bars and Lounges In Durango, the hot spot is the **Diamond Belle Saloon** (Strater Hotel, 699 Main Ave., tel. 303/247–4431), whose antique gold-leaf filigree bar, honky-tonk piano player, and waitresses dressed as 1880s saloon girls pack them in.

In Telluride, **Leimgruber's** (*see* Dining, *above*) and the elegant turn-of-the-century bar at the **Sheridan Hotel** (231 W. Colorado Ave., tel. 303/728–4351) are the popular après-ski hangouts. In the Mountain Village, **Village Bar & Grille** (113 Lost Creek La., tel. 303/728–4449) is an overlit, overloud joint with chrome and blacktop tables, and redwood chairs at the marble bar, but it does get some good bands and offers $1 happy-hour snacks that can make a filling meal.

In Crested Butte, **Kochevar's** (127 Elk Ave., tel. 303/349–6756), a hand-hewn 1896 log cabin, is a classic pool-hall saloon. The other popular bar in town is the **Wooden Nickel** (222 Elk Ave., tel. 303/349–6350), which has two happy hours daily 3–6 and 10:30–midnight.

Casinos Colorado's first tribal gaming facility, offering limited-stakes gambling—slots, poker (video and live), bingo, and 21—is the **Ute Mountain Casino** (Hwys. 160 and 666, Towaoc, tel. 303/565–8800; open daily 8 AM–4 AM). **The Casino Express** (tel. 303/385–4711) runs trips from Durango.

Country and Western In Durango, **Sundance Saloon** (601 E. 2nd St., tel. 303/259–2985) is a foot-stomping place to "scoot your boot."

In Mancos, the **Mancos Social Club** (Main St., no tel.) is a fun but frankly redneck spot that can get wild and sometimes hairy.

Dinner Shows **Bar D Chuckwagon** (8080 C.R. 250, East Animas Valley, tel. 303/247–5753) serves barbecued beef, beans, and biscuits, along with a heaping helping of their Bar D Wranglers singing group.
Cowboy Ranch (11920 C.R. 240, 12 mi east of Durango, tel. 259–0008) offers BBQ and bands.
Durango Jamboree (Iron Horse Inn, 5800 Main Ave., Durango, tel. 303/259–1290) presents "hand-clappin', knee-slappin' down-home music and country corn," along with its BBQ.

Discos **Yesterdays** (Holiday Inn, 800 S. Camino del Rio, Durango, tel. 303/247–5393) has a dance floor and a DJ nightly.

Jazz Clubs In Durango, the **Pelican's Nest** (656 Main Ave., tel. 303/247–4431) is a cool joint for hot jazz, with a sedate Victorian decor. The funky clientele wears anything from cowboy hats to berets.

Rock Clubs **Farquahrt's** (725 Main Ave., Durango, tel. 303/247–5440) is decorated with antiques, but attracts a lively youthful crowd that likes to rock and roll to the best local bands. There's also a "ski lodge" version at **Purgatory Mountain Village** (tel. 303/247–9000, ext. 3123).

In Mountain Crested Butte Village, **Rafters** (tel. 303/349–2298) is packed to the rafters of this big barn with cheap eats, strong drinks, and loud music (often live on weekends).

In Telluride, **One World Café** (114 E. Colorado Ave., tel. 303/728–5530) is an eclectic club: Japanese fans and lanterns contrast intriguingly with the building's original, corrugated-tin roof and stone- and brickwork. Tasty Thai is served in the front restaurant/art gallery. Exquisite stained-glass doors lead to the Conga Room disco, where the DJ spins everything from Motown to salsa, and hot funk and ska bands perform regularly. **Last Dollar Saloon** (100 E. Colorado Ave., tel. 303/728–4800) couldn't be less chic (and couldn't care less); when it's not a pool-hall saloon, it's the best venue for local rock bands. **Excelsior Café** (200 W. Colorado Ave., tel. 303/728–4250) is the spot to hear the best in folk rock.

Singles **Rafters** in Crested Butte and **Farquahrt's** (*see* Rock Clubs, *above*) in Purgatory/Durango are the closest things to classic pickup joints in Southwest Colorado.

Southcentral Colorado

The contented residents of Colorado's southcentral region believe they live in an ideal location, and it's hard to argue with them. To the west, the Rockies form a majestic backdrop; to the east, the plains stretch for miles. Together, the settings ensure a mild, sunny climate year-round and make skiing and golfing on the same day feasible with no more than a two- or three-hour drive. This diversity and accessibility to the outdoors attracts tourists seeking a varied vacation: They can climb the Collegiate Peaks one day, and go white-water rafting on the Arkansas River the next.

Equally alluring are cities such as Colorado Springs and Pueblo, numbered among the most contemporary in the West, with sleek shining arts and convention centers.

The region also abounds in natural and man-made wonders, such as the yawning Royal Gorge and its astounding Suspension Bridge; the eerie sandstone formations of the Garden of the Gods; and the space-age architecture of the U.S. Air Force Academy. However, the most indelible landmark is unquestionably Pikes Peak, from whose vantage point Katherine Lee Bates penned "America the Beautiful." The song's lyrics remain an accurate description of Southcentral Colorado's many glories.

Important Addresses and Numbers

Tourist Information Buena Vista Chamber of Commerce (Hwy. 24, Buena Vista 81211, tel. 719/395–6612); **Canon City Chamber of Commerce** (Bin 749, Canon City 81215, tel. 719/275–2331); **Colorado Springs Convention and Visitors Bureau** (104 S. Cascade, Suite 104, Colorado Springs 80903, tel. 719/635–7506 or 800/DO VISIT); **Cripple Creek Chamber of Commerce** (Box 650, Cripple Creek 80813, tel. 719/689–2169); **Florissant/Lake George Chamber of Commerce** (Box 507, Florissant 80816, tel. 719/748–3395); **Heart of the Rockies Chamber of Commerce** (406 W. Rainbow Blvd., Salida 81201, tel. 719/539–2068); **Huerfano County Chamber of Commerce** (Box 493, Walsenburg 81089, tel. 719/738–1065); **La Junta Chamber of Commerce** (110 Santa Fe Ave., La Junta 81050, tel. 719/384–7411); **La Veta/Cuchara Chamber of Commerce** (Box 32, La Veta 81055, tel. 719/742–3676); **Lamar Chamber of Commerce** (Box 860, Lamar 81052, tel. 719/336–4379); **Manitou Springs Chamber of Commerce** (354 Manitou Ave., Manitou Springs 80829, tel. 719/685–5089 or 800/642–2567); **Pueblo Chamber of Commerce and Convention & Visitors Bureau** (302 N. Santa Fe Ave., Pueblo, 81003, tel. 719/542–1704 or 800/233–3446); **Trinidad/Las Animas Chamber of Commerce** (309 Nevada St., Trinidad 81082, tel. 719/846–9285).

Hospitals **Arkansas Valley Regional Medical Center** (1100 Carson Ave., La Junta, tel. 719/384–5412); **Colorado Springs Memorial Hospital** (1400 E. Boulder Ave., Colorado Springs, tel. 719/475–5000); **Heart of the Rockies Regional Medical Center** (448 E. 1st St., Sailda, tel. 719/539–6661); **Mt. San Rafael Hospital** (410 Benedicta St., Trinidad, tel. 719/846–9213); **Parkview Episcopal Medical Center** (400 W. 16th St., Pueblo, tel. 719/584–4000); **St. Thomas More Hospital** (1019 Sheridan St., Canon City, tel. 719/275–3381).

Arriving and Departing by Plane

Airports and Airlines Colorado Springs: **Colorado Springs Municipal Airport** (tel. 719/596–0188) is serviced by American Airlines (tel. 800/433–4700), America West (tel. 800/247–5692), Continental (tel. 800/525–0280), Delta (tel. 800/221–1212), TWA (tel. 800/221–2000), and United (tel. 800/241–6522).

Pueblo: **Pueblo Airport** (tel. 719/948–3355) is serviced by America West, Continental Express, TWA, and United Express.

Between the Airport and the Hotels/Downtown
By Bus or Shuttle **Airport Transportation Service** (tel. 719/635–3518) offers regular shuttles from the Colorado Springs airport to hotels. **Colorado Springs/Pueblo Airporter** (tel. 719/578–5232) services the stretch of I–25 between the two cities. **Pueblo Shuttle Express** (tel. 719/545–8687) offers shuttles from Pueblo Airport.

By Taxi In Colorado Springs: **Yellow Cab** (tel. 719/634–5000). In Pueblo: **City Cab** (tel. 719/543–2525).

Arriving and Departing by Car, Train, and Bus

By Car Interstate 25, which bisects Colorado and runs north–south from New Mexico to Wyoming, is the major artery accessing the area.

By Train **Amtrak** (tel. 800/USA–RAIL) stops in Trinidad and La Junta.

By Bus **Greyhound/Trailways** (tel. 800/752–4841) serves most of the major towns in the region.

Getting Around

By Bus **Colorado Springs Transit** (tel. 719/475–9733) serves most of the Colorado Springs metropolitan area, including Manitou Springs.
Pueblo Transit (tel. 719/542–4306) services Pueblo and outlying areas.
The **Trinidad Trolley** stops at parks and historical sites, departing from the parking lot next to City Hall (for information, call the chamber of commerce, tel. 719/846–9285).

By Taxi In Colorado Springs: **Yellow Cab** (tel. 719/634–5000). In Pueblo: **City Cab** (tel. 719/543–2525). In Trinidad: **City Cab** (tel. 719/846–2237).

By Car Pueblo and Colorado Springs are both on I–25. Florissant and Buena Vista are reached via U.S. 24 off I–25; Canon City and the Royal Gorge via U.S. 50. Salida can be reached via CO 291 from either U.S. 24 or U.S. 50. La Junta can be reached via U.S. 50 from Pueblo or U.S. 350 from Trinidad.

Guided Tours

Orientation **Gray Line** (tel. 719/633–1181) offers tours of the Colorado Springs area, including Pikes Peak and Manitou Springs, as well as jaunts to Cripple Creek.

Special-Interest **Gentle Earth Tours** (tel. 719/633–2301) leads hikes into the
Tours Pikes Peak area. **Ghost Town Tours** (tel. 719/689–3000) offers in-depth tours through the Cripple Creek and Victor mining districts.

Exploring Colorado Springs and Environs

This tour takes in an array of attractions in the Colorado Springs/Manitou Springs and Pikes Peak area.

Numbers in the margin correspond to points of interest on the Colorado and Colorado Springs maps.

㊸ **Colorado Springs,** the state's second-largest city, unfortunately made headlines in 1992 when it was identified as the headquarters of several right-wing groups that were behind the controversial Amendment 2, which outlawed antidiscrimination legislation, targeting the gay community. With active and retired military personnel and their families comprising nearly a third of the population, it's no surprise that the Springs is staunchly conservative. Although for a brief time a state boycott was called and the Springs continues to be recognized as the place where the controversy snowballed, the political situation hasn't affected tourism significantly. The '92–'93 winter season was phenomenal, and the Springs, after all, boasts a dazzling array of tourist attractions. Pikes Peak, for instance, is the state's most famous landmark, but only one of the city's many natural and man-made wonders. Other tourist draws include the Cave of the Winds, Garden of the Gods, and historic neighborhoods such as Manitou Springs and Old Colorado City.

Colorado Springs was created by General William Palmer, president of the Denver & Rio Grande Railroad, as a utopian vision of fine living in the 1870s. The original broad, tree-lined boulevards still grace the southwest quadrant of the city. With the discovery of hot springs in the area, the well-to-do descended on the bustling resort town to take the waters and enjoy the mild climate and fresh air. It soon earned the monikers "Saratoga of the West" and "Little London," the latter for the snob appeal of its considerable resident and visiting English population. The discovery of gold at nearby Cripple Creek toward the end of the century signaled another boom for the Springs. In the early part of the 1900s, until the mines petered out just before World War I, the residents' per-capita wealth was the highest in the nation.

After World War II, the city fathers invited the military to move in, and the city's personality changed drastically. Ironically, the **U.S. Air Force Academy,** which set up camp in 1954, has become one of Colorado's largest tourist attractions. A portion of the academy is most notable for its striking futuristic design; but even more extraordinary are the 18,000 beautiful acres of land that's been dedicated as a game reserve and sprinkled with antique and historic aircraft. Most of the campus is off-limits to civilians, but a 13.5-mile self-guided tour will take you to the visitor center, with photo exhibits, a model of a cadet's room, a gift shop, a snack bar, and short videos on air force history, cadet training, athletics, and academics. Other attractions include a B-52 display, sports facilities, planetarium, parade ground (the impressive cadet review takes place daily at noon), and the chapel. The controversially designed house of worship is easily recognized by its unconventional design, whose 17 spires resemble sharks' teeth or billowing sails. Catholic, Jewish, and Protestant services can be held simultaneously without the congregations disturbing each other. *Exit 156B, off I–25 north, tel. 719/472–2555. Admission free. Open daily 9–5.*

Directly across I–25 from the north gate of the academy is the **Western Museum of Mining and Industry,** preserving the rich history of mining through comprehensive exhibits of equipment and techniques and hands-on demonstrations, including gold panning. This attraction is an oasis during the summer season, thanks to its stunning mountain setting. *1025 N. Gate Rd., tel. 719/488–0880. Admission: $4 adults, $3.50 students and senior citizens, $1.50 children. Open Mar.–Nov., Mon.–Sat. 9–4; Sun. noon–4.*

Continue along I–25 south toward downtown and get off at Exit 147. A bronze rodeo bull lures visitors to the **Pro Rodeo Hall of Fame and Museum of the American Cowboy.** Even a tenderfoot would get a kick out of this museum, which includes changing displays of Western art; permanent photo exhibits that capture both the excitement of broncobustin' and the lonely life of the

Colorado Springs

cowpoke; gorgeous saddles and belt buckles; and multimedia tributes to rodeo's greatest competitors (including the unsung clowns who often save their butts!). *101 Pro Rodeo Dr., off Exit 147 of I–25), tel. 719/528–4764. Admission: $5 adults, $2 children 5–12. Open daily 9–5.*

Time Out   **Old Chicago** (7115 Commerce Center Dr., tel. 719/593–7678) is one of many "concept restaurants" popular throughout Colorado. This one features a sports bar in front and a pleasant enclosed atrium and outdoor patio in back. It's a pizza, pasta, and beer (110 varieties) joint, and scores on all counts.

Now take I–25 or Nevada Avenue to the southern end of the city for a glimpse of its posher neighborhoods, of which the pink-stucco, Italianate **The Broadmoor,** built in 1918, stands as the most aristocratic symbol. One of the world's great luxury resorts, its 30 buildings and three championship 18-hole golf courses cover 3,500 acres of prime real estate and create a minicity unto itself. It stands as a tribute to the foresight of its original owner, the enterprising Spencer Penrose, one of Colorado Springs's wealthiest (and conspicuously consuming) philanthropists. Having constructed the zoo, the Cheyenne Mountain Highway, and Pikes Peak Cog Railway, Penrose is credited with making the town the tourist mecca it is today.

Two superb museums are included in The Broadmoor complex: the **International Skating Hall of Fame and Museum** (20 1st St., tel. 719/635–5200; admission free; open June–Sept., Mon.–Sat. 10–4; Oct.–May, weekdays 10–4), which documents the history of the sport and immortalizes its greatest practitioners such as Sonja Henie and the Springs's own Peggy Fleming; and the exquisite **Carriage House** (Lake Circle, no tel.; admission free; open daily 9–noon and 1–5), which displays Penrose's prodigious carriage collection, from broughams (closed carriages with driver outside) to opera buses.

From The Broadmoor, take the Cheyenne Mountain Zoo Road to begin the ascent of Cheyenne Mountain. Aside from stunning panoramic views of the city and Pikes Peak in the distance, the road also offers two major attractions. First up is the

㊼ Cheyenne Mountain Zoo, America's highest zoo, at 7,000 feet, with more than 800 animals amid mossy boulders and ponderosa pines. *Cheyenne Mt. Zoo Rd., tel. 719/475–9555. Admission: $5.50 adults, $4.50 senior citizens, $3 children 3–11. Open June–Sept., daily 9–7; Oct.–May, daily 9–5.*

㊽ Continue up the spiraling road to the **Will Rogers Shrine of the Sun,** the other big attraction off the zoo road. This "singing" tower guarded by two carved Chinese dogs was dedicated in 1937 after the tragic plane crash that claimed Rogers's life. Its interior is painted with all manner of Western scenes (in which Rogers and Spencer Penrose figure prominently) and plastered with photos and the homespun sayings of America's favorite cowboy. *Cheyenne Mt. Zoo Rd., no tel. Admission free with zoo ticket. Open Memorial Day–Labor Day, daily 9–5:30; Labor Day–Memorial Day, daily 9–4:30.*

At the base of the mountain, turn west on Cheyenne Road and
㊾ follow the signs to **Seven Falls.** The road up to this transcendent series of seven cascades is touted as the "grandest mile of scenery in Colorado." Considering the state's splendors, that may be an exaggeration, but the red-rock canyon *is* stunning—though no more so than the falls themselves, plummeting into a tiny emerald pool. A set of 265 steep steps leads to the top, but there is an elevator for those who don't wish to walk. *Tel. 719/632–0765. Admission: $4 adults, $2 children under 12. Open daily 9–5.*

Take Cheyenne Mountain Zoo Road back into town and turn north on Nevada Avenue. Colorado Springs's handsome downtown contains many historically significant buildings, including the old El Paso County Courthouse, now the admirable
㊿ **Pioneers Museum.** This repository of artifacts relating to the entire Pikes Peak area is most notable for the wonderful special exhibits it mounts (or is loaned on tour from institutions such as the Smithsonian), such as a quilt competition commemorating the 100th anniversary of the song "America the Beautiful." *215 S. Tejon St., tel. 719/578–6650. Admission free. Open Mon.–Sat. 10–5, Sun. 1–5.*

㉿ A few blocks north is the **Colorado Springs Fine Arts Center,** an exemplary space that includes a performing-arts theater, an art school, and a room devoted to the work and life of famed Western artist Charles Russell. Also at the venue are a handsome sculpture garden, a surprisingly fine permanent collection of modern art, and rotating exhibits that highlight the cultural contributions of the area's diverse ethnic groups. *30 W. Dale St., tel. 719/634–5581. Admission: $3 adults, $1.50 senior citizens and students, $1 children 5–12. Open Tues.–Fri. 9–5, Sat. 10–5, Sun. 1–5.*

Cross under I–25 to Colorado Avenue and take it west, turning left on 21st Street, which you'll follow to the cluster of three wildly different attractions: Ghost Town, Van Briggle Art Pottery Factory and Showroom, and the Hall of Presidents Living Wax Studio.

52 If you can't make it to Buckskin Joe Park and Railway (*see* What to See and Do with Children, *below*), than visit **Ghost Town,** a complete, authentic Western town with a sheriff's office, general store, saloon, and smithy. You can play a real player piano and nickelodeon. *21st St., exit Hwy. 24 W, tel. 719/634–0696. Admission: $3.75 adults, $2 children 6–16, children under 6 free. Open Mon.–Sat. 9–6, Sun. 1–6 (hrs. may vary during winter so call ahead).*

53 Right across the way is the famous **Van Briggle Art Pottery Factory and Showroom,** in operation since the turn of the century. Van Briggle ceramic work is admired for its graceful lines and pure, vibrant glazes. A free tour of the facility is offered, culminating—naturally—in the mind-boggling showroom. *600 S. 21st St., tel. 719/633–7729. Admission free. Open Mon.–Sat. 8:30–5.*

54 One block south is the admittedly hokey but enjoyable **Hall of Presidents Living Wax Studio,** with more than 100 wax figures crafted at the famed Madame Tussaud's in London. The exhibits run from Washington at Trenton through Jefferson signing the Declaration of Independence, right up to the Reagans (there are surprising omissions, such as Herbert Hoover, for example). There's also an Enchanted Forest, alive with storybook characters from Peter Pan to Pinocchio. *1050 S. 21st St., tel. 719/635–3553. Admission: $4 adults, $2 children 5–12. Open Oct.-May, daily 10–5; June–Sept., daily 9–9.*

55 Back on Colorado Avenue you'll find yourself in **Old Colorado City,** once a separate, rowdier town where miners caroused, today a National Historic Landmark District whose restored buildings house the city's choicest galleries and boutiques. Continue west along Colorado Avenue to one of the region's most riveting sights: the gnarled jutting spires and sensuously **56** abstract monoliths of the **Garden of the Gods.** These magnificent, eroded red-sandstone formations were sculpted more than 300 million years ago.

Follow the road as it loops through the Garden of the Gods, past such oddities as the Three Graces, the Siamese Twins, and the Kissing Camels. High Point, near the south entrance, provides camera hounds with the ultimate photo-op: the jagged formations framing Pikes Peak.

As you exit the park, take U.S. 24 west; on your right are two admittedly touristy sights: the Cliff Dwellings Museum and the **57** Cave of the Winds. The **Cliff Dwellings Museum,** an obvious tourist trap, is something of an embarrassment to locals. It's replete with Indian flute music piped through the chambers, but this minireplica of Mesa Verde is a decent (and educational) substitute if you haven't seen the real thing. *U.S. 24, tel. 719/685–5242. Admission: $3 adults, $2 children under 12. Open June–Aug., daily 9–8; May and Sept., daily 9–6; rest of year, daily 9–5.*

58 The **Cave of the Winds** was discovered by two boys in 1880 and has been exploited as a tourist sensation ever since. The entrance is through the requisite "trading post," but once inside the cave you'll forget the hype and commercialism. You'll pass through grand chambers with such names as the Crystal Palace, Oriental Garden, Old Curiosity Shop, Temple of Silence, and the Valley of Dreams. The cave contains examples of every major sort of limestone formation, from the traditonal stalactites and stalagmites to delicate cave flowers, rare anthracite crystals, flowstone (rather like candle wax), and cave coral. Enthusiastic guides, most of them members of the Grotto Club (a spelunking group), also run more adventurous cave expeditions, called Wild Tours. The entrance to the cave is via **Williams Canyon,** off the highway. Summer evenings, a laser show transforms the canyon into an unsurpassed sound-and-light show of massively hokey, yet undeniably effective, proportions. *U.S. 24, tel. 719/685–5444. Admission: $8. Open daily 9–5; 45-minute tours conducted continuously.*

59 On the left of U.S. 24 is the lovely **Manitou Springs,** home of Manitou Springs mineral water. The **chamber of commerce** (354 Manitou Ave., tel. 719/685–5089) offers free walking tours of the springs, set in this quaint National Historic Landmark District, which exudes a slightly shabby but genteel charm. Antique trolleys also ply the streets in summer. Among the must-see attractions in town is William Packer's grandiose estate, **Glen Eyrie** (north of Garden of the Gods, 30th St., tel. 719/598–1212; admission: $5; tours June–Aug., weekdays twice daily; Sept.-May, Sun.; hours vary so call ahead).

Another Manitou Springs attraction, albeit an unusual one, is **60** **Miramont Castle Museum**—a wonderfully Byzantine extravaganza commissioned in 1895 as the private home of French priest Jean-Baptiste Francolon. The museum is more Disneyland than anything else, with 46 rooms offering a wide variety of displays, from original furnishings to doll and railroad museums. *9 Capitol Hill Ave., tel. 719/685–1011. Admission: $2. Open June–Aug., daily 10–5; Sept.–May, daily noon–3.*

61 The **Pikes Peak Cog Railway,** the world's highest cog railway, departs from Manitou and follows a frolicking stream up a steep canyon, through copses of quaking aspen and towering lodgepole pines, before reaching timberline and the 14,100-foot summit. *Ruxton Ave. (depot), tel. 719/685–5401. Round-trip fare: $20.50 adults, $9 children 5–11. Runs May–Oct., daily 9–6.*

You can also drive the 19-mile **Pikes Peak Highway,** which rises nearly 7,000 feet in its precipitous, dizzying climb to the **Summit House,** a pit-stop café and trading post. This is the same route that leading race-car drivers follow every July at 100 miles an hour in the famed Race to the Clouds.

The Collegiate Peaks and the Arkansas River This tour loops through stunning alpine and desert scenery, passing thrilling natural attractions such as the Florissant Fossil Beds and Royal Gorge.

Leave Manitou Springs on U.S. 24 north and west, and travel 15 miles to the town of **Florissant.** Three miles south of town (follow signs) is the little-known **Florissant Fossil Beds National Monument,** a treasure trove for would-be paleontologists, where volcanic ash has perfectly preserved the remains of a 35-40-million-year-old primeval rain forest. The visitor center offers guided walks into the monument, or you can follow the well-marked hiking trails and lose yourself amid the Oligocene period, among 300-foot petrified redwoods. *U.S. 24, follow signs, tel. 719/748–3253. Admission: $3. Open daily, 10–5.*

62 From the town of Florissant a dirt road leads to **Cripple Creek,** Colorado's third legalized gambling town. (The paved CO 67 also connects with Divide, 8 miles east on U.S. 24.) Cripple Creek once had the most lucrative mines in the state—and 10,000 boozing, brawling, bawdy citizens. Today, its old mining structures and the stupendous curtain of the Collegiate Peaks are marred by slag heaps and parking lots. Although the town isn't as picturesque as Central City or Black Hawk, the other gambling hot spots, Cripple Creek—a little rougher and dustier than the others—feels more authentic.

There are a few worthwhile attractions here: The **Cripple Creek District Museum** (east end of Bennett Ave., tel. 719/689–2634; admission: $2; open late May–mid-Oct., daily 10–5; mid-Oct.– May, weekends noon–4) provides a fascinating glimpse into mining life at the turn of the century. The **Mollie Kathleen Mine Tour** (CO 67, north of town, tel. 719/689–2466; admission: $6; open May–Oct., daily 9–5) descends 1,000 feet into the bowels of the earth in a mine that operated continuously from 1892 to 1961. **Imperial Hotel and Casino** (123 N. 3rd St., tel. 719/689–7777) offers a peek into the era's high life and a chance spin on the wheel of fortune.

A narrow-gauge railroad (depot at Cripple Creek District Museum, tel. 719/689–2640; fare: $6; runs Memorial Day–Oct., daily 10–5) weaves past abandoned mines to Cripple Creek's former rival **Victor.** In bygone days more than 50 ore-laden trains made this run daily. Today, however, Victor is a sad town, virtually a ghost of its former self; walking the streets— of several abandoned or partially restored buildings—is an eerie experience that does far more to evoke the mining (and postmining) days than does walking the streets of its tarted-up neighbor.

63 Back on U.S. 24 west, continue on to **Buena Vista** (or as locals pronounce it, BYOO-na VIS-ta), a town ringed by sky-scraping mountains, the most impressive being the **Collegiate Peaks.** The 14,000-foot giants attract alumni climbers from Yale, Princeton, Harvard, Columbia, and Oxford. A small mining town turned resort community, Buena Vista offers the usual historic buildings alternating with motels.

The most compelling reason to visit this area is for the almost unequaled variety of recreational activities. Hiking, biking, and climbing in the **Collegiate Peaks Wilderness Area** are among the favorite jaunts. Also, Buena Vista bills itself as "The Whitewater Rafting Capital of the World" and offers numerous excursions down the Arkansas River.

Time Out   After a full day of activities, check out the **Mt. Princeton Hot Springs** (5 mi west of Nathrop, C.R. 162, tel. 719/395–2447), for a restorative soak. The springs has three swimming pools and several private tubs.

Before leaving downtown Buena Vista, meander through the four rooms of **The Buena Vista Heritage Museum.** Each is devoted to a different aspect of regional history: One concentrates on mining equipment and minerals, another is devoted to fashions and household utensils, a third to working models of the three railroads that serviced the area in its heyday, and the last to historical photos. *E. Main St., tel. 719/395–2515. Admission: $1 adults, 50¢ children under 16. Open Memorial Day–Labor Day, daily 9–5.*

If Buena Vista has any competition in the beautiful scenery and outdoors activities departments, it comes from **Salida,** approximately 25 miles south along U.S. 24 and CO 291 and situated along the Arkansas River. It, too, is dominated by imposing peaks, with fourteener **Mt. Shavano** its landmark.

Head east on U.S. 50 to reach one of the Rockies' most powerful sights. The 1,053-foot-deep **Royal Gorge,** often called the Grand Canyon of Colorado, was carved by the Arkansas River over three million years ago. It's a tribute to the powers of nature, but it's spanned by no less monumental an achievement: the world's highest **suspension bridge.** Near the bridge, hubristic signs trumpet WHO SAYS YOU CAN'T IMPROVE ON NATURE? Never intended for transport, it was originally constructed in 1929 as a commercial enterprise. It now attracts more than half a million visitors annually, causing not a small amount of exploitation to the area. Families love crossing the bridge, particularly on gusty afternoons when it sways, adding to the thrill. Other activities at the gorge are: riding the astonishing aerial tram (2,200 feet long and 1,178 feet above the canyon floor) and descending the **Scenic Railway** (the world's steepest incline rail), to stare at the sun and the bridge 1,000 feet above. There is also a theater presenting a 25-minute multimedia show, outdoor musical entertainment in the summer, and the usual assortment of food concessions and gift shops. *Royal Gorge Complex, tel. 719/275–7507. Admission: $9.50 adults, $7.50 children 4–11. Open Oct.–May, daily 9–5; June–Sept., daily 8–8.*

This site boasts its share of history, too: The famed Royal Gorge War between the Denver & Rio Grande and Santa Fe railroads occurred here in 1877. The battle was over right-of-way through the canyon, which could only accommodate one rail line. Rival crews would lay tracks during the day and dynamite each other's work at night. The dispute was finally settled in court—the Denver & Rio Grande won.

Cañon City, an undeniably quirky town—and proud of it—is the gateway to the gorge. Where else would you find a shop named Fluff 'em, Buff 'em, Stuff 'em? Would you have guessed the services it provides: hairstyling, car waxing, and taxidermy? From its aggressive, even tacky strip-mall veneer (softened, fortunately, by some lovely old buildings) you'd think Cañon City existed solely for tourism. Nothing could be further from the truth. Cañon City's livelihood stems from its lordly position as "Colorado's Prison Capital." There are 10 prisons in the vicinity, all of which the citizens lobbied to get! It might seem a perverse source of income to court, but consider that the prisons have pumped nearly $200 million into the local economy, and, as the affable former mayor and current director of tourism states, "You got these people walking around Denver and the Springs, here at least they're locked up."

Morbid curiosity seekers and sensationalists will revel in the **Colorado Territorial Prison Museum,** which formerly housed the Women's State Correctional Facility. Now, it exhaustively documents prison life in Colorado, through old photos and newspaper accounts, as well as confiscated inmates' weapons, contraband, and one warden's china set. The individual cell exhibits were, of course, funded by local businesses and civic organizations. There's also a video room where you can view titles such as *Prisons Ain't What They Used to Be* and *Drug Avengers*. The original gas chamber sits in the courtyard. This museum is grim, grisly, gruesome, and admittedly fascinating. *1st and Macon Sts., tel. 719/269–3015. Admission: $3. Open May–Oct., daily 8:30–8; Nov.–Apr., Wed.–Sun. 10–5.*

To be fair, Cañon City is also called the Climate Capital of Colorado, for its temperate year-round conditions that attract retirees in droves. Set 12 miles north of town, amid glorious terrain, is the city-owned **Redrock Park,** a magnet for hikers and climbers—thanks to its twisted sandstone formations. **Garden Park,** also city-owned, boasts rich deposits of dinosaur fossils.

A four-wheel-drive gravel-and-dirt road (open only in summer) follows the old tracks that were used to transport ore, running through both parks and north to Cripple Creek. The route winds through red-rock canyons and the **Rampart Range,** over rickety (but reinforced) wooden trestle bridges, and mountain, meadow, and sky in vivid primary colors.

What to See and Do with Children

Buckskin Joe Park and Railway. Not only is this the largest Western-style theme park in the region, but it's actually an authentic ghost town that was literally moved here from its original site 100 miles away. Famous films such as *True Grit* and *Cat Ballou* were shot in this place that vividly evokes the Old West, especially during the re-creation gunfights and hangings that occur daily. Children love the horse-drawn trolley rides, horseback rides, and gold panning, while adults appreciate live entertainment in the Crystal Palace and Saloon. The complex includes its own scenic railway that travels to the rim of the Royal Gorge, as well as a Steam Train and Antique Car Museum. *Off Hwy. 50, Cañon City, tel. 719/275–5485. Combination ticket for all attractions: $12 adults, $10 children 5–11. Open May–Sept., daily 9–9.*

North Pole and Santa's Workshop. Energetic elves bustle about this colorful shrine to the commercialization of Christmas. Kids can feed deer, ride a Ferris wheel and carousel, try their luck in an arcade, visit Santa at the height of summer, and stuff themselves in the Candy Kitchen, Sugar Plum Terrace, or old-fashioned ice-cream parlor. *Exit 141 of Hwy. 24 west, tel. 719/684–9432. Admission: $7.95. Open May, Fri.–Wed. 9:30–6; June–Aug., daily 9:30–6; Sept.–Dec. 24, Fri.–Tues. 10–5.*

Royal Gorge and suspension bridge (*see* Exploring, *above*).

Shopping

Shopping Districts and Malls In Colorado Springs, the areas to shop are **Old Colorado City,** with numerous charming boutiques and galleries, and the very upscale **Broadmoor Shopping Arcade.** The streets of **Manitou Springs** and **Cripple Creek** offer one souvenir shop and gallery after another.

Specialty Stores **Art of the Rockies** (135 W. 3rd St., Salida, no tel.) is a co-op col-
Art Galleries lective showcasing the work of 70 regional artists.
Michael Garman Gallery (2418 W. Colorado Ave., Colorado
Springs, tel. 719/471–1600) carries Western-style paintings
and unusual figurines and dioramas.

Boutiques **Helstrom Studios** (330 N. Institute St., Colorado Springs, tel.
719/473–3620) showcases beads, textiles, silks, and batiks.

Ceramics **Van Briggle Pottery** (21st and Colorado Ave., Colorado
Springs, tel. 719/633–7729) offers free tours of its world-famous facility, winding up in the showroom.

Crafts **Simpich Character Dolls** (2413 W. Colorado Ave., Colorado
Springs, tel. 719/636–3272) fashions wonderfully detailed ceramic figurines and fabric dolls, including extraordinary mari-
onettes.

Food **Rocky Mountain Chocolates** (2431 W. Colorado Ave., Colorado
Springs, tel. 719/635–4131), with branches also in Pueblo, Castle Rock, and Boulder.

Western **Old West Co.** (645 E. U.S. 50, Salida, tel. 719/539–3422) offers
Paraphernalia Western gifts and taxidermy.

Sports and the Outdoors

Camping Camping is superb in the **San Isabel** and **Pike national forests.**
The forest service (tel. 719/265–4119 or 719/636–1602) or
Bureau of Land Management (tel. 719/275–0631) can provide
more information.

Climbing **Garden of the Gods** is a popular place to test your skills, thanks
to its stark spires and cliffs. Register with the visitor center at
the entrance. Also, **Collegiate Peaks** around Buena Vista and
Salida offer a variety of ascents from moderate to difficult. The
Royal Gorge, Redrocks Park, and **Garden Park,** outside Canon
City, are alive with intrepid clamberers.

Cycling Pueblo has an extensive **bike trail system,** which loops the city
following the Arkansas River partway, then goes out to the
reservoir. The **Pueblo Parks and Recreation Department** (tel.
719/566–1745) can provide more information.

Cycling is popular in the **Collegiate Peaks Wilderness Area,**
around Buena Vista and Salida. **American Adventure Expeditions** (228 N. F St., Buena Vista, tel. 719/395–2409) and **Rocky
Mountain Tours** (tel. 719/395–4101) provide rentals and tours.

Fishing Pike, bass, and trout are plentiful in this region. Favorite fishing spots include **Spinney Mountain Reservoir** (between Florissant and Buena Vista) and the **Arkansas** and **South Platte rivers.**
For more informaton, call the Colorado Division of Wildlife,
Southeast Region (tel. 719/473–2945).

Golf In Colorado Springs, **The Broadmoor** (Broadmoor Complex,
tel. 719/634–7711) offers 54 splendid holes to guests and members. **Colorado Springs Country Club** (3333 Templeton Gap Rd.,
tel. 719/4734–1782) is another fine 18-hole course, as is the public **Pine Creek Golf Course** (9850 Divot Dr., tel. 719/594–9999).

Hiking Canon City–owned **Redrocks Park,** 12 miles north of town, offers splendid hiking among the sandstone spires. There are numerous trails in the **Pikes Peak area,** including **Barr Trail** up the
mountain and **North Cheyenne Canyon Trail. Garden of the**

Gods, outside Colorado Springs, is also popular. Call the El Paso Parks and Recreations Department (tel. 719/520–6375) for further information about the Colorado Springs/Pikes Peak area.

Horseback Riding   **Academy Riding Stables** (Colorado Springs, tel. 719/633–5667) offers trail rides through the Garden of the Gods. **Buckskin Joe's** (Canon City, tel. 719/275–5149) offers rides in the Canon City area, from one hour to all day; rates begin at $20.

Skiing   **Cuchara Valley.** Four chairs; 24 trails; 250 acres; 1,562-foot ver-
Downhill   tical drop. *CO 12, Cuchara, tel. 719/742–3163 or 800/227–4436. Open Dec.–Apr., daily 9–4.*

Monarch. Four chairs; 54 trails; more than 670 acres; 1,160-foot vertical drop. The service, which has garnered numerous Tourism Hospitality Achievement Awards, is exceptional. Lift lines and lift tickets are of microscopic proportions, by most standards. *U.S. 50 (18 mi from Salida), tel. 719/539–3573. Open mid-Nov.–mid-Apr., daily 9–4.*

White-water   **Arkansas River Outfitters** (Canon City, tel. 719/275–3229),
Rafting   **Brown's Royal Gorge Rafting and Helicopter Tours** (Canon City, tel. 719/275–5161), **Royal Gorge River Adventures** (Canon City, tel. 719/269–3700), and **Sierra Outfitters** (Canon City, tel. 719/275–0128) are but a few of the reliable outfits that line U.S. 50, between Canon City and the Royal Gorge.

Buena Vista is the other major rafting center, with **American Adventure Expeditions** (tel. 719/395–2409) and **Rocky Mountain Tours** (tel. 719/395–4101).

Spectator Sports

Horse Racing   **Pikes Peak Meadows** (Exit 122 off I–25, Fountain, tel. 719/382–7805; open mid-Mar–early Sept.).

Dining

Steak houses and Mexican cantinas are usually the most dependable restaurants throughout Southcentral Colorado, though Colorado Springs and Pueblo offer a wide variety of fine eateries. For rates, *see* Towns and Country price chart in Chapter 1, Essential Information.

Highly recommended restaurants are indicated by a star ★.

Cañon City   **Merlino's Belvedere.** This Italian standby has ritzy coffee-shop decor, with floral banquettes, centerpieces, and a "running-water rock grotto." Locals swear by the top-notch steaks, seafood, and pasta. It's the usual choice for a big evening out. *1330 Elm Ave., tel. 719/275–5558. Reservations advised. Dress: casual. AE, MC, V. Moderate–Expensive.*

★   **Janey's Chile Wagon.** Owner Janey Workman is a former New Yorker who fled the big city. *The National Enquirer* did a feature on her: "Waitress Builds Diner into $350,000 Restaurant!" Her food is haute greasy spoon, with huge portions of delicious burritos and the like, smothered in "green chili that won't stay with you all night, hon." The decor favors neon parrots, velvet paintings, and other tchotchkes, but nothing is as colorful as Janey herself. *0807 Cyanide Ave., tel. 719/275–4885. Reservations accepted. Dress: casual. No credit cards. Closed Sun. and Mon. Inexpensive.*

Colorado Springs   **Briarstone Manor.** The symphony of cherrywood wainscoting,
★   balustrades and furnishings, Van Briggle wood-and-ceramic
fireplaces, tapestries, chinoiserie, and hand-painted glass
make this one of the most exquisitely romantic restaurants in
Colorado. There are several dining rooms, each with its own
look and mood. Among the most charming are the converted library and the garden room (a converted private chapel with
granite walls). To complete the picture, classical quartets play
on the patio in summer. Chef Sigi Krauss is to be commended
for literally rescuing this gorgeous old Victorian from the
wrecker's ball, and his international clientele appreciates his
diversified menu as much as the unparalleled ambience. Start
with the house-smoked Rocky Mountain trout mousse or alligator pear (avocado stuffed with seafood, topped with both hollandaise and bordelaise sauces), then try the perfectly
prepared rack of Colorado lamb or chateaubriand. *404 Manitou
Ave., Manitou Springs, tel. 719/685–1864. Reservations advised. Jacket and tie advised. AE, D, DC, MC, V. Closed for
lunch and Sun. Expensive.*

★   **Craftwood Inn.** This intimate, restful spot has been in operation as a restaurant for more than 50 years: It once regularly
hosted such luminaries as Cary Grant, Bing Crosby, and
Liberace. To start, try the wild mushroom and hazelnut
soup, black-bean ravioli, or warm pheasant salad. The mixed
game bird and wild grill are particularly memorable entrées,
especially when accompanied by a selection from the well-
considered and fairly priced wine list. *404 El Paso Blvd., Manitou Springs, tel. 719/685–9000. Reservations advised. Jacket
and tie advised. MC, V. Closed for lunch. Expensive.*

Pepper Tree. Due to its elevated position upon a hill, the Pepper
Tree enjoys smashing views of the city that combine nicely with
the restaurant's note of quiet sophistication. Interior decor
features a pink-and-maroon color scheme and mirrored wall.
Table-side preparations (including the inevitable and delectable pepper steak) are its stock-in-trade, though the chef will go
out on a limb with such daily specials as calamari stuffed with
crabmeat and bacon. Still, this is one of those old-fashioned
places where flambé is considered the height of both elegance
and decadence. *888 W. Moreno Ave., tel. 719/471–4888. Reservations advised. Jacket and tie advised. AE, MC, V. Closed for
lunch and Sun. Expensive.*

Margarita. Plants, adobe walls, terra-cotta tile, and mosaic tables lend an air of refinement to this fine eatery, whose constantly changing menu is an intriguing hybrid of Mexican and
Continental influences. *7350 Pine Creek Rd., tel. 719/598–
8667. Reservations advised. Dress: casual. AE, MC, V. Closed
Sun. for dinner and Mon. Moderate.*

Henri's Mexican. Don't be fooled by the name: Henri's is the
oldest and best *Mexican* restaurant in town. The food is as
bright and festive as the interior design (lots of murals and
sombreros). Among the appetizing standards are shrimp-
stuffed relleños and chimichangas. *2427 W. Colorado Blvd., tel.
719/634–9031. Reservations accepted. Dress: casual. AE, MC,
V. Closed Mon. Inexpensive–Moderate.*

Salida   **First Street Café.** Occupying a late-19th-century building in the
historic district is this café, with creative heart-healthy and
vegetarian specials, in addition to the expected robust
Mexican-American fare. Breakfast is served here, as well as
lunch and dinner. *137 E. 1st. St., tel. 719/539–4759. Reserva-*

tions accepted. Dress: casual. AE, D, MC, V. Inexpensive–Moderate.

Lodging

Colorado Springs boasts some of the higher-end chain properties, but, in general, the choice is usually among bed-and-breakfasts, guest houses, and motels on the strip. Unless otherwise noted, all accommodations listed below include phones, cable TVs, and private baths. For rates, *see* Towns and Country price chart in Chapter 1, Essential Information.

Highly recommended lodgings are indicated by a star ★.

Buena Vista **Adobe Inn.** This adobe hacienda has five charming rooms, each named for the predominant decorative motif: antique, Mexican, Indian, Mediterranean, and wicker. Some rooms have a fireplace. Complimentary gourmet breakfast is offered to guests. *303 N. Hwy. 24, 81211, tel. 719/395–6340. 5 rooms. Facilities: hot tub. MC, V. Inexpensive.*

Cañon City **Cañon Inn.** A host of famous people have stayed here, including
★ John Belushi, Tom Selleck, Jane Fonda, John Wayne, Glenn Ford, and Goldie Hawn; their names emblazon the doors to their rooms. Spacious and ultracomfortable accommodations are offered in two wings. Rooms in the new section are nicest, although the old wing has been completely refurbished. All are decorated in muted pastels and earth tones. *Hwy. 50 and Dozier St., 81215, tel. 719/275–8676; fax 719/275–8675. 104 rooms. Facilities: restaurant, lounge, outdoor pool, hot tub. AE, D, DC, MC, V. Inexpensive.*

Colorado Springs **The Broadmoor.** Here's one of America's truly great hotels.
★ Completely self-contained—more a village than a resort—its 30 buildings sprawl majestically across 3,500 acres. The property celebrated 75 years of deluxe service in 1993, and it maintains its exalted status through continual upgrading and refurbishment. The pink-and-ocher main building, crowned by Mediterranean-style towers, serenely commands a private lake. Rooms here are the loveliest, with period furnishings; accommodations in the other complexes are more contemporary in style. The Broadmoor is renowned for its three world-class championship golf courses, and the indoor ice-skating arena has remained the premier training facility in Colorado ever since Peggy Fleming started practicing her figure eights here. There are eight restaurants, of which the Tavern, with its original Toulouse-Lautrec posters, the elegant cranberry-and-silver Penrose Room, and the romantic primrose, mint, and buff Charles Court rank among the state's finest. *Box 1439, 80901, tel. 719/634–7711 or 800/634–7711; fax 719/577–5779. 483 rooms, 67 suites. Facilities: 8 restaurants, 3 lounges, 54 holes of championship golf, riding stables, 4 indoor and 8 outdoor tennis courts, 3 squash courts, health club, skeet and trap-shooting ranges, 3 swimming pools, 21 shops, beauty salon, movie theater, rental-car desk, 100,000 sq. ft. of meeting space. AE, D, DC, MC, V. Very Expensive.*

★ **Antlers Hotel.** Two previous incarnations of this hotel once competed with The Broadmoor for the rich and famous, thanks to its superb, historic location downtown. This third Antlers was completely renovated and expanded in 1991. The large airy lobby strikes an immediate note of class when you enter, and the handsome rooms sport hunting-lodge decor with mountain colors. *4 S. Cascade Ave., 80904, tel. 719/473–5600 or 800/ 528–0444; fax 719/389–0259. 274 rooms, 16 suites. Facilities: 2 restaurants, lounge, health club, Jacuzzi, shopping arcade, meeting space. AE, D, DC, MC, V. Moderate.*

★ **Embassy Suites.** This is one of the original properties in this chain, and it's among the best. The airy atrium lobby, crawling with plants, is watched over by the resident talkative birds (in cages). Suites are comfortable, favoring teal and dusty rose. To complete the tropical motif, a waterfall tumbles lavishly into the indoor pool. The pool deck boasts quite a view of Pikes Peak; jazz groups play here every Thursday night in season. Complimentary breakfast is offered to all guests. *7290 Commerce Center Dr. 80919, tel. 719/599–9100; fax 719/599–4644. 207 suites. Facilities: restaurant, lounge, indoor pool, exercise room, Jacuzzi, meeting facilities. AE, D, DC, MC, V. Moderate.*

Sheraton Hotel. The ugly cinder-block exterior gives no clue to the attractive space within: Pleasing spacious, rooms done up in southwestern pastels, all feature the standards and full bath including double vanities. There are plenty of facilities and activities to keep guests happy. *2886 S. Circle Dr. 80906, tel. 719/ 576–5900; fax 719/576–7695. 502 rooms, 16 suites. Facilities: restaurant, deli, lounge, health club with sauna, indoor/outdoor pool (with waterfall), Jacuzzi, 4 lighted tennis courts, meeting space. AE, D, DC, MC, V. Moderate.*

The Hearthstone. Two Victorian houses joined by a carriage house comprise this famed bed-and-breakfast, listed on the National Register of Historic Places. The 25 nonsmoking guest rooms (most with private bath), are resplendent with furnishings from the 1880s; each is individually decorated around a theme, such as Author's Den, replete with vintage typewriter, and Solarium, brightened by plants and an expansive skylight. Included in the room rate is a complimentary gourmet breakfast. *506 N. Cascade Ave. 80903, tel. 719/473–4413 or 800/ 521–1885. 25 rooms. No facilities. AE, MC, V. Inexpensive–Moderate.*

★ **Holden House.** Genial innkeepers Sallie and Welling Clark realized their dream when they impeccably restored this 1902 Victorian home transformed into a B&B. Three charming rooms in the main house and two in the adjacent carriage house are filled with family heirlooms and antiques. Fireplaces, oversize or clawfoot tubs in the private baths, and down pillows and quilts make guest rooms even more cozy. Complimentary breakfasts are truly a gourmet's delight. *1102 W. Pikes Peak Ave., 80904, tel. 719/471–3980. 5 rooms. No facilities. AE, D, MC, V. Inexpensive–Moderate.*

Salida **The Poor Country Farm Inn.** Situated on the Arkansas River, this cozy Victorian home boasts breathtaking mountain prospects. Rooms are filled with antiques and family memorabilia. Complimentary gourmet breakfast is offered to guests. *8495 C.R. 60, 81201, tel. 719/539–3818. 5 rooms, 4 with shared bath; coed dorm sleeps 8. No facilities. MC, V. Inexpensive.*

Victor **Victor Hotel.** In 1991, more than a million dollars was dedicated to renovating this hotel, listed on the National Register of Historic Places. Public spaces have been restored to their Victorian splendor, adding to the list of reasons why Victor Hotel is the nicest place to stay in the Cripple Creek area. Other attributes include tastefully decorated rooms with stunning mountain views. Unfortunately, aside from the original open brickwork and a few old-fashioned tubs and radiators, the accommodations' decor and furnishings are prosaically modern, and bathrooms are tiny. *4th and Victor Sts., 80860, tel. 719/ 689–3553. 30 rooms. Facilities: restaurant, complimentary shuttle to and from Cripple Creek. AE, D, MC, V. Inexpensive–Moderate.*

The Arts

Colorado Springs's **Pikes Peak Center** (190 S. Cascade Ave., tel. 719/520–SHOW) presents the **Colorado Springs Symphony**, as well as touring theater and dance companies.

Music Salida draws some of the musicians from the Aspen Music Festival during the summer, becoming the **Aspen-Salida Music Festival,** July–August.

Theater **Air Force Academy, Arnold Hall** (Colorado Springs, tel. 719/ 472–4497) present touring and local companies.

Powerhouse Players (200 W. Sackett St., Salida, tel. 719/539– 2455), a community theater based in Dallas, presents a variety of musical revues and straight plays throughout the summer in the town's historic steam plant.

Nightlife

Bars and Lounges In Buena Vista, head to **The Lariat** (206 W. Main St., tel. 719/ 395–6308), where they "sell and service hangovers"; or **The Green Parrot** (304 Main St., tel. 719/395–8985), which has live music weekends.

In Colorado Springs, the **Golden Bee** (International Center, The Broadmoor, tel. 719/634–7711) is an institution. The gloriously old-fashioned bar with pressed-tin ceilings and magnificent woodwork features a piano player leading sing-alongs. **Judge Baldwin's** (4 S. Cascade Ave., Antlers Hotel, tel. 719/ 473–5600) is a lively brew pub.

Casinos Cripple Creek has several casinos offering limited-stakes gambling.

Comedy Clubs **Jeff Valdez' Comedy Corner** (204 N. Union St., Colorado Springs, tel. 719/578–0496) features live stand-up comedy, including several nationally known comics.

Country and Colorado Springs has several C&W spots. **Cowboys** (Rustic
Western Hills North Shopping Ctr., tel. 719/596–1212) is for hard-core two-steppers. **Gambler's Dance Hall and Saloon** (3958 N. Academy St., tel. 719/574–3369) attracts a younger, family-oriented clientele. **Rodeo** (3506 N. Academy St., tel. 719/597–6121) tends to have a Yuppie crowd.

Dinner Shows Cripple Creek's **Imperial Hotel Theater** (123 N. 3rd. St., tel. 719/689–2922) is renowned for its Victorian melodramas.

In Colorado Springs, **Flying W Ranch** (Flying W Ranch Rd., tel. 719/598–4000), open mid-May–October, has been roping them in for the sensational Western stage show and chuckwagon dinner. **Iron Springs Dinner Theater** (Manitou Springs, across from Pikes Peak Cog Railway, tel. 719/685–5104), in Colorado Springs, offers melodrama.

Discos In Colorado Springs, you can dance part of the night away at **Studebaker's** (7852 N. Academy St., tel. 719/594–0778) and **Top of the Rock** (3506 N. Academy St., tel. 719/591–2100).

In Pueblo, try **Images** (4001 N. Elizabeth St., tel. 719/543–8080).

Jazz Clubs In Colorado Springs, **McKenna's Pub** (3725 Austin Bluffs Pkwy., tel. 719/599–3020) presents live jazz several nights weekly.

Singles In Colorado Springs, try **Old Chicago** (118 N. Tejon Ave., tel. 719/634–8812).

Northcentral Colorado

Northcentral Colorado is an appealing blend of Old West and New Age. More a ranching than a mining area, it's strewn with rich evocations of pioneer life, as well as turn-of-the-century resort towns such as Estes Park and Grand Lake. Yet the region is anchored by Boulder, one of the country's most progressive cities and a town virtually synonymous (some might say obsessed) with environmental concern and physical fitness. As the local joke goes, even the dogs jog.

Boulderites take full advantage of the town's glorious natural setting, nestled amid the peaks of the Front Range, indulging in everything from rock climbing to mountain biking. A short drive south brings them to the ski areas along I–70. To the west and north, the Roosevelt and Arapahoe national forests and the Great Lakes of Colorado provide a host of recreational opportunities from hiking to fishing to cross-country skiing and snowmobiling. To the northeast, Estes Park stands as the gateway to America's alpine wonderland—Rocky Mountain National Park—which spans three ecosystems that 900 species of plants, 250 species of birds, and 25 species of mammals, including elk, muletail deer, moose, bobcats, and even black bears, call home.

Important Addresses and Numbers

Tourist Information **Boulder Convention & Visitors Bureau** (2440 Pearl St., Boulder 80302, tel. 303/442–2911 or 800/444–0447); **Estes Park Area Chamber of Commerce** (Box 3050, Estes Park 80517, tel. 303/586–4431 or 800/44–ESTES); **Fort Collins Area Convention & Visitors Bureau** (420 S. Howes, Suite 101, Fort Collins 80522, tel. 303/482–5821 or 800/274–FORT); **Grand Lake Area Chamber of Commerce** (Box 57, Grand Lake 80447, tel. 303/627–3402); **Greeley Convention & Visitors Bureau** (1407 8th Ave., Greeley 80631, tel. 303/352–3566); **Loveland Chamber of Commerce** (114 E. 5th St., tel. 303/667–6311); **Poudre Canyon Visitor Information** (9940 Poudre Canyon Rte., Bellvue 80512, tel. 303/484–3013 or 800/462–5870).

Hospitals **Boulder Community Hospital** (1100 Balsam Ave., Boulder, tel. 303/440–2037); **Estes Park Medical Center** (555 Prospect Ave., Estes Park, tel. 303/586–2317); **North Colorado Medical Center** (1801 16th St., Greeley, tel. 303/352–4121); **Poudre Valley Hospital** (1024 S. Lemay Ave., Fort Collins, tel. 303/482–4111).

Arriving and Departing by Plane

Airports and Airlines Boulder and Estes Park are served by **Denver International Airport** (*see* Arriving and Departing by Plane in Denver, *above*); regular shuttles are available from Denver (*see* By Shuttle, *below*). **Fort Collins-Loveland Municipal Airport** (tel. 303/221–1300) welcomes flights from **America West, Continental**, and **Delta**.

Between the Airport and the Hotels/Downtown
By Bus or Shuttle **Airport Express** (Fort Collins, tel. 303/482–0505) runs shuttles from Denver and the Fort Collins airport. **Boulder Airporter** (tel. 303/321–3222) and **Boulder Ground Transportation** (tel. 303/444–4410) provide transportation from Denver. **Charles Limousine Service** (tel. 303/586–5151 or 800/950–3274) offers rides to Estes Park from Denver and Boulder. Costs run from $10 to $30 depending on pickup location.

By Taxi **Boulder Yellow Cab** (tel. 303/442–2277) costs $1.50 for first ⅙ mile and 20¢ for subsequent ⅙ mile.

Arriving and Departing by Car and Bus

By Car The region is easily accessed via I–25, which runs north–south.

By Bus **Greyhound/Trailways** (tel. 800/752–4841) serves most of the major towns in the region.

Getting Around

By Car U.S. 36 north accesses Boulder and Estes Park from Denver. Fort Collins and Longmont can be reached from Denver, via I–15 north. The main thoroughfare through Rocky Mountain Park, connecting Grand Lake with Estes Park, is U.S. 34, which is partially closed October–May. Grand Lake can also be reached by U.S. 40 into U.S. 34, out of Georgetown on I–70.

By Taxi **Boulder Yellow Cab** (tel. 303/442–2277) costs $1.50 for the first ⅙ mile and 20¢ for each subsequent mile; **Charles Taxi** (Estes Park, tel. 303/586–8440) quotes individual rates; and **Shamrock Taxi** (Fort Collins, tel. 303/224–2222) costs $2.30 for the first mile, $1.40 for each mile thereafter.

By Bus or Trolley In Estes Park: A public trolley runs throughout the area during the summer.

In Fort Collins: **Transfort** (tel. 303/221–6620) runs along major thoroughfares, charging 75¢.

Guided Tours

Orientation **Doo-Dah Tours** (tel. 303/449–0433) and **Explore Tours** (tel. 303/530–5116) offer tours of the Boulder area and other nearby attractions, including Rocky Mountain National Park and the Peak to Peak Highway.

Special-Interest Tours **Boulder Historical Tours** (tel. 303/444–5192) sponsors tours of various Boulder neighborhoods during the summer.

Charles Taxi and Tours (tel. 303/586–8440) runs trips to Rocky Mountain National Park, as does **Rocky Mountain National Park Tours** (tel. 303/586–8687).

Exploring Northcentral Colorado

Boulder and Rocky Mountain National Park

Numbers in the margin correspond to points of interest on the Colorado map.

🟤 No place in Colorado better epitomizes the state's outdoor mania than **Boulder.** There are more bikes than cars in this uncommonly beautiful and beautifully uncommon city, embroidered with 25,000 acres of parks and greenbelts laced with jogging tracks and bike trails. You're also more likely to see ponytails than crew cuts: Boulder is a college town with an arty, liberal reputation. Physically fit and environmentally hip, it's a city of cyclists and recyclers who, when they're not out enjoying their natural surroundings, enjoy nothing more than sitting at a sidewalk café, watching the rest of the world jog by.

Boulder's heartbeat is the **Pearl Street Mall,** a mind-boggling, eye-catching array of chic shops and trendy restaurants where all of Boulder hangs out. As an added bonus, the mall slices through Mapleton Hill, a historic district of great charm.

On the outskirts of the city there are three free attractions worth visiting. The first is the **Celestial Seasonings Plant** (4600 Sleepytime Dr., tel. 303/530–5300), offering free tours of its facility, weekdays three times daily, 11–2 on the hour. Its unmistakable aroma permeates the parking lot, and inside you can see the ingredients in their raw form (the Mint Room is isolated due to its potent scent) and how they're blended. The tour ends up in the gift shop for a tea tasting. Also aromatic is the free tour of the **Boulder Beer Company** (2880 Wilderness Pl., tel. 303/444–8448). These run Monday–Saturday, at 2 PM, and culminate in a tasting. The last free attraction is **The Leanin' Tree Museum of Western Art** (6055 Longbow Dr., tel. 303/530–1442; open weekdays 8–4:30)—brought to you by the folks who make the wildly popular and humorous, Western-themed greeting cards—whose superlative collection ranges from traditionalists in the Remington and Bierstadt manner to stylistic innovators in the Western genre. One room is devoted to the paintings of the original greeting-card genius, Lloyd Mitchell.

Take Broadway north to the **Colorado University** (tel. 303/492–6301) campus, its handsome collection of stone buildings with red tile roofs separated by spacious lawns. Tours are available weekday afternoons. A favorite nearby student hangout is the bohemian neighborhood called The Hill (around 13th and College steets, west of the campus), home to lots of coffee houses and hip boutiques, and always happening day or night.

Time Out   **Alfalfa's** (Broadway and Arapahoe St., tel. 303/442–0082) is a New Age organic supermarket, where one-stop shopping will net you everything from "cruelty-free" cosmetics to herbal and homeopathic remedies. The deli offers expected healthful fare, with a crisp fresh salad bar, homemade muffins, and soups (usually something like tofu miso) and custom-blended vegetable and fruit juices.

The prettiest views of town can be had by following Baseline Drive (off Broadway) up to **Chatauqua Park,** site of the Colorado Music Festival, and a favorite oasis of locals on weekends. Continue farther up Flagstaff Mountain to Panorama Point and Boulder Mountain Park, where people jog, bike, climb, and rarely remain still. The admirable parks system also includes the trademark red-sandstone **Flatirons,** which can be seen from nearly every vantage point in town. The massive structures, so named because of their flat rock faces, are popular among rock climbers and hikers.

The most direct route to Rocky Mountain National Park is along U.S. 36 north, via the quaint town of **Lyons.** The scenery gives little hint of the grandeur to come when you reach **Estes Park.** If ever there was a classic picture-postcard Rockies view, Estes Park has it. Even the McDonald's boasts glorious views and a facade that complements its surroundings, thanks to strict zoning laws that require all businesses to present a rustic exterior. The town itself is very family-oriented: Many of the small hotels lining the country roads are mom-and-pop outfits that have been passed down through several generations.

Time Out At **Ed's Cantina**'s (362 E. Elkhorn Ave., tel. 303/586–2919) the walls are festooned with pennants and neon signs advertising beers and ball clubs. Huge, filling breakfast burritos and burgers are the more reliable choices at this popular locals' hangout.

If you would rather explore Estes's environs than the park, you have a number of options. As a resort town, Estes attracted the attention of genius entrepreneur F. O. Stanley, inventor of the Stanley Steamer automobile and several photographic processes. In 1905, having been told by his doctors he would soon die of tuberculosis, he constructed the regal **Stanley Hotel,** on a promontory overlooking the town. Stanley went on to live another 30-odd years, an extension that he attributed to the fresh air. The hotel soon became one of the most glamorous resorts in the Rockies, a position it still holds to this day. Incidentally, the hotel was the inspiration for Stephen King's spooky book, and later movie, *The Shining.*

From the Stanley take Elkhorn Avenue and turn right on Route 36. In two blocks you'll see the **Estes Park Area Historical Museum,** which makes an eloquent case to support the theory that Native Americans used the area as a summer resort, attested to by the archaeological evidence that's displayed here. The museum also offers the usual assortment of pioneer artifacts and interesting changing exhibits. *200 4th St., tel. 303/586–6256. Admission: $2 adults, $1 children. Open May–Sept., Mon.–Sat. 10–5; Sun. 1–5.*

Double back on Route 36 where it intersects with Route 34; follow Route 34 to MacGregor Avenue and take it for a mile. **The MacGregor Ranch Museum,** in the National Register of Historic Places, offers spectacular views of the Twin Owls and Longs Peak (towering more than 14,000 feet). Although the original ranch was homesteaded in 1873, the present house was built in 1896 and provides a well-preserved record of typical ranch life, thanks to a wealth of material discovered in the attic. *MacGregor Ave., tel. 303/586–3749. Admission free. Open June–Sept., Tues.–Sat. 10–5.*

These sights give you a good education about the history of the area, but the real attraction in the neighborhood is **Rocky Mountain National Park** (tel. 303/586–2371; admission, $5 weekly per vehicle), sculpted by violent volcanic uplifts and receding glaciers that savagely clawed the earth in their wake. There are three distinct ecosystems in the park, including ver-

Rocky Mountain National Park

ROOSEVELT NATIONAL FOREST

COMANCHE PEAK WILDERNESS

N

Long Draw Reservoir

Cache la Poudre River

Mummy Range

Black Canyon

West Creek

Alpine Visitor Center

Old Fall River Rd.

Big Thompson River

Forest Canyon

Trail Ridge Rd.

Fall River Entrance Station

34

Gorge Lakes

Estes Park

36

Continental

Visitor Center Park Headquarters

Timber Creek

Never Summer Ranch

Moraine Park

Moraine Park Museum

Spruce Canyon

Cub Lake

Divide

34

Bear Lake

Sprague Lake

7

Kawuneeche Visitor Center

North Inlet

Alva Adams Tunnel

Colorado River

Grand Lake

East-Inlet Trailhead

Grand Lake

Adams Falls

Shadow Mountain Lake

East Inlet

Wild Basin

Calypso Cascades

Lake Granby

ARAPAHO NATIONAL RECREATION AREA

34

72

KEY	
	Highways
	Minor Roads
	Unpaved Road
	Trail
	Ranger Station
	Campground
	Picnic Area

0   6 miles

0   6 km

dant subalpine—a cathedral of towering proud ponderosa pines; alpine; and harsh unforgiving tundra, with wind-whipped trees that grow at right angles, and microscopic doll-house versions of familiar plants and wildflowers. The park also teems with wildlife, from beaver to bighorn sheep, with the largest concentrations of sheep and majestic elk in Horseshoe Meadow.

The fine visitor centers at the east and west ends of the park, on U.S. 34 (also called Trail Ridge Road, the world's highest continuous paved highway; open only in summer), offer maps, brochures, newsletters, and comprehensive information on the park's statistics and facilities. The park is a spendid place to wander. The scenery, accessed by various trails, can be similar, but still inspiring. Trail Ridge Road accesses several lovely hikes along its meandering way, through terrain filigreed with silvery streams and turquoise lakes. The views around each bend—of moraines and glaciers, and craggy hills framing emerald meadows carpeted with columbine and Indian paintbrush—are truly awesome: nature's workshop on an epic scale.

Take U.S. 36 south for about 4 miles to the **Moraine Park Museum** (open May–Sept., daily 10–6), which offers lectures, slide shows, and displays on the park's geology and botany. Turn onto Bear Lake Road, which winds past shimmering waterfalls, perpetually shrouded with rainbows, and a series of other sapphire lakes. From the museum you can take the twisting, 9-mile-long Bear Lake Road, which offers superlative views of Longs Peak (Colorado's highest) and the glaciers surrounding Bear Lake.

If you choose not to follow Bear Lake Road, head west from the museum on Trail Ridge. Many Peaks Curve affords breathtaking views of the crest of the Continental Divide and of the Alluvial Fan, a huge gash created in 1982 by a vicious flood after an earthen dam broke. Erosion occurred immediately, rather than over the millions of years that nature usually requires, and today it resembles a lonely lunar landscape.

Grand Lake is the western gateway to the park, and it, too, enjoys an idyllic setting on the shores of the state's largest natural lake of the same name; this is the highest-altitude yacht anchorage in America. According to Ute legend, the fine mists that punctually shroud the lake at dawn are the risen spirits of women and children whose raft capsized as they were fleeing a marauding party of Cheyennes and Arapahoes. Grand Lake feeds into two much larger man-made reservoirs, **Lake Granby** and **Shadow Mountain Lake,** forming the "Great Lakes of Colorado." The entire area is a paradise for hikers and fishermen. Even the town, while it boasts the usual assortment of souvenir shops and motels, seems less spoiled than many other resort communities.

What to See and Do with Children

Estes Park Area Historical Museum (*see* Exploring *above*)

The MacGregor Ranch Museum (*see* Exploring *above*)

Shopping

Shopping Districts and Malls	Boulder's **Pearl Street Mall** is a shopping extravaganza, with numerous upscale boutiques and galleries. **The Hill**, by Colorado University, is a great place for hip duds and CDs.

Main Street, in the tiny town of **Niwot** (northeast of Boulder on CO 119), is one long strip of antiques stores. Main Street in **Lyons** (north of Boulder on U.S. 36) also boasts several fine antiques shops.

In Estes Park, the **Park Theatre Mall** and **Old Church Shops Mall** feature a wide variety of upmarket stores, hawking primarily indigenous crafts.

Specialty Stores
Art Galleries Pearl Street Mall, in Boulder, features a number of art galleries and boutiques that carry crafts. **Art Source International** (1237 Pearl St., Boulder, tel. 303/444–4080) is Colorado's largest antique print and map dealer. **Handmade in Colorado** (1426 Pearl St., Boulder, tel. 303/938–8394), and **Boulder Arts & Crafts Cooperative** (1421 Pearl St., tel. 303/443–3683) handle only the best Colorado-made goods. **McLaren & Markowitz Gallery** (1011 Pearl St., Boulder, tel. 303/449–6807) features fine jewelry, sculpture, and pottery—primarily with a Southwestern feel. **White Horse Gallery** (1218 Pearl St., Boulder, tel. 303/443–6116) offers top-of-the-line Native American and Southwestern art and artifacts.

Children **The Christmas House** (Park Theatre Mall, Estes Park, tel. 303/586–2882) delights kids of all ages with every conceivable ornament, doll, curio, and knickknack related to Noël, from around the world.

The Printed Page (1219 Pearl St., Boulder, tel. 303/443–8450) presents unique and exquisite old-fashioned toys.

Clothing In Boulder, **Alpaca Connection** (1326 Pearl St., tel. 303/447–2047) offers Indian silks, Bolivian alpaca, and Ecuadorian merino. In Estes Park, **JB Sweaters** (140 E. Elkhorn Ave., tel. 303/586–6101) features hand-knit sweaters, shirts, and ties for men and women.

Food **Celestial Seasonings** (4600 Sleepytime Dr., Boulder, tel. 303/530–8300) creates soothing blends of tea in a variety of exotic New Age flavors.

Outdoor Gear In Boulder, vist **Hangouts** (1328 Pearl St., tel. 303/442–2533) for their splendid handmade hammocks. **Mountain Sports** (821 Pearl St., tel. 303/443–6770), also in the city, provides four seasons' worth of outdoor equipment and clothing. **McGuckin's Hardware** (Village Shopping Ctr., tel. 303/443–1822) is a Boulder institution that features a mind-boggling array of equipment and tools.

Western Paraphernalia **Rocky Mountain Comfort** (116 E. Elkhorn Ave., Estes Park, tel. 303/586–0512) has home accessories with the lodge look, including furniture, quilts, baskets, and throws, and even local foodstuffs.

Stage Western Family Clothing (104 Moraine Ave., Estes Park, tel. 303/586–3430), permeated by the pungent aroma of leather, offers imaginative cowboy hats, boots, and belts.

Sports and the Outdoors

Camping Camping facilities abound in the 800,000 acres of **Roosevelt National Forest** (tel. 303/498–1100). There are five top-notch sites in **Rocky Mountain National Park** (tel. 303/586–2371).

Cycling The **Boulder Creek path** winds for 16 miles from Eben G. Fine Park, at the base of Boulder Canyon, to 55th Street, passing gardens and a fish observatory along the way. There is excellent cycling throughout the **Roosevelt National Forest** (tel. 303/498–1100).

Fishing The best fishing can be found on **Grand Lake, Lake Granby,** the **Big Thompson River** near Estes Park, and the **Horsetooth Reservoir, Red Feather Lakes,** and **Cache la Poudre River** west of Fort Collins. For more information, call the Colorado Division of Wildlife, Northeast Region (tel. 303/484–2836).

Golf **Collindale Golf Course** (1441 E. Horsetooth St., Fort Collins, tel. 303/221–6651) is an 18-hole public course.

Estes Park Golf Course (1080 S. St. Vrain St., tel. 303/586–8146) is one of the oldest and prettiest 18-hole courses in the state.

In Boulder, **Flatirons Golf Course** (5706 Arapahoe Ave., Boulder, tel. 303/442–7851) is an 18-hole public course at the foot of the eponymous mountains; and **Lake Valley Golf Club** (Neva Rd., 5 mi north of Boulder, tel. 303/444–2144) is another 18-hole course with fine views.

Grand Lake Golf Course (C.R. 48, Grand Lake, tel. 303/627–8008) is an 18-hole course standing 8,240 feet above sea level.

Hiking The premier hiking, of course, is within **Rocky Mountain National Park.** The **Colorado Mountain Club** (Estes Park, tel. 303/586–6623) sponsors day and overnight trips into the park. Other splendid hiking is within the superb **Boulder Mountain Parks** system, including Chatauqua Park and Sunshine Canyon. **Roosevelt National Forest** (tel. 303/498–1100) offers fine backcountry hiking in the Estes Park area. For information, call the **Boulder Parks and Recreation Department** (tel. 303/441–3000).

In Grand County, near Lake Granby, **Indian Peaks Wilderness Area** (tel. 303/887–3331) is another prime location.

West of Fort Collins, in truly unspoiled surroundings, the **Colorado State Forest** (tel. 303/723–8366) offers superb hiking.

Horseback Riding **National Park Village Stables** (tel. 303/586–5269) and **Sombrero Stables** (tel. 303/586–4577) offer trail rides through one Estes Park region, including Rocky Mountain National Park.

In-line Skating *See* Cycling, *above.*

Skiing
Cross-Country The lower valleys of **Rocky Mountain National Park** (tel. 303/586–2371) are accessible year-round and provide miles of trails. The **Grand Lake Touring Center** (tel. 303/627–8008) offers 32 miles of trails with breathtaking vistas of the Never Summer Range and the Continental Divide. The **Never Summer Yurt System** (Box 1254, Fort Collins 80522, tel. 303/484–3903) is a hut-to-hut system.

Downhill **Eldora Mountain Resort.** 43 trails; 5 chairs and 1 tow; 386 acres; 1,400-foot vertical drop. There is night skiing Wednesday–Saturday. *CO. 119, Nederland, tel. 303/440–8700. Open mid-Nov.–mid-Apr. 9–4.*

Silver Creek Ski Area. 25 runs on 200 acres; 3 chairs, 1 T-bar; 1,500-foot vertical. Excellent for family skiing. *U.S. 40, Silver Creek, tel. 303/887–3384. Open Dec.–early Apr. 9–4.*

Water Sports **Grand Lake** and **Lake Granby** are the premier boating centers. Call the **Spirit Lake Marina** (tel. 303/627–8158) for information on renting boats and Windsurfers.

Dining

Boulder boasts almost as impressive a range of ethnic eateries as the much larger Denver. By and large, prices are quite reasonable, thanks to the large student population that can't afford very expensive meals. There is far less diversity elsewhere in the region, although you can count on finding solid American or Continental restaurants throughout. For rates *see* Towns and Country price chart in Chapter 1, Essential Information.

Highly recommended restaurants are indicated by a star ★.

Boulder **The Flagstaff House.** This refined restaurant atop Flagstaff
★ Mountain is one of Colorado's finest. Sit on the enclosed patio and drink in the sublime views of Boulder to go with a selection from the remarkably comprehensive wine list. Chef Mark Monet is noted for his exquisite combinations of ingredients and fanciful, playful presentations. The menu changes daily, but sample inspirations might include lobster ravioli and shrimp in shiitake broth; potato roll of smoked rabbit and duck with sautéed foie gras; mesquite-smoked alligator and rattlesnake; and elk dumplings with ginger and sweet onion. Those are just appetizers. Opt for the daily tasting menu. *Baseline Rd., tel. 303/442–4640. Reservations required. Dress: neat but casual. AE, DC, MC. V. Very Expensive.*

★ **Gold Hill Inn.** This humble log cabin 10 miles west of Boulder hardly looks like a bastion of haute cuisine, but the six-course, $19.50 prix-fixe dinner is to rave about. Sample entrées may be paella or lamb venison marinated for four days in buttermilk, juniper berries, and cloves. *Sunshine Canyon, 10 mi from Boulder, tel. 303/443–6461. Reservations advised. Dress: casual. No credit cards. Closed for lunch and Tues. Moderate.*

The Imperial Mataam Fez. You eat with your hands at this lavish Moroccan restaurant that looks like it came straight from *The Arabian Nights.* The prix-fixe dinner includes five courses, with such fragrant dishes as lamb with honey and almond and hare paprika and couscous. There are branches in Denver, Colorado Springs, and Vail, but this is the original. *2226 Pearl St., tel. 303/440–4167. Reservations advised. Dress: casual. AE, MC, V. Closed lunch. Moderate.*

★ **Sushi Zanmai.** The restaurant section is a cool, sleek place to enjoy delectable seafood and very good hibachi items, but the action's really at the zany sushi bar, where the chefs periodically burst into song: "If you knew Sushi" is a popular request. It's always karaoke here, although the official night is Saturday. *1221 Spruce St., tel. 303/440–0733. Reservations advised. Dress: casual. AE, MC, V. Closed for weekend lunch. Moderate.*

Bangkok Cuisine. This very pretty restaurant looks more like a French bistro than a typical Thai place, with cut-glass lamps, brass fixtures, and mauve tablecloths. In addition to expertly prepared staples such as satay, lemon-grass soup, pad Thai (Thai noodles), and the inimitable curries, try less familiar items such as Gung Pao—juicy shrimp charbroiled with red chili paste. *2017 13th St., tel. 303/440–4830. Reservations accepted. Dress: casual. AE, D, MC, V. Inexpensive–Moderate.*

Pasta Jay's. The name says it all: Homemade pastas in every size and shape dominate the menu, as well as traditional favorites such as veal parmigiana. The outdoor patio is the perfect place to watch Boulder go by. *925 Pearl St., tel. 303/444–5800. Reservations accepted. Dress: casual. AE, MC, V. Inexpensive–Moderate.*

L.A. Diner. This temple of chrome and Formica calls itself the Last American Diner and is open 24 hours. Good ol' rock and roll blasts from the speakers, waiters zip by on roller skates, and the menu runs to classic diner food, from meatloaf to malts. *1955 28th St., tel. 303/447–1997. Reservations accepted. Dress: casual. MC, V. Inexpensive.*

Estes Park **Nicky's Cattleman Restaurant.** Elegant wood beams, oak paneling, maroon carpeting and upholstery, and a huge picture window fronting the mountain and river make this one of the most sophisticated dining spots in town. They age and cut their own meat here, and specialties include sensational sirloin prepared Greek style with onions, peppers, and feta, and prime rib broiled in rock salt. Nicky's also offers motor-lodge rooms with shag carpeting. *1350 Hwy. 34, tel. 303/586–5376. Reservations accepted. Dress: casual. AE, D, MC, V. Closed for lunch. Moderate.*

Friar's. The name refers to the fact that part of the restaurant occupies a former church. The back room is woodsier and more elegant; the front room sunnier, with blackboard tables (chalk is supplied). The food ranges from dependable salads and sandwiches to fine daily fish and chicken specials. *157 W. Elkhorn Ave., tel. 303/586–2806. Reservations accepted. Dress: casual. AE, D, DC, MC, V. Inexpensive–Moderate.*

Lodging

There is a wide selection of accommodations, from charming Victorian B&Bs and guest houses to family-run motels and lodges to dude ranches. Unless otherwise noted, all accommodations include phones, cable TV, and private bath. For rates *see* Towns and Country price chart in Chapter 1, Essential Information.

Highly recommended lodgings are indicated by a star ★.

Boulder **Hotel Boulderado.** It's hard to believe that this elegant 1909
★ beauty had deteriorated into a flophouse by the late 1970s; fortunately, though, new ownership restored it to its former glory in 1980. The public spaces are wonderful places to idle: Spend some time in the gracious lobby, which resembles a private men's club; or on the second floor, with romantic nooks galore—especially suitable for enjoying a quiet drink (or you can head to the always-hopping Catacomb Blues Bar). When choosing your accommodations, opt for the old building, with spacious rooms filled with period antiques and reproductions, over the new wing, which is plush and comfortable but has less character. The gourmet restaurant, Q's, features the stylish New American cuisine of David Query, who was once a personal chef to Malcolm Forbes. *2115 13th St. 80302, tel. 303/442–4344 or*

800/433-4344; fax 303/442-4378. 103 rooms. Facilities: 3 restaurants, 2 lounges, boutique, access to health club, free parking. AE, DC, MC, V. Moderate–Expensive.

★ **Victoria B&B.** This ideally situated, restored 1870s Victorian offers the most exquisite accommodations in the area. Large rooms, each named after a present or former owner and all with private bath, run toward the Laura Ashley English country-home look. Brass beds, down comforters, terry-cloth robes, lace curtains, rocking chairs, dried flowers, and period antiques complete the picture. In addition to the complimentary Continental breakfast, baked goods (try the scones or ginger snaps) and tea are served every afternoon in a sunny parlor scented with potpourri. *1305 Pine St. 80302, tel. 303/938-1300. 7 rooms. Facilities: sun deck. AE, MC, V. Moderate–Expensive.*

Briar Rose B&B. Innkeeper Margaret Weisenbach makes guests feel completely at home at this appealing bed-and-breakfast. Perhaps the fact that she and her husband also live here accounts for the lived-in feel. There are five rooms in the sturdy 1890s brick main house and four in the adjacent carriage house. The individually decorated rooms abound in froufrou, like floral carpeting and flowers stenciled above the headboards. All rooms feature down comforters and private bath; the most expensive have wood-burning fireplaces. *2151 Arapahoe Ave. 80302, tel. 303/442-3007. 9 rooms. No facilities. AE, DC, MC, V. Moderate.*

★ **Clarion Harvest House.** This relatively large property sports an unusual semicircular design, set amid immaculate gardens dotted with splashing fountains. Spacious rooms are done up in light woods and pastel colors, and some have full baths with a mountain view. In keeping with Boulder's environmental concerns, 32 rooms have been designated as ecologically sound, with all trash recycled and water recirculated and treated. *1345 28th St. 80302, tel. 303/443-3850; fax 303/443-1480. 259 rooms. Facilities: restaurant, 2 lounges, 15 lighted tennis courts (5 enclosed in winter), indoor/outdoor pool and hot tub, exercise room, basketball court, 2 sand volleyball courts, gift shop, rental-car desk, children's playground, fish observatory, laundry facilities, 10,000 sq. ft. of meeting space. AE, D, DC, MC, V. Moderate.*

Pearl Street Inn. The decor is reserved and refined at this striking bed-and-breakfast, favoring subtle shades of purple, plush carpeting, wildlife prints and antiques, and brass or mahogany four-poster beds. The dining alcove and outdoor patio are lovely places to enjoy the complimentary gourmet breakfasts. For dinner the restaurant serves lovely meals and is open to the public. *1820 Pearl St. 80302, tel. 303/444-5584 or 800/232-5949. 7 rooms. Facilities: restaurant. AE, MC, V. Moderate.*

★ **Foot of the Mountain Motel.** The motel is a series of connecting wood cabins and is conveniently located across from the city park where the bike path originates. It is seemingly far away from Boulder's bustle, yet only a few minutes' walk from downtown. Each cozy cabin boasts either a mountain or stream view and is outfitted with TV, heater, minifridge, hot plate, and large bath. *200 Arapahoe Ave. 80302, tel. 303/442-5688. 18 units. No facilities. AE, D, MC, V. Inexpensive.*

Estes Park
★ **Aspen Lodge Ranch Resort and Conference Center.** The main building is the largest log structure in Colorado, a majestic edifice of lodgepole pine. The imposing reception area boasts

cathedralesque ceilings, antler chandeliers, and a vaulted stone fireplace. Balconies jut from the rustic lodge rooms and open onto thrilling views of Long's Peak or the Twin Sisters. While the decor is similar throughout, each has distinctive touches, such as Native American weavings and original artwork by the owners' friends. There are also 20 nicely appointed maroon-, jade-, and smoke-colored cabins with gingerbread trim. Rides are offered to a 2,000-acre working ranch and to Roosevelt National Forest. Children will love the elaborately themed programs, including a national park tour and Native American lore and crafts. You can two-step or square dance in the homey lounge after sampling the excellent Colorado cuisine of chef Ross Kamens. The resort is named for the unusually high number of aspens, which according to Ute and Arapahoe lore signify a sacred, special place. It certainly is. *6120 Hwy. 7, 80517, tel. 303/440–3371. 32 rooms, 20 cabins. Facilities: restaurant; lounge; pool; hot tub; riding stables and livery; snowmobiling; cross-country skiing; fishing; sports center with fitness room, sauna, basketball court, 2 racquetball courts; 4 lighted tennis courts; laundry facilities; conference center. American Plan in summer. AE, D, DC, MC, V. Very Expensive.*

Boulder Brook. Units at this secluded retreat are on the river, and individually decorated in either contemporary-rustic or country-provincial style. All feature full kitchen or kitchenette, private deck, gas fireplace, double-headed showers, cable TV, and VCR. Half the units have whirlpool tubs, for which you'll pay a great deal more. *1900 Fall River Rd., 80517, tel. 303/586–0910. 16 units. Facilities: outdoor hot tub. AE, D, MC, V. Moderate–Expensive.*

Best Western Lake Estes Resort. All the rooms have been remodeled within the last three years. They're a good size and outfitted with a hodgepodge of furniture, some extremely nice mahogany pieces mixed with others that are better left in someone's attic. All rooms include minifridge and hair dryer, as well as the usual amenities. The new suites also feature gas or wood-burning fireplaces and baths with jets. Ask for a lakeview unit. *1650 Big Thompson Hwy., 80517, tel. 303/586–3386. 58 rooms. Facilities: restaurant privileges at Antlers restaurant, outdoor pool, Jacuzzi, sauna, playground, videogame room, laundry facilities. AE, D, DC, MC, V. Moderate.*

★ **Hearthside Inn.** The cheerful rooms in this 1928 house, each named for an artist (Renoir, Monet, Rembrandt), feature fourposter or brass beds, gas fireplaces, lace curtains and doilies, down comforters, stenciled walls, tapestries, wicker furniture, hand-carved cherry armoires, and family heirlooms. The house is decorated with European flair: carefully coordinated carpets and fabrics, flowery but not overwhelmingly so. To complete the idyllic picture, deer nibble on the lawn (and flower beds). Complimentary gourmet breakfast is offered. *Box 442, Estes Park 80517, tel. 303/586–3100. 3 rooms. Facilities: lounge. AE, MC, V. Moderate.*

Stanley Hotel. Perched regally on a hill commanding the town, the Stanley is one of Colorado's great old hotels. As is often the case, the sunny rooms, decorated with antiques and period reproductions, are not as sumptuous as they once were. Still, there is an incomparable air of history, along with all modern conveniences. The McGregor Room is the classiest restaurant in town. *333 Wonderview Ave., 80517, tel. 303/586–3371 or 800/ ROCKIES; fax 303/586–3673. 92 rooms. Facilities: heated* *outdoor pool, hot tub, croquet, 2 tennis courts. AE, MC, V. Moderate.*

Trails West. This homey property has been in the same family for three generations, and repeat business is high. Though it's one of the older properties, the owners consistently upgrade and refurbish the units, which are decorated in mountain colors, with wood-burning fireplace, cable TV, full bath, and either full or efficiency kitchenette. Several have tiny extra rooms, making this a good bet for families. *1710 Fall River Rd., 80517, tel. 303/586–4629. 19 units. Facilities: hot tub. AE, D, DC, MC, V. Moderate.*

YMCA Estes Park Center of the Rockies. This self-contained property is so huge it's easy to get lost. In fact, it even has its own zip code! Both lodge rooms and cabins are simple, clean, and attractive, and all are constructed of sturdy oak. Cabins also have a fully stocked kitchen. *2515 Tunnel Rd., 80511, tel. 303/586–3341. 230 cabins, 565 rooms. Facilities: 4 restaurants, gift shop, 2 auditoriums, playground, indoor pool, basketball courts, roller-skating rink, exercise room, first-aid clinic. No credit cards. Inexpensive.*

Grand Lake   **Grand Lake Lodge.** This rustic retreat, built of lodgepole pine in 1925, calls itself "Colorado's favorite front porch," thanks to its stupendous views of Grand and Shadow Mountain lakes. Cabins are simply but comfortably furnished. The restaurant offers the same gorgeous vistas, in addition to fine mesquite-grilled fish. *Off U.S. 34 north of Grand Lake, tel. 303/627–3967. 66 cabins. Facilities: restaurant, lounge, heated swimming pool. AE, MC, V. Open Apr.–Oct. Inexpensive.*

The Arts

Music   There are concerts throughout the summer in Boulder's peaceful **Chatauqua Community Hall,** including the superb Colorado Music Festival. **The Boulder Theater** (2032 14th St., tel. 303/444–3600) is a venue for top touring bands.

Theater   The **Mary Rippon Theater** on the Colorado University campus (tel. 303/492–8181) offers excellent student productions throughout the year, as well as the Colorado Shakespeare Festival each summer.

In Estes Park, concerts and top-notch semiprofessional theatrical productions are given periodically at the **Stanley Hotel** (tel. 303/586–3381; or Creative Ensemble Productions, tel. 303/586–6864).

Nightlife

Bars and Lounges   In Boulder, **The West End Tavern** (926 Pearl St., tel. 303/444–3535) and **Potter's** (1207 Pearl St., tel. 303/444–3100) are popular after-work hangouts, both with fine pub grub. Potter's also periodically offers live bands and dancing. The microbreweries, **Boulder Brewing** (2880 Wilderness Pl., tel. 303/444–8448), **Walnut Brewery** (1123 Walnut St., tel. 303/447–1345), and **Oasis Brewery** (1095 Canyon St., tel. 303/449–0363) are also hot spots. The **Mezzanine Lounge** (tel. 303/442–4344) in the Boulderado has Victorian-style love seats and is a romantic place for an after-dinner drink.

In Estes Park, the watering holes of choice are the venerable **Wheel Bar** (132 E. Elkhorn Ave., tel. 303/586–9381), the **Gas-**

light Pub (246 Moraine Ave., tel. 303/586–0994), which has occasional live music, and the locals' favorite **Aspens Lounge** (Holiday Inn, 101 S. St. Vrain Ave., tel. 303/586–2332).

Country and Western **Boulder City Limits** (47th St. and Diagonal Hwy., tel. 303/444–6666) has dancing nightly.

Lonigans (110 W. Elkhorn Ave., Estes Park, tel. 303/586–4346) offers live blues and country-and-western bands several nights weekly.

Dinner Shows **Boulder Dinner Theater** (5501 Arapahoe Ave., tel. 303/449–6000) presents Broadway-style productions.

Discos **The Broker** (301 Baseline Ave., Boulder, tel. 303/449–1752) is the closest thing to a disco in these parts. In Fort Collins, try the collegiate **Fort Ram** (450 N. Linden St., tel. 303/482–5026).

Jazz Clubs In Boulder, the **Catacombs Blues Bar** (Hotel Boulderado, 2115 13th St., tel. 303/443–0486) and **'Round Midnight** (1005 Pearl St., tel. 303/442–9427) offer the best in local and national talent.

Rock Clubs In Boulder, the **Marquee Club** (1109 Walnut St., tel. 303/447–1803) favors house music.

5 Idaho

By Brian Alexander

Brian Alexander is a free-lance journalist and travel writer. His work has appeared in magazines such as Outside, Science, *and* Details *and in newspapers across North America.*

Sure, now everybody is talking about Idaho. They talk about escaping cities for the simple life. They talk about mountain biking in summer on mountains they ski on during winter. They talk about fishing the Salmon and Snake rivers and about rafting the white water through tremendous chunks of wilderness. They talk about Cecil Andrus, longtime governor of Idaho, and how he never seems to be without a fly-fishing vest.

They won't let you into this state unless you do something outdoors. That's the official state religion, and it has been embraced by thousands of new immigrants from California, Washington, New York, and elsewhere. It's why they say that if God doesn't live here, He at least has a vacation home.

The popularity was a long time coming, however. Until the 1980s, Idaho may well have qualified as the most ignored state in the Union. Native American tribes like the Nez Percé, the Coeur d'Alene, and the Shoshone-Bannock settled here because they found the rivers full of fish, the land fertile, and the game abundant, but, despite Lewis and Clark's trip through the state in 1805, white folks didn't show up in numbers until the 1840s, when pioneers on the Oregon Trail came, saw, and kept heading west. It wasn't until 1860, when a few Mormons came up from Utah at the direction of Brigham Young and settled in Franklin, that a true settlement was established.

No wonder. At first glance Idaho is an inhospitable place. The Snake River plain in southern Idaho is high-plateau desert, largely made up of a thin layer of soil over the ancient lava flows. It's hot in summer and cold in winter. The Sawtooth Mountains, with peaks as high as 11,800 feet, loom to the north. Northern Idaho is covered in alpine forest and glacier-carved lakes, a pleasant sight when the heavy winter snow melts.

These days, though, we have Gore-Tex and down and waterproofing, and what looked like misery to pioneers looks like fun to us. So, despite the cries of native Idahoans about all the newcomers arriving in their Volvos and bringing their espresso shops with them, people keep coming. Still, Idaho has just over 1 million people spread over its 83,564 square miles. That's 12 people per square mile. Considering that 350,000 Idahoans live in just 10 towns—125,000 in Boise alone—there's a lot of land out there with nobody on it. Only 0.4% of the state (215,000 acres) is considered urban or built-up, and virtually the entire eastern two-thirds is wilderness or national forest. Point all this out to Idahoans, and they'll shoot back that the population increased by 62,000 from 1980 to 1990 and that you ain't from around here, else you'd feel how crowded it's gotten.

The fact is, Idahoans do feel some pressure. They lived a certain way for nearly 150 years: They fished, hunted, did a little skiing, trapped furbearing animals, and cut down trees. Now people, including many newcomers, are telling them that way of life is all wrong. There is a palpable cultural rift between new arrivals and old-timers, and one can't help feeling that the new arrivals will eventually carry the day.

For now, though—aside from celebrity-filled Sun Valley, which some Idahoans look upon as a completely different planet—this is a meat-and-potatoes, cowboys and fishermen, back-to-basics kind of place. It is a conservative agricultural state despite the growth of manufacturing. There are the famous potatoes, of course, but also barley, sugar beets, hops, and beans. Idaho raises 70% of the nation's trout, and the dollar value of cattle outstrips even that of potatoes. Lumber, too, is still a tremendous industry in Idaho. That's why small boxes of "Spotted Owl Helper" decorate more than one small-town bar.

Things still operate very informally here. Unless you are conducting business, it is possible to go into any restaurant sans coat and tie and feel completely at home. This is a state where the lieutenant governor could enter a local tight jeans contest, win it, travel out of town to the national finals, and hear little more from his constituents than a chuckle.

Essential Information

Visitor Information

Idaho Travel Council (700 W. State St., Boise 83720, tel. 208/334–2470 or 800/635–7820).

In addition, almost every town of any size in Idaho has a small visitor information booth set up on the main road at the edge of town. Many rest stops along major arteries and the visitor centers at prime attractions offer a new system with touch-screen computer terminals for planning where to stay and what to see.

Emergencies

In emergency situations, call 911 (almost everywhere in the state) or visit a hospital emergency room (*see* Emergencies sections in individual regions, *below*). For nonemergencies, check in telephone directories, with chambers of commerce, or at your lodging for names of doctors, dentists, or late-night pharmacies.

Tour Groups

Most tourism in Idaho is related to the outdoors. Packagers can combine different sites, such as the Salmon and Snake rivers, or activities, such as fishing and rafting, on their trips. It is against the law for anyone who is not a member of the **Idaho Outfitters and Guides Association** (Box 95, Boise 83701, tel. 208/342–1919) to provide guiding or outfitting services; contact it for a free directory of members.

Package Deals for Independent Travelers

By far the most popular packages in Idaho are ski packages. Lodgings near most ski hills offer ski-lodging combinations with discounted rooms or discounted lift tickets. Delta Air Lines has traditionally offered an air, lodging, and ski package to Sun Valley. Package deals are easier to come by in shoulder seasons like early December, late January, and summer.

When to Go

Climate Idaho goes through some of the most dramatically delineated seasonal changes in the nation. In winter, parts of the state can have days below zero, but the average in Boise is about 30°F. Some mountain areas receive 200 inches of snow or more, and while that makes Idaho one of the best places in the world to ski, it also results in road closures that make travel difficult. In summer, temperatures in southern Idaho can soar over 100°F, but nights are usually cool and refreshing. Northern Idaho is in the Pacific Northwest's weather pattern and receives abundant rainfall and cooler temperatures. Spring and fall are mild, with the mercury reaching the high 60s in the lowlands and 50s in the mountains. In addition, Idaho has many microclimates, and conditions can change in an hour's drive.

Festivals and Seasonal Events

Winter **Sandpoint Winter Carnival,** Sandpoint, mid-January: a 10-day festival of winter activities. **Winter Olympics Week,** Sun Valley, mid-January: a winter carnival complete with celebrity ski racing, food fair, and dances. **McCall Winter Carnival,** McCall, last weekend in January/first week in February: winter sports with a little snowman and ice-sculpture making thrown in. **Lionel Hampton/Chevron Jazz Festival,** Moscow, last weekend in February: some of the best jazz musicians in the world.

Spring **Riggins Rodeo,** Riggins, first weekend in May: the rodeo that starts the season and makes this tiny town burst with visitors.

Summer **Idaho Shakespeare Festival,** Boise, all summer: Shakespeare under the stars. **National Old-Time Fiddlers Contest,** Weiser, last week in June: the nation's most prestigious fiddlers summit. **Sun Valley Music Festival,** Sun Valley, July–mid-August: classical and jazz performers. **Festival at Sandpoint,** Sandpoint, first two weeks in August: a celebration of music that includes classical, pop, and jazz, under the direction of famed maestro Gunther Schuller. **Art on the Green,** Coeur d'Alene, first weekend in August: arts, crafts, and dance in one of Idaho's largest festivals. **Three Island Crossing,** Glenns Ferry, first weekend in August: a re-creation of the pioneers' treacherous Snake River crossing. **Shoshone-Bannock Indian Festival,** Fort Hall, mid-August: includes an all-Indian old-timers' rodeo, one of the best in the state.

Fall **Pocatello Dixieland Jamboree,** Pocatello, September: Dixieland bands from across the country. **Swing and Dixie Jazz Jamboree,** Sun Valley, mid-October: big-band and Dixieland music.

What to Pack

What you pack will be sport specific, of course, but, in general, take layers. Even in summer, nights can be cool and you'll want a sweater or jacket. The closest most folks in Idaho get to wearing a tie is their bolos, or string ties. Be sure to pack some rain gear, and if you plan to be outdoors in summer, especially in southern Idaho, bring a hat and sunblock. If you'll be in the backcountry in winter, remember the two most important rules: Keep warm and stay dry. Pack long underwear made of polypropylene or another high-tech fabric, seam-sealed waterproof pants, and pile jackets that will keep insulating even if they get wet. If you hire an outfitter, ask for a packing list and follow it.

Traveling with Children

Resorts have become much more accommodating toward children than they were just a decade ago. Most ski areas, for example, offer day care that includes ski lessons or other outdoor activities as well as indoor games, and since most are now four-season destinations, children's programs carry over into summer. Other spots in Idaho may be problematic for children, however. Wilderness areas are normally inappropriate for the very young, though there are exceptions. Some outfitters welcome children, say, over 10 years old, if some advance notice is given and any special needs can be planned for.

Hints for Travelers with Disabilities

A disability need not keep people from enjoying Idaho. There are ramps or other provisions for wheelchairs at the prime attractions. The larger ski resorts now offer handicapped programs, including blind-skier escorts. Even some wilderness trips are possible, depending on the traveler's disability. For example, excursions into Hells Canyon have been made by scores of disabled persons. It's best to consult with a guide or outfitter, who can advise on a particular trip's feasibility or suggest alternatives.

Hints for Older Travelers

Happily for senior citizens, most chain establishments in Idaho give discounts to those with the AARP card (*see* Chapter 1, Essential Information). Adventurous seniors have a full range of options for wilderness travel, including many raft trips that are not as white-knuckle dangerous as the more famous ones. Because Idaho sees many seniors who travel after September, their needs are well known.

Getting Around Idaho

By Plane   Commuter airlines serve airports in Boise, Idaho Falls, Lewiston, Pocatello, Sun Valley, and Twin Falls (*see* Arriving and Departing sections in individual regions, *below*). In addition, there are many airstrips scattered around Idaho, especially in wilderness areas. These strips, open only in summer and early fall, are used by private planes and those chartered by outfitters.

By Car   A car is really the best way to see the state. This is the West, after all, and interesting sights are sometimes spread out over the landscape. Remember that Westerners often have an expanded view of distance. So when an Idahoan says "right around the corner," translate that as under an hour's drive. The good news is that the words "traffic jam" have not yet entered the state's vocabulary. Interstates and the much more interesting two-lane state and U.S. routes are uncrowded, with rare exceptions (like Boise to McCall on Friday at 5:30). Best of all, a car allows you to travel the state's back roads, where some of Idaho's truly unique sights are waiting. There are two caveats, however. First, be sure to keep an eye on your gas gauge; in some parts of the state, the next gas station may be no closer than "right around the corner." Second, many Idaho roads, usually roads leading into the wilderness, simply shut down for the winter. Others experience periodic snow closures. Major newspapers carry road condition reports on their weather pages, or you can call the state's road report hot line (tel. 208/336–6600) or those for specific regions: Boise (tel. 208/334–

3731), Coeur d'Alene (tel. 208/765–2323), Idaho Falls (tel. 208/522–5141), Lewiston (tel. 208/743–9546), Pocatello (tel. 208/232–1426), and Twin Falls (tel. 208/733–7210).

By Train Amtrak's *Pioneer* (tel. 800/USA–RAIL) roughly parallels I–84 and stops in Boise, Shoshone, and Pocatello.

By Bus Major Idaho towns are served by **Greyhound/Trailways** (tel. 800/231–2222) and by **Boise-Winnemucca Stages** (tel. 208/336–3300).

Opening and Closing Times

Many places in Idaho don't have firm opening and closing times. Hours and even seasons depend on the weather or on the number of visitors or simply on when folks feel like opening up. You might want to call attractions to confirm times before embarking on a long pilgrimage.

Shopping

Every city in Idaho has the generic mall, but luckily most also have unique districts with flavors not found elsewhere. The state is an excellent place for antiques hunters. Although towns like Coeur d'Alene and Boise have antiques shops, often Idaho's antiques are still being used as store signs or restaurant condiment containers. In some parts of Idaho, whole towns are antiques.

Sports and the Outdoors

There's a reason Hemingway liked Idaho so much. It has some of the best fly-fishing in the world and is known for its steelhead and sturgeon. (Unfortunately, sockeye salmon have been dammed out of existence, and chinook are barely hanging on.) Locals will tell you the fishing is always good in Idaho. Maybe, but some spots are better than others. An excellent publication, *The Official Guide to Fishing in Idaho*, which details boat ramp locations, regulations, the best spots for various species, and even filleting instructions, is available from the Department of Fish and Game (*see below*).

One reason so many Native Americans lived in Idaho was the plentiful game. White folks have been hunting since the first French-Canadian trappers came down from the north in the early 1800s. Today hunters have a bewildering choice of game and sites. Top game animals include deer, elk, bighorn sheep, bear, moose, cougar, mountain goat, upland birds, and waterfowl. Elk is especially plentiful, but permits are not. Locals have first take at permits and licenses, but clients of Idaho outfitters receive a special allotment, so there is rarely a problem if you sign on with a professional hunting guide.

There are certain rules and codes about fishing and hunting that Idahoans take very seriously. Hunting only for trophies is frowned upon. Meat is meant to be consumed. Taking undersize fish or not releasing in a catch-and-release area is not only frowned upon, it's against the law. Also, always be sure to obtain the proper licenses. (In McCall, the biggest scandal in recent years was when a local resort owner deceptively obtained a hunting license. Folks around there would sooner forgive selling nuclear secrets.) For details on fishing and hunting and to obtain licenses, contact the **Idaho Department of Fish and Game** (600 S. Walnut St., Box 25, Boise 83707, tel. 800/635–7820) or the Idaho Outfitters and Guides Association (*see* Tour Groups, *above*).

Because the state falls in the Northwest's weather pattern, it receives plenty of winter precipitation, but as elsewhere in the West, the snow is often dry and powdery. For skiers, it's the best of both worlds. Idaho, especially Sun Valley, is known for Alpine skiing. The popularity of Nordic skiing has soared, however, and many Alpine resorts now offer groomed cross-country tracks at their hill's base or near the principal lodge. Idaho's Department of Parks and Recreation (*see* National and State Parks, *below*) makes trails in many of the state parks.

In addition, since ski resorts are trying to make themselves attractive year-round, mountain biking is now available on Idaho's major ski hills. Most resorts run their lifts in summer to carry bikers to the top of the hills.

Aficionados will tell you there is no better state for canoeing and rafting, with the possible exception of Alaska. Canoe and raft trips range from placid to suicidal, and because the state is so outdoor conscious, the public has access to virtually every body of water.

The golf courses listed have 18 holes and require reservations for tee times. Prices vary but are in the $20–$50 range unless otherwise stated.

National and State Parks

National Parks Surprisingly, there is only one national park in Idaho, the **Nez Percé National Historic Park** (*see* Exploring Northern Idaho, *below*). The park is really a scattered group of individual sites where events of the Nez Percé War took place. However, the state is virtually covered in federal lands, including the largest contiguous wilderness in the lower 48 states.

State Parks Idaho has 21 state parks spread throughout the state. Though they contain everything from a mission to an RV campground, most are on a river or lake. Primitive campsites cost $5 per day, basic sites $7, and developed sites $8. Electric and sewer hookups cost an additional $4. There is an entrance fee of $2 for motorized vehicles at most parks, but it is incorporated into camping fees. For $25, annual passports provide unlimited entrance to all state parks for a calendar year. Group facilities are available at some parks. For a complete guide, contact the **Idaho Department of Parks and Recreation** (Statehouse Mail, Boise 83720, tel. 208/327–7444 or 800/635–7820).

Dining

It is virtually impossible to go hungry in Idaho, especially if you like basic American cooking. What restaurants lack in Continental flair, they make up for in volume. Meals are often served on platters big enough to be mistaken for UFOs. But what Idaho does, it does well: A bad steak is a sin here. There are a few standouts in places like Boise, Coeur d'Alene, Sandpoint, and, of course, Sun Valley, where it's possible to find food prepared with as much sophistication as you'd find in any U.S. city. Dining is very informal, and unless otherwise noted in the reviews, dress is casual and reservations aren't taken. Almost all restaurants take major credit cards.

Highly recommended restaurants in each price category are indicated by a star ★.

Category	Cost*
Expensive	over $20
Moderate	$10–$20
Inexpensive	under $10

per person, excluding drinks, service, and 5% state sales tax

Lodging

Although there are a few bed-and-breakfasts, including one or two very good ones, for the most part lodging in southern Idaho is in Best Westerns, AmeriTels, and other national and regional motel chains on the I–84 corridor. Boise itself has 2,500 motel rooms, but from Boise north, lodging becomes more diverse: B&Bs, guest ranches, grand old hotels, and resort lodges. Long-term condominium, apartment, and home rentals are available in the Ketchum/Sun Valley area. Guest ranches near wilderness areas offer complete vacation packages, including horseback riding, rodeos, and even cattle herding; a list is available from the Idaho Outfitters and Guides Association (*see* Tour Groups, *above*). Unless otherwise noted in the reviews, rooms have private baths.

Highly recommended lodgings in each price category are indicated by a star ★.

Category	Cost*
Expensive	over $95
Moderate	$50–$95
Inexpensive	under $50

All prices are for a standard double room.

Pioneer Country

During the 1840s, westbound pioneers on the Oregon Trail seemed to lose their way in southeastern Idaho. They tried several routes, the remnants of which now crisscross the region, attempting to find the best way out. Now if you tell people in Boise, for example, that you plan to spend time in this area, they'll look at you cross-eyed and ask why. What's here is a kind of time capsule. Those living in larger towns may have forgotten what it's like in hamlets of 230 or 407 or even 103, but they still exist in the southeast. Here women drive pickups with bumper stickers declaring WRANGLER BUTTS DRIVE ME NUTS. One village is locally renowned for its automatic car wash. The towns, collectively known as pioneer towns, were usually founded by hardy souls from Utah who trapped or hunted or farmed. Today they are almost unchanged since the days when folks like Pegleg Smith opened trading posts; often the only modern building is the local Mormon church.

Important Addresses and Numbers

Tourist Information	**Pioneer Country Travel Council** (Box 668, Lava Hot Springs 83246, tel. 208/776–5273 or 800/423–8597), **Yellowstone/Teton Territory** (Box 50498, Idaho Falls 83402, tel. 208/523–1010 or 800/634–3246).
Emergencies	In an emergency, dial 911 except in Franklin County, where you should call 208/852–1234.
Hospital Emergency Rooms	In Idaho Falls, there is the **Eastern Idaho Medical Center** (3100 Channing Way, tel. 208/529–6111) and in Pocatello, **Pocatello Regional Medical Center** (777 Hospital Way, tel. 208/234–0777).

Arriving and Departing by Plane

Airports and Airlines The commuter carriers **Horizon** (tel. 800/426–0333), the Alaska Airlines partner, and **SkyWest** (tel. 800/453–9417), the Delta Air Lines partner, have service to **Idaho Falls** and **Pocatello.** In addition, **American** (tel. 800/433–7300) and **Delta** (tel. 800/221–1212) have flights to Idaho Falls.

Arriving and Departing by Car, Train, and Bus

By Car From the south, I–15 connects Salt Lake and other Utah cities to southeastern Idaho; from the north, it comes from western Montana. In Idaho, I–15 runs through Idaho Falls and Pocatello, where it intersects I–86 (the main route west), and along the edge of the pioneer towns in the southeast corner. From the east, the most scenic route into the region descends from Wyoming's Teton Pass and connects with Idaho's Routes 33 and 31 at Victor in the Targhee National Forest. Route 31 runs to Swan Valley and U.S. 26, which goes to Idaho Falls.

By Train **Amtrak** (tel. 800/USA–RAIL) connects Pocatello's **Union Pacific Station** (300 S. Harrison Ave., tel. 208/234–2150) to points east and west.

By Bus **Greyhound/Trailways** (tel. 800/231–2222) has regular service along the Boise–Idaho Falls corridor. To the east, buses run to Rexburg and West Yellowstone, Montana.

Getting Around

By Car A car is the only way to see most of the region. The major rental companies have booths at both the Pocatello and Idaho Falls airports. Be aware, however, that rentals in Idaho, especially during ski season, can be pricey.

By Bus Pocatello has an urban bus service. Schedules can be obtained from the chamber of commerce (tel. 208/233–1525).

Guided Tours

Special-Interest Tours The **Idaho National Engineering Laboratory** (INEL), on 890 square miles of sage desert northwest of Idaho Falls and site of more nuclear reactors (52) than anywhere else on earth, conducts research on subjects ranging from nuclear-powered naval vessels to radioactive-waste management. Tours of the facility, including EBR-1 (*see* Exploring Pioneer Country, *below*) can be arranged through **INEL Public Affairs** (785 DOE Pl., MS 3516, Idaho Falls 83401, tel. 208/526–0050).

Exploring Pioneer Country

Numbers in the margin correspond to points of interest on the Idaho map.

If you're coming from Wyoming or you just want to drive in some beautiful countryside, a good place to start a tour of Pioneer Country is along a stretch of the **Teton Scenic Byway,** Route 33 to Route 31 through **Tetonia, Driggs,** and **Victor.** Strictly farming and ranching towns until the Grand Targhee ski resort (just across the Wyoming border) was built in 1969, they're now part Western ski town, part ranching community.

Continue south on Route 31 through the Snake River valley, one of the state's most beautiful drives in any season. In winter, hoofprints of elk, deer, and smaller animals zigzag across the hills, and in spring and summer, wildflowers coat the mountains. At **Swan Valley,** you'll meet up with U.S. 26, which crosses the Snake River, the artery that gives life to all of southern Idaho, and continues into Idaho Falls.

1 **Idaho Falls** sits at the edge of the Snake River plain, which arcs across southern Idaho. This town of 50,000 people sprouted when an industrious stagecoach worker figured a bridge across a narrow section of the Snake would be much faster for overland stages than the ferry used upstream. He completed the bridge in 1866, and a community, called Eagle Rock, developed at the site. Later the name was changed to Idaho Falls, despite the lack of natural falls. In 1911 a weir was built in the river to generate power, lending some legitimacy to the name.

The town's history is illustrated at the **Bonneville Museum,** which is small but more impressive than most small-town museums. Somehow the volunteer historical society that operates it has managed to re-create early Eagle Rock in the basement. The faux street is complete with a dentist's office, dry-goods store, and other facades. Upstairs, displays include objects and photos from the early days of Bonneville County, including an extensive selection of Shoshone-Bannock artifacts. *Eastern and Elm Sts., tel. 208/522–1400. Admission: $1 adults, 25¢ children 5–18. Open weekdays 10–5, Sat. 1–5. Closed holidays. (In winter, hours are slightly irregular.)*

Time Out If the weather is warm and the skies blue, take a break on the **greenbelt,** which runs along the Snake River from Market Street north to U.S. 20. Locals take lunch breaks and bike, walk, or roller-skate along the paved paths. Picnic tables are set up at intervals.

Today Idaho Falls is almost completely dependent on income generated by INEL. Back in 1951, when the atom was our **2** friend, **EBR-1** became the nation's first nuclear reactor to generate usable amounts of electricity. When you're driving on U.S. 20 to the site, near the aptly named Atomic City, it's easy to see why makers of B movies thought odd things might crawl out of the desert around nuclear facilities. EBR-1 is now a National Historic Landmark. *35 mi west of Idaho Falls on U.S. 20,*

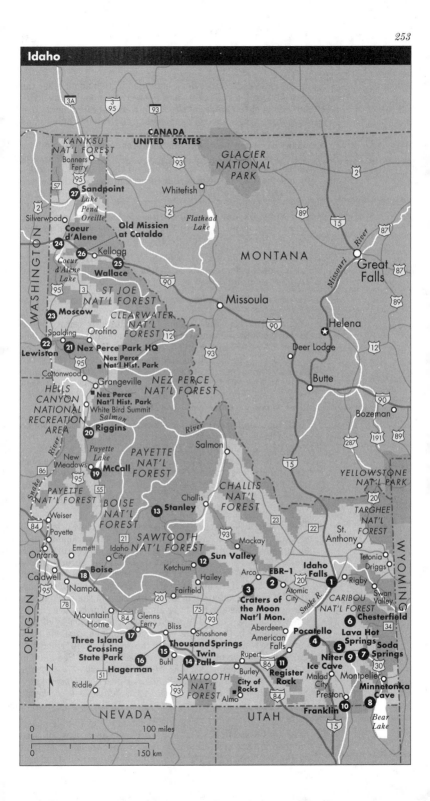

Idaho

tel. 208/526–0050. Admission free. Open Memorial Day–Labor Day, daily 8–4.

In case movie directors need more inspiration about what the world might look like post–nuclear war, they could travel still farther west to **Craters of the Moon National Monument.** Just 15,000 years ago, the earth opened up to the north of here and poured molten rock over the landscape. The flows pushed the Snake River south and left this part of the Snake River valley a ghostly plain punctuated by lava tubes and mysterious-looking formations. The visitor center, just off the highway, provides an introduction to the area, but those wanting to learn and see more can drive the 7-mile loop road on a self-guided tour. *20 mi west of INEL on U.S. 93, tel. 208/527–3257. Loop admission: $3 per vehicle. Visitor center open June 15–Labor Day, daily 8–6; Labor Day–June 14, daily 8–4:30. Loop road closed to cars Nov. 1–Apr. 15 (approximately).*

A smaller version of Craters of the Moon, the **Hell's Half Acre Lava Flows,** is located about 25 miles south of Idaho Falls on I–15. They include a rest stop and interpretive sign.

To see more of what Idaho was like a long, long time ago, continue on I–15 to the other good-size town in the southeast, **Pocatello.** Here, on the campus of Idaho State University, is the **Idaho Museum of Natural History.** The museum has a fine collection of Ice Age animal skeletons and the Fujii Western Rock Collection. Take U.S. 91 to Yellowstone Avenue and follow the signs to the campus. *S. 5th Ave. and E. Dillon St., tel. 208/236–3366. Admission: $3 adults, $2.50 senior citizens, $2 children 2–12. Open Mon.–Sat. 9–5, Sun. noon–5. Closed Thanksgiving, Christmas, and New Year's Day.*

Head south on 4th Avenue about 2 miles until you reach Avenue of the Chiefs. Turn right and head up the hill. There you'll find Ross Park and the **Old Fort Hall Replica;** Fort Hall was a major pioneer outpost northeast of Pocatello on what is now the Fort Hall Indian Reservation. *In front of Bannock County Historical Museum, tel. 208/234–1795. Admission: $1 adults, 50¢ youths 13–18, 25¢ children 6–12. Open Apr. 1–Sept. 15; hours vary.*

Take I–15 south and then U.S. 30 east to **Lava Hot Springs,** one of the funkiest little towns in Idaho. Lava, with a population of about 400, has one main street, turn-of-the-century brick buildings, and some of the most desirable **hot springs** in the United States. The springs passed from Native American hands to the U.S. Army to the state of Idaho and are now operated by a state foundation, which has turned the pools into a garden spot. The springs have almost no sulfur but are rich in other minerals. This brings people who, for a variety of reasons, believe in the powers of mineral springs. You can soak here in the water that comes out of the ground at 110°F or swim in the pool at the other end of town (*see* What to See and Do with Children, *below*). *430 E. Main St., tel. 208/776–5221 or 800/423–8597. Admission: $3.50 ages over 11. Open Apr.– Sept., daily 8 AM–11 PM; Oct.–Mar., weekdays 9–10, weekends 9–11.*

About 7 miles east of Lava Hot Springs is the 16-mile paved road to **Chesterfield.** Virtually a ghost town now, it was founded in 1880 by Mormons, complete with the Mormon grid system for blocks. Many of the original buildings still stand as if waiting for the inhabitants to return. Chesterfield is listed on the National Register of Historic Places.

❼ Soda Springs, about 18 miles farther east on U.S. 30, is home to another regional landmark. No, not the Monsanto slag pour, which the town lists as a tourist attraction, but the only **man-made geyser** on earth, a sight that's more reputation than reality. It seems the town fathers were drilling for a swimming pool when they hit carbon dioxide, a gas that permeates this region. The carbon dioxide mixed with groundwater under pressure and started shooting out of the ground. Local boosters capped the geyser with a valve. Now, every hour during daylight, they turn the geyser on, unless, that is, the wind is coming from the west, which would douse the parking lot. From U.S. 30, turn left onto Main Street. The geyser is right behind the Statesman's Lounge and Enders Café on the left side of the street.

At this point in the tour, adventurous travelers may want to take a side trip on U.S. 30 east to Montpelier, another interesting pioneer town, and then U.S. 89 south to St. Charles. Just west of St. Charles, first on a county highway and then on a U.S. Forest Service road (both numbered 30012), lies the **❽ Minnetonka Cave,** a classic nine-room limestone cavern dotted with stalactites and stalagmites. The forest service gives 90-minute tours throughout the summer. Take a jacket. The cavern is naturally a constant 40°F. *1.2 mi west of St. Charles, tel. 208/523–3278. Admission: $2.50 adults, $1.50 children 6–15. Open for tours mid-June–Labor Day (approximately, depending on weather), daily 10:30–5, leaving every half hour.*

Nearby Bear Lake, famous for its odd turquoise color, is a local favorite with anglers and campers. From here, backtrack north on U.S. 89 and west on U.S. 30 past Soda Springs, and pick up Route 34 south. Drive through Grace, population 970, toward the village of Niter, population under 100 (and probably not listed on any map you have). About 3 miles beyond Grace, you'll see a small sign directing you left onto Ice Cave Road, to **❾ the Niter Ice Cave.** It may look like a small hole in the ground, but the cave, used by pioneers to keep food cold, is nearly half a mile long. You can climb in if you want, but be sure to have a flashlight and be prepared to get dirty.

Continue south on Route 34 through rolling ranch lands that were the object of range wars between farmers, who wanted to put up fences, and sheepherders and cattlemen, who wanted an open range. The land around here has been owned by some of the local families for over 100 years.

❿ At Preston, take U.S. 91 south to **Franklin,** the oldest town in Idaho. It was established on April 14, 1860, by order of Brigham Young, who sent settlers north from Utah. At first the pioneers struggled, but eventually a sawmill was installed and more cash flowed in. Today the town, population 478, contains the Franklin Historic District along Main Street. Turn left off U.S. 91; the **village hall,** built in 1904, is on the right. Across the street, the **Lorenzo Hatch house** (1870) is a fine example of Greek Revival architecture, popular in many Western pioneer towns. The exterior masonry is a marvel, considering how primitive the town was in 1870. Nearby stands the **Franklin Cooperative Mercantile Institution,** a great stone structure; it was built to house the local cooperative store and now contains a museum.

Continue south out of town on U.S. 91, and just before the Utah border you'll see the town **cemetery.** Many grave sites are over 100 years old.

Cross into Utah, take Route 61 to Cornish, and drive north on Route 23 toward Weston, where you pick up Route 36 to Malad City. From here, you can either take I–15 north back to Pocatello, or, if the weather is good and all roads are open, head south on I–15 to Route 38 west, follow it to Holbrook, and turn north on Route 37. This road winds through the Curlew National Grasslands and past abandoned homestead cabins sitting lonely on the rolling hills.

This is the most scenic way to the final stop in Pioneer Country. When Route 37 meets I–86, drive west. After about 8 miles, ⑪ signs for **Register Rock** lead you into a canyon where wagons on their way west often stopped to camp. During the night, pioneers, like the cave painters of Lascaux, left proof of their passage by painting or carving their names into the stone. The rock is now protected by a roofed and fenced enclosure. *Admission free. Open daylight hours.*

What to See and Do with Children

At the other end of **Lava Hot Springs** is a giant **swimming and diving complex.** Here the water is kept at 86°F. Suits, towels, and lockers are available. *U.S. 30 exit at Center St., tel. 208/ 776–5221. Admission: $3.50 ages over 11. Open Memorial Day–Labor Day, Sun.–Fri. 11–8, Sat. 10–9.*

Shopping

Shopping Malls **Grand Teton Mall** (17th St., 3 mi e. of central Idaho Falls) has helped pull small shops out of downtown Idaho Falls, creating empty storefronts along its main street. The mall has a variety of specialty and department stores, including **The Bon Marché** and **Made in Idaho,** which, as its name suggests, sells a variety of Idaho-based products.

Sports and the Outdoors

Biking The **greenbelt** in Idaho Falls is an excellent place to pedal. For information on bike rentals, call **Idaho Falls City Parks** (tel. 208/ 529–1478).

Fishing **Bear Lake** and **Henry's Lake** (the latter near the Montana border) are known for cutthroat trout.

Golf Area courses include **Pinecrest** (701 E. Elva St., Idaho Falls, tel. 208/529–1485), **Sandcreek** (5230 Hackman Rd., Idaho Falls, tel. 208/529–1115), **Teton Lakes** (N. Hibbared Hwy., Rexburg, tel. 208/359–3036), and **Thunder Canyon** (9898 E. Merrick Rd., Lava Hot Springs, tel. 207/776–5048).

Skiing An especially interesting spot for Nordic skiing is **Craters of the**
Cross-Country **Moon National Monument,** near Arco. In this eerie landscape, the National Park Service makes a trail on the loop road.

Dining and Lodging

Idaho Falls **Dolores Casella's Downtowner.** This tiny, sparsely decorated
Dining restaurant on the street level of an office building is operated

by a local food aficionado who also writes for the local paper on matters gastronomical. Meals are themed, but the accent is usually Continental. *447 Shoup St., tel. 208/524-2524. Reservations accepted. MC, V. Closed Sat.-Mon. for lunch and Sun.-Wed. for dinner. Moderate.*

Sandpiper. While the nautical theme may have gone a little overboard (pun intended), this seafood and steak establishment is one of the better dining spots in town. Since it sits on the bank of the Snake River, there are lovely views out the back windows. *750 Lindsay Blvd., tel. 208/524-3344. Reservations accepted. AE, DC, MC, V. Closed for lunch. Moderate.*

Mama Inez. The Idaho Falls outpost of this popular Mexican restaurant chain is regarded as the best ethnic food in town. *338 Park Ave., tel. 208/525-8968. MC, V. Inexpensive.*

Smitty's. The waitresses still call you "honey" in this cross between a Big Boy and a roadhouse. The pancakes are meals in themselves, and if you don't want it fancy, the burgers, steaks, and chicken are reliable. Local businesspeople come in for breakfast, which is served all day. According to waitresses, this place is packed in summer with families heading for Yellowstone National Park. *645 W. Broadway, tel. 208/523-6450. No credit cards. Inexpensive.*

Lodging **Best Western AmeriTel.** The newest motel in town, this immediately became the best choice. It has lots of extras, including fitness equipment and such business amenities as a fax. A Continental breakfast served in the lobby is included. *900 Lindsay Blvd., 83402, tel. 208/523-6000 or 800/528-1234, fax 208/523-0000. 94 rooms. Facilities: indoor pool, spa, exercise facilities. AE, D, MC, V. Inexpensive-Moderate.*

Best Western Driftwood. Although a little tattered around the edges, this motel, located on the bank of the Snake just behind the Lindsay motel strip, has a nice lawn area in summer. Rooms have coffee makers, and some have refrigerators. *575 River Pkwy., 83402, tel. 208/523-2242 or 800/528-1234, fax 208/523-2242. 74 rooms. Facilities: laundry room. AE, D, MC, V. Inexpensive.*

Lava Hot Springs **Blue Moon.** This place has the most impressive sign in town,
Dining and the sandwiches and burgers are solid. At night, the smoke gets heavy, the pool tables see a lot of use, and the beer flows pretty freely. Some of the miners and cowboys have even been known to mix it up. *89 1st St., tel. 208/776-5806. MC, V. Inexpensive.*

Silver Grill Café. If you want nouvelle cuisine, head for Sun Valley. This is strictly "food that won the West." The seats are covered in vinyl, the tabletops are Formica (and just what are you gonna do about it?), but the sandwiches, burgers, and steaks are pretty good. *78 E. Main St., tel. 208/776-5562. D, MC, V. Inexpensive.*

Dining and Lodging **Royal Hotel.** Lisa Toly fell into inn keeping by accident but has since managed to take an old miners' rooming house and turn it into a cozy bed-and-breakfast. Renovated in 1993, the interior is decorated in turn-of-the-century colors and furnishings. Rooms are small, but the second floor has one especially for guests to make snacks. The full breakfast, including Toly's home-baked apple turnovers and frittata, is the best in town, or, if you're in time for lunch—and especially if you've got a hungry brood—stop in for a pizza. As improbable as it sounds, Toly makes pizza that would make any New Yorker smile. *11 E.*

Main St., 83246, tel. 208/776–5216. 8 rooms, 6 share bath. Facilities: dining room, snack room. AE, MC, V. Inexpensive–Moderate.

Lodging **Lava Hot Springs Inn.** This grand old building was a hospital, a retirement/nursing-home facility, and now, after a complete renovation in the late 1980s, a European-style bed-and-breakfast inn. (A buffet breakfast is included.) The interior is done in pink and black art deco, and the rooms are neat and well appointed. Two Jacuzzi suites have private baths. A hot pool, just steps away from the back door, overlooks the Portneuf River. *5 Portneuf Ave., 83246, tel. 208/776–5830. 17 rooms, 15 share bath. Facilities: dining room, sitting room/library, hot pool. AE, D, MC, V. Moderate.*

Riverside Inn and Hot Springs. Also located by the Portneuf River, this 1914 inn, which has mineral hot tubs, was once quite the romantic getaway. Over time, it fell into disrepair but was restored in the 1980s and now has an immaculate interior. Some of its neighbors have not yet caught the renovation bug sweeping this tiny town, however. A Continental breakfast is included. *255 Portneuf Ave., 83246, tel. 208/776–5504. 16 rooms, 4 share bath. Facilities: library, 4 mineral baths. D, MC, V. Moderate.*

Pocatello **Best Western Cotton Tree Inn.** This motel is conveniently lo-
Lodging cated off I-15 Exit 71. Some rooms have kitchenettes. *1415 Bench Rd., 83201, tel. 208/237–7650 or 800/528–1234, fax 208/238–1355. 147 rooms. Facilities: restaurant, lounge, hot tub, racquetball, laundry room. AE, D, DC, MC, V. Moderate.*

The Arts

The **Idaho Falls Symphony** (tel. 208/529–1080) presents a five-concert series each year, often with renowned special guests. Each August the **Shoshone-Bannock Indian Festival** celebrates the culture of the region's original inhabitants; for information, contact the Pioneer Country Travel Council (*see* Important Addresses and Numbers, *above*).

Southcentral Idaho

Southcentral Idaho was a sleepy backwater, home to a few ranchers and Basque sheepherders until 1935, when W. Averell Harriman, head of the Union Pacific Railroad, realized he needed more riders for his trains. He hired a European count, who presumably understood what makes for a good ski area, to scout the West and come up with a site for a resort. The site turned out to be Ketchum, Idaho, and the result was Sun Valley. Although Twin Falls and the Magic Valley around it are still largely agricultural, growing beans and hops, there is considerable tourism, spurred by Sun Valley's presence 80 miles north. Still, the Oregon Trail and the scenic Thousand Springs area in the Snake River valley are interesting stops in their own right.

Important Addresses and Numbers

Tourist **South Central Idaho Travel Committee** (858 Blue Lakes Blvd.
Information N, Twin Falls 83301, tel. 800/255–8946), **Twin Falls Chamber of Commerce** (same address, tel. 208/733–3974).

Emergencies
Hospital Emergency Rooms   In Sun Valley, there is **Wood River Medical Center** (Sun Valley Mall, near resort golf course, tel. 208/622–3323), and in Twin Falls, **Magic Valley Regional Medical Center** (650 Addison Ave. W, tel. 208/737–2000, TDD 208/737–2114).

Arriving and Departing by Plane

Airports and Airlines   **Twin Falls** and **Sun Valley** are served by **Horizon** (tel. 800/426–0333) and **SkyWest** (tel. 800/453–9417). Because the Sun Valley airport—actually located in Hailey, south of Ketchum—is at a high elevation, be prepared for delays or diversions. In winter, the same snow that attracts skiers can also close the airport. The alternate route is to land in Twin Falls (or Boise) and rent a car. Sun Valley hotels often offer guests free shuttle service from Hailey; ask when making reservations.

Arriving and Departing by Car, Train, and Bus

By Car   The region's main highway, I–84, stretches from Boise in the west, through Twin Falls, and then east and south into Utah. However, a much more scenic route from Boise to Twin Falls is U.S. 30, which turns off at Bliss and follows the Snake River canyon. From Boise to Sun Valley, there are several options. In summer, Routes 21 and 75 through the Sawtooth National Recreation Area make for a long but very beautiful drive. In winter, the road is often closed, so be sure to check road conditions. The shortest route is to head east on I–84 to Mountain Home and then take U.S. 20 east to Route 75 north.

By Train   Shoshone's **Union Pacific Station** (N. Rail St., no phone), north of Twin Falls, receives **Amtrak** service from Boise and Pocatello.

By Bus   **Greyhound/Trailways** offers service into Twin Falls from Boise or Idaho Falls.

Getting Around

By Car   From Twin Falls, take U.S. 93 north to Route 75 north to reach Sun Valley. For a scenic route west, take U.S. 30.

By Bus   Sun Valley and Ketchum offer free service on **KART** (Ketchum Area Rapid Transit) to most major lodgings, downtown Ketchum, and the River Run and Warm Springs ski lifts. Buses run about every 20 minutes from Sun Valley and Elkhorn resorts and about every hour from central Ketchum. Call KART (tel. 208/726–7140) for schedules and routes.

Guided Tours

Orientation Tours   **Sun Valley Stages** (119 S. Park Ave. W, Twin Falls 83303, tel. 208/733–3921) can arrange tours or charters of the Sun Valley area. **Town and Country Scenic Tours and Transportation** (319 4th Ave., Hailey 83333, tel. 208/788–2012 or 800/234–1569) arranges tours throughout south central Idaho.

Special-Interest Tours   About 10 miles west of Buhl, where several swimming-pool operators have set up hot-springs pools and river-swimming areas, **Thousand Springs Tours** runs a 2½-hour excursion. Tour boats leave from Sligar's and motor about 5 miles up the Snake; they stop at various points, including eddies in which the water is a clear green, a favorite spot for scuba divers. The tour is by reservation only. *State and Hagerman Sts., Box 117, Hagerman 83332, tel. 208/837–9006. Cost: $16 adults, $11 children under 7. Runs mid-Apr.–Sept., daily; first tour at 10.*

Exploring Southcentral Idaho

Numbers in the margin correspond to points of interest on the Idaho map.

⑫ Since the late 1930s and especially after World War II, **Sun Valley** has been one of the premier ski destinations in the country (*see* Sports and the Outdoors, *below*). The precursor of later resorts, it helped create the idea that the slopes used for skiing in the winter could also draw visitors for summer activities. Today Sun Valley and its neighbor, **Ketchum,** are gold-plated resort towns with a gentrified Western feel. "Lifestyles of the Rich and Famous" could do a whole season just on people who have homes in the area. The nearby Wood River is also a haven for outdoor activities, which residents pursue with manic energy.

Sightseeing in the area is largely limited to Hemingway's grave site in the Ketchum cemetery (off Rte. 75 near 10th St.), a small memorial to him just north of the Sun Valley resort up Sun Valley Road, and Arnold Schwarzenegger's Humvee.

⑬ A brief side trip, about an hour's drive north on Route 75, lands you in the very genuine town of **Stanley.** In the middle of the Sawtooth National Recreation Area, it's about as old-time Idaho as you can get. Trappers, guides, boatmen, and dropouts from the world live here, and on weekend nights, especially in summer, the music starts up in the saloons and the "Stanley Stomp" takes over. Beer and two-stepping in the shadow of the jagged Sawtooths can make you feel as though you've stepped into a John Ford Western.

⑭ Return south on Route 75 and U.S. 93 to **Twin Falls,** flanked by the Snake River and the bridges that cross it. Taking U.S. 93 leads across the Perrine Bridge and into the heart of Twin Falls. A few miles east of town, off I–84, Route 50 runs across the Hansen Memorial Bridge. Either way, unsuspecting drivers may feel a sudden sense of vertigo. Both bridges cross the massive Snake River canyon, justly known for its drama. The flat plain to the north simply falls away into the chasm below, as if the hand of nature took a stick and gouged the earth.

That's basically what happened. About 15,000 years ago, a massive inland sea, Lake Bonneville (the remnant of which is the Great Salt Lake), crashed through its natural dikes in southeast Idaho and poured into the Snake. For about six weeks, a volume of water many times greater than the flow of the Amazon acted like a giant plow as it thundered down the Snake and carved the canyon.

Driving into Twin Falls feels like putting on a comfortable sweater. It is perhaps as all-American a city as you'll find anywhere. After a shopping mall was built just on the town side of the Perrine Bridge, downtown merchants banded together to take on the new competition. The result is a downtown straight out of the 1950s, with neon signs, a score of small shops, and some new eateries and bars. The massive Greek Revival courthouse (Shoshone St.) faces a band shell in the park across the street, home to summertime concerts. The downtown's only drawback is its maddening adherence to the classic Mormon street grid. There are, for example, four 3rd avenues, one for each point on the compass.

Time Out Locals who eat downtown often stop in for a pastry dessert and espresso or other specialty coffee at **Metropolis** (125 Main Ave., tel. 208/734-4457). The Echo and the Bunnymen (a rock group) poster hanging in this sunny downtown bakery and café tells you right away that Eric and Susan Ettesvold aren't from around here. Both are formally trained chefs from Los Angeles, and, for her prowess with dough, Susan represented the United States at a recent culinary competition. The café carries a complete line of baked goods, from baguettes to blintzes, and serves a light lunch. (There is also a monthly dinner, for which there is a long waiting list.)

Twin Falls used to be famous as the site of Shoshone Falls, a waterfall higher than Niagara, and for the Twin Falls, just to the east. Snake River dams have greatly reduced the flow over these once-majestic attractions, but, for a short period in the spring, during the height of the snowmelt in the Snake River watershed in the Tetons, the falls sometimes return to their former glory. In any case, follow signs off Route 30 east of town for the **canyonside park by Shoshone Falls.** The drive gives you a good look at the canyon's geology, an added bonus, especially if the falls are tame. The park is open in daylight hours.

From Twin Falls, take U.S. 30 west; past Buhl, the road gradually tumbles into the Snake River canyon until it is nearly level **⓯** with the river at the **Thousand Springs** area. Here, dozens of springs literally pour out of the north canyon wall. Geologists think the water comes from mountains to the north and that it may take up to 100 years for it to make the underground journey to the Snake. It's possible to tour the area by boat (*see* Guided Tours, *above*).

⓰ U.S. 30 crosses the Snake and continues into **Hagerman,** a favorite getaway spot for Boiseites and home of the "world-famous" Idaho state fossil, a complete skeleton of a small Ice Age horse. On the way, look for large, round boulders scattered over the landscape. These "melon rocks" were eroded into that shape and dumped here by the Bonneville flood.

Stop in at the **Idaho State Bank building** (State and Hagerman Sts.), which dates from 1887, when it served as a general store. The teller area has been restored to a wooden and brass showplace, just the way a bank would have looked in the 1880s. Around the back of the building and down the stairs in the basement is the tiny Rose Creek Winery, where you can taste a product of Idaho's booming wine industry.

Farther down State Street is the tiny **Hagerman Valley Historical Museum,** known locally as the fossil museum. It's home to the fossil horse as well as artifacts from the area's past. *State and Main Sts., tel. 208/837-6288. Admission free. Open Wed.–Sun. 1–4.*

Across the street, the **Fossil Beds National Monument headquarters** provides detailed information on the fossils in the area. The Pliocene fossil beds along the river were declared a national monument in 1988, and plans are in the works for a new visitor center and a visitor program, so tourists will be able to see these incredibly rich fossil fields. To date, over 100 species have been identified. *221 N. State St., tel. 208/837–4793. Admission free. Open weekdays 8–5.*

Frank Lloyd Wright, perhaps the greatest architect of the 20th century, believed that buildings should harmonize with their sites. An excellent example of this philosophy, Idaho's only **Frank Lloyd Wright house** is about 2 miles west of Hagerman off U.S. 30. At the Snake River Pottery sign, turn left and go 1.1 miles. It's to the left, overlooking the Snake River and its magnificent canyon. For the best view, go as far as the driveway of Snake River Pottery (the oldest producer of pottery in Idaho) and head back up the road. (The house can also be seen from an overlook a mile farther uphill on U.S. 30.) Since it's a private home, please don't disturb the occupants.

The bad news is that U.S. 30 melds into I–84 at Bliss. The good news is that the town of Glenns Ferry is only a 30-minute drive. **⑰** Here you'll find **Three Island Crossing State Park,** site of one of the most dangerous Snake River crossings on the Oregon Trail. The pioneers were forced to cross channels separated by the three islands, often losing stock and belongings in each one. It's doubtful they would have made it without their Shoshone guides. The trail itself, winding down the hills on the opposite bank, stands out like a dark vein on the landscape.

What to See and Do with Children

Bill Mason Outfitters (Sun Valley Village, tel. 208/622–9305) boasts that its classes can teach even a novice to fly-fish in just 15 minutes, and it's true. You may not be a champion, but you'll be able to cast and even catch fish. Classes for kids (Tuesday, Thursday, and Saturday noon–4) include equipment, instruction, transportation, and fishing on a private, stocked pond. Reservations are required.

Shopping

Shopping Districts/Malls Central **Ketchum** is made up almost completely of small shops, art galleries, and cafés. Everything from Ralph Lauren designs to Indian beadwork beckons from shop windows.

Sun Valley Village, located in the Sun Valley Resort's pedestrian mall, offers 13 mostly upscale specialty shops ranging from **Bill Mason Outfitters,** for anglers, to **Towne and Park Jewelers.**

Downtown **Twin Falls** has a variety of small stores. Shopping along **Main Avenue** around the intersection with **Shoshone Street** is much the way shopping in small American towns used to be before malls arrived. If you're hankering for a mall, however, the **Magic Valley Mall** (1485 Pole Line Rd.) is near the Perrine Bridge.

Specialty Stores
Galleries There are no fewer than 19 art galleries in central **Ketchum,** offering a range of art from the wildly esoteric to traditional Western. For more information on gallery tours or a map, contact **Sun Valley Gallery Association** (Box 1241, Sun Valley 83353, tel. 208/726–2602).

Sports and the Outdoors

Biking A public biking/in-line skating/walking trail runs most of the length of the Wood River valley in the **Sun Valley** area. It's possible to ride all the way from Hailey to a point about 2 miles north of the Sun Valley Resort, a distance of about 18 miles. Maps are available from the **Blaine County Recreation District** (Box 297, Hailey 83333, tel. 208/788–2117). **Pete Lane's Sports** (Sun Valley Mall, tel. 208/622–2276) has rentals by the hour or the day.

Fishing The Sun Valley area on the **Wood River** (also known as the Big Wood but not to be confused with the Little Wood) and **Silver Creek** are known worldwide for dry fly-fishing. For tackle and classes, try **Bill Mason Outfitters** (*see* What to See and Do with Children, *above*).

Golf Without question, two of Idaho's three premier golf courses are at the **Radisson Elkhorn** (Sun Valley, tel. 208/622–4511) and **Sun Valley Resort** (Sun Valley, tel. 208/622–2251). They are both expensive (over $50), but a number of golf packages can lower the cost. Other area courses include **Blue Lakes Country Club** (1940 Blue Lakes Grade, Twin Falls, tel. 208/733–2330) and **Canyon Springs** (Canyon Springs Rd., Twin Falls, tel. 208/734–7609).

Rock Climbing The **City of Rocks**, southeast of Twin Falls, draws European and American rock climbers to its sheer faces. The rock formations towering out of the desert are considered some of the most challenging in the American West.

Skiing
Cross-Country The **Sun Valley Resort** has trails evenly divided among beginner, intermediate, and advanced. Most trails run along the golf course, and classical and skating lanes are groomed into the tracks. In addition, there are trails throughout the valley; for information on these, contact the **Sun Valley Cross Country Ski Association** (Box 2420, Sun Valley 83353, tel. 208/726–3423).

Downhill There's no doubt that **Sun Valley** (tel. 800/635–8261), when it has snow—which it now always does, thanks to a multimillion-dollar investment in snowmaking equipment—is one of the best ski resorts in the country. Bald Mountain, primarily an intermediate and advanced hill, has one small area, Seattle Ridge, essentially for beginners. However, because of the mountain's steep 3,400-foot vertical drop, an intermediate run here might earn a black diamond elsewhere. Dollar, a much smaller teaching hill near the Radisson Elkhorn, is almost completely beginner terrain. Together they have 75 runs serviced by three quads, five double chairs, and seven T-bars. On-hill facilities include four restaurants, and the children's program is among the most complete of any ski resort. Some purists might find Baldy a little crowded with glittery lodge sitters, but they add color and lend a festive atmosphere to the day.

Dining and Lodging

Hagerman **The Riverbank.** People drive all the way from Twin Falls for this
Dining small restaurant's fried catfish. Located near the Snake River and formerly the branch of a bank, this cement-block building has an interior that is about as soothing as, well, a bank's, but locals swear by the food. *191 State St., tel. 208/837–6462. MC, V. Closed Mon. and for lunch Tues.–Sat. Inexpensive.*

Lodging
★

The Cary House. Just outside town on a site that extends to the cliffs overlooking the Snake is this restored and updated farmhouse. Built in 1908, it is listed on the National Register of Historic Places. Owners Linda and Darrell Heinemann have recreated a 1900s feel without sacrificing today's comforts. Horses graze outside the windows. Rooms are decorated with antiques from the region but are fully carpeted. Linda's complete gourmet breakfast varies but emphasizes local ingredients. *17985 U.S. 30, 83332, tel. 208/837-4848. 4 rooms. Facilities: dining room, sitting room, horse boarding, horseback riding. No credit cards. Moderate.*

Sun Valley
Dining

Peter's. This local favorite is a casual, bright bistro offering northern Italian and Austrian dishes. Veal, pork, fresh fish, and other seafood get some exotic treatments. *6th St. and 2nd Ave., Ketchum, tel. 208/726-9515. Reservations accepted. AE, MC, V. Closed for lunch weekends. Expensive.*

A Winter's Feast. No doubt about it, this is different. The owner calls it gourmet yurt dining. Okay, well, this is Sun Valley. The idea here is to cross-country ski along an easy trail for about half a mile, take the skis off, enter a Mongolian yurt, and indulge in a five-course gourmet meal. You're supposed to feel as if you're eating in the wilds, but the lights shining from million-dollar homes on the hill detract from the intended ruggedness. The food is expertly created by Colleen Crain. Entrées include home-smoked salmon, beef tenderloin, and rack of lamb. *Near Warm Springs condo/resort complex, Ketchum, tel. 208/726-5775. Reservations required. MC, V. Expensive.*

The Christiana. This is as old-line as Sun Valley gets. Hemingway had cocktails here during his final months. The menu reflects that heritage with beef fillets in béarnaise sauce, salmon in hollandaise, and other traditional favorites. *Sun Valley Rd. and Walnut St., Ketchum, tel. 208/726-3388. Reservations advised. Dress: upscale casual. AE, MC, V. Moderate-Expensive.*

Gretchen's. This rustic, cozy restaurant offers breakfast, lunch, and dinner. The salmon and trout are fresh and especially well prepared, and the hamburgers are enormous. The young staff is very enthusiastic. *Sun Valley Village, tel. 208/622-2097. AE, MC, V. Inexpensive-Moderate.*

Perry's. The Belgian waffles in this café are favorites of local skiers who want a carbohydrate and sugar rush. Hot oatmeal, cereals, fresh fruits, yogurts, and muffins round out the breakfast menu, while hot and cold sandwiches and a selection of salads are offered for lunch. Eat-in and take-out service are available. *131 W. 4th St., Ketchum, tel. 208/726-7703. MC, V. Closed for dinner. Inexpensive.*

Dining and Lodging

Sun Valley Resort. This is, of course, what started it all, and it's still the most complete year-round vacation option in Idaho. Lodge, inn, condominium, and cottage accommodations are available, and the list of facilities is almost endless. The lodge's poured-concrete exterior is almost indistinguishable from wood (from a slight distance), while the interior decor has a traditional European feel. Lodge apartments, primarily for families, are more modern. **The Lodge Dining Room,** a dramatic, circular, two-level room, is Sun Valley's signature restaurant. A large chandelier hangs above the dance floor, booths are tucked along the wall, and a soft jazz trio plays nightly. The Continental menu features old standards and fresh fish, and there is an extensive wine list. Sunday brunch is a mammoth affair. *Sun Valley Co., 83353, tel. 800/786–8259. Restaurant: tel. 208/622–2097; reservations required; dress: jacket and tie or upscale casual; closed for lunch Mon.–Sat. 600 units. Facilities: 5 restaurants, 1 unheated and 2 heated pools, year-round outdoor ice rink, indoor hockey rink, bowling alley, Nordic trails, gun club, stables, 6 tennis courts, movie theater. AE, MC, V. Expensive.*

Lodging **Idaho Country Inn.** This quiet inn in a residential neighborhood looks like a tremendous log home with a river-rock foundation. Inside, the wood accents continue. Four-poster beds made of local wood, such as pine or willow, furnish the spacious, rustic rooms. The building is new, however, so the works are modern. The river-rock fireplace in the sitting room is tempting, as is the plate of cookies kept at fireside. Breakfast is included. *134 Latigo La., 83353, tel. 208/726–1019. 10 rooms. Facilities: dining room, sitting room. AE, MC, V. Expensive.*

Knob Hill Inn. With lots of wood and log furnishings, the interior of this exclusive inn suits Ketchum's Western character, but, since this is a brand-new building, everything that should be modern is. All rooms have large tubs, wet bars, and balconies with mountain views. Intermediate rooms, suites, and penthouse suites have fireplaces. A full breakfast, afternoon refreshments, and fresh baked goods are included. *960 N. Main St., Ketchum 83340, tel. 208/726–8010 or 800/526–8010, fax 208/726–2712. 20 rooms. Facilities: restaurant, indoor pool, spa, sauna, workout room. AE, MC, V. Expensive.*

Radisson Elkhorn Resort. This is Sun Valley's "other" resort, a large hotel and affiliated condominiums just over the hill from the Sun Valley Resort. The Elkhorn's lodge has fully appointed hotel rooms with modern decor and refrigerators. Upgraded rooms have fireplaces, kitchens, and Jacuzzis. The resort offers a variety of year-round activities but is best known for its massive 7,100-yard, Robert Trent Jones–designed golf course. *Box 6009, 83354, tel. 208/622–4511 or 800/333–3333. Facilities: 3 restaurants, lounge, nightclub, outdoor Olympic-size pool, golf course, 18 tennis courts. AE, D, MC, V. Moderate–Expensive.*

Lift Tower Lodge. Don't let the rusting lift tower outside the front door put you off. Here's a casual, homey place about three minutes by car from the River Run lift of Baldy. Recent remodeling has spruced up this old establishment and upgraded some of the simple and utilitarian rooms, which have single, double, or queen beds; TVs; and small refrigerators. Some have small cooking facilities. There is a free Continental breakfast but no restaurant. *Box 185, Ketchum 83340, tel. 208/726–5163 or 800/462–8646. 14 rooms. Facilities: outdoor hot tub. AE, D, MC, V. Moderate.*

Twin Falls **Rock Creek.** This steak, prime rib, and seafood house west of
Dining downtown is a throwback to the days before cholesterol and red meat became taboo. With a dark red interior, thick booths, and a massive salad bar, it's known for its wide selection of single-malt whiskies and vintage ports and probably the most complete wine list in town. *200 Addison Ave. W, tel. 208/734–4154. Dress: upscale casual. AE, MC, V. Moderate–Expensive.*

Aroma. Opened by Mark and Dawn Makin in 1985, when downtown Twin Falls was struggling, this small Italian restaurant has become a local favorite by serving such standards as lasagna, ravioli, and pizza. Tablecloths are plastic and the decor simple in what amounts to a storefront operation, but service is friendly and the food reliable. *147 Shoshone St. N, tel. 208/733–0167. Reservations accepted. MC, V. Closed Sun., Mon. Moderate.*

★ **Buffalo Café.** Ask anybody in town where to go for breakfast, and you'll get the same answer. This tiny café, with a twin in Sun Valley, is a shack squeezed next to a tire store, across from a truck lot surrounded by barbed wire. You can sit at the counter or at one of 10 tables, but if you go on Sunday, expect to wait. The house specialty is the Buffalo Chip, a concoction of eggs, fried potatoes, cheese, bacon, peppers, and onion. (The brave can ask for a Mexi-chip, made with spicy chorizo sausage.) A half order should fill most stomachs. *218 4th Ave. W, tel. 208/734–0271. No credit cards. Closed for dinner. Inexpensive.*

Lodging **AmeriTel Inn.** This is the newest of the motels. Kitchenettes are available. *1377 Blue Lakes Blvd., 83301, tel. 208/736–8000 or 800/822–TWIN. 88 rooms. Facilities: restaurant, lounge, indoor pool, spa, fitness center, conference room. AE, D, MC, V. Moderate.*

Best Western Canyon Springs Inn. This property is slightly less expensive than the AmeriTel next door. Rooms are larger than most other motels' and very well kept. *1357 Blue Lakes Blvd., 83301, tel. 208/734–5000 or 800/528–1234. 112 rooms. Facilities: restaurant, lounge, outdoor pool. AE, MC, V. Moderate.*

Best Western Apollo. This smaller motel offers clean, reliable rooms but no restaurant or lounge. A Continental breakfast is served in the lobby, and restaurants are a short walk away. *296 Addison Ave. W, 83301, tel. 208/733–2010 or 800/528–1234. 50 rooms. Facilities: hot tub. AE, MC, V. Inexpensive.*

The Arts

Sun Valley In addition to the Sun Valley Music Festival and Swing and Dixie Jazz Jamboree (*see* Festivals and Seasonal Events in Essential Information, *above*), Sun Valley plays host to a number of arts programs. From January through May, the **Sun Valley Center for the Arts and Humanities** (Box 656, Sun Valley 83353, tel. 208/726–9491) puts on concerts, a film festival, readings by such luminaries as Allen Ginsberg, and art exhibits.

Nightlife

Sun Valley *The* night spot for a decade has been **Whiskey Jacques** (Main St. and Sun Valley Rd., Ketchum, tel. 208/726–5297). It's a cross between a nightclub and a cowboy bar. Live music, Western dancing, and lots of drinking help create a rowdy crowd and a few red eyes on ski slopes the next day. The Sun Valley Resort's **Duchin Room** (tel. 208/622–2097) is more subdued and features live jazz trios.

Twin Falls **Dunken's** (102 Main Ave., tel. 208/733–8114), Tim Jones's homage to microbreweries, has become a regular stop for downtown workers. There are 19 taps, covering most of the better Northwest brews. Many regulars come for a beer, some good conversation, and a few games of cribbage, dominoes, or chess. If you bring an out-of-town newspaper, Jones will be your friend for life.

Boise

"It's tough to be the object of so much swooning, so much rosy wooing . . . ," wrote *Idaho Statesman* reporter Marianne Flagg in 1992. "Now please stop writing about us." With a river running through it, a ski hill towering over it, and hundreds of square miles of nature all around it, including a desert to the south and alpine forests to the north, Boise is worried that its "discovery" will bring an end to its old (and pretty good) quality of life. A number of major corporate headquarters, including Boise Cascade and Ore-Ida, are here, and things have been moving along swimmingly for a number of years.

Make no mistake, though: Even with 125,000 people and a university, Boise is still a small town. People know one another and exchange waves as they whiz by on their in-line skates or mountain bikes. A murder, a very rare event, is shattering news. And while it hasn't got the nightlife or great restaurants of other cities, there are a few notables.

Important Addresses and Numbers

Tourist Information Boise Convention and Visitors Bureau (168 N. 9th St., Suite 200, 83701, tel. 208/344–7777), Southwest Idaho Travel Association (Box 2106, 83701, tel. 800/635–5240).

Emergencies Boise has two full-service hospitals: St. Alphonsus Regional Medical Center (1055 N. Curtis Rd., tel. 208/378–2121, emergency room 208/378–3221) and St. Luke's Regional Medical Center (190 Bannock St., tel. 208/386–2222, emergency room 208/386–2344).

Arriving and Departing by Plane

Airport and Airlines Jet service into Boise Municipal Airport (tel. 208/383–3110) is provided by American (tel. 800/433–7300), Delta (tel. 800/221–1212), and United (tel. 800/241–6522). Most flights originate in Salt Lake City, although United flies direct from Chicago. The commuter carriers Horizon (tel. 800/426–0333) and SkyWest (tel. 800/453–9417) also serve Boise.

Between the Airport and Downtown
By Bus The city's bus service, Boise Urban Stages (tel. 208/336–1010), called simply "the Bus," runs frequently from the airport to major points around the city. The cost is approximately $1.25 to downtown.

By Taxi Boise has several cab companies. A taxi stand is just outside the terminal building. The cost is $6–$7 to downtown, depending on the destination.

Arriving and Departing by Car, Train, and Bus

By Car Interstate 84 is the primary east–west route into Boise. From the north, take Route 55. From the south, you may find it easier to take U.S. 93 through Jackpot, Nevada, which joins U.S. 30 near Twin Falls, rather than taking the smaller and twisting Routes 225 (Nevada) and 51 (Idaho).

By Train Morrison-Knudsen Depot (1701 Eastover Terr., tel. 208/336–5992) is a stop for the Amtrak *Pioneer,* which connects Boise to Oregon in the west and to Pocatello and Wyoming in the east.

By Bus **Boise-Winnemucca Stages** (tel. 208/336–3300) serves the U.S. 95 corridor from Nevada to Boise, with stops in towns around Boise. **Greyhound/Trailways** has service to the **Boise Bus Depot** (1212 W. Bannock St., tel. 208/343–3681).

Getting Around

By Bus **The Bus** is cheap, runs frequently, and provides good service throughout the city.

By Taxi Local cab companies include **Ace** (tel. 208/867–1414), **Blue Line** (tel. 208/384–1111), **Boise City Taxi** (tel. 208/890–4800), and **Metro Cab** (tel. 208/866–0633).

Guided Tours

The **Boise Tour Train** is a re-created motorized locomotive that takes sightseers on a tour of Boise. *Julia Davis Park, tel. 208/ 342–4796 or 800/999–5993. Fare: $5.50 adults, $5 senior citizens, $3 children 3–12. Hours of operation vary by day and season, and it doesn't run in winter.*

Exploring Boise

Numbers in the margin correspond to points of interest on the Idaho map.

18 The best place for you to start your exploration of **Boise** is at the **state capitol** (Capitol Blvd.), which is a scale replica of the capitol in Washington, D.C. You can walk in the main rotunda during business hours. The rest of the city fans out from the capitol steps. From here, walk northwest to 8th Street, the heart of downtown. Streets on both sides of 8th are lined with cafés, businesses, and shops (*see* Shopping, *below*).

Time Out **Bar Guernica** (Grove St. and Capitol Blvd.), a popular bar and café, is a convenient downtown window to Idaho's long history of Basque culture. Many people come for the exotic Basque food, which features spicy meats, but burgers are also served, as are specialty coffees. You may have to squeeze yourself into this narrow, redbrick, corner café if you go on a weekend night.

After exploring the capitol area, head east on Warm Springs Avenue through the **Warm Springs** neighborhood, where the houses are heated by underground hot springs.

Turn left on Old Penitentiary Road for a visit to the **Old Idaho Penitentiary,** one of only three territorial pens still standing. The jail, built in 1870, was used until 1974 without much improvement in conditions. Things became so intolerable that prisoners staged a series of rebellions starting in the 1960s. The final revolt, in 1973, prompted the move to a more modern facility. The cell blocks have been left exactly as they were after the riot. Scorched stone walls, tiny cells with calendars still in place, and metal bunks evoke the ghosts of prisoners. A self-guided tour takes at least 90 minutes. *2445 Old Penitentiary Rd., tel. 208/334–2844. Admission: $3 adults, $2 senior citizens and children 6–12. Open Memorial Day–Labor Day, daily noon–5; Labor Day–Memorial Day, daily noon–4. Closed state holidays.*

Returning to Warm Springs Avenue, head back toward downtown, but turn left onto Walnut Avenue. Behind the state's Department of Fish and Game, the **Morrison-Knudsen Nature Center** features a man-made Idaho stream—a kind of outdoor natural museum in a park. The stream has been constructed so that viewers can look from above and below the water's surface to see fish swimming, laying eggs, and doing what fish do. The exhibit is completely self-maintaining. Whatever happens, happens. *600 S. Walnut Ave., no phone. Admission free. Open daily sunrise–sunset.*

From Walnut Avenue, follow Park Boulevard into **Julia Davis Park,** home of the **Idaho Historical Museum.** The museum surveys Idaho's past and includes very detailed reconstructions of building interiors that make accompanying text about the pioneer days come to life. *610 Julia Davis Dr., tel. 208/334–2120. Admission free. Open Mon.–Sat. 9–5, Sun. 1–5. Closed Christmas, Thanksgiving, and New Year's Day.*

Julia Davis Park is also the spot to pick up the Boise Tour Train (*see* Guided Tours, *above*), but perhaps it's most notable as a key gateway to the city's renowned **greenbelt,** which runs along both banks of the Boise River and stretches 4 miles in either direction from downtown. In all, there are about 19 miles of paved pathways linking parks and attractions, and it's not unusual to see deer and other wildlife browsing along the way. The trails are also favorites of in-line skaters, bicyclists, walkers, and joggers.

Continue west and cross the river at Americana Boulevard. In the 1000 block is **Kathryn Albertson Park** (local magnates named the parks for their wives), a tiny wilderness in the middle of Boise. A walking trail nearly a mile long leads visitors through lagoons and a grassland. An urban wildlife area, the park is home to many varieties of birds and the occasional large game animal.

Short Excursions from Boise

It wasn't easy, but after a fight, the federal government set aside the 482,640-acre **Birds of Prey Natural Area,** 30 miles south of Boise along the Snake River's northern shore. Although not easily accessible, it has become a key stop for those fascinated by North American raptors. A good place to start is the **World Center for Birds of Prey.** Species like the harpy eagle and peregrine falcon are on view here. Tours are by appointment only. Take Exit 50 off I–84, head south for 6 miles on South Cole Road, and follow the signs. *5666 W. Flying Hawk La., tel. 208/362–8687. Admission: $4 adults, $3 senior citizens, $2 children 4–16. Open Mar.–Oct., Tues.–Sun. 9–5; Nov.–Feb., Tues.–Sun. 10–4. Closed holidays.*

The natural area itself is another 24 miles south. Take I–84 west to Route 69 south, but past Kuna the road is unimproved. You can get a closer look from the river. Day trips through **Whitewater Shop River Tours** (252 N. Meridian Rd., Kuna 83634, tel. 208/922–5285) run $50 to $99 per person.

What to See and Do with Children

The **Discovery Center of Idaho** has joined the list of hands-on science museums for children (and adults who act like children). Almost every exhibit moves, talks, or otherwise acts up in response to a child's interaction with it. *131 Myrtle St., tel. 208/343–9895. Admission: $3 adults, $2 senior citizens and children 5–18. Open Memorial Day–Labor Day, Wed.–Fri. 10–5, weekends noon–5; Labor Day–Memorial Day, Wed.–Fri. 9–5, Sat. 10–5, Sun. noon–5.*

Off the Beaten Track

Idaho has its own small wine industry, which, say proud locals, is catching up to Oregon's and Washington State's, especially in the white varietals. You can see for yourself how successful the wineries have become by visiting them; five of the 12 are located west of Boise in Nampa and Caldwell, and one is in Hagerman (*see* Exploring Southcentral Idaho, *above*). Admission to all wineries is free. For a map, contact **Idaho Grape Growers and Wine Producers Commission** (Box 790, Boise 83701, tel. 208/334–2227).

Shopping

Shopping Districts/Streets

A rich selection of stores line 8th Street downtown. **The 8th Street Shops** (8th St., between Grove and Broad Sts.) make up a restored turn-of-the-century block with specialty shops and small restaurants. **The 8th Street Marketplace** (Capitol Blvd. and Front St.), a brick warehouse converted into stores, sits on the east side of 8th Street. **Boise Center** (Front St., between 8th and 9th Sts.), the city's new convention center, also houses a **St. Chapelle Winery** tasting room and a shop called **Taters,** stuffed with all manner of things spud.

In **Hyde Park,** around the intersection of 13th and Eastman streets, just northwest of the state capitol, antiques shops line the streets, and several cafés and specialty stores vie for attention with classic awnings and decorated windows.

Specialty Stores
Books and Magazines

The Book Shop (908 Main St.) has a huge selection of books, including the best array of books about Idaho in the state. **Hannifin's** (1024 Main St.) is a block away but about 90 years in the past. The men who work in this cigar and magazine shop are as old and grizzled as the building, which opened in 1907. You can buy just about any magazine published, including a rather colorful selection of pornography discreetly placed behind glass windows in the back of the store.

Fishing Gear

Wherever more than 10 people live in Idaho, there is a store that sells fishing gear and permits, but **Moon's Café and Criner's Tackle and Cutlery** (815 Bannock St.) is one of a kind. It may be the only store in the country to combine hamburgers and milk shakes with fishing tackle.

Sports and the Outdoors

Biking

The **greenbelt** is a great place to cycle. Mountain biking is popular on the hills just outside central Boise. Trails include the **8th Street Extension** (north on 8th St. to where the pavement ends) and **Cartwright Road** (Harrison Blvd. north to Hill Rd., to Bogus Basin Rd., then left on Cartwright). **Willow Lane Athletic Complex** (end of Willow La., off W. State St.) and **Wheels R Fun** (831 S. 13th St., at Shoreline Park) have bicycle rentals.

Golf Courses include **Quail Hollow** (4520 N. 36th St., tel. 208/344–7807), **Shadow Valley** (15711 Rte. 55, tel. 208/939–6699), and **Warm Springs** (2495 Warm Springs Ave., tel. 208/343–5661).

Skiing Only 16 miles north of town, **Bogus Basin** (2405 Bogus Basin
Downhill Rd., 83702, tel. 208/336–4500) is Boise's winter backyard playground. It's known for night skiing, which leads suit-clad executives to climb in their 4×4s and change into ski gear on the way. There are some serious black diamond runs as well as a healthy proportion of tame beginner trails. The vertical drop is 1,800 feet; six double chairs and four rope tows serve 45 runs.

Tubing In summer, thousands of people go tubing—sitting in an inner tube and floating down the river. A special bus service from **Ann Morrison Memorial Park** (Americana Blvd.) carries tubers to **Barber Park**, about 6 miles to the east across the Ada County line. From there, floaters drift back to Ann Morrison Park. Across from the park, **Wheels R Fun** (*see* Biking, *above*), open April–October, carries inner tubes for floating the river.

Dining

★ **Peter Schott's.** The dining room in the Sun Valley Resort might argue the point, but this small restaurant on the first floor of the Idanha Hotel is generally regarded as the best restaurant in Idaho. Its light walls, fireplace, and bookshelves create an intimate feel. Schott used to run the restaurants at Sun Valley Resort after immigrating from Austria. Now a local celebrity with his own two-minute cooking show, Schott calls his food New American cuisine, but he also throws in a little northern Italian. Fresh fish dominates the menu, and the wine list is complete (155 selections) but not extravagant. It's possible for two people to have dinner and a bottle of wine for $50 (not including tip). *928 Main St., tel. 208/342–3611. Reservations advised. Dress: jacket and tie or upscale casual. AE, D, DC, MC, V. Closed for lunch and Sun. Moderate–Expensive.*

Manly's Prime Rib and Pies. Your instinct will tell you not to try this white clapboard roadhouse about a mile south of Boise State University, but it didn't become a local legend on its looks. Rather, this classic greasy spoon with an attitude is known for great slabs of prime rib stretched over a platter and served with french fries. Many patrons eat at the small counter, others wait for tables, but they all eat. *1225 Federal Way. No credit cards. Closed Sun., Mon. Inexpensive–Moderate.*

Table Rock Brew Pub and Grill. This microbrewery makes the second-best beer in Idaho, and it has managed to turn that skill into a happening restaurant, especially on weekend nights. Neon lights; long, high tables; an energetic staff; and loud pop music create a kinetic atmosphere. Food is basic—onion rings, chili, salads, and burgers—but it is served in great heaps. *705 Fulton St., tel. 208/342–0944. AE, D, DC, MC, V. Inexpensive–Moderate.*

Harrison Hollow Brewhouse. This brew pub is a favorite stop for skiers heading to or returning from Bogus Basin. It's decorated like a cross between a sports bar and a Western cabin. TVs keep patrons up-to-date on scores and games. Speakers pour forth blues and R&B, because an owner loves them, and photos of great blues guitarists adorn a wall in the bar area. The menu offers sandwiches, bar food, and ribs. *24555 Harrison Hollow Rd., tel. 208/343–6820. AE, MC, V. Inexpensive.*

Lodging

The Owyhee Plaza. Several Hawaiians got lost in the Idaho wilderness in the 1800s and became local legend. Idahoans, not knowing how to spell Hawaii, settled on Owyhee, now the name of a county and this hotel, built in 1910. Refurbished during the '50s, the building lost a little of its charm, but its old glory can still be seen in the carpets, giant light fixtures, and especially the dark wood paneling. An adjacent motel offers moderately priced rooms. *1109 Main St., 83702, tel. 208/343–4611. 100 rooms. Facilities: 2 restaurants, lounge, beauty salon, conference rooms. AE, D, DC, MC, V. Moderate–Expensive.*

★ **Idaho Heritage Inn.** Tom and Phyllis Lupher operate this B&B in a former governor's mansion about a mile east of downtown. Each room is very different, but all have names with political themes. Antiques, wallpaper, and old-style bed frames retain an early 1900s feel. The top-floor room, carved out of the attic, is very private. A full breakfast is included. *109 W. Idaho St., 83702, tel. 208/342–8066. 5 rooms. Facilities: dining room, sun room. MC, V. Moderate.*

★ **The Idanha.** Built in 1901 and once Boise's showplace, this hotel is recommended with a very large grain of salt. Today the brown shag carpeting is a little ratty. TV reception depends on a set of rabbit ears and luck. The steam heat is piped in from three blocks away through old-style radiators, accompanied by a symphony of clangs and hisses, if, that is, the night clerk remembers to turn the heat on. On the second floor, a sign with a large red arrow reads ROOM 206/FIRE ESCAPE. It's to be hoped that the person in 206 will be willing to unlock the door. On the other hand, in what hotel would a kitchenette feature appliances from 1939? There is even a cast of odd hotel residents. Movies have been made based on less. This is a true classic that deserves to be brought back to life. *928 Main St., 83702, tel. 208/342–3611. 45 rooms. Facilities: restaurant, lounge, validated parking. AE, MC, V. Inexpensive–Moderate.*

The Arts

The **Morrison Center for the Performing Arts** (2101 Campus La., tel. 208/385–1609) offers one of the most extensive arts programs in any city this size. The **Boise Opera Company,** the American Festival Ballet, the **Boise Philharmonic,** and the **Boise Master Chorale** all have full season programs. In summer, an outdoor theater is home to the **Idaho Shakespeare Festival** (400 Parkcenter Blvd., tel. 208/336–9221).

Nightlife

Bars and Lounges In addition to the lively brew pubs **Harrison Hollow** and **Table Rock** (*see* Dining, *above*), there are several bars that offer live jazz and pop on weekends in the neighborhood around 6th and West Idaho streets, downtown.

Northern Idaho

Most Idahoans consider the Salmon River the unofficial boundary between north and south, since it bisects the state almost perfectly and separates the Pacific and Mountain time zones. The Salmon is also one of the state's great scenic attractions. It is the longest wild river left in the United States, outside of Alaska, and the Middle Fork, which begins as runoff from the Sawtooths and flows through the River of No Return Wilderness Area, is recognized around the world for one of the wildest, most gorgeous river raft trips on earth. The river system is a magnet for anglers, too. Riggins, near its western end; Stanley, high in the Sawtooths near the Middle Fork; and Salmon, to the east near Montana, are the gateways to the Salmon and its wilderness.

Another informal dividing line crosses the White Bird Summit, north of Riggins. Over the summit, Idaho begins to feel more like the Northwest, as opposed to the West. Lewiston, for example, is an inland port whose traffic comes from the Columbia River; it's also the portal to Hells Canyon, a natural wonder that forms the border between Oregon and Idaho.

The panhandle of Idaho is a logging region that has been "discovered" by refugees from larger cities in California, Washington State, and elsewhere. The resort towns of Coeur d'Alene and Sandpoint are just the sort of places that drive visitors to look up the words "Real Estate" in the Yellow Pages.

Important Addresses and Numbers

Tourist Information
For regional information: **North Central Idaho Travel Committee** (2207 E. Main St., Suite G, Lewiston 83501, tel. 800/473–3543), **North Idaho Travel Committee** (Box 928, Sandpoint 83864, tel. 208/263–2161). For towns: **Greater Coeur d'Alene Convention and Visitors Bureau** (202 Sherman Ave., Box 1088, Coeur d'Alene 83814, tel. 208/664–0587 or 800/232–4968), **McCall Area Chamber of Commerce** (116 N. 3rd St., McCall 83638, tel. 208/634–7631).

Emergencies
Hospital Emergency Rooms
In Coeur d'Alene, there is the **Kootenai Medical Center** (2003 Lincoln Way, tel. 208/667–6441); in Lewiston, **St. Joseph Hospital** (5th Ave. and 6th St., tel. 208/743–2511); and in Sandpoint, **Bonner General Hospital** (3rd and Fir Sts., tel. 208/263–1441).

Arriving and Departing by Plane

Airports and Airlines
Horizon (tel. 800/426–0333) serves **Lewiston/Clarkston,** the only commercial airport north of Boise. Air travelers heading for Moscow fly to Pullman, Washington, and those going to the Idaho panhandle fly to Spokane, a 35-minute drive from Coeur d'Alene.

Arriving and Departing by Car, Train, and Bus

By Car
From Boise, Route 55 heads north to McCall. From Spokane in the west or western Montana in the east, take I–90 to Coeur d'Alene and U.S. 2 to Sandpoint.

By Train **Amtrak** serves **Sandpoint Depot** (Railroad Ave., tel. 208/265–9940) from Montana to the east and Spokane and Seattle to the west.

By Bus **Greyhound/Trailways** stops at the **Coeur d'Alene Bus Depot** (1527 Northwest Blvd., tel. 208/667–3343).

Getting Around

By Car A car is essential here. The primary north–south highway is U.S. 95, while I–90 and U.S. 2 run east–west.

Guided Tours

Hells Canyon tours are a thriving business. Most tour operators give historical and geological information on one- or two-day trips on the Snake. Some outfitters run jet boats upriver from Lewiston into the Hells Canyon National Recreation Area, while others put rafts in near Oxbow Dam and float downstream. Some offer lodging inside the canyon in cabins or lodges. One, **Beamer's Landing Hells Canyon Tours** (Box 1223, Lewiston 83501, tel. 800/522–6966), has the contract to deliver the U.S. mail to remote ranches in the canyon and offers a two-day mail-run trip that includes a stop at a sheep ranch. Other outfitters are **Northwest Voyagers** (Box 373G, Lucile 83542, tel. 800/727–9977) and **Snake Dancer Excursions** (614 Lapwai Rd., Lewiston 83501, tel. 800/234–1941).

Exploring Northern Idaho

Numbers in the margin correspond to points of interest on the Idaho map.

19 While the town of **McCall** is close to Boise and falls within the capital's sphere of influence, it has the alpine feel of the northern half of the state. The 108-mile drive north from Boise on Route 55 is one of the most beautiful in Idaho, if not the country. The road runs along the shore of the Payette River as it jumps down the mountains, over boulders, and through alpine forests. The arid plains of the Snake River give way to higher and higher mountains covered by tremendous stands of pines.

Long a timber town, McCall was known as a hunting and fishing spot in summer and, thanks to a nearby mountain and prodigious winter snows, a ski destination in winter. The film *Northwest Passage* was shot here in 1938. In 1948, a lodge was built on the shore of Payette Lake as a sort of manly hideaway, but during the 1980s, the area was discovered by Californians. Now espresso shops dot the main street, and the lodge, bought by a San Diego developer, has been remodeled and gone upscale. Locals are a little ambivalent about all this, but there's no doubt the changes have made McCall one of the most popular resort destinations in the state.

Route 55 reaches its peak a few miles outside McCall and then gradually snakes its way down hillsides. It joins U.S. 95 and the Little Salmon River at New Meadows and heads into mining territory, where gold and silver, and rumors of both, brought hundreds of mostly disappointed men to the region. About 50 miles north of the junction, where the Little Salmon flows into **20** the main Salmon River, the tiny town of **Riggins** is a wide spot in the road. It's also the last stop in the Mountain Time Zone;

across the river, it's an hour earlier. Hunters and anglers flock here for chukar, elk, and steelhead.

Immediately outside Riggins, U.S. 95 crosses the Salmon and begins the 40-mile climb toward **White Bird Summit,** which rises 4,245 feet above sea level. There were no roads from north to south Idaho until 1915, when the White Bird Grade was finished. It climbed nearly 3,000 feet in 14 miles of agonizing hairpins and switchbacks. The new road was finished in 1975.

A little over halfway up the new grade, a small scenic overlook sits above the valley where the Nez Percé War started. In 1877, Chief Joseph and his band of Nez Percé, who had not signed a treaty with the whites as had other bands, were nevertheless on their way to resettle at the nearby reservation when trouble broke out. About 80 Native Americans, using guerrilla tactics and surprise, decimated a much larger white force without losing a person. The army retreated, but the legendary pursuit of Joseph's band across 1,500 miles of Idaho and Montana began. An interpretive shelter tells the story of the battle.

From White Bird Summit, U.S. 95 plunges rapidly into the Camas Prairie and into Grangeville, a farming town. Here, the Nez Percé dug the roots of the camas plant, a dietary staple. About 20 miles past Grangeville, the road enters the modern **Nez Percé Indian Reservation,** home to treaty and nontreaty Nez Percé. (There is still some minor antagonism between the groups.) The road heads through Lapwai and enters Spalding.

㉑ Though the park itself is really a series of sites spread over three states, the **Nez Percé National Historic Park headquarters** is in Spalding. The headquarters building gives a detailed look at the Nez Percé, or Ne-Mee-Poo, as they called themselves, and their history, including a 30-minute film about the tribe, their contacts with Lewis and Clark, and their lives today. A small museum exhibits artifacts from Chiefs Joseph and White Bird, including textiles, pipes, and, poignantly, a ribbon and a coin given to the tribe by Meriwether Lewis as thanks for help. *Follow signs on U.S. 95, tel. 208/843-2261. Admission free. Open daily 8–4:30.*

㉒ Just 10 miles farther up U.S. 95, which joins U.S. 12, the hard-working mill town of **Lewiston** is tucked into the hills at the junction of the Snake and Clearwater rivers. It was once the capital of the Idaho Territory but is now known regionally for its relatively mild temperatures and early golf season. Its blue-collar economy is based on its inland seaport and the giant paper mill located just on its eastern edge.

Lewiston and Clarkston (its twin city in Washington), named for you know whom, are also known as the gateways to **Hells Canyon,** a geologic wonder deeper than the Grand Canyon. Canyon tours have become big business in Lewiston (*see* Guided Tours, *above*). The hills in the canyon resemble ancient Mayan temples as they rise high above the waterway. Columnar basalts, rock formations that look like giant black pencils standing next to one another, frame the river. In some spots, ancient Native American pictographs can be seen on smooth rock faces. Bald eagles swoop down from cliffs to hunt for food, and deer scatter along the hillsides.

Miners tried to exploit the area, but they gave up. Today a few hardy sheep and cattle ranchers are all that's left of the pioneers who first settled here. The **Kirkwood Historic Ranch,** a 6-mile walk from Pittsburgh Landing or a four-hour jet-boat ride from Lewiston, has been preserved to show how the pioneers lived. Aside from making homes from cut lumber instead of logs, ranchers today live in nearly the same style. *Admission free. Ranch house open daily during daylight.*

From Lewiston, U.S. 95 climbs 2,000 feet virtually straight up out of the valley and into rolling farmland. About 40 miles later, **②** it cuts through the middle of **Moscow,** home of the University of Idaho. Students often joke that the university was placed in Moscow because there is absolutely nothing to do here except study. The city does feature a fine set of late-19th-century buildings, however, and one of the best jazz festivals in the country (*see* Festivals and Seasonal Events in Essential Information, *above*).

From Moscow, U.S. 95 winds its way through tiny farm towns to the **Coeur d'Alene Indian Reservation.** French-Canadian trappers mingled with the local Native Americans in the early 1800s and found them to be astute traders. Because of their tough bargaining skills, the trappers called them Coeur d'Alenes (Pointed Hearts). Today the tribe has found another way to get money: a new bingo gaming hall.

② **Coeur d'Alene** itself is just 10 miles farther north. Idaho's second-most-famous resort town sits on the shores of Coeur d'Alene Lake, surrounded by pine-covered hills. Although the town was originally a Native American settlement, then a U.S. Army fort, and, in the 1880s, an entrepôt for mining and timber in this part of Idaho, it has always attracted visitors. Now it does so with a vengeance, but the town, especially along Sherman Avenue, the main drag, still has a pleasant village atmosphere. Although primarily known as a summer destination and as Spokane's Playground, Coeur d'Alene has recently boosted the number of winter visitors by promoting Silver Mountain, a ski area about 50 miles to the east (*see* Sports and the Outdoors, *below*). The city also makes a good base from which to explore the historic mining towns of Wallace and Kellogg, both east on I–90.

② **Wallace,** the quainter of the two, is one of the few towns to be included in its entirety on the National Register of Historic Places. About 50 miles east of Coeur d'Alene, it was first settled in the 1880s mining rush, and today much of the town center looks exactly as it did at the turn of the century.

② One of the best historical attractions in the area is the **Old Mission at Cataldo,** 24 miles east of Coeur d'Alene on I–90. Influenced by trappers and visited by missionaries, a group of Coeur d'Alenes took up Roman Catholicism. In 1850, together with Father Anthony Ravalli, they began construction of the mission, now the oldest building in Idaho. The mission church is massive, considering it was built almost totally by hand with an ax and a few other old hand tools. Behind the altar you can see the mud and stick construction used on the walls. The giant beams overhead were dragged from the forest, and rock for the foundation was quarried from a hill half a mile away. The adjacent mission house, home to generations of priests, is furnished the way it would have been at the turn of the century. An interpretive center provides more details about the Coeur d'Alenes and the site, which is disabled accessible. *Old Mission State*

Park, Cataldo, tel. 208/682–3814. Admission: $2 per vehicle. Open Memorial Day–Labor Day, daily 8–6; Labor Day–Memorial Day, daily 9–5.

Time Out On the way back from Wallace and Kellogg, Silver Mountain, or the mission, take Exit 43 off I–90 and head north along the river. After about 1½ miles you'll see **The Snakepit.** Its proper name is Enaville Resort, but nobody calls it that. Now a restaurant, the 1880s-era log building was once a notorious bordello for loggers and miners. The bartender will be happy to show you the small dumbwaiter behind the bar, used to send drinks up to the rooms, or the bullet holes in the ceiling made by a disgruntled customer. The menu offers burgers, fish, Rocky Mountain oysters (bull testicles), and steak, including a 40-ounce number that, believe it or not, sells big around here.

㉗ Northern Idaho's other resort town, **Sandpoint,** lies just 40 miles north of Coeur d'Alene on the shores of Lake Pend Oreille, the second-deepest lake in the United States. Nestled between the lake and the Selkirk and Cabinet mountain ranges, Sandpoint has been a railroad depot and a mining town, but now it survives on tourism and lumber. The town is small— five blocks of shops and restaurants form its core—and the brick and stone buildings are almost unchanged since the early 1900s. Locals say the town is 20 years behind Coeur d'Alene. They mean it as a compliment. Like Coeur d'Alene, this is a summer destination with fine lake beaches, extensive woodlands, and nearby mountains. However, now the local ski hill, Schweitzer (*see* Sports and the Outdoors, *below*), is transforming itself into a first-class ski area, and Sandpoint, it has been said, is where places like Vail and Jackson, Wyoming, were just before they expanded.

What to See and Do with Children

In between shopping, swimming, sailing, and fishing in Coeur d'Alene, visit **Tubbs Hill,** adjacent to the parking lot just east of the resort's tower. A 2-mile loop trail winds around the hill. Small wooden signs describe plant and rock types found in the area as well as the remnants of historical buildings. An interpretive guide is available from the city's parks department (221 S. 5th St., tel. 208/769–2252).

The man who owned Schweitzer Mountain, originally purchased to be logged, also liked cars. Now his collection of about a dozen antique vehicles, along with artifacts from the region's logging industry and a couple of historical exhibits, is on display at the **Vintage Wheel Museum,** located in the Company Store in Sandpoint. Included are a U.S. mail wagon, a 1913 Stanley Steamer, a 1907 International horseless carriage, and a giant steam engine. *3rd and Cedar Sts., tel. 208/263–7173. Admission: $2.50 adults, $2 senior citizens, $1 students and children. Open daily 9:30–5:30.*

Shopping

Shopping Malls **The Shops at Coeur d'Alene** (2nd St. and Sherman Ave.) is an enclosed minimall with small shops and resort-wear retailers.

Sandpoint has turned an old footbridge into the **Cedar Street Bridge Public Market** (foot of Cedar St.). Cafés, souvenir stands, and specialty shops, including the only retail outlet of the **Coldwater Creek** mail-order operation, line the two-level structure, which is open daily.

Specialty Stores
Books   **Wilson's Variety** (4th St. and Sherman Ave.), in Coeur d'Alene, carries a wide selection of books about Idaho, including guides on geology and history, and topographical maps.

Candy   **The Original Penny Candy Store** (4th St. and Sherman Ave.), in Coeur d'Alene, is a re-created turn-of-the-century dry-goods and candy store with an array of exotic candies from around the world, from sour-green-apple balls to strawberry bonbons.

Esoterica   The next time you need a custom Mongolian yurt, try **Little Bear Trading Company** (1st St. shops, three doors west of Cedar St. Bridge) in Sandpoint. The shop owner, Bear (that's it, just Bear), makes tepees and yurts for clients around the country. The small store also carries Native American crafts, beads, and feathers, as well as materials from Africa and Central and South America.

Sports and the Outdoors

Biking   The premier cycling journey is the **Centennial Trail,** a new paved path leading from east of Coeur d'Alene all the way to Spokane. **Silver and Schweitzer ski areas** (*see* Skiing, *below*) are especially renowned for mountain biking. In Coeur d'Alene, bikes can be rented at the **Coeur d'Alene Resort's activities desk** (*see* Dining and Lodging, *below*) or from **Coeur d'Alene Surrey Cycles** (Box 14, Hayden Lake, tel. 208/664–6324); in Sandpoint, rent cycles at **Sandpoint Recreational Rentals** (209 E. Superior St., tel. 208/265–4557).

Fishing   Despite the river's name, don't look for too many salmon. Most runs have been dammed away, and a total of two sockeye made it back up the Salmon to Red Fish Lake near Stanley in 1991. **Coeur d'Alene Lake** was successfully stocked with chinook a few years ago, and people have been pulling out some large fish there.

Lake Pend Oreille is renowned for kamloops, a large variety of rainbow trout, and the **Middle Fork of the Salmon** is known for cutthroat trout. Significant populations of steelhead, one of the state's trophy fish, are found in the **Clearwater** and northern sections of the **Snake.** The Snake and **Kootenai** rivers are famous for sturgeon, an ancient species that can grow to well over 6 feet; however, sturgeon may not be removed from the water, even for weighing.

Golf   Northern Idaho courses include **Bryden Canyon Golf Course** (445 O'Connor Rd., Lewiston, tel. 208/746–0863); **Coeur d'Alene Golf Club** (2201 Fairway Dr., Coeur d'Alene, tel. 208/765–0218); **Coeur d'Alene Resort** (2255 Mullan Ave., Coeur d'Alene, tel. 800/688–5253), among the nation's loveliest but very expensive (greens fees: $150 per person, but packages can lower cost); **Hidden Lakes Country Club** (8838 Lower Pack River Rd., Sandpoint, tel. 208/263–1642); **the Highlands Golf and Country Club** (701 N. Inverness Dr., Post Falls, tel. 208/773–3673); **Kimberland Meadows** (New Meadows, tel. 208/347–2164); and **McCall Golf Course** (Davis St., McCall, tel. 208/634–7200).

Rafting The three premier raft trips in Idaho are on the **Selway, Lochsa,** and the **Middle Fork of the Salmon.** Rafting these rivers should not be undertaken casually. While the Lochsa parallels U.S. 12, the Selway and the Middle Fork run ferociously through true wilderness. Unless you are an expert, it's a good idea to pick a recognized outfitter. Even then, you should be a good swimmer and in solid general health. Permits from the U.S. Forest Service are usually required to run these rivers, but they're often hard to get and may require waiting periods (another good reason to use an outfitter). Call 800/635–7820 for permit information.

Skiing In addition to a commercial cross-country trail at **Schweitzer**
Cross-Country **Mountain,** there are several Nordic trails in and around **McCall, Coeur d'Alene,** and **Priest Lake,** north of Sandpoint. Contact the **Idaho Department of Parks and Recreation** (*see* National and State Parks in Essential Information, *above*) for information and maps.

Downhill **Brundage Mountain** (Box 1062, McCall 83638, tel. 208/634–4151), a small hill outside McCall, is in the snowiest area in Idaho. While the runs are a little short and black diamond speed freaks may want to test their sanity elsewhere, Brundage does have enough to keep intermediates and beginners interested. Advanced skiers find solace in the powder glades. On top of the hill are spectacular views of the Seven Devils peaks and Payette Lake. With a vertical drop of 1,800 feet, Brundage has a triple and two double chairs and a platter tow.

For years, only people in Spokane and Sandpoint knew much about **Schweitzer** (Box 815, Sandpoint 83864, tel. 800/831–8810), but it's on the way to becoming a top Western ski destination. It offers on-hill accommodations, children's programs, and a full-service ski school, in addition to two mountain bowls with spine-tingling black diamond runs so steep your elbows scrape the snow on turns. Open-bowl skiing is available for the intermediate and advanced, and beginners can choose from among half a dozen tree-lined runs. There is a vertical drop of 2,400 feet. A quad and five double chairs access 48 runs.

Silver Mountain (610 Bunker Ave., Kellogg 83737, tel. 208/783–1111) solved an accessibility problem by installing the world's longest single-stage gondola. Adjacent to Kellogg, the hill offers a complete family learning program. Locals think the advanced terrain at Schweitzer is better, but Silver offers some excellent wooded powder skiing and some steep runs. Fifty trails cover a vertical drop of 2,200 feet and are reached by a quad, two triple chairs, two double chairs, and a surface lift in addition to the gondola.

Water Sports Boating on the lakes of northern Idaho is one reason many people go there. **Coeur d'Alene** and **Pend Oreille lakes** have miles and miles of shoreline with small coves, bays, and stream inflow points. Though each has popular beaches, you can find your own secluded spot within minutes of leaving the boat dock.

Dining and Lodging

Coeur d'Alene **Jimmy D's.** This comfortable downtown spot is a favorite of lo-
Dining cals, including several inn owners who have their food catered. Redbrick walls decorated with art, candlelit tables, and a small

bar forge a bistrolike atmosphere. The menu is uncomplicated but well done: pastas, steaks, chicken, and fish. There is also a strong selection of wines, perhaps because Jimmy D's runs a wine store across the street. *320 Sherman Ave., tel. 208/664–9774. Reservations accepted. D, MC, V. Moderate.*

Hudson's Hamburgers. When they say hamburgers, they mean it. It's burgers, ham and cheese, or egg sandwiches, and that's it. These folks have been in business since 1907, and even local rivals have been forced to admit that Hudson's basic burgers are the town favorites. Sit at the counter and watch how burgers used to be made. The most expensive item on the six-item menu is a double cheeseburger for $3.50. *207 Sherman Ave., tel. 208/664–5444. No credit cards. Closed for dinner and Sun., Mon. Inexpensive.*

Toro Viejo. Yes, you can get the real enchilada in northern Idaho. This family-run restaurant offers authentic Mexican food prepared hot and spicy. Mama Briseno cooks all the food, and the kids wait tables. It can get crowded in this new eatery, so consider a reservation. *117 N. 2nd St., tel. 208/667–7676. Reservations accepted. MC, V. Inexpensive.*

T.W. Fisher's Brewpub. Fisher's microbrewery offers the best beer made in Idaho, along with a solid menu of burgers, chicken, salads, and other bar food. The pub is a lively place, with sports on TV, a wood and brass U-shaped bar, and a mainly young crowd. Brewery tours are given at 1:30 and 5:30 daily. *204 N. 2nd St., tel. 208/664–2739. AE, D, MC, V. Inexpensive.*

Dining and Lodging **Coeur d'Alene Resort.** Since its re-creation in 1986, the resort has become a favorite getaway for people in the Pacific Northwest. Construction of the tall modern tower was controversial, but its effect has been mitigated somewhat by the long floating boardwalk around the marina. Inside, the lobby area is stuffed with small eateries and shops. The restaurant, **Beverly's**, sits atop the tower and serves up commanding views of the lake as well as primarily Continental cuisine and a broad wine selection. Standard rooms, especially in the former motel section, are small, with very basic amenities dating from the 1960s; more expensive tower rooms are more spacious. A concierge service can arrange a wide range of activities, from horseback riding to mountain-bike rentals. In winter, buses to Silver Mountain cost $15, and ski packages are available. *2nd and Front Sts., 83814, tel. 208/765–4000 or 800/826–2390. Restaurant: reservations advised; dress: jacket and tie or upscale casual. 338 rooms. Facilities: restaurant, café, espresso/pastry bar, 2 lounges, indoor pool, weight room, game areas, shops. AE, D, DC, MC, V. Expensive.*

Lodging **Clark House on Hayden Lake.** This giant house, half hidden in
★ the trees across the street from Hayden Lake, is a B&B on steroids. The structure was built in 1910 by F. Lewis Clark, an eccentric millionaire, as a copy of one of Kaiser Wilhelm's palaces. By the late 1980s, the local fire department was ready to torch it for practice. Two local B&B operators wanted to buy it but were scared off by the massive restoration required. In stepped Monty Danner, his partners, and nearly $1 million in restoration funds. The result is a giant wedding cake of a place with wide-open rooms, an art deco feel, hardwood floors in public areas, and an expansive walled garden. The luxurious guest suites all have queen or king beds, three have fireplaces, and three overlook the garden or a small cedar forest. A formal, four-course breakfast is served, and an on-site chef has begun

full dinner service. *E. 4550 S. Hayden Lake Rd., Hayden Lake 83835, tel. 208/772–3470. 5 suites. Facilities: dining room, garden. AE, D, DC, MC, V. Expensive.*

Anderson's Country Cabin. Frank and Katie Anderson's place is a little more upscale than the name implies. Frank, a builder by trade, has transformed a traditional log house into a B&B with two upstairs suites. A separate log cabin contains another room and an upstairs loft perfect for kids. Both are decorated with Old West antiques, wood-burning stoves, and Native American crafts. It's on a wooded hillside near hiking and mountain-biking trails, about 1 mile from Coeur d'Alene Lake and 5 miles from the center of town. Full breakfast is served. *E. 6495 Sunnyside Rd., 83814, tel. 208/667–2988. 3 rooms. Facilities: dining room. MC, V. Moderate–Expensive.*

The Warwick Inn. This wood frame house, on a quiet street near the Ft. Sherman grounds, a block from the lakefront and a quarter mile from town center, was built about 1900. Rooms are stuffed with lace, floral fabrics, and country French antiques, and all are immaculate. Bonnie Warwick's breakfasts are enormous affairs, usually featuring local fare such as huckleberry waffles. Wine and snacks are served in the afternoon, and each room has sherry. *303 Military Dr., 83814, tel. 208/765–6565. 3 rooms (2 share bath). Facilities: breakfast room. MC, V. Moderate–Expensive.*

Lewiston
Dining

Bojack's. Frankly, the pickings are slim for good dining spots in Lewiston, but Bojack's, located downtown, is renowned locally for good steaks, spaghetti, and salads. From the outside it doesn't look like much more than a dark lounge, but inside, it's, umm, a dark lounge with a restaurant added on. *311 Main St., tel. 208/746–9532. AE, MC, V. Closed for lunch. Moderate.*

Dining and Lodging

Sacajawea Motor Inn. The basic motel-type rooms are clean, quiet, and a good bargain. Also, lots of locals eat at the attached restaurant, **The Helm,** because they know exactly what to expect: good, reliable, simple food for breakfast, lunch, or dinner. It is much like a Denny's with its counter and vinyl booths. The menu carries steaks, burgers, chops, chicken, pancakes, and a variety of sandwiches. *1824 Main St., 83501, tel. 208/746–1393 or 800/333–1393. 90 rooms. Facilities: outdoor pool, spa. AE, D, MC, V. Inexpensive–Moderate.*

Lodging

Ramada Inn. On the east side of town, this is as dependable as most other links in the national chain. It's often used for local meetings. *621 21st St., 83501, tel. 208/799–1000 or 800/232–6730. 134 rooms. Facilities: restaurant, lounge, disco, indoor pool, spa. AE, D, MC, V. Moderate–Expensive.*

McCall
Dining

The Pancake House. At the south edge of town, this breakfast spot has become a skiers' favorite thanks to its massive pancakes. It offers counter or table service, but you may have a short wait since everybody in McCall seems to eat here. *201 N. 3rd St., tel. 208/634–5849. MC, V. Closed for dinner. Inexpensive.*

Dining and Lodging

The Shore Lodge. Thanks to its lakefront location, the lodge has become almost synonymous with McCall. The interior is decorated with lots of hunter green, dark wood, and plaid upholstery—an English hunting lodge moved to Idaho. In the public areas, the theme works well, but some guest rooms painted with dark green ceilings can feel almost cavelike. Lakefront suites are large, with high ceilings and excellent views, whereas street-side units are like small motel rooms. In keeping with the lodge's mood, **The Narrows,** its restaurant, has chandeliers made of intertwined antlers, burled-wood furniture, and a dramatic view of the lake. Game selections include elk, venison, and duck, and the sharp-cheddar and beer soup with red pepper and potato is warming and smooth. Service is friendly, but some diners may feel the restaurant is overreaching its grasp. In summer, there is outdoor lakefront dining. *501 W. Lake St., 83638, tel. 208/634–2244 or 800/657–6464. Restaurant: reservations advised; dress: jacket and tie or upscale casual; closed for lunch. 117 rooms. Facilities: restaurant, café, lounge, hot pool, sauna, workout room, gift shop. AE, D, MC, V. Restaurant: Expensive. Lodge: Moderate–Expensive.*

Lodging **Hotel McCall.** This hybrid between a hotel and a B&B is in the center of town. The building, constructed in 1939, is more attractive outside than in. Rooms (and prices) vary widely; six are small, dark, and share a bath, while others are almost grand and have lots of light and antique furnishings. A Continental breakfast is included. *3rd and Lake Sts., Box 1778, 83638, tel. 208/634–8105. 22 rooms (6 share bath). Facilities: dining room, parlor, sun deck, garden patio. AE, MC, V. Moderate–Expensive.*

Riggins **The Lodge at Riggins Hot Springs.** This lodge, named for hot
Lodging springs that have been harnessed into pools on the bank of the
★ Salmon River, is just over 10 miles upriver from Riggins along a narrow, winding road. Inside, Western antiques and Native American crafts abound, and a sitting room is dominated by a large rock fireplace. Rooms feature pine paneling and wooden bed frames. Full country breakfasts, snack lunches, and gourmet dinners, such as lamb in raspberry sauce, are included. Kate Bradbury, a novice innkeeper, already knows how to do it right. The lodge works with Exodus outfitters, owned by Bradbury's brother, to create package excursions for hunters, anglers, and rafters. *Box 1247, 83549, tel. 208/628–3785. 10 rooms. Facilities: dining room, sitting room, pool, outdoor hot pools, sauna, Jacuzzi, billiards. MC, V. Expensive.*

Salmon River Motel. The rooms are clean, comfortable, and spare, but they offer TVs and sounds of the river. One of Riggins's four restaurants is on site. *1203 U.S. 95, 83549, tel. 208/628–3231. 16 rooms. Facilities: restaurant. MC, V. Inexpensive.*

Sandpoint **The Bistro.** Nouvelle cuisine in a converted auto-repair garage
Dining may sound improbable, but Al and Kelly Czap, who began this
★ bistro after tiring of local offerings, pull it off. Now they serve salmon in a light cream sauce as well as other fresh fish, chicken, and pasta. The wine list is small but discriminating. *1st and Pine Sts., tel. 208/265–2260. Reservations advised. MC, V. Closed for lunch and Sun., Mon. Moderate.*

The Garden Restaurant. This restaurant overlooking Lake Pend Oreille has been the Sandpoint standard since 1971, thanks to its wandering menu and greenhouse feel. Fare ranges from sandwiches, pastas, and steaks to sophisticated items like owner (and expert mushroom hunter) Richard Hollars's exotic mushroom soups. The wine list features West Coast and European varietals. Sunday brunch is very popular. *115 E. Lake St., tel. 208/263–5187. AE, D, MC, V. Moderate.*

Dining and Lodging **Connie's Best Western.** This may be the best-maintained motel
★ in Idaho. Rooms are spotless and tastefully decorated for a mo-

tel, with special touches like marbleized wallpaper. Most rooms come with a small refrigerator and two sinks. Family suites offer microwaves. A two-room Jacuzzi suite with a wet bar feels downright decadent. At **Connie's Café**, locals gather for breakfast at the counter, but the basic fare—pancakes, eggs, cereal, sandwiches (often big enough for two), steaks, and chicken—is also served in the café, cocktail lounge, or dining room with fireplace. *323 Cedar St., 83864, tel. 208/263–9581 or 800/528–1234. 54 rooms. Facilities: restaurant, outdoor pool, whirlpool, meeting/banquet rooms. AE, D, MC, V. Restaurant: Inexpensive. Motel: Moderate.*

Lodging **Green Gables Lodge.** At ski resorts you pay for location, and that's what this lodge 50 yards from Schweitzer's ski lift offers. There is a cozy, European-chalet feel in the public areas. Standard rooms are basic, motel-type units, while more deluxe rooms, like Jacuzzi suites, are bigger and offer microwave/wet-bar facilities. *Box 815, 83864, tel. 208/265–0257. 82 rooms. Facilities: 2 restaurants, 2 outdoor Jacuzzis, gift shop. AE, MC, V. Expensive.*

Quality Inn. The rooms are clean and pleasant, and units on the second floor have water views. *807 N. 5th Ave., 83864, tel. 208/263–2111 or 800/635–2534. 57 rooms. Facilities: restaurant, lounge, indoor pool, Jacuzzi. AE, D, MC, V. Inexpensive-Moderate.*

Super 8 Motel. There's nothing fancy here except a hot tub and free in-room coffee, but ski freaks who want to schuss their brains out and collapse at night without breaking a budget can stay at this reliable motel a mile north of town. *3245 U.S. 95 N, 83864, tel. 208/263–2210 or 800/843–1991. 60 rooms. Facilities: hot tub. AE, D, MC, V. Inexpensive.*

The Arts

A number of art and music festivals take place around northern Idaho (*see* Festivals and Seasonal Events in Essential Information, *above*).

Nightlife

Bars and Lounges Out of season, locals hunt and drink at the **Shortbranch Bar**
Riggins (U.S. 95), that rare establishment that gives drinks on credit to folks it knows (but please pay off the tab when you hit $100). Yes, it's a small-town dive, but a dive of the best kind.

Sandpoint The **Kamloops** (302 N. 1st St., tel. 208/263–6715) often leaves its mike open for blues and R&B musicians during the week, so you never know what you'll hear. On weekends, it has live rock and blues acts.

6 Montana

By Jim Robbins

Jim Robbins is a freelance writer and the author of Last Refuge— Environmental Showdown in the American West.

They call it Big Sky Country, but that's only part of the story; the land is big, too: The fourth-largest state stretches from North Dakota on the eastern side to Idaho on the west, 600-and-some-odd miles. From north to south, meanwhile, is a distance of some 400 miles. Not only is this a massive chunk of land, but it's also barely peopled. There are some 800,000 Montanans on all this ground, most of them in the major cities of Billings, Great Falls, Missoula, and Helena.

Montana is divided into two regions: the Rocky Mountain cordillera, which enters Montana in the northwest corner, taking up most of the western half of the state with timbered mountains and broad, grassy river valleys; and the plains and rolling hills to the east.

When night comes down, the skies are so dark and clear, the stars look like shiny glass beads suspended in a midnight sky. Northern lights shimmer like red and green curtains against velvet black skies and at other times scream across the full scope of the sky, ending only when the light of dawn erases them. If there is a factor that makes Montana so unusual, it is this light. Sometimes it shoots down from behind the clouds in long, radiant spotlight shafts, outlining the clouds in gold. There is a pink and orange light that falls gently like dust on Western slopes. A brilliant crimson takes over clouds at sunset. A fiery red and orange light of sunset in the desert Rockies illuminates the mountains so intensely, they appear to be lit from within like a glowing coal.

As intense as the sky is, so is the land teeming with wildlife. Bald eagles soar by the thousands and zero in on streams that seethe with spawning salmon. Cougars scream in the night. With manes flapping, wild horses gallop over red hillsides; thousands of elk move from the high country to the lowlands in the fall, and back to the high country come summer.

Long gone, but not forgotten, is some of Montana's most famous wildlife, whose skeletons remain as evidence of their greatness. Some of the richest dinosaur fossil beds in the world are found in the Rocky Mountain Front Range, where the mountains meet the plains. Recently, "thunder lizards," or dinosaur remains, have been found here, challenging the notion of the thunder lizards as lumbering cold-blooded beasts with the idea that they were warm-blooded animals that cared for their young.

Evidence of early human occupation dates back 12,000 years, and for generations before the Europeans arrived here, natives inhabited what is now Montana. In 1804–1805, the Lewis and Clark Expedition came through, seeking a transcontinental route to the Pacific and expanded trade relations with the natives.

Montana remained a remote place, however, through much of the 19th century and was valued for its rich fur trade in buffalo hides and beaver pelts. It was the discovery of gold at Gold Creek, Montana (between Missoula and Helena), in 1858 that began to change the region dramatically. After large gold strikes at Grasshopper Creek and Alder Gulch, miners came to the southwest mountains of Montana by the thousands. In 1862, the Territory of Montana was created. Pressure by miners and settlers for native lands in the area was unrelenting; inhabitants were forced from their traditional homelands and restricted to reservations. Major events in the West's Indian wars—the Battle of the Little Bighorn and the Flight of the Nez Percé—were played out in Montana, indelibly shaping the history of this region and the nation.

The state of Montana entered the Union in 1889, and its motto "Oro y Plata" (Gold and Silver) stands. With the landscape relatively untouched, history remains alive here. Ranching and farming, mining and logging are still the ways of life, and a small-town atmosphere and friendly outlook greet travelers even in the state's larger towns and cities. The natural splendor, the state's free-running rivers, vast mountain ranges, and large populations of wildlife make this what Montanan's call "The Last Best Place."

Essential Information

Visitor Information

Travel Montana (Dept. of Commerce, 1424 9th Ave., Helena 59620, tel. 406/444–2654 or 800/541–1447) provides information and free publications, including a comprehensive directory of lodgings, guest ranches, campgrounds, outfitters, and special events.

Tour Groups

Glacier Park, Inc. (tel. 406/226–5551) operates a fleet of vintage-1930s red-and-black buses that navigate along the Sun Highway. **Sun Tours** (tel. 406/226–9220) offers tours of Glacier from a Native Blackfoot perspective.

Package Deals for Independent Travelers

Bridger Bowl (tel. 406/587–2111), near Bozeman, offers ski packages, as does **Big Mountain** (tel. 406/862–3511), near Whitefish.

When to Go

Montana is most accessible in summer (June, July, and August), although the parks are inundated with tourists. To avoid the crowds, visit during the shoulder seasons of spring and fall. As for the winter months of December, January, and February, more and more people are taking advantage of Montana's cold-weather opportunities. Some park facilities remain open and, of course, ski areas are in full swing.

Climate Montana's climate can change dramatically with a passing storm front, but summer and fall are generally warm during the day and cool at night, with little rain. Summer temperatures range 75°–95°F; fall temperatures are 60°–75°F. Spring is less predictable. Regardless, the possibility of a winter storm is never far off at any time, even in the summer: Snow has been reported in Montana every month of the year.

Festivals and Seasonal Events

In mid-January, Great Falls hosts the **Montana Pro Rodeo Circuit Finals** (tel. 406/727–8115), which has a barbecue, rodeo dance, and auction in addition to the competition. The **"Race to the Sky" Dogsled Race** (tel. 406/442–2335), the longest event of its kind in the lower 48 (500 miles), goes along the Continental Divide and takes 4 to 5 days. There is viewing at check-in points.

The three-day **Whitefish Winter Carnival** (tel. 406/862–3501) with sidewalk sales, parades, dinners, and other activities, is held annually early in February.

In June, Helena has the **Montana Traditional Jazz Festival** (406/449–7969), five days in which Dixieland jazz bands from around the country play at various locations in downtown Helena.

The first full weekend of August is Bozeman's **Sweet Pea Festival** (tel. 406/586–4003), a four-day festival of music, children's art activities, Shakespeare in the park, dance workshops, and evening concerts. Also in August, the Crow Nation holds its annual **Crow Fair** (tel. 406/638–2228) in Crow Agency, an eight-day celebration featuring parades, crafts displays, and a nightly rodeo.

In early October, Flathead Valley hosts the **Flathead International Balloon Festival** (tel. 800/543–3105 or 406/755–6100), which consists of activities throughout the valley, including a competition, games, and, of course, hot-air balloons.

In late October, Billings hosts the **Northern International Livestock Exposition** (tel. 406/256–2495), featuring a rodeo, horse and cattle shows and sales, art shows and a cowboy revue.

From mid-November through mid-December more than 400 eagles feed on spawning salmon below the Canyon Ferry Dam. The visitor center is staffed by volunteers who answer questions seven days a week during this time, and there are spotting scopes on weekends for the **Eagle Watch** (tel. 406/444–4720).

Towns throughout the state hold **Christmas strolls** and other holiday activities during December. Contact Travel Montana for details.

What to Pack

Bring clothes for all kinds of weather: In summer, you may find yourself in shorts and a T-shirt one day and in heavily insulated foul-weather gear the next. Layered clothing is a good idea, as is sound footwear for walking over wet, uneven terrain. Rain gear is also a must, since thunderstorms can develop at any time. Also, don't forget to bring insect repellent.

Traveling with Children

In the past several years, resorts have latched on to the family market, providing day care and children's programs. These facilities began primarily with the ski resorts, but most run year-round. The national parks are a great place to take children because of the family-oriented educational programs they now offer. However, some park activities may not be appropriate for children, who would be required to hike long distances or even climb steep terrain.

Hints for Travelers with Disabilities

Since the passing of the ADA, attractions in Montana have been working to become wheelchair accessible. Areas and activities previously inaccessible to people with mobility or other impairments may now be more accommodating, but your best bet is to call ahead to be sure changes have been implemented.

The **Montana Independent Living Project,** or MILP (38 SW Chance Gulch, Helena, 59601, tel. 406/442–5755), is a non-profit agency that provides assistance to Montanans with disabilities. Though it's not a travel promotion agency, MILP can answer travelers' questions. There are similar organizations in other parts of the state: **Summit Independent Living Center** (1280 S. 3rd St. W, Missoula, 59801, tel. 406/782–1632); **North Central Independent Living Services** (104 2nd St. S, Great Falls, 59405, tel. 406/452–9834); and **Living Independently for Today and Tomorrow,** or **LIFT** (1925 Grand Ave., Suite 104, Billings, 59102, tel. 406/259–5981).

For information about accessible lodging at **Glacier National Park,** call tel. 406/226–5551 (May–Sept.) or tel. 607/207–6000 (Oct.–Apr.); for information on accessible trails and activities call Dennis Holden (tel. 406/888–5441; 406/888–5790 TDD). **Yellowstone National Park** (tel. 307/344–2021) has an accessibility coordinator.

Hints for Older Travelers

The altitude in much of western Montana is over 3,500 feet; some people may suffer altitude sickness, causing them to be short of breath or dizzy. Give yourself a little time to get used to higher elevations by not overexerting yourself.

Getting Around Montana

By Plane Billings's **Logan Field International Airport** is the largest in the state and is serviced by Continental (tel. 800/525–0280), Delta/SkyWest (tel. 800/221–1212), Northwest (tel. 800/225–2525), and United (tel. 800/241–6522). **Gallatin Field Airport,** just outside Bozeman, **Glacier International Airport** in Kalispell, and **Johnson Bell Airport** in Missoula are other major facilities in the state.

By Car Going east to west, I–94 runs from the North Dakota border and into I–90 near Billings, where it becomes I–90 all the way to the Idaho border. Interstate 90, meanwhile, comes up from Wyoming to join I–94. From north to south, I–15 comes into southern Montana from Idaho, and runs through Dillon, Butte, Helena, and Great Falls on its way to the Canadian border.

By Train Amtrak's *Empire Builder* (tel. 800/USA–RAIL) runs east-west across Montana's Highline, the most northern part of the state. Major stops along the route, which parallels Highway 2, include Havre, Shelby, Glacier National Park, and Whitefish.

By Bus **Greyhound** (tel. 800/231–2222) services the southern part of the state. **Rimrock Stages** (tel. 406/549–2339) runs regular bus service between Missoula, Bozeman, and Billings.

Shopping

Montana is the place to stop for everything from fine cowboy boots to Western hats to handmade saddles. There are also some unique finds here, such as "turd bird," figures made from horse manure; or a Frisbee shaped like a cowpat.

Sports and the Outdoors

Montana is very fitness-oriented, as are most of the Rockies states. Cycling, hiking, fishing, and skiing opportunities abound, and outfitters are available for almost every sport.

This state is home to almost 1,000 species of animals, from deer to dippers, mountain lions to moose. The **Montana Department of Fish, Wildlife and Parks** (1420 E. 6th Ave., Helena 59620, tel. 406/444–2535; cost: $5) publishes the *Montana Wildlife Viewing Guide*, keyed to sites throughout the state marked with an icon that represents a pair of binoculars. These signs along the highway indicate 100 of the best places to see some of the state's wildlife.

Camping   Some 30% of Montana's land is publicly owned, and there is camping on much of it—in national forests and parks. The Montana state highway map, which is free from gas stations, hotels, and Travel Montana (*see* Visitor Information, *above*), lists many of the campgrounds. The regional office of the U.S Forest Service (Aerial Fire Dept., 5765 Hwy. 10 W, Box 6, Airport Terminal, Missoula 59802, tel. 406/329–4934) or any of the district offices around the state can provide information on camping in Montana's forests.

Cycling   For information on cycling in the state, contact **Bikecentennial** (tel. 406/721–1776 or 406/721–8719).

Fishing   Montana has the best rainbow, brown, and brook trout fishing in the country. The Yellowstone, Missouri, Madison, Beaverhead, Gallatin, and Bighorn rivers are the cream of the crop, and there are numerous lakes and small streams. State law says that all land along rivers to the high-water mark is publicly owned and access is guaranteed. Montana has numerous outfitters who can take you fishing for a day or a week.

Licenses are required for fishing. An annual, nonresident season license costs $45 and is good until the end of February of the season it was purchased. A two-day license is $15 for the first two days and $10 for every two days after that. For more information, contact the **Montana Department of Fish, Wildlife, and Parks** (1420 E. 6th Ave., Helena 59601, tel. 406/444–2535).

Golf   There are more than 70 public and private golf courses all over the state of Montana. The season is short, running from mid-May to October. Chambers of commerce in most cities can give you information on nearby courses.

Hiking and Backpacking   Hiking opportunities abound in Montana, almost anywhere you travel. Many of the trails involve arduous climbing, changeable weather, and wild animals: It's best to know what you are getting into before you go. *The Hiker's Guide to Montana*, by Bill Schneider, offers a lot of useful, basic information, and is available from most bookstores.

Spectator Sports

Baseball The **Billings Mustangs,** the **Butte Copper Kings,** the **Great Fall Dodgers,** and the **Helena Brewers** are major-league farm teams that play in June and July. Call the chamber of commerce in each city for information.

Rodeo Every city and most towns in Montana have a summer rodeo. Check with the chamber of commerce in each city.

National Parks

Montana has more than its share of parks. All of **Glacier** and a little of **Yellowstone National Park** (*see* Chapter 8, Wyoming) are in Montana. The **Little Bighorn Battlefield National Monument,** where George Armstrong Custer met his fate, and the **Big Hole National Battlefield,** where the Nez Percé fought one of their most ferocious battles with the U.S. cavalry, are also found here.

Dining

No matter where you eat in Montana, dress is casual. Leave your ties at home. Good ethnic cuisine is a rarity, but beef and wild game are available at most restaurants. For Dining rates *see* the Towns and Country chart in Chapter 1, Essential Information.

Lodging

Montana's lodging falls generally into two categories: historic hotels and bed-and-breakfasts, and newer motels along commercial strips. For Lodging rates *see* the Towns and Country chart in Chapter 1, Essential Information. Unless otherwise noted, hotel rooms have private baths.

Billings to Helena

Interstate 90, near Billings, travels through much of the heart of Montana, including the grasslands, foothills, and full-blown mountain ranges. Highway 287, which loops through Helena, affords a tour of Montana's historic capital.

Important Addresses and Numbers

Tourist Information Local tourism information is available from the Billings Chamber of Commerce (Box 31177, Billings 59107, tel. 406/245–4111); Bovey Restorations, Inc. (Box 338, Virginia City, 59755, tel. 406/843–5331 or 800/648–7588); Bozeman Convention and Visitors Bureau (Box B, Bozeman 59715, tel. 406/587–2111 or 800/228–4224); Helena Chamber of Commerce (201 E. Lyndale, Helena 59601, tel. 406/442–4120 or 800/743–5362); Livingston Chamber of Commerce (212 W. Park St., Livingston 59047, tel. 406/222–0850); Miles City Chamber of Commerce (901 Main St., Miles City 59301, tel. 406/232–2890); and Red Lodge Chamber of Commerce (Box 998, Red Lodge 59068, tel. 406/446–1718).

Emergencies For **police, ambulance,** or **other emergencies,** dial 911. The **Montana Highway Patrol** can be reached at 800/525–5555.

Emergency Rooms Area hospitals with emergency rooms include **Billings Deaconess Medical Center** (Box 31000, Billings 59107, tel. 406/657–4000); **Bozeman Deaconess Medical Center** (915 Highland Blvd., Bozeman 59715, tel. 406/585–5000); and **Helena St. Peter's Community Hospital** (2475 Broadway, Helena 59601, tel. 406/442–2480).

Arriving and Departing by Plane

Airports and Airlines **Logan Field International Airport** is the largest in the state and is serviced by **Continental** (tel. 800/525–0280), **Delta** (tel. 800/221–1212), **Northwest** (tel. 800/225–2525), and **United** (tel. 800/241–6522). Farther west, **Gallatin Field Airport** is also serviced by **Delta, Continental,** and **Northwest,** as well as **SkyWest** (tel. 800/453–9417). Butte is served by the **Bert Mooney Airport.**

Arriving and Departing by Car, Train, and Bus

By Car Use I–90 for Billings, Livingston, Bozeman, and Butte. U.S. 89 and U.S. 212 link this region with Yellowstone. Interstate 15 passes through Helena.

By Train **Amtrak's** (tel. 406/226–4452) *Empire Builder* stops daily in Havre, Matta, and Whitefish.

By Bus **Intermountain Transportation Co.** has buses that stop in Helena (tel. 406/442–5860) and Butte (tel. 406/723–3287). **Greyhound** (tel. 800/231–2222) and **Rimrock Stages** (tel. 406/442–5860) serve Billings and Bozeman. In summer, **Karst Stage** (tel. 406/586–8567 or 800/332–0504) runs between Bozeman, Livingston, Billings, and Yellowstone.

Getting Around

Public transportation in Montana is basically limited to the options previously listed (*see* Arriving and Departing, *above*). Renting a car is the only effective way to follow the Exploring tours.

Guided Tours

Orientation **Karst Stage** (*see* Arriving and Departing by Bus, *above*), in Bozeman, does group tours of the state and one-day tours of Yellowstone National Park for individuals.

Exploring Billings to Helena

Numbers in the margin correspond to points of interest on the Montana map.

This 460-mile tour runs from the high plains of eastern Montana along the meandering Yellowstone River and finally into the timber-draped mountains of the West and the state capital, Helena. As you drive east along the interstate, the landscape will get larger and larger. Give the trip at least three or four days.

❶ This tour begins in **Billings,** the regional capital of the coal and oil industry, whose population of 100,000 makes it not only the largest city in Montana but also the largest city for 500 miles in any direction. The "Magic City" was developed with the coming of the railroad in 1882, and named after one of its board of direc-

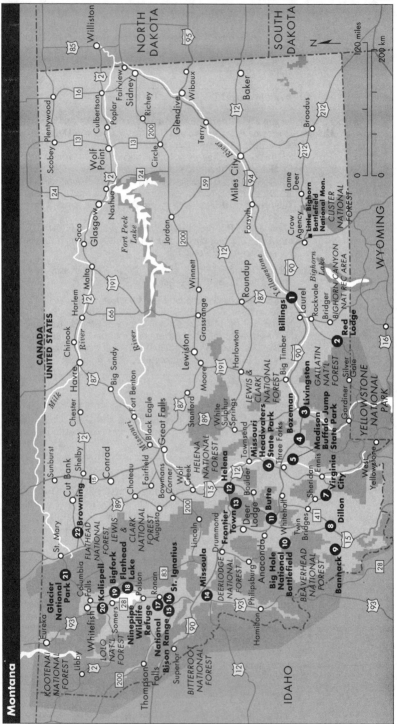

Montana

tors Frederick Billings. Billings is situated in the middle of the rolling plains of eastern Montana, beneath what are known as rimrocks—buckskin-colored cliffs The Bighorn Mountains are about an hour's drive south and offer hiking, fishing, camping, and all kinds of recreation.

The inspiring **Moss Mansion,** at 3rd and Division Streets, was built in 1903 for businessman P. B. Moss by Dutch architect Henry Hardenbergh (designer of the original Waldorf-Astoria Hotel in New York City). It still contains many of the elaborate original furnishings, ranging in style from Moorish to Art Nouveau Empire. *914 Division St., tel. 406/256–5100. Admission: $5 adults, $4 senior citizens, $3 children. Open Labor Day– May, Mon.–Sat. 10–5, Sun. 1–3; June–Labor Day, daily 1–3. Group tours by appointment.*

A worthwhile attraction that offers insight into the history and culture of the Yellowstone River region is the **Western Heritage Center,** located on the corner of 29th and Montana Avenues. Its four galleries feature antique clothing and photographs, crafts, and art pertinent to the area. *2822 Montana Ave., tel. 406/256–6809. Admission free. Open Tues.–Sat. 10–5, Sun. 1–5.*

From the Western Heritage Center go to North 27th Street and 4th Avenue—in the heart of downtown—to the **Yellowstone Art Center** in the original county jail. Its five galleries hold the best collection of contemporary art in Montana, including works by regional and nationally known artists living in the west. *401 N. 27th Ave., tel. 406/256–6804. Admission free. Open Memorial Day–Labor Day, Tues.–Sun. 10–5; Thursday 10–8.*

Time Out Have a bowl of black-bean chili at **Café Jones** (2712 2nd Ave., tel. 406/259–7676), a small downtown bistro. The chrome tables and unusual lamps are reminiscent of the 1950s. Try the special coffee drinks.

Just a few miles east of town, off I–90, is **Pictograph Cave,** a state monument with ochre, black, and white early drawings of humans, tepees, guns, and wildlife. *Follow signs from Lockwood exit of I–90, tel. 406/855–0255. Admission: 50¢ per person or $3 per car. Open May–Oct., daily 8–7:30.*

Take U.S. 212 from Billings and travel 60 miles southwest to **❷ Red Lodge.** Nestled against the foot of the pine-draped Pryor Mountains, Red Lodge was named for a band of Cheyenne who marked their settlement with paintings of red earth. It became a town in the late 1880s when the Northern Pacific Railroad laid tracks here to bring coal back to Billings. At one time, "Liver Eatin'" Jeremiah Johnson was sheriff here. Now the historic little burg is listed on the National Register of Historic Places and is in the process of becoming a full-blown resort town, complete with a ski area, trout fishing, horseback riding, and a golf course. Each August, the town holds a nine-day **Festival of Nations** to celebrate the numerous ethnic heritages of people who worked in the mines nearby.

From Red Lodge, you can continue south on U.S. 212 over the precipitous **Beartooth Pass,** which winds its way through lush alpine country, to the "back door" of Yellowstone National Park in Wyoming. The highway is usually open from May to September, but bad weather can close it at any time.

To continue the original tour, take Route 78 back to I–90, and follow the interstate west to the town of **Livingston.** The stunning mountain backdrop to this town was once Crow territory, and a chief called Arapooish said about it: "The Crow country is good country. The Great Spirit has put it in exactly the right place. When you are in it, you fare well; when you go out of it, you fare worse."

The railroads brought white people to settle, and Livingston, along the banks of the beautiful Yellowstone River, was built to service the railroad. The railroad has been replaced by small businesses that cater to tourists, but the town of 12,000 has retained much of its turn-of-the-century flavor. Perhaps you'll recognize it from Robert Redford's movie *A River Runs Through It* (adapted from the book of the same title by Norman Maclean), which was filmed here.

From the interstate take the second exit, turn right, and come through town on Park Street to the **Northern Pacific Depot,** an Italian villa-style structure with mosaic trim, terrazzo floor, and wrought-iron ticket windows. The museum now houses displays on Western and railroad history, and artwork by artists from the region and around the country. *200 W. Park St., tel. 406/222–2300. Admission: $3 adults, $2 senior citizens and children, $8 families. Open mid-May–mid-Oct., Mon.–Sat. 9–5, Sun. 1–5.*

Two blocks away, on the north side of town and housed in a historic schoolhouse, is the **Park County Museum,** which features an old caboose, a sheep wagon, a stagecoach, and other pioneer memorabilia. *118 W. Chinook St., tel. 406/222–3506. Admission: $2 adults, $1 senior citizens and children 6–17. Open June–Labor Day, daily 12–5 and 7–9.*

Just south of town, the **Yellowstone River** comes roaring down the Yellowstone Plateau, just north of Yellowstone Park, and flows through Paradise Valley. Primitive, public campsites (available on a first-come, first-served basis) and fishing access sites are situated at various places along the river, which is especially popular for trout fishing, rafting, and canoeing.

Get back on I–90 and drive about 25 miles west of Livingston to **Bozeman,** a college town of 25,000. In 1864, a trader named John Bozeman led his wagon train through this valley en route to the booming gold fields at Virginia City and throughout southwest Montana. For several years it was the site of Fort Ellis, established to protect settlers making their way west along the Bozeman Trail, which extended into Montana Territory. Recently the city has become a recreation capital for everything from trout fishing to white-water river rafting to backcountry mountain biking. Arts and culture have also flowered here in the home of the state's second-largest university. Each April, for example, members of New York's Metropolitan Opera stage a performance. The town has a strong Western heritage, and each June the **College National Rodeo Finals** (tel. 406/994–4221) are held at the Montana State University (MSU) fieldhouse.

At the southeast corner of the campus is the inspirational **Museum of the Rockies,** which celebrates the history of the Rockies region, including southern Montana. Eclectic exhibits include everything from prehistory to pioneers and a planetarium. There are dinosaur displays, complete with bones and eggs dug up in Montana, and a room where visitors can watch workers clean dinosaur fossils. Children love the hands-on science activities in the Martin Discovery Room and the Tensley Homestead, with home-crafts demonstrations including butter churning, weaving, and blacksmithing. *S. 7th Ave. and Kagy Blvd., tel. 406/994-2251. Admission: $5 adults, $3 youths 13-18, $2 children 5-12. Open Memorial Day-Labor Day, daily 9-9; Labor Day-Memorial Day, Mon.-Sat. 9-5, Sun. 12:30-5.*

Continue west on I-90 for about 20 miles to the Logan exit; from that exit you'll turn onto a gravel road. Follow signs south **❺** for about 7 miles to the **Madison Buffalo Jump State Park.** Within the park is a preserved cliff where Plains natives stampeded bison to their deaths more than 2,000 years ago. An interpretive center explains how the technique enabled Native Americans to gather food and hides. *Tel. 406/994-4062. Admission: 50¢ per person or $3 per vehicle (includes admission to Missouri Headwaters State Park). Open year-round, daily dawn-dusk.*

Travel a few more miles along I-90, exit at Three Forks, and **❻** drive north about 3 miles to the **Missouri Headwaters State Park,** a National Historic Landmark. This is where the Madison, Jefferson, and Gallatin rivers come together to form the mighty Missouri River. Lewis and Clark named the three forks after Secretary of the Treasury Albert Gallatin, Secretary of State James Madison, and President Thomas Jefferson. There are historical exhibits, interpretive signs, picnic sites, hiking trails, and camping. *406/994-4042. Admission: $3 per vehicle (included in Madison Buffalo Jump State Park admission, see above). Open year-round, daily dawn-dusk.*

Take U.S. 287 south from the state park and at Ennis turn onto **❼** Montana Route 287 (a state road) heading west to **Virginia City,** and its smaller neighbor, Nevada City. These remnants of Montana's frontier days are two of the most unusual attractions the state has to offer. When miners stampeded into the state in the 1860s, one of the places where the diggings were rich was in Virginia City's Alder Gulch; the city prospered and eventually became the capital of Montana Territory. The success of the city enticed criminals, who held up miners; in turn, vigilance committees—eager to maintain order—grew, held lightning-fast trials, and strung up the bad guys. Some of the graves of those hung by vigilantes remain atop a hill overlooking town. Today Virginia City is a real tourist attraction where you can tour town on an old-time fire truck, walk along a boardwalk, wander through stores stocked with 19th-century goods, and ride a narrow-gauge railroad.

Nevada City has a smaller collection of historic buildings, a music hall with fascinating coin-operated instruments, and all sorts of restaurants and shops.

From Nevada City, take Route 287 north to Route 41 south to **❽** **Dillon.** (More direct routes involve unpaved and unmarked roads.) Dillon is a capital of southwestern Montana's ranch country and was a shipping point for cattle and sheep on the Union Pacific Railroad. There is hiking and mountain biking in the nearby Ruby and Tendoy mountains, and the fishing on the Beaverhead River is very good. The **Beaverhead County Museum** exhibits Native American artifacts, ranching and mining memorabilia, a homesteader's cabin, mining equipment and agricultural artifacts, and a boardwalk imprinted with the area's ranch brands. *15 S. Montana St., tel. 406/683–5027. Admission free. Open Memorial Day–Labor Day, weekdays 10–8, weekends 1–5; Labor Day–Memorial Day, weekdays 10–12, weekends 1–5.*

Follow Route 278 out of Dillon and watch for a sign just before Badger Pass. Take the well-maintained gravel road for 3 miles to **Bannack,** Montana's first territorial capital. Today the town, which is protected as a state park, is a good example of a frontier boom town, and is fortunately off the beaten tourist path. Montana's vigilantes were active here, and one of the most notorious was Henry Plummer, the sheriff, himself. The gallows on which he was hanged still stands in Bannack. Rumors persist that Plummer's stash of stolen gold was hidden somewhere in the mountains near here and never found.

Return to Route 278 and take it about 40 miles northwest to Route 43. Go west on Route 43 to **Big Hole National Battlefield,** where part of one of the West's greatest and most tragic stories played out. In 1877, Nez Percé warriors in central Idaho killed some white settlers, claiming it was retribution for earlier killings by whites. The Nez Percé, knowing the army would make no distinction between the guilty and innocent, fled—the beginning of a 1,700-mile odyssey. They engaged 10 separate U.S. commands in 13 battles and skirmishes. One of the fiercest of those was here at Big Hole Battlefield, where both sides suffered serious losses. From here, the Nez Percé headed toward Yellowstone.

A visitor center overlooks the meadows of the Big Hole, which remain as they were at the time of the battle. Tepee poles erected by the park service mark the site of the Nez Percé village and serve as haunting reminders of what transpired here.

Double back along Route 43 and pick up I–15 north to its junction with I–90. The two roads run together into the city of **Butte.** Coined the "Richest Hill on Earth," Butte was once a wealthy and rollicking copper-, gold-, and silver-mining town. The underground copper mines were dug up in the 1950s, creating the **Berkeley Open Pit Mine,** which extends more than a mile across and reaches 1,800 feet deep. A viewing platform allows you to look into the now-abandoned, mammoth pit. *Continental Dr., tel. 406/782–8117. Admission free. Open daily 8AM–9PM, weather permitting.*

Adjacent to the pit is downtown Butte, a National Historic Landmark area with numerous ornate buildings, reminiscent of the Old West days. While meandering through the streets, consider this: Butte has the dubious distinction of being the largest toxic waste site in the country—thanks to the old mining wastes.

Keeping watch over the city—as seen from the east ridge of the Rocky Mountains—is **Our Lady of the Rockies,** a 90-foot-tall, 80-ton statue of the Virgin Mary, situated on the Continental Divide and lit up at night. For tours, stop by the visitor center. *434 N. Main St., tel. 406/782–1221. Admission: $10 adults, $9* *senior citizens and youths 13–17, $5 children 12–5. Open Sept.–Apr., daily 10–4, May–Aug., daily 9–5.*

From Butte, continue north on I–15 for about 65 miles to **Helena,** Montana's capital. This jewel of a town where the prairie meets the mountains started as a rowdy mining camp in 1864 and became a banking and commerce center in the nascent Montana Territory. With statehood came a fight between the town of Anaconda and Helena over which would be the capital. In a notoriously corrupt campaign in which both sides bought votes, Helena won. The iron ball of urban renewal robbed the town of much of its history, but Helena still has ornate brick and granite historic buildings along the Last Chance Gulch, of early mining fame. Some gambling is still legal in Montana—a legacy of frontier days.

Across from the state capitol, the **Montana Historical Society Museum** displays one of the most important collections of Western artist Charles M. Russell's work in its MacKay Gallery. Early black-and-white photos of Yellowstone National Park taken by F. Jay Haynes are on display in the Haynes Gallery. The expansive Montana Homeland exhibit, which features nearly 2,000 historical artifacts, documents, and photographs, gives visitors a thorough look at Montana from the time of the first Native settlers to the present. The venue also hosts special events and "family days" during the summer, including programs on folk music, Native American culture, and cowboys. Call ahead for information on upcoming events. *225 N. Roberts St., tel. 406/444–2694. Admission free. Open Memorial Day–Labor Day, weekdays 8–6, weekends and holidays 9–5; Labor Day–Memorial Day, weekdays 8–5, Sat. 9–5, closed Sun. and holidays.*

Out in front of the Historical Society Museum catch the *Last Chancer*, an hour-long tour train that threads through Helena's historic neighborhoods, from the stately miners' mansions on the west side to the site where four miners made their first discovery on the gulch. It runs from May until September on the half hour. *Tel. 406/442–4120. Admission: $3.50 adults, $3 senior citizens, $2.50 children 2–12.*

Walk a few blocks down Sixth Avenue to the center of historic downtown Helena. Ask at the Downtown Helena Office (121 N. Last Chance Gulch, tel. 406/442–9869) for **"The Heart of Helena,"** a self-guided walking tour of historic downtown. On the corner of Last Chance Gulch and Lawrence Street, the lobby of the **Norwest Bank** holds a gold collection featuring nuggets taken from area diggings. *350 N. Last Chance Gulch, tel. 406/447–2000. Admission free. Open weekdays 9:30–4.*

The **Holter Museum of Art,** a block off Last Chance Gulch, houses both permanent and changing exhibits of visual arts. The emphasis is on Montana artists, folk art, crafts, photography, painting, and sculpture. *12 E. Lawrence Ave., tel. 406/442–6400. Admission free. Open Memorial Day–Labor Day, Tues.–Sat. 10–5, Sun. noon–5; Labor Day–Memorial Day, Tues.–Sun. noon–5. Closed Mon.*

If you're tired of looking at attractions and want to stretch your legs, consider taking an hour-long hike to the top of **Mount Helena,** the centerpiece of the **Mount Helena City Park,** on the edge of town. From the summit, you'll have panoramic views of Helena, the Helena Valley, and the Rocky Mountains to the west. To reach the park, drive to the Adams Street parking lot on the city's west side or ask at the chamber of commerce (*see* Important Addresses and Numbers, *above*) for directions.

Time Out For an old-fashioned sweet treat, pull up a stool at the **Parrot,** a soda fountain and candy store built in the 1920s that sells everything from chocolate malts with homemade ice cream to hand-dipped chocolates. *42 N. Last Chance Gulch, tel. 406/442–1470. Open Mon.–Sat. 9–5:30.*

Fifteen miles west of town, atop the Continental Divide at McDonald Pass, is **Frontier Town,** a kitschy eccentric tourist attraction built in the 1950s. Frontier-style buildings handmade from huge trees and mammoth boulders are filled with reproduction and antique furnishings. Swager into the saloon and order a beer at the long bar cut from a single huge tree. There is also a good restaurant. *U.S. Hwy. 12, tel. 406/442–4560. Admission free. Open Apr.–Oct., daily 9 AM–10 PM.*

What to See and Do with Children

Frontier Town (*see* Exploring Billings to Helena, *above*).

The Montana Historical Society Museum (*see* Exploring Billings to Helena, *above*).

Museum of the Rockies (*see* Exploring Billings to Helena, *above*).

Off the Beaten Track

History buffs may want to travel on I–94 east from Billings for 145 miles to see some more of Montana's Old West. There you'll find the ranch town of **Miles City** (population 10,000), situated at the confluence of the cottonwood-lined Tongue and the Yellowstone rivers. The federal Treaty of 1868 said this would be native country "as long as the grass is green and the sky is blue." That promise changed, however, when gold was found in the Black Hills of South Dakota to the east, and white settlers streamed into this part of the world. Ranchers eventually took over, and in 1884, the last of the great herds of buffalo was slaughtered near here to make room for cattle. Ranching has been a way of life ever since.

In May, locals hold the **Bucking Horse Sale** (tel. 406/232–2890) a three-day event downtown, with a rodeo and a giant block party. The **Range Rider's Museum** is jammed to the rafters with saddles, chaps, spurs, guns, and other cowboy paraphernalia, some of it dating back to the days of the Open Range when cattlemen from Texas drove beeves here. *Exit 135 off I–94 to Old Hwy. 10 W, tel. 406/232–6146. Admission: $3.50 adults, 50¢ children. Open Apr.–Oct., daily 8–8.*

Sixty miles southeast of Billings, off I–90, is the **Little Bighorn Battlefield Monument,** on the Crow Indian Reservation. When the smoke cleared on June 25, 1876, neither Lieutenant Colonel George Armstrong Custer nor his 200 or so blue-shirted troopers were alive to tell the story of their meeting with several thousand Northern Plains natives on this rolling, windswept prairie along the Little Bighorn River. It was a Pyrrhic victory for the tribes; the loss would force the U.S government to redouble its efforts to clear them off the plains. Now a national monument, the site has a new interpretive display that includes material from recent archaeological excavations. The display explains what led to the momentous clash of two cultures and speculates on what might have happened during the battle. *Tel. 406/638–2621. Admission free. Open Memorial Day–Labor Day, daily 8–7:45; Sept.–Oct., daily 8–5; Nov.–Memorial Day, daily 8–4:30.*

Shopping

Specialty Stores
Art Galleries

Red Lodge's beauty has inspired artists, as evidenced by the many fine art galleries in town. Paintings, sculptures and works in other mediums can be found at the **Wishing Tree Gallery** (113 W. Callender St., tel. 406/222–7528), **Chatham Fine Art** (120 N. Main St., tel. 406/446–1601), the **Danforth Gallery** (106 N. Main St., tel. 406/222–6510), and the **Visions West Gallery** (104 N. Main St., tel. 406/222–0337).

Books

The floorboards creak as you walk through **Sax and Fryer's** (109 W. Callender St., Red Lodge, tel. 406/222–1421), an old-time bookstore specializing in Western literature. It also sells gifts.

Ceramics

Many of the nation's best ceramic artists come to work in residency at the **Archie Bray Foundation** (2521 Country Club Rd., Helena, tel. 406/443–3502). Wander between the antiquated beehive brick kilns on a self-guided walking tour and visit the gift shop, which sells energetic sculptures as well as functional plates and cups. The venue is open daily 9–5.

Home Furnishings

Kibler and Kirch (22 N. Broadway, Red Lodge, tel. 406/446–2802) sells lodgepole pine beds, cowboy pillows, antiques, and original artwork.

Western
Paraphernalia

Rand's Custom Hats (2205 1st Ave. N, Billings, tel. 406/259–4886 or 800/346–9815) creates cowboy hats for working cowboys as well as the celluloid variety and will make a felt fur hat exactly the size and shape of your head. Prices range from $200 to $2,000. They also produce custom leather carrying cases.

A charming little store in downtown Billings, **Stillwater Traders** (2821 2nd Ave. N, tel. 406/252–6211) specializes in the Western theme, corralling unique items such as nightlights shaped like trout, cowboy dishware, Western-style clothing, and themed toys and T-shirts.

Sports and the Outdoors

Canoeing/Rafting

Glacier Wilderness Guides and its affiliate **Montana Raft Company** (tel. 800/521–RAFT) lead trips through stomach-churning white water, and often combine the adventure with horseback riding or hiking.

Cycling

Backcountry Bicycle Tours of Bozeman (Box 4209, Bozeman, 59772, tel. 406/586–3556) offers touring all over the state. Old logging roads running through the mountains of western Montana and on national forest lands offer some of the best mountain biking in the state. Trail biking is not allowed in the national parks. For route information, call the **Helena National Forest** (tel. 406/449–5201).

Fishing

High Plains Outfitters of Helena (31 Division St., tel. 406/442–9671) offers guided trips on various rivers in Montana, including the Missouri, the Big Hole, and the Blackfoot, and wading on smaller rivers and streams.

Golf The **Red Lodge Golf Course** (828 Upper Continental St., tel. 406/446–3344) offers a beautiful view of the mountains. In Billings, try **Lake Hills** (1930 Clubhouse Way, tel. 406/252–9244).

Hiking and Backpacking **Wild Horizon Expeditions** (West Fork Rd., Darby 59829, tel. 406/821–3747) is a wilderness guide service that specializes in six–eight day backpack trips into some of Montana's remotest wild places, where you're not likely to see other people. Expert guides interpret the plants, wildlife, and geology.

Skiing *Cross-Country* This region of the state has a lot of opportunities for cross-country skiers, and the sport's popularity has grown immensely. One of the best Nordic ski places is the Big Sky resort's **Lone Mountain Guest Ranch** (U.S. Hwy. 191, between Bozeman and West Yellowstone, tel. 406/995–4644).

Downhill One of the nicest things about skiing in Montana is short lift lines. There are 25 miles of trails at **Red Lodge Mountain** (101 Ski Run Rd., tel. 406/446–2610), an hour south of Billings. Near Bozeman, **Bridger Bowl** (15795 Bridger Canyon Rd., tel. 406/587–2111) is a top-ranked ski area. There's a variety of terrain, from steep, rocky chutes to gentle slopes and meadows. **Big Sky Resort** (Box 1, Big Sky, tel. 800/548–4486), 45 miles from Bozeman, is a good, family resort with 55 miles of groomed trails.

Dining

Billings **Fuddruckers.** Although this is a national chain restaurant, the three sizes of burgers taste great and are made with quality beef that's cut and ground on the premises. Other menu items include hot dogs, salad, fish, and steak sandwiches. Children love this huge (seats 200) brightly lit place. *2011 Overland Ave. (near the King Ave. exit, off I–90), tel. 406/656–5455. No reservations. AE, DC, MC, V. Inexpensive.*
Jake's. This pleasant downtown fern bar features steaks, seafood, and an inspired salad bar. The dimly lit restaurant, decorated with brass and wood, can seat 130 guests. *2701 1st Ave. N, tel. 406/259–9375. Reservations advised. No credit cards. Closed Sun. Inexpensive.*

Bozeman ★ **John Bozeman's Bistro.** It may be small, but the menu—from hot seafood stir-fry and Cajun cookery to creative sandwiches and soups—is one of the best in the state. Bozeman's Bistro is also known for its setting in a National Historic Register building, with a brick interior and well-preserved wood floors. Located in bustling downtown Bozeman, the bistro isn't far from some good antiques and furniture shops. *242 E. Main St., tel. 406/587–4100. Reservations recommended. A, D, MC, V. Closed Sun. Inexpensive.*
Mackenzie River Pizza. Zesty gourmet pizzas featuring tomato or pesto sauces, sun-dried tomatoes, artichoke hearts, and more are baked in a brick oven before your eyes. Eat here in this bustling joint, or take it to go. *242 E. Main St., tel. 406/587–4100. No reservations. AE, MC, V. Inexpensive.*

Helena ★ **Great Rocky Mountain Oyster Company at Yacht Basin Marina.** Tucked away on Canyon Ferry Lake, 20 minutes from town, this restaurant remains a well-kept secret. Gourmet steaks and seafood are featured, and the panoramic view of the lake and surrounding hills provides a romantic setting. The more adventurous should try the Rocky Mountain oysters (bull testicles deep-fried in garlic and placed in an oyster shell to bake) and go all out with flaming bananas Foster (bananas flambayed at table, and served with rum, sugar, and vanilla ice cream). *7035 Canyon Ferry Rd., tel. 406/475–3125. Reservations advised on weekends. No credit cards. Inexpensive–Moderate.*

On Broadway. Wooden booths, discreet lighting, and brick walls contribute to the comfortable ambience at this Italian restaurant. Popular dishes include New York strip steak, scampi fra diablo (Scampi with mushrooms, peppers, spicy wine and tomato sauce), and chicken prosciutto. On Broadway is a nice place to chat, with a leisurely dining pace. *106 Broadway, tel. 406/443–1929. No reservations. AE, DC, MC, V. Closed Sun. Inexpensive.*

★ **Windbag Saloon & Grill.** This historic restaurant in the heart of downtown was a sporting house called Big Dorothy's until 1973, when a crusading county attorney forced Dorothy to close up shop. Now it's a family restaurant that serves burgers, quiche, and sandwiches for lunch and dinner. Inside the historic building is a bounty of cherry wood, highlighted by a dark green detail to give this place a cozy, public feel. It also has a large selection of imported beers, on tap and in bottles. *19 S. Last Chance Gulch, tel. 406/443–9669. Reservations accepted. AE, DC, MC, V. Closed Sun. for lunch. Inexpensive.*

Livingston **Livingston Bar and Grill.** Just across the main thoroughfare from this quiet, homey restaurant is the town's railway depot, where the trains once rolled in. The pleasant ambience inside, with lots of artwork and rustic details, matches the historic setting. Among the menu items are buffalo burgers, chicken sandwiches and seafood dishes including deep-sea trout and bass. *130 N. Main St., tel. 406/222–7909. Reservations advised. MC, V. Closed for dinner except Sun. Inexpensive.*

Red Lodge **17 Broadway.** This cozy, unpretentious little restaurant on Red Lodge's main street has an award-winning chef who offers casual gourmet cuisine. Try the campfire trout (pan-fried trout with rosemary-and-pecan breading) or shrimp akumal (shrimp sauteed in tequila). *17 Broadway, tel. 406/446–1717. Reservations accepted. AE, MC, V. Closed Mon. Memorial Day–Labor Day. Inexpensive.*

Townsend **Rosario's.** If this place looks like a converted gas station, that's
★ because it is. Don't let the decor fool you, though, as it's been turned into one of Montana's finest Italian restaurants. On the edge of the little Missouri River town of Townsend, between Bozeman and Helena, this is home to some of the tastiest veal and pasta dishes, pizza, and calzones on the east side of the Continental Divide. *316 N. Front St., 406/266–3603. Reservations recommended. No credit cards. Closed Mon.–Tues. Inexpensive–Moderate.*

Lodging

Big Timber **The Grand Hotel.** This is a renovated classic Western hotel in
★ the middle of downtown Big Timber—on I-90 between Billings and Livingston. The rooms are small, clean, and comfortable and furnished in antiques—the kind of accommodations you might find over the Longbranch Saloon in "Gunsmoke." A full breakfast is included in the daily room rate. *139 McLeod St.,*

59011, tel. 406/932–4459. 7 rooms, 2 with private bath. Facilities: dining room, saloon, banquet facilities. DC, MC, V. Inexpensive.

Billings **The Olive Hotel.** This turn-of-the-century accommodation has been well restored and now features a vintage Gus McRae Room, named after the character in *Lonesome Dove*, the television miniseries based on Larry McMurtry's popular novel about an 1880s cattle drive that ended in Miles City. In the large standard room is a brass bed and private bath with a pull-chain toilet. The hotel is in historic downtown, next to a city park. *501 Main St. 59301, tel. 406/232–2450 or 800/424–4777. 59 rooms, all with private bath. Facilities: restaurant. AE, D, DC, MC, V. Inexpensive.*

Ponderosa. Just down the street from the Radisson (*see below*) is this comfortable, more modern motel. All the rooms have carpets and are painted in pastel colors. There's a heated pool in the courtyard, surrounded by plenty of greenery. *2511 1st Ave. N, 59101, tel. 406/761–3410 or 800/528–1234. 130 rooms. Facilities: outdoor pool, spa, 24-hour café. AE, D, DC, MC, V. Inexpensive.*

Radisson Northern Hotel. This historic 1905 building in downtown Billings was destroyed by fire in 1940, then rebuilt. Although recently remodeled, it still provides a sense of the city's past. Rooms were recently redecorated and follow an American-West theme, with woven rugs, bedspreads, and a gaming table. Views are glorious. The massive fireplace is the centerpiece of a comfortable lobby—a common gathering place for guests and locals. *Broadway at 1st Ave. N, Box 1296, 59101, tel. 406/245–5121 or 800/221–2222. 160 rooms. Facilities: restaurant, lounge, gift shop. AE, D, DC, MC, V. Inexpensive.*

Bozeman **The Voss Inn.** This bed-and-breakfast occupies an elegant 1883
★ Victorian house and is lavishly furnished with antiques. Stop by the parlor for afternoon tea or to catch up on the news with other guests who drop in to watch TV or to chat. The knowledgable owners run day and overnight fishing trips to Yellowstone for interested guests. *319 S. Willson Ave, 59715, tel. 406/587–0982, 6 rooms. MC, V. Moderate.*

Gallatin Gateway Inn. Built in 1882 by the Milwaukee Railroad as a stopping-off point for visitors to Yellowstone National Park, this sumptuous inn remains conveniently situated, just 10 miles from town on U.S. 191, and 30 minutes from Big Sky Ski Resort. It did have its dog days, however, when it fell into disrepair and became a seedy bar that featured female Jell-O wrestling (honest). After a recent renovation, the inn has returned to its original glory, with a wonderful restaurant and an outdoor swimming pool. The uniquely furnished, contemporarily decorated rooms feature modern Western decor and are painted in soothing pastels. The bathrooms, with original tilework and brass fixtures, exude simple elegance. *Hwy. 191, Box 376, Gallatin Gateway 59730, tel. 406/763–4672. 35 rooms, including 3 2-room combos with shared bath; 29 rooms with private bath. Facilities: restaurant, outdoor pool, tennis courts. AE, DC, MC, V. Inexpensive–Moderate.*

Butte **Fairmont Hot Springs.** If you have children, you should bring
★ them to this resort near Anaconda and not far from Butte. Although it's not much as far as architecture goes, it's on beautiful property and has naturally heated indoor and outdoor swimming pools and a water slide in a beautiful setting. For

golfing enthusiasts, there's an 18-hole course on the grounds. *1500 Fairmont Rd., Gregson 59711, tel. 406/797–3241 or 800/ 443–2381. 153 rooms. Facilities: restaurant, coffee shop, lounge, gift shop, massage parlor, salon, tennis and volleyball courts, petting zoo. AE, D, DC, MC, V. Inexpensive.*

Helena **The Sanders Bed and Breakfast.** This three-story Victorian
★ mansion was built by Colonel Wilbur Sanders, the prosecuting attorney at some of the summary trials hosted by the Montana vigilantes. The colonel's rock collection is still in the front hall, and the B&B has retained his furnishings. Most of the rooms have beautiful views overlooking mountain-ringed downtown Helena, and the breakfasts are something to behold. *328 N. Ewing St. 59601, tel. 406/442–3309. 6 rooms with private, adjoining bath; 1 room with private bath down the hall. MC, V. Inexpensive.*

Livingston **Mountain Sky Guest Ranch.** Not only is this accommodation situated 30 miles north of lovely Yellowstone National Park, but it also rests in the middle of scenic Paradise Valley. This full-service guest ranch has riding, tennis, fishing, a heated pool, and a sauna. Seven-night bookings are arranged mid-June– Labor Day; there's a 3-night minimum during the low season. *Box 1128, 59715 , tel. 406/587–1244. 80-person occupancy in varying units; some with private bath. Facilities: Dining room, tennis courts, pool. No credit cards. Moderate.*

63 Ranch. This ranch, located 12 miles south of Livingston, is one of Montana's oldest, and rests on 2,000 acres of land. It has been a family-owned dude ranch by the present proprietors since 1929. A full range of activities is offered, from horseback riding to fishing to pack trips, but only 7-night (Sunday–Sunday) packages are offered. *Box 979A, 59047. 30-person occupancy in varying units; some with private bath. MC, V. Moderate.*

★ **The Murray Hotel.** In the old days, this hotel in downtown Livingston catered to early visitors to Yellowstone who came by train. It has been remodeled, and the simple, elegant dining room, now called the Winchester Café, is second to none. Rooms are modest and awaiting renovation, but they are clean and have the charm of another era. *201 W. Park St. 59047, tel. 406/222–1350. 43 rooms, 35 with private bath. Facilities: restaurant, lounge. AE, DC, MC, V. Inexpensive.*

Red Lodge **Pollard Hotel.** This landmark in the heart of Red Lodge's historic district was undergoing renovations at press time, but should be open by early 1994. Refurbishment should renew this building to its former glory. *2 N. Broadway, Box 1217, 59068, tel. 800/765–5273. Facilities: restaurant, lounge. AE, DC, MC, V. Inexpensive.*

Rock Creek Resort. This brand-new resort, just 4½ miles south of town on U.S. 212, is built along a babbling, rock-strewn creek and decorated in a native Southwestern motif. It has a wonderful restaurant—the Old Piney Dell—in a historic old cabin. The Continental cuisine features simple American, Mexican, and regional fare. *Rte. 2, Box 3500, 59068, tel. 406/446– 1111. 75 rooms. Facilities: restaurant, lounge, indoor pool, spa. AE, DC, MC, V. Inexpensive.*

Three Forks **The Sacajawea Inn.** This carefully restored, 33-room historic hotel—built in 1910—is named after the Native American woman who guided Lewis and Clark on their journey to map the West. Rooms, which were renovated in 1991, are decorated with arts and crafts reminiscent of the early 1900s. On summer evenings, the owners serve iced tea to guests who can sit in a line of wooden rockers on the expansive front porch. The headwaters of the Missouri River—where the Madison, Gallatin, and Jefferson rivers flow together—is just a few miles away. The restaurant serves a fine meal. *5 N. Main St., Box 648, 59752, tel. 406/285–6515 or 800/821–7326. 33 rooms. Facilities: restaurant, Continental breakfast, meeting room. No smoking. Inexpensive–Moderate.*

The Arts and Nightlife

The Arts   The largest theater for performing arts between Minneapolis and Spokane is the **Alberta Bair Theater for the Performing Arts** (Broadway and 3rd Ave. N, Billings 59105, tel. 406/255–6052). Presentations are by orchestras, chorale groups, and theater and dance troupes, among others.

In Helena, an oasis for the arts is the **Myrna Loy Center for the Performing Arts** (15 N. Ewing, tel. 406/443–0287). Located in a remodeled historic jail, the center—named after the Montana-born actress—offers live performances by national and internationally recognized musicians and dancers. There are also two theaters here that show foreign and independent films.

Nightlife   On summer nights you can watch cowboys coming out of the chute at the **Billings Night Rodeo,** at the Four Cross Arena. There's everything from professional rodeo, to Indian rodeo, to rodeo schools. *Admission: $6. Rodeo runs June–Aug., daily 7 PM–10 PM.*

Missoula to Glacier National Park

Important Addresses and Numbers

Tourist   Local information is available from the following sources:
Information   **Blackfoot Nation** (Box 850, Browning 59417, tel. 406/338–7276), **Glacier National Park** (West Glacier 59936, tel. 406/888–5441), and **Missoula Chamber of Commerce** (Box 7577, Missoula 59807), tel. 406/543–6623 or 800/526–3465).

Emergencies   For **police, ambulance, or other emergencies,** dial 911. The **Montana Highway Patrol** can be reached at tel. 800/525–5555.

Emergency Rooms   Area hospitals with emergency rooms include Missoula's **St. Patrick's Hospital** (500 W. Broadway, tel. 406/543–7271) and **Kalispell Regional Hospital** (310 Sunnyview La., tel. 406/752–5111).

Arriving and Departing by Plane

Airports and   **Johnson Bell Airport** (tel. 406/728–4381), on U.S. 93 just north
Airlines   of Missoula, is serviced by **Continental** (tel. 800/525–0280), **Delta** (tel. 800/221–1212), **Northwest** (tel. 800/225–2525), and **United** (tel. 800/241–6522). **Glacier International Airport** (tel. 406/752–1028), 8 miles northeast of Kalispell on U.S. 2, is serviced by **Delta, Northwest,** and **United.**

Arriving and Departing by Car, Train, and Bus

By Car I–90 and U.S. 93 pass through Missoula. U.S. 93 and Route 35 lead off I–90 to Kalispell in the Flathead Valley; from there, U.S. 2 leads to Glacier Park .

By Train **Amtrak** (tel. 406/226–4452) stops in East Glacier Park.

By Bus **Greyhound/Trailways** (tel. 406/549–2339 or 800/231–2222) serves Missoula. **Intermountain Bus Company** (tel. 406/755–4011) stops in Kalispell.

Getting Around

A car is the only effective way to follow the Exploring tour.

Exploring Missoula to Glacier National Park

Numbers in the margin correspond to points of interest on the Montana map.

⑭ This trip starts in **Missoula** and makes its way through the heart of Montana's mountainous western half, with its long, finger-shaped lakes and towering pines framing the snow-mottled peaks of mountain range after mountain range. Some 30% of Montana is publicly owned land, and the national forests, national parks, and state parks on this drive have plenty of campgrounds and hiking and biking trails.

If you are continuing from Helena, take U.S. 12 west and follow it about 40 miles to I–90; stay on I–90 all the way to Missoula. The aptly nicknamed "Garden City" is one of the most beautiful in Big Sky Country, and its population of 80,000 makes it the largest city in western Montana. Chestnut and maple trees line the residential streets, the Clark Fork River slices through the center of town, and the University of Montana is set against the cliffs of Mount Sentinel. A gravel trail along the river is ideal for walking and cycling.

North of town, a short way on U.S. 93 and not far from the airport, is the **Smoke Jumpers' Center,** which has exhibits, motion pictures, and murals that detail and explain various fire-fighting techniques. *5765 Hwy. 10 W, tel. 406/329–4934. Admission free. Open Memorial Day–Labor Day, daily 8:30–5; Labor Day–Memorial Day, weekdays 7:30–4.*

Where West Broadway intersects with Pattee Street, go a block to the **Missoula Museum of the Arts** with its changing exhibitions of contemporary work and a small permanent collection. *335 N. Pattee St., tel. 406/728–0447. Admission free. Open Mon.–Sat. 12–5.*

Time Out Take a break while touring downtown Missoula and have a cappuccino or a glass of fresh-squeezed juice at **Butterfly Herbs** (430 Higgins Ave., tel. 406/728–8780). If you can't decide what you fancy, try the "Over the Rainbow"—a drink with flavors including strawberry, hot pepper, orange, ginger, and mint. The shop also sells baked goods, gourmet candies, soaps, candles, china, and other odds and ends.

Travel north on U.S. 93 to its junction with Route 200 in **⑮** Ravalli, and follow signs to the **National Bison Range** at Moiese. This 20,000-acre refuge at the foot of the Indigo Mission Mountains was established in 1908 by President Theodore Roosevelt. Today the U.S. Fish and Wildlife Service ranches a herd of several hundred bison. A visitors center explains the life, habitat, and history of the buffalo. *Tel. 406/644-2211. Admission free. Open Memorial Day–Labor Day, daily 8–8; Labor Day–Memorial Day, weekdays 8–4:30.*

⑯ Return to U.S. 93 and continue north to the town of **St. Ignatius.** The **St. Ignatius Mission**—a church, cabin, and collection of other buildings—was built in the 1890s with bricks made with local clay by missionaries and Native Americans. The 58 murals on the walls and ceilings of the church were used to teach Bible stories to the natives. In the St. Ignatius Mission Museum—an old log cabin—is an exhibit of early artifacts and arts and crafts. *Tel. 406/745-2768. Admission free. Open May–mid-Oct., daily 9–5.*

⑰ Farther north on U.S. 93 is the **Ninepipe Wildlife Refuge,** *the* place for bird-watchers. This sprawling wetland complex in the shadow of the Mission Mountains is home to everything from marsh hawks to kestrels to red-winged blackbirds. Different parts of the refuge are open during various seasons; call ahead. *Tel. 406/644-2211.*

⑱ About 20 minutes from the wildlife refuge, where U.S. 93 meets Route 35, are the glassy waters of **Flathead Lake.** One of the largest freshwater lakes west of the Continental Divide, this body of water is a wonderful place for sailing, fishing, or swimming. Toward the end of July, on the east side of the lake, farmers harvest cherries and sell them at roadside stands.

⑲ The Swan River empties into Flathead Lake at the small, idyllic resort community of **Bigfork.** There is a host of vacation activities in the area: boating, hiking, horseback riding, golf, and cross-country skiing.

⑳ Follow Route 82 west from Bigfork back to U.S. 93 and go north to **Kalispell,** a lumber town and burgeoning tourist destination of about 12,000. This city is considered the center of Montana's "Banana Belt," but farmers harvest other produce as well, including Christmas trees, peppermint, and sweet cherries. The mild climate of the Flathead Valley makes the area recreation capital of northwest Montana, with opportunities for rafting, hiking, mountain biking, downhill skiing, and fishing, among other sports.

One of Kalispell's highlights is the **Conrad Mansion National Historic Site Museum,** a 26-room Norman-style mansion that was the home of C. E. Conrad, the manager of a freighter on the Missouri River and the founder of the town of Kalispell. Come Christmas, the mansion is lavishly decorated and filled with the wares of local artisans. *4th St. (6 blocks east of Main St.), tel. 406/755-2166. Open mid-May–mid-June, 10–5:30; mid-June–mid-Sept., 9–8; mid-Sept.–mid-Oct., 10–5:30. Admission: $4 adults, $1 children.*

Also in Kalispell is the **Hockaday Center for the Arts,** housed in the renovated Carnegie Library. National and international contemporary art exhibits are featured here on a rotating basis. *2nd Ave. E and 3rd St., tel. 406/755-5268. Admission free. Open Tues.–Fri. 10–5, Sat. 10–3.*

Return to U.S. 93 where it meets Route 40, then follow Route 40 to the small village of Apgar, where you'll begin a loop

㉑ through **Glacier National Park.** The view into the park's interior from Apgar has few equals: Its majestic, snowcapped peaks look like an illusion rising in the distance at the end of Lake McDonald.

Glacier is known as the "Crown of the Continent," for good reason. About a 100 million years ago, continents collided and this part of the world was thrust skyward. The last of the glaciers swept through here 10,000 years ago, acting like a giant rasp on the landscape, moving huge amounts of soil and rock and etching details such as waterfalls, some 200 lakes, knife-edge ridges, and spires into the mountains. Rivers, gravity, and the yearly cycle of freezing and thawing put the finishing touches on the landscape. The only glaciers that remain here now are relatively tiny year-round patches of ice and snow hidden, like refugees, in the dark, cool, high-altitude recesses of the northern mountains.

Triple Divide Peak in the backcountry north of the park is a real curiosity. When the snow from most mountains melts, the water drains to either the Pacific or Atlantic. This peak provides water to the Atlantic, Pacific, and the Arctic oceans.

In spring and summer, the alpine wildflowers make up for their short season with an unmatched intensity of color. As the sun warms Glacier in the spring, lilies grow up next to the lip of receding snowbanks. Then the mountain meadows explode in the pinks and reds of devil's paintbrush, white phlox, lavender shooting stars, pale blue wild irises, moss campion, and mountain heather—all blooming together in a high-mountain Expressionist painting. Later in the summer, the fragrant white balls of bear grass bloom, looking like lightbulbs on the end of a stick.

Glacier is one of the last enclaves of the grizzly bear, and the wild country in and around the park is home to the largest population of grizzlies in the lower 48 states. Snow-white mountain goats with their wispy white beards and curious stares are often seen in alpine areas, and surefooted bighorn sheep graze the high meadows during the short summers.

A haven for outdoor enthusiasts, Glacier National Park offers white-water river rafting, horseback riding, bird-watching, and scenery gazing, to name a few activites. Glacier is also a backpacker's heaven, and more than 700 miles of maintained trails twist and switchback through towering pines, steel gray mountains, and valleys, past turquoise high-alpine lakes, and over wind-whipped ridges that command vast expanses of wilderness.

Head east along the shore of finger-shaped Lake McDonald on the serpentine, 52-mile, Going-to-the-Sun Highway, one of the most scenic drives in the world. If you want a little exercise, stop near **Avalanche Creek,** where you can pick up a 3-mile trail leading to **Avalanche Lake,** one of many mountain-ringed lakes in the park. The walk is relatively easy, making this one of the most accessible backcountry lakes in the park.

At **Logan Pass,** at the top of Going-to-the-Sun Highway, there's a visitor center, with crystalline Hidden Lake a short hike from its parking lot. Mountain goats climb rocky cliffs at the lake, wildflowers bloom, and ribbons of water pour off the rocks. Before you set out on any hike in the park, however, re-

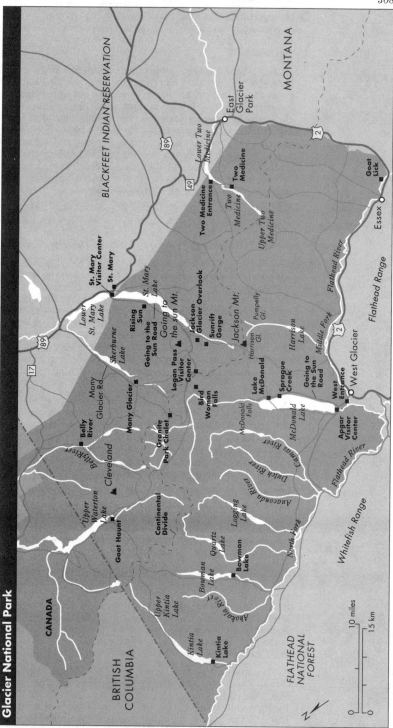

member to grab a jacket: Locals say there are only two seasons here, winter and the Fourth of July, and the only one you can really count on is winter.

When you drive over the highway to the east side of the Continental Divide, you might want to stop in **Browning.** This is the center of the Blackfoot Nation, which comprises three bands of native peoples: the Piegan, Blackfoot, and Blood. Until the late 19th century, the Blackfoot hunted the great northern buffalo herd, moving with them across the vast northern plains of Canada and the United States. At one time Blackfoot homeland stretched all the way from the Missouri River north to the Bow and Red Deer rivers in Canada, and from the Rocky Mountains to 300 miles east. Rugged terrain and remoteness left Blackfoot territory some of the last Native American country in the continuous United States to be opened to whites.

The **Museum of the Plains Indian,** on the north end of town, has been in operation since the 1930s. Now run by the Blackfoot, the museum houses a stunning collection of ancient artifacts from the Blackfoot and other Plains peoples. *Near jct. of Hwys. 2 and 89, tel. 406/338–2230. Admission free. Open daily 9–5.*

Half-day and full-day tours of the historic and prehistoric sites of the rugged and beautiful Blackfoot Nation are available through **Blackfoot Historic Site Tours** (tel. 406/338–7406). During the second week of July, the Blackfoot host **North American Indian Days** (tel. 405/338–7276) in Browning. This gathering of tribes is a pageant of drumming, chanting, and tepees as far as the eye can see.

Leave Browning and head west on U.S. 2. On this route you'll travel over Marias Pass. At 5,216 feet, this is the lowest major pass over the Rocky Mountains, and the spot where the Great Northern Railroad crossed the Great Divide in 1891. Near Essex is a goat lick—a natural salt formation along the highway that attracts mountain goats. It's a good place to watch these animals.

U.S. 2 brings you around to West Glacier, near the start of the loop in Apgar (*see above*).

Shopping

Specialty Stores **Rockin' Rudy's** (237 Blaine, tel. 406/721–9250; Univ. Ctr.,
Gifts Univ. of MT, tel. 406/542–0077) could be called the store that has everything, including new and used records, CDs, and tapes; T-shirts; imported dresses, hats, and accessories; postcards; greeting cards; and other gifts.

Want to bring an unusual gift home? How about an indoor trout stream? Steve Fisher of **Indoor Trout Streams** (6640 Hwy. 10 E., Missoula, tel. 406/258–6800) builds custom-made streams from 5 to 30 feet long, complete with insects and trout to match the new drapes. You can make an appointment to see his creations.

Home Furnishings Lodgepole pine furniture was used for practical purposes at the ranch, and now it's all the rage. Stop at **Darv's Log Connections** (4039 U.S. Hwy. 93 S, Kalispell, tel. 406/756–3092) to see lamps, beds, dressers, and other furniture made from pine trees.

Sports and the Outdoors

Canoeing Glacier National Park has an abundance of waters for good canoeing.

Cycling The folks at **Bikecentennial** (tel. 406/721–1776 or 406/721–8719), near Missoula, have good suggestions for nearby bike routes.

Fishing Within Glacier National Park is an unlimited range of fishing options.

Golf The 27-hole golf course near **Whitefish Lake** (Box 666, Hwy. 93 N, tel. 406/862–4000) is among the most beautiful in the state, with 36 holes. On the east side of Glacier, there is the **Glacier Golf Course** (Box 147, E. Glacier, tel. 406/226–9311) with 9 holes. Near Missoula, the **Highlands Golf Club** (102 Ben Hogan Dr., tel. 406/728–7360), with 9 holes, and the **Larchmont Golf Course** (tel. 406/721–4416) are fine courses.

Hiking and Backpacking Maps for hiking are available at the Apgar Visitor Center, (tel. 406/888–5441) near the western entrance of Glacier. If you want to backpack, you must pick up a backcountry permit at the same location. Trails of various lengths and levels are well marked within the park. Novices and those who want the help of an experienced guide can sign up with **Glacier Wilderness Guides** (1 Highline Dr., tel. 406/888–5333 or 800/521–7238), located just outside the park in West Glacier. This service runs daylong to weeklong trips and also combines hiking and rafting expeditions (*see* Rafting, *below*).

Rafting **Montana Raft Company** (U.S. 2, across from the Amtrak station in West Glacier) will take you on a raft trip through the stomach-churning white water of the Middle Fork of the Flathead and combine it with a hike or horseback ride.

Skiing *Downhill* **Big Mountain** (Box 1400, Whitefish 59937, tel. 406/862–3511 or 800/858–4439), 28 miles from Glacier National Park, has 50 runs; a 2,170-foot vertical rise; 3,000 skiable acres—plus out-of-bounds for cat skiing—and eight lifts, including a high-speed quad. During summer, the gondola continues to operate high above the mountains, exposing the resort's beauty.

Dining

Bigfork **Coyote Roadhouse.** Cajun, Sicilian, and Mexican dishes are served in this simply decorated restaurant *8083 Rte. 35, tel. 406/837–4250. Reservations advised. AE, MC, V. Moderate.*

Missoula ★ **Alley Cat.** As the name suggests, this quaint little eatery in downtown Missoula is located in an alley. The wooden booths provide privacy and coziness while you dine on the usual Continental fare, including seafood, steaks, and chicken dishes. *125½ Main St., tel. 406/728–3535. Reservations advised. MC, V. Moderate.*

Zimorino's Red Pies over Montana. Some of the best pizza that has ever been tossed anywhere is tossed here. Eat in, take out, or call for a delivery. Beer and wine are served. *424 N. Higgins St., tel. 406/728–6686 or 406/549–7434. Reservations advised. Closed for lunch. MC, V. Inexpensive.*

Lodging

Glacier National Park and Environs

Izaak Walton Inn. This small, out-of-the-way inn is set along the Marias Pass, between East and West Glacier. Originally built as a dormitory for railroad workers, the inn has a historic presence and is a convenient lodging for cross-country skiers mountain bikers, and hikers. Just outside the front door are more than 18 miles of groomed trails for such activities. Also, for those who don't have a car, Amtrak trains stop right outside the inn, whose front overlooks the train yard. Ask for a room in the back where it's quieter. For train buffs, four cabooses have been renovated and are available for cabin-style lodging. *U.S. 2, Essex 59916, tel. 406/888–5700. Facilities: 31 rooms, 11 with private bath, restaurant, sauna, gift shop, laundry, rec room. MC, V. Inexpensive.*

Glacier National Park–Owned Properties

The three massive stone and timber structures described below were built in the early part of this century by the Great Northern Railroad, and today are owned by Glacier Park, Inc. They are available June–Labor Day and must be reserved far in advance because they book up early. *For all hotels contact: 147 East Glacier 59434, tel. 406/226–5551 (May–Sept.); Greyhound Tower, Station 1210, Phoenix, AZ 85077, tel. 602/248–6000 (Sept.–June). D, MC, V.*

Glacier Park Lodge. Situated on the east side of the park and across from the Amtrak station is this beautiful hotel made of giant timbers. *154 rooms. Facilities: restaurant, lounge, snack bar, golf course, outdoor pool, playground, gift shop. Moderate–Expensive.*

Many Glacier Hotel. Also on the east side of the park is this hotel with commanding views of Swiftcurrent Lake. *208 rooms. Facilities: restaurant, ice cream parlor, lounge, gift shop, hiking trails, boat launch. Moderate–Expensive.*

Lake McDonald Lodge. This resort is located on the shore of Lake McDonald and offers cabins, which sleep up to four and don't have kitchens; motel rooms which are the largest; and units that are in the lodge itself. *100 rooms. Facilities: restaurant, coffee shop, lounge, gift shop, boat rentals, hiking, fishing. Inexpensive–Moderate.*

Missoula
★

Goldsmith's Bed and Breakfast. Built in 1911 for the first president of the University of Montana, this lodging is situated on the shore of the Clark Fork River, at the end of a footbridge that leads to the campus. Within the prairie-style building, with big white eaves and a huge porch, are period furnishings, wool carpets, and fresh flowers. Each private room is unique, and public rooms include a library and TV sitting area. An added bonus to staying at this B&B is that it's right next to Goldsmith's Premium Ice Cream, a café that features homemade ice cream and gourmet coffee, in addition to breakfast, lunch, and dinner. *809 E. Front St. 59801, tel. 406/721–6732. 7 rooms. No facilities. AE, D, MC, V. Moderate.*

Red Lion Motor Inn. Stretching along the Clark Fork River, this reliable chain offers inviting rooms, some of which face the mountains; others overlook the pool. Also on the grounds, which is close to the campus, is a lovely garden. *100 Madison Ave. 59802, tel. 406/728–3100 or 800/547–8010. 172 rooms. Facilities: restaurant, lounge, pool, gift shop. AE, D, DC, MC, V. Moderate.*

Holiday Inn. The Missoula member of this chain is a large, comfortable hotel with a lush atrium in the center, and comfortable, modern rooms. However, the property's most valued asset is its location in Missoula's riverfront park, a stone's throw from the Clark Fork. *200 S. Pattee St. 59801, tel. 406/721–8550 or 800/HOLIDAY. 200 rooms. Facilities: restaurant, lounge, pool, gift shop. AE, D, DC, MC, V. Inexpensive.*

Polson **Kwa-Taq-Nuk.** On the shore of crystalline Flathead Lake in ★ Polson, is this brand-new resort owned by the Confederated Salish and Kootenai Indians. In addition to the deluxe accommodations, guests enjoy sweeping views of the lake and the majestic Mission Mountains from their rooms. The hotel is well situated to provide visitors with golfing, rafting, and lake cruise adventures. *303 U.S. Hwy. 93 E 59860, tel. 406/883–3636 or 800/882–6363. 112 rooms. Facilities: restaurant, lounge, full-service marina, gift shop, indoor and outdoor pool, whirlpool, gallery. AE, D, DC, MC, V. Moderate.*

7 Utah

By Scott Warren

Scott Warren is a photographer and writer specializing in the four-corners states. His work has appeared in Travel and Leisure, National Geographic World, *and* Outside *magazines.*

Although 10 other states exceed Utah's 84,990-square-mile area, few if any can match the breadth and diversity of its topography. Around virtually every bend, mountains pierce the skyline. Spacious oceans of sagebrush roll out to the horizon. Improbable canyons score the earth. Snow-white salt flats shimmer, lush evergreen forests rim alpine meadows, and azure lakes glisten in the sun.

Given that spectacular scenery pervades virtually every corner of Utah, visitors can be thankful that much of the state falls under public domain. Federally owned lands include five national parks, six national monuments, a national historic site, two national recreation areas, seven national forests, and more than 22 million acres held by the Bureau of Land Management (BLM). Add to this some four dozen state parks, and it's easy to see why there are unlimited opportunities for enjoying the great outdoors. Whether your interest is hiking a trail, touring a scenic byway, skiing a powdery slope, fishing a lake, setting sails to the wind, watching wildlife, shooting the rapids, or capturing a scenic panorama on film, you can find it in Utah.

Its natural beauty notwithstanding, Utah is unique in other respects. Prior to 1847, Utah was like many other western areas. It was home to the Ute, Navajo, Paiute, Gosiute, and Shoshone Indians. It had witnessed the birth and eventual disappearance of the Fremont and Anasazi peoples. Spanish expeditions had come and gone, and streams and river valleys were stalked by rough-and-ready mountain men.

But on July 24, 1847, an event took place that would set Utah on a unique course. On that day, a small band of Mormons led by Brigham Young got its first look at the Great Salt Lake valley. Casting his gaze over the arid land, Young declared to his followers: "This is the right place." Within hours the pioneers began planting crops and diverting water for irrigation, and within days Brigham Young drew up plans for what would become one of the most successful social experiments ever.

As members of the relatively new Church of Jesus Christ of Latter-day Saints (LDS), these pioneers had migrated west to escape religious intolerance. Establishing a new promised land adjacent to the Great Salt Lake, they were joined by tens of thousands of other Mormons in the two decades that followed. Many settled in Salt Lake City, while others were directed by Young to establish smaller towns in distant corners of the territory. To populate this particularly harsh land took an effort that was no less than heroic, but the reward was to be a society free from outside influence and control. Or so the pioneers had hoped.

Although the Mormons were determined to keep to themselves, their land of Zion was not to be. In 1862, U.S. troops were dispatched to Salt Lake City to keep an eye on them. In 1868, the discovery of silver in the nearby Wasatch Mountains led to a flood of prospectors and miners and, as a result, to the growth of riotous mining camps. In the year following, the completion of the first transcontinental railroad ushered in additional waves of non-Mormon ("gentile" in LDS terminology) settlers. By the turn of the century, Utah's religious and social homogeneity had been effectively destroyed.

Today, because 70% of all Utahns count themselves as members of the Mormon church, Utah is decidedly conservative. Utah was, for instance, the only state in the nation that placed Bill Clinton third behind George Bush and Ross Perot in the 1992 presidential election. Politics aside, Utah is not nearly as provincial as many nonresidents have come to believe. When it comes to hotels, restaurants, the arts, and other worldly pleasures, places like Salt Lake City, Park City, and Ogden are as contemporary as any town in the nation. A legislative overhaul of Utah's infamous drinking laws has rendered the beast essentially harmless. However, there are a few towns in the state where it's necessary for patrons of a bar or restaurant to purchase a two-week "membership" for a mere $5, and then diners may freely order their favorite cocktail or bottle of wine along with their meal. Combine this with the state's natural splendor, wealth of recreational opportunities, and growing list of guest services and facilities, and it can safely be said that having fun is not prohibited in Utah.

Essential Information

Visitor Information

Utah Travel Council (Council Hall, Capitol Hill, Salt Lake City 84114, tel. 801/538–1030) distributes brochures and answers questions on tourism.

Emergencies

In most towns, call 911 for police, fire, and ambulance service. In rural areas, the Utah Highway Patrol (tel. 801/965–4518) has jurisdiction, as do county sheriff departments.

Major towns have hospitals with emergency rooms. In nonemergencies, ask at your lodging for recommendations of doctors and dentists. Outside Salt Lake, pharmacies don't tend to stay open late, but major supermarket chains have pharmacy departments that are often open to 9 PM or so.

Tour Groups

General-Interest Tours **Gray Line Tour** (553 W. 100 South St., Salt Lake City 84101, tel. 801/521–7086) operates tours of the greater Salt Lake City area and beyond. Destinations include downtown Salt Lake City, the Great Salt Lake, the Bingham Canyon mine, and several national parks.

Scenic West Tours, Inc. (Box 369, Draper 84020, tel. 801/572–2717 or 800/723–6429) offers one- to 12-day trips throughout Utah. In addition to regularly scheduled tours, customized itineraries are available.

Getting Around Utah

By Plane Commuter service between Salt Lake City and smaller Utah cities, such as St. George, Cedar City, and Moab, is available through **Alpine Air** (tel. 801/575–2839) and **SkyWest** (tel. 801/575–2508 or 800/453–9417).

By Car By far the best way to see Utah is by car; in fact, beyond Salt Lake City and the Wasatch Front, it's basically the only way. Interstate 80 crosses Utah east to west, and I–15 runs the length of the state, from Idaho to Arizona. These two routes intersect in Salt Lake City. In addition, U.S. 191 accesses eastern Utah, and U.S. 666 enters the southeast from Colorado. Front-wheel drive is suggested on the snowy roads of winter.

By Train **Amtrak** (tel. 801/364–8562 or 800/872–7245) has daily service from the Rio Grande Depot in Salt Lake City and also serves Helper, Milford, Ogden, Provo, and Thompson.

By Bus **Greyhound/Trailways** (tel. 801/355–4684 or 800/231–2222) runs several buses each day through Salt Lake City. In addition, there are stations in Beaver, Brigham City, Cedar City, Logan, Ogden, Parowan, Price, Provo, St. George, Tremonton, and Vernal.

Shopping

Shopping is not a big attraction in Utah. Malls are everywhere, and specialty stores carry much the same items you'd find throughout the West: Western wear, outdoor gear, and Indian jewelry, especially in the south. Shoppers should be warned, however, that more stores close on Sundays here than elsewhere.

Sports and the Outdoors

In the winter, skiing is king, and a number of first-class resorts bring skiers from all over the country and the world. In the summer, Utah is filled with hikers, campers, and, increasingly, mountain bikers. Perhaps most surprising in this second-driest state, boating on the many lakes, rafting on the rivers in the south, and fishing for bass, pike, kokanee salmon, and cutthroat trout, are extremely popular activities. Fishing licenses are available from the **Utah Division of Wildlife Resources** (1596 W. North Temple St., Salt Lake City 84116, tel. 801/533–9333). Golf courses are located throughout the state, and reservations are generally necessary.

National and State Parks

With five, Utah has more national parks than any other state except Alaska and California. Though Bryce and Zion are the best known, fascinating landscape can be seen at Arches, Canyonlands, and Capitol Reef national parks. For information, contact the individual parks: **Arches National Park** (Moab 84532, tel. 801/259–8161), **Bryce Canyon National Park** (Bryce Canyon 84717, tel. 801/834–5322), **Canyonlands National Park** (Moab 84532, tel. 801/259–7164), **Capitol Reef National Park** (Torrey 84775, tel. 801/425–3791), and **Zion National Park** (Springdale 84767, tel. 801/772–3256). Entrance fees are $5 at Bryce and Zion, and $3 at the others.

State parks range from historic monuments to recreation areas, many of which have public lakes, often reservoirs, that are popular spots for camping as well as boating and other water sports. Admission is generally $1.50 for adults and $1 for children under 13 to the historical monuments and $3 per vehicle to the recreational parks. Although some state parks take reservations for campsites, many are first come, first served. Write to the individual parks for information.

Officially, national and state parks are open 24 hours a day, but visitor centers are usually open 8–sunset.

Dining

The gourmet restaurants of Salt Lake and Park City rival those in any U.S. city, while elsewhere, more traditional, family-style eateries serve up meat and potatoes (and a little fresh fish). Having a drink with dinner is not a problem, nor, at most places, is getting a table. Reservations aren't necessary, and dress is casual unless otherwise noted in the reviews.

Highly recommended restaurants in each price category are indicated by a star ★.

Category	Cost*
Very Expensive	over $25
Expensive	$20–$25
Moderate	$12–$20
Inexpensive	under $12

per person, excluding drinks, service, and approx. 6½% sales tax.

Lodging

Chains are everywhere. Other than that, accommodations are varied—from the ski villages under one roof at some of the resorts and the tall, modern business hotels in downtown Salt Lake City to historic bed-and-breakfast inns and modest motels that simply provide a good place to rest after a day of sightseeing. Nonsmoking rooms are now generally available; ask when making reservations. Rooms have private baths unless otherwise noted in the reviews.

Highly recommended lodgings in each price category are indicated by a star ★. Note that some accommodations may come with breakfast, three meals, or even lift tickets included in the price, so compare accordingly.

Category	Cost*
Very Expensive	over $100
Expensive	$75–$100
Moderate	$50–$75
Inexpensive	under $50

All prices are for a standard double room, excluding approx. 6¼% sales tax and 1% tourist tax.

Salt Lake City

Nestled at the foot of the rugged Wasatch Mountains and extending to the south shore of the body of water for which it's named, Salt Lake City features one of the most scenic backdrops in the country. As the capital of progress-minded Utah, it is emerging as a prominent population and economic center of the Rocky Mountains. Within the last decade, the number of people living in the Salt Lake valley has climbed to over three-quarters of a million. As a reflection of this growth, a small but dynamic skyline has sprouted, along with ever-widening rings of suburbia. Smog occasionally bedevils the town, and crime is on the upswing, but for all intents and purposes, Salt Lake maintains the charm of a small, personable city. It is still an easy place to get around, and its residents are as down-to-earth as you will find anywhere.

Just as Salt Lake has grown considerably in recent years, so too has it come of age. The downtown now features several high-rise hotels, Salt Lake restaurants serve up a whole world of tastes, and there is finally a nightlife worthy of discussion. The Salt Lake arts scene is as prodigious as you'd expect to find in a city twice its size. All over town, fashionable retail enclaves are springing up. The community takes great pride in its NBA team, the Utah Jazz, and is taking very seriously its role as America's bid for the Winter Olympics in 2002.

Important Addresses and Numbers

Tourist Information The **Salt Lake Convention and Visitors Bureau** (180 S. West Temple St., 84101, tel. 801/521–2868) is open weekdays 8–5 and Saturdays 9–4.

Emergencies
Hospitals Salt Lake hospitals include **HCA St. Mark's Hospital** (1200 E. 3900 South St., tel.801/268–7111), **Holy Cross Hospital** (1050 E. South Temple St., tel. 801/350–4725), **LDS Hospital** (8th Ave. and C St., tel. 801/321–1100), **Primary Children's Medical Center** (100 N. Medical Dr., tel. 801/588–2000), and **University Hospital and Clinics** (50 N. Medical Dr., tel. 801/581–2121).

Late-Night Pharmacies The pharmacy at **Harmon's Supermarket** (3200 S. 1300 East St., tel. 801/487–5461) is open 24 hours a day. **Crossroads Drug** (Crossroads Plaza, 50 S. Main St., tel. 801/355–5823) is open until 9 on weekdays.

Arriving and Departing by Plane

Airport and Airlines **Salt Lake International Airport** (tel. 801/575–2400) is located 7 miles west of downtown Salt Lake City. It is served by **American** (tel. 801/521–6131 or 800/433–1790); **America West** (tel. 801/539–7918 or 800/247–5692); **Continental** (tel. 801/359–9800 or 800/525–0280); **Delta** (tel. 801/532–7123 or 800/221–1212), which maintains a hub here; **Northwest** (tel. 800/225–2525); **TWA** (tel. 801/363–0624 or 800/221–2000); and **United** (tel. 801/328–8011 or 800/241–6522).

Between the Airport and City Center All major car rental agencies have desks at Salt Lake International. From the airport, drive 7 miles east on I–80 to 600 South Street and follow signs for city center.

By Bus The **Utah Transit Authority** (tel. 801/262–5626 or 801/287–4636) runs bus service between the airport and downtown. Buses run regularly and are less expensive than cabs. In addition, most downtown hotels offer free airport pickup for guests.

By Taxi **Yellow Cab** (tel. 801/521–2100 or 800/826–4746) provides 24-hour service to all of the Salt Lake valley. The cost of a ride into town is about $11.

Arriving and Departing by Car, Train, and Bus

By Car From I–80, take I–15 north to 600 South Street to reach the city center. Salt Lake City's streets are extra wide and typically not congested. Most are two-way.

By Train The **Rio Grande Depot** (300 S. Rio Grande St., tel. 800/872–7245) has daily **Amtrak** service.

By Bus **Greyhound/Trailways** (tel. 800/231–2222) runs several buses each day to the terminal at 160 West South Temple.

Getting Around

By Bus Salt Lake has a very workable public transportation system in the **Utah Transit Authority** (tel. 801/262–5626 or 801/287–4636). A Free Fare Zone covers a 15-block area downtown and on Capitol Hill. Most other routes cost 65¢ per ride or $1.25 for all day.

Guided Tours

Orientation Tours **Lewis Brothers Tours** (Box 510247, 84151, tel. 801/359–8677 or 800/826–5844) conducts tours of Salt Lake City sights in *Old Salty*, an open-air, rubber-tired train. Tours depart from Temple and Trolley squares.

Special-Interest Tours **Utah Heritage Foundation** (355 Quince St., 84103, tel. 801/533–0858) offers the most authoritative tours of Salt Lake's historic sights. Two-week advance notice is required.

Exploring Salt Lake City

Numbers in the margin correspond to points of interest on the Utah and Salt Lake City/Salt Lake City Vicinity maps.

❶ As with most Utah municipalities, **Salt Lake City** is based on a grid plan that was devised by Brigham Young in the 19th century. Most street names have a directional and a numerical designation, which describes their location in relation to one of two axes. Streets with "East" or "West" in their names are east or west of (and parallel to) Main Street, which runs north–south, while "North" and "South" streets run parallel to South Temple Street. The numbers tell how far the streets are from the axes. (For example, 200 East Street is two blocks east of Main Street.) To confuse the matter further, addresses typically include two directional references and two numerical references; 320 East 200 South Street, for instance, is located in the east 300 block of 200 South Street. As an added complication, three of Salt Lake's most prominent streets are named after the Mormon Temple: North Temple, South Temple, and West Temple.

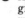 If for no other reason than to orient yourself to Salt Lake's street system, **Temple Square** is a good place to begin a walking tour of the city. Brigham Young chose this spot for a temple upon arriving in the Salt Lake valley, but work on the building

Utah

did not begin for another six years. Constructed with blocks of granite hauled by oxen and then train from Little Cottonwood Canyon, the Mormon Temple took 40 years to the day to complete. Its walls measure 16 feet thick at the base, and perched 210 feet above ground level is a golden statue of the trumpeting angel Moroni. Off-limits to all but faithful followers of the Mormon religion, the temple is used for marriages, baptisms, and other religious functions. Non-Mormons can learn more about the activities within the temple at the North and South visitor centers. Dioramas, photos of the temple interior, a baptismal font, and other displays offer considerable insight into the Mormon religion. *50 W. North Temple St., tel. 801/240-3318. Admission free. Open Memorial Day-Labor Day, daily 8-10; Labor Day-Memorial Day, daily 9-9.*

Other buildings of interest at Temple Square include the **Assembly Hall,** which was completed in 1882 with leftover granite from the temple, and the **Tabernacle,** home of the world-renowned Mormon Tabernacle Choir (*see* The Arts, *below*). This unusual dome-shaped structure was built in the 1860s as a meeting place. Void of interior supports, the 8,000-seat building is known for its exquisite acoustics.

As impressive as the architectural trappings of Temple Square are, don't forget to enjoy the quiet environs of the grounds themselves. But don't be surprised if a member of the church politely inquires about any interest you might have in learning more about Mormonism.

Across West Temple Street from Temple Square are two Mormon-owned and -operated institutions. The first of these, ❸ the **Museum of Church History and Art,** houses a variety of artifacts and works of art related to the history of the Mormon faith. *45 N. West Temple St., tel. 801/240-2331. Admission free. Open weekdays 9-9, weekends 10-7.*

❹ Nearby, the **Family History Library** is home to the largest collection of genealogical data in the world. Genealogy is important to Mormons because they believe in baptizing their ancestors, even after death. Anyone can use the facility, however. *35 N. West Temple St., tel. 801/240-2331. Admission free. Open Mon. 7:30-6, Tues.-Fri. 7:30-10, Sat. 7:30-5.*

❺ Dominating the block east of Temple Square is the **LDS Church Office Building.** Standing 28 stories high, this is Salt Lake's tallest structure. Although there is not a lot to see here, tours do include a visit to an observation deck on the 26th floor. Indicative of the breadth of the church's business dealings, this building has its own zip code just to deal with the volume of mail it receives. *50 E. North Temple St., tel. 801/240-2452. Admission free. Open weekdays 9-4:30.*

Around the corner from the Church Office Building is the ❻ **Beehive House,** Brigham Young's official residence. Now a national historic landmark, the home was constructed in 1854 and is topped with a replica of a beehive, symbolizing industry. In order to house his 27 wives and 56 children, Young built the **Lion House** next door, but unlike the Beehive House, it is not open for tours. *67 E. South Temple St., tel. 801/240-2671. Admission free. Open Mon.-Sat. 9:30-4:30, Sun. 10-1.*

The pervasiveness of the Mormon religion notwithstanding, Salt Lake City is not and was not devoid of representation by other faiths, especially in its early years. In the blocks east of downtown are three impressive houses of worship. Dating back to 1871, the Episcopal **Cathedral Church of St. Mark** (231 E. 100 South St.) is Salt Lake's oldest non-Mormon church. The Gothic-inspired **Catholic Cathedral of Madeleine** (331 E. South Temple St.) features twin spires, gargoyles, and plenty of stained-glass windows. Nearby, the **First Presbyterian Church** (E. South Temple at C St.) features beautifully crafted red sandstone construction.

In addition to being home to the Mormon church's competition, East South Temple Street was also a favored neighborhood for early Salt Lake's well-to-do. Among its many splendid homes is **7** the **Kearns Mansion.** Built by silver-mining tycoon Thomas Kearns, the impressive structure is now the governor's mansion. *603 E. South Temple St., tel. 801/538–1005. Admission free. Open for tours June–Nov., Tues. and Thurs. 1–4.*

Another impressive turn-of-the-century structure, half a block **8** south of the Beehive House, houses the **Hansen Planetarium.** This stargazer's delight features various exhibits, including a moon rock display. There is a great book/gift shop and, of course, a domed theater. Special events include laser shows set to music and live stage performances. *15 S. State St., tel. 801/ 538–2098. Admission free; shows are $1–$5. Open weekdays 9–8, Sat. 10 AM–midnight, Sun. 1–5.*

Continue south on State Street to the middle of the south 300 **9** block, and turn right to see the **Exchange Place Historic District.** Reminiscent of early Chicago, this cluster of buildings reaching 11 stories includes Salt Lake's first skyscrapers. As the city's center for non-Mormon commerce, it was one of the West's leading business centers early in this century.

Time Out | If you're ready for a break, stop for a picnic on the beautiful grounds of the impressive **City and County Building** (State St., between 400 and 500 South Sts.). Construction of this large structure, once the state capitol, began in 1892 and took two years to complete, at a cost of $900,000. The building was recently renovated at a cost of nearly $35 million.

A few blocks west of downtown are additional relics of Salt Lake's colorful past. Two train stations, enormous edifices built a year apart, underscore the two railroads' fierce competition for dominance in the region. At the west end of 300 South **10** Street, the 1910 **Rio Grande Depot** (300 S. Rio Grande St.) is still in operation, handling Salt Lake's Amtrak service and also housing the Utah State Historical Society Museum. The 1909 **11** **Union Pacific Railroad Depot** at South Temple and 4th West, on the other hand, stands vacant. Adorned with western murals and stained glass, it's a vivid monument to the importance that the railroad played in the settling of Utah and the West.

Heading back toward Temple Square, you'll see two buildings in sharp contrast to the turn-of-the-century train depots. The **12** enormous glass cube known as the **Delta Center** (301 W. South Temple St., tel. 801/325–2000) is home court for the Utah Jazz (*see* Spectator Sports, *below*). Previously, the Jazz played at **13** the **Salt Palace** (100 S. West Temple St.), a distinctive round, 14,000-seat facility, which is now the centerpiece of one of the West's premier convention centers.

(14) North of downtown Salt Lake, but still within walking distance, is the **Utah state capitol.** Topping Capitol Hill, this marvelous structure was begun in 1912, after the state happened upon $800,000 in inheritance taxes from the estate of Union Pacific Railroad president Edward Harriman. Taking less than three years to complete, the structure is considered one of the finest examples of Renaissance Revival architecture in the nation. Beneath the 165-foot-high rotunda is a series of murals, commissioned during the Depression, that depict the state's history. From the steps outside, you get a marvelous view of the entire Salt Lake valley. *Capitol Hill, tel. 801/538–3000. Admission free.*

(15) Also on Capitol Hill is the **Pioneer Memorial Museum.** Featuring 38 rooms of exhibits, many of which relate to the area's settlement by Mormon pioneers, the museum has one of the more extensive collections of settlement-era relics in the West. *300 N. Main St., tel. 801/538–1050. Admission free but donations accepted. Open Mon.–Sat. 9–5.*

Northwest of Capitol Hill are the small Victorian homes of the
(16) **Marmalade Historic District.** So called because its streets were named after fruit trees, this small but interesting neighborhood has been restored thanks to the efforts of the Utah Heritage Foundation. In contrast to most of Salt Lake City's streets, these avenues are steep and narrow. The Utah Heritage Foundation (*see* Guided Tours, *above*) sells a brochure about the district, including a self-guided tour, for $2.

At this point, you'll probably want to switch to a car to visit sights outside central Salt Lake City. Located a few blocks southeast of downtown is another of Salt Lake's unique historical treasures, **Trolley Square** (600 S. 700 East St., tel. 801/521–
(17) 9877). From 1908 to 1945, this sprawling redbrick structure housed nearly 150 trolleys and electric trains for the Utah Light and Railway Company. In the face of more contemporary modes of transport, however, the facility was closed. After a complete overhaul, the mission-style edifice reopened in 1972 and today is home to a collection of more than 100 boutiques, shops, and restaurants, making it one of the more intriguing retail centers in the West.

A few blocks south of Trolley Square is the expansive Liberty
(18) Park, home to the **Tracy Aviary.** Set on 11 acres, this facility features some 250 species of birds from around the globe: ostriches, bald eagles, flamingos, parrots, several types of waterfowl, and many more. *700 E. 900 South St., tel. 801/596–5034. Admission: $1.50 adults, 75¢ senior citizens, 50¢ children. Open Apr.–Oct., daily 9–6; Oct.–Apr., daily 9–4:30.*

A short distance east of downtown is the **University of Utah** campus. Dating to 1850, this large institution was relocated to its present site in 1900 and now has an enrollment of 25,000. Among the school's accomplishments are headline-grabbing advancements in artificial-organ research and cold fusion.

For the public, there's a pair of museums worth a visit. The
(19) **Utah Museum of Natural History** contains a number of exhibits about the state's prepioneer past. In addition to collections of rocks, minerals, dinosaurs, and other fossils, there are displays about prehistoric Indians of the West. Utah wildlife is well represented, and you can even learn why Utah is so enamored of seagulls. *President's Circle at 200 South St. entrance to cam-*

*pus, tel. 801/581–4303. Admission: $2 adults, $1 children.
Open Mon.–Sat. 9:30–5:30, Sun. and holidays noon–5.*

㉒ The **Utah Museum of Fine Arts** features both venerable and
contemporary art from around the world. Included in the permanent collection are ancient Egyptian relics, Italian Renaissance paintings, Chinese ceramics, traditional Japanese
screens, Navajo weavings, and American art from the 17th
century to the present. Special exhibits are regularly mounted.
*South Campus Dr. (continuation of 400 South St.), just s. of
Marriott Library, tel. 801/581–7332. Admission free. Open
weekdays 10–5, weekends 2–5.*

㉑ Just east of the U of U campus is **Ft. Douglas.** Established in
1862, this former military post resulted from strained relations
between the U.S. government and the Mormon settlers. Under
the premise that Brigham Young might side with the Confeder-
ates during the Civil War, a brigade of California and Nevada
volunteers set up shop on this site to keep an eye on things.
During their free time, the soldiers took to prospecting in the
nearby mountains, which in turn led to the establishment of
mining camps like Park City (*see* The Wasatch Mountains, *below*). Today Ft. Douglas showcases several examples of military architecture spread out across manicured grounds. There
is also a museum. *Off Wasatch Dr., tel. 801/524–4154. Admission free. Museum open Tues.–Fri. 10–4, Sat. 10–noon and
1–4. Closed federal holidays.*

㉒ Just beyond Ft. Douglas, the **Red Butte Garden and Arboretum**
not only features a fascinating collection of flora from various
corners of the earth but also is a great respite from the bustle of
the city. With 16 acres of gardens and 150 acres of natural areas, the grounds can provide many pleasurable hours of strolling. Trails access the nearby mountain terrain. *University of
Utah at mouth of Red Butte Canyon, tel. 801/581–5322. Admission free. Open daily 9–sunset.*

㉓ Farther east, at the mouth of Emigration Canyon, is **Pioneer
Trail State Park.** As the site where Brigham Young first looked
out upon the Great Salt Lake valley, this park features the This
Is the Place Monument, a 12-foot bronze statue of Young and
two cohorts, as well as Old Deseret, a collection of original pioneer homes. Inside the visitor center, displays relate the toils
of those who followed the 1,300-mile Mormon Trail (now a national historic trail) from Nauvoo, Illinois, to Salt Lake City.
*2601 Sunnyside Ave., tel. 801/584–8391. Admission: $1.50
adults, $1 children. Open May–Sept., daily 8 AM–10 PM; Sept.–
May, daily 8–5.*

What to See and Do with Children

The **Children's Museum of Utah** opened in 1983 with the mission
to "create the love of learning through hands-on experience,"
and that's exactly what it does. Kids can operate a TV station,
pilot a jetliner, draw with computers, perform heart surgery,
or unearth a saber-toothed tiger as part of the many interactive
exhibits. *840 N. 300 West St., tel. 801/328–3383. Admission: $3
adults, $2.50 senior citizens and children. Open Mon. 9:30–9,
Tues.–Sat. 9:30–5, Sun. noon–5.*

Hogle Zoo features 1,200 animals, big and small, from all over
the world. There is a children's zoo in the summer months, plus

a miniature train that conducts young visitors on make-believe journeys. *2600 Sunnyside Ave., tel. 801/582–1631. Admission: $4 adults, $2 senior citizens and children. Open Oct.–Apr., daily 9–4:30; May–Sept., daily 9–6.*

With nearly a dozen pools, 20 water slides, and the world's first water roller coaster, **Raging Waters** will delight kids of all ages. *1200 W. 1700 South St., tel. 801/973–4020. Admission: $12.95 ages 12 and over, $9.95 children 4–11. Open Memorial Day–Labor Day, Mon.–Sat. 11–8, Sun. 11–6.*

At **Wheeler Historic Farm,** visitors can experience early farm life. They can take an "afternoon chores tour," try their hand at milking a cow, or ride a draft horse–drawn wagon. *6351 S. 900 East St., tel. 801/264–2212. Admission: $1 adults, 50¢ senior citizens and children. Open daily 8–dusk.*

Off the Beaten Track

Depending on one's point of view, the **Bingham Canyon Copper Mine** is either a marvel of human engineering or simply a great big eyesore. At any rate, this enormous open-pit mine is touted as the world's largest excavation. Measuring nearly 2½ miles across and ½ mile deep, it is the result of the removal of 5 billion tons of rock. Since operations began 80 years ago, some 12 million tons of copper have been produced. Visitors may view the mine from an overlook, but be sure to check on hours before making the 22-mile trip out there. The site also has a visitor center. *Rte. 48 w. from I–15 past Copperton, tel. 801/322–7300. Admission: $2 per vehicle. Open Apr.–Oct., daily 8–dusk.*

As one of the West's most unusual natural features, the **Great Salt Lake** is second only to the Dead Sea in saltiness. (It is up to eight times saltier than the ocean.) Ready access to this natural wonder is possible at the **Great Salt Lake State Park,** 17 miles west of Salt Lake City, on the lake's south shore. Here a marina and beach allow you to set sail—either by boat or by floating on your back—across the buoyant water. What makes the lake so salty? Because there is no outlet to the ocean, salts and other minerals carried down by rivers and streams become concentrated in this enormous evaporation pond. *From Exit 104 on I–80, follow the n. frontage rd. e. to park entrance. Admission: $3 per vehicle. Open daily, 7AM–10PM.*

Head west from town on I–80, past the Great Salt Lake, and you'll eventually reach the **Bonneville Salt Flats,** an area nearly as devoid of life as the surface of the moon. Left behind by the receding waters of ancient Lake Bonneville, these extremely level salt flats support precious little in the way of plants and animals. One thing you will find here, however, is the Bonneville Speedway. First used in 1896, vehicles of varying designs have topped 600 miles per hour on the 80-foot-wide, 9-mile-long track. The BLM, managing agency of the salt flats, has seen an alarming 30% reduction in salt volume in the last 30 years.

Jordan River State Park (1084 N. Redwood Rd., tel. 801/533–4496) is an 8½-mile riverside complex offering jogging paths, canoeing, picnic facilities, a golf course, and bicycling. Like the river for which it's named, the Jordan River runs from fresh water (Utah Lake) to salt (Great Salt Lake).

Shopping

Shopping Districts **Crossroads Plaza** (50 S. Main St., tel. 801/531–1799) offers an all-inclusive downtown shopping experience. Among its 140 stores and restaurants are **Nordstrom** and **Mervyn's.**

Under the commission of Brigham Young, Archibald Gardner built a flour mill in 1877. Today you can visit the mill and stroll among a number of stores in the adjacent **Gardner Historic Village** (1095 W. 7800 South St., tel. 801/566–8903). Items for sale include furniture, collectibles, and knickknacks.

Founded by Brigham Young in 1868, the Zions Cooperative Mercantile Institution was America's first department store. The cast-iron facade on the Main Street entrance of the **ZCMI Center Uptown** (36 S. State St., tel. 801/321–8743) dates to 1902. History notwithstanding, this thoroughly modern shopping center features not only a **ZCMI** store but also **Eddie Bauer** and **Gart Brothers** outlets. The center is closed Sundays.

Specialty Stores
Antiques **Honest Jon's Hills House Antiques** (126 S. 200 West St., tel. 801/359–4852) carries a nice collection of Early American furniture. **State Street Antiques Mall** (251 S. State St., tel. 801/359–1956) features a wide array of collectibles in 12 different shops.

Books **Sam Weller's Zion Book Store** (254 S. Main St., tel. 801/328–2586) stocks over half a million new and used books.

Sports and the Outdoors

Biking Salt Lake City is a comparatively easy city to tour by bicycle, thanks to extra-wide streets and not-so-frenetic traffic. An especially good route is **City Creek Canyon,** east of the state capitol. On odd-numbered days from mid-May through September the road is closed to motor vehicles.

Golf Salt Lake is home to numerous golf courses, and the city itself operates seven facilities throughout the valley. Some good 18-hole courses include **Bonneville** (954 Connor Rd., tel. 801/596–5041), **Meadow Brook** (4197 S. 1300 West St., Murray, tel. 801/266–0971), **Rose Park** (1385 N. Redwood Rd., tel. 801/596–5030), **University** (100 S. 1900 East St., tel. 801/581–6511), and **Wingpointe** (Salt Lake International Airport, tel. 801/575–2345).

Jogging Salt Lake has a number of areas ideal for jogging. **City Creek Canyon** is always popular, as are **Liberty Park, Sugarhouse Park,** and **Jordan River State Park.**

Spectator Sports

Basketball The **Utah Jazz** (301 W. South Temple St., tel. 801/355–DUNK) is Salt Lake City's NBA team and a real crowd pleaser, having enjoyed a string of winning seasons in recent years. Home games are played at the Delta Center.

Hockey The **Salt Lake Golden Eagles** match sticks with NHL rivals at the Delta Center (301 W. South Temple St., tel. 801/532–GOLD).

Dining

American/Continental **Lamb's Restaurant.** Having opened its doors in 1919, Lamb's claims to be Utah's oldest operating restaurant. The decor is reminiscent of a turn-of-the-century diner, and the menu has beef, chicken, and seafood dishes, plus a selection of sandwiches. *169 S. Main St., tel. 801/364–7166. Reservations advised. Dress: casual. AE, D, DC, MC, V. Closed Sun. Moderate.*

★ **Squatter's Pub Brewery.** It seems delightfully sinister to enjoy home-brewed beer in a state like Utah, but that's exactly what you'll find here. The pub is on the first floor of the old Boston Hotel; the brewery occupies the floors above. Combining a lively atmosphere with great food and drink, Squatter's comes highly recommended by locals and visitors alike. In addition to the popular Squatterburger, the Sicilian-style pizza, and the generous plate of fish-and-chips, it also serves killer bread pudding, plus six different ales. Because it bases production on demand, the brew pub promises the freshest ales in town; no preservatives are used. Casual beer drinkers enjoy the light City Creek Pale Ale, while stout lovers savor the Millcreek Cream Stout. *147 W. Broadway, tel. 801/363–BREW. Reservations advised. Dress: casual. AE, MC, V. Inexpensive.*

French **La Caille at Quail Run.** It's hard to imagine a dining experience
★ as interesting and tasty as the one here. Start with the escargots à la Bourguignonne, followed by the best wilted-spinach salad anywhere. Then choose from such treats as sautéed swordfish, Chateaubriand, and rack of New Zealand lamb. Add personable servers dressed in period costume, the stately surroundings of an 18th-century French château replica, and a 22-acre nature preserve. The result is a dinner worth every penny. *9565 Wasatch Blvd., tel. 801/942–1751. Reservations required. Jacket suggested. AE, DC, MC, V. Very Expensive.*

Italian **Nino's.** In one of downtown Salt Lake's most spectacular settings, atop the University Club Building, the restaurant offers stunning nighttime views. A variety of wonderful chicken, veal, seafood, and pasta dishes highlight the northern Italian cuisine. *136 E. South Temple St., tel. 801/359–0506. Reservations advised. Jacket suggested. AE, D, DC, MC, V. Closed Sun. Expensive.*

Spaghetti Factory. Located in historic Trolley Square, this animated restaurant serves a lot of spaghetti for very little money. It's a good place to take a hungry family. *189 Trolley Sq., tel. 801/521–0424. No reservations. Dress: casual. MC, V. Inexpensive.*

Seafood **Market Street Grill.** Known for its fresh and well-prepared sea-
★ food, this restaurant has a lively atmosphere. It is owned by Gastronomy, Inc., a Salt Lake chain that transforms historic buildings into tasteful dining spots. Although you can count on every entrée being a winner, be sure to check the daily fish specials before ordering. *48 Post Office Pl., tel. 801/322–4668. Reservations advised. Jacket suggested. AE, MC, V. Moderate.*

Southwest **The Santa Fe Restaurant.** This restaurant, located in scenic Emigration Canyon, has earned acclaim for its cuisine. The extensive menu offers a variety of appetizers, salads, American selections, and specialties of the Southwest. Also available are regional dishes: buffalo steak and rainbow trout, to name just two. A brunch is served on Sunday. *2100 Emigration Canyon,* *tel. 801/582–5888. Reservations advised. Dress casual. MC, V. Closed Sat. for lunch and Sun. for dinner. Moderate.*

★ **Café Pierpont.** Tasty Southwestern cuisine is served in a fun, family-oriented setting. Kids small enough to walk through the wrought-iron cactus at the door eat for free. The menu includes four fajita, nine combination, and several enchilada plates; in addition to beef and chicken, seafood is liberally scattered in the listings. *126 W. Pierpont Ave., tel. 801/364–1222. Reservations advised. Dress casual. AE, MC, V. Closed for lunch weekends. Inexpensive.*

Thai **Bangkok Thai.** With a wide selection of authentic Thai dishes, this is a good place to find something different. Categories include curry, wok-fried, seafood, rice and noodle, and vegetarian dishes. *1400 S. Foothill Dr., tel. 801/583–7840. Reservations required Fri., Sat. Dress: casual. AE, MC, V. Closed for lunch weekends. Inexpensive.*

Lodging

Downtown **Brigham Street Inn.** If you love historic bed-and-breakfasts,
★ this is the place to stay. Situated on East South Temple (formerly Brigham Street), this turn-of-the-century mansion was carefully restored by Salt Lake architect John Pace. Each of the nine guest rooms was decorated by a different interior designer. The end result: a collection of superbly appointed rooms, each with its own personality. The original woodwork has been preserved throughout, one example of the special attention paid to preserving the home's character. The breakfast is Continental. *1135 E. South Temple St., 84102, tel. 801/364–4461, fax 801/521–3201. 9 rooms. Facilities: dining room. AE, D, MC, V. Very Expensive.*

Red Lion Hotel. Like most links in the Red Lion chain, this hotel is surprisingly glitzy. Within walking distance of many downtown attractions, it is also within a block of several great restaurants, though a complimentary Continental breakfast is offered. The hotel caters to skiers, making available such things as lift tickets and complimentary ski storage. *255 S. West Temple St., 84101, tel. 801/328–2000 or 800/547–8010, fax 801/532–1953. 503 rooms. Facilities: 2 restaurants, 2 lounges, heated outdoor pool, Jacuzzi, saunas, exercise room, laundry room, airport shuttle. AE, D, DC, MC, V. Expensive.*

★ **Little America Hotel & Towers.** Inside Salt Lake's largest hotel are such niceties as brass railings, chandeliers, and marble tubs. Perhaps because Little America is a small regional chain (six properties in all), it can afford to pay close attention to details. *500 S. Main St., 84101, tel. 801/363–6781 or 800/453–9450, fax 801/322–1610. 850 rooms. Facilities: 2 restaurants, lounge, indoor pool, hot tub, exercise room, laundry room, free airport shuttle. AE, D, DC, MC, V. Moderate.*

Peery Hotel. Constructed in 1910, the Peery is a salute to a bygone era, though the entire structure has been carefully renovated. Rooms are nicely appointed, service is personal, and, what's more, the front door is within two blocks of 25 restaurants and nightclubs. A free Continental breakfast is served. *110 W. 300 South St., 84101, tel. 801/521–4300 or 800/331–0073, fax 801/575–5014. 77 rooms. Facilities: 2 restaurants, lounge, Jacuzzi, exercise room, laundry room, free airport shuttle. AE, D, DC, MC, V. Moderate.*

Shilo Inn. Located a couple of blocks from Temple Square, this hotel combines the convenience of being right downtown with good rates. Service is reasonable, and the amenities are better than what you'd expect for the price. For example, there is a complimentary Continental breakfast. *206 S. West Temple St., 84101, tel. 801/521–9500 or 800/222–2244, fax 801/359–6527. 200 rooms. Facilities: 2 restaurants, lounge, outdoor pool, hot tub, saunas, laundry room, free airport shuttle. AE, D, DC, MC, V. Moderate.*

The Avenues. In a historic neighborhood, this is the best bet for hostel-style accommodations. Bed areas are clean and comfortable. *107 F St., 84103, tel. 801/363–8137. 14 multibed rooms share bath. Facilities: laundry room. No credit cards. Inexpensive.*

Deseret Inn. This '60s-style motor inn offers a basic room at a good price but little else. Rooms are somewhat plain, and the exterior trim could use some paint. Nevertheless, it would be hard to beat the price unless you look outside downtown. *50 W. 500 South St., 84101, tel. 801/532–2900. 88 rooms. Facilities: restaurant, hot tub. AE, D, DC, MC, V. Inexpensive.*

Airport and Greater Salt Lake Valley ★

Radisson Hotel Airport. A relatively new addition to the Radisson lineup, this hotel is typically elegant and very comfortable. Rooms include a wet bar and refrigerator. Try the free Continental breakfast and the Club Room for fun dining possibilities. This is the best bet near the airport. *2177 W. North Temple St., 84116, tel. 801/364–5800 or 800/333–3333, fax 801/364–5823. 127 rooms. Facilities: restaurant, lounge, heated outdoor pool, hot tub, exercise facility, free airport shuttle. AE, D, DC, MC, V. Expensive.*

Hampton Inn. Because this facility is new, and because Hampton Inns generally offer pleasant rooms with nice furnishings for a moderate price, this is a worthwhile place to stay if you're just passing through. It's located by I–15, so there are no attractions nearby. *10690 S. Holiday Park Dr., Sandy 84070, tel. 801/571–0800 or 800/426–7806, fax 801/571–0800. 131 rooms. Facilities: indoor pool, hot tub, laundry room. AE, D, DC, MC, V. Moderate.*

The Arts

Dance
Salt Lake's three main dance companies also perform at the historic **Capitol Theatre** (50 W. 200 South St.). **Ballet West** (tel. 801/355–ARTS) is considered one of the nation's top ballet companies, performing both classical and original works. **Repertory Dance Theatre** (tel. 801/534–6345) presents modern-dance performances. **Ririe-Woodbury Dance Company** (tel. 801/328–1062) is Salt Lake's premier modern-dance troupe. It's recognized for its innovation and commitment to community education.

Music
The **Mormon Tabernacle Choir** (Temple Sq., tel. 801/240–3318) may be heard in performance in the Tabernacle on Sunday mornings at 9:30 (be seated by 9:15) or during rehearsals on Thursdays at 8 PM. The **Utah Symphony** (123 W. South Temple St., tel. 801/533–5626) performs 260 concerts annually, both at home in the acoustically acclaimed Maurice Abravanel Concert Hall (part of the Salt Palace Convention Center) and in cities across the nation and abroad.

Opera
Utah Opera Company (Capitol Theatre, 50 W. 200 South St., tel. 801/355–ARTS) produces four operas a year, which often

feature nationally recognized stars. If you don't care for opera, check out the ornate facade of the Capitol Theatre anyway.

Theater **Desert Star Playhouse** (4861 S. State St., tel. 801/266–7600) specializes in musical-comedy melodrama. You are encouraged to hiss at the bad guy and cheer for the hero. **Pioneer Theatre Company** (300 S. 1340 East St., tel. 801/581–6961) features several different classic and contemporary musicals during its season, which runs from September through May. At **Promised Valley Playhouse** (132 S. State St., tel. 801/364–5696), performances are given in a renovated 19th-century theater. **Salt Lake Acting Company** (168 W. 500 North St., tel. 801/363–0525) is nationally recognized for its development of new plays. Performances run year-round.

Nightlife

Bars and Lounges **The Green Parrot Café** (155 W. 200 South St., tel. 801/363–3201) has been a favorite local hangout for years. Lunch and dinner are served, and the small stage occasionally hosts bands. In the downtown Marriott, **Solitude Lounge** (75 S. West Temple St., tel. 801/531–0800) offers a relaxed and intimate respite from the city.

Comedy Clubs Also in the downtown Marriott, **Bentley's Comedy Club** (75 S. West Temple St., tel. 801/531–0800) hosts stand-up comedy on weekends. South of town, **The Comedy Circuit** (10 N. Main St., Midvale, tel. 801/561–7777) is Utah's best choice for stand-up comedy. Some of the nation's top acts stop here while on tour.

Nightclubs **Club Max** (255 S. West Temple St., tel. 801/328–7047) is a high-energy dance club in the Red Lion Hotel. The **Dead Goat Saloon** (165 S. West Temple St., tel. 801/328–GOAT) features live music nightly. The tempo is upbeat, and the grill is fired up every day for lunch and dinner. **The Zephyr Club** (301 S. West Temple St., tel. 801/355–5646) showcases both local and nationally recognized bands in a lively atmosphere. The decor is art deco.

The Wasatch Mountains

Rising to elevations of over 11,000 feet and stretching some 160 miles from the Idaho border to central Utah, the Wasatch Range is an imposing and important geographic feature in the western United States. From a geologic perspective, the mountains are a complex assemblage of igneous, sedimentary, and metamorphic formations. From a demographic one, these mountains or, more precisely, their western base—a corridor known as the Wasatch Front—is home to three-quarters of all Utahns. Not only Salt Lake City residents but also those in Ogden, Logan, and Provo are greeted each morning with a spectacular view of the Wasatch.

Scientific and social implications aside, the Wasatch Range is one of the nation's premier mountain playgrounds. Uppermost in many visitors' minds is the legendary skiing found at resorts like Snowbird, Alta, and Park City. What many don't realize, however, is that these same ski towns double as wonderful summer destinations. Picturesque mountain communities, miles of hiking and bicycling trails, bright blue lakes, and truly spectacular alpine scenery add up to a vacation that's hard to beat.

Important Addresses and Numbers

Tourist Information Regional travel offices are **Bridgerland** (160 N. Main St., Logan 84321, tel. 801/752–2161 or 800/657–5353), **Golden Spike Empire** (2501 Wall Ave., Ogden 84401, tel. 801/627–8288 or 800/255–8824), **Great Salt Lake Country** (180 S. West Temple St., Salt Lake City 84101, tel. 801/521–2822), **Mountainland** (2545 N. Canyon Rd., Provo 84604, tel. 801/377–2262), and **Panoramaland** (250 N. Main St., Box 820, Richfield 84701, tel. 801/896–9222 or 800/748–4361).

Community information centers include **Brigham City Chamber of Commerce** (6 N. Main St., Brigham City 84302, tel. 801/723–3931), **Heber Valley County Chamber of Commerce** (475 N. Main St., Heber 84032, tel. 801/654–3666 or 800/858–2655), **Orem/Provo Chamber of Commerce** (777 S. State St., Orem 84058, tel. 801/224–3636), **Park City Chamber of Commerce/Convention and Visitors Bureau** (Box 1630, Park City 84060, tel. 801/649–6100 or 800/453–1360), **Sanpete County Travel Council** (345 W. 100 North St., Ephraim 84627, tel. 801/283–4321), and **Springville Chamber of Commerce** (175 S. Main St., Springville 84663, tel. 801/489–3263).

Arriving and Departing by Car, Train, and Bus

By Car If you're driving into the area, chances are you'll be coming on either I–15 or I–80. Even if you fly into Salt Lake City, it's a good idea to rent a car at the airport and drive to the section of the Wasatch you want to visit.

By Train **Amtrak** (tel. 800/872–7245) has service to both Ogden and Provo.

By Bus **Greyhound/Trailways** (tel. 800/231–2222) serves many towns along the Wasatch Front: Tremonton, Logan, Brigham City, Ogden, and Provo. In addition, the **Utah Transit Authority** (*see* Getting Around by Bus, *below*) connects Salt Lake City to many spots in the area.

Getting Around

By Car The main thoroughfare along the Wasatch Mountains is I–15. From this trunk, I–80 heads east toward Park City, U.S. 89 branches to the far north, U.S. 189 runs up Provo Canyon, and Route 132 winds into Sanpete County. Though most of the driving is urban, mountain views are spectacular. Winter visitors should be versed in driving on snowy roads and should be prepared with snow tires or chains.

By Bus The **Utah Transit Authority** (tel. 801/262–5626 or 801/287–4636) has frequent service to all of Salt Lake valley, Davis and Weber counties, and Utah Valley. Buses, with ski racks, also make several runs a day to the ski areas in Little and Big Cottonwood canyons.

Exploring the Ski Resorts

Numbers in the margin correspond to points of interest on the Utah map.

From Salt Lake City, follow I–15 south and I–215 east to the turnoff for Little Cottonwood Canyon. Situated 9 miles up the canyon is Utah's oldest—and the nation's second-oldest—ski

24 area: **Alta.** Alta actually began as a silver-mining camp in the 1800s. So frenzied was the pace back then that the year-round population topped 1,000. The eventual crash of the silver market, however, left the canyon virtually empty until it was recognized for its potential as a winter sports area. A lift was pieced together from an old mine tram, and in January of 1939 the Alta Lifts Company was in business. Today Alta is widely acclaimed for both what it has and what it doesn't have. The ski area (*see* Sports and the Outdoors, *below*) promises a generous helping of Wasatch powder—up to 500 inches a year. What you won't find is the glitz and pomp that other resorts exude.

A mile down Little Cottonwood Canyon is a study in contrasts.

25 Since the early '70s, **Snowbird,** or more simply "the Bird," has taken skiing to new heights. The Snowbird Ski and Summer Resort (*see* Sports and the Outdoors, *below*) is one of the nation's most modern ski facilities, and at the base area, a cluster of modern structures house elegant guest rooms, exquisite restaurants, and pleasurable nightclubs. The largest of these buildings, the Cliff Lodge (*see* Dining and Lodging, *below*), is like an entire ski town under one roof.

During the summer, Little Cottonwood Canyon is still the place to be for outdoor fun. From Memorial Day weekend to October, Snowbird fires up its tram to ferry sightseers and hikers to the top. From here you get one of the most spectacular views in the West.

Up range (i.e., north) from Little Cottonwood Canyon is Big Cottonwood Canyon—home to two smaller ski areas, **Brighton** and **Solitude** (*see* Sports and the Outdoors, *below*).

Although not far from Big and Little Cottonwood canyons as

26 the crow flies, **Park City** is best accessed by following I–80 east from Salt Lake City through Parley's Canyon. On the back side of the Wasatch Mountains, it is Utah's only real ski town, and because it is a mere 40-minute drive from Salt Lake International Airport, it is the most accessible ski town in the country.

Historically, Park City was a rip-roaring mining town like no other. Silver was discovered here in 1868, and in the years immediately following, the town's population grew by leaps and bounds. In the process it earned the nickname "Sin City." Certainly, it was uncommon for any municipality within spitting distance of Salt Lake to have more than two dozen saloons and a thriving red-light district. Despite the generosity of the mountains, Park City eventually fell victim to depressed silver prices. It was not until 1946 that its current livelihood began to take shape in the form of the small Snow Park ski hill, which opened a few miles north. In 1963, Treasure Mountains Resort began operations with its skier's subway—an underground train and hoist system that ferried skiers to the mountain's top. In the years since, facilities were upgraded, and Treasure Mountains became the Park City Ski Area (*see* Sports and the Outdoors, *below*).

Today, because Park City includes a mind-numbing collection of condominiums, it could be considered just another ill-conceived resort town. At its heart, however, is a historic downtown district that rings with authenticity. "Charming" is a word that comes to mind when describing the buildings that line Main Street, but, what's more important, this collection of turn-of-the-century edifices reminds visitors that Park City is a real town with real roots.

While it's the skiing that attracts most visitors to Park City, the town also serves as an excellent base camp for summer activities. Hiking trails are plentiful. A scenic drive over Guardsman Pass (via a gravel road that is passable for most vehicles) reveals incredible mountain vistas and a plethora of alpine wildflowers. There are some acclaimed golf greens, hot-air ballooning is taking off (pun intended), and an increasing number of mountain bikers are finding that the ski slopes make for truly exceptional pedaling. ParkWest, a smaller ski area in town (*see* Sports and the Outdoors, *below*), hosts an impressive concert series, which has brought such acts as Bob Dylan, the Grateful Dead, and Muddy Waters to its outdoor stage.

Exploring the Northern Wasatch Mountains

In the 35 miles along I–15 from Salt Lake to Ogden (the next large city north) are a string of municipalities that serve as bedroom communities for the larger towns. Although there are not many sights to take in along this stretch of road, a side trip west at Exit 335 takes you to **Antelope Island State Park.** The largest island in the Great Salt Lake, this water-bound mountain appears deserted and desolate from shore, but it is home to a variety of wildlife, including a herd of 600 bison. In 1983, the lake level rose dramatically and flooded the causeway that leads to the island. The water has since receded, and the island's beaches, campground, and hiking areas are again accessible. *Rtes. 108 and 127 to causeway, tel. 801/538–7220. Admission: $5 per vehicle including fee for causeway. Open daily 7AM–10PM.*

With a population of 65,000, **Ogden** combines a small-town feel with the infrastructure of a larger city. Upon the site of a stockade and trading post built by mountain man Miles Goodyear, Brigham Young directed the settlement of Ogden in 1850. Despite its Mormon roots, however, Ogden was to change radically with the arrival of the transcontinental railroad in the area in 1869. The town quickly became a major Western crossroads, and it received a great influx of non-Mormons. With the advent of World War II, the military began to have a considerable presence in town, which, with Hill Air Force Base nearby, it still has today. Ogden is also a college town; Weber State University is within the city limits.

On your way into town from the south, at Exit 341 off I–15, are Hill Air Force Base and the **Hill Aerospace Museum.** Among the many interesting planes housed in this large hangar are the SR-71 Blackbird (a reconnaissance aircraft that made a transatlantic flight in under two hours) and a B-17 Flying Fortress. *Hill Air Force Base, tel. 801/777–6818. Admission free. Open Tues.–Fri. 9–4:30, weekends 9–5:30.*

Given Ogden's history, it's safe to assume that it has a number of vintage buildings and museums. The best of these are found in the **Ogden Union Station.** Built in 1924, this impressive Spanish Revival structure demonstrates the considerable esteem railroad travel once enjoyed and houses some interesting museums: the Utah State Railroad Museum, the Browning-Kimball Car Museum, and the Browning Firearms Museum. (Browning is a renowned gun manufacturer.) *25th St. and Wall Ave., tel.*

801/629–8535. Admission: $2 adults, $1 children under 12.
Open Oct.–May, Mon.–Sat. 10–6; June–Sept., Sun. 1–5.

Highlighting a chapter in history that unfolded decades prior to the railroad era, **Fort Buenaventura State Park** is an 84-acre tract with exact replicas of the stockade and cabins that Miles Goodyear built in 1846. Guides in period costume interpret the ways of the early trappers, and hundreds of mountain-man enthusiasts gather at the fort in September, at Thanksgiving, and over Easter weekend for rendezvous. Camping and picnicking facilities are available. *2450 A Ave., tel. 801/621–4808. Admission: $3 per vehicle. Open daily 8–sunset.*

Back in downtown Ogden, the recently completed **Ogden River Parkway** follows the banks of the Ogden River for 3 miles to the mouth of Ogden Canyon. A real people place, this urban greenway hosts a number of outdoor activities, including bicycling, walking, jogging, tennis, baseball, and fishing. What really distinguishes it, however, are the two parks found along the way: the MTC Learning Park, which has botanical gardens and pavilion facilities, and the **George S. Eccles Dinosaur Park,** which features 26 life-size dinosaur replicas, one of the largest collections of its kind in the nation. *1544 E. Park Blvd., tel. 801/ 393–DINO. Admission: $2.50 adults, $1 youths 6–17, 50¢ children 2–5. Open Apr.–Nov., daily 10–dusk.*

With the Ogden River Parkway pointing the way, follow Route 39 into scenic **Ogden Canyon.** A few miles beyond the canyon mouth, the mountains open up to make room for **Pineview Reservoir.** During the summer, this 2,000-acre lake is festooned with the colorful sails of Windsurfers and the graceful arcs of water-skiers. The fishing is good, and some nice beaches, campgrounds, and marinas dot the shore. Anderson Cove, along the southern end of the lake, is quite popular, as is Middle Inlet, along the eastern shore. During the winter, Ogden Canyon reveals some great (and inexpensive) alternatives to the Salt Lake City ski scene, including Snowbasin and Powder Mountain (*see* Sports and the Outdoors, *below*).

Time Out   For what some consider to be the best burger in the country, if not the most down-home barroom atmosphere in Utah, visit the **Shooting Star Saloon** (7350 E. 200 South St., tel. 801/745–2002) in Huntsville. From the dollar bills pinned to the ceiling to the stuffed head of a 300-pound St. Bernard on the wall to the graffiti in the bathrooms, there is something to look at in every corner.

After you return to I–15 north, the next point of interest is **Willard Bay State Park.** About 10,000 acres in size, the bay is actually a freshwater arm of the Great Salt Lake. Fed by canals in the spring, it is effectively protected from saltwater intrusion by dikes, and because it is fresh water, Willard Bay is a popular fishing, boating, and bird-watching area. *15 min. of Ogden off I–15, tel. 801/734–9494. Admission: $3 per vehicle. Open 6 AM– 10 PM daily.*

If you happen to be passing through in the fall, drive up U.S. 89/91 from Ogden to Brigham City to enjoy Utah's **Fruitway.** You'll find many produce stands and the peach, apple, cherry, plum, pear, and apricot orchards from which the fruit came.

Upon reaching Brigham City, this tour turns northeast to follow U.S. 89/91 up and over Sardine Summit to Cache Valley. A brief detour to the west, however, takes you to two worthwhile

30 attractions. **Bear River Migratory Bird Refuge,** 17 miles from Brigham City, was originally a series of freshwater lagoons ideally suited for waterfowl, but in 1983 the 65,000-acre preserve was inundated by the rising Great Salt Lake. Ice floes destroyed all facilities at the refuge, but a considerable amount of work by the U.S. Fish and Wildlife Service has resurrected a driving-tour route that follows various dikes. The habitat has been reclaimed, and the refuge once again hosts seasonal influxes of ducks, geese, and shorebirds. Plans for a new visitor center and a 17,000-acre expansion are in the works. *16 mi west of Brigham City on Forest St., which becomes Bird Refuge Rd., tel. 801/723–5887. Admission free. Open daily 9–sunset.*

31 The second attraction, near Promontory, is the **Golden Spike National Historic Site.** It was here that the Union Pacific and Central Pacific railroads met on May 10, 1869, completing the first transcontinental route. Under the auspices of the National Park Service, Golden Spike features a visitor center, an auto tour, and some vintage locomotives on display. Every May 10, a reenactment of the driving of the golden spike is held, and the second Saturday in August brings the annual Railroaders Festival. *29 mi west of I–15, Exit 368, on Rtes. 13 and 83, tel. 801/471–2209. Admission: $3 per vehicle. Open daily 8–4:30.*

East of Brigham City, U.S. 89/91 tops Sardine Summit before dropping into the highly scenic **Cache Valley.** Walled in to the west by the imposing Wellsville Mountains (often touted as the steepest range in the world) and by the Bear River Range (a subrange of the Wasatch) to the east, Cache Valley is 15 miles wide and 60 miles long. Although first successfully settled in 1856 by Mormon pioneer Peter Maughan, during the 1820s Cache Valley was a favorite haunt for mountain men, who held a rendezvous here. These early trappers often stashed their furs in the valley, hence the name.

Today Cache Valley is one of the most important agricultural regions in Utah, and topping the list of foods produced here is cheese. Of the three cheese factories in the valley, Cache Valley Cheese is the nation's largest producer of Swiss cheese. To learn about agriculture's early days in the valley, visit the

32 **Ronald V. Jensen Living Historical Farm,** a 1917 dairy farm. Numerous antique farm implements are on display. Draft horses still pull their weight. Workers dressed in period clothing demonstrate such tasks as sheepshearing and quilting, and a variety of special events takes place throughout the year. *4025 S. U.S. 89/91, Wellsville, tel. 801/245–4064. Admission: $2 adults, $1 senior citizens, 50¢ children. Open June–Aug., Tues.–Sat. 10–4, and on special occasions year-round.*

While agriculture is Cache Valley's primary industry, the re-

33 gion's largest city, **Logan,** follows the beat of a different drummer. It's home to **Utah State University,** a land-grant college that began in 1888. Today, USU has an enrollment of 13,000 and is a leader in such diverse fields as agriculture, natural resources, and space technology. Located on a benchland just east of downtown Logan, the USU campus is best toured by starting at the historic **Old Main** administration building. Across campus, the Chase Fine Arts Center includes the **Nora Eccles Art Museum** (tel. 801/750–1412), which features exhibits by local and nationally recognized artists. For further information about USU, contact the University Public Relations Department (tel. 801/750–1000).

Time Out No visit to USU would be complete without a stop at the **Food Science Building** (12 East and 750 North; open 9–9.) for a scoop of the university's famous ice cream. You can also get soup and sandwiches here.

Just as Old Main's bell tower signifies that Logan is a college town, the twin towers of Logan's **Mormon Temple** (100 North and 200 East Sts.) remind all that it's also a somewhat conservative community with Mormon roots. Rising from a grassy knoll, this impressive limestone edifice took settlers seven years to complete. The site was chosen by Brigham Young in 1877, and the work was directed by architect Truman O. Angell, designer of the Salt Lake temple. As with all Mormon temples, this structure is open only to followers of the faith.

A Mormon landmark that can be visited by all is the **LDS Tabernacle** (Center and Main Sts.). Holding court over downtown Logan, the Tabernacle is one of several structures featured on a walking tour of historic Main Street. A nicely illustrated brochure, available from the chamber of commerce (160 N. Main St.), guides you along both sides of Main Street and up a few cross streets. The more interesting buildings along the walk include St. John's Episcopal Church, representing Cache Valley's first non-Mormon denomination; the Ellen Eccles (formerly Capitol) and Lyric theaters; and the Cache County Courthouse, with its recently restored cupola.

㉞ If you happen to be passing through in the winter, be sure to drive up Blacksmith Fork Canyon to **Hardware Ranch.** Here the state Division of Wildlife Resources feeds several hundred head of elk throughout the snowy months. A 20-minute sleigh ride takes you up close to the majestic creatures for some great pictures. There is also a visitor center and café. *tel. 801/245–5869. Sleigh rides: $3 ages over 3; open mid-Dec.–mid-Mar., daily 10–5, snow conditions permitting.*

From Logan, U.S. 89 continues for 30 miles up the scenic **Logan Canyon** before topping out at the crest of the Bear River Range. Within the canyon are a number of campgrounds and picnic areas administered by the Wasatch-Cache National Forest. For a particularly satisfying excursion, climb the 7 miles to **Tony Grove Lake.** At over 8,000 feet, this subalpine jewel is surrounded by beautiful scenery. A short trail circles the lake, and other backcountry routes enter the Mt. Naomi Wilderness Area to the west. Summer is the most popular season in Logan Canyon, but fall and winter are also worthwhile times to visit.

㉟ A mile beyond the summit, a turnoff reveals a spectacular view of **Bear Lake.** Some 8 miles wide and 20 miles long, the lake is an unusual shade of blue, thanks to calcium carbonate in the water. It is home to four species of fish found nowhere else, including the Bonneville cisco, which draws fishermen with nets during spawning in January. Water-sports enthusiasts can best access Bear Lake at one of three state parks (*see* State Parks, *below*). Among the lake's more discreet inhabitants is the Bear Lake Monster, which, like its Loch Ness counterpart, has lurked in local lore for many years. Beyond Bear Lake, a high sagebrush desert stretches east into Wyoming, and the Wasatch Mountains effectively end at the Idaho border.

Exploring the Southern Wasatch Mountains

South of Salt Lake City, around Point of the Mountain (a popular hang-gliding haven and site of the Utah State Prison), I–15 drops into Utah Valley, much of which is covered by **Utah Lake.** Although this freshwater lake is 11 miles wide and 24 miles long, it averages a scant 9 feet in depth. A state park is sited on the lake's eastern shore. Boating is popular, but the cloudy (some would say polluted) water makes swimming and fishing questionable.

Utah Valley's other chief natural feature is the soaring, 11,750-foot **Mt. Timpanogos.** Rising abruptly to the east, this imposing landmark is the centerpiece of a wilderness area of the same name and towers over **Timpanogos Cave National Monument,** located along Route 92 within American Fork Canyon. After walking a 1½-mile trail to the cave entrance, visitors may explore three separate caves connected by tunnels. A variety of well-preserved stalactites and stalagmites, plus other formations, make the three-hour tour well worth the effort. *Rte. 92, American Fork, tel. 801/756–5238. Tours: $2 adults, $1 children 12–15. Open daily 9–sunset.*

36

Beyond Timpanogos Cave, Route 92 continues up American Fork Canyon before branching off to climb behind Mt. Timpanogos itself. Designated the **Alpine Scenic Byway,** this twisting mountain road reveals some stunning mountain scenery before dropping into Provo Canyon to the south. Closed in the winter, the Alpine Loop is not recommended for recreational vehicles.

Within the last 3 miles of the Alpine Scenic Byway is the **Sundance Resort** (*see* Sports and the Outdoors, *below*). Best accessed from Provo Canyon, this small but distinctive resort came into being when Robert Redford purchased a ski hill in 1969. Reflecting the actor's interests in the environment, the arts, and outdoor recreation, the resort was designed to blend in with the natural surroundings. In the summer, a number of hiking trails, as well as theater productions, entice visitors.

37

While the Alpine Scenic Byway provides a roundabout way to get to scenic Provo Canyon, a more direct route follows U.S. 189 east from Orem. Within the canyon is **Bridal Veil Falls,** which drops a total of 607 feet in two tiers. The Skytram—touted as one of the steepest aerial trams in the world—climbs nearby, giving riders a spectacular view of the falls below. *Skytram: 4 mi up the canyon, tel. 801/225–4461. Admission: $4 adults, $2 children. Open Memorial Day weekend–Oct., daily 9–dusk.*

38

Beyond Bridal Veil Falls, U.S. 189 passes Deer Creek Reservoir before entering Heber Valley. Running along this route are railroad tracks, part of the scenic **Heber Valley Historic Railroad.** Following a line that first ran in 1899, the "Heber Creeper" takes passengers on a nostalgic trip through beautiful Provo Canyon. Each car has been carefully restored, and one of the engines—no. 618—is a fully operational, steam-powered locomotive. *450 S. 600 West, St., Heber City, tel. 801/*

39

654–5601 or 800/982–3257. Tickets begin at $8 for adults and $5.50 for children under 10.

40 While the scenic resources in and around Utah Valley are considerable, the region, **Provo** in particular, is probably best known as the home of **Brigham Young University.** As one of the largest religiously affiliated universities in the world, BYU reflects the conservative nature of the Mormon church. Students must adhere to a strict dress code, and they are supposed to refrain from alcohol, tobacco, and caffeine. The university is known for a variety of undergraduate and graduate programs, is a considerable force in regional athletics, and serves as a cultural center for the southern Wasatch area.

Heading up BYU attractions is a trio of museums. A fourth, the **Museum of Fine Arts** (Campus Dr., tel. 801/378–2819) is scheduled to open by early 1994. The **Monte L. Bean Life Science Museum** includes exhibits on wildlife from around the world plus live reptile displays. *E. of Marriott Center, tel. 801/378–5051. Admission free. Open Tues.–Sat. 10–5.*

The **Earth Sciences Museum** features dinosaur bones, fossils, and various hands-on activities. *Across from Cougar Stadium, tel. 801/378–3680. Admission free. Open Mon. 9–9, Tues.–Fri. 9–5, Sat. noon–4.*

The **Museum of Peoples and Cultures** is an interesting collection of artifacts relating to cultures from all over the earth. *700 N. 100 East St., tel. 801/378–6612. Admission free. Open Mon. 9–9, Tues.–Fri. 9–5, Sat. noon–4.*

One other museum of interest in Provo is the **McCurdy Historical Doll Museum.** Covering global themes, this collection of more than 3,000 dolls was started by Laura McCurdy Clark. The facility includes a doll hospital (for repairs) and a gift shop. *246 N. 100 East St., tel. 801/377–9935. Admission: $2 adults, $1 children. Open Jan.–Apr., Tues.–Sat. 1–5; May–Dec., Tues.–Sat. noon–6.*

41 South of Provo in **Springville,** known for its support of the arts, is a stop that's a must for fine-arts fans: the **Springville Museum of Art.** Beginning as a warehouse for works produced at the local high school, the museum later began to accept gifts from major artists. The present facility was built in 1937 and features mostly works by Utahns. *126 E. 400 South, St., tel. 801/489–2727. Admission free. Open Tues.–Sat. 10–5, Sun. 2–5.*

Continuing south on I–15, you will soon leave behind the more populated area of the state for more rural surroundings. Towering over this area is Mt. Nebo, which at 11,877 feet is the tallest peak in the Wasatch Range. The 43-mile **Mt. Nebo Scenic Byway** circles east of the summit to access both impressive panoramas and some alluring hiking trails. A ¼-mile walk leads to the Devil's Kitchen Geologic Area, a collection of strangely eroded spires and ridges.

The Mt. Nebo Scenic Byway returns to I–15 at Nephi, a small town that provides basic services. To complete the final leg of this tour, however, follow Route 132 east and south to U.S. 89 and the small but colorful towns of **Sanpete County.** Nicknamed "Little Denmark," Sanpete County was settled mainly by Mormon pioneers of Scandinavian extraction. The county seat, **Manti,** is Sanpete's largest community and one of Utah's oldest, established in 1849. Several buildings date back more than a century, including the Manti Temple, completed in 1888. The town of **Ephraim** is home to Snow College, a two-year institution that also dates to 1888; several historic buildings; and turkey farms. Nearly all of nearby **Spring City** is listed on the National Register of Historic Places.

Because the Wasatch Mountains reach their southern terminus in the area around Mt. Nebo, Sanpete County marks the end of this tour. To return to Salt Lake City, either backtrack on I–15 or follow U.S. 89 north to Spanish Fork, just south of Provo. On U.S. 89 near Thistle, a ghost town, watch for a view of the **landslide** that caused considerable damage in 1983. A new stretch of highway was subsequently built around the slide, and an interpretive sign describes the event in some detail.

What to See and Do with Children

The **Alpine Slide** (1345 Lowell Ave., Park City, tel. 801/649–7150) is a big attraction during the summer at the Park City Ski Area. Kids of all ages can fly down the curving track on a sled that is easy to control.

Camp Snowbird actually provides summer activities for children to enjoy without their parents. An array of day and overnight camps include hiking, tennis, swimming, panning for gold, nature studies, and guest speakers. *Snowbird, tel. 801/ 742–2222. Prices range from $24 for a full day to $175 for a two-night stay. Open Memorial Day–Labor Day.*

Children's Theatre features outdoor musicals performed especially for children. *Sundance Resort, Sundance, tel. 801/225–4107 or 800/892–1600. Admission: $6 adults, $4 children under 13. Open mid-June–early Sept.*

Calling itself the largest amusement park between Kansas City and the West Coast, **Lagoon** includes all of the rides and attractions you'd expect, plus the adjacent Lagoon-A-Beach water park. In operation for over a century, Lagoon is a Utah landmark. *375 N. Lagoon Dr., Farmington, tel. 801/451–8000. Admission: $19.75 adults, $15.75 children. Open Memorial Day–Labor Day, noon–8.*

Seven Peaks Resort Water Park includes 26 acres of waterborne fun. *E. Center St., Provo, tel. 801/373–8777. Open mid-May–Labor Day, 10:30–8:30 Mon.–Sat., closed Sun. Admission: $10.95 adults, $8.95 children 4–9, 3 and under free.*

Off the Beaten Track

For a bit of the beach (minus the water, of course), travel west from Nephi to the **Little Sahara Recreation Area.** Originating as sandbars in Lake Bonneville, these expansive sand dunes have moved 150 miles in the 10,000 years since the lake receded. Although much of this 20,000-acre sandbox is popular with off-road vehicle enthusiasts, the BLM has established three campgrounds and an area especially for children. Some 9,000 acres in the western portion of the recreation area have been set aside as a nature preserve. *Tel. 801/743–6811. Admission: $5 per vehicle, open April–Oct.*

Shopping

**Shopping
Streets/Malls**
In **Ogden,** east of the train depot, **25th Street** first served as a center for immigrants before becoming the town's shadiest avenue in the 1870s. Today the historic street is a fashionable shopping district. Behind the old brick fronts that once housed gambling halls, saloons, opium dens, and the like is a variety of antiques shops, gift boutiques, and restaurants.

Within the colorful structures that line **Main Street** in **Park City** are a number of clothing boutiques, sporting goods stores, and gift shops. Check out **Wyoming Woolens** (518 Main St., tel. 801/645–9427) for regional favorites in stylish outdoor clothing and **Christmas on Main Street** (442 Main St., tel. 801/645–8115) for a year-round supply of ornaments.

A few miles north of Park City, next to I–80, are the **Factory Stores at Park City** (6699 North Landmark Dr., tel. 801/645–7078). Represented in this collection of 48 outlets are **Nike, American Tourister, Capezio,** and **Corning,** among others.

Specialty Stores
Catalogue Stores
The General Store (Sundance Resort, tel. 801/225–4107) features distinctive home furnishings, clothing, and jewelry reflecting the Sundance ethic and taste. The shop is home base for the award-winning Sundance catalogue.

Sporting Goods
When in Rome, do what the Romans do, and when you're in Park City, you visit **Jan's Mountain Outfitters** (1600 Park Ave., tel. 801/649–4949) to pick up skiing, bicycling, camping, and fly-fishing gear. It carries everything you need to get out the door and into the woods.

Sports and the Outdoors

Biking
There are countless bike routes, both on and off the pavement, along the Wasatch Mountains. Many trails access the higher reaches of the Wasatch-Cache National Forest from **Alta.** The trail over Katherine Pass will put you at the head of Big Cottonwood Canyon at the Brighton Ski Area. Down the road, at **Snowbird,** off-road cyclists are discovering that ski slopes make for some excellent riding.

Around **Logan,** road cyclists will enjoy heading out into scenic Cache Valley on country roads or up Logan and Blacksmith Fork canyons. Mountain bikers can enjoy the 7-mile ride to White Pine Lake near the Mt. Naomi Wilderness Area or the strenuous climb to the top of Logan Peak.

Several mountain bike trails are accessible from the Guardsman Pass Road in **Park City.** Deer Valley Ski Resort runs one of its lifts in the summer to facilitate fun descents by bike.

In the **Provo** area, road cyclists may make a 100-mile circumnavigation of Utah Lake or tackle the Alpine Scenic Byway. Farther to the south, near **Nephi,** they can tackle laborious grades of the Mt. Nebo Scenic Byway.

Camping
Across the Wasatch-Cache and Uinta national forests are a number of wonderful campgrounds. Between **Big and Little Cottonwood canyons** there are four higher-elevation camping facilities. Of the nine facilities in **Logan Canyon,** Guinavah-Malibu and Tony Grove campgrounds are the nicest. Near **Nephi** a pair of campgrounds are found along the Mt. Nebo Scenic Byway. All 11 campgrounds in the Huntsville area up **Og-**

den Canyon offer swimming and fishing. In the **Provo** area, American Fork, Provo Canyon, and the Hobble Creek drainage hold dozens of possibilities. In **Sanpete County,** most campground facilities are found to the east in the Manti–La Sal National Forest (tel. 801/259–7155 for information). Additional campgrounds await visitors at the region's state parks and national monuments (*see* the Exploring sections, *above*, and State Parks, *below*) and at the Little Sahara Recreation Area (*see* Off the Beaten Track, *above*).

Canoeing While you can canoe on virtually any body of water in the region, the best places include **Tony Grove Lake** in Logan Canyon (*see* Exploring the Northern Wasatch Mountains, *above*) and the **Bear River,** northwest of Logan. Winding in serpentine fashion through Cache Valley, the Bear River features several nice stretches, including a particularly satisfying one that runs 11 miles from Amalga to Tremonton. Canoeists pass a blue heron rookery along the way, so this is a good float for birdwatchers.

Fishing Good fishing is to be found at the following locations: **Bear Lake;** the **Logan** and **Blacksmith Fork** rivers, outside Logan; **Willard Bay** and **Pineview Reservoir,** near Ogden; and **Deer Creek Reservoir,** northeast of Provo.

Golf The Wasatch Mountains are home to a variety of spectacular courses, some municipally owned and all with a wealth of natural scenery. Eighteen holes are found at **Ben Lomond Golf Course** (1600 N. 500 West St., Ogden, tel. 801/782–7754); **Homestead Golf Course** (700 N. Homestead Dr., Midway, tel. 801/654–1102 or 800/327–7200); **Jeremy Ranch Golf Course** (8770 N. Jeremy Ranch Rd., Park City, tel. 801/649–9693); **Logan River Municipal Golf Course** (1000 S. U.S. 89/91, Logan, tel. 801/750–9877); **Park City Municipal Golf Course** (1541 Thaynes Canyon Dr., Park City, tel. 801/649–8701); **Park Meadows Golf Club** (2000 Meadows Dr., Park City, tel. 801/649–2460); **Wasatch Mountain State Park** (1281 Warm Springs Dr., Midway, tel. 801/654–0532); and **Wolf Creek Resort** (3900 N. Wolf Creek Dr., Eden, tel. 801/745–3365). In addition, there is a nine-hole course at **Bear Lake Golf Course** (Garden City, tel. 801/946–3306) and 27 holes at **East Bay Golf Course** (1860 S. East Bay Blvd., Provo, tel. 801/377–2042).

Hiking Several trails originating at **Alta** climb to the surrounding peaks. The trail to Katherine Pass is relatively easy and quite scenic. Down the canyon from **Snowbird** is the trailhead for the Red Pine Lake and White Pine Lake trails. Located 3½ and 5 miles in, respectively, these mountain lakes make for great day hikes.

There is wonderful hiking in the **Cache Valley/Logan Canyon** area. Of the trails that access the Mt. Naomi Wilderness Area northeast of Logan, a good pick is the 3-mile route from Tony Grove Lake to the summit of Naomi Peak. The Limber Pine Trail is a popular and easy hike (1-mile round-trip) at the summit between Logan Canyon and Bear Lake. In the Wellsville Mountains, a 2-mile trail climbs steeply from Maple Bench to Stewart Pass, a lofty ridge top with a spectacular view.

A challenging 6-mile route climbs **Mt. Nebo** from a trailhead along the Mt. Nebo Scenic Byway. It is administered by the Uinta National Forest.

The best trails in **Provo Canyon** take off from the Alpine Scenic Byway. The 9-mile Timpooneke Trail and the 8-mile Aspen Trail both reach the summit of Mt. Timpanogos. Trails on the slopes of Sundance Resort are accessible by chairlift.

Skiing   **Alta** (Box 8007, Alta 84092, tel. 801/742–3333) is noted for both steep runs and ski-where-you-please openness. From the lifts to lodging, everything here is unpretentious. Fortunately, so is the price. Where other major ski resorts will charge upward of $40 for a lift ticket, Alta comes in at nearly half that rate.

With 850 and 1,100 skiable acres, respectively, **Brighton** (Brighton Ski Resort, Brighton 84121, tel. 801/532–4731 or 800/873–5512) and **Solitude** (Solitude Ski Resort, Box 21350, Salt Lake City 84121, tel. 801/534–1400) are roughly half the size of Alta and Snowbird, but they still offer the same fluffy powder that has made Utah skiing so exemplary. Because these resorts are less crowded, locals often purchase their season passes here and save the bigger resorts for special occasions.

Opening its slopes in 1981, **Deer Valley** (Box 3149, Park City 84060, tel. 801/649–1000 or 800/424–DEER), just south of Park City, broke new ground in the ski industry by providing such amenities as ski valets, on-slope telephones, grooming fit for a king, and slope-side dining of the highest caliber. For such pampering, the resort has won rave reviews from virtually every ski and travel magazine. However, for these added touches you pay about $3 extra for a lift ticket. Because Deer Valley has elevated grooming to an art, don't come looking for extreme terrain.

Front and center in Park City is the **Park City Ski Area** (Box 39, Park City 84060, tel. 801/649–8111 or 800/222–PARK), Utah's largest ski area. Featuring 83 trails and 650 acres of open bowls, the mountain is accessed by 11 chairlifts (two of which are high-speed quads) and a four-passenger gondola. Roughly half of Park City's terrain is rated as intermediate, but the slopes that line Jupiter Mountain are revered by experts as well. Snowmaking covers 375 acres, and night skiers will delight in Pay Day, the longest artificially lighted run in the Rockies. If you want to ski Park City but your youngsters do not, **Professional Sitters' Service** (Box 1673, Park City 84060, tel. 801/649–0946), a bonded and licensed service, will dispatch mature, well-trained care providers to your hotel room for $9 per hour for the first child and $1 for each extra child.

Park City's third ski area is a bit smaller than the others and has struggled with financial problems in years past; nevertheless, locals find an inexpensive alternative to Utah's larger ski areas in **ParkWest** (4000 ParkWest Dr., Park City 84060, tel. 801/649–5400). As Park City's only mountain that allows snowboarding, it is especially popular among younger crowds. The ski area includes a vertical drop of 2,200 feet (equal to that of Deer Valley) and is serviced by seven double chairlifts.

Rising north of Ogden Canyon's Pineview Reservoir is **Powder Mountain** (Box 450, Eden 84310, tel. 801/745–3772). As the name suggests, Powder Mountain receives a generous helping of the white stuff for which Utah is known. It offers just under 2,000 vertical feet, three chairlifts, and three surface tows. Skiable acreage totals 1,600, and night skiing is an option 4:30–10. Four slope-side eateries provide après-ski diversions.

With a vertical drop of 2,400 feet, **Snowbasin** (Box 348, Huntsville 84317, tel. 801/399–1135) is ready to host the downhill ski races should Utah win its bid for the 2002 Winter Olympics. With five chairlifts accessing some 1,800 acres of skiable terrain, this is northern Utah's largest ski hill. Only 17 miles from Ogden, Snowbasin has no base area accommodations.

Like Alta, **Snowbird** (Snowbird Ski and Summer Resort, Snowbird 84092, tel. 801/742–2222 or 800/453–3000) features plenty of powder-filled chutes, bowls, and meadow areas. Like its neighbor, it's known for its expert runs; 50% of Snowbird is black diamond terrain. In contrast, however, an extra $15 for a lift ticket will get you the speed, convenience, and impressive vertical drop (2,900 feet in one fell swoop) that only Snowbird's 125-passenger aerial tram can provide.

Winter visitors to the **Sundance Resort** (R.R. 3, Box A-1, Sundance 84604, tel. 801/225–4107 or 800/892–1600) will find 41 runs across 450 acres of terrain and four lifts that access the mountain's 2,150 vertical feet.

Water Sports Water-sports enthusiasts will find a surprising number of places to boat, windsurf, water-ski, and sail. The most popular of these are accessed by state park facilities. They include **Bear Lake, Willard Bay, Pineview Reservoir, Rockport Reservoir, Deer Creek Reservoir, Hyrum Reservoir,** and **Utah Lake** (*see* Exploring sections, *above*, and State Parks, *below*).

State Parks

In addition to those listed in the Exploring sections above, there are a number of state parks in the Wasatch.

Bear Lake State Park (2 mi north of Garden City on U.S. 89, tel. 801/946–3343 or 800/322–3770), one of three state parks on the lake, contains a marina, beach, picnic area, campground, and visitor center.

Deer Creek State Park (11 mi northeast of Provo on U.S. 189, tel. 801/654–0171) is popular with anglers and boaters.

East Canyon State Park (5535 S. Rte. 66, Morgan, tel. 801/829–6866) is on a 680-acre reservoir in the mountains northeast of Salt Lake City.

Eastside State Park (10 mi north of Laketown) is another of Bear Lake's parks. Because the lake bottom drops off quickly here, this site is a favorite among anglers and scuba divers. Facilities include a primitive campground and boat ramp.

Hyrum State Park (405 W. 300 South St., in the northwest corner of Hyrum, tel. 801/245–6866) features boating on a 450-acre reservoir.

Palisade State Park (southeast of Manti off U.S. 89, tel. 801/835–7275) has a small reservoir and nine-hole golf course.

Rendezvous Beach State Park (Rte. 30, near Laketown) is located on the south shore of Bear Lake and features more than a mile of sandy beaches, three campgrounds, and picnic areas. Getting its name from the mountain-man gatherings that took place here in 1827 and 1828, Rendezvous Beach hosts a reenactment of the events each September.

Rockport State Park (9040 N. Rte. 302, Peoa, 7 miles south of Wanship on S.R. 32, tel. 801/336–2241) is northeast of Park City and is quite nice for boating and fishing. There are nine campgrounds.

Utah Lake State Park (4400 W. Center St., Provo, tel. 801/375–0731) is the best access point for Utah's largest freshwater lake. In addition to a boat ramp, campgrounds, picnic areas, and a marina, the park has an ice-skating rink in the winter and a fishing area for the disabled.

Wasatch Mountain State Park (1281 Warmsprings Dr., off Rte. 224, Midway, tel. 801/654–1791) is known for its 27-hole golf course but also offers hiking and riding trails in the summer and Nordic skiing in the winter. It is Utah's largest state park.

Dining and Lodging

Alta
Dining

The Shallow Shaft. For fine beef, seafood, poultry, and pasta dishes, Alta's only base area sit-down restaurant that is not part of a lodging property is the place to go. Homemade pizza is also served, as is liquor. *Across from the Alta Peruvian, tel. 801/742–2177. Reservations advised. D, MC, V. Moderate.*

Lodging
★

Alta Peruvian Lodge. Comfortably rustic is the best way to describe the Alta Peruvian. Guest rooms range from simple dormitory style to two-bedroom suites. Breakfast, lunch, and dinner at the in-house restaurant are included in all lodging packages. Combine this American meal plan with complimentary lift tickets and you have one-stop shopping—Alta style. *84092, tel. 801/742–3000 or 800/453–8488. 80 rooms, 25 rooms with shared bath. Facilities: restaurant, lounge, heated outdoor pool, hot tub, laundry room. AE, D, MC, V. Very Expensive.*

Rustler Lodge. Offering some of Alta's most elegant rooms, this property has nice furnishings such as sofas and seating areas in deluxe rooms and a pleasant atmosphere. As at all of Alta's lodges, breakfast and dinner are included in the price. Choose from dorms to one-bedroom suites. *84092, tel. 801/742–2200 or 800/451–5223. 52 rooms, 8 with shared bath. Facilities: restaurant, lounge, heated outdoor pool, hot tub, state liquor store, laundry room, free shuttle to Snowbird. AE, DC, MC, V. Very Expensive.*

Bear Lake
Lodging

Inn of the Three Bears at Bear Lake. This quaint, turn-of-the-century abode features comfortable accommodations in a wonderfully rural setting. It's a five-minute walk from the front door to Bear Lake. A complimentary Continental breakfast is included. *135 S. Bear Lake Blvd., Garden City 84028, tel. 801/946–8590. 3 rooms. Facilities: hot tub. MC, V. Moderate.*

Logan
Dining

Gia's Italian Restaurant. Upstairs you will find sit-down service and carefully prepared Italian dishes. Downstairs, in the Factory, the service is strictly cafeteria style, the food includes pizza and sandwiches, and the atmosphere is lively. As any college student will tell you, the basement is where you go to meet friends for a beer, while upstairs is reserved for entertaining a date or parents. *119 S. Main St., tel. 801/752–8384. AE, MC, V. Moderate.*

Bluebird Restaurant. A favorite dining spot in downtown Logan for decades, this restaurant serves steak, seafood, and such standbys as prime rib in a setting that's straight out of a

Norman Rockwell painting. It's also known for its chocolates. *19 N. Main St., tel. 801/752–3155. AE, D, MC, V. Inexpensive.*

Lodging
★

Center Street Bed & Breakfast. This wonderful B&B on Logan's most prestigious historic boulevard is actually three separate buildings on one city lot: the 22-room mansion that dates to the late 1800s; the Carriage House; and the White House. Guest rooms range from smaller models to full suites, but each has different decor. Honeymooners enjoy the Garden Suite, but travelers will perhaps find the Arabian Nights Suite, the Jungle Bungalow, or Aphrodite's Court more to their liking. A Continental breakfast is included, and there is no smoking in the rooms. *169 E. Center St., 84321, tel. 801/752–3443. 12 rooms. Facilities: hot tub. AE, MC, V. Moderate.*

Baugh Best Western Motel. These basic yet comfortable accommodations are one of the best deals in town. Because it is locally owned, the service is personable. *153 S. Main St., 84321, tel. 801/752–5220 or 800/462–4145, fax 801/462–4154. 78 rooms. Facilities: restaurant, heated outdoor pool. AE, D, DC, MC, V. Inexpensive.*

Manti
Lodging

Manti House Inn Bed & Breakfast. This 1880 home was built by the same workers who built the Manti Temple. Known as the McAllister House, the inn is now a state historic site. Breakfast is included, and, for snacks, there is an ice-cream parlor on the premises. Rooms are nonsmoking. *401 N. Main St., 84642, tel. 801/835–0161. 6 rooms. Facilities: hot tub, exercise facilities. AE, MC, V. Moderate.*

Midway
Dining and Lodging
★

The Homestead. The Homestead combines the facilities of a complete resort with the charm of a country inn. The centerpiece is a natural hot spring that was first developed in 1895. A recent expansion has turned the property into a rustic yet elegant year-round resort. In addition to a soak in the hot spring, you can enjoy a championship golf course, cross-country ski touring, hot-air ballooning, snowmobiling, and exceptionally fine dining. The restaurant menu includes such dishes as crab cakes with a shrimp sauté, rack of lamb, and breast of duck, all meticulously prepared and served. *700 N. Homestead Dr., 84049, tel. 801/654–1102 or 800/327–7220, fax 801/654–5785. Restaurant: reservations required. Dress: neat but casual. 100 rooms. Facilities: restaurant, lounge, outdoor pool, hot tub, sauna. AE, MC, V. Restaurant: Expensive. Hotel: Very Expensive.*

Nephi
Lodging

Whitmore Mansion Bed & Breakfast. Built at the turn of the century, this opulent Queen Anne–style home is now listed on the National Register of Historic Places. Antiques and fine woodwork add to its charm. Breakfast is complimentary, and there is no smoking in the rooms. *110 S. Main St., 84648, tel. 801/623–2047. 6 rooms. Facilities: parlor, breakfast room, living room. MC, V. Inexpensive.*

Ogden
Dining

Gray Cliff Lodge Restaurant. Set in scenic Ogden Canyon, this local favorite features Utah trout, prime rib, lamb, and seafood as well as great atmosphere. *508 Ogden Canyon, tel. 801/392–6775. Reservations advised. Dress: neat but casual. DC, MC, V. Expensive.*

Prairie Schooner. The atmosphere might be overkill for some, but it's fun nevertheless. Steaks, prime rib, and seafood are served in a re-created Western setting; each table is enclosed in a covered wagon. Underneath it all, however, the food is good.

445 Park Blvd., tel. 801/392-2712. AE, D, DC, MC, V. Moderate.

Lee's Mongolian Barbecue. In a simple setting, the purely ethnic (and occasionally spicy) fare reflects both Mongolian and Mandarin roots. The food is as exotic as the way in which it is prepared. After selecting your ingredients, you hand over your dish to the chef, who stir-fries the meal before your eyes on a large hot plate. *2866 Washington Blvd., tel. 801/621-9120. MC, V. Inexpensive.*

Lodging
★ **Radisson Suite Hotel Ogden.** Combining the luxurious suites for which Radisson is known with the allure of a historic downtown building, this hotel is one of Ogden's most visually important structures and is listed on the National Register of Historic Places. In addition to its elegant rooms, the hand-painted ceiling tiles and chandeliers in the lobby area are worth a look. A full breakfast and cocktails are included. *2510 Washington Blvd., 84401, tel. 801/627-1900 or 800/333-3333, fax 801/394-5342. 144 rooms. Facilities: restaurant, lounge, hot tub, fitness room. AE, D, DC, MC, V. Expensive.*

Snowberry Inn. Overlooking Pineview Reservoir in the Wasatch Mountains above Ogden, this cozy bed-and-breakfast is everything a rural B&B should be. The rooms are rustic yet comfortable, and the breakfast is complete and country good. The inn is located near three ski areas. *1315 N. Rte. 158, Eden 84310, tel. 801/745-2634. 5 rooms. Facilities: hot tub, laundry room. MC, V. Moderate.*

Best Western High Country Inn. Conveniently located near I–15, this motel is comfortable and surprisingly complete. Rooms are spacious, and there are many exercise facilities. *1335 W. 12th St., 84404, tel. 801/394-9474 or 800/594-8979, fax 801/392-6589. 110 rooms. Facilities: restaurant, heated outdoor pool, hot tub, exercise room, laundry room. AE, DC, MC, V. Inexpensive.*

Park City
Dining
★ **Glitretind.** A source of Deer Valley's unsurpassed reputation in ski-resort dining, this fabulous restaurant is worth breaking open the piggy bank for. Selections include various seafood, beef, and poultry dishes, which are prepared with a creative selection of ingredients. How does saffron sauce and Caspian caviar with your New England lobster sound? Or what about grilled chicken breast stuffed with goat cheese? This is the stuff that travel, food, and ski magazines rave about when Deer Valley is the topic of discussion. *Stein Eriksen Lodge, Deer Valley, tel. 801/645-6455. Reservations advised. Dress: neat but casual. AE, DC, MC, V. Very Expensive.*

★ **Bistro Royale.** Some locals insist that this is Park City's best restaurant, and that's quite a statement considering that it's relatively new in town. The menu includes such entrées as grilled ahi tuna and Alpine Hunter's Elk Plate. Everything is prepared with low-fat or nonfat ingredients. Actress Kate Jackson is a co-owner. *U.S. Ski Team Bldg., Bonanza St. and Kearns Blvd., tel. 801/649-1799. Reservations advised. Dress: neat but casual. AE, D, MC, V. Moderate.*

★ **Café Terigo.** This airy café serves several well-prepared pasta and seafood dishes from fresh ingredients. Good picks include chicken tequila pasta and ginger coconut prawns. Be sure to top your meal off with a helping of bread pudding or mud pie. *424 Main St., tel. 801/645-9555. AE, DC, MC, V. Moderate.*

Lodging **Washington School Inn.** Although it is hard to imagine an old
★ schoolhouse making a great bed-and-breakfast, this circa 1890
inn proves that it can be done. The exterior of this three-story
stone structure was carefully restored, and the inside was completely gutted to make way for the guest rooms, kitchen, and
common areas. Each room is appointed with Victorian-era furnishings and down pillows and comforters. Of course, breakfast
is included. *236 Park Ave., Box 536, 84060, tel. 801/649–3800 or
800/824–1672, fax 801/649–3802. 15 rooms. Facilities: sauna,
hot tub, laundry room. AE, D, MC, V. Very Expensive.*

Olympia Resort Hotel. As one of Park City's largest, this hotel
includes a full array of amenities. On the premises are two popular restaurants plus a nice atrium area with pool. A free
breakfast is offered. *1895 Sidewinder Dr., Box 4439, 84060, tel.
801/649–2900 or 800/SKI–EASY, fax 801/649–4852. 235 rooms.
Facilities: 2 restaurants, lounge, indoor pool, hot tub, sauna,
exercise room, gift shop. AE, D, DC, MC, V. Expensive.*

Shadow Ridge Resort. Few other hotels in town can match the
Shadow Ridge for convenience and comfort. Located just a few
feet from the Park City Resort Center, you can amble to the
slopes in less time than it takes to warm up your car. Accommodations range from a single hotel room to a two-bedroom condominium suite. With full kitchens, these suites are a sweet deal
for families. All rooms are attractively furnished, and the staff
is friendly and experienced. *50 Shadow Ridge St., Box 1820,
84060, tel. 801/649–4300 or 800/451–3031, fax 801/649–5951.
150 rooms. Facilities: restaurant, lounge, heated outdoor pool,
hot tub, sauna, laundry room. AE, DC, MC, V. Expensive.*

Best Western Landmark Inn. Located out by the interstate, this
property makes a great stopover for travelers. The rooms are
nicely furnished, and the location is convenient for those visitors splitting their time between Park City and Salt Lake. *6560
N. Landmark Dr., 84060, tel. 801/649–7300 or 800/548–8824,
fax 801/649–1760. 106 rooms. Facilities: restaurant, indoor
pool, hot tub, exercise room, state liquor store, laundry room,
free ski-area shuttle. AE, D, DC, MC, V. Moderate.*

Provo **Magelby's.** Steaks, seafood, and chicken are served in a Euro-
Dining pean ambience. *1675 N. 200 West St., tel. 801/374–6249. AE, D,
MC, V. Closed Sun. Moderate.*

Panda Chinese Restaurant. Provo has a large number of Asian
restaurants. If you're looking for Szechuan, this is the place to
try. *138 W. Center St., tel. 801/377–3323. AE, MC, V. Closed
Sun. Moderate.*

Brick Oven. Cooking up what many consider to be the best pizza in town, this restaurant also offers sandwiches and pasta as
well as a salad bar. *150 E. 800 North St., tel. 801/374–8800. AE,
D, MC, V. Closed Sun. Inexpensive.*

Lodging **Holiday Inn Provo.** Like other Holiday Inns, this one has clean
and comfortable rooms plus an array of facilities. *1460 S. University Ave. 84601, tel. 801/374–9750 or 800/HOLIDAY, fax
801/373–4451. 52 rooms. Facilities: restaurant, heated outdoor
pool, laundry facilities. AE, D, DC, MC, V. Moderate.*

Seven Peaks Resort Hotel. A large facility, this hotel is close to
the downtown area and includes an expansive water park and
golf course. *101 W. 100 North St., 84601, tel. 801/377–4700 or
800/777–7144, fax 801/377–4708. 233 rooms. Facilities: restaurant, heated outdoor pool, hot tub, sauna, golf course, water
park, exercise room. AE, D, DC, MC, V. Moderate.*

Snowbird **Aerie.** In what may just be Utah's most scenic dining spot, this
Dining restaurant serves sumptuous seafood, beef, and poultry
★ dishes. In keeping with the elegance of its 10th-floor setting,
much attention is paid to preparation and presentation. There
is a sushi bar, and drinks are available to members of the Club
at Snowbird. (Upon checking in at the Cliff Lodge, you may
purchase drinking rights at this and other Snowbird restaurants for $5.) Even if you are staying for only one night, it's
worth dining here simply to be able to select from the impressive wine list. *Top floor of Cliff Lodge, tel. 801/742–2222, ext.
5500. Reservations advised. Dress: neat but casual. AE, D,
DC, MC, V. Expensive.*

Lodging **Cliff Lodge.** To some, this 10-story structure with bare con-
★ crete walls initially looks a bit bland, but it doesn't take long to
realize that the real beauty of its design is that it blends nicely
with the surrounding scenery. The rooms in this large hotel are
very nice—done mainly in mountain colors and desert pastels.
Wonderful views are to be found from every window, and service is friendly and helpful. Even in summer, guests may use
the Cliff Spa, on the top two floors, with its rooftop pool, massage rooms, hot tubs, and steam rooms. In addition, you have
your choice of several fine restaurants in the Snowbird base
area if you join the "Club at Snowbird" upon registration. This
is one of the finest ski resort accommodations to be found in the
Rocky Mountains. *Snowbird Ski and Summer Resort 84092,
tel. 801/521–6040 or 800/453–3000, fax 801/742–3304. 532
rooms. Facilities: restaurants, lounges, heated outdoor pools,
hot tubs, sauna, exercise rooms, laundry facilities. AE, D,
DC, MC, V. Very Expensive.*

Sundance **The Tree Room.** In addition to serving up great Continental
Dining cuisine, this restaurant has a special ambience. The place is
★ filled with exquisite Native American art and Western memorabilia collected by Robert Redford. The man does have good
taste. *Sundance Resort, tel. 801/225–4107. Reservations advised. Dress: neat but casual. AE, DC, MC, V. Expensive.*

Lodging **The Sundance Cottages.** Ranging in size from one to three bed-
★ rooms, these cottages lie in an appealing forest setting. Units
feature natural wood trim, rock fireplaces, decks, and handmade furniture. This is a great place to get away, especially in
the summer. *R.R. 3, Box A-1, 84604, tel. 801/225–4107 or 800/
892–1600, fax 801/226–1937. 65 cottages. Facilities: restaurant, lounge, hot tub, laundry facilities. AE, DC, MC, V. Very
Expensive.*

The Arts

Logan Thanks to both the presence of Utah State University and the
community's keen interest in the arts, Logan is home to many
fine productions. USU's theater and music departments host a
variety of exciting performances. In downtown Logan, the recently refurbished **Ellen Eccles Theatre** (43 S. Main St., tel.
801/752–0026) hosts the newly formed **Utah Festival Opera
Company,** and the **Lyric Theatre** (28 W. Center St., tel. 801/
750–3046) features repertory performances.

Ogden The **Eccles Community Art Center** (2580 Jefferson Ave., tel.
801/392–6935) displays a permanent art collection plus special
showings in an impressive Victorian mansion. **Weber State Uni-**

versity (3750 Harrison Blvd., tel. 801/626–6000) regularly offers theater, music, and dance performances by students and visiting artists at the **Val A. Browning Center for the Performing Arts.**

Park City Park City hosts a variety of performing arts events throughout the summer. Running for seven weeks is the **Deer Valley International Chamber Music Festival** (tel. 801/649–5309 or 800/472–6073). The historic **Egyptian Theatre** (328 Main St., tel. 801/649–9371), in downtown Park City, stages many different plays. The town also produces an outdoor **Shakespeare Festival** in July and August.

Provo Because **Brigham Young University** (tel. 801/378–7447) has a considerable interest in the arts, Provo is a great place to catch a play, dance performance, or musical production. There are a dozen performing groups in all. Of special note are the BYU International Folk Dancers and Ballroom Dancers.

Snowbird As part of the **Snowbird Institute for the Arts and Humanities** (tel. 801/742–2222, ext. 4150), the resort puts on a variety of musical and dance events throughout the summer. Included are performances by the **Ririe-Woodbury Dance Company,** a **String Chamber Music Festival,** and several **artist-in-residence programs.**

Sundance Held under the auspices of the Sundance Institute (tel. 801/225–4107 or 800/892–1600), the **Sundance Film Festival** is a renowned showcase for independent filmmakers. It takes place at Sundance and in Park City in January. Sundance Resort also hosts the **Sundance Summer Theatre** from mid-June through early September. Broadway musicals are staged in a spectacular outdoor theater.

Nightlife

In the northern reaches of the state, there are a great many places to cut loose and have fun. At Snowbird, you can join the **"Club at Snowbird"** and enjoy a drink at any of several lounges spread about the base area. Park City features such lively bars as **Cicero's** (306 Main St., tel. 801/649–6800) and **Sneakers** (1200 Little Kate Rd., tel. 801/649–7742). Ogden has **Toones** (2410 Wall Ave., tel. 801/399–5729) for dancing, billiards, and big-screen TV.

Northeastern Utah

With the western portion of Dinosaur National Monument within its borders, northeastern Utah counts the remains of Jurassic giants as its primary attraction. While the monument and related sites explore the lives of long-extinct creatures, the region also showcases some beautiful landscape: colorful slickrock canyons and deserts, a scenic stretch of the Green River, and the Uinta Mountains—Utah's highest mountain range. Add to these natural wonders some Fremont rock art, relics of 19th-century pioneers and outlaws, and a good dose of outdoor recreational activities, and you have a worthwhile tour to a remote corner of the West.

Important Addresses and Numbers

Tourist Information **Dinosaurland** (235 E. Main St., Vernal 84078, tel. 801/789–6932 or 800/477–5558).

Arriving and Departing by Car and Bus

By Car The best way to reach the area is by car, whether you're coming from Salt Lake or Colorado on U.S. 40 or Wyoming on U.S. 191.

By Bus **Greyhound/Trailways** (tel. 800/231–2222) serves Vernal.

Getting Around

By Car Both U.S. 40 and U.S. 191, the tour's main routes, are well maintained; however, there are some curvy, mountainous stretches. If you're headed for the wilderness, be prepared for dirt roads.

Guided Tours

Orientation Tours **Dinosaur River Tours** (540 E. Main St., Vernal 84078, tel. 801/ 649–8092 or 800/247–6197) offers half- or full-day van tours from Vernal to Dinosaur National Monument and surrounding areas. The cost is $20 and up.

Exploring Northeastern Utah

Numbers in the margin correspond to points of interest on the Utah map.

From I–80, take U.S. 40 south. Along the way, you'll pass the **Strawberry** and **Starvation reservoirs,** both popular lakes providing a variety of recreational facilities (*see* Other Recreation Areas, *below*), and the towns of **Duchesne** and **Roosevelt.** With a population of 4,000, Roosevelt is the second-largest town on the tour. It was named for President Theodore Roosevelt, who signed a declaration in 1902 allowing whites to settle on Ute lands. The town of Duchesne, 28 miles west, was originally called Theodore, but the community eventually adopted the name of a French nun instead.

Travel north from Duchesne or Roosevelt, and you'll soon cross portions of the **Uinta and Ouray Indian Reservation.** Nearly 1 million acres in size, this sovereign land is spread out across northeastern Utah in several units. Visitors are asked to stay on the main roads, although camping and hiking are allowed with a permit. The tribe hosts the Northern Ute Indian Pow Wow in early July at tribal headquarters in Fort Duchesne (tel. 801/722–5141).

42 Return to U.S. 40, and drive 30 miles northeast from Roosevelt to **Vernal.** The largest town (population 6,500) in this corner of the state, Vernal serves as a hub for visiting the area, which was frequented by mountain man William Ashley in the 1820s and first settled during the 1870s.

Because Vernal was so isolated in its early days, shipping was expensive. One businessman, in order to avoid high freight costs, had a bank facade shipped in brick by brick by U.S. mail. Nicknamed the **Parcel Post Bank,** the 1916 structure still stands and is part of the Zions First National Bank building in downtown Vernal.

Other historic sites in and about Vernal include an 1877 **log post office and store** (1255 W. 2000 North St.) and the old **Oscar Swett Ranch** (½ mi north on U.S. 191). Additionally, three museums feature relics and memorabilia from Vernal's yesteryear. The **Daughters of Utah Pioneers Museum** (158 S. 500 West St.) offers some perspective on what pioneer life was like. The **Thorne Studio** (18 W. Main St., tel. 801/789–0392) is a private collection of settlement-era firearms, Ute Indian artifacts, and photographs. The recently completed **Western Heritage Museum** (302 E. 200 South St., tel. 801/789–7399) highlights, among other Old West themes, 19th-century outlaws of the Vernal area.

While Vernal proudly draws attention to its last 150 years of history, the community is especially quick to point out the region's more distant past. Go back 150 million years and this land was the stomping ground of dinosaurs, both large and small. A good place to initiate an investigation is the **Utah Field House of Natural History State Park.** In its museum, numerous rock samples and fossils (including dinosaur bones) are housed; a large mural depicts the last 2.7 billion years of the Uinta Basin's geologic history; and Fremont and Ute artifacts offer insight into the early presence of humans in the area. Outside, the Dinosaur Garden features 14 life-size dinosaur models in a primordial setting. *235 E. Main St., tel. 801/789–3799. Admission: $1.50 adults, $1 children 6–15. Open June–Sept., daily 8 AM– 9 PM; Oct.–May, daily 9–5.*

With a visit to the Utah Field House under your belt, it's time to visit the focal point of dinosaur mania: **Dinosaur National Monument** park, which straddles the Utah–Colorado border. Located 20 miles east of Vernal are the monument's visitor center and astounding **Dinosaur Quarry,** where, inside a large enclosure, there are some 2,000 dinosaur bones encased in a 200-foot-long sandstone face. This collection of fossils resulted when floods brought the bodies of several dinosaurs to rest on a sandbar; subsequent deposits covered the carcasses where they lay, becoming part of the Morrison Formation. The cache of paleontological treasures was discovered by Earl Douglass in 1909. Today visitors must ride a shuttle bus from the visitor center to the quarry during busy times of the year. *20 mi east of Vernal on Rte. 149. Quarry: tel. 303/374–2216. Admission: $5 per vehicle, summer only. Open June–Sept., 8–7; rest of the year, 8–4:30.*

Although most people visit Dinosaur National Monument to see dinosaur bones, this 200,000-acre park also offers a generous supply of alluring backcountry to explore, either on foot or by vehicle. An especially scenic drive runs 6 miles east from the quarry to the **Josie Morris Cabin.** A rugged individualist, Ms. Morris kept company with the likes of Butch Cassidy. For wonderful vistas along the Utah-Colorado border, take the Harpers Corner Road. The drive into Rainbow Park not only passes some impressive Fremont petroglyph panels but also reaches a put-in point for rafters, who will find a variety of white-water thrills on the Green and Yampa rivers (*see* Sports and the Outdoors, *below*).

For more recreational opportunities, return to Vernal and head north on U.S. 191. **Steinaker Lake** and **Red Fleet state parks** (*see* Other Recreation Areas, *below*) both have reservoirs ideally suited for water sports and fishing. Past Red Fleet Reservoir, U.S. 191 begins to ascend the eastern flank of the Uinta uplift. This section of the tour follows what is known as the **Drive through the Ages.** Within a distance of 30 miles, the road passes 19 geologic formations, with signs identifying and describing them. A brochure is available at the Vernal Welcome Center.

U.S. 191 then reaches the truly spectacular **Flaming Gorge National Recreation Area.** Named for its "flaming, brilliant red" color by the explorer John Wesley Powell in 1869, Flaming Gorge was plugged with a 500-foot-high wall of concrete in 1964. The end result is a 90-mile-long reservoir that twists and turns among canyon walls. Although much of the lake stretches north into Wyoming, most facilities lie south of the state line in Utah.

44 Upon reaching Greendale Junction, 36 miles north of Vernal, stay right on U.S. 191 if you wish to visit the **Flaming Gorge Dam** itself. Displays at the nearby visitor center explain aspects of this engineering marvel, and the dam is open for self-guided tours. *Open Memorial Day–Labor Day, daily 9–5.*

45 If, on the other hand, you turn left on Route 44 at Greendale Junction, you will shortly arrive at the turnoff for the **Red Canyon Visitor Center.** Inside are displays covering the geology, flora and fauna, and human history of the Flaming Gorge area, but the most magnificent thing about the center is its location. Sitting atop a cliff that towers 1,300 feet above the lake makes for outstanding views. *Open Memorial Day weekend–Sept., daily 9:30–5.*

To conclude the tour, try one of the numerous hiking trails or the scenic drive through the Sheep Creek Canyon Geological Area, which is full of upturned layers of rock. The quickest route to Salt Lake City cuts northwest across Wyoming to I–80, or, of course, you can return the way you came and enjoy the attractions of Northeastern Utah once again.

What to See and Do with Children

Not surprisingly, since Northeastern Utah is chock-full of dinosaurs, it's a good place for traveling with kids. **Dinosaur National Monument** and **Utah Field House of Natural History State Park** (*see* Exploring Northeastern Utah, *above*) are both good choices for children.

Off the Beaten Track

If visiting the back of beyond is your interest, then drive 40 miles northeast from Vernal to **Browns Park.** Lying along a quieter stretch of the Green River and extending into Colorado, this area features plenty of high desert scenery and a fascinating historic site, the **John Jarvie Ranch** (follow signs off Rte. 191). Operated by the BLM, it includes four original buildings constructed by Scotsman John Jarvie more than a century ago. Because the road into Brown's Park can be rough at times, be sure to check on conditions first.

Sports and the Outdoors

Camping Campgrounds abound in the **Ashley National Forest** (*see* Other Recreation Areas, *below*) north of Duchesne and Roosevelt and west of Flaming Gorge. **Flaming Gorge National Recreation Area** (administered by the Ashley National Forest) contains more than a dozen campgrounds within the Utah portion, including those in the Dutch John and Antelope Flat areas. **Dinosaur National Monument** (Box 210, Dinosaur, CO 81610, tel. 303/374–2216) has two campgrounds, one near the quarry and the other in a more remote section of the monument.

Fishing While anglers can try their luck at all of the region's reservoirs, the best lakes are **Flaming Gorge** and **Starvation reservoirs.** For the best river fishing, experts suggest the **Green River** below the Flaming Gorge Dam. Fed by cold water from the bottom of the lake, this stretch has been identified as one of the best trout fisheries in the world.

Hiking Numerous trails access the high country of **Ashley National Forest,** the lower deserts of **Dinosaur National Monument,** and the beauty of **Flaming Gorge National Recreation Area.** Check with each for the best bets.

Rafting White-water enthusiasts find challenging stretches on the **Green and Yampa rivers** in **Dinosaur National Monument.** Joining forces near Echo Park, in Colorado, the two waterways have each carved spectacular canyons through several aeons' worth of rock, and they are still at it in rapids like Whirlpool Canyon, SOB, Disaster Falls, and Hell's Half Mile. Daytrippers will enjoy a float down the **Green River** below the **Flaming Gorge Dam.**

Guided river trips are available from **Adrift Adventures** (Box 192, Jensen 84035, tel. 801/789–3600 or 800/824–0150), **Dinosaur River Expeditions** (540 E. Main St., Vernal 84078, tel. 801/649–8092 or 800/247–6197), and **Don Hatch River Expeditions** (55 E. Main St., Box 1150, Vernal 84078, tel. 801/789–4316 or 800/342–8243). Trips cost $25 and up.

Water Sports Boating, waterskiing, and windsurfing are popular at **Flaming Gorge Reservoir, Red Fleet Reservoir, Starvation Reservoir, Steinaker Lake,** and **Strawberry Reservoir.** All feature boat-ramp facilities. At Flaming Gorge, three marinas offer boat rentals and supplies: **Cedar Springs Marina** (Box 337, Dutch John 84023, tel. 801/889–3795), near the dam; **Lucerne Valley Marina** (Box 356, Manila 84046, tel. 801/784–3483), east of Manila; and the **Buckboard Marina** (Star Rte. 1, Green River, WY 82935, tel. 307/875–6927) in Wyoming.

Other Recreation Areas

Red Fleet State Park (13 mi north of Vernal off U.S. 191, tel. 801/789–4432), like the other reservoirs in the region, is great for boat and bait. The real attraction here, though, is the colorful sandstone formations in which the lake is nestled. In addition, a section of 200-million-year-old dinosaur tracks can be reached by a short hike or by boat.

Although **Starvation Reservoir** (4 mi northwest of Duchesne on U.S. 40, tel. 801/738–2326) is only 3,500 acres, it does have a state park, and anglers successfully cast for walleye, German brown trout, and bass. The waters are a few degrees warmer than those at Strawberry.

Boating and waterskiing enthusiasts will love **Steinaker Lake State Park** (6 mi north of Vernal on U.S. 191, tel. 801/789–4432). Over 2 miles long, Steinaker Reservoir also relinquishes a fair number of largemouth bass and rainbow trout.

Today the **Strawberry Reservoir** (25 mi south of Heber City on U.S. 40, tel. 801/548–2285) covers 17,000 acres. Construction on the original reservoir, part of a federal project designed to bring water from the Colorado River basin to the Wasatch Front, began in 1906. In 1973, the Soldier Creek Dam was built downstream, and the original Strawberry Reservoir dam was eventually removed. The result was a much larger storage facility, which boaters and anglers alike now relish. Ice fishing is also popular. Four U.S. Forest Service campgrounds and three marinas dot the lakeshore.

Although the Wasatch may be Utah's best-known mountain range, the **Uinta Mountains**, the only major east–west mountain range in the Rockies, are its tallest, topped by 13,528-foot Kings Peak. Though the mountains lie north of the Uinta and Ouray Indian Reservation, the quickest, easiest (read: paved) route to Uinta country is the Mirror Lake Scenic Byway, which begins in Kamas. The 65-mile drive follows Route 150 into the heavily wooded canyons of the **Wasatch-Cache National Forest** (50 E. Center St., Box 68, Kamas 84118, tel. 801/783–4338), cresting at 10,687-foot Bald Mountain Pass. At nearby Mirror Lake, campgrounds provide a base for hikes into the surrounding mountains, and Highline Trail accesses the 460,000-acre **High Uintas Wilderness Area** to the east. Still farther east, accessible by dirt roads from the reservation, are several recreation areas in the **Ashley National Forest** (W. U.S. 40, Box 338, Roosevelt 84066, tel. 801/722–5018). One of these, Moon Lake, features a U.S. Forest Service campground and private resort. Another, along the Yellowstone River, has five campgrounds. These areas also have trails that lead to the High Uintas Wilderness Area.

Dining and Lodging

Duchesne
Lodging

Rio Damian Motel. Small and unassuming, this motel provides clean and comfortable rooms. *23 W. Main St., Box 166, 84021, tel. 801/738–2217. 10 rooms. Facilities: gift shop. AE, MC, V. Inexpensive.*

Flaming Gorge
Lodging

Flaming Gorge Lodge. Probably the best accommodations in the vicinity of Flaming Gorge, the lodge has a great restaurant, plus a store, raft rentals, and fishing guide service. *Greendale, U.S. 191, Dutch John 84023, tel. 801/889–3773. 44 rooms. Facilities: restaurant, store. AE, D, MC, V. Moderate.*

Grubb's Flaming Gorge Motel. A good place to check in if you find yourself on this end of the lake when night falls. *Rtes. 43 and 44, Box 398, Manila 84046, tel. 801/784–3131. 15 rooms. Facilities: restaurant. AE, MC, V. Inexpensive.*

Roosevelt
Dining
★

Frontier Grill. This family restaurant is known for its great sandwiches and salads during the noon hour, its prime rib and seafood at night, and its homemade pies any time of the day. *75 S. 200 East St., tel. 801/722–3669. AE, DC, MC, V. Inexpensive.*

Lodging **Best Western Inn.** Clean and comfortable rooms, plus a pool, make this the place to stay in Roosevelt. *E. Hwy. 40, Box 2860, 84066, tel. 801/722–4644 or 800/354–7803. 40 rooms. Facilities: restaurant, outdoor pool. AE, D, DC, MC, V. Moderate.*

Vernal **Great American Café.** Serving food that's a bit different from
Dining the standard fare at other Vernal restaurants, the café is known
★ for its deep-fried catfish. *13 S. Vernal Ave., tel. 801/789–1115. D, MC, V. Moderate.*

Casa Rios. If you're in search of south-of-the-border flavors, this is a good bet. Try the special beef burrito or the chimichangas. *W. Rte. 40, tel. 801/789–0103. MC, V. Closed Sun. and Mon. Inexpensive.*

Last Chance Saloon. You wouldn't expect to find Vernal's best breakfast at a bar, but that's exactly what locals have come to expect here. Lunch and dinner are also served. *3340 N. Vernal Ave., tel. 801/789–5657. MC, V. Inexpensive.*

Lodging **Best Western Antlers Motel.** Locals rate this as Vernal's best accommodations. The motel offers clean and very comfortable rooms, and the staff is friendly and helpful. *423 W. Main St., 84078, tel. 801/789–1202 or 800/524–1234. 49 rooms. Facilities: restaurant, outdoor pool. AE, D, DC, MC, V. Moderate.*

Weston Lamplighter Inn. For in-town convenience and amenities, this is another good pick in Vernal. *120 E. Main St., 84078, tel. 801/789–0312, fax 801/789–4874. 165 rooms. Facilities: restaurant, outdoor pool. AE, D, MC, V. Moderate.*

Southeastern Utah

Characterized by multihued buttes, bizarre rock formations, deep canyons, and lonesome plateaus, southeastern Utah stirs the imagination as few other places can. The broad and open desert topography provides grand vistas, where scale is often an intangible element. Storm clouds billow high into the sky, and spectacular sunsets routinely light up an already colorful landscape. Add to this incredible natural beauty a wealth of paleontological, archaeological, and historical treasures, plus a broad range of outdoor recreational opportunities, and you have one of the most alluring travel destinations to be found anywhere.

If you do set out for this distant corner of the state, be prepared for some of the most desolate stretches of highway in the country. In addition to stocking up on extra supplies and making sure that your vehicle is in good mechanical condition, you should also prepare yourself mentally for the vast stretches of nothingness that lie ahead. While some travelers thrive on the extra elbow room, others may become a bit unnerved when they learn just how spacious the West really is.

Important Addresses and Numbers

Tourist **Canyonlands/North** (Center and Main Sts., Moab 84532, tel.
Information 801/259–8825 or 800/635–6622), **Canyonlands/South** (117 S. Main St., Box 490, Monticello 84535, tel. 801/587–3235 or 800/574–4FUN), **Castle Country** (155 E. Main St., Box 1037, Price 84501, tel. 801/637–3009 or 800/464–3790).

Arriving and Departing by Plane

You can fly to Moab's airport, **Canyonlands Field** (tel. 801/259–7421), from Salt Lake City on Alpine Air (tel. 800/748–4899).

Arriving and Departing by Car, Train, and Bus

By Car   To reach southeastern Utah, take I–15 to U.S. 6 from Salt Lake City and the northwest, I–70 or U.S. 666 from Colorado and the east, and U.S. 191 from Wyoming and the northeast or Arizona and the south.

By Train   Amtrak has service to Helper and Thompson.

By Bus   Price is served by **Greyhound/Trailways** (tel. 800/231–2222).

Getting Around

By Car   Most roads on this tour are well-maintained two-lane highways. Be sure your car is in good working order, as there are long stretches of empty road between towns, and keep the gas tank topped off.

Guided Tours

Adrift Adventures (378 N. Main St., Box 577, Moab 84532, tel. 801/259–8594 or 800/874–4483) and **Canyonland Tours** (543 N. Main St., Moab 84532, tel. 801/259–5865) offer guided jeep tours into rugged wilderness areas. The **Canyonlands Field Institute** (1350 S. U.S. 191, Moab 84532, tel. 801/259–7750) sponsors seminars and nature walks. Rates vary.

Exploring Southeastern Utah

Numbers in the margin correspond to points of interest on the Utah map.

46   If you're headed into the area from the north, making a brief stop in **Helper** yields a worthwhile tribute to the local area's history. The **Western Mining and Railroad Museum**, housed in a former hotel that is part of a national historic district, features displays on the development of mining in Castle Country, Depression-era paintings, an archive room for researchers, and an outdoor display of trains and mining equipment. *296 S. Main St., tel. 801/472–3009. Admission: $1 suggested donation. Open mid-May–Sept., Mon.–Sat. 9–5; Oct.–mid-May, weekdays 10–4.*

47   The tour begins in earnest, however, in **Price,** the hub of Utah's Castle Country (so called because many rock formations resemble castles). As with virtually every other community in southern Utah, Price began as a Mormon farming enclave in the latter part of the 19th century. Shortly after it was established, however, the town took on a noticeably different character. In 1883 the railroad arrived, bringing with it immigrants from around the world. Nearby coal reserves were tapped, and the town has counted mining, not agriculture, as its primary industry ever since. Today, because many of Price's 10,000 residents are still employed in the coalfields, there are strong labor union ties in the community, a fact that makes Price and nearby Helper bastions of liberalism and the Democratic party in an otherwise conservative state.

While in many ways a modern town, Price has not forgotten its heritage and celebrates its ethnic diversity with two summer festivals. Song, dance, and food reminiscent of old Greece are the highlights of **Greek Days** in mid-July. **International Days,** which takes place during the first or second week in August in conjunction with the county fair, is a real local's event. If you should miss these colorful festivals, then be sure to visit the **Price Mural** in the Municipal Building (185 E. Main St.). A Works Progress Administration project, this 200-foot-long mural was painted between 1938 and 1941 by Lynn Fausett. It narrates the modern history of Price and surrounding Carbon County, beginning with the first white settlers.

As in other parts of Utah, the past in Castle Country extends at least a few years prior to the arrival of Mormon farmers in the 19th century—to about 150 million years ago. Housing one of the best collections of dinosaur memorabilia in the region is the **College of Eastern Utah Prehistoric Museum,** located next to the Price Municipal Building. Front and center in the museum's recently added Hall of Dinosaurs are several complete skeletons. A rare dinosaur egg is on display, as are dinosaur tracks unearthed by miners in nearby coal beds. *155 E. Main St., tel. 801/637–5060. Admission: $1 suggested donation. Open year-round, Mon.–Sat. 9–5; June–Sept., Sun. noon–5.*

From Price, drive southeast on U.S. 6/191 through the town of Wellington to the turnoff for **Nine Mile Canyon.** Known for the hundreds of petroglyphs etched into its boulders and cliffs, this enormous outdoor gallery is the handiwork of the Fremont Indians, who lived in much of what is now Utah from AD 300–1250. Indeed, the meaning of these images is one of the most mystifying puzzles of the area, but almost as confounding is how a canyon 40 miles long came to be named "Nine Mile." One explanation points to John Wesley Powell's epic float down the nearby Green River in 1869. It seems the expedition's mapmaker drew up a 9-mile triangulation, which he titled Nine Mile Creek. It's important not to disturb the fragile petroglyphs in any way. Additionally, because most of this 100-mile round-trip is on a gravel road, plan on taking most of a day to complete it.

Beyond the turnoff for Nine Mile Canyon, U.S. 6/191 continues southeast into some of the most desolate terrain anywhere. Known as the **San Rafael Desert,** this barren landscape can be a bit overwhelming, but views of the Book Cliffs to the east do lessen the monotony somewhat. Because this drive includes some lengthy straightaways, you may find yourself developing a heavy foot, but beware: The Utah Highway Patrol watches this stretch closely.

Nearly 60 miles from Price, U.S. 6/191 intersects I–70. Continue 5 miles east on the four-lane interstate to the town of **Green River.** Today travelers can avoid Green River completely, but not so long ago the highway traffic cruised right through town, because the town fathers fought a bypass in the name of commerce. Although no longer compulsory, a visit to Green River can be a pleasant experience. Thanks to irrigation water siphoned from the river of the same name, the town is known for its melons—watermelons, to be exact—and its annual **Melon Days** celebration. Held the third weekend in September, this small-town event features a parade and fair, plenty of music, and a canoe race.

Green River's claim to agricultural fame notwithstanding, the town is also known as a base for several river-running outfits— and for good reason. To the north, the Green River has carved two spectacular canyons, Desolation and Gray, whose rapids make them a favorite haunt of rafters. South of town, it drifts at a lazier pace through Labyrinth and Stillwater canyons, and the 68-mile stretch of river that runs south to Mineral Bottom in Canyonlands National Park is best suited for canoes and motorized boats.

While exploring Utah's wild waterways may seem like a thoroughly contemporary pastime, it actually enjoys a rich history—more than a century's worth, in fact. As the largest tributary of the Colorado River, the Green was the last major river in the continental United States to be explored. John Wesley Powell and a party of nine men rectified the situation with an epic voyage in 1869. Commemorating this feat is the **John Wesley Powell River History Museum.** In addition to various exhibits, artifacts, and works of art concerning 19th-century Western exploration, it also houses the River Runner's Hall of Fame, a tribute to those who have followed in Powell's wake. *Rte. 19 and the Green River, tel. 801/564–3427. Admission: $1. Open June–Sept., daily 8 AM–9 PM; Oct.–May, daily 9–5.*

For a bit of exploring on "dry" land, drive out to **Crystal Geyser,** 10 miles south of town on good, graded road. Reaching up to 60 feet high, this cold-water eruption blows three or four times a day and usually lasts for seven minutes. The staff at the Green River Information Center, which is located in the John Wesley Powell River History Museum, can provide approximate eruption times, detailed directions, and updated road conditions.

Another worthwhile excursion is the **Green River Scenic Drive,** which descends into the lower portion of Gray Canyon. Following the west bank of the river, this 10-mile route provides spectacular views of the Beckwith Plateau. After passing some sandy beachfront and a set of rapids, you'll know you're nearing the end as the aptly named landmark Nefertiti comes into view. A primitive campground is located here, and it is possible to hike upstream for several miles along old cattle trails. Because all but 1½ miles of this drive is on dirt road, be sure to check on conditions beforehand. Wet weather renders the drive impassable, but when dry it's suitable for cars with good clearance. From Main Street, follow the Hastings Road (1200 East St.) north.

From Green River, drive 20 miles east on I–70, turn south on **50** U.S. 191, and continue 32 miles to **Moab.** Established in the 1870s adjacent to the Colorado River, Moab was supposed to be a Mormon farming community. The discovery of uranium in the early 1950s, however, made the plan moot. Within a few years the town's population tripled, as prospectors armed with Geiger counters flooded in. One of these was Charlie Steen, a penniless young man from Texas. Striking it very rich with his Mi Vida mine, Steen built a mansion overlooking town in which he threw lavish parties. Although he may have been a bit more eccentric than most of his neighbors, Steen and his lifestyle were characteristic of the town's freewheeling ways, which led to the saying that Moab stands for "Mormons on a binge."

Moab is still quite lively and enjoys a greater-than-average influx of outsiders, but it is no longer mineral wealth that draws visitors. Rather, it is the beauty of the surrounding canyons, mesas, and mountains. First lured to Moab by the establishment of Canyonlands National Park in 1964, a small but dedicated corps of outdoor enthusiasts has long known of the area's outstanding rafting and hiking opportunities (*see* Sports and the Outdoors, *below*). Similarly, four-wheelers have rallied in Moab every Easter since 1966 to participate in the Moab Jeep Safari. Within the last few years, however, Moab's tourism industry has grown by leaps and bounds. A number of new motels have sprung up, seemingly overnight. A McDonald's was built on South Main. A brew pub now serves homemade beer, and one of the banks has even installed an automatic teller machine. What could bring such unprecedented change to this distant corner of the state? Move over, boaters, hikers, and Jeepers; meet the mountain bike.

All-terrain bicycles are well suited for the many miles of rugged back roads left behind by uranium prospectors. What has really put Moab on every mountain biker's map, though, is a simple matter of geology; the asphalt-smooth sandstone, or slickrock, that characterizes much of canyon country is to mountain biking what powder snow is to skiing (*see* Sports and the Outdoors, *below*).

If you happen to visit Moab sans raft, backpack, four-wheel-drive vehicle, or mountain bike, don't despair. The area still offers plenty of places that require nothing more than a car and your own two feet to explore. Perhaps the handiest of these is **Arches National Park,** located a few miles north. Boasting the largest collection of natural arches in the world, the park is a geologic wonderland unlike any other. Although the process by which these spans of red rock were formed is complex, geologists do point to an underlying bed of salt as the main impetus. As this material shifted, fissures formed in the overlying layer of sandstone. Wind and water then eroded this rock into free-standing fins, which were in turn sculpted into the arches and formations seen today. Many of the park's premier sights, including the Courthouse Towers, Balanced Rock, the Windows, and Skyline Arch, are found along the park's 21-mile paved road. Others, such as Delicate Arch, the Fiery Furnace, and Devil's Garden, are accessible only by foot. Other than the visitor center at the park entrance and the 50-site Devil's Garden Campground, which lies at road's end, there are no services in Arches. *5 mi north of Moab on U.S. 191, tel. 801/259–8161. Admission: $3 per vehicle. Visitor center open daily 8–sunset.*

A bit more remote but spectacular in its own right is **Canyonlands National Park.** Encompassing some 500 square miles of rugged desert terrain, Canyonlands is naturally divided by the Colorado and Green rivers into three districts. While the Needles and Maze districts are accessible from points farther on in this tour, the **Island in the Sky District** is reached from Moab. As the name suggests, this portion of the park features a high plateau ringed by thousand-foot cliffs. A favorite among photographers is Mesa Arch, which is reached by hiking a ¼-mile trail. A number of scenic overlooks, each of which is precariously perched at land's end, are accessed by 20 miles of paved road. From the Shafer Canyon Overlook, you gaze down upon the twisted Shafer Trail—an early 1900s cattle route that was later upgraded for high-clearance vehicles. From Grand View Point, you can take in spectacular views of the meandering Colorado and Green rivers, the sandstone pinnacles of the Needles District far to the south, and the labyrinths of the Maze District to the southwest. *33 mi from Moab on U.S. 191 north and Rte. 313 west, tel. 801/259–7164. Admission: $3 per vehicle. Visitor center open daily 8–sunset.*

51 Nearly matching the breadth of the view from Grand View Point is the panorama to be had at nearby **Dead Horse Point State Park.** One of the finest of Utah's state parks, it overlooks a sweeping oxbow of the Colorado River, some 2,000 feet below. Dead Horse Point itself is a small peninsula connected to the main mesa by a narrow neck of land. As the story goes, cowboys used to drive wild horses onto the point and pen them there with a brush fence. Some were accidentally forgotten and left to perish. Facilities at the park include a modern visitor center and museum, a campground with drinking water, and an overlook. *34 mi from Moab at end of Rte. 313, tel. 801/259–6511. Admission: $3 per vehicle. Open daily 8–sunset.*

Although the stretches of the Colorado River visible from the Island in the Sky and Dead Horse Point can be accessed only by boat, other portions can be enjoyed up close along two scenic drives. Branching off from U.S. 191 2 miles north of Moab is the **Colorado River Scenic Byway.** Also known as Route 128, this paved road follows the Colorado River northeast to I-70. First passing through a high-walled corridor, the drive eventually breaks out into Professor Valley, home of the monoliths of Fisher Towers and Castle Rock, which you may remember from various car commercials. The byway also passes the single-lane Dewey Bridge, in use from 1916 to 1986. Near the end of the 44-mile drive is the tiny town of Cisco. Although a thriving community during the uranium boom, Cisco is today all but abandoned. It is worth a visit just to see what has to be one of the smallest post offices in the nation.

A second interesting drive follows the Potash Road, or Route 279, 15 miles downstream. After entering the Portal (a break in the high cliffs west of town), the **Potash Scenic Byway** continues through a gorge with a number of petroglyphs etched by the Fremont Indians. The canyon's walls are also a favorite of rock climbers. At the end of the pavement is the Moab Salt Plant, formerly known as the Potash Plant. This facility extracts salt and potash from deposits hundreds of feet below by injecting a solution into drill holes and then pumping it out to large evaporation ponds. Beyond the plant, a rough dirt road continues on to the previously mentioned Shafer Trail.

Although Moab is best known for its slickrock desert, it is also the gateway to the second-highest mountain range in the state—the 12,000-foot **La Sal Mountains.** Because these peaks remain snowcapped a good part of the year, they provide a striking contrast to the red-rock desert of lower elevations. Exploring them is easy, thanks to the paved **La Sal Mountain Loop.** Beginning 8 miles south of town, this 62-mile drive climbs up and over the western flank of the range before dropping into Castle Valley and Route 128 to the north. Along the way a number of scenic pull offs and hiking trails are accessible. Long a favorite haunt of locals, the La Sal Mountain Loop is now being discovered by out of towners as both a retreat from the heat in the summer and a wonderful place to cross-country ski in the winter.

On those rare days when the weather may not be conducive to outdoor fun, pay a visit to the **Hollywood Stuntmen's Hall of Fame.** Recalling Moab's long association with Hollywood, from John Ford's *The Wagonmaster* in 1949 to *Thelma and Louise,* this collection of movie memorabilia highlights the important but often risky role of the stunt person in bringing life to the silver screen. A theater regularly runs stunt footage and occasionally features live performances. *100 N. 100 East St., tel. 801/259-6100. Admission: $3. Open weekdays 10-9, weekends 7-9.*

For a taste of history in the Moab area, stop by the **Dan O'Laurie Museum.** The Fremont and Anasazi Indians are remembered in exhibits of sandals, baskets, pottery, and other artifacts. The Ute, a Native American group that has lived in the region during more recent times, command some attention here. A display on the 1776 Dominguez–Escalante Expedition reveals the role that the Spanish played in exploring this part of the West, and the variety of rocks, fossils, and dinosaur bones speaks of the influence that geology has had in shaping life in southeastern Utah. *118 E. Center St., tel. 801/259-7985. Admission free. Open Apr.–Oct., Mon.–Sat. 1-5 and 7-9; Nov.–Oct., Mon.–Thurs. 3-5 and 7-9, Fri. and Sat. 1-5 and 7-9.*

Having had your fill of Moab, continue south on U.S. 191 toward Monticello. Along the way, you might stop for a quick scramble to the base of **Wilson Arch.** With a few hours to spare, you can enjoy the two remarkable vistas featured in the **Canyon Rims Recreation Area.** Located 22 miles west of the highway, the Needles Overlook takes in the southern end of Canyonlands National Park. Less than 20 miles farther is the Anticline Overlook, which encompasses the Colorado River, Dead Horse Point, and other locales to the north.

Shortly after the turnoff for the Canyon Rims Recreation Area is the road to the **Needles District** of Canyonlands National Park, a land of countless spires and monoliths, not to mention several interesting canyons that are fun to hike. Four-wheelers can delight in tackling Elephant Hill, one of the most challenging Jeep routes in the West. A visitor center and campground are the only facilities in the Needles District. *35 mi west of U.S. 191 on Rte. 211, tel. 801/259-7164. Admission: $3 per vehicle. Open daily 8-sunset.*

Either on your way in or as you leave the Needles District, be **52** sure to stop at **Newspaper Rock State Park.** Beginning 2,000 years ago, prehistoric inhabitants of the region began etching cryptic images on a large rock face. In the centuries following, subsequent chapters of an undecipherable history were added, resulting in an impressive collection of petroglyphs that archaeologists cite as one of the most comprehensive in the Southwest. An interpretive trail and small campground are provided. *12 mi west of U.S. 191 on Rte. 211, tel. 801/624-3268. Admission: free. Always open.*

53 Back on U.S. 191, it's a quick 14 miles to **Monticello,** the seat of San Juan County. A mostly Mormon community, this quiet town has seen some growth in recent years, mostly in the form of new motels. Situated at 7,000 feet, Monticello provides a cool respite from the summer heat of the desert, and it's at the doorstep of the **Abajo Mountains.** The highest point in the range, 11,360-foot **Abajo Peak,** is accessed by a road that branches off the graded, 22-mile Blue Mountain Loop. Although it's suited for most four-wheel-drive, high-clearance vehicles, be sure to first inquire with the **Manti–La Sal National Forest** (tel. 801/587–2141) about up-to-date road conditions.

Beyond Monticello, U.S. 191 continues south for 21 miles to the slightly larger town of **Blanding.** A tad more conservative, Blanding is dry: That is, there is no state liquor store, and no beer is sold in grocery or convenience stores. What Blanding does offer, however, is the **Edge of the Cedars State Monument.** Here, one of the nation's foremost museums dedicated to the Anasazi Indians displays a variety of pots, baskets, spear points, and such. Interestingly, many of these artifacts were donated by guilt-ridden pot hunters, or archaeological looters. Behind the museum, you can visit an actual Anasazi ruin. Having recently undergone extensive renovation, the monument is now bigger and better than ever. *660 W. 400 North St., tel. 801/678–2238. Admission: $1.50 adults, $1 children 6–15, under 6 free. Open June–Sept., daily 9–6; rest of year, daily 9–5.*

A few miles south of Blanding, a right-hand turn on Route 95 heads west on what promoters alternately call the Bicentennial Highway and the Trail of the Ancients. So as not to miss some interesting sights, however, first continue your tour south on U.S. 191 to **Bluff,** situated on the San Juan River. One of southeastern Utah's oldest towns, Bluff began as a farming community in the 1880s. Reminders of its past include several historic homes that were skillfully fashioned from blocks of local sandstone. The area also includes small kivas and cliff dwellings that attest to the presence of the Anasazi centuries ago. Their descendants, residents of the **Navajo Indian Nation,** the largest Indian reservation, visit Bluff to shop, gas up, or eat out. Today Bluff witnesses a steady stream of boaters setting out for a float down the San Juan from the **Sand Island Recreation Site** (3 mi west of Bluff). In addition to a developed launch site, this BLM facility includes a primitive campground and one of the largest panels of rock art in the Four Corners area.

Head east to U.S. 160 and take a right to reach the **Four Corners Monument,** the only place in the country where four states (Utah, Arizona, Colorado, and New Mexico) meet. Administered by the Navajo tribe, Four Corners offers not only a geography lesson but also a great opportunity to buy Indian jewelry directly from the Navajos themselves.

Return to Bluff and continue west. The next stop is **Mexican Hat,** another small community situated on the north bank of the San Juan River. Named for a nearby rock formation, which you can't miss on the way into town, Mexican Hat is a jumping-off point for two geological wonders.

By crossing the river and driving 21 miles south on U.S. 163 across Navajo land, you will reach the **Monument Valley Tribal Park.** Thanks to its striking red-rock spires, buttes, and mesas, Monument Valley has earned international recognition as the setting for dozens of movies and television commercials. Just as memorable as the scenery, though, is the taste of Navajo culture you can get here. In addition to visiting the historic Gouldings Trading Post (*see* Shopping, *below*) and shopping at its rows of arts and crafts booths, plan on taking a Navajo-guided tour of the valley. These informative excursions invariably include a stop at a hogan, the traditional Navajo home.

Guide services can be acquired at park headquarters (Box 93, Mountain Valley 84536, tel. 801/727–3287) and vary in cost.

58 A second local, must-see natural wonder is the **Goosenecks of the San Juan River** (10 mi northwest of Mexican Hat off Rte. 261). From the overlook, you can peer down upon what geologists claim is the best example of an "entrenched meander" in the world. The river's serpentine course resembles the necks of geese in spectacular 1,000-foot-deep chasms. Although the Goosenecks of the San Juan River is actually a state park, no facilities other than pit toilets are found here, and no fee is charged.

From the turnoff for the Goosenecks, Route 261 heads north toward what looks to be an impregnable 1,200-foot wall of rock. In actuality, the road climbs this obstacle in a steep, 3-mile ascent known as the **Moki Dugway**. Unpaved but well graded, the series of tight curves is manageable by passenger car. At a pull off near the top, be sure to take in the superb view of the **Valley of the Gods.** Featuring scattered buttes and spires, this lonesome valley is accessed by a 17-mile dirt road that begins just south of the dugway.

At the top of the Moki Dugway, the drive returns to pavement as Route 261 tracks north across Cedar Mesa—relatively flat terrain that is thick with piñon pine and juniper, but not cedar. On occasion, you might spy a canyon break in the distance. Actually, several canyons divide this plateau land. Once home to the Anasazi, these drainages feature hundreds if not thousands of their cliff dwellings. **Grand Gulch,** the largest of these drainages, is today protected as a primitive area and is quite popular among backpackers.

Thirty-five miles north of Mexican Hat, Route 261 connects up with the Trail of the Ancients (Route 95). A short distance west **59** is the turnoff for **Natural Bridges National Monument.** Different from an arch, a natural bridge, which spans a drainage or streambed, is created by water's erosion. Three natural bridges—Sipapu, Kachina, and Owachomo—are visible from a scenic drive that loops through the small monument. A second item of interest is the monument's impressive bank of solar panels. Upon completion in 1980, it was the largest solar-energy system in the world. *Rte. 275 off Rte. 95, tel. 801/259–7164. Admission: $3 per vehicle. Open daily 8–sunset.*

Shortly beyond Natural Bridges National Monument, a choice must be made. What lies ahead is the Colorado River, a major obstacle for the Mormon settlers of the 1800s. Today, however, this mightiest of Western rivers has been stilled by the Glen Canyon Dam and **Lake Powell.** Your decision is whether to cross the lake quickly by bridge or take the longer way around and cross by ferry. If you choose the latter, turn left on Route 276 and drive 40 miles to the Hall's Crossing Marina. Like all four marinas on Lake Powell, Hall's Crossing includes a gas station, campground, motel, general store, and boat docks. Since 1985, however, it has also served as the eastern terminus of the **Lake Powell Ferry.** From here the 100-foot *John Atlantic Burr* will float you and your car across a 3-mile stretch of the lake to the Bullfrog Basin Marina, from which it's an hour's drive north to rejoin Route 95. *Hall's Crossing Marina, Rte. 276, tel. 801/ 684–2261. No reservations. Ferry fees: $2 per foot passenger;*

*$9 per car, including all passengers. Crossings: mid-May–
Sept., 6 per day; Oct.–mid-May, 4 per day.*

Of course if you have even more time, you can explore Lake
Powell itself (although as the second-largest man-made lake in
the United States, it would take years to explore fully). Certainly, the most pleasurable way to see the lake is to rent a
houseboat at any of the four marinas and set out across the
lake's intriguing blue waters. However, guided day tours are
also available. A popular excursion sets out from the Bullfrog,
Hall's Crossing, or Wahweap (in Arizona) Marina to Rainbow
Bridge. The largest natural bridge in the world, this 290-foot-
high, 275-foot-wide span is breathtaking. *For rentals and
tours: Lake Powell Resorts and Marinas, 2916 N. 35th Ave.,
Phoenix, AZ 85017, tel. 800/528–6154. Houseboat rentals begin
at $507 for 3 days in off-season; day trip to Rainbow Bridge
starts at $160.*

If you don't even have the extra two to four hours for the ferry,
then follow Route 95 to **Hite Crossing.** (Just before the bridge, a
left turn leads to Hite Marina—the only services for miles
around.) Upon crossing the bridge, continue north past the
11,000-foot Henry Mountains to Hanksville, a good place to gas
up. Here, pick up Route 24, and head northeast toward I–70.
About a dozen miles out of town, signs point the way to **Goblin
Valley State Park.** As the name implies, the area is filled with
hundreds of gnomelike rock formations, and there's a small
campground with modern rest rooms and showers. *12 mi n. of
Hanksville on Rte. 24, tel. 801/564–3633. Admission: $3 per ve-
hicle. Open daily 8–sunset.*

A bit north of Goblin Valley, you may notice a long line of flat-
iron-shape cliffs jutting from the desert floor to the west. This
is the San Rafael Reef—the front of the 80-mile-long **San
Rafael Swell.** Rugged and quite expansive, the San Rafael Swell
is a popular destination for outdoor lovers of various persua-
sions. After turning west on I–70, you can get an up-close look
at this impressive landform from a turnoff located where the interstate passes through the sawtooth ridge.

A little more than 50 miles west of the Route 24 interchange,
turn north on Route 10 to complete the last leg of this tour. After passing through the small towns of Emery (the first outpost
of civilization since Hanksville) and Ferron, you'll reach **Castle
Dale,** where you may notice that the surrounding countryside
is beginning to look familiar. That's because you have re-en-
tered Castle Country, the northern half of which includes
Price. In Castle Dale, the **Emery County Museum** reveals more
about 19th-century life, through period rooms, and more about
the Anasazi and Fremont Indians. As further proof that you
are indeed closing in on Price, there are a number of dinosaur
bones on display. *City Hall, 64 E. 100 North St., tel. 801/381–
2115. Admission: $1 adults. Open Mon.–Sat. 9–5.*

Two scenic byways climb west from Castle Country into the
nearby **Manti Mountains.** The first travels for a little over 20
miles on Route 29 from Castle Dale to the subalpine setting of
Joe's Valley. The second begins in Huntington, to the north,
and follows Route 31 for 50 miles to Electric Lake. Both drives
offer stunning fall colors in late September and early October.

As a nearby power plant suggests, the town of **Huntington**
counts its coal reserves as its most valuable resource. It is also

home to Huntington State Park, with a 250-acre reservoir, and
Ⓖ is the nearest sizable community to the **Cleveland-Lloyd Dinosaur Quarry.** Reached by Route 155 and a series of graded
roads, the quarry features, in addition to an enclosed quarry, a
visitor center and an outdoor nature trail. Having produced
more complete skeletons than any other site in the world, the
Cleveland-Lloyd Quarry is one of the state's premier destinations for dinosaur aficionados. *20 mi east of Huntington on Rte.
155, tel. 801/637–4584. Admission free. Open Easter–Memorial Day, weekends 10–5; Memorial Day–Labor Day, daily
10–5.*

What to See and Do with Children

Hole 'n the Rock is a 14-room home carved into a solid rock wall.
It would be just another roadside attraction if it didn't represent 20 years of toil for Albert and Gladys Christensen. Kids
can run around all over it. *15 mi south of Moab on U.S. 191, tel.
801/686–2250. Admission: $1.50. Open June–Sept., daily 8–8;
Oct.–May, daily 9–5.*

Off the Beaten Track

For anyone with an abiding interest in the Anasazi Indians, a
visit to **Hovenweep National Monument** is a must. Located
along a remote stretch of the Utah–Colorado border southeast
of Blanding, Hovenweep features several unusual tower structures that may have been used for making astronomical obser-
vations. By marking the summer solstice, these early farmers
knew the best times of the year to plant their crops. Because
Hovenweep is accessible only by graded gravel road, you can
count on having the monument pretty much to yourself. *21 mi
east of U.S. 191 on Rte. 262, tel. 303/529–4465. Admission free.
Open daily 8–sunset.*

Of the three districts within Canyonlands National Park, the
Maze is by far the most remote. Requiring a four-wheel-drive
vehicle and a steady hand at the wheel, the route into the Maze
begins north of Hanksville. After nearly 50 miles of high-
clearance dirt road, you must then drive the incredibly rugged
Flint Trail. At road's end, intrepid travelers will find not only a
wonderful view of the Maze but also a trail of sorts that runs to
the bottom. A scrambled collection of sandstone canyons, the
Maze is one of the most appropriately named features in Southern Utah. If you do make the drive into the Maze, consider a
visit to nearby Horseshoe Canyon. Featuring pictographs that
possibly date back several thousand years, this annex of Canyonlands National Park is well worth the 4-mile hike in. *50 mi.
from Rte. 24 on a dirt road; take the turn off near Globin Valley
State Park. Tel. 801/259–7164. Admission: $4 per vehicle or $2
for individuals.*

Shopping

Specialty Stores   When in Monument Valley, be sure to stop at **Gouldings Trad-**
Native American   **ing Post** (tel. 801/727–3231) for a wide selection of fine hand-
Arts and Crafts   crafted jewelry, Navajo rugs, pottery, and such. You can be
sure everything sold here is authentic, as the store has a reputation that extends back to 1923 to protect.

Rocks and Minerals In Moab, be sure to check out the **Moab Rock Shop** (600 N. Main St., tel. 801/259–7312) for one of the most interesting rock collections in the state. The shop is owned by Lin Ottinger, a long-time resident of Moab and backcountry tour guide.

Sporting Goods For outdoor sports enthusiasts, a visit to Moab would not be complete without stopping by **Rim Cyclery** (94 W. 100 North St., tel. 801/259–5333). A fixture in town long before Moab was ever "discovered," it offers a wide array of bicycles, plus a full line of accessories, parts, and outdoor clothing.

Sports and the Outdoors

Biking Mountain bikes are the bicycle of choice in southeastern Utah and are at home on most any back road or trail (provided they are allowed). In the slickrock desert that surrounds **Moab,** the possibilities are inexhaustible. The most popular off-road cycling route is the **Slickrock Trail,** a few miles east of Moab. Beginners should master the 2½-mile practice loop before tackling the longer and more difficult 10.3-mile main loop. Another popular ride is the one to **Gemini Bridges,** which begins a few miles north of town along U.S. 191. For expedition-length rides, try either the 100-mile **White Rim Trail** in Canyonlands National Park or the 140-mile **Kokopelli Trail,** which runs from Grand Junction, Colorado, to Moab.

Price also has a fair number of mountain-biking routes from which to choose. The **San Rafael Swell** features many Jeep trails ideal for exploring on bicycle, and **Nine Mile Canyon** is also popular. For information on both areas, check with the BLM (900 N. 700 East St., Price 84501, tel. 801/637–4584).

Camping Of the many appealing campgrounds found in the **Moab** area, **Devil's Garden** in Arches National Park, **Squaw Flat** in the Needles District of Canyonlands National Park, and **Dead Horse Point State Park** are the best bets for finding good facilities along with interesting vistas or hiking trails nearby. Another nice spot is the **Wind Whistle Campground** in the BLM's Canyon Rims Recreation Area.

Outside of **Price** check out the **Price Canyon Recreation Area** (18 mi northwest of Price along U.S. 6). It is operated by the BLM.

Canoeing **Green River** serves as a put-in point for those headed into **Labyrinth Canyon.** Here canoeists are king, for there is barely a ripple along the entire route. For information, contact the BLM in Price (*see* Biking, *above*).

Fishing Although it doesn't figure that you should bring your tackle box to the desert, **Lake Powell** is known for its bass fishing. A Utah fishing license and further information may be obtained at any of the marinas.

Four-Wheeling With routes like the White Rim Trail, Elephant Hill, and the Moab Rim, **Moab** has been a mecca for off-road lovers for decades. Tours are available through **Lin Ottinger Tours** (600 N. Main St. 84532, tel. 801/259–7312) and **Tag-A-Long Expeditions** (452 N. Main St., Box 1206, 84532, tel. 801/259–8946 or 800/453–3292), among others.

Gaining in popularity among four-wheelers is the **San Rafael Swell,** west of Green River. In the same area, **Buckhorn Draw, Hidden Splendor,** and the **San Rafael Desert** are also favored destinations. Contact the BLM in Price (*see* Biking, *above*) for information.

Golf   Two 18-hole courses are **Blue Mountain Meadows Golf Course** (549 S. Main St. Monticello, tel. 801/587–2468 or 800/225–1898) and **Moab Golf Club** (2750 S. East Bench Rd., Moab, tel. 801/259–6488).

Hiking   There are countless hiking trails around **Moab.** In **Arches National Park,** good routes access the Courthouse Towers, Windows, and Devil's Garden areas. Of the many trails in the **Needles District** of Canyonlands National Park, the Joint Trail is very interesting, and on BLM land just outside of Moab, the **Mill Creek Canyon** and **Hidden Valley** trails are popular.

Rafting   As it flows through **Moab,** the **Colorado River** is misleadingly calm; white-water adventures await rafters both upstream and down. Upriver, near the Colorado state line, is **Westwater Canyon,** an exciting one- or two-day float that includes legendary rapids. Moab's **Daily** river run, which begins along Route 128, offers somewhat tamer waters just out of town. Downstream from Moab, in the heart of Canyonlands National Park, is **Cataract Canyon,** which features more than two dozen rapids in a 14-mile stretch. A permit is required from the BLM (Grand Resource Area, Box M, Moab 84532, tel. 801/259–8193) to run Westwater, and a trip down Cataract Canyon requires one from Canyonlands National Park (*see* National and State Parks in Essential Information, *above*).

If you want to hook up with a raft-outfitting company, try **Adrift Adventures** (378 N. Main St., Box 577, Moab 84532, tel. 801/259–8594 or 800/874–4483) or **Tag-A-Long Tours** (452 N. Main St., Box 1206, Moab 84532, tel. 801/259–8946 or 800/453–3292). They have both been in Moab for many years and have good reputations.

While somewhat calmer than the Colorado, the **San Juan River** offers some truly exceptional scenery. It can be run in two sections: from Bluff to Mexican Hat and from Mexican Hat to Lake Powell. For permits, contact the BLM (San Juan Resource Area, Box 7, Monticello 84535, tel. 801/587–2141).

Water Sports   **Lake Powell** is a water-sports area like no other. Although sailing is not a particularly worthwhile endeavor thanks to the high sandstone walls, waterskiing, pleasure cruising, and houseboating are (*see* Exploring Southeastern Utah, *above*).

Dining and Lodging

Blanding   **Comfort Inn.** The fact that a national chain built in remote
Lodging   Blanding suggests that southeastern Utah is gaining prominence as a travel destination. Because this is a new property, it includes a variety of amenities. A complimentary Continental breakfast is included. *711 S. Main St., 84511, tel. 801/678–3271 or 800/622–3250. 52 rooms. Facilities: restaurant, indoor pool, hot tub, exercise room, laundry room. AE, D, DC, MC, V. Moderate.*

Bluff   **Sunbonnet Café.** The café serves a variety of American food in a
Dining   Western log-cabin setting, but is best known for the Navajo taco: an oversize flap of Indian fry bread piled high with pinto beans, red or green chili, lettuce, tomatoes, and cheese. *Rte.*

163, along the Bluff's Historic Loop, tel. 801/672-2201. MC, V. Inexpensive.

Lodging **Recapture Lodge.** In addition to comfortable rooms, this locally owned motel provides guided tours into the surrounding canyon country. Slide shows are presented at night. *U.S. 191, Box 309, 84512, tel. 801/672-2281. 36 rooms. Facilities: heated outdoor pool, hot tub, laundry room. AE, D, MC, V. Inexpensive.*

Green River **Ray's Tavern.** Because man (and woman) cannot live on melons
Dining alone, stop here for one of the best burgers in the state. Topped
★ with a thick slice of onion, tomato, and lettuce, this all-beef monstrosity is nestled in a large helping of steak fries. Although a draw of cold beer is optional, interesting conversation is not. That's because Ray's is a favorite hangout for river runners. Although at times a surly bunch, they're always ready with some great tale about working on the river. If you have time, be sure to rack up a game of pool. *25 S. Broadway, tel. 801/564-3511. No credit cards. Inexpensive.*

Tamarisk Restaurant. New in Green River, this sit-down eatery features homemade pies and fudge in addition to dinner specials. The riverside setting makes dining here a treat. *870 E. Main St., tel. 801/564-8109. AE, D, DC, MC, V. Inexpensive.*

Lodging **Best Western River Terrace Hotel.** The setting, on the banks of the Green River, is conducive to a good night's rest. Comfortable rooms are furnished with large beds, and the premises are clean. *880 E. Main St., tel. 801/564-3401 or 800/528-1234, fax 801/564-3403. 51 rooms. Facilities: restaurant, outdoor pool, hot tub, exercise room. AE, D, DC, MC, V. Moderate.*

Moab **Center Café.** This is Moab's version of nouvelle cuisine, and a
Dining successful one at that. It features the likes of cioppino, roast
★ game hen, and prawns and pasta baked in paper. Such tempting dishes have been a long time in coming to this meat-and-potatoes town. A prix fixe menu and a wine list are also available. *92 E. Center St., tel. 801/259-4295. Reservations advised. Dress: neat but casual. AE, MC, V. Closed for lunch. Moderate.*

Cattleman's. If you follow the premise that truckers know all the best places to eat, then you might give this truck stop a try. It cooks up burgers, sandwiches, prime rib, steaks, and breakfast 24 hours a day. *1991 S. U.S. 191, tel. 801/259-6585. AE, D, MC, V. Inexpensive.*

La Hacienda. Since opening its doors in 1981, this restaurant has earned a reputation for serving good south-of-the-border meals at an equally good price. The helpings are generous and the service is friendly. And yes, you can order a margarita, too. *574 N. Main St., tel. 801/259-6319. AE, MC, V. Inexpensive.*

Poplar Place. This local landmark for fun and lively dining is known for its appetizers, pizzas, and sandwiches. If you're not too hungry, just stop in for a drink and some Poplar Hot Wings. *100 N. Main St., tel. 801/259-6018. MC, V. Inexpensive.*

Rumors Gourmet Café. This new café is the perfect place to sit down with friends. The atmosphere is completely casual, and the food is tasty. From the lunch menu, the Philly steak sandwich is a good choice, but so, too, is the chef's salad topped with homemade dressings. Breakfasts are reputed to be the best in town. *606 S. Main St., tel. 801/259-5908. No credit cards. Closed for dinner. Inexpensive.*

Lodging ★ **Pack Creek Ranch.** A real treat, this out-of-the-way (and glad of it) guest ranch sits beneath the snowcapped summits of the La Sal Mountains. Wildlife abounds in this natural setting off the southern end of the La Sal Mountain Loop. Rooms are spacious and luxurious, including woven rugs, bent-willow furnishings, and refrigerators; most have stone fireplaces. This is one of those places that can get away with no TVs in the rooms; the main feature here is peace and solitude in a spectacular setting. Meals (all of which are included in the price) are served in a rustically cozy dining hall, replete with wagon-wheel chandeliers and oil lamps. The menu echoes the ranching life with such meals as barbecue chicken and French pepper steak. The pool is located within earshot of the creek. *Box 1270, 84532, tel. 801/259-5505, fax 801/259-8879. 12 rooms. Facilities: restaurant, outdoor pool, hot tub, trail rides. AE, D, MC, V. Very Expensive.*

Comfort Suites. Moab's newest major hotel is somewhat of an anomaly in town—and a sign of things to come. It has nice suites, an attractive lobby area, and a fitness facility impressive for Moab. *800 S. Main St., 84532, tel. 801/259-5252 or 800/221-2222, fax 801/259-7110. 53 rooms. Facilities: indoor pool, hot tub, exercise room. AE, D, DC, MC, V. Moderate.*

Landmark Motel. Newly remodeled, this motel offers deluxe rooms in a convenient location near many downtown restaurants and shops. *168 N. Main St., 84532, tel. 801/259-6147 or 800/441-6147, fax 801/259-5556. 36 rooms. Facilities: outdoor pool, hot tub, laundry room. AE, D, DC, MC, V. Moderate.*

Monticello
Lodging ★ **Grist Mill Inn.** A bed-and-breakfast like this deserves more than the usual accolades. Housed in a 1933 flour mill—yes, a flour mill—are six beautiful suites that are superbly appointed. There is a library on the third floor, a sitting room with a fireplace, and plenty of charm to spare. Additional guest rooms are located next door. No smoking is allowed in the rooms, and a full breakfast is included. *64 S. 300 East St., Box 156, 84535, tel. 801/587-2597 or 800/645-3762. 9 rooms. Facilities: dining room, library, sitting room, hot tub. AE, DC, MC, V. Moderate.*

Monument Valley
Lodging **Gouldings Lodge.** This is the best place from which to tour Monument Valley and the surrounding Navajo Nation. Rooms are nice and the service is friendly. Part of the 1923 Gouldings Trading Post, the lodge gives guests a good feel for the history of the area. Be sure to peruse the shop for Native American arts and crafts. *Box 360001, 84536, tel. 801/727-3231 or 800/874-0902, fax 801/727-3344. 64 rooms. Facilities: restaurant, outdoor pool. AE, D, DC, MC, V. Moderate.*

Price
Dining **Greek Streak.** For the real McCoy (or Mykonos) in Greek food, this is the place in Price. Family owned, the restaurant serves up gyros, lamb stew, and roast lamb, among other authentic dishes. *84 S. Carbon Ave., tel. 801/637-1930. MC, V. Closed Sun. Moderate.*

Lodging **Carriage House Inn.** Unlike some locally owned motor inns, which can disappoint, this one in downtown Price outpaces the big national chains in all respects. For a good price, you get a clean and comfortable room, plus personal service. *590 E. Main St. 84501, tel. 801/637-5660 or 800/228-5732, fax 801/637-5660. 41 rooms. Facilities: restaurant, indoor pool, hot tub. AE, D, DC, MC, V. Inexpensive.*

Nightlife

Most nightlife is concentrated in Moab. **Poplar Place** (*see* Dining and Lodging, *above*) offers live music, usually folk or soft rock. On weekends, there's live country music at **Rio Colorado Restaurant** (2 S. 100 West St., tel. 801/259–6666) and the **Sportsman's Lounge** (1991 S. U.S. 191, tel. 801/259–9972).

Southwestern Utah

When Mormon pioneers came to this distant corner of Utah in the early 1860s, it was determined that they could and would grow cotton. Given the warm temperatures, the crop was a viable one, and, thanks to the economic independence it promised to bring to the territory, it was to be an important one as well. After 1869, however, the newly completed transcontinental railroad provided a cheaper source of the fiber, rendering Utah's cotton farms unnecessary. Today "Utah's Dixie" still attracts people with the promise of warm weather—so much so that the largest community in the area, St. George, is also the state's fastest-growing one. In addition to this enviable climate, there is a wealth of scenic wonders, from desert to sierra, and boundless opportunities to hike, bike, and tee off.

Important Addresses and Numbers

Tourist Information The following regional travel offices cover the southwest: **Color Country** (906 N. 1400 West St., Box 1550, St. George 84771, tel. 801/628–4171 or 800/233–8824) and **Panoramaland** (250 N. Main St., Box 820, Richfield 84701, tel. 801/896–9222 or 800/748–4361).

Eight counties also maintain tourism bureaus: **Beaver County Travel Council** (Box 272, Beaver 84713, tel. 801/438–2975), **Garfield County Travel Council** (Box 200, Panguitch 84759, tel. 801/676–8826 or 800/444–6689), **Iron County Tourism and Convention Bureau** (Box 1007, Cedar City 84720, tel. 801/586–5124), **Kanab County Travel Council** (41 S. 100 East St., Kanab 84741, tel. 801/644–5033 or 800/644–KANAB), **Piute Tourism Board** (Piute County Courthouse, Junction 84740, tel. 801/577–2840), **Sevier Travel Council** (220 N. 600 West St., Richfield 84701, tel. 801/896–6904), **Washington County Travel and Convention Bureau** (425 S. 700 East St., St. George 84770, tel. 800/869–6635), and **Wayne County Travel Council** (County Clerk, Courthouse, Loa 84747, tel. 801/836–2731).

Arriving and Departing by Plane

Airports and Airlines SkyWest (tel. 801/575–2508 or 800/453–9417) flies to **Cedar City** and **St. George** municipal airports.

Arriving and Departing by Car, Train, or Bus

By Car Interstate 15 is the main route into the region: from Las Vegas to the southwest and Salt Lake City to the northeast.

By Train **Milford** receives Amtrak service (tel. 800/872–7245).

By Bus **Greyhound/Trailways** (tel. 800/231–2222) runs buses along the I–15 corridor, making stops in **Beaver** (El Bambi Café, 935 N. Main St., tel. 801/438–2229), **Parowan** (20 N. Main St., tel. 801/

477–3421), **Cedar City** (1355 S. Main St., tel. 801/586–9465), and **St. George** (Trafalga Restaurant, 76 W. St. George Blvd., tel. 801/673–3933).

Getting Around

By Car This tour follows I–15 before continuing on various well-maintained two-lane highways. Some mountain curves can be expected, and winter months may see hazardous conditions in the higher elevations. Be sure that your car is in good working order, and keep the gas tank topped off.

Guided Tours

Bryce-Zion Trail Rides (Zion National Park Lodge, Springdale 84767, tel. 801/586–7686) offers mule tours in these two national parks.

Exploring Southwestern Utah

Numbers in the margin correspond to points of interest on the Utah map.

62 Begin by taking I–15 south from Nephi to the town of **Fillmore.** Given its central location, Fillmore was designated the territorial capital in 1851, before the town even existed. In 1855, after the first wing of the capitol building was completed, the state legislature convened here, but the capital was eventually moved back to Salt Lake for want of better facilities. Although the entire building was never completed, the portion that does stand is counted as Utah's oldest government building. Today it is included in the **Territorial Statehouse State Park.** *50 W. Capitol St., tel. 801/743–5316. Admission: $1.50 adults, $1 children under 15. Open daily 8–sunset.*

63 A stop in the town of **Beaver,** farther south on I–15, will reveal more historical haunts. Established by the Mormons in 1856, Beaver soon became an unsettled melting pot when gold and silver were discovered in the mountains to the west. To keep the calm between gentile miners and pious Mormons, the army established Ft. Cameron here in 1872. Part of the town is included in a national historic district, and the old Beaver County Courthouse is now a museum. Beaver served as the county seat from 1882 to 1975.

East of Beaver rise the spectacular **Tushar Mountains.** Reaching elevations of over 12,000 feet, they are Utah's third-highest mountain range, but because of their out-of-the-way location, they are not as well known as the Wasatch, Uinta, or La Sal mountains. Those who venture east from Beaver on Route 153 will find uncrowded trails and campgrounds, some beautiful mountain lakes, and a small ski resort known as Elk Meadows (*see* Sports and the Outdoors, *below*).

To reach southern Utah's other ski resort, continue on I–15 and then on Route 143 south from Parowan for a dozen miles to Brian Head (*see* Sports and the Outdoors, *below*). It is also a favored summertime retreat.

A few miles beyond Brian Head is one of the region's better-**64** known scenic wonders, **Cedar Breaks National Monument.** Cutting deep into the western end of the lofty Markagunt Plateau, uplift and erosion by wind, rain, and river have etched an amphitheater awash in shades of pink, gold, and lavender. Two especially nice backcountry strolls (each 2 miles long) follow the Spectra Point and Alpine Pond trails, and although winter snows do close the road, the monument is a favorite among cross-country skiers. By the way, there are no cedars at Cedar Breaks. Rather, early pioneers misidentified junipers growing in the area. *Rte. 143, tel. 801/586–9451. Admission: $3 per vehicle. Open May–Oct., daily 8–sunset.*

From the west, the gateway to Brian Head and Cedar Breaks is ⑥⑤ **Cedar City,** which lies where Route 14 meets I–15. With a population of about 12,000, this is southern Utah's second-largest community. Cedar City was first settled in 1851 by Mormons sent to mine iron-ore deposits. The going was rough, though, and very little iron was produced before a more feasible supply line was established with the East. This chapter in the town's history is today embodied at the **Iron Mission State Park.** It displays the usual collection of Native American and pioneer artifacts, plus a number of horse-drawn wagons, one of which was reportedly shot up by Butch Cassidy and his bunch. *585 N. Main St., tel. 801/586–9290. Admission: $3 per vehicle. Open daily 8–sunset.*

In 1897, Cedar City was awarded a branch of Utah's teacher-training school. In the years since, the school has evolved into **Southern Utah University** (351 W. Center St., tel. 801/586–7700), a four-year college offering strong programs in education, business, science, and, most conspicuously, performing arts. From late June through the first week of September, the **Utah Shakespearean Festival** is held. What began in 1962 as an attempt to keep the town from dying has developed into a major production requiring hundreds of actors (students and professionals) and workers, drawing tens of thousands, and involving much more than just Shakespeare (*see* The Arts, *below*). The university auditorium includes a fascinating replica of the Tiring House Theater from Shakespeare's time, showcasing Shakespearean costume and set displays during the season.

⑥⑥ From Cedar City, it is roughly 50 miles on I–15 to **St. George.** It was here that 300 Mormon families were sent to grow cotton in 1861. Named after the group's leader, George A. Smith, the colony faced many hardships, among them disease, drought, and floods. After the railroad rendered their cotton farms insignificant, the settlers stayed on and built a tabernacle. In 1877, the **St. George Temple** (250 E. 400 South, tel. 801/673–3533) was completed, and starting in 1873, Brigham Young spent his last five winters in a **home** (89 W. 200 North St., tel. 801/673–5181) he had built here. Free tours of the temple grounds and the home are given daily. Today these venerable structures, plus many others, bring some historical perspective to a city that is growing by leaps and bounds. St. Georgians now number 30,000, of whom a burgeoning number are retirees. The town has many hotels and restaurants and even some interesting convention sites. The **St. George Chamber of Commerce** (97 E. St. George Blvd., tel. 801/628–1658), housed in the 1876, brick Old Washington County Courthouse, puts out a walking-tour map that covers 22 sights, including those above.

While St. George does proffer a handful of interesting sights, it is the surrounding natural landscape that is the area's primary draw. Best known, of course, is Zion National Park, which lies 40 miles east. Before taking in the park, however, it would be prudent to visit some of the less-heralded spots west and north of town. First on the list is **Snow Canyon State Park** (11 mi northwest of St. George on Rte. 18, tel. 801/628–2255), where red Navajo sandstone walls topped by a cap of volcanic rock make for some rather scenic canyon terrain. There are the **Pine Valley Mountains**, with a recreation area and wilderness trails, and the **Beaver Dam Wash**, south of the small town of Shivwits. At 2,350 feet, this is Utah's lowest point, but more important, the area marks the spot where the Colorado Plateau, the Great Basin, and the Mojave Desert converge. In this overlapping of ecosystems, you'll find a great variety of plants and animals, especially birds.

If your itinerary allows for only a quick visit to the St. George area, then you should spend most of your time exploring **Zion National Park,** a wonderland of vividly hued, sheer, steep canyons; monumental monoliths; and spindly spires. First established as Mukuntuweap National Monument in 1909, it became Zion National Park a decade later. Now the 147,000-acre park welcomes some 2.5 million visitors annually. Front and center is Zion Canyon, which contains the park's main road (a 6½-mile scenic loop), a historic lodge, and a visitor center. Some 2,500 feet deep, Zion Canyon is rimmed by such naturally sculpted landmarks as the Sentinel, East Temple, the Temple of Sinawava, and the Great White Throne. At road's end is the Gateway to the Narrows. As its name suggests, the Narrows is a slender passageway, in places only a couple of dozen feet wide, carved by the Virgin River. A mile-long trail heads into the abyss, but hikers often wade up the stream beyond. *30 mi east of I–15 on Rte. 9, Springdale, tel. 801/772–3256. Admission: $5 per vehicle. Open daily 8–sunset.*

From the depths of Zion Canyon, this tour climbs east along the Zion–Mount Carmel Highway. After several switchbacks, the road enters a mile-long tunnel, complete with portals. Constructed in 1930, the tunnel is too small for large RVs to pass without having rangers stop traffic. Beyond the tunnel's east entrance, Route 9 continues out of the park to Mount Carmel Junction, passing through the park's slickrock territory, including Checkerboard Mesa, which resembles an enormous sandstone playing board. From here, U.S. 89 heads south for 17 miles to **Kanab,** a picturesque town with considerable ties to Hollywood. Since the 1920s, the Kanab area has played a cameo role in more than 100 movies and television shows.

Travel north from Mount Carmel Junction on U.S. 89 to the turnoff for Route 12. Head east through Red Canyon, and you'll get a taste of what's to come at **Bryce Canyon National Park.** Not actually a canyon, Bryce is a series of amphitheaters carved into the eastern rim of the Paunsaugunt Plateau. Exposed and sculpted by erosion are pink and cream-color spires, or hoodoos, visible from many overlooks along the park's 21-mile paved road. Among the stunning sights are the Silent City, named for the eerie rock profiles and figures, and the "chessmen" of Queen's Garden. Because early-and late-day sunlight casts such an unusual glow on these rock formations, many folks count Bryce as their favorite of Utah's national parks. Given its 8,000-foot elevation, winter turns the area into a wonderland for cross-country skiers. *Rtes. 12 and 63, Bryce*

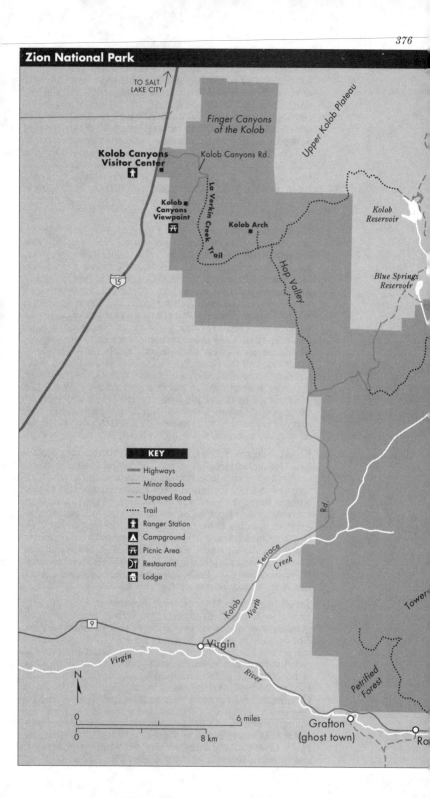

Zion National Park

TO SALT
LAKE CITY

*Finger Canyons
of the Kolob*

Upper Kolob Plateau

**Kolob Canyons
Visitor Center**

Kolob Canyons Rd.

**Kolob
Canyons
Viewpoint**

La Verkin Creek Trail

*Kolob
Reservoir*

Kolob Arch

Hop Valley

*Blue Springs
Reservoir*

15

KEY

Highways
Minor Roads
Unpaved Road
Trail
Ranger Station
Campground
Picnic Area
Restaurant
Lodge

Kolob Terrace Rd.

North Creek

Tower

9

Virgin

Virgin

River

N

0   6 miles
0   8 km

*Petrified
Forest*

Grafton
(ghost town)

Ra

ava Point

West Rim Trail

Horse Pasture Plateau

Deep Creek

North Fork Virgin River

The Narrows

West Rim Trail

Gateway to the Narrows Trail

Temple of Sinawava

East Mesa Trail

Weeping Rock

East Rim Trail

Emerald Pools Trail

Zion Canyon

Red Arch Mountain

Grotto

Emerald Pools

Zion Lodge

Echo Canyon Trail

East Entrance Trail

the Virgin

Zion Canyon Scenic Dr.

9

East Entrance

ion Canyon isitor Center

Canyon Overlook

Checkerboard Mesa

Zion–Mt. Carmel Hwy.

th Entrance

South

Watchman

Springdale

East Fork Virgin River

ille

Bryce Canyon National Park

Bryce Canyon Airport

12

Sevier River

East Fork

East Creek

63

Ruby's Inn

Visitor Center

North Campground

Sunset Campground

Dixie National Forest

Tropic Reservoir

Bryce Amphitheater

Fairyland Point

Fairyland Loop Trail

Tropic Canyon

Tropic

Sunrise Point

Queen's Garden

Sunset Point

Inspiration Point

Bryce Creek

Bryce Point

Rim Trail

Paria View

Under The Rim Trail

Whiteman Bench

Piracy Point

Fairview Point

Natural Bridge

Pink Cliffs

Agua Canyon

Ponderosa Point

Pink Cliffs

Riggs Spring Loop Trail

Yovimpa Point

Rainbow Point

Pink Cliffs

N

KEY

Highways
Minor Roads
Unpaved Road
Trail
Ranger Station
Campground
Picnic Area

0   4 miles

0   4 km

Canyon, tel. 801/834–5322. Admission: $5 per vehicle. Open daily 8–sunset.

Just east of Bryce, Route 12 passes through the tiny town of Tropic before reaching Cannonville and the turnoff for
68 **Kodachrome Basin State Park.** Here, among a spectacular but little-known geological display, are unusual petrified geysers and peculiar formations called sand pipes. The basin was named for Kodak's classic color film after pictures of it appeared in a 1949 *National Geographic* article. *9 mi south of Rte. 12, tel. 801/679–8562. Admission: $3 per vehicle. Open daily 8–sunset.*

69 Farther on, the tour reaches **Escalante.** Although home to **Escalante State Park** (Rte. 12, tel. 801/826–4466), with its collection of rainbow-colored, 150-million-year-old petrified wood, the town is best known as the gateway to the most remote region of the state. While en route to southeastern Utah in 1879, Mormon pioneers chipped and blasted a narrow passageway in solid rock, through which they lowered their wagons. Known as **"Hole-in-the-Rock,"** much of it is now covered by Lake Powell. The 60-mile gravel road to the site, however, does access the interesting Devil's Garden Natural Area, plus some beautiful canyons and gulches.

East of Escalante, Route 12 crosses the Escalante River, which has carved an extensive canyon system highly favored by backpackers. The road passes the **Calf Creek Recreation Area,** highlighted by 126-foot Calf Creek Falls (a 5½-mile-round-trip
70 hike), and reaches the small enclave of **Boulder.** So remote is this outpost that, in 1942, it was the last U.S. community to receive its mail by mule. Today the town is home to **Anasazi Indian Village State Park.** One of the largest Anasazi sites west of the Colorado River, the village predates AD 1200. *Rte. 12, tel. 801/335–7308. Admission: $3 per vehicle. Open daily 8–sunset.*

Beyond Boulder, Route 12 continues north up and over Boulder Mountain, in Dixie National Forest. Because the road reaches 9,200 feet, it encounters some lush pine, spruce, and aspen forests. In addition, magnificent views of the Escalante River canyon to the south and the Henry Mountains to the east open up along the way.

Also visible from the drive over Boulder Mountain are the sandstone monuments of **Capitol Reef National Park.** Named for a formation that resembles the U.S. Capitol, the preserve extends north for 75 miles from Glen Canyon National Recreation Area. The most heavily visited corridor of the park follows the Fremont River in the northern section. Here various short hikes allow for different views of the cliffs and domes in surrounding canyons, and the Mormon village of Fruita offers a historical perspective on the region. Reached by a high-clearance road that leads to the northernmost section of the park is the aptly named Cathedral Valley. Waterpocket Fold, a giant wrinkle of rock running south for many miles, contains some spectacular hikes, especially in Muley Twist Canyon. It is accessed by the 66-mile Burr Trail, which is passable by most cars when dry and offers motorists the chance to explore some wonderful terrain. *12 mi east of Torrey on Rte. 24, tel. 801/425–3791. Admission: $3 per vehicle. Open daily 8–sunset.*

From Capitol Reef, return west to Torrey and then continue on through the towns of Bicknell and Loa before getting to the

71 turnoff for **Fish Lake.** At 8,800 feet, this 1-by-6-mile natural lake is known for, not surprisingly, its fishing. But you needn't have tackle box in hand to enjoy its beautiful environs. Some great hikes explore the higher reaches of the area, and there are several campgrounds as well as some wonderful lodges. The 1.4 million–acre Fishlake National Forest was named after it.

From Fish Lake, this tour heads due north toward Salt Lake City but detours for a side trip west on Route 119 to the fertile farmlands of the Sevier River valley and the town of **Richfield.** Close to town is the Monroe Hot Springs (tel. 801/527–4014),

72 and 21 miles south, along I–70, is **Fremont Indian State Park.** During construction of the highway in 1983, this largest of Fremont sites was discovered. Today the park features a visitor center with a museum and three interpretive trails. Originally the site included a village of pit houses, but that was obliterated by construction after archaeologists completed excavation. Most of the hundreds of rock art panels are intact and on display, however. *11550 Clear Creek Canyon Rd., Sevier, tel. 801/527–4631. Admission: $1.50 adults, $1 children. Open daily 8–sunset.*

If you have the time, you might continue south into tiny **Piute County.** Along the drive you'll pass Big Rock Candy Mountain, a colorful landmark made famous in a song by Burl Ives. In the town of Junction, you can't miss the bright red Piute County Courthouse. Built in 1902, the adobe structure is on the National Register of Historic Places. Additionally, it was near the small town of Circleville that Robert LeRoy Parker—alias Butch Cassidy—grew up.

From Junction, you can backtrack to Richfield and return to Salt Lake by way of U.S. 50 and I–15. Or, if you're up for a little adventure, you can drive the Kimberly Scenic Backway (passable by most cars in the summer) over the Tushar Mountains to Beaver, I–15, and civilization.

What to See and Do with Children

Coral Pink Sand Dunes State Park (12 mi west of Kanab off U.S. 89, follow turn-off, tel. 801/874–2408) is a giant playland of tinted sand. Big kids play on the dunes with their ATVs, but an area has been set aside for families to explore.

Lopeman's Frontier Movie Town is jam-packed with Old West movie memorabilia. Some of the buildings in its replica of a frontier town were actually used in movie sets, and photos on the walls inside reveal many familiar faces. *297 W. Center St., Kanab, tel. 801/644–5337. Admission: $2 adults. Open Apr.–Oct., varying hours.*

Off the Beaten Track

Besides being the closest town to the Intermountain Power Project (said to be the world's largest coal-fired generating station), **Delta** is also Utah's gateway to the lonesome yet beautiful **Great Basin,** a desert region that covers much of the West. Within the city limits is the **Great Basin Museum** (328 W. 100 North St., tel. 801/864–5031), with its collection of pioneer relics, old mining equipment, and mineral samples. A few miles south of Delta are the crumbling adobe remains of **Ft. Deseret,** and west of town are the remains of **Topaz.** During World War

II, some 9,000 Japanese-Americans were interned here; at the time it was Utah's fifth-largest city. The area also has a number of mountain ranges and sagebrush valleys to explore.

Sports and the Outdoors

Biking Given its colorful desert terrain and its forested plateaus, Southwestern Utah makes for some rather alluring bicycling—both on the road and off.

Claiming to have the highest number of bike shops per capita—four shops in a town of 75—**Brian Head** is a good place to base cycling excursions. The area's most popular ride is the 12-mile **Bunker Creek Trail,** which winds its way through forests and meadows to Panguitch Lake. Road cyclists will enjoy stretches of Routes 14, 143, and 148 in the **Cedar Breaks National Monument** area.

A good long-distance mountain-bike ride in the isolated **Escalante** region follows the 44-mile **Hell's Backbone Road** from Escalante to Boulder. The grade is steep, but the views of Box Death Hollow make it worthwhile. Mountain bikers may also want to pedal a portion of the **Burr Trail,** a 66-mile backcountry route (usable by most vehicles when dry) that crosses into the southern portion of Capitol Reef National Park.

Near **St. George,** Snow Canyon State Park and Zion National Park are popular among road cyclists. The scenery is great, but watch for heavy traffic during peak season. For safety reasons, the Zion–Mount Carmel tunnel in Zion is closed to bicycles.

Camping In this region of Utah, campers have their choice from low desert to high mountain facilities. Campgrounds in **Bryce, Capitol Reef,** and **Zion national parks** fill up fast. Most of the area's state parks have camping facilities, and the region's two national forests offer many wonderful sites. In the **Dixie National Forest** (Box 580, Cedar City 84721, tel. 801/865–3700), the Panguitch Lake, Pine Valley, and Boulder Mountain areas are especially nice. In **Fishlake National Forest** (115 E. 900 N., Richfield 84701, tel. 801/896–9233), Beaver Canyon and Fish Lake are good picks.

Fishing A number of nice trout streams lace the region. These include **Panguitch Creek,** below the lake of the same name; **Mammoth Creek,** south of Hatch; the **Beaver River;** and the **Sevier River,** which flows north through Richfield and Salina. As for lake fishing, anglers favor **Otter Creek Reservoir, Yuba Reservoir,** and **Panguitch Lake.** Of course, with a name like **Fish Lake,** how can you go wrong? Mackinaw and rainbow trout have both made the lake famous.

Golf The same feature of this corner of the state that allowed early Mormon farmers to grow cotton now draws golfers in every month of the year. Among the dozen or so golf courses found in the region are the nine-hole courses **Canyon Breeze** (E. Canyon Rd., Beaver, tel. 801/438–2601) and **Dixie Red Hills** (1000 N. 700 West St., St. George, tel. 801/634–5852), as well as 18-hole courses **Cedar Ridge** (200 E. 900 North St., Cedar City, tel. 801/586–2970), **Green Spring** (588 N. Green Spring Dr., St. George, tel. 801/673–7888), and **St. George Golf Club** (2190 S. 1400 East St., St. George, tel. 801/634–5854).

Hiking Hiking trails abound in southwestern Utah. In **Bryce Canyon National Park,** the Rim Trail features nonstop scenery, while the Fairyland Loop and Queen's Garden trails lead hikers among the park's fantastic hoodoos. At **Capitol Reef National Park,** the strenuous route to the Fremont Overlook and the Hickman Bridge Trail are good picks. **Zion National Park** is home to the Narrows, but the walk to Emerald Pools is similarly worthwhile. In southwestern Utah's two national forests, the **Boulder** area includes the hike to Calf Creek Falls, and **Fish Lake** features a trail to the 11,633-foot summit of Fish Lake Hightop Plateau. West of St. George, the 50,000-acre **Pine Valley Wilderness** is laced with several backcountry routes, including the 6-mile Whipple National Recreation Trail and the 35-mile Summit Trail. The **Tushar Mountains** are accessed by several paths near Beaver.

Skiing Known for its abundance of snow, **Brian Head Resort** (Brian Head 84719, tel. 801/677–2035 or 800/272–7426) is a favorite among California skiers who eschew the crowded megaresorts of their own state. Seven lifts service 55 runs and a vertical drop of 1,250 feet.

Elk Meadows Ski and Summer Resort (Box 511, Beaver 84713, tel. 801/438–5433 or 800/248–SNOW) has 30 runs with five lifts and a vertical drop of 1,200 feet.

State Parks

In addition to the many state parks described in the tour of the area, a few others, each with its own lake, are of interest:

Gunlock State Park (15 mi northwest of St. George, tel. 801/628–2255) includes a 240-acre reservoir.

Minersville State Park (12 mi west of Beaver on Rte. 21, tel. 801/438–5472) provides boating facilities on a 1,130-acre reservoir.

Otter Creek State Park (4 mi north of Antimony on Rte. 22, tel. 801/624-3268) has a 3,120-acre lake known for rainbow trout.

Piute State Park (12 mi south of Marysvale off U.S. 89, tel. 801/624–3268) promises excellent fishing and boating on a 3,360-acre reservoir.

Quail Creek State Park (3 mi east of I–15 on Rte. 9, tel. 801/879–2378) includes a 590-acre reservoir north of St. George.

Yuba State Park (30 mi south of Nephi off I–15, tel. 801/758–2611) is on the shores of the expansive Sevier Bridge Reservoir.

Dining and Lodging

Beaver **Paradise Inn Garden of Eat'n.** This small-town eatery serves
Dining sandwiches, burgers, steaks, and more, and it's open for breakfast, lunch, and dinner. *324 W. 1425 North St., tel. 801/438–5464. AE, D, MC, V. Moderate.*

Lodging **Best Western Paradise Inn.** There are a fair number of facilities in this I–15 stopover. Rooms are comfortable and clean. *1451 N. 300 West St., Box 1137, 84713, tel. 801/438–2455 or 800/528–1234, fax 801/743–6892. 53 rooms. Facilities: restaurant, pool, hot tub. AE, D, DC, MC, V. Inexpensive.*

Brian Head **The Edge.** This is the place to eat lunch and dinner in Brian
Dining Head. The Edge Burger is a half-pound monstrosity draped

with cheese. Deli sandwiches are similarly sizable, while dinners include delicious steaks, seafood, soups, and salads. And, as you'd expect, the views are great. *406 S. Rte. 143, tel. 801/677-3343. AE, MC, V. Moderate.*

Lodging **Brian Head Hotel.** Located on the north end of town, the hotel features large studio rooms and suites with kitchens in desert pastels. The atmosphere is casual, and the service is friendly and helpful. *223 Hunter Ridge Rd./Rte. 143, Box 190218, 84719, tel. 801/677-3000 or 800/468-4898, fax 801/677-2211. 170 rooms. Facilities: restaurant, lounge, hot tub, exercise facilities. AE, D, DC, MC, V. Expensive.*

Bryce Canyon **Best Western Ruby's Inn.** Located just north of the park en-
Lodging trance and housing a large restaurant and gift shop, this is Grand Central Station for visitors to Bryce. A nightly rodeo takes place nearby. *Rte. 63, Box 1, 84717, tel. 801/834-5341 or 800/528-1234, fax 801/834-5265. 316 rooms. Facilities: restaurant, store, indoor pool, hot tub. AE, D, DC, MC, V. Expensive.*

Bryce Canyon Lodge. Located inside the park, this historic property is a few feet from rim views. Guests have their choice of standard rooms or cozy cabins. The lodge organizes horseback rides and park tours. *Box 400, Cedar City 84720, tel. 801/586-7686, fax 801/586-3157. 114 rooms. Facilities: restaurant. AE, D, MC, V. Expensive.*

Cedar City **Milt's Stage Stop.** Locals and an increasing number of tourists
Dining have discovered the terrific food and inviting atmosphere of
★ this dinner spot in beautiful Cedar Canyon. It's known for its 12-ounce rib-eye steak, its prime rib, and its fresh crab, lobster, and shrimp dishes. In the winter, deer feed in front of the restaurant as a fireplace blazes away inside. A number of hunting trophies decorate the rustic building's interior, and splendid views of the surrounding mountains delight patrons year-round. *5 mi e. of town on Rte. 14, tel. 801/586-9344. Reservations advised. AE, D, DC, MC, V. Moderate.*

Pancho & Lefty's. This is a great place for Mexican cuisine. Locals like the chimichangas, flautas, and fajitas, and those who imbibe can order margaritas. *2107 N. Main St., tel. 801/586-7501. AE, MC, V. Moderate.*

Lodging **Holiday Inn Cedar City.** This property offers clean and comfortable accommodations, plus a nice lineup of facilities. It's a convenient departure point to Bryce and Zion National Parks and Cedar Breaks National Monument in the summer and Brian Head Ski Resort in the winter. *1575 W. 200 North St., 84720, tel. 801/586-8888 or 800/432-8828, fax 801/586-1010. 100 rooms. Facilities: restaurant, pool, indoor hot tub. AE, D, DC, MC, V. Moderate.*

Willow Glen Inn. This real country bed-and-breakfast sits amid a 10-acre farm that is home to peacocks, ducks, sheep, and other farm animals. Despite its rural character, it's only 5 miles from town, and, as you might expect on a farm, a full breakfast is included. *3308 N. Bulldog Rd., 84720, tel. 801/586-3275. 8 rooms, 2 with shared baths. Facilities: dining room, 2 sitting rooms. No credit cards. Inexpensive.*

Fish Lake **Fish Lake Lodge.** Situated at lakeside, this large log structure
Lodging was built in 1932 and today exudes rustic charm and character. Guests stay in cabins—some old, others new. There is a dance hall and store, and the views are wonderful. *10 E. Center St.,*

Rte. 25, 84701, tel. 801/638–1000. 25 rooms. Facilities: restaurant, dance hall, store. AE, MC, V. Open Memorial Day–Sept. Moderate.

Hurricane **Pah Tempe Hot Springs Bed & Breakfast.** Located in a small
Lodging town along the Virgin River between St. George and Zion National Park, this B&B counts outstanding scenery and natural mineral springs as primary attributes. The springs were thought to have healing powers by the Paiute Indians. A small gourmet restaurant serves vegetarian food and nonalcoholic drinks, and a Continental breakfast is complimentary. Rooms are nonsmoking. *825 N. 800 East St., Box 35-4, 84737, tel. 801/ 635–2879. 8 rooms. Facilities: restaurant, outdoor pool, hot tub. MC, V. Moderate.*

Kanab **Chef's Palace.** This restaurant is a local favorite for rib-eye
Dining steaks, prime rib, and seafood. For added atmosphere, dine in the Dude Room. *151 W. Center St., tel. 801/644–5052. AE, D, DC, MC, V. Moderate.*

Lodging **Parry Lodge.** Back in the 1930s, movie stars stayed here. The names of who slept in each room are listed above the doors of the older units, and Hollywood-related photos decorate the lobby. Despite the age of the hotel, rooms are nice. *89 E. Center St., 84741, tel. 801/644–2601 or 800/748–4104, fax 801/644– 2605. 89 rooms. Facilities: restaurant, outdoor pool. AE, DC, MC, V. Moderate.*

Loa **Road Creek Inn.** This pleasurable bed-and-breakfast offers
Lodging such treats as a trout pond and a game room in addition to a Continental breakfast. Guest rooms, in which there is no smoking, are decorated in Victorian-era motifs. This is a good bet in this hideaway town. *90 S. Main St., Box 310, 84747, tel. 801/ 836–2485 or 800/38–TROUT, fax 801/836–2489. 12 rooms. Facilities: hot tub, exercise facilities. AE, D, MC, V. Moderate.*

Richfield **Topsfield Lodge.** Aside from Richfield's docket of national chain
Lodging motels, you might try this locally owned one. In addition to basic yet clean rooms and friendly service, there is an on-site steak house that is quite popular among locals and visitors alike. *1200 S. Main St., 84701, tel. 801/896–5437. 20 rooms. Facilities: restaurant. AE, MC, V. Inexpensive.*

St. George **Andelin's Gable House.** This nice sit-down restaurant features a
Dining varied menu upstairs in the Garden Room and five-course dinners downstairs in the Captain's Room. Entrées cover such fare as fish, ribs, stir-fries, brisket, and homemade chicken pot pie. *290 E. St. George Blvd., tel. 801/673–6796. Reservations advised. Dress: neat but casual. AE, MC, V. Moderate.*
J. J. Hunan Chinese Restaurant. The service is good, and the Oriental dishes are tasty. *2 W. St. George Blvd., tel. 801/628– 7219. Dress: neat but casual. AE, D, MC, V. Moderate.*
Sullivan's Rococo. Specializing in beef and seafood, the restaurant is known for its prime rib. Because it sits atop a hill overlooking town, you can enjoy spectacular views from tableside. *511 Airport Rd., tel. 801/628–3671. Dress: neat but casual. AE, D, DC, MC, V. Moderate.*

Lodging **Days Inn Four Seasons Convention Center.** For comfortable rooms and an inviting array of amenities, this is a good bet. It has both indoor and outdoor pools, plus tennis courts, and provides a complimentary Continental breakfast. *747 E. St. George Blvd., 84770, tel. 801/673–6111 or 800/635–4441. 96* *rooms. Facilities: restaurant, 2 pools, tennis courts, hot tub, laundry facilities. AE, D, DC, MC, V. Moderate.*

★ **Green Gate Village Historic Bed & Breakfast Inn.** This inn is named for a gate that reportedly dates back to 1877. As legend has it, Brigham Young had the fence and gate around the St. George Temple painted green. He then gave the excess paint to church members so that they, too, could paint their own gates and fences. Local lore notwithstanding, this collection of eight vintage homes offers elegantly comfortable accommodations in downtown St. George. There is no smoking in the rooms, and a full breakfast is included. *76 W. Tabernacle St., 84770, tel. 801/ 628–6999 or 800/350–6999. 16 rooms. Facilities: garden room, outdoor pool, hot tub. AE, MC, V. Moderate.*

Ramada Inn. Because this is St. George's newest all-inclusive hotel, it may very well be its nicest. The rooms and furnishings are up-to-date, and the facilities are impressive. *1440 E. St. George Blvd., 84770, tel. 801/628–2828 or 800/228–2828. 90 rooms. Facilities: lounge, heated outdoor pool, hot tub, game room, gift shop. AE, D, DC, MC, V. Moderate.*

★ **Seven Wives Inn.** Two historic homes constitute this bed-and-breakfast. It is said that Brigham Young slept here and that one of the structures may have been used to hide polygamists after the practice was prohibited in the 1880s. Antiques are liberally used in the decor, and guest rooms, most of which boast fireplaces or woodburning stoves, are named after the wives of owner Donna Curtis's great-great-grandfather. A full breakfast is served. *217 N. 100 West St., 84770, tel. 801/628–3737. 12 rooms. Facilities: dining room, outdoor pool. AE, D, MC, V. Moderate.*

The Arts

Music The **Southwest Symphony** (Dixie Center, St. George, tel. 801/ 673–6290) performs from October to May. Also at the Dixie Center, an intermittent **Celebrity Concert Series** lures top acts.

Theater The **Pioneer Players** (Dixie College, St. George, tel. 801/628–3121) perform comedies and melodramas at the Arena Theatre during the months of July and August.

The **Utah Shakespearean Festival** features several stage productions, Shakespearean and otherwise; the Greenshow, with jugglers, puppet shows, and folks dressed in period costume; workshops and literary seminars; and the Renaissance Feaste, a popular feed for guests. *351 W. Center St., Cedar City, tel. 801/586–7878. Admission: $10–$24, depending on seating and show times. Runs late June–early Sept.*

Nightlife

In St. George, **The Blarney Stone** (800 E. St. George Blvd., tel. 801/628–3121) is a beer-only joint with country and rock bands on weekends. In Cedar City, you can scoot your boot on weekends at the **Sportsmen's Lounge** (900 S. Main St., tel. 801/586–9036) and **The Playhouse** (1027 N. Main St., tel. 801/586–9010).

8 Wyoming

By Geoffrey O'Gara and Michael McClure

Geoffrey O'Gara writes for National Geographic Traveler *and other publications; hosts "Main Street, Wyoming" on Wyoming Public Television; and is the author of* A Long Road Home. *Michael McClure is a photographer, writer, and graphic designer whose work has appeared in books such as* Native Home of Hope.

Touring Wyoming's unpaved roads by Model T in the 1930s, writer Agnes Wright Spring found it easy to imagine the covered wagons and Native American bands of the 1800s. "The past presses so closely on the present!" she wrote, and even today her words hit the mark. Antelope still graze nonchalantly by highways, bull riders still bite the dust at Cheyenne's Frontier Days, and towering peaks, bearded with glaciers, stand as timeless sentinels in the west.

The closest Wyoming comes to big cities is Cheyenne and Casper, neither of which has more than 100,000 residents. Like most of the country, the state has tried to lasso high-tech industries, but you won't find General Motors or Boeing here. Even the oil and natural gas industries, centered in Casper and long a staple of the state's economy, have declined of late. Increasingly, Wyoming residents have recognized that the state's most valuable resource is the same wild and unspoiled country that astonished explorers 50, 100, and 200 years ago. Of that, there is no shortage.

In most people's minds, wild Wyoming is synonymous with its northwest section and its cluster of parks, forests, and ski resorts. Yellowstone National Park, the most popular destination, does not disappoint. Geysers spout, elk bugle, mud pots boil, and larkspur blooms. The scars of 1988's severe fires show here and there, but park officials have capitalized on them, making the park a giant ecological classroom. Just to the south, the Grand Tetons rise abruptly from the Snake River plain, above the lively community of Jackson, where efforts are being made to retain working ranches and open space in the face of a tide of second-homers.

Incomparable as the northwest is, there is much more to Wyoming. The other most-visited regions of the state, the northeast and southeast, have a mixture of mountain and plain, mine and ranch, and country towns and Western cities that is all their own.

Wyoming has fewer full-time residents (around 460,000) than any other state, but you'll find no inferiority complex. Whether they're riding the tram at Teton Village's world-class ski resort or haying the horses at a ranch in the Bighorn Mountains, Wyomingites take ornery pride in being just specks on an uncluttered landscape, five people per square mile. They know they have something that is fast disappearing elsewhere in the world, and, with a hint of pride on a weather-beaten face, they're willing to share it.

Essential Information

Visitor Information

Contact the **Wyoming Division of Tourism** (I–25 at College Dr., Cheyenne 82002, tel. 307/777–7777, or 800/225–5996 for a recording).

Emergencies In most areas, call 911 for **police, fire,** and **medical** emergencies. Call the Wyoming Highway Patrol (tel. 800/442–9090) for **accidents.** For **poison control,** call 800/955–9119. Ask at your lodging for suggestions of doctors, dentists, or late-night pharmacies.

Tour Groups

General-Interest Tours **Rocky Mountain Holiday Tours** (Box 8411, Fort Collins, CO 80525, tel. 303/482–5813 or 800/237–7211, fax 303/482–5815) offers various packages of lodging, transportation, and tours with a range of itineraries, including Cheyenne Frontier Days and Yellowstone.

Special-Interest Tours **Equitour** (Bitterroot Ranch, Box 807, Dubois 82513, tel. 307/455–2778) coordinates equestrian tours the world over, but home base is in Wyoming, where trips explore areas such as Butch Cassidy's Hole in the Wall country and the route of the Pony Express.

Off the Beaten Path (109 E. Main St., Bozeman, MT 59715, tel. 406/586–1311, fax 406/587–4147) specializes in individualized vacations throughout Wyoming. They're well connected with the outdoor recreation community, work with the best, and charge $60 an hour for their services.

Package Deals for Independent Travelers

Packages that include airfare, lodging, and a variety of activities abound in the Yellowstone/Grand Teton area. From its base at the resort, **Jackson Hole Central Reservations** (Box 510, Teton Village 83025, tel. 307/733–4005 or 800/443–6931) offers packages covering a variety of seasonal activities, including skiing, horseback riding, and visits to the parks. **Jackson Hole Vacations** (Box 423, Jackson 83001, tel. 307/733–7131 or 800/223–4059) has packages for dude ranching, rock climbing, hunting, and sightseeing, among others. **Pan-O-Rama West, Inc.** (Box 3130, Cody 82414, tel. 800/227–8483, fax 307/587–8025) provides air and ground packages for a variety of vacations in Wyoming and throughout the Rockies.

When to Go

The two faces of Wyoming most visitors see are the white-clad skiing months of winter and the alpine wildflower fests of summer. If you don't consider it winter until there's a dependable snowpack and ski lifts running full bore, it's best to visit between January and March. For wilderness lovers, summer isn't firmly in place until June, and some higher elevations can't be reached until July. There's no time busier than July and August, especially during Cheyenne's Frontier Days, the West's nonpareil rodeo, but what appears busy to locals may seem like virtual solitude to survivors of Disney World and other tourist meccas.

Anglers and hunters love the fall, but others come as well for the lower prices, splashy sunsets, and blinking gold of aspen groves. Spring bursts suddenly in Wyoming, clothing the plains in sagebrush green and wildflowers, as the streams fill up with snowmelt. Locals are at their friendliest in these rump seasons, and while the weather is changeable, the pace is unhurried and the experience is all your own.

Climate Wyoming, a high plateau broken by mountain ranges, has a reputation for wind in the south, changeable mountain weather in the north, and everything else in between. The weather is so diverse that the National Weather Service divides the state into over 50 distinct climatic zones. A few generalizations are possible, though: It is a dry and relatively sunny state, even in the winter. Summer weather on the high plains of eastern Wyoming brings temperatures in the 80s and 90s, sometimes prompting afternoon thundershowers; mountain temperatures are cooler, dropping at night into the 40s. Moisture—either snow or rain—is heavier on the western side of the ranges, but sudden downpours and peak-rattling thunderstorms can happen anytime in the high country. In the winter, the fabled winds can turn snowstorms on the plains into blinding blizzards.

Festivals and Seasonal Events

Spring **Pole, Pedal, and Paddle Race,** Teton Village, second Sunday in April: Contestants ski, bicycle, and kayak or canoe in what is one of the first signs of spring.

Summer **The Woodchoppers' Jamboree,** Saratoga, Father's Day weekend: Lumberjacks show off skills such as logrolling; there's also a rodeo, a dance, and other festivities. **The National High School Rodeo Finals,** Gillette (until 1995), last week in July: Nearly 1,400 young U.S. and Canadian cowboys and cowgirls ride broncs and rope calves. **Cheyenne Frontier Days,** Cheyenne, last full week in July: This is the rodeo world's big event. **Grand Teton Music Festival,** Teton Village, July and August: Musicians from the nation's finest orchestras play in a symphony and smaller chamber groups.

What to Pack

Whether you bring a suitcase or a backpack, make it large. You must prepare for heat (light, airy clothing), glare (a visor, dark glasses), heavy rain (waterproof gear and boots), cold (long underwear, a warm sweater), and wind (a sturdy parka), but leave the tuxedo in the closet. The thin atmosphere at this altitude makes sunscreen a must, winter or summer. If you are planning a wilderness trip, get an equipment list from an outfitting store or a book, and don't scrimp.

Traveling with Children

Children who love the outdoors—and most do, given the chance—will love Wyoming, where campgrounds, lakes, and wildlife are plentiful. However, straight, uncrowded roads may not please a child as much as they do an adult urban refugee. So on the long drives, bring car games and books, and plan ahead for stops at the widely spaced highway rest areas and perhaps longer breaks at spots such as Hobo Hot Springs in Saratoga or the Teton overlooks on Togwotee Pass.

Hints for Travelers with Disabilities

Highway rest stops are generally disabled accessible, but many smaller towns lack curb breaks and other amenities. **Access Tours** (Box 2985, Jackson 83001, tel. 307/733–6664) provides leisurely tours in the Yellowstone area on small buses with wheelchair lifts; priority is given to people with disabilities.

Hints for Older Travelers

Though the weather can be harsh, Wyoming attracts many senior citizens, who praise its natural beauty, small towns, and unhurried pace. There are senior citizen centers in most communities. An extensive **Elderhostel** program (University of Wyoming, Box 3972, Laramie 82071) combines learning and vacation in weeklong programs covering the region's history, flora, and fauna.

Getting Around Wyoming

By Plane An oddity of Wyoming is that you can fly directly from Jackson to Chicago, but to get by commercial flight from Jackson to Casper, within the state, requires a change of planes in Denver. Commuter airlines connect a few towns—Riverton and Cody, for instance, on **Continental Express** (tel. 800/525–0280)—but these intrastate routes change fairly often.

By Car Interstate 80 traverses Wyoming's southern tier, connecting Cheyenne to Salt Lake City; be weather-watchful in the winter, when wind and snow can cause major problems. Entering the northeast corner from the east, I-90 passes through Gillette and Sheridan before exiting north into Montana. Interstate 25 runs north from Denver through Cheyenne and Casper to join I-90 at Buffalo. Major natural attractions keep their distance from the interstates, however, so travelers can expect to cross Wyoming's wide-open spaces on smaller, well-maintained highways. Snowplows do a Herculean job of keeping most roads clear in winter.

By Train The **Amtrak** *Pioneer* (tel. 800/USA–RAIL) travels across Wyoming's southern tier, with one stop daily eastbound and westbound in Evanston, Green River, Rock Springs, Rawlins, Laramie, and outside Cheyenne. Rock Springs and Evanston are the stops for those heading to Yellowstone; cars can be rented at the stations.

By Bus **Greyhound/Trailways** (tel. 800/231–2222) serves the southern tier from Cheyenne to Evanston, while **Powder River Transportation** (tel. 800/442–3682) concentrates on the northeast, including Sheridan and Gillette. There is no service to the northwest.

Shopping

Wyoming, to put it bluntly, is not a shopping state. The larger towns have malls and chain discount stores, and the state's one bona fide tourist town, Jackson, has a range of specialty stores that sell everything from Western clothing to art to recreational equipment. There are also a few gems tucked away elsewhere.

Sports and the Outdoors

There is no shortage of mountains and rivers and all kinds of trails for the intrepid outdoor lover. Jackson and the parks just to the north are the focus of intensive summer and winter outdoor recreation, whether it's bagging peaks in the Tetons in August or snowcat skiing in the fresh powder at Grand Targhee. There is a lot of outdoors in Wyoming, however, and the adventurous visitor may want to try some less-well-known areas and activities, from dude ranching around Sheridan to camping in national forests all over the state; to reserve campsites for a small fee, call **U.S. Forest Reservations** (tel. 800/283–2267). Local chambers of commerce can provide lists of guides and outfitters.

National and State Parks

National Parks   Wyoming's two national parks are clustered together in the path of the Rocky Mountains. **Yellowstone National Park,** with its geothermal wonders, is the state's most popular destination. Just to the south, **Grand Teton National Park** protects the spectacular Tetons, which jut along the skyline above the Snake River. *Yellowstone: National Park Service, Mammoth 82190, tel. 307/344–7381. Grand Teton: National Park Service, Moose 83012, tel. 307/543–2851, or 307/733–2220 for a recording. Admission to both: $10 adults, $25 for yearlong pass. Yellowstone closed to automobiles in winter.*

State Parks   Wyoming's state parks and historic sites range from recreations of 19th-century towns to state-run mineral baths. The **Division of Parks and Cultural Resources** (Barrett Bldg., 24th St. and Central Ave., Cheyenne 82002, tel. 307/777–7013) provides a brochure that describes them all.

Dining

For Dining rates see Towns and Country price chart in Chapter 1, Essential Information.

The greatest variety of fine dining is in Jackson, and no other community in Wyoming comes close. However, in almost every small town you'll find a place that does wonders with the regional specialty: steak. Some have even gained national reputations. Dining is casual; jackets and ties are simply not needed. Reservations, especially outside Jackson, are generally accepted but not required unless otherwise stated in reviews. A dinner in some Jackson restaurants can cost up to $50 per person with wine, but prices throughout the state are usually inexpensive to moderate.

Lodging

For Lodging rates see Towns and Country price chart in Chapter 1, Essential Information.

Accommodations in Wyoming range from practical roadside motels—not surprising, since most visitors come by car—to exclusive dude-ranch retreats. The *Wyoming Vacation Guide*, available from the Wyoming Division of Tourism (*see* Visitor Information, *above*) provides listings of motels, bed-and-breakfasts, dude ranches, and campgrounds and RV parks, along with major attractions. Summer traffic slackens after Labor Day, and many motels drop their fees from then until June. (In Jackson, however, prices go up again from late December through March, for the ski season.) Summer reservations for the better accommodations in Yellowstone National Park, Jackson, and Cody should be made three months in advance; Cheyenne reservations during Frontier Days should be made six months ahead. The accommodations available all around Yellowstone are growing exponentially, and the few remaining older, more primitive establishments (bathrooms down the hall, no air-conditioning) are refurbishing. The turn-of-the-century Lake Yellowstone Hotel, for instance, has prepared for the future by installing television jacks (but no TVs yet).

Northwest Wyoming

By now, most Americans realize that the geysers and wilderness of Yellowstone were not destroyed by the fires of 1988. What damage was done—a few areas of bare black tree trunks with colorful fireweed blooming underfoot—has, in fact, become another lure to ecologically curious travelers. The hysterical media coverage of that crispy summer failed to convey what is at the heart of the public's love affair with Yellowstone: a blind faith that here, amid our most extraordinary wildlands, nature can be trusted to run its course.

The number of visitors to Yellowstone continues to increase, pushing above 3 million annually. More and more, travelers are recognizing that the wild beauty extends beyond the artificial boundaries of the park. They hike in June among the colorful explosions of wildflowers near Togwotee Pass in the Bridger-Teton National Forest north of Dubois or ride horses in the Wapiti Valley near Cody. They raft down the white water of the Hoback River south of Jackson and shoot—with a camera—the herds of elk that gather at the National Elk Refuge.

Nor are diversions limited to the natural world. Yellowstone's so-called "gateway" towns, including Jackson, Cody, and Dubois, are friendly hosts to this increasing interest, developing their own attractions, some of them cultural, and improving their accommodations. They are also dealing with their own mini–population booms, as more and more people decide to settle in the country they love to visit. Attempting to cope with growth, communities debate how much and what kind of development are desirable, in an ongoing effort to control their destiny. The effort to find a balance between saving the untrammeled wonders of the region and playing host to a curious, eager—and sometimes jealous—tide of visitors will be an ongoing drama during the 1990s.

Important Addresses and Numbers

Tourist Information   **Cody Country Chamber of Commerce** (836 Sheridan Ave., Box 2777, Cody 82414, tel. 307/587–2297), **Jackson Hole Chamber of Commerce** (Box E, Jackson 83001, tel. 307/733–3316), **Jackson Hole Visitors Council** (Box 982, Dept. 8, Jackson 83001, tel. 800/782–0011), and **Wapiti Valley Association** (1231 Yellowstone Hwy., Cody 82414, tel. 307/587–3963).

Emergencies   In Yellowstone, the **Lake Clinic and Hospital** (behind the Lake Hotel, tel. 307/242–7241) is open May 24–September 15; clinics are also located in Mammoth (in upper Mammoth, next to the post office, tel. 307/344–7965), open June–August, and at Old Faithful (in back of the parking lot behind Old Faithful Inn, tel. 307/545–7325), open May 7–October 10. **Grand Teton Medical Clinic** (next to Jackson Lake Lodge, tel. 307/543–2514) is open May 23–October 3, and in Jackson there's **St. John's Hospital** (625 E. Broadway Ave., tel. 307/733–3636).

Arriving and Departing by Plane

Airports and Airlines   **Jackson Hole Airport** (tel. 307/733–7682) lies north of Jackson in Grand Teton National Park, about 40 miles south of Yellowstone National Park. **American** (tel. 800/433–7300), **Continental** (tel. 800/525–0280), **Delta** (tel. 800/221–1212) and its commuter partner **SkyWest** (tel. 800/453–9417), and **United** (tel. 800/241–6522) provide daily service, with connections in Denver, Salt Lake City, and Chicago. Smaller commuter airlines also serve the airport from Denver, Salt Lake City, and Boise. There are seasonal variations; for example, scheduled jet service increases during the ski season. Flights may also be booked—often at a discount—through **Central Reservations** (tel. 307/733–4005 or 800/443–6931).

Jackson Hole Transportation (tel. 307/733–3135) meets incoming flights at the airport, delivers guests to their accommodations, and returns for departures.

East of Yellowstone, at Cody, **Yellowstone Regional Airport** (tel. 307/587–5096) is served by commuter airlines out of Denver. There is also service to the Yellowstone area through Bozeman and West Yellowstone, both in Montana.

Arriving and Departing by Car

The Yellowstone area is well away from the interstates, so drivers make their way here on two-lane highways that are long on miles and scenery. From I–80, take U.S. 191 north from Rock Springs; it's about 177 miles to Jackson. From I–90, drive west from Sheridan on U.S. 14 or 14A to Cody, and cross over beautiful Sylvan Pass to Yellowstone's East Entrance. It's about 200 miles from Sheridan to the park. Alternatively, you can take U.S. 89 from the north or U.S. 191/287 from the west, both from Montana.

Getting Around

By Car   To best see the area, go by car. You can drive the road loops within the parks and stop at will for a hike or a view. Be extremely cautious in the winter when whiteouts and ice are not uncommon. If you didn't drive to Wyoming, you'll probably want to rent a car; Jackson Hole Airport has major car-rental agencies, which offer four-wheel-drive vehicles and ski racks.

Guided Tours

Orientation Tours **Powder River Tours** (565 N. Cache St., Box 7748, Jackson 83001, tel. 307/733–4152 or 800/343–2755) offers motor-coach tours of the region, including meals and float trips. **TW Recreational Services** (Yellowstone National Park, Mammoth 82190, tel. 307/344–7311) offers lodging and bus tours of Yellowstone in the summer; in the winter, packages include snowmobiling, skiing, and group tours by motorized snow coach.

Special-Interest Tours **Absaroka Outfitters** (Box 929, Dubois 82513, tel. 307/455–2275), from its scenic ranch, offers hunting and horseback-riding trips of up to seven days in the remote wilderness to the southeast of Yellowstone. **Backcountry Bicycle Tours** (Box 4029, Bozeman, MT 59772, tel. 406/586–3556) offers mountain-bike tours in the area's parks and forests, mixing in rafting and hiking for variety. **Barker-Ewing River Trips** (Box 3032, Jackson 83001, tel. 307/733–1000) conducts gentle scenic floats or white-water trips, either half-day journeys or longer trips that include cookouts and camping. **Flagg Ranch Village** (Box 187, Moran 83013, tel. 307/733–8761 or 800/443–2311), between Grand Teton and Yellowstone parks, runs snowmobiling and fishing trips. **Great Plains Wildlife Institute** (Box 7580, Jackson 83001, tel. 307/733–2633) takes guests on wildlife photography tours by van, accompanied by biologists. **Off the Deep End Travels** (Box 7511–WT, Jackson 83001, tel. 307/733–8707 or 800/223–6833) offers bicycle touring in both Grand Teton and Yellowstone, with rafting and other diversions. **Togwotee Mountain Lodge** (Box 91, Moran 83013, tel. 307/543–2847 or 800/543–2847 outside WY) has a large snowmobile-guiding operation in the winter and switches to horse packing in summer.

Exploring Cody and Yellowstone

Numbers in the margin correspond to points of interest on the Wyoming map.

❶ **Cody,** founded in 1887 and named for Pony Express rider, army scout, and entertainer William F. "Buffalo Bill" Cody, lies 52 miles from the East Entrance to Yellowstone National Park. It's within easy reach of Shoshone National Forest, the Absaroka Range, the Washakie Wilderness, and the Buffalo Bill Reservoir. A brochure with a self-guided walking tour of the town's historic sites is available from the chamber of commerce (*see* Important Addresses and Numbers, *above*) for a $1 donation.

At the west end of this quiet little gateway town is one of the finest museums in the West: the **Buffalo Bill Historical Center,** sometimes called the Smithsonian of the West. The center actually houses four museums in one: the Whitney Gallery of Western Art, with works by traditional Western artists, including Charlie Russell and Frederic Remington; the Buffalo Bill Historical Center, which has memorabilia of the scout and showman; the Plains Indian Museum, housing art and artifacts of the Plains tribes; and the Cody Firearms Museum, with the world's largest collection of American firearms. *720 Sheridan Ave., tel. 307/587–4771. Admission (2 days): $7 adults, $6 sen-*

ior citizens, $4 youths over 12, $2 children 6–12. Open Mar. and Nov., Tues.–Sun. 10–3; Apr., Tues.–Sun. 8–5; May and Sept., daily 8–8; June–Aug., daily 7–10; Oct., daily 8–5; Dec.–Feb., tours on request.

On Cody's western outskirts, just off the West Yellowstone Highway, is **Trail Town,** a collection of historic buildings from Wyoming's frontier days. It features a cemetery of famous local mountain men, besides Native American and pioneer artifacts. *1831 Demaris Dr., tel. 307/587–5302. Admission: $3. Open May 1–"until the snow flies."*

The road from Cody to Yellowstone climbs through Shoshone Canyon, skirts the Buffalo Bill Reservoir, and runs through the wide, forested Wapiti Valley, which has many dude ranches.

Almost everyone who comes any distance to visit Wyoming has **Yellowstone National Park** in mind. Few places in the world can match the park's collection of accessible wonders, from grazing bison and cruising trumpeter swans to rainbow-colored hot springs and thundering geysers. As you visit the park's hydro-thermal areas, you'll be walking on top of the Yellowstone Caldera—a 28-mile-by-47-mile collapsed volcanic cone, which last erupted about 600,000 years ago. The park's geyser basins, hot mud pots, fumaroles (steam vents), and hot springs are kept bubbling by an underground pressure cooker filled with magma. One geophysicist describes Yellowstone as "a window on the earth's interior."

Before you start visiting the sights, assess your desires and abilities. Would you rather hike, drive the roads, or buy a seat on a tour bus? You can sleep in solitude at a backcountry campsite or in luxury at a historic lakeside hotel. Choose between geysers and wildlife or between fishing hip-deep in the Firehole River and boating on Yellowstone Lake. If time is limited, pick a single area, such as the Grand Canyon of the Yellowstone or the Norris Geyser Basin, and don't try to do everything.

The 370 miles of public roads in the park are both a blessing and a curse. They provide access to extraordinary landscapes and wildlife but are often potholed, overcrowded, and dotted with motor homes that have been pulled over on narrow shoulders so that their occupants can photograph grazing elk or buffalo cows with calves. As a result, roads become choked with slow-moving caravans led by big RVs. With budgets dwindling and visitation growing, this situation will only get worse.

There are summer-staffed visitor centers throughout the park and a busy schedule of guided hikes, evening talks, and campfire programs. (Check *Discover Yellowstone*, a park newsletter available at entrances and visitor centers, for dates and times.) Pamphlets describing hot-spring basins are available for 25¢ at each site or visitor center. The park has numerous picnic areas and campgrounds, as well as restaurants and lodgings (*see* Dining and Lodging, *below*).

The road from Cody slips through **Sylvan Pass** and arrives at Yellowstone's **East Entrance,** one of five park entrances. (Each entrance road links up to the 142-mile figure-eight Grand Loop Road at the heart of the park, which connects the most accessible attractions.) In the winter, this is a favorite, if rather harrowing, entrance for snowmobilers, who come in increasing numbers to ride the park's snow-packed roads. The East En-

Yellowstone National Park

trance Road meets the Lower Loop at **Fishing Bridge,** where the Yellowstone River drains Yellowstone Lake. Although you can't fish here anymore—it's too popular with grizzly bears— it's a nice place for a stroll.

Head north toward the magnificent **Grand Canyon of the Yellowstone,** where water draining from Yellowstone Lake has cut deep into an ancient lava flow. Just shy of Canyon is a road to the 109-foot **Upper Falls,** not as high as the more spectacular Lower Falls (*see below*) but well worth a visit. You can also drive across Chittenden Bridge above the Upper Falls to view the canyon from a paved road that runs about 2 miles along the **South Rim.** A short hike brings you to **Artist Point,** and adventurous hikers can go farther along the South Rim on various trails. The Grand Loop Road continues along the **North Rim** to **Canyon,** where there is a lodge and campground. From here you can backtrack along the one-way North Rim Drive to see more of the canyon. Short paths lead to a number of scenic overlooks, including **Inspiration Point,** which provide great views of the canyon and of the breathtaking 308-foot **Lower Falls.** From Inspiration Point, you can also hike 3 miles along the **North Rim Trail,** with still more river and falls views.

Return to the Grand Loop Road and head north to where the Lower and Upper loops join. Drive west toward Norris, and you'll see the remains of the **North Fork Fire,** which left a moonscape on this plateau. At **Norris,** the hottest and oldest geyser basin in the park, changes occur every year: new geysers erupt, steam vents hiss to life, hot springs suddenly stop flowing. The names of the features—Whirligig Geyser, Whale's Mouth, Emerald Spring, and Arch Steam Vent—describe them. Visit the **Norris Museum** for a history of Yellowstone's watchdogs, from turn-of-the-century army troops to today's rangers. Walk west through **Back Basin,** where the huge, unpredictable **Steamboat Geyser** has come dramatically to life in recent years, but don't wait for it. It blows 300 feet about once a year. To the east, the smaller, colorful **Porcelain Basin** has a 1-mile boardwalk and, usually, a lot of people. You can sometimes see the whitish basin floor bulge and pulsate from underground pressure.

From Norris, head north on the Upper Loop to **Mammoth Hot Springs.** Many travelers skip this section of the loop, though it includes some spectacular views, including those of **Roaring Mountain,** which looks like a giant pile of melted vanilla ice cream. Mammoth is the gateway for the North Entrance. Here you'll find full services; the colony of old, stone military buildings that is now the park headquarters; and the **Horace Albright Visitor Center,** with the park's largest assemblage of information, exhibits, and publications about the park as well as historic archives for researchers. Antlered elk wander on the grass, and during the fall, bugling bulls collect their harems. The hot springs drop down terraces on the mountainside just west of the headquarters and hotel. Though the springs' flow has diminished in recent years, the **Minerva Terrace** is worth a look. You can hike a boardwalk from the top to the bottom of the huge white hot-spring constructions.

Continue clockwise on the Upper Loop. You'll pass the 60-foot **Undine Falls** and, farther along the road, a short trail to the huge stump of a petrified redwood tree before reaching **Tower Junction.** Here you can take the Northeast Entrance Road up the **Lamar River valley,** a favorite haunt of bison, for a nice side trip outside the park on the 68-mile **Beartooth Highway,** U.S. 212. The highest highway in the state, it runs in and out of Montana and over 10,947-foot Beartooth Pass. Switchbacks cut into steep cliffs ferry autos up to spectacular views of granite peaks, snowfields, and lakes. You can make the trip even better, and longer, by taking the **Chief Joseph Scenic Highway,** Route 296, south from the Beartooth Highway toward Cody. There are sections of well-kept gravel road on this route, and no services, but you'll see the beautiful Sunlight Basin and the dramatic gorge carved by the Clarks Fork of the Yellowstone River.

Back on the Upper Loop, head south toward Canyon. If you drive a short way up Chittenden Road, you can hike an easy 3 miles to the top of **Mt. Washburn** (10,243 feet). Back on the Upper Loop, you'll cross over **Dunraven Pass;** in recent years, two grizzlies have often been seen in a meadow here. When you rejoin the Lower Loop, you can return south toward Yellowstone Lake or head west again to Norris and south toward Madison Junction.

This area was hard hit by the 1988 fires, but park scientists contend that the fires corrected ecological imbalances caused by generations of fire suppression. Although there are still areas burned to a ghostly crisp—here and along the **Lewis River** toward the South Entrance—they only add to the variety of this unparalleled preserve.

At **Madison Junction,** traffic from the popular West Entrance joins the loop, and just to the south, a one-way circuit branches off through the **Firehole River canyon,** which features a spring-warmed swimming hole. Continuing south, the Lower Loop follows the steaming Firehole River, and there are often elk and bison grazing in the distance.

As you approach Old Faithful, you'll pass through three distinct geyser areas, beginning with **Lower Geyser Basin,** which features the fumaroles, blue pools, pink mud pots, and mini-geysers of **Fountain Paint Pots,** small in scale but great in variety, as well as the **Great Fountain Geyser.** The **Midway Geyser Basin** has some beautiful, richly colored, bottomless pools— former geysers—**Grand Prismatic Spring** and **Excelsior Geyser Crater.**

Last but not least is the **Upper Geyser Basin** and its centerpiece, **Old Faithful.** The mysterious plumbing of Yellowstone has lengthened the geyser's cycle somewhat in recent years, but Old Not-So-Faithful spouts a powerful 140-foot spume that pleases faithful spectators every 80 minutes or so. A visitor center nearby posts the time of the next eruption. Marked trails and bridges lead across the river to **Geyser Hill.** You can wander downriver, too, away from crowds, to **Castle Geyser** and **Morning Glory Pool,** which has recently been cleaned of coins and trash. Also in the Old Faithful area are two geysers famous for huge, but very rare, eruptions: **Giantess Geyser** and **Giant Geyser.**

At the heart of the tourist development here is **Old Faithful Inn** (*see* Dining and Lodging, *below*), worth a visit even if you aren't staying here. An architectural marvel built in 1903 and later expanded, the log building has a six-story lobby with huge rock fireplaces and wraparound balconies high in the rafters.

Traveling east over Craig Pass was once the slowest section of the Lower Loop. A recent upgrade and widening are a significant improvement. At West Thumb, you reach **Yellowstone Lake** and the South Entrance Road. If it's the lake you're interested in, drive north along the shore and stop to stroll along it or visit mud pots and steam vents. The South Entrance Road passes **Lewis Lake,** follows along the sometimes steep-sided path of the **Lewis River,** and connects the park to Grand Teton National Park and Jackson.

Exploring Grand Teton

Just to the south of Yellowstone, connected by the John D. Rockefeller Memorial Parkway (U.S. 89/191/287) is **Grand Teton National Park.** One might think this smaller park with a shorter history is dwarfed by its neighbor to the north, but nothing overshadows peaks like these. Presumably no translation of the French is necessary. The peaks—Mt. Moran, Teewinot Mountain, Mt. Owen, the Grand, and Middle Teton— form a chesty front along the west side of the Teton Valley. Lakes large and small are strung along the range's base, draining north into Jackson Lake, which in turn drains south into the Snake River. Grand Teton was put together from ranches John D. Rockefeller, Jr., bought up in the 1920s. It has a few oddities within its boundaries, such as a commercial airport and a dam to hold water for Idaho irrigators, but for fishing, hiking, climbing, boating, and rugged beauty, it's hard to match.

At the north end of the park is **Jackson Lake.** The biggest of the park's glacier-scooped lakes, it was made larger still by a dam, farther south, built in 1919. The lake is popular with sailors, anglers, and even windsurfers. Campgrounds and lodges dot the shore (*see* Dining and Lodging, *below*).

Near Jackson Lake Junction, the **Snake River** emerges from the Jackson Lake Dam and winds east and then south through the park. Whether you're on the water or on shore, **Oxbow Bend,** below the dam, is an excellent place to see waterfowl and other wildlife. U.S. 26/89/191 does run the full length of the park, with the Tetons on display all the way, but at this point, a better, more leisurely route is the smaller Teton Park Road, which runs south to Moose, where it rejoins the highway heading to Jackson.

Not far from Jackson Lake Junction on the Teton Park Road, you can take a brief side trip up narrow **Signal Mountain Road** to its summit, where you can see the valley and mountains on all sides.

South of Jackson Lake is **Jenny Lake,** right below the Grand Teton. You can hike 2 miles around the lake from the parking area at the south end to **Inspiration Point,** near the bottom of Cascade Canyon, or make the walk shorter by taking a boat ride from the dock near the parking area to the Cascade Canyon Trailhead. The boats run June 5–September 20, 8–6.

There are many easy hikes heading off toward the mountains from Teton Park Road. (They're shown on the map in "Teewinot," the free publication handed out at the entrances.) One of the nicest, south of Jenny Lake, is to **Taggart Lake.** Hikers as well as canoeists enjoy **Leigh** and **String lakes,** just north of Jenny Lake; turn west at North Jenny Lake Junction.

Grand Teton National Park

TO YELLOWSTONE

Flagg Ranch

89

287
191

Lizard Creek

JEDEDIAH SMITH
WILDERNESS AREA

Ranger Peak

Jackson
Lake

Waterfalls
Canyon

Eagles
Rest Peak

Colter Bay Visitor Center

Two
Ocean
Lake

Rolling Thunder
Mountain

Colter Bay

Emma
Matilda Lake

Bivouac
Peak

Moran
Creek

Half Moon
Bay

Moran
Bay

Elk
Island

TARGHEE
NATIONAL
FOREST

Mount
Moran

Signal
Mountain
Lodge

Moran Junction

Jackson
Lake Lodge

287 26

Signal Mountain

River

Grand Targhee
Resort Ski Area

Leigh Canyon

Leigh
Point

Spalding
Bay

Paintbrush Canyon

Leigh
Lake

String
Lake
Trailhead

Mount Moran
Turnout

191

Teton

Hidden Falls

Teton Park Rd.

Cascade
Canyon

Inspiration
Point

Teewinot
Mountain

Jenny
Lake

Jenny
Lake Lodge

26
89

Triangle X Ranch

Mount
Owen

Jenny Lake

Snake River
Overlook

South
Teton

Grand Teton
Middle Teton

Glacier
Gulch
Turnout

Snake

Teton
Point
Turnout

Teton Crest Trail

Nez
Perce
Peak

Bradley
Lake

Taggart
Lake

Taggart
Lake
Trailhead

Glacier
View
Turnout

Hole Antelope Flats Rd.

BRIDGER-TETON
NATIONAL FOREST

Death
Canyon

Menor's Ferry
Historic Site

Death.
Canyon
Trailhead

Moose
Visitor Center

Moose

Teton
Science School

Open Canyon

Phelps
Lake

Jackson

Lower
Slide Lake

Granite Canyon

River

Gros
Ventre

Granite
Canyon
Trailhead

Teton
Village

NATIONAL
ELK REFUGE

Moose-Wilson Road

Gros
Ventre
Junction

Gros

Ventre

River

22

West Gros Ventre Butte

East Gros Ventre Butte

191

KEY

Highways
Minor Roads
Unpaved Road
Trail
Ranger Station
Campground
Picnic Area
Restaurant
Lodge

Jackson

0   50 miles

0   75 km

N

Near the end of Teton Park Road, take a road to the left to visit the nondenominational **Chapel of the Transfiguration;** the view of the Tetons induces couples from all over the world to say their vows here. A short hike from this road on a marked trail brings you to the **Menor's Ferry.** It shows a technique used to carry people across the Snake River around the turn of the century, before bridges were built; there is a historic photo collection in one of the cabins.

At **Moose,** site of another visitor center, traffic rejoins the highway, leaves the park, and heads toward Jackson.

Exploring Jackson and Vicinity

2 **Jackson** remains a small Western town, howdy in the daytime and hopping in the evening. For outdoor types, it's a place to stock up on supplies before heading out for white-water rafting, backpacking, mountain climbing, or, in the winter, skiing. For tourists, there's a wealth of galleries and Western-wear shops and, at night, varied cuisines and no shortage of bars and music.

Jackson's charm and popularity put it at risk. On busy summer days, traffic can slow to a crawl as the highway doglegs through downtown. Proposals for new motels and condominiums sprout like the purple asters in the spring, as developers vie for a share of the vacation market. Old-timers suggest that the town—in fact, the entire Teton Valley—has already lost the dusty charm it had when horses parked around the Town Square. However, with national parks and forests and state lands occupying some of the most beautiful real estate, there's only so much ground to build on. These limitations, along with the cautious approach of locals, may keep Jackson on a human scale.

Start a tour of Jackson at the **Town Square,** which has tall shade trees and, at the corners, arches woven from hundreds of elk antlers. In the winter, Christmas lights adorn the arches, and during the summer, there's a melodramatic "shootout" every evening at 6:30. Stagecoach rides originate here during the day.

Nearby, the **Wildlife of the American West Art Museum** (110 N. Center St., tel. 307/733–5771) is just what it sounds like. Among the paintings and sculptures of bighorn sheep, elk, and other animals of the West are works by famous artists such as George Catlin and Charles M. Russell. For local history, visit the **Jackson Hole Museum** (tel. 307/733–2414).

South of Jackson, concerted local and national efforts have preserved both the wildlands and the ranches that dot the Teton Valley floor. The Snake River turns west and the contours steepen; by Hoback Junction there's white-water excitement. From the highway, there are good views of the river's twists and turns and the life-jacketed rafters and kayakers who float the canyon.

About 13 miles south of Jackson at Hoback Junction, turn east on U.S. 189/191 and follow the **Hoback River** south up its beautiful canyon. A tributary canyon 10 miles south of the junction is followed by a well-maintained and marked gravel road to
3 **Granite Hot Springs** in the Bridger-Teton National Forest. Visitors come for the shady campground along a creek, a pool fed

by hot springs, and moderate hikes up Granite Canyon to passes where you get panoramic views of the mountains. In the winter, there is a popular snowmobile excursion from the highway. *10 mi east of U.S. 189/191 on Granite Creek Rd., tel. 307/ 733–2752.*

What to See and Do with Children

Children love the outdoors and animals, and they'll find plenty of both here. In the parks, a dip at the **Firehole River swimming hole** (*see* Exploring Cody and Yellowstone, *above*) will please most any child, whereas older kids might like a white-water-rafting trip on the Snake River (*see* Sports and the Outdoors, *below*).

Outside the parks, there are still many activities for kids. **Cody Nite Rodeo,** more dusty and intimate than big rodeos like Frontier Days, has children's events, such as goat roping, and audience participation. Contact the Cody Country Chamber of Commerce (*see* Important Addresses and Numbers, *above*) for information. *Admission: $7 and $9 adults, $4 and $5 children 7–12. June–Aug., daily at 8:30 PM.*

Over 7,000 elk, many with enormous antler racks, winter in the **National Elk Refuge,** just north of Jackson. Horse-drawn sleigh rides to visit the huge herd are offered in the winter. The elk sit calmly as sleighs loaded with families and alfalfa pellets move in their midst. Dress warmly. Throughout the year, visitors drive up Refuge Road (well east of the herd in winter) for a view of Teton Valley and sometimes camp at Curtis Creek Campground. *Elk Refuge Visitor Center, tel. 307/733–8084. Admission: $7.50 adults, $3.50 children. Open Dec. 15–Apr.*

Off the Beaten Track

The nonprofit **Yellowstone Institute** (Box 117, Yellowstone National Park 82190, tel. 307/344–7381), housed in primitive cabins moved up to the pastoral Lamar Valley from Old Faithful, offers a wide range of courses about the ecology, history, and wildlife of Yellowstone. Search with a historian for the trail the Nez Percé took in their flight a century ago, or get tips from professional photographers on how to capture a trumpeter swan on film. Facilities are fairly primitive: Guests do their own cooking and camp during some of the courses, but prices are reasonable. Besides, there's no better way to get out from behind the windshield and learn what makes the park tick. Some programs are specifically designed for young people and families. Down the road in Grand Teton, similar programs are offered by the **Teton Science School** (Box 68, Kelly 83011, tel. 307/733–4765).

Shopping

Shopping Districts/Streets Jackson's peaceful **Town Square** is surrounded by storefronts with a mixture of specialty and outlet shops—most of them small-scale—with prices moderate to expensive. Just north is a small cluster of fine shops in **Gaslight Alley** (N. Cache St.). In Teton Village (the cluster of buildings at the base of the Jackson Hole Ski Resort, 15 mi northwest of Jackson), the **Mountainside Mall,** not to be mistaken for a big suburban mall (to its credit), serves the resort crowd.

Specialty Stores **Books**	In Jackson's Gaslight Alley, **Valley Books** (125 N. Cache St., tel. 307/733–4533) ranks among the best bookstores in the region, with a big selection and salespeople who can talk Tolstoy while guiding you to the best publications on local subjects.
Galleries	Jackson's art galleries serve a range of tastes. The fine nature photography of Tom Mangelson is displayed at his **Images of Nature Gallery** (125 N. Cache St., 2nd floor, tel. 307/733–6179). Some of the best regional and local artists, including Russell Chatham, are represented at **Partners Gallery** (125 W. Pearl St., tel. 307/733–0870). **Trailside Galleries** (105 N. Center St., tel. 307/733–3186) has more traditional Western art and jewelry.
Hats	Cody's **Wind River Hat Company** (144 W. Yellowstone Ave., tel. 307/ 527–5939) designs personalized hats for work or dress.
Leather	In Cody, **Creations in Leather** (1212 Sheridan Ave., tel. 307/ 587–6461) boasts a complete line of custom leather goods for the working cowboy; beyond chaps, you'll find elk and deer jackets as well as shirts, vests, and skirts with matching belts and purses. **Hide Out Leather** (40 N. Center St., tel. 307/733–2422), in Jackson, carries many local designs.
Outdoor Equipment	Jackson is well stocked with the best in outdoor equipment, winter and summer, including standouts **Jack Dennis Sports** (50 E. Broadway Ave., tel. 307/733–3270), **Skinny Skis** (65 W. Deloney Ave., tel. 307/733–6094), and **Teton Mountaineering** (86 E. Broadway Ave., tel. 307/733–3595). **Westbank Anglers** (Box 523, Teton Village, tel. 307/733–6483) fulfills fly-fishing dreams.
Western Wear	In downtown Cody, women shop at the **Plush Pony** (1350 Sheridan Ave., tel. 307/587–4677) for "uptown Western clothes" and **Flight West** (1155 Sheridan Ave., tel. 307/527–7800) for embroidered shirts and Navajo print vests as well as Wyoming-made bent-willow furniture and other items to spice up any Western decor. On the Town Square in Jackson, try **Jackson Hole Clothiers** (45 E. Deloney Ave., tel. 307/733–7211), for women's Western wear and sweaters; **Wyoming Outfitters** (12 Center St., tel. 307/733–3877); or **Cattle Kate** (120 E. Broadway Ave., tel. 307/ 733–4803), who produces some of the best designs in contemporary Western wear.

Sports and the Outdoors

Biking	Wyoming roads do not offer wide shoulders, but that doesn't stop cyclists from pedaling the area's two-lane highways, either in the midst of cross-country tours or on day trips. Bikers need to be alert for motorists, who are often distracted and sometimes negligent. In addition, mountain bikes are increasingly climbing the trails that hikers favor, and there are sometimes conflicts.
	In Yellowstone, the road from Grant Village over **Craig Pass** to Old Faithful is roomier and in better shape than most other park roads, though there is no designated bike path. In the Jackson area, cyclists ride the **Spring Gulch Road,** part pavement, part dirt, off Route 22, along the base of Gros Ventre Butte, rejoining U.S. 26/89/191 near the Gros Ventre River. The trip up to **Lower Slide Lake,** north of town, is also a favorite. Turn east off U.S. 26/89/191 to Kelly, and then take the Slide Lake Road.

Various outfitters guide and supply bicyclists as well as provide advice and trail maps (*see* Guided Tours, *above*).

Camping This is a camper's paradise, a place where even mattress-lovers deign to spend a night or two on the ground for the pleasure of a sky full of stars and the quiet sounds of the night. There are plenty of choices, but campgrounds in the parks tend to fill up quickly, often by midday. There are no reservations; every day it's first come, first served. In **Yellowstone,** there are 11 campgrounds (under $10) and one RV park, Fishing Bridge ($16), open May to October with some variations. The **Grant Village** campground is as well designed as the resort (*see* Dining and Lodging, *below*) is ill designed, and **Madison** is another favorite. **Grand Teton** has five public campgrounds. The most popular is at **Jenny Lake** (Teton Park Rd. at S. Jenny Lake), and the most luxurious is **Colter Bay** (on Jackson Lake, 7 mi north of Jackson Lake Lodge), which has showers, RV hookups, and laundry facilities. **Gros Ventre Campground** (4 mi east of U.S. 26/89/191 at Gros Ventre Junction), on the far eastern side of the park, is big enough (360 sites) that it doesn't fill up as fast as the others. Fees are $8 per night.

U.S. Forest Service campgrounds are less quick to fill, and there are some beauties in **Bridger-Teton National Forest** (340 N. Cache St., Box 1888, Jackson 83001, tel. 307/733–2752), including **Curtis Creek,** east of the National Elk Refuge, and **Granite Creek,** just below the hot springs near the Hoback River (*see* Exploring Jackson and Vicinity, *above*). Most campgrounds are open June–September, and fees are under $10. For an extra charge, you can reserve a campsite by calling **U.S. Forest Reservations** (tel. 800/283–2267). In the forest backcountry, you can camp where you like at no charge.

Canoeing, Kayaking, and Rafting For river runners, there are peaceful, scenic stretches of the upper **Snake River** in Grand Teton National Park, including the beautiful Oxbow; you can navigate them yourself by canoe or kayak or float as a passenger on a guided raft. Be sure to check current conditions and ability recommendations with park rangers before you launch. Farther down the river past Jackson, where the Hoback joins the Snake and the canyon walls become steep, there are lively white-water sections. Guided raft trips here will thrill and douse you. Experienced paddlers run the **Hoback,** too.

If you want instruction in the fine art of paddling, contact **Snake River Kayak and Canoe** (Box 3482, Jackson 83001, tel. 307/733–3127). Take lessons or rent canoes and kayaks from **Teton Aquatics** (145 W. Gill Ave., Jackson 83001, tel. 307/733–3127). If you'd rather be a passenger, traveling the peaceful parts of the river looking for wildlife, contact **Barker-Ewing Scenic Float Trips** (Box 100–J, Moose 83012, tel. 307/733–1800 or 800/365–1800) or **Triangle X Float Trips** (Moose 83012, tel. 307/733–5500). For wet and wild stretches of river, get in touch with **Lewis & Clark Expeditions** (145 W. Gill St., Box 720, Jackson 83001, tel. 307/733–4022 or 800/824–5375) or **Mad River Boat Trips** (1060 S. U.S. 89, Box 2222, Jackson 83001, tel. 307/733–6203 or 800/458–RAFT).

In Cody, family river trips on the **Shoshone River** are offered by **River Runners** (1491 Sheridan Ave., 82801, tel. 307/527–7238) and **Wyoming River Trips** (Buffalo Bill Village, Box 1541-TC, 82414, tel. 307/587–6661).

Fishing Lake and stream fishing in Wyoming is legendary. Record Mackinaw trout have been taken at **Jackson Lake,** and the trout population in **Yellowstone Lake** has been revived. Inside and outside the parks, the rivers are teeming with rainbow, native cutthroat, brook, brown, and Mackinaw trout, as well as whitefish and catfish at some lower elevations. The **Snake River** has its own unique cutthroat strain. Fishing aficionados often trek south into the **Wind River Mountains,** where glacier-fed lakes yield all of the above plus golden trout.

Limits and restrictions on fishing in the parks change from year to year. A free park license is required. Outside the parks on state, private, or national forest lands, Wyoming fishing licenses are required and are usually available at sporting goods stores and drugstores. Nonresidents can purchase a one-day license for $5; five-day, $20; ten-day, $30; and season, $50. Children under 14 may fish without a license when with a licensed adult. Contact **Wyoming Game and Fish Department** (5400 Bishop Blvd., Cheyenne 82006, tel. 307/777–4600) for information. You can get licenses at sporting goods stores throughout the state. The **Wind River Indian Reservation** has some of the best fishing in the Rockies. A separate license is required here. Contact **Shoshone and Arapaho Tribes** (Fish and Game Dept., 1 Washakie, Fort Washakie 82520, tel. 307/332–7207).

Golf In Cody, **Olive Glenn Golf and Country Club** (802 Meadow La., tel. 307/587–5551) is a highly rated 18-hole course, with Jacuzzi, pool, and tennis courts available after a round of golf. Jackson has two fine 18-hole courses: **Jackson Hole Golf Club** (tel. 307/733–3111), a championship course with tennis and swimming facilities near the Jackson Hole Airport, and **Teton Pines Golf Club** (3450 N. Clubhouse, tel. 307/733–1733), just south of the Jackson Hole Ski Resort.

Mountain Climbing Mountain climbers get a leg up in the Grand Tetons from **Jackson Hole Mountain Guides** (165 N. Glenwood St., Box 7477, Jackson 83001, tel. 307/733–4979) or **Exum Mountain Guides** (south end of Jenny Lake, Box 56, Moose 83012, tel. 307/733–2297).

Skiing Cross-country skiing and snowshoeing are permitted in parts
Cross-Country of Yellowstone and Grand Teton national parks and surrounding forests. Among the best places is **Togwotee Pass,** east of Jackson on U.S. 26/287, in Bridger-Teton and Shoshone national forests. Lessons and groomed trails are available for a fee at **Spring Creek Ranch** (*see* Dining and Lodging, *below*) and **Jackson Hole Nordic Center** (Teton Village, tel. 307/733–2292).

Downhill About a 45-minute drive from Jackson, on the far side of the Tetons, is **Grand Targhee Ski and Summer Resort** (Box SKI, Alta 83422, tel. 307/353–2304 or 800/443–8146), a resort famed for its deep powder and its family atmosphere. Targhee's slopes—predominantly intermediate—never feel crowded, but to experience complete solitude, try a day of snowcat skiing in untracked powder. There are four lifts and 2,200 vertical feet. The resort was rebuilt recently and has a handsome, natural-wood look as well as an outdoor pool and hot tub for overnight guests. Lift prices are moderate ($24 for adults, $12 for senior citizens and children under 13).

The **Jackson Hole Ski Resort** (Box 290, Teton Village 83025, tel. 307/733–2292 or 800/443–6931) boasts the longest vertical drop among American ski areas: 4,139 feet. Especially rich in intermediate and advanced terrain, it has nine lifts and a tram to the top of Rendezvous Mountain. Few resorts have views to match the one of Teton Valley, and in good snow years, like 1993, Jackson Hole provides some of the best skiing in the Rockies. Plans for expansion and faster lifts are afoot. The ski school is run by Olympic medalist Pepi Stiegler. Tickets are pricey: $38 per day for adults.

Snowmobiling Snowmobiling is increasingly popular and is allowed on snow-packed roads within Yellowstone Park. The state of Wyoming grooms an extensive network of trails in the forests of the northwest, including the **Continental Divide Snowmobile Trail,** which runs from Lander to Grand Teton. For information on trails, contact the **Wyoming State Snowmobile Program** (tel. 307/777–7550).

Among the bigger snowmobile operations are **Flagg Ranch Village** and **Togwotee Mountain Lodge;** in Yellowstone, **TW Recreational Services** rents snowmobiles at the Mammoth Hot Springs Hotel or Old Faithful Snow Lodge for $95 per day (*see* Guided Tours, *above*, for all). Additional information on snowmobile rentals and guides is available from the Jackson Hole Chamber of Commerce (*see* Important Addresses and Numbers, *above*).

Water Sports On Yellowstone Lake, boaters embark from **Bridge Bay** (tel. 307/344–7311); rentals are available. If you want to get out on Jackson Lake but you didn't bring your own boat, you can hire canoes and powerboats at **Colter Bay Marina** (north of Jackson Lake Junction, tel. 307/733–2811) or **Signal Mountain Marina** (Teton Park Rd. at the south end of the lake, tel. 307/543–2831). Boats must be licensed by the parks. Seven-day permits, good in both parks, cost $7 for motorboats and $5 for nonmotorized boats.

Dining and Lodging

Cody **Franca's Italian Dining.** Serving authentic northern Italian
Dining gourmet fare, this restaurant has a single nightly menu. Entrées vary—pork, poultry, beef, seafood, or veal—and are complemented by a wine list of some 90 selections. The small room (maximum 24) is filled with artwork from Italy. *1421 Rumsey Ave., tel. 307/587–5354. Reservations required. No credit cards. Closed for lunch and Mon., Tues. Moderate.*
La Comida. Making no claim to authentic Mexican cooking, this restaurant nevertheless recently received the Five Star Diamond Award as one of the top 50 Mexican restaurants in the country from the Academy Awards of the Restaurant Industry and has been reviewed in numerous national newspapers and magazines. Instead, the owners prefer to describe their recipes as "Cody-Mex," but the decor is authentic Mexican and the atmosphere festive. *1385 Sheridan Ave., tel. 307/587–9556. Reservations advised. AE, D, DC, MC, V. Inexpensive.*
Proud Cut Saloon. At this popular downtown eatery and watering hole, owner Del Nose claims to serve "kick-ass cowboy cuisine": steaks, prime rib, shrimp, fish, and chicken. The Western decor includes paintings, vintage photographs of Cody country, and large game mounts. *1227 Sheridan Ave., tel. 307/527–6905. AE, D, DC, MC, V. Inexpensive.*

Lodging **Buffalo Bill Village.** This downtown development comprises three lodgings, which share many facilities. The **Buffalo Bill**

Village Resort, consisting of log cabins with modern interiors, and the Holiday Inn Convention Center, a typical two-story brick hotel, are most noteworthy. *1701 Sheridan Ave., 82414, tel. 307/587–5544. Resort: 85 cabins. Inn: 184 rooms. Facilities: restaurant, lounge, outdoor heated pool, conference rooms. AE, D, DC, MC, V. Resort and Inn: Expensive.*

The Irma Hotel. Named for Buffalo Bill's daughter, this hotel has some of the flavor of earlier days, when Buffalo Bill still ranched nearby. With brass beds and period furniture in many rooms, a huge restaurant, and an elaborate cherrywood bar, it retains its old charm. During the summer, locals stage a gunfight on the porch Wednesday–Friday at 7 PM. *1192 Sheridan Ave., 82414, tel. 307/587–4221. 41 rooms. Facilities: restaurant, bar. AE, D, DC, MC, V. Moderate–Expensive.*

Pahaska Teepee Resort. Two miles from Yellowstone's East Entrance, these cabins are a good base for summer and winter recreation, both inside and outside the park. This was Buffalo Bill's original getaway in the high country. *183 Yellowstone Hwy., Cody 82414, tel. 307/527–7701. 48 cabins. Facilities: restaurant, snowmobile rentals, horseback riding, gift shop. AE, MC, V. Moderate.*

★ Parson's Pillow. Built in 1902 as Cody's first church, this B&B serves big, delicious breakfasts. Innkeepers Lee and Elly Larabee are founts of information about the area's sights and history. *1202 14th St., 82414, tel. 307/587–2382 or 800/377–2348. 4 rooms, 2 share bath. MC, V. Moderate.*

Grand Targhee
Dining and Lodging

Grand Targhee Ski and Summer Resort. Perched on the west side of the Tetons, this small but modern facility has the uncrowded, stroll-around atmosphere of a small village in the Alps, rather than the speedy, noisy scene of many American resorts today. The motel-style rooms are simply furnished and clustered around common areas with nestled fireplaces; the condominum rooms have more space and a brighter look inside. Expansion plans are on the drawing board, but the permit process with the U.S. Forest Service may take several years. Skadi's, the resort's foremost restaurant, is a relaxing, well-lighted place with Southwestern-style decor, high ceilings, and a general feel of roominess. On the menu are tenderloin beef with *pablano* chile sauce and regional game dishes including venison and pheasant. For quicker, less expensive fare, there is the Cactus Kitchen. *Box SKI, Alta 83422, tel. 307/353–2300 or 800/443–8146. Skadi's and Cactus Kitchen: AE, D, MC, V. Inexpensive. 97 rooms: 65 motel-style, 32 condos. Facilities: 5 restaurants, outdoor pool, indoor and outdoor hot tubs, gift shops, boutiques, pro shop, cross-county trails. Motel/condo: reservations recommended. AE, D, MC, V. Inexpensive to Moderate.*

Grand Teton National Park
Dining

Dornan's. This popular local hangout has Old West decor and mountain views. In the summer, it cooks up an outdoor Dutch-oven buffet (steak, ribs, and cowboy beans) and a friendly atmosphere to go with it. In the winter, gourmet sit-down dinners are served. A good wine shop is adjacent. *U.S. 191, Moose, tel. 307/733–2415. Reservations required. MC, V. Moderate.*

Dining and Lodging
★

Jenny Lake Lodge. In this most exclusive of the park's resorts, elegant yet rustic cabins are bedecked with handmade quilts (and electric blankets). Overnight guests are on the American plan; two meals a day are included, as are horseback riding, bicycling, and other outdoor activities. The lodge dining room offers a set dinner menu with a choice of entrées emphasizing Rocky Mountain cuisine, including roast prime rib of buffalo or breast of pheasant with pheasant sausage. *Jenny Lake Rd., Grand Teton Lodge Co., Box 240, Moran 83013, tel. 307/733–2811. Restaurant: Expensive. 30 cabins. Facilities: restaurant, lounge. AE, DC, MC, V. Closed mid-Sept.–early June. Expensive.*

Jackson Lake Lodge. Outside, the resort has a 1950s look, dark brown and low-slung. Inside, two large fireplaces adorn the lounge, Native American designs decorate the walls, and huge picture windows look out at Willow Flats, below Jackson Lake Dam. There are 30 smaller rooms in the main lodge; the others, in one-story motor-lodge-style buildings, are preferable. The lodge boasts the only swimming pool in the park. Rotating four dinner menus, the **Mural Room** often features buffalo, popular with the largely tourist clientele, as well as local game dishes such as venison or antelope. *U.S. 89 north of Jackson Lake Junction, Grand Teton Lodge Co., Box 240, Moran 83013, tel. 307/733–2811. Restaurant: Moderate–Expensive. 385 rooms. Facilities: 2 restaurants, pool. AE, DC, MC, V. Closed Oct.–early June. Moderate–Expensive.*

Signal Mountain Lodge. Built of volcanic stone and pine shingles, the lodge sits on the eastern shore of Jackson Lake. The lobby has a fireplace, a piano, and Adirondack furniture, and guest rooms are clustered in cabinlike units, some with kitchenettes. **The Aspens** restaurant offers up views of the lake and the Tetons as well as a menu with buffalo sirloin and lots of fish. *Teton Park Rd., Box 50, Moran 83013, tel. 307/543–2831. 79 units. Facilities: restaurant, bar, marina. AE, DC, MC, V. Closed mid-Oct.–early May. Restaurant: Expensive. Lodge: Moderate–Expensive.*

Colter Bay Village. Less expensive than its posher cousins, the resort, near Jackson Lake, has splendid views and an excellent marina and beach for the windsurfing crowd. (You'll need a wet suit.) The **Chuckwagon** is family oriented, serving lasagna, trout, and barbecue spare ribs. *Off U.S. 89, Grand Teton Lodge Co., Box 240, Moran 83013, tel. 307/543–2855. 250 cabins (30 share bath). Facilities: 2 restaurants, bar, Laundromat. AE, DC, MC, V. Closed late Sept.–mid-May. Restaurant: Moderate–Expensive. Village: Inexpensive–Moderate.*

Jackson Dining **The Blue Lion.** Consistently excellent fare is served in this blue clapboard house two blocks from the Town Square. Dishes ★ range from grilled elk tenderloin served with apple-currant chutney to a wine-basted trout stuffed with Canadian snow crab. Lunch on the deck is a treat in summer. *160 N. Millward St., tel. 307/733–3912. AE, MC, V. Expensive.*

★ **The Bunnery.** Lunch and dinner are served here in the summer, but it's the breakfasts that are irresistible, whether it's an omelet with blue cheese, mushrooms, and sautéed spinach or home-baked pastry. It's elbow to elbow inside and a brief wait to be seated on busy mornings, but it's worth it. *130 N. Cache St., Hole-in-the-Wall Mall, tel. 307/733–5474. No reservations. MC, V. Moderate.*

Nani's. The ever-changing menu at this cozy, almost cramped, restaurant may contain braised veal shanks with saffron risotto or other regional Italian cooking. Almost hidden behind a motel, it's designed to attract gourmets, not tourists. *240 N. Glenwood St., tel. 307/733–3888. DC, MC, V. Moderate.*

Sweetwater Restaurant. Mediterranean meals are served in a log cabin atmosphere, and it works. Start with humus or a Montrechet tart (goat cheese with caramelized onions in pastry); then go on to lamb dishes, chicken Bombay, or shrimp spetses (simmered in tomato and garlic with feta cheese). *King and Pearl Sts., tel. 307/733–3553. MC, V. Moderate.*

Mangy Moose. Folks pour in off the ski slopes for a lot of food and talk. Two levels, plus a bar with an outdoor deck, are decorated with antiques and a biplane hanging from the ceiling. There's a high noise level but decent fare at fair prices. *Teton Village, tel. 307/733–4913. AE, MC, V. Inexpensive–Moderate.*

Jedediah's House of Sourdough. This restaurant a block east of the Town Square, makes breakfast and lunch for the big appetite. There are plenty of "sourjacks" (sourdough flapjacks) and biscuits and gravy and a friendly, elbow-knocking atmosphere. *135 E. Broadway Ave., tel. 307/733–5671. No reservations. AE, MC, V. Closed for dinner. Inexpensive.*

Off Broadway. This restaurant emphasizes seafood and pasta (Cajun shrimp with black linguine), with a little Thai, wild game, and snazzy neon thrown in. Seating is indoors or out. *30 King St., tel. 307/733–9777. AE, MC, V. Inexpensive.*

Vista Grande. At this popular spot, you sometimes have to wait for generous portions of Mexican-style food. Lovers of hot food will find it a little bland, and at times, it's too crowded and noisy. *Teton Village Rd. near Wilson turnoff, tel. 307/733–6964. No reservations. MC, V. Inexpensive.*

Dining and Lodging ★ **The Wort Hotel.** This brick Victorian hotel near the square seems to have been around as long as the Tetons, but it feels fresh inside. A fireplace warms the lobby, and a sitting area is just up the stairs. You can sip a drink in the Silver Dollar Bar or sit down for a gourmet meal. Try the mixed grill of buffalo and elk medallions or the nightly veal special. *50 N. Glenwood St., 83001, tel. 307/733–2190 or 800/322–2727. 60 rooms. Facilities: restaurant, bar, 2 Jacuzzis, exercise room. AE, D, DC, MC, V. Expensive.*

Spring Creek Ranch. Outside of town on Gros Ventre Butte, this luxury resort offers beautiful views of the Tetons and a number of amenities, including cooking in some units, horseback riding, tennis, and cross-country skiing and sleigh rides in winter. Aside from 36 hotel rooms, there's a changing mix of studios, suites, and two-bedroom condos with lofts, called "Choates." The comfortable restaurant, **The Granary,** serves fine food; lead off with Dungeness crab and Havarti cheese wrapped in phyllo dough, followed by poached salmon in cucumber dill sauce with wild rice. *1800 Spirit Dance Rd., Box 3154, 83001, tel. 307/733–8833 or 800/443–6139. 117 units. Restaurant: reservations required; expensive. Facilities: restaurant, pool, tennis courts, horseback riding. AE, D, DC, MC, V. Moderate–Expensive.*

Lodging You can make reservations for most motels through two reservation services: **Central Reservations** (tel. 800/443–6931) or **Jackson Hole Vacations** (tel. 800/223–4059).

Painted Porch Bed and Breakfast. Cozy, clean, and comfortable, this traditional red and white farmhouse built in 1901 is nestled on 3½ acres of pine and aspen 8 miles out of town. There are actually four porches and a white picket fence, along with Japanese soaking tubs. Full breakfast is included. *Box 7453,*

83001, tel. 307/733–1981. 1 suite, 1 room. Facilities: living room. MC, V. Expensive.

Days Inn. Like other chains, this motel is something familiar, but the lodgepole swing out front, the lobby's elk-antler chandelier, and the rooms' Teton, Wind River, or Snake River range views remind you where you are. Some rooms have microwaves and fridges, and a Continental breakfast is included. *1280 W. Broadway Ave., 83001, tel. 307/739–9010. 78 rooms. Facilities: sauna, Jacuzzi. AE, D, DC, MC, V. Moderate–Expensive.*

Pony Express. Rooms are standard motel rooms, but some have mountain views, while others have patios. The center of town is just two blocks away. *Box 972, 83001, tel. 307/733–2658. 41 rooms. Facilities: pool, Jacuzzi. AE, D, MC, V. Moderate–Expensive.*

Virginian Motel. Part of a larger complex that occupies a few blocks, this shingle-roof motel is near restaurants, an Old West saloon, a beauty shop, a Laundromat, and an outdoor heated pool. Though it looks much as it did when it opened 30 years ago, it's been upgraded since. Some units have cooking. *750 W. Broadway Ave., 83001, tel. 307/733–2792. 158 rooms. Facilities: pool. AE, DC, MC, V. Moderate–Expensive.*

Alpenhof. This small Austrian-style hotel is in the heart of the Jackson Hole Ski Resort next to the tram. The dining room features such entrées as wild game loaf, and Dietrich's Bar and Bistro is a relatively quiet night club, considering its proximity to the slopes. *Box 288, Teton Village 83025, tel 307/733–3242. 44 rooms. Facilities: dining room, bar, pool, ski room, masseuse. AE, D, DC, MC, V. Closed Oct., Nov., part of Apr.–May. Moderate.*

Motel 6. On the outskirts of town, it's big, cheap, and standard for the chain. It's often filled with kids and tour-bus groups. *1370 W. Broadway Ave., 83001, tel. 307/733–9666. 155 rooms. Facilities: pool. AE, D, DC, MC, V. Inexpensive.*

Yellowstone National Park
Dining and Lodging

The park has six areas with lodges and full-scale restaurants open during the summer. They are operated by **TW Recreational Services** (*see* Guided Tours, *above*), and all accept major credit cards (AE, D, DC, MC, and V). Ask about size of beds, bathrooms, thickness of walls, and room location when you book, especially in the older hotels, where accommodations vary and upgrades are ongoing. Telephones have been put in some rooms, but no TVs yet.

Lake Lodge. Less regal than its neighbor, the Lake Yellowstone Hotel, the lodge is ½ mile away along the lakeshore. Accommodations are in the lodge and in cabins, and there's cafeteria service. Pets are allowed. *Lake Village. 186 units. Facilities: cafeteria. Moderate–Expensive.*

★ **Lake Yellowstone Hotel.** Built in 1889 on the north end of Yellowstone Lake, the hotel, which has neoclassical Greek columns and huge lakefront windows, is one of the oldest and most elegant park resorts. Afternoon chamber music in the sunny lobby provides a refreshing reminder of old-style luxury tourism in the "wilderness." You can rent rather primitive cabins, with pine beds and paneling, or hotel rooms, some of which have brass beds and historic fixtures. The dining room menu includes Thai curry shrimp and fettuccine with smoked salmon and snow peas. *Lake Village. Restaurant: reservations required; Inexpensive–Moderate. 194 rooms, 102 cabins. Facilities: restaurant. Closed late Sept.–mid-May. Moderate–Expensive.*

Canyon Lodge. The park's biggest, it consists of a large number of nondescript cabins and motel rooms perched above the Grand Canyon of the Yellowstone. A cafeteria fills up with a lunchtime crowd interested in sandwiches, chili, and lasagna, and the restaurant features pastas, prime rib, and trout almandine. *Canyon. Restaurant: reservations required for dinner. 572 cabins, 37 annex rooms. Facilities: restaurant, cafeteria, lounge, gift shop, horseback riding. Closed late Aug.–mid-June. Moderate.*

Grant Village. The least appetizing accommodation in the park is also the newest. It's dull and gray and in standard motel style but has a view of the lake. The steak house and restaurant serves steak, chicken, and seafood. *Grant Village. Restaurant: reservations required. 300 rooms. Facilities: restaurant, marina. Closed mid-Sept.–May. Moderate.*

Mammoth Hot Springs Hotel. Sharing its grounds with park headquarters, this is farther from some of the park's favorite attractions than other hotels but also less crowded. Rooms are small, and cabins, four of which have hot tubs, are ranged around "auto courts," a 1950s touch. The lobby and restaurant, which serves regional American fare as prime rib and chicken with Brie and raspberry sauce, have art deco touches. Elk and tourists sometimes graze between the hotel and the **Terrace Grill,** an airy room with large windows offering fast-food and cafeteria-style service. *Mammoth. 140 cabins. Facilities: 2 restaurants, lounge, horseback riding. Closed mid-Sept.–mid-Dec., mid-March–late May. Inexpensive–Moderate.*

★ **Old Faithful Inn.** You can loll in front of the lobby's roaring fire and look up at wooden balconies that seem to disappear into the night sky; on those deep balconies, guests play cards, scribble at writing desks, or just relax above the hubbub. Guest-room decor ranges from brass beds to Victorian cherrywood to inexpensive motel-style furniture. More expensive rooms face the geyser. The dining room is a huge hall centered on a fireplace of volcanic stone and offers up shrimp scampi and chicken Forestière. *Old Faithful. Restaurant: reservations required. 327 rooms (77 share bath). Facilities: restaurant, lounge, gift shop. Closed mid-Oct.–mid-Dec., mid-Mar.–mid-May. Inexpensive.*

Old Faithful Snow Lodge. This compact motel tucked off to the side in the Old Faithful complex is drab-looking, but it stays open for winter visitors. The cozy lobby is warmed by a wood-stove, and the small restaurant serves family fare. *Old Faithful. Restaurant: closed for lunch. 32 rooms (30 share bath), 34 cabins. Facilities: restaurant, gift shop. Closed mid-Oct.–mid-Dec., mid-Mar.–mid-May. Inexpensive.*

Roosevelt Lodge. Located near the beautiful Lamar Valley in the park's northeast corner, this is a simple, log-cabin alternative to more expensive accommodations. The dining room dishes up barbecued ribs, Roosevelt beans, and more Western fare. *Tower-Roosevelt. Restaurant: reservations required. 86 cabins, 8 with bath. Facilities: restaurant, lounge, gift shop. Closed early Sept.–early June. Inexpensive.*

The Arts

Wyoming is not the place to come for sophisticated performances, lacking both the facilities and the population to support major groups. Touring productions do visit occasionally, and every summer at the Teton Village resort, the **Grand Teton Music Festival** (Box 490, Teton Village 83025, tel. 307/733–1128) brings symphonic and chamber music.

Nightlife

Bars and Lounges There is never a shortage of live music in **Jackson,** where local performers play country, rock, and folk. Two of the most popular bars are on the Town Square: the **Million Dollar Cowboy Bar** (25 N. Cache St., tel. 307/733–2207), where everyone dresses up in cowboy garb and tries to two-step into the Old West, and the **Rancher Bar** (20. E. Broadway Ave., tel. 307/733–3886), where the renowned Wyoming band Bruce Howser and Sawmill Creek often performs.

A special treat is down the road at the **Stagecoach Bar** (Rte. 22, Wilson, tel. 307/733–4407), which fills to bursting Sundays when the house band—a motley bunch that includes a novelist, the first man to ski down the Grand Teton, and a changing cast of guitar aces—is playing.

The Cheyenne Area

Cheyenne sits apart from the mountainous magnet of western Wyoming. Some detractors say it's more a part of Colorado's Front Range, which runs north across the nearby border, but the area is no Colorado wanna-be. While the rest of Wyoming struggles to get by, Cheyenne is a dynamic city, thriving on a mixture of state government, the military, and new industry. The University of Wyoming, the state's only four-year university, is just over the Medicine Bow Mountains in Laramie, and outside city limits, cattle grazing on rolling hills are a reminder that the area's century-old ranching community still survives.

Born in 1867 as the Union Pacific Railroad inched its way across the plains, Cheyenne began as a rowdy camp for railroad gangs, cowboys, prospectors heading for the Black Hills, and soldiers. It more than lived up to its nickname: "Hell on Wheels." Among the eager entrepreneurs who spent time here were Frank and Jesse James and Butch Cassidy's Hole in the Wall Gang. In the late 19th century, the region's enormously wealthy cattle barons, many of them English, settled in Cheyenne. They sipped brandy at the Cheyenne Social Club and hired hard cases like Tom Horn to take care of their competitors on the open range. Those brief years of wealth and glory—and the hardworking ranches that endure today—are remembered in the area slogan "Live the Legend" and celebrated with Western élan in Frontier Days.

During Frontier Days, Cheyenne is up to its neck in bucking broncs and bulls and joyful bluster. There are pancake breakfasts put on by locals, parades and pageantry, and parties that require the endurance of a cattle hand on a weeklong drive. The event, almost a century old, is now the world's largest outdoor rodeo extravaganza, dubbed "The Daddy of 'Em All." Reservations are a must; for tickets and information, contact **Cheyenne Frontier Days** (Box 2477, Cheyenne 82003, tel. 307/778–7222; 800/22–RODEO; in WY, 800/54–DADDY).

Important Addresses and Numbers

Tourist Information Cheyenne Area Convention and Visitors Bureau (309 W. Lincolnway [16th St.], Cheyenne 82001, tel. 307/778–3133 or 800/426–5009); **Laramie Area Chamber of Commerce** (800 S. 3rd St., Laramie 82070, tel. 307/745–7339).

Emergencies Area hospitals include **Ivinson Memorial Hospital** (255 N. 30th St., Laramie, tel. 307/742–2141) and **United Medical Center** (300 E. 23rd St., Cheyenne, tel. 307/634–2273).

Arriving and Departing by Plane

Airports and Airlines **Cheyenne Airport** (200 E. 8th Ave., tel. 307/634–7071) is served by **Continental Express** (tel. 800/525–0280) and **United Express** (tel. 800/241–6522). Many visitors prefer to fly into Denver's Stapleton International Airport and drive the 90 miles north.

Arriving and Departing by Car, Train, and Bus

By Car Cheyenne is at the intersection of I–80 and I–25.

By Train **Amtrak** (tel. 307/778–3912 or 800/872–7245) has stops both in Laramie and outside Cheyenne, where a free shuttle bus takes passengers on a 15-minute ride to and from the city. Trains connecting to Denver and Salt Lake City run once a day in each direction.

By Bus **Greyhound/Trailways** (1503 Capitol Ave., tel. 307/634–7744) connects Cheyenne to such hubs as Denver and Salt Lake City.

Getting Around

By Car Unless you will just be in downtown Cheyenne, you'll need to rent a car or bring your own.

By Cab If you only need to get to and from the airport or bus station and the capitol area, you can make do with cabs: **Checker Cab** (tel. 307/635–5555) or **Yellow Cab** (tel. 307/638–3333).

Guided Tours

Orientation Tours The **Cheyenne Trolley** takes a two-hour tour of the historic downtown area and Frances E. Warren Air Force Base, including 20–25 minutes at the Old West Museum. Tickets are sold at the Cheyenne Area Convention and Visitors Bureau (*see* Important Addresses and Numbers, *above*) on weekdays and at Wrangler (16th and Capitol Sts.) on weekends. *16th and Capitol Sts. Fare (museum admission included): $6 adults, $3 children under 12. Runs mid-May–mid-Sept., Mon.–Sat. 10 and 1:30, Sun. 11:30.*

Walking Tours For a self-guided walking tour of the downtown and capitol area, contact the **Cheyenne Area Convention and Visitors Bureau** (*see* Important Addresses and Numbers, *above*).

Exploring the Cheyenne Area

Numbers in the margin correspond to points of interest on the Wyoming map.

 Start a tour of **Cheyenne** with the **Old West Museum,** which has 30,000 pieces in all, including 125 carriages. Guided tours are aimed at children. During Frontier Days, the museum hosts the Governor's Invitational Western Art Show and Sale, in which top Western wildlife and landscape artists from around the country exhibit. *4501 N. Carey Ave., tel. 307/778–7290. Admission: $6 families, $3 adults, $2 senior citizens, $1 per person at group rate. Open winter, weekdays 9–5, Sat. 11–4; summer, weekdays 8–6, weekends 10–5.*

The **Wyoming State Museum** has areas devoted to Plains and prehistoric tribes and to Wyoming history and development. A gallery has revolving exhibits of regional artists, and a gift shop carries Wyoming books and crafts. *24th and Central Sts. Admission free. Open weekdays 8:30–5, Sat. 9–5 and in summer, Sun. 1–5.*

The **Wyoming State Capitol** is a Corinthian-style structure, authorized by the Ninth Territorial Legislative Assembly in 1886 and now on the National Register of Historic Places. The dome, covered in 24-carat gold leaf and visible from all roads leading into the city, is 50 feet in diameter at the base and 146 feet high at the peak. Standing in front is a statue of Esther Hobart Morris, the nation's first female governor and a proponent of women's suffrage. In fact, Wyoming is nicknamed the "Equality State" because it was the first state to give women the vote, due largely to the persuasive powers of Esther Hobart Morris. As a result of Wyoming's small population and informal ways, it's not unusual to find the governor wandering the halls of the capitol in blue jeans and in-state visitors hailing him by his first name. *Tel. 307/777–7220. Admission free. Open weekdays 8–5 and May–Aug., Sat. 9–5. Tours (self-guided) of state offices and Senate and House chambers: year-round; tours of dome: May–Aug.*

The **Historic Governor's Mansion** was the residence of 19 Wyoming first families from 1905 to 1976. Ornate chandeliers in nearly every room are just some of the interesting appointments. *300 E. 21st St. Admission free. Open Tues.–Sat. 9–5.*

Time Out	On your way west, midway between Cheyenne and Laramie, north of I–80 and south of Happy Jack Road (Route 210), is **Vedauwoo,** a particularly unusual area and a great place for a picnic. Springing out of high plains and open meadows are glacial remnants in the form of huge granite boulders piled skyward with reckless abandon. These one-of-a-kind rock formations, dreamscapes of gray stone, excite the imagination and are great for hiking, climbing, and photography.

Continuing on, 40-odd miles to the west of Cheyenne in a valley between the Medicine Bow Mountains and the Laramie Range, ❺ you come to **Laramie.** First settled when the railroad reached here in 1867, it was for a time a tough "end-of-the-rail" town.

Perhaps due to the bedlam of the early days, Laramie became the site of the Wyoming Territorial Prison in 1872. Until 1903, it was the region's federal and state penal facility, housing the likes of Butch Cassidy and other infamous frontier outlaws. Today the restored prison is the gem of **Wyoming Territorial Park,** giving life to the legends of frontier law and justice. In addition, the park contains a 19th-century railroad display, a U.S. marshals' museum, a replica of a frontier town, a living-history program, and the Horse Barn Dinner Theater. *975 Snowy Range Rd., tel. 307/745–6161 or 800/845–2287. Admission: $20* *family, $7.50 adults, $7 senior citizens, $6.50 children 6–12. Dinner theater: $20 adults, $18 senior citizens, $10 children 6–12, $5 children under 6. Open Memorial Day–Labor Day, daily 9–6; dinner theater Tues.–Sun. 6–8:30.*

For more area history, visit the **Laramie Plains Museum,** in the Ivinson mansion. Built in 1892 by Edward Ivinson, a businessman, philanthropist, and one of Laramie's first settlers, the estate houses a growing collection of historical artifacts from the Laramie Plains area. *6th St. and Ivinson Ave., tel. 307/742–4448. Open June–Aug., Mon.–Sat. 9–8; Sept.–May, Mon.–Sat. 1–3.*

The **University of Wyoming** (13th St. and Ivinson Ave.) offers year-round events—from concerts to football—and a number of attractions. The best place to start, for a tour or just for information, is the **UW Visitor Center** (tel. 307/766–4075). Depending on your interests, you might want to visit the **Anthropological Museum** (tel. 307/766–5136), **Planetarium** (tel. 307/766–6150), **Entomology Museum** (tel. 307/766–2298), **Rocky Mountain Herbarium** (tel. 307/766–2236), or other campus museums of note.

The **Geological Museum** contains the skeleton of an apatosaurus (brontosaurus) 15 feet high and 75 feet long and believed to weigh in at 30 tons. Other exhibits explore the dinosaur family tree, meteorites, fossils, and earthquakes. *University, in the northwest corner of campus, the building with a dinosaur statue out front, tel. 307/766–4218. Admission: free. Open weekdays 8–5, weekends 10–3.*

New in 1993, the **American Heritage Center** houses more than 10,000 photographs, rare books, collections of papers, and memorabilia related to American and Western history, the petroleum industry, conservation movements, transportation, and the performing arts. *2111 Willet Dr., tel. 307/766–4114. Admission: free. Open Mon.–Fri. 8–5, Sat. 11–5.*

In the summer, you can get away from the interstates by taking Route 130, the **Snowy Range Scenic Byway,** west of Laramie. This paved road in excellent condition runs over 10,847-foot Snowy Range Pass through the **Medicine Bow National Forest,** providing views of Medicine Bow Peak. Along the way, there are 10 campgrounds (six right on the road), 10 hiking trails (from 1.5 to 8.2 miles), and 100 alpine lakes and streams. For the more adventurous, take any of the several gravel roads that lead into the forest. Maps are available from the **U.S. Forest Service** (2468 Snowy Range Rd., Laramie, tel. 307/745–8971).

At the end of the scenic byway, Route 130 joins Route 230 and heads north to **Saratoga.** The main attraction in this small community is **Hobo Hot Springs** and the adjacent swimming pool heated by the springs. *Admission free. Springs open year-round, but pool hrs. change.*

For a quicker, though less scenic, trip back to Laramie and Cheyenne, continue north and pick up I-80 east.

What to See and Do with Children

Take a one-day scenic excursion on the **Wyoming-Colorado Railroad,** which runs from Laramie through the Centennial Valley, stops for an hour in Centennial (population 100) for a barbecue and live music, continues through "muleshoe" curves into the Snowy Range, and turns around at Fox Park. Open-air gondolas on all cars provide 360° views. For parents, the nonsmoking train provides complimentary champagne and a cash bar along with delicious hors d'oeuvres in first class. *452 Snowy Range Rd., tel. 307/742–9162. Fare: $49.95 1st class, $32.95 adults, $29.95 senior citizens, $17.95 children under 12. Runs Apr., May, Nov. (weather permitting), weekends; June, Wed.–Mon.; July–Sept., daily. Departure time: 10.*

The **Wyoming Children's Museum and Nature Center,** in the Laramie Plains Civic Center, is a hands-on place in which children and families can explore, make noise, experiment, play, imagine, discover, and invent. *710 Garfield St., Room 254, Laramie, tel. 307/745–6332. Admission: $1.50 adults, 75¢ children. Open Tues. 8:30–12:30, Thurs. 1–5, Sat. 10–4.*

Shopping

Shopping Streets/Malls Cheyenne's **Frontier Mall** (1400 Dell Range Blvd., tel. 307/638–2290) houses 75 specialty shops and four major department stores. It's as typical an American mall as you'll find.

Laramie's most unusual shopping is found in the 100 blocks of Ivinson Avenue and, one block south, Grand Avenue, where a shopping district called Landmark Square is being created.

Specialty Stores
Books **The Second Story** (105 Ivinson Ave., tel. 307/745–4423), in an old, antiques-laden upstairs suite of offices in Laramie, stocks only "personally recommended books," some of them signed by visiting authors.

Specialty Foods Laramie's **Whole Earth Granary** (111 Ivinson Ave., tel. 307/745–4268) sells organic whole grains and flours, 50 varieties of coffee, herbal extracts, essential oils, and fresh seafood flown in weekly, including live Maine lobster.

Western Wear Catercorner from each other in downtown Cheyenne are **Cheyenne Outfitters** (210 W. 16th St., tel. 307/775–7550) and **Wrangler** (16th and Capitol Sts., tel. 307/634–3048).

Sports and the Outdoors

Biking Mountain-biking trails are scattered throughout, especially in the **Medicine Bow National Forest** and **Happy Jack** area, neighboring Laramie. For information, trail maps, and rentals, see Mike or Doug Lowham at the **Pedal House** (207 S. 1st St., Laramie, tel. 307/742–5533).

Camping As everywhere in Wyoming, camping opportunities are abundant. Cheyenne has the new **Terry Bison Ranch** (I–25 Service Rd. near Colorado state line, tel. 307/634–4171) and, 15 minutes east, the **Wyoming Campground and Mobile Home Park** (I–80, Exit 377, tel. 307/547–2244). Laramie has a **KOA** (I–80 at Curtis St. Exit, tel. 307/742–6553). **Curt Gowdy State Park** (off Happy Jack Rd.) is a good camping spot away from the metropolis.

Canoeing and Rafting **Great Rocky Mountain Outfitters** (216 E. Walnut, Saratoga 82331, tel. 307/326–8750) offers guided canoe and raft expeditions on the North Platte River or canoe and raft guide/rental packages. River floats are available through **Platte Valley Anglers** (*see* Fishing, *below*).

Fishing Brook trout are prevalent in the lakes and streams of **Medicine Bow National Forest,** but you can find rainbow, golden, cutthroat, and brown trout and splake, too. Anglers can also drop a fly in the North Platte River near Saratoga. **Platte Valley Anglers** (1st and Bridge Sts., Saratoga 82331, tel. 307/326–5750) rents tackle and runs fishing trips on the Upper North Platte near Saratoga.

Golf Tee times are not hard to get at the local public courses: in Cheyenne, **Airport Course** (4801 Central Ave., tel. 307/637–6418), **Prairie View** (3601 Windmill Rd., tel. 307/637–6420), and the nine-hole executive course at **Little America Hotel and Resort** (2800 W. Lincolnway, tel. 307/775–8400); and in Laramie, **Jacoby Park Golf Course** (off N. 30th St., tel. 307/745–3111).

Skiing Downhill and cross-country skiing are available 32 miles southwest of Laramie at the **Snowy Range Ski Area** (1420 Thomas, Laramie 82070, tel. 307/745–5750 or 800/602–SNOW). Cross-country trails are also scattered throughout the **Happy Jack** and **Medicine Bow National Forest** areas. For information and rentals, contact **Cross Country Connection** (100 block of Ivinson Ave., Laramie, tel. 307/721–2851).

Dining and Lodging

Cheyenne **Poor Richard's.** In an interior of stained glass and dark wood,
Dining steaks, prime rib, formula-fed veal, pasta, chicken, fresh fish and seafood, soup and salad, and buffalo are served, as is Cheyenne's only Saturday brunch. *2233 E. Lincolnway, tel. 307/635–5114. AE, D, DC, MC, V. Moderate.*

★ **Lexie's Café.** Located in the oldest home in Cheyenne, a brick building over a century old, the café has delightful breakfast and lunch menus and offers up heaping platters of Mexican, Italian, and American food. *216 E. 17th St., tel. 307/638–8712. No reservations. AE, D, DC, MC, V. Closed for dinner and Sun. Inexpensive.*

Los Amigos. Mexican decorations on the walls complement the south-of-the-border fare at this local favorite south of downtown. *620 Central Ave., tel. 307/638–8591. MC, V. Closed Sun. Inexpensive.*

Lodging **A. Drummond's Ranch Bed and Breakfast.** Halfway between Cheyenne and Laramie and bordered by Curt Gowdy State Park lands, this B&B is on 120 acres and has a 100-mile view of the Laramie Range and the Colorado Rockies. Cross-country skiers and mountain bikers are welcome; in fact, the ranch conducts two- to six-hour tours for both. It also caters to runners who want to train at the 7,500-foot elevation and to horseback riders; stalls are available to board a horse or other pet during your stay. For those on extended stays, three meals a day are provided for an extra charge. (Special diets can be accommodated.) *399 Happy Jack Rd., Cheyenne/Laramie 82007, tel. 307/634–6042. 3 rooms, 2 with shared bath. Facilities: dining room, living room, outdoor hot tub, indoor riding arena, 4 stalls. No credit cards. Moderate.*

The Best Western Hitching Post Inn. Because of its location and facilities, this is the favorite haunt of Wyoming's citizen legislature when it gathers in the capital city. *1700 W. Lincolnway, 82001, tel. 307/638–3301 or 800/528–1234. 175 rooms. Facilities: 3 restaurants, lounge, indoor and outdoor pools, saunas, Jacuzzi, exercise facility. AE, D, DC, MC, V. Moderate.*

Little America Hotel and Resort. At the intersection of I–80 and I–25, the resort has an executive golf course. *2800 W. Lincolnway, 82001, tel. 307/775–8400 or 800/445–6945. 189 rooms. Facilities: dining room, lounge, heated Olympic-size pool, 9-hole golf course. AE, D, DC, MC, V. Moderate.*

Laramie
Dining
★

Café Jacques. Though the interior is inspired by French cafés, including a bar counter made of wine corks, this downtown restaurant dishes up innovative American cuisine. Entrées include chicken Alaska (chicken breast stuffed with cream cheese and crabmeat in a cheese sauce), coco shrimp (shrimp covered in coconut, deep-fried, and served on pineapple), steaks, and stir-fry specials. *216 Grand Ave., tel. 307/742–5522. Weekend reservations advised. AE, DC, MC, V. Closed for lunch. Moderate.*

The Cavalryman Supper Club. This old-fashioned restaurant with a large local clientele is on the plains, a mile south of Laramie on U.S. 287. Prime rib, steak, and lobster are on the menu. *4425 S. 3rd St., tel. 307/745–5551. Reservations accepted. AE, DC, MC, V. Closed for lunch except Easter, Thanksgiving, and New Year's Day. Moderate.*

The Overland Restaurant. This restaurant in the historic district, right on the railroad tracks, cooks up breakfast, lunch, and dinner. Patio dining and a superb wine list enhance the food: pasta, chicken, quiche, beef, and seafood. For Sunday breakfast, you might find such entrées as yellowfin tuna and eggs, a buffalo chili omelet, or avocados Benedict. *100 Ivinson Ave., tel. 307/721–2800. AE, D, MC, V. Inexpensive.*

Lodging
★

Annie Moore's Guest House. This historic home across from the University of Wyoming campus has been a fraternity, a sorority, an apartment building, and now a B&B, so it has great ghosts. Terra-cotta tiles, hardwood floors, the sounds of nesting owls, and a cat named Archina, who greets guests, make it cozy, though. Continental breakfast with homemade goodies comes with good conversation. *819 University, tel. 307/721–4177. 6 rooms, all share baths. Facilities: dining room, living room, TV room. AE, D, DC, MC, V. Moderate.*

Foster's Country Corner. On the western edge of town at the Snowy Range Road Exit off I–80 is this white-brick Best Western with a convenience store, 24-hour restaurant, and liquor store. *Box 580, exit 311 off I–80, 82070, tel. 307/742–8371 or 800/528–1234. 112 rooms. Facilities: restaurant, lounge, indoor pool, spa. AE, MC, V. Moderate.*

The University Inn. This motel near the university comprises four buildings surrounded by gardens. Most rooms are on the ground floor, and all have minirefrigerators. A complimentary Continental breakfast is included. *1720 Grand Ave. 82070, tel. 307/721–8855. 37 rooms. AE, D, DC, MC, V. Moderate.*

Saratoga
Lodging

The Saratoga Inn. This is a rustic, 1950s fishing, hunting, and golfing lodge. Hotel-style rooms are in a main building and two adjacent wings. There's a nine-hole public golf course, where cottonwoods, conifers, and the North Platte River also come into play. *E. Pic-Pike Rd., 82331, tel. 307/326–5261. 58 rooms. Facilities: hot tub, outdoor pool, 9-hole golf course. AE, DC, MC, V. Moderate.*

Wolf Hotel. This downtown hotel, on the National Register of Historic Places, has been recently renovated. It offers fine dining, especially steak and chicken. *101 E. Bridge, 82331, tel.*

307/326–5525. 3 suites, 5 rooms. Facilities: restaurant, lounge. AE, DC, MC, V. Inexpensive–Moderate.

The Arts

In Laramie, the **University of Wyoming's fine arts program** (tel. 307/766–5249) brings classical and popular performers.

Nightlife

Cheyenne For an evening of live country music; two-, three-, and four-chord songs; a large dance floor; and ample beverage service, try **The Cheyenne Club** (1617 Capitol Ave., tel. 307/635–7777) and **The Cowboy South** (312 S. Greeley Hwy., tel. 307/637–3800).

Laramie Country-and-western nightlife is found at **The Buckhorn** (114 Ivinson Ave., tel. 307/742–3554) and **The Cowboy Saloon** (108 S. 2nd St., tel. 307/721–3165). For more on the rock-and-roll side, you might chance the **Shooters Saloon** (303 S. 3rd St., tel. 307/745–7676) or hang out where the college students gather: **Mingles** (3206 Grand Ave., tel. 307/721–2005) and **The Drawbridge Tavern** (1622 Grand Ave., tel. 307/745–3490).

Northeast Wyoming

Separated from Yellowstone by the Bighorn Basin, the Bighorn Mountains should not be overlooked by lovers of high places. Topped by the 200,000-acre Cloud Peak Wilderness Area, the mountains offer good fishing, good hiking, plenty of wildlife, and some fascinating relics of ancient aboriginal residents.

Friendly little towns dot the Bighorns' eastern slope, but the "big" town is Sheridan. When Queen Elizabeth visits the Rockies, she comes to this area, not just because she has relatives here, which she does, but also because it has its own polo-playing "mink and manure" set.

The area has not been heavily promoted, though it has a rich history, especially of 19th-century warfare between the cavalry and Native Americans. Even richer is its lode of coal, which lies just below the surface mostly east of Sheridan and has brought huge multinational companies' strip mines. It's the topsoil above the coal seams, however, that maintains the area's most characteristic and enduring element—ranches. Dude ranching had its start here, and many of the dudes were so loyal to this country that they married locals and moved west permanently.

Heading east, the landscape becomes starker. By the time you reach Gillette, you are in a different world. This is the heart of energy-boom country, not far from nowhere and surrounded by coal mines and oil fields. Gillette has worked hard to make itself presentable, but you don't have to go far to find a shovel bigger than a house at one of the giant strip mines nearby.

Farther to the east, the Black Hills rise from the Powder River basin and lead into South Dakota.

Important Addresses and Numbers

Tourist Information **Gillette Chamber of Commerce** (314 S. Gillette Ave., Gillette 82716, tel. 307/682–3673); **Sheridan Chamber of Commerce** (Box 707, Sheridan 82801, tel. 307/672–2485).

Emergencies Area hospitals include **Campbell County Memorial Hospital** (501 S. Burma St., Gillette, tel. 307/682–8811) and **Sheridan County Memorial Hospital** (1401 W. 5th St., Sheridan, tel. 307/672–1000).

Arriving and Departing by Plane

Airports and Airlines **Sheridan** and **Gillette** are served by commuter airlines out of Denver. Flight times and carriers—currently **Continental Express** (tel. 800/525–0280) and **United Express** (tel. 800/241–6522)—have varied in recent years.

Arriving and Departing by Car and Bus

By Car Two interstates join at Buffalo: I–25 comes up from Denver, Cheyenne, Casper, and points south; I–90 comes from South Dakota and the Black Hills in the east and from Montana to the north.

By Bus The northeast corner is well served by **Powder River Transportation** (1700 E. U.S. 14/16, Gillette, tel. 800/442–3682), which connects with **Greyhound/Trailways** in Cheyenne.

Getting Around

By Car To get around northeastern Wyoming, you'll have to rent a car or bring your own. Sights are spread out along and off the interstates.

Exploring Northeast Wyoming

Numbers in the margin correspond to points of interest on the Wyoming map.

❼ **Sheridan** is what you'd expect a Western town to be. Main Street, unlike so many downtowns, is still vital and bustling, crowded with false-fronted stone and brick buildings, some of which date back to the turn of the century. The refurbished art deco **Wyo Theater** (42 N. Main St., tel. 307/672–9048) hosts special events from time to time. A narrow storefront on Main holds **King's Ropes and Saddlery** (*see* Shopping, *below*) and behind it a free museum with a collection of cowboy memorabilia assembled by owner Don King.

Time Out If you like your coffee with atmosphere, stop in at **Ritz Sporting Goods** (135 N. Main St., tel. 307/674–4101). It may be the only sporting goods store in the country with a coffee counter, and this one is never bare. A lineup of old-timers, cowboys, and outdoor types provides a bottomless cup of stories, opinions, and gossip. Never mind that locals call it the "whine line"; keep quiet and listen. There's even a bonus for anglers: a chance to meet owner and local fly-fishing legend Sam Mouvrakis, who is likely to be doctoring a reel or tying a fly.

Not far from the center of town is the **Sheridan Inn**, on the National Register of Historic Places, with 69 gables sprouting all over its long roof. The inn was once considered the finest between Chicago and the Pacific, luring the likes of Herbert Hoover, Will Rogers, and Ernest Hemingway. Cowboys no longer ride their horses into the bar, but lunch is now served there during the summer and tours are led by local volunteers. *856 Broadway, tel. 307/674–5440. Open Memorial Day–Labor Day, daily 9–8; Labor Day–Memorial Day, daily 9–5.*

The **Trail End Historic Center** is the former home of Wyoming governor, U.S. senator, and rancher John B. Kendrick and is the closest Sheridan comes to a historical museum (a surprising shortcoming in an area so rich in history). Built in the Flemish style, the 1913 house features elegant hand-carved woodwork and a third-floor ballroom. Turn-of-the-century furnishings and Kendrick's memorabilia decorate the house. Out back is a sod-roof log cabin built in 1878. *400 E. Clarendon Ave., tel. 307/674–4589. Admission free. Open June–Aug., daily 9–6; Sept.–May, daily 2–5.*

❽ Drive southwest of Sheridan on U.S. 87 and Route 335. Continue west beyond the town of **Big Horn** on Route 28, and you'll come to the **Big Horn Equestrian Center** (near state bird farm, tel. 307/674–5179), a huge expanse of green fields where locals play polo—yes, polo—on Sundays in the summer. English and Scottish families brought polo to this area in the 1890s, and now the Big Horn Polo Club is opening its 65 acres of turf to other summer events as well, from youth soccer to bronc riding.

If you're not staying at a ranch and want to get a look at one of the West's finest, visit the **Bradford Brinton Memorial** on the old Quarter Circle A Ranch. It, too, is located near Big Horn, southwest of Sheridan on U.S. 87 and Route 335. The Brinton family didn't exactly rough it in this 20-room clapboard home, complete with libraries, fine furniture, and silver and china services. A reception gallery hangs changing exhibits from the Brinton art collection, which features such Western artists as Charles M. Russell and Frederic Remington. *239 Brinton Rd., tel. 307/672–3173. Admission free. Open May 15–Labor Day, daily 9:30–5.*

❾ Head south on U.S. 87 or I-90 to **Buffalo,** a treasure trove of history and a hospitable little town in the foothills below Big Horn Pass. This is the area where cattle barons, who wanted free grazing, and homesteaders, who wanted to build fences, fought it out in the Johnson County Wars of the 1890s. Nearby are the sites of several skirmishes between the U.S. military and Native Americans along the Bozeman Trail, such as the **Wagon Box Fight** (17 mi north of Buffalo on U.S. 87, near Story) and the **Fetterman Massacre Monument** (20 mi north of Buffalo, just off I-90).

The **Jim Gatchell Memorial Museum,** in Buffalo, is the kind of small-town museum one ought to stop for. It contains Native American, military, outlaw, and ranching artifacts collected by a local druggist. *100 Fort St., tel. 307/684–9331. Admission free. Open June–Aug., daily 9–8; Sept., daily 9–5; Oct. 1–15, daily 1–5.*

Driving across the Powder River basin east of the Bighorns toward Gillette may seem a bore and a chore to people more accustomed to four lanes of bumper-to-bumper traffic. It helps to be able to read the history in the landscape: the draws where the Sioux hunted and hid from white interlopers, the uplifts where coal seams rise to the surface, and the ranches where cattle barons once grazed their steers. The rolling countryside may look as if it's been turned back to the deer and antelope, but on back roads such as U.S. 14/16 and around eye-blink towns such as Ucross and Spotted Horse, some of the country's wealthiest people have built ranch retreats.

⑩ In **Gillette,** check the schedule at **Camplex** (1635 Reata Dr., tel. 307/682–0552), a theater and convention hall with a rodeo arena, racetrack, and parks. National acts book here, but local ones fill the gaps. You might actually learn more about Wyoming by seeing Gillette high school kids dance with a Denver dance troupe than by listening to Garth Brooks warble.

If you want to see what fuels America's power plants, check out the **AMAX Belle Ayre Coal Mine,** where big shovels and haul trucks dwarf anything in a science fiction movie. There's a surprising amount of wildlife, from falcons to deer to bobcats, dwelling in and around the huge pits. *1901 Energy Ct., tel. 307/ 687–3200. Free tours: summer mornings by appt.*

Another 60 miles east of Gillette, I–90 begins rising into the **⑪** Black Hills. A side trip north takes in **Devils Tower,** a butte that juts upward 1,280 feet above the plain of the Belle Fourche River. Native American legend has it that the tower was corrugated by the claws of a bear trying to reach a maiden on top, but unimaginative geologists say it's the core of a defunct volcano. The tower was a tourist magnet long before a spaceship landed here in the movie *Close Encounters of the Third Kind.* In fact, Teddy Roosevelt made it the nation's first national monument in 1906. *6 mi off U.S. 14 on Rte. 24, tel. 307/467–5283. Admission: $1 adults. Visitor center open June–Labor Day, daily 8–8; Labor Day–June, daily 8–5.*

What to See and Do with Children

There's plenty for kids here: the cowboy charm of Sheridan, the giant earth-moving machines of the strip mines, and the wide open spaces everywhere.

Shopping

Shopping Streets The suburban malls that have drained so many downtowns are absent in **Sheridan,** where **Main Street** is lined with fascinating, mostly homegrown, businesses. Don't miss **King's Ropes and Saddlery** (184 N. Main St., tel 307/672–2702 or 800/443–8919), where hardcore cowboys the world over shop for the tools of the trade—and now and then a British queen drops by. From Stetson hats to bridle bits, you can get an entire rancher's repertoire, including a hand-carved saddle costing thousands of dollars. Enormous racks in the back hold every kind of rope imaginable, and professional cowboys are often here trying out the hemp on a dummy steer. For an excellent selection of both local and general-interest books, try the **Book Store** (122 N. Main St., tel. 307/672–6505). Anglers will want to visit the **Fly Shop of the Big Horns** (377 Coffeen Ave., tel. 307/672–5866).

Sports and the Outdoors

Camping **Bighorn National Forest** has several campgrounds, or camp anywhere from the highways for free; contact the **Bighorn National Forest** (1969 S. Sheridan Ave., Sheridan 82801, tel. 307/672–0751) for more information. Like many Wyoming towns, Sheridan makes campers welcome for a night of free tenting in **Washington Park,** along Little Goose Creek. The **Big Horn Mountain KOA Campground** (63 Decker Rd., Box 35A, Sheridan 82801, tel. 307/674–8766) has 35 tent sites and 80 trailer slots.

Dining and Lodging

Gillette **Boot Hill Night Club.** This steak and seafood place is a good one.
Dining Located a little north of town, it has music and dancing, too. _910 N. Gurley Ave., tel. 307/682–1600. AE, D, MC, V. Moderate._

★ **Bailey's Bar & Grill.** This handsome, shadow-filled restaurant in an old brick building turns out delicious sandwiches in the afternoon and dinners that include some Mexican dishes. _301 S. Gillette Ave., tel. 307/686–7678. AE, D, MC, V. Inexpensive–Moderate._

Bazel's Restaurant. Decorated like an old-fashioned diner and serving the requisite burgers, shakes, and hearty breakfasts, this eatery is infectiously '50s. Retro poster art adorns the walls, and a model train runs around the ceiling, above your head. _408 S. Douglas Hwy., tel 307/686–5149. No reservations. DC, MC, V. Inexpensive._

Dining and Lodging **Gillette Holiday Inn.** Having had a recent face-lift, this is now
★ the best place to stay in town. Rooms are decorated in soft teals and mauves. Travelers with a yen for exercise will appreciate a pool of lap-swimming proportions. Steak and seafood are on tap at **The Sugarland** restaurant, while lighter fare is offered next to the waterfall at **The Greenery.** _2009 S. Douglas Hwy., 82716, tel. 307/686–3000 or 800/HOLIDAY. Restaurant: Moderate. 213 rooms. Facilities: 2 restaurants, pool, sauna. AE, D, DC, MC, V. Moderate–Expensive._

Lodging **Best Western Towers West Lodge.** The biggest in town and currently undergoing renovation, the motel provides good value. _109 N. U.S. 14/16, 82716, tel. 307/686–2210 or 800/528–1234. 190 rooms. Facilities: restaurant, pool. AE, D, DC, MC, V. Moderate._

Thrifty Inn. Right off I–90, the motel has large rooms but no frills, except for a free Continental breakfast. Antelope are often grazing nearby. _1004 E. U.S. 14/16, 82716, tel. 307/682–2616 or 800/621–2182. 74 rooms. Facilities: breakfast room. AE, D, DC, MC, V. Inexpensive._

Sheridan **Golden Steer.** Four dining rooms, including one Western room,
Dining ensure that Sheridan is not without the Wyoming staples— steak and prime rib—as well as imported shrimp and lobster. _2071 N. Main St., tel. 307/672–2749. AE, D, DC, MC, V. Closed for lunch on weekends. Moderate–Expensive._

★ **Ciao.** Eight tables are squeezed into this European-style café's cramped quarters, but it gets an impressive array of gourmet food on the menu. Prawns in cognac cream are served at dinner, and the Ciao salad, with avocado and coconut-flavored chicken, is as good to look at as it is to eat. _120 N. Main St., tel. 307/672–2838. No credit cards. Moderate._

Silver Spur. You have to look closely to spot this breakfast place. It appears a little dingy, but the helpings are cowboy size and the omelets gently constructed. *832 N. Main St., tel. 307/672–2838. No credit cards. Closed for dinner. Inexpenisve.*

Lodging **Eaton's Guest Ranch.** This is the place that gets credit for creating the dude ranch, and it's still going strong after nearly a century as a working cattle ranch that takes guests. Located west of Sheridan on the edge of the Bighorn National Forest, it offers horseback riding, fishing, cookouts, and pack trips. The ranch can accommodate 125 guests, and reservations should be made by March. *270 Eaton Ranch Rd., Wolf 82844, tel. 307/655–9285. Facilities: horseback riding. MC, V. Closed Oct.–May. Expensive.*

Sheridan Holiday Inn. This five-floor lodging is five minutes from downtown. Rooms are done in earth tones. *1809 Sugarland Dr., 82801, tel. 307/672–8931 or 800/HOLIDAY. 214 rooms. Facilities: restaurant, indoor pool, hot tub, game room, putting green. AE, D, DC, MC, V. Expensive.*

★ **Spahn's Big Horn Mountain Bed and Breakfast.** Ron and Bobbie Spahn have guest rooms and cabins at their soaring log home 15 miles west of Sheridan. They offer far more than a traditional B&B: horseback riding, cookouts, and guided tours that include an eyes-only "moose safari." Full breakfasts are provided, and other meals are available by arrangement. *Box 579, Big Horn 82833, tel. 307/674–8150. 4 rooms. Facilities: hot tub, horseback riding. MC, V. Expensive.*

Best Western Sheridan Center Motor Inn. A favorite with bus tours, this motel has four buildings connected by a sky bridge over Main Street. Though building exteriors vary from alpine to block-type styles, rooms are all about the same. *612 N. Main St., 82801, tel. 307/674–7421 or 800/528–1234. 138 rooms. Facilities: 2 restaurants, lounge, indoor and outdoor pools, spa, sauna. AE, D, DC, MC, V. Moderate–Expensive.*

Mill Inn Motel. An old mill by a bridge is incorporated into this motel on old farm grounds on the east side of town. The building is six stories, but only the first two have remodeled guest rooms; the others have offices. *2161 Coffeen Ave., 82801, tel. 307/672–6401. 43 rooms. D, DC, MC, V. Inexpensive–Moderate.*

The Arts

Pop and country performers make occasional appearances at Gillette's **Camplex** (1635 Reata Dr., tel. 307/682–0552).

Index

Personal Itinerary

Departure *Date*

Time

Transportation

Arrival *Date*   *Time*

Departure *Date*   *Time*

Transportation

Accommodations

Arrival *Date*   *Time*

Departure *Date*   *Time*

Transportation

Accommodations

Arrival *Date*   *Time*

Departure *Date*   *Time*

Transportation

Accommodations

Personal Itinerary

Arrival *Date* *Time*

Departure *Date* *Time*

Transportation

Accommodations

Arrival *Date* *Time*

Departure *Date* *Time*

Transportation

Accommodations

Arrival *Date* *Time*

Departure *Date* *Time*

Transportation

Accommodations

Arrival *Date* *Time*

Departure *Date* *Time*

Transportation

Accommodations

Personal Itinerary

Arrival *Date*   *Time*

Departure *Date*   *Time*

Transportation

Accommodations

Arrival *Date*   *Time*

Departure *Date*   *Time*

Transportation

Accommodations

Arrival *Date*   *Time*

Departure *Date*   *Time*

Transportation

Accommodations

Arrival *Date*   *Time*

Departure *Date*   *Time*

Transportation

Accommodations

Personal Itinerary

Arrival *Date*   *Time*

Departure *Date*   *Time*

Transportation

Accommodations

Arrival *Date*   *Time*

Departure *Date*   *Time*

Transportation

Accommodations

Arrival *Date*   *Time*

Departure *Date*   *Time*

Transportation

Accommodations

Arrival *Date*   *Time*

Departure *Date*   *Time*

Transportation

Accommodations

Personal Itinerary

Arrival   *Date* _____   *Time* _____

Departure *Date* _____   *Time* _____

Transportation _____
_____
_____

Accommodations _____
_____
_____

Arrival   *Date* _____   *Time* _____

Departure *Date* _____   *Time* _____

Transportation _____
_____
_____

Accommodations _____
_____
_____

Arrival   *Date* _____   *Time* _____

Departure *Date* _____   *Time* _____

Transportation _____
_____
_____

Accommodations _____
_____
_____

Arrival   *Date* _____   *Time* _____

Departure *Date* _____   *Time* _____

Transportation _____
_____
_____

Accommodations _____
_____
_____

Addresses

Name	*Name*
Address	*Address*
Telephone	*Telephone*
Name	*Name*
Address	*Address*
Telephone	*Telephone*
Name	*Name*
Address	*Address*
Telephone	*Telephone*
Name	*Name*
Address	*Address*
Telephone	*Telephone*
Name	*Name*
Address	*Address*
Telephone	*Telephone*
Name	*Name*
Address	*Address*
Telephone	*Telephone*
Name	*Name*
Address	*Address*
Telephone	*Telephone*
Name	*Name*
Address	*Address*
Telephone	*Telephone*

Addresses

Name   *Name*

Address   *Address*

Telephone   *Telephone*

Name   *Name*

Address   *Address*

Telephone   *Telephone*

Name   *Name*

Address   *Address*

Telephone   *Telephone*

Name   *Name*

Address   *Address*

Telephone   *Telephone*

Name   *Name*

Address   *Address*

Telephone   *Telephone*

Name   *Name*

Address   *Address*

Telephone   *Telephone*

Name   *Name*

Address   *Address*

Telephone   *Telephone*

Name   *Name*

Address   *Address*

Telephone   *Telephone*

Notes

Fodor's Travel Guides

Available at bookstores everywhere, or call 1–800–533–6478, 24 hours a day.

U.S. Guides

Alaska

Arizona

Boston

California

Cape Cod, Martha's Vineyard, Nantucket

The Carolinas & the Georgia Coast

Chicago

Colorado

Florida

Hawaii

Las Vegas, Reno, Tahoe

Los Angeles

Maine, Vermont, New Hampshire

Maui

Miami & the Keys

New England

New Orleans

New York City

Pacific North Coast

Philadelphia & the Pennsylvania Dutch Country

The Rockies

San Diego

San Francisco

Santa Fe, Taos, Albuquerque

Seattle & Vancouver

The South

The U.S. & British Virgin Islands

The Upper Great Lakes Region

USA

Vacations in New York State

Vacations on the Jersey Shore

Virginia & Maryland

Waikiki

Walt Disney World and the Orlando Area

Washington, D.C.

Foreign Guides

Acapulco, Ixtapa, Zihuatanejo

Australia & New Zealand

Austria

The Bahamas

Baja & Mexico's Pacific Coast Resorts

Barbados

Berlin

Bermuda

Brazil

Brittany & Normandy

Budapest

Canada

Cancun, Cozumel, Yucatan Peninsula

Caribbean

China

Costa Rica, Belize, Guatemala

The Czech Republic & Slovakia

Eastern Europe

Egypt

Euro Disney

Europe

Europe's Great Cities

Florence & Tuscany

France

Germany

Great Britain

Greece

The Himalayan Countries

Hong Kong

India

Ireland

Israel

Italy

Japan

Kenya & Tanzania

Korea

London

Madrid & Barcelona

Mexico

Montreal & Quebec City

Morocco

Moscow & St. Petersburg

The Netherlands, Belgium & Luxembourg

New Zealand

Norway

Nova Scotia, Prince Edward Island & New Brunswick

Paris

Portugal

Provence & the Riviera

Rome

Russia & the Baltic Countries

Scandinavia

Scotland

Singapore

South America

Southeast Asia

Spain

Sweden

Switzerland

Thailand

Tokyo

Toronto

Turkey

Vienna & the Danube Valley

Yugoslavia

Special Series

Fodor's Affordables
Caribbean
Europe
Florida
France
Germany
Great Britain
London
Italy
Paris

Fodor's Bed & Breakfast and Country Inns Guides
Canada's Great Country Inns
California
Cottages, B&Bs and Country Inns of England and Wales
Mid-Atlantic Region
New England
The Pacific Northwest
The South
The Southwest
The Upper Great Lakes Region
The West Coast

The Berkeley Guides
California
Central America
Eastern Europe
France
Germany

Great Britain & Ireland
Mexico
Pacific Northwest & Alaska
San Francisco

Fodor's Exploring Guides
Australia
Britain
California
The Caribbean
Florida
France
Germany
Ireland
Italy
London
New York City
Paris
Rome
Singapore & Malaysia
Spain
Thailand

Fodor's Flashmaps
New York
Washington, D.C.

Fodor's Pocket Guides
Bahamas
Barbados
Jamaica
London

New York City
Paris
Puerto Rico
San Francisco
Washington, D.C.

Fodor's Sports
Cycling
Hiking
Running
Sailing
The Insider's Guide to the Best Canadian Skiing
Skiing in the USA & Canada

Fodor's Three-In-Ones (guidebook, language cassette, and phrase book)
France
Germany
Italy
Mexico
Spain

Fodor's Special-Interest Guides
Accessible USA
Cruises and Ports of Call
Euro Disney
Halliday's New England Food Explorer

Healthy Escapes
London Companion
Shadow Traffic's New York Shortcuts and Traffic Tips
Sunday in New York
Walt Disney World and the Orlando Area
Walt Disney World for Adults

Fodor's Touring Guides
Touring Europe
Touring USA: Eastern Edition

Fodor's Vacation Planners
Great American Vacations
National Parks of the East
National Parks of the West

The Wall Street Journal Guides to Business Travel
Europe
International Cities
Pacific Rim
USA & Canada

WHEREVER YOU TRAVEL, *H*ELP IS NEVER FAR AWAY.

From planning your trip to

providing travel assistance along

the way, American Express®

Travel Service Offices* are

always there to help.

For the office nearest you, call

1-800-YES-AMEX.